SEARCHING FOR ALTERNATIVES

SEARCHING FOR ALTERNATIVES

Drug-Control Policy in the United States

EDITED AND WITH
AN INTRODUCTION BY
MELVYN B. KRAUSS
AND EDWARD P. LAZEAR

HOOVER INSTITUTION PRESS

STANFORD UNIVERSITY
STANFORD, CALIFORNIA

www.hoover.org

Hoover Institution Press Publication No. 406

First printing, 1991
97 96 95 94 93 92 91   9 8 7 6 5 4 3 2 1
First paperback printing, 1992
06 05 04 03 02 01 00   9 8 7 6 5 4

Manufactured in the United States of America

The paper used in this publication meets the minimum requirements
of the American National Standard for Information Sciences—
Permanence of Paper for Printed Library Materials, ANSI Z39.48–1984.

Library of Congress Cataloging-in-Publication Data
Searching for Alternatives : drug-control policy in the United States /
Edited by Melvyn B. Krauss and Edward P. Lazear.
        p.   cm.
    Includes bibliographical references and index.
    ISBN 0-8179-9141-7 — ISBN 0-8179-9142-5(pbk.)
    1.   Narcotics, Control of—United States. 2. Drug legalization—
United States. I. Krauss, Melvyn B. II. Lazear, Edward P.
HV5825.S396 1991   91-20103
363.4'5'0973—dc20   CIP

CONTENTS

PART TWO: ECONOMIC IMPLICATIONS

PART THREE: LESSONS FROM ABROAD

PART FOUR: SOCIAL COSTS OF DRUG USE

PART FIVE: LEGAL IMPLICATIONS

PART SIX: MEDICAL AND HEALTH IMPLICATIONS

CONTRIBUTORS

GARY S. BECKER is a professor of economics at the University of Chicago. After receiving his Ph.D. there, he taught at Columbia University until he joined the University of Chicago faculty in 1970. He is also affiliated with the Department of Sociology at Chicago and is a research associate at the NORC Economics Research Center. He is the author of many monographs and articles on the family, human behavior, the economics of crime and punishment, and the economics of discrimination, as well as other related subjects. In addition to his university duties, he is a columnist for *Business Week* and is or has been a member of the Domestic Advisory Board for the American Enterprise Institute, an associate member of the Institute of Fiscal and Monetary Policy for the Ministry of Finance in Japan, and a senior research associate and research policy advisor for the National Bureau of Economic Research. Professor Becker has received numerous academic honors including membership in the National Academy of Sciences and the American Academy of Arts and Sciences.

KILDARE I. CLARKE, M.D., is associate medical director of the Kings County Hospital Center Department of Emergency Medicine. He received his medical degree from the State University of New York Downstate Medical College in 1974, his J.D. from Pace University School of Law in 1982, and in 1988 earned an M.S. in industrial relations and management from Cornell University. From 1977 to 1979 he served as director of Community Mental Health Service at New York Medical College, Lincoln Hospital. Dr. Clarke is a medicolegal consultant to the Brooklyn District Attorney's Office and a forensic psychiatric consultant. He is a Fellow of the American College of Legal Medicine.

HOPE CORMAN is an associate professor of economics at Rider College in Lawrenceville, New Jersey, and a research associate in the Health Economics Program at the National Bureau of Economic Research. She received her B.A. from the University of Illinois at Champaign and her Ph.D. from the City University of New York Graduate Division. Professor Corman has published numerous articles on the economics of crime in New York and on the economics of health and education. She is currently participating in the National Bureau of Economic Research's Drug Research Program.

EDDY L. ENGELSMAN, a sociologist, holds a position in the Ministry of Welfare, Health and Cultural Affairs in the Netherlands. He is a recent recipient of the Bing Spear Award for Drug Enforcement.

MILTON FRIEDMAN, a 1976 Nobel Price winner for excellence in economics, has been a Senior Research Fellow at the Hoover Institution since 1977. He earned his Ph.D. from Columbia University in 1946 and taught for many years at the University of Chicago, where he holds an endowed chair as professor emeritus. He was a member of the research staff of the National Bureau of Economic Research from 1937 to 1981 and is a past member of the President's Commission on an All-Volunteer Armed Force and the President's Commission on White House Fellows. Professor Friedman has authored many books on monetary economics and has also written extensively on public policy. He has received honorary degrees from universities worldwide and has served as president of the American Economic Association, the Western Economic Association, and the Mont Pelerin Society. He is a member of the American Philosophical Society and the National Academy of Sciences.

VICTOR R. FUCHS is the Henry J. Kaiser, Jr., Professor at Stanford University, with a joint appointment in the Department of Economics and Department of Health Research and Policy. He has authored or edited books, and has published more than a hundred articles in professional and popular journals. Professor Fuchs twice was a Fellow at the Center for Advanced Study in the Behavioral Sciences and has been a research associate of the National Bureau of Economic Research since 1962. He is a member of the American Philosophical Society, the Institute of Medicine of the National Academy of Sciences, and the American Academy of Arts and Sciences.

IRA GLASSER has been executive director of the American Civil Liberties Union since 1978. He received his B.S. in mathematics from Queens College and his

M.A., also in mathematics, from Ohio State University. He did graduate work in sociology and philosophy at the New School for Social Research. Before joining the American Civil Liberties Union in 1967, he taught mathematics at the City University of New York (Queens College) and at Sarah Lawrence College and was the associate editor and editor of *Current* Magazine. He is the author of many articles on various aspects of civil liberties and rights. Mr. Glasser received the Martin Luther King, Jr., Award from the Association of Black School Supervisors and Administrators and the Silver Gavel Award from the American Bar Association. In 1970 he was a member of the Association of Black School Supervisors and Administrators. From 1970 to 1972 he served as chair of the St. Vincent's Hospital Community Advisory Board. He is currently a member of the board of directors of the Asian-American Legal Defense and Education Fund.

AVRAM GOLDSTEIN, M.D., is professor emeritus of pharmacology at Stanford University. He received both his undergraduate and medical degrees from Harvard University, where he served on the faculty of the Pharmacology Department for eight years. In 1974 he formed the Addiction Research Foundation of Palo Alto, which he directed until its dissolution in 1987. Dr. Goldstein has authored or coauthored books on biostatistics and drug action and has published many research papers. He is an honorary professor of the Beijing Medical University and the Institute of Materia Medica of the Academia Sinica, Shanghai, and has received the Franklin Medal, the Nathan B. Eddy Award, the Sollman Award, and the Pacesetter Award for Research from the National Institute on Drug Abuse. Currently he is chairman of the Section of Physiology and Pharmacology of the National Academy of Sciences.

LESTER GRINSPOON, M.D., is an associate professor of psychiatry at the Harvard Medical School. After receiving his M.D. from Harvard, he was an assistant in medicine at the University of Southern California for two years before returning to Harvard in 1958. Dr. Grinspoon has also held numerous nonacademic appointments, including present service as an examiner for the American Board of Psychiatry and Neurology, executive director of the Massachusetts Mental Health Research Corporation, a member of the Board of Directors of Physicians for Human Rights, and others. He is the editor of several scientific journals and has authored, coauthored, or edited many scholarly publications. He is a Fellow of the American Psychiatric Association for the Advancement of Science. In 1990 he received the Alfred R. Lindesmith Award from the Drug Policy Foundation.

MICHAEL GROSSMAN is Distinguished Professor of Economics at the City University of New York Graduate School. He received his Ph.D. from Columbia University in 1970 and was on the faculty of the Graduate School of Business, University of Chicago, and Hunter College of the City University of New York before joining the graduate school in 1972. He is the author of numerous publications in the field of health economics and has received funded research in that field as principal or coprincipal investigator. Professor Grossman received a Ford Foundation Fellowship in 1966–1967 and and an Earheart Foundation Fellowship in 1967–1968. He is a member of the Institute of Medicine of the National Academy of Sciences.

GORDON HAWKINS is a Senior Research Associate at the Earl Warren Legal Institute at the University of California at Berkeley. He is also retired director of the Institute of Criminology at Sydney University.

JOEL W. HAY is a Senior Research Fellow at the Hoover Institution. After earning his Ph.D. in economics from Yale University in 1980, he served as a senior policy analyst for Project HOPE at the Center for Health Affairs before joining the Hoover Institution in 1985. In addition, Dr. Hay has been a consultant for the U.S. Food and Drug Administration, the U.S. Department of Health and Human Services, the U.S. Environmental Protection Agency, and state and foreign governments and private foundations as well as corporations. He was recently a consultant on AIDS in the United States to the Center for Disease Control and to the Public Health Service on AIDS cost projections. Dr. Hay is the author of many journal articles in the fields of health economics, health policy, and econometrics. He held a Yale University fellowship from 1974 to 1978 and was a reviewer for the National Science Foundation's economics section in 1982 and 1987.

THEODORE JOYCE has a Ph.D. in economics from the City University of New York Graduate Center. He is currently an associate professor in the Department of Economics and Finance at Baruch College, the City University of New York, and a research associate with the National Bureau of Economic Research. His present research explores the clinical and cost outcomes of material substance abuse in New York City.

MARK A.R. KLEIMAN is a lecturer in public policy and a research fellow with the Program in Criminal Justice Policy and Management at the Kennedy School of Government, Harvard University. He holds a Master's and Ph.D. in public policy from the Kennedy School. From 1979 to 1983 he was with the Office of Policy and Management Analysis in the Criminal Division of the U.S. Department of Justice, of which he was the director in 1982–1983. At that time he was also a member of the National Organized Crime Planning Council. From 1977 to 1979 Dr. Kleiman served as deputy director for Management and director of Program Analysis for the Office of Management and Budget of the City of Boston.

He recently published a book on federal marijuana enforcement policy and is currently writing a book on drug policy.

MELVYN B. KRAUSS is a Senior Fellow at the Hoover Institution. He holds a Ph.D. in economics from New York University and has been a professor of economics at that university since 1976. Dr. Krauss's areas of expertise include taxation and tax reform, U.S. aid to foreign nations, international trade, economic development, the economics of alliances, and the North Atlantic Treaty Organization. He is widely published in these areas.

EDWARD P. LAZEAR, Senior Fellow at the Hoover Institution, Isidore Brown and Gladys J. Brown Professor of Urban and Labor Economics at the University of Chicago, received his Ph.D. from Harvard University in economics. Dr. Lazear is founding editor of the *Journal of Labor Economics*.

MELVYN LEVITSKY is the assistant secretary of state for International Narcotics Matters. He entered the foreign service after receiving his B.A. from the University of Michigan and his M.A. in Soviet studies from the State University of Iowa. His overseas assignments included Germany, Brazil, and the USSR. Mr. Levitsky became officer in charge of Bilateral Relations in the Office of Soviet Union Affairs in 1975. From 1978 to 1980 he was deputy director of the Office of U.S. Political Affairs in the Department of State and director of the same office from 1980 to 1982. In 1982 he became deputy assistant secretary for Human Rights and Humanitarian Affairs. From 1983 to 1984, he was deputy director at the Voice of America. In 1984 he was appointed ambassador to Bulgaria, where he served until 1987. Upon his return to the United States he was appointed executive secretary and special assistant to the secretary of state, which post he held until his present position. Mr. Levitsky is the recipient of both the Meritorious Honor Award and the Superior Honor Award from the Department of State. He has also won the department's Senior Foreign Service Performance Award four times and the Presidential Meritorious Service Award twice.

JOSEPH D. MCNAMARA became chief of police in San Jose, California, in 1976. His law-enforcement career began with the New York Police Department, where he served for many years before becoming chief of police in Kansas City, Missouri, in 1973. Chief McNamara holds a Ph.D. from Harvard University and was a Criminal Justice Fellow at Harvard Law School in 1969. He has published law-enforcement articles in numerous magazines and newspapers and has held many television interviews regarding the importance of citizen education on matters of crime reporting, serving as witnesses, and taking precautions against personal violence. In 1980, the Civil Rights Commission commended the San Jose Police Department for greatly improved community relations. As well as authoring professional books and articles, Chief McNamara has written two detective fiction best-sellers and has recently completed another novel. In 1991, Dr. McNamara joined the Hoover Institution as a Research Fellow.

EDWIN MEESE III, former attorney general of the United States (1985–1988), is presently a Distinguished Visiting Fellow at the Hoover Institution. He holds a law degree from the University of California at Berkeley and a B.A. from Yale University. After serving as deputy district attorney of Alameda County, California, he became Governor Reagan's legal affairs secretary from 1967 to 1968 and his executive assistant and chief of staff from 1969 to 1974. During the 1980 presidential campaign, he was chief of staff and senior issues advisor for the Reagan-Bush Committee. Before his appointment as attorney general, Mr. Meese was counselor to the president from 1981 to 1985 and a member of the president's Cabinet and the National Security Council. From 1977 to 1981, Mr. Meese was a professor of law at the University of San Diego, where he was also director of the Center for Criminal Justice Policy and Management. During 1975 and 1976 he was vice-president for administration of Rohr Industries.

ROBERT B. MILLMAN, M.D., is the Saul P. Steinberg Distinguished Professor of Psychiatry and Public Health at Cornell University and director of Drug and Alcohol Abuse Treatment and Research programs at New York Hospital. He received his M.D. from the New York Hospital–Cornell Medical Center and worked in the field of drug and alcohol abuse at Rockefeller University and New York Hospital before joining the faculty at Cornell. He has developed a number of treatment programs for drug abusers and has established a network of employee-assistance programs for New York City workers. His research interests include the characterization and treatment of mentally ill substance abusers and the pharmacotherapy of heroin and cocaine dependence. He has served on a number of local and national advisory bodies involved in the development of policy and programs with respect to drug and alcohol abusers.

JEFFREY A. MIRON is a professor of economics at Boston University. His Ph.D. from MIT was aided by a Social Science Research Council Fellowship, and he has since been awarded a Rackham Faculty Fellowship, an Olin Fellowship, and a Sloan Fellowship. From 1985 to the present, Professor Miron has been a Faculty Research Fellow in the National Bureau of Economic Research's Program in Financial Markets and Monetary Economics. Since 1988, he has been an NBER Faculty Research Fellow in the Economic Fluctuations Program. Professor Miron has published extensively in leading professional journals and books.

NACI MOCAN received his B.A. in economics from Bosphorus University, Istanbul, in 1984. He received his Ph.D. in economics from the City University of New York in 1989. He is currently assistant professor of economics at the University of Colorado at Denver and Faculty Research Fellow at the National Bureau of Economic Research. His research interests include the economics of health, labor, and public policy.

JOHN P. MORGAN, M.D., is a professor of pharmacology at the City University of New York Medical School. He is also an Adjunct Scholar in the Center for the Study of Drug Development at Tufts University and associate professor of pharmacology at Mt. Sinai School of Medicine in New York. He received his M.D. from the University of Cincinnati College of Medicine and taught at SUNY Syracuse, the University of Rochester, and SUNY Buffalo before assuming his present duties. Besides his research on the cultural and social context of drug use, Dr. Morgan's interests include a review of the uses of drug analysis in the workplace and studies that attempt to document the impact of employee drug use. He has instituted a large-scale toxicity trial of the drug phenylpropanolamine and explored the portrayal of alcohol and alcoholism in country music, as well as examining pharmacist behavior in filling prescriptions with generic versus brand-name drugs. He is a member of many professional societies and has reviewed for and contributed to numerous medical publications.

STEPHEN K. MUGFORD is a senior lecturer in sociology at the Australian National University. After receiving his Ph.D. from Bristol University, he taught at Bristol, then moved to New Zealand, where he lectured in sociology at Victoria University. Since joining the Australian National University in 1979, he has held positions in the Australian Institute of Criminology and the Australian Institute of Health. In 1982 he was acting head of the Department of Sociology at ANU. Among many professional activities, Dr. Mugford was a member of the ANU Postgraduate Medical Education Committee from 1975 to 1985 and a member of the Commonwealth Department of Health's National Drug Education Project Research Working Group. He is widely published in the fields of drug use and policy, violence and social control, and social aspects of consumption and consumer society and is the associate editor of the *International Journal on Drug Policy*.

KEVIN M. MURPHY is an associate professor in the Graduate School of Business at the University of Chicago, where he has taught since receiving his Ph.D. at that university. He has published on the family and the state, addiction, government regulation of cigarette health information, unemployment, and the use of survey data in predicting behavior, among other subjects. His work has been heavily supported by fellowships, including a Getty Oil Fellowship, a Departmental Fellowship, and two Earhart Fellowships.

ETHAN A. NADELMANN is an assistant professor of politics and public affairs at
the Woodrow Wilson School of Public and International Affairs, a position he
has held since 1987. His education included both a J.D. and a Ph.D. in political
science from Harvard, as well as a Master's Degree in international relations from
the London School of Economics. Professor Nadelmann's research interest in
the international aspects of crime and law enforcement led him to prepare a
classified report on drug trafficking and money laundering for the U.S. State
Department. He has published many scholarly articles relating to the failures of
U.S. drug policy and the wisdom of considering the controlled legalization of
drugs as a policy alternative. His work has been supported by the John M. Olin
Foundation, the Ford Foundation, and the National Science Foundation, among
many others.

JAMES OSTROWSKI received his Doctorate of Jurisprudence from Brooklyn Law
School in 1983. A member of the New York and New Jersey bars, he is also an
associate policy analyst of the Cato Institute. From 1986 to 1988 he was vice-
chairman of the Committee on Law Reform of the New York County Lawyers'
Association. He has written articles and memoranda concerning drug legalization
and drug-related AIDS.

ROBERT E. PETERSON received his law degree at SUNY Buffalo and is engaged
in the private practice of law and government policy consulting and authoring a
book on the drug culture in the United States. He formerly served as an assistant
district attorney and chief of intergovernmental affairs in Buffalo, then was put
on special assignment to the U.S. Department of Justice, where he wrote the
U.S. attorney training manual on drug-legalization issues. He was also executive
advisor to two attorneys general in Pennsylvania, where he was the chief liaison
to the National Association of Attorneys General and the Executive Working
Group for Prosecutorial Relations. He played a key role in putting together a
state program on drug enforcement, prevention, education, and legislation that
was commended by President Bush in the 1990 National Drug Control Strategy
and was cited in former President Reagan's White House Conference for a Drug-
Free America Final Report.

PETER REUTER is senior economist in the Washington Office of the Rand Cor-
poration and co-director of Rand's Drug Policy Research Center. He earned his
Ph.D. in economics from Yale University and was Guest Scholar at the Brookings
Institution before joining Rand in 1981. His research has resulted in the publi-
cation of a number of papers and studies on drug enforcement and drug policy.
His early research has resulted in the publication of *Disorganized Crime: The
Economics of the Visible Hand*. Since 1985 his research has focused on drug
policy.

MITCHELL S. ROSENTHAL, M.D., is president and founder of Phoenix House, the nation's largest private, nonprofit substance abuse services agency. He received his medical degree at Downstate Medical Center, State University of New York, and served from 1965 to 1967 at the Naval Hospital in Oakland, California, where he established the first service-sponsored therapeutic community. From 1967 to 1970 he was deputy commissioner of New York City's Addiction Services Agency. Dr. Rosenthal is a special consultant to the Office of National Drug Control Policy and has advised the White House Office of Drug Abuse Policy during previous administrations. Since 1985 he has been chairman of the New York State Advisory Council on Substance Abuse.

ROBERT W. SWEET has been United States district judge for the Southern District of New York since 1978. After earning his law degree from Yale University, he served as assistant U.S. attorney for the Southern District of New York from 1953 to 1955 and as deputy mayor of New York from 1966 to 1969.

PAUL TAUBMAN is a professor of economics at the University of Pennsylvania and head of the National Bureau of Economic Research's program on the economics of illegal drugs. His Ph.D. is from the University of Pennsylvania. He is a Fellow of the Econometric Society, the International Society for Twin Studies, and the American Association for the Advancement of Science, Section K. He has published five books and numerous articles in a variety of areas including human capital, health, public finance, and consumption behavior.

DAVID TURNER is director of the Standing Conference on Drug Abuse, the national representative organization for drug services in the United Kingdom. He has held this post since 1977.

E. LEONG WAY is a professor emeritus of pharmacology, toxicology, and pharmaceutical chemistry at the University of California, San Francisco. He is also a Senior Staff Fellow of the National Institute of Drug Abuse for the year 1990–1991. After receiving his Ph.D. from the University of California, he was a pharmaceutical chemist with Merck and Company and instructed in pharmacology at George Washington University before joining the faculty at UCSF. He was chairman of his department from 1973 to 1978 and has held visiting professorships at the University of Berne, Guangzhou Medical College in China, Gunma University Medical School in Japan, and the University of Hong Kong. He has authored or contributed to many publications in drug metabolism, analgetics, developmental pharmacology, and drug tolerance and dependence. In 1962 he was the first recipient of the American Pharmaceutical Foundation's Achievement Award in Pharmacodynamics and also the recipient of the Nathan B. Eddy Award for excellence in drug abuse research. Among more recent awards, he received the Chancellor's Award for Public Service from UCSF in 1986. He has served on numerous scientific committees.

BARBARA R. WILLIAMS is a vice-president of the Rand Corporation and co-director of its Drug Policy Research Center. Since 1982 she has been a member of the Advisory Board of the Rand Graduate School and since 1989 has been vice-president of planning of the Senior Health and Peer Counseling Center. Dr. Williams received her Ph.D. in sociology from the University of Illinois and joined Rand in 1971. From 1962 to 1967, she taught at St. Lawrence University and was professor of sociology at Vassar College from 1969 to 1971. While on leave from St. Lawrence, she served for two years in the Research and Plans Division of the Office of Economic Opportunity, authoring numerous reports on crime, poverty, and juvenile issues. Her publications at Rand cover a variety of urban policy problems. A member of the American Sociological Association, she has been chairman of its Committee on Applied Sociology and a member of its Committee on Certification.

KEVIN B. ZEESE is vice-president and counsel of the Drug Policy Foundation and an adjunct professor in the Department of Justice, Law, and Society, School of Public Affairs, the American University. He holds a J.D. degree from the George Washington University National Law Center. From 1980 to 1986 he served as chief counsel to the National Organization for the Reform of Marijuana Laws, and from 1983 to 1986 was the organization's national director. He is the author or editor of numerous criminal defense manuals.

FRANKLIN E. ZIMRING has been professor of law and director of the Earl Warren Legal Institute at the University of California, Berkeley, since 1985. After gaining his J.D. at the University of Chicago, he was on the faculty of that university for many years and served as director of the Center for Studies in Criminal Justice. He has published on the changing legal world of adolescence, capital punishment, gun control, and other subjects relating to criminal and family law and the empirical study of legal institutions.

FOREWORD

The serious drug problem in the United States poses exceedingly complex questions about the health, economic, legal, social, and international implications of alternative drug policies. Indeed, the complexity is such that it may cause us to accept the status quo by default, which would be a shameful indictment of public policy.

That complexity notwithstanding, my reading and my discussions with Hoover scholars have shown that drug policy experts fall into two essentially divergent camps: those who feel that the distribution and use of at least some now-contraband drugs should be decriminalized and those who urge not only that the current laws not be relaxed but that, in some cases, they be made more stringent.

Within both camps there is a certain continuum. Classically liberal thinkers believe that the choice of what one does to one's body should not be dictated by the state, that is, the decision to use drugs should be a personal one. Others, viewed by many as more moderate, believe that case-by-case studies are necessary to determine whether controlled (along the lines of our current alcohol and nicotine laws) drug use is acceptable.

Those who oppose relaxing the laws calculate and describe the lost lives, the increased medical and rehabilitation costs, and the economic and personal losses associated with increased addiction, which they believe will inevitably follow any easing of current drug laws. Some strongly feel that, to truly discourage use, the penalties associated with drug violations should be more severe.

This lively debate is of critical importance to the future welfare of this country.

Accordingly, the Hoover Institution convened top drug policy experts to discuss, debate, present new evidence, and clarify the drug policy issue at the Hoover Conference on U.S. Drug Policy at Stanford University on November 15 and 16, 1990. We at the Hoover Institution hope that our contribution will ultimately improve public policy decision making.

The success of the Hoover conference owes a great deal to the work of many people, but I would like to single out Hoover overseer Bruce Kovner, who supplied both the inspiration and financial support for the conference. I am also grateful to Donald Sussman and the Eldorado Foundation for their support. Finally, Associate Director Richard Sousa and Hoover senior fellows Melvyn Krauss and Edward Lazear proved invaluable in realizing the conference.

John Raisian
Director, Hoover Institution

INTRODUCTION

Melvyn B. Krauss
and Edward P. Lazear

The Hoover Institution's conference on drug policy in the United States was the result of two forces. First, growing frustration with current drug policy in this country and the perceived effect on crime rates have led many to speak out against prohibition of drugs. At the same time, a substantial number of respected thinkers and policymakers believe that drugs should be prohibited and that sellers should be severely prosecuted. Second, a number of influential Americans have taken an interest in U.S. drug policy and they encouraged Hoover to organize the conference of which this volume is an outgrowth.

The conference brought together some of the most thoughtful, and perhaps outspoken, proponents of the various views on drug policy. As will become clear, there are far more than two positions. All those who favor drug decriminalization do not envision the same policy and do not expect the same results. Nor are those who are opposed to drug legalization of one mind. Some would permit legal use of some currently prohibited drugs; others would allow use of drugs only for well-defined medical purposes.

In this Introduction, we will select some of the more important points made in each presentation. We will offer our own thoughts when we believe they are relevant. What follows reflects the views of the editors. Our discussion is not meant to be a summary. We expect that a number of authors may disagree not only with our discussion of their work, but also with our own views on some of their points. Further, the two editors have two minds on many subjects. We have attempted to integrate those views in this essay.

Historical Overview

Franklin Zimring opened the conference by arguing three points. First, both sides of the debate on drug prohibition were argued eloquently at least as far back as the nineteenth century. Second, the drug-decriminalization issue has split the U.S. right wing into two factions—those who favor the libertarian approach and those who favor the cautionary approach. Third, the policy debate has focused on the wrong issue. There should be a discussion of what kind of, not whether there should be, criminal law regulating drug use.

The second and third points are the most interesting for our purposes. Libertarians favor individual liberty so long as it does not harm anyone else. This casts the discussion in terms of externalities, or the harmful effects that drugs cause to others. Most obvious among the injured are infants whose fetal development is affected by the drug use of the mother. Highway victims make up another major group; to the extent that drugs impair an individual's ability to operate a vehicle, those who share the roads are adversely affected.

To argue against the libertarian view, two key empirical points must be made. First, it must be demonstrated not simply that the harm caused by drug use to others is substantial, but that such harm is greater than that caused by legal products for which drugs are close substitutes—alcohol, for example. If drug prohibition shifts demand to close substitutes whose negative consequences on others are as bad as if not worse than those of drugs, the case for drug prohibition is substantially weakened. Second, it must be shown that decriminalization of drugs would lead to increased use. If not, libertarians argue, there can be no objective reason to prohibit drug use.

The other view among conservatives is what Zimring terms the "cautionary" view. This view is best characterized as a desire for continuity. In the absence of convincing information, laws should not be changed in ways that deviate strongly from the past. There are reasons to prohibit drug use. The current prohibition of certain substances grows out of a long history of such prohibitions. Prohibition of cocaine but legalization of tobacco and alcohol are not arbitrary ideas; they reflect the degree of certainty about the negative effects of the drug. This, argues Zimring, is the basis for the cautionary view.

Implicit in both the cautionary and libertarian views are cost-benefit calculations. "The question is not whether there are costs or benefits of legalization," writes Jeffrey Miron, "but whether the costs outweigh the benefits." The libertarians assume the benefits of legalization outweigh the costs, whereas those following the cautionary approach assume the opposite.

The final point that Zimring makes is extremely important. He points out that the issue is not whether laws should regulate drug use, but rather what kind of laws should be enacted. Even in an environment of decriminalization, some kinds of use may be prohibited. For example, it is unlikely that legal use of cocaine would extend down to ten-year-olds. Additionally, the penalties and level of enforcement associated with use are policy variables. Even where purchase of tobacco by minors is prohibited, little public money is spent to enforce the prohibition. Further, the taxes associated with drug use are tools that can be used to prohibit even when there is no outright legal prohibition. Key here is the elasticity of demand for drugs and the responsiveness of black market supply to high prices of legal drugs.

Some policies will result in a gray market. For example, legalization of drugs for nonminors may not prevent minors from obtaining drugs, but the drugs that are obtained will be those that are sold legally to adults. As a result, some feel that the gray market at least will remove some of the negative effects that result from minors being sold particularly dangerous low-quality drugs—a current concern.

Stephen Mugford argues that the drug debate in the United States is a "dialogue of the deaf." The United States, he states, has the strongest prohibition *and* the worst drug problem. Further, the policy has not prevented many from using drugs in a serious way. Mugford argues that the probability of apprehension is more important than the penalties in deterring drug use.

These statements are subject to challenge. First, the United States does not have the world's strongest antidrug policy. Singapore, where use of drugs brings the death sentence, and Moslem countries with similarly severe punishment, have virtually eliminated drug use. Further, it is exactly the severity of punishment and not the probability of detection that is doing the work in these societies. Although a well-dressed tourist carrying drugs into Singapore is very unlikely to be caught, few cocaine-using tourists are willing to risk the death penalty.

The obvious point here is that such extreme punishments may be effective, but they are irrelevant. The United States is not about to adopt such severe measures. Even if we did, the court and jury system is unlikely to hand out harsh punishments for minor drug offenses. From a practical standpoint, extreme policies are simply not on the menu in the United States.

Mugford recognizes this reality and uses the metaphor of Goldilocks. The search is for the policy that is analogous to the baby bear's chair—neither too hard nor too soft, but just right. To pursue this search, Mugford makes the following points:

First, drug usage is normal. There are no drug-free societies.

Second, drugs are not always demanded for reasons of escape. Some drugs are used for excitement.

Third, Mugford claims that the prohibitionist argument is contradictory. The idea that drugs are addictive might suggest that the demand for drugs is inelastic. The argument against legalization, however, is based on the view that usage would increase significantly. This, Mugford argues, requires an elastic demand. It cannot be both ways.

The point is an interesting one, but it is not quite accurate as it stands. There is a distinction between long-run and short-run demand. It may be possible for the demand by nonusers to be quite elastic, even if the demand by users is inelastic. An individual's willingness to become involved with drugs may depend significantly on their price, even if he recognizes that once he starts he will find his future demand quite inelastic. If the long-run price is to remain low, the concern that he will be addicted may be of little consequence. The discussion in the Becker, Grossman, and Murphy paper makes this distinction clear.

Mugford, like Zimring, pushes the point that the discussion should not be over legalization per se, but over what kind of laws should regulate drug usage. He argues that there are different avenues of control, and defines intrinsic and extrinsic costs of drug usage. One point that Mugford argues convincingly is that social norms are important in the control of drug usage. He suggests that society needs the appropriate social relations to control drug usage. This raises two questions. First, how can this be done effectively and does it take a great deal of time to implement? Second, what role does the law play in affecting social values? Specifically, are prohibitions helpful or harmful in creating a value system that eschews drug usage?

ECONOMIC IMPLICATIONS

The papers presented in the economics portion of the conference were most useful in terms of conceptual clarifications and the presentation of important and, in some instances, new empirical information. For economists, the drug-policy issue needs to be evaluated in terms of cost-benefit analysis. The costs of drug legalization are calculated along with its benefits and a balance is struck. If the costs are greater than the benefits, then drug legalization is judged a bad thing, and vice versa.

In evaluating costs and benefits, certain economic effects are critical. First, there is the effect drug legalization can be expected to have on drug use. Would legalization increase, decrease, or be irrelevant for drug use? Second, there is the potential harmful effect that expected increased use of drugs would have on others—the so-called "externalities" issue. Finally, there is the question of the effect drug legalization would have on crime, its victims, and the resources society presently devotes to fighting drug-related crime.

Conceptually, drug legalization can be expected to affect drug use in at least two different ways. First, by lowering the price of drugs, legalization will increase drug use. Legalization also may affect attitudes toward, or taste for, drugs in a more fundamental way: For some—the young in particular—not only is there the kick from taking illegal drugs themselves, but also the challenge to authority implied by participating in an illegal activity. Making drugs legal will take some of the fun out of drugs for these people. Legalization, thus, can be expected to induce both movements along the demand curve for drugs, and shifts in the demand curve itself. The combined effect of the two changes on drug use is not clear-cut. Milton Friedman made this point in his luncheon address.

Friedman also presented to the conference interesting data on U.S. homicides and prisoners received during President Nixon's and Bush's "war on drugs," to argue that this war has had an enormous human cost in terms of lives lost and lives destroyed. In the decade of the 1950s, homicides averaged 4.8 per 100,000 people; the 1960s, 5.7; the 1970s, 9.5; and the 1980s, 9.1. For prisoners received, the figures were 47.2 per 100,000 population during the 1950s; 43.7 during the 1960s; 54.3 during the 1970s; and 79.7 during the 1980s. "There seems little doubt," said Friedman, "that the war on drugs is the single most important factor that produced such drastic increases."

Alcohol prohibition produced a similar pattern of homicides, according to Friedman. There was a steady rise in the homicide rate through World War I, and then an even steeper rise when prohibition became effective. That rise peaked in 1933, the year in which the prohibition amendment was repealed. The homicide rate then fell, at first rapidly, and then more slowly to the mid-1950s.

Friedman was not the only speaker at the conference to relate the U.S. experience during prohibition to present drug-policy questions. Jeffrey Miron (with Jeffrey Zwiebel) used data from the prohibition period to argue that drug legalization would cause only a small increase in drug use. They found that the death rate from cirrhosis of the liver, the death rate from alcoholism, the drunkenness arrest rate, and the number of first admittances to mental hospitals—all are good proxies for the consumption of alcohol during prohibition. At the beginning of prohibition, alcohol consumption declined significantly to approximately 25 to 45 percent of its pre-prohibition level. Beginning in the early 1920s, however, alcohol consumption increased steadily, and by 1928 it had returned to about 70 percent of its pre-prohibition level. Over the remaining five years of prohibition, consumption increased still further, although not as quickly as after the inception of prohibition. Most importantly, alcohol consumption increased only slightly after the removal of prohibition, rising about 10 percent from its value in 1928, and even less from its value in 1933.

Miron's conclusion: "There are theoretical reasons to anticipate small increases in consumption from legalization, and the evidence from prohibition confirms these expectations."

Michael Grossman disagrees. In a paper coauthored with Gary Becker and Kevin Murphy, Grossman attacks what he calls the conventional wisdom—that the consumption of illegal addictive substances is not responsive to price. Not only does Becker and Murphy's theoretical model of rational addiction contradict the conventional wisdom, but empirical application of the model to the demand for such legal addictive substances as cigarettes and gambling also supports the view that addictive substances are quite responsive to price.

The three authors fit models of rational addiction to cigarettes in a time series of state cross sections for the period 1955 to 1985 and find a long-run price elasticity of demand ranging from between $-.7$ and $-.8$ (meaning that a 10 percent decrease in price yields between a 7 and 8 percent increase in demand). They refer to a study by Mobilia, which applies the rational addiction framework to the demand for gambling at horse-racing tracks and finds the long-run price elasticity of demand for gambling at horse tracks to be $-.7$. Grossman considers a large, permanent reduction in the price of drugs. His conclusion: "Lower prices could significantly expand use even in the short run, and it would surely stimulate much greater addiction in the long run (long-run elasticities are greater than short-run ones). He adds: "If drug legalization is coupled with a drug education program, since drug use among the poor would be relatively more sensitive to the price fall than to greater information about harmful longer-run effects, drug addiction among the poor is likely to become more important relative to addiction among the middle classes and rich. For similar reasons, addiction among the young may rise more than among other segments of the population."

Victor Fuchs does not find the Grossman-Becker-Murphy conclusion of a substantial price elasticity of demand for drugs surprising. He points out that high demand elasticity for an addictive commodity necessarily implies that there is a good substitute for that commodity. What are these substitutes? Could they be other addictive commodities? Fuchs writes: "If, for instance, illegal drugs and alcohol are substitutes, the implications for public policy are different than if the substitution is between illegal drugs and bran muffins. We need to know more about the specifics of substitution that underlie these high elasticities."

From an economic perspective, a compelling line of argument to restrict drugs is that the consumption of drugs creates negative externalities—that is, does harm to others. Miron makes an important point when he notes that it is the differential externality that counts for public policy purposes. "Raising the price of marijuana relative to that of alcohol may result mainly in substitution from marijuana to alcohol. Since consumption of alcohol impairs one's ability to drive as much or more than does marijuana, the total reduction in externalities arising from the decrease in marijuana consumption may be substantially offset by the externalities created by increased consumption of alcohol. . . . More generally, prohibition of drugs may not significantly reduce externalities because it simply results in a substitution toward consumption of other goods that also create externalities." This is an extension to externalities of the above point made by Victor Fuchs.

No man (or woman) is an island, and the drug taker least of all. Those who are negatively impacted by the drug taker's usage are unborn babies, victims of automobile and other accidents, society at large . . ., and so on. Paul Taubman surveyed ad hoc evidence of the external effects of drug usage. The picture he paints is not a happy one. He predicts "a noticeable increase in the use of drug and new users and addicts. People other than the users will be affected, with children being one of the largely impacted groups." The costs to make these children "whole" will be large. There will probably be an increase in homelessness, which will impose health and other costs on society and its members. An increase in child, spouse, and parental abuse is likely, especially if cocaine and crack arc used more heavily.

Taubman may be right, but it is the size of the elasticity that is of interest. In his conclusion, Taubman writes: "Although the quality and quantity of the available research . . . should be improved, it seems likely that the price elasticity of demand is not zero." The critical question, of course, is precisely how much above zero is the price elasticity. A rational society may be willing to ban drugs for a price elasticity of -1 but not $-.1$. Taubman also ignores the differential externalities issues.

In the Corman, Joyce, and Mocan paper, weak evidence is found of any significant upturn in murders and murder rates since the introduction of crack in New York City. Murders increased from 151 per month in 1980 to 161 per month in 1989, a 6 percent increase in 9 years. If correct—and the Corman results were greeted with considerable skepticism—this finding is important and undermines Milton Friedman's point that drug prohibition leads to higher homicide rates.

Peter Reuter's paper is concerned with whether the punitive approach to drug control works. Reuter questions whether the 1980s constituted a period of tough drug-law enforcement as commonly assumed. To Reuter, the drop in marijuana sales to high-schoolers is related more to changed perception of health dangers than to enforcement risks.

Reuter reminds us that the range of policy options available to society is broader than the two extremes of "war on drugs" or complete permissiveness (Ethan Nadelmann made this same point). It is wrong to think that the simple retention of prohibition is equivalent to a war on drugs. It is the enforcement that really counts. He warns that vigorous enforcement against high-level dealers, smugglers, and refiners does little to raise the retail price but may engender corruption in transit nations and instability in producer countries (Milton Friedman agrees), arguing that there is no justification for what the United States has done in Colombia and Peru, where many lives have been lost. Instead, he favors enforcement moving to the fringes of drug policy, aimed at getting dependent users into treatment and making drug dealing less conspicuous so as to discourage novice users. He admits his case is far from proven.

LESSONS FROM ABROAD

The drug policy of the Netherlands stands at the more liberal fringe of the wide range of options open to society. Possession of and trafficking in all drugs are prohibited in the Netherlands. According to Eddy Engelsman, a Dutch government official, the Dutch do not enforce the prohibition as concerns the possession and sale of small quantities of drugs. People can sell and use cannabis products openly. Much attention to all drugs is paid in school education programs as part of an integrated approach aimed at the promotion of healthy life-styles. Drug use is not considered primarily a problem for police and the courts, but rather a matter of public health and social well-being.

As for the results of what the Dutch call their "pragmatic approach" to drug policy, Engelsman claims that in the age group up to 19 years, only 2.7 percent used cannabis during October 1990. (Mitchell Rosenthal disputes this figure. He claims that a subsequent study shows about one-third of Dutch boys 16 to 19 years old had smoked marijuana, and 25 percent of this same group had smoked marijuana within the month.) For heroin and cocaine, the Dutch figure is .5 percent. Approximately .15 percent of the national population are drug addicts, according to Engelsman—20,000 of the 15 million inhabitants. (Rosenthal argues, however, that since the adoption of more liberal policies in 1976, heroin addiction in the Netherlands has more than tripled, from an estimated 5,000 addicts in 1977 to between 15,000 to 20,000 today.) In 1988 there were 42 drug-related deaths in all of the Netherlands. Only 11 of the estimated 5,000 to 6,000 drug addicts died in Amsterdam in 1989. The percentage of intravenous drug users among the total group of AIDS patients (1,313 in July 1990) stands at 9.2 percent—a relatively low figure.

David Turner characterizes British drug policy as "pragmatic incoherence." On the one hand, there is the political policy on the national level, which is punitive, penal, and bellicose. On the other hand, there is the service policy on the local level, which is accommodating, individual-based, and liberal. The political policy stresses the criminal aspects of the drug problem, whereas the service policy stresses the social and medical dimensions of the problem. The political policy is strictly for public consumption, according to Turner. It contradicts and is meant to camouflage the service policy.

Turner champions the service policy, which he argues better meets the needs of the individual drug user and society. He claims that the political policy of the 1980s failed to reduce the drug supply. In fact, supply and use continued to rise. Demand reduction is viewed with considerable skepticism when it consists in penal sanctions, refusal of or loss of employment, eviction from housing, education, and the like. The danger is that such policies exasperate rather than mitigate the harm to the individual, society, and to public health. Implicitly, Turner's vision of the optimal drug policy comes closer to what the Dutch are doing rather than the actions of the British. Turner feels that U.S. drug policy has adversely affected that of Britain in that it has served as a model for the political policy he disdains.

Social Costs of Drug Use

The papers presented in this section are similar to the economics papers in that considerable emphasis is placed on the external consequences of drug use. Mark Kleiman justifies drug laws by arguing the "drug consumption leads some drug users to behave in ways that damage other people." He defines three categories of externalities: crimes, accidents, and public nuisances. He also notes involuntary exposure to drugs as a problem; the spread of communicable diseases; the problem when drug-using parents fail in their responsibility so that maladjusted children become a public charge; the drain drug-users make on public resources, and so on. Kleiman rejects the notion that present criminal and civil tort law can adequately deal with the externality problem because such laws are "very costly, very inefficient, and have limited capacity."

Kleiman does not favor outright drug prohibition. Rather, in the spirit of conventional "welfare economics," he seeks to define the "optimal set of control policies" or the optimal mix of taxes and regulations.

Implicitly, Kleiman appears to recognize that most of the arguments he makes about the external consequences of drug use apply with equal force to alcohol and tobacco use. Thus, he favors an optimal set of control policies for their use as well as the use of drugs—a universal nondiscriminating approach, so to speak.

As is often the case with those who seek to design optimal policies, Kleiman does not consider the problem of (1) whether government subscribes to the same welfare function as he does, and (2) whether government is competent to design and enforce these optimal policies, even if it does agree with the experts' social welfare function. Moreover, as Joel Hay points out, the taxes required to compensate for externalities in certain drug categories could be so high as to guarantee a flourishing black market. The bottom line in describing Mark Kleiman's drug-policy views would appear to be that he favors legalization for most drugs but with considerably more taxes and controls than the conventional legalization advocates would agree to.

This is not the case with Joel Hay, whose paper also deals with the externalities issue. He writes, "I would definitely prefer a real drug war, with swift and certain punishment of casual drug users, to a drug-legalization surrender." Yet, Hay's 1990 estimates of the yearly externality costs of substance abuse in the United States are $21.79 billion for cocaine, $1.21 billion for heroin, $116.19 billion for tobacco, and $52.24 billion for alcohol. The externalities problem for alcohol and tobacco, based on this evidence, would appear far more serious than for drugs.

According to Hay, one reason for the high externality-cost figures for tobacco and alcohol is precisely that they are legal. If drugs were legal, too, their consumption would skyrocket and drug-externality costs would rival those of alcohol and tobacco. The evidence on high elasticities has not been persuasive, however. A further problem raised by Hay's paper is whether it is proper for society's drug policy to focus exclusively on the minimization of externality costs. To be sure, external costs are important, but they are not—or, at least, should not be—the sole factor driving a nation's drug policy.

In his paper, Mitchell Rosenthal first tries to explain the acrimony over U.S. drug policy, which he relates to the different perspectives of various analysts, as well as to the symbolism attached to policy alternatives. He, too, is concerned with drug-use externalities, and charges that drug-legalization advocates downplay the social disorder that results from drug abuse. Drug abuse is high among the homeless (particularly homeless women with children), teenage runaways, mentally ill, child abusers, and so on. But is drug abuse the cause of homelessness, teenage runaways, mental illness, or is it the result? Rosenthal clearly believes the former, and more. He writes: "Drug abuse is to blame for rising levels of violence, and not only murder, rape, robbery, and assault."

A further reason Rosenthal favors continued criminalization is that the criminal justice system puts pressure on drug users to seek treatment. "Dysfunctional drug abusers, leading lives of extraordinary dangers and disorder (and, therefore, most in need of treatment), are least likely to come to treatment by any route other than the criminal justice system," he writes. Rosenthal notes that he would prefer treating drug abuse as a health rather than a criminal issue— and favors mandatory treatment via civil commitment. Mandatory treatment, he notes, is likely to be quite controversial.

Ethan Nadelmann points out the wide variety of drug-policy alternatives from the very harsh Malaysian and Singaporean models to the more tolerant models found in the Netherlands. He argues that both the "legalization advocates" and "prohibitionists" are split among themselves, as well as one another, on moral, ideological, and political grounds. Moreover, objective analysis is made difficult by the fact that the analyses of the costs and benefits of any given policy proposal "are powerfully shaped by the ideological and moral values of the analysts." A common middle ground, Nadelmann suggests, is having minimization of loss of life and physical pain as a drug-policy objective.

LEGAL IMPLICATIONS

Ira Glasser began this session with a discussion that clarified a number of the issues—focusing on the goal of drug prohibition. Are we trying to improve health by making drugs illegal? He suggests that this is unlikely and quotes a survey result in which 54 percent answered negatively to the health concern. Instead, he argues, the issue is crime. Most Americans are upset with drugs and drug policy because of the apparent crime that results from drug use, not because of the tragic consequences for cocaine babies. The average American is bothered by increased lawlessness, and particularly by random violence. Much of this random violence, Glasser asserts, is drug-related. There is a need to get money, and the specific drugs involved are cocaine and crack.

There is evidence, Glasser argues, that laws do not change usage. Instead, he agrees with Mugford that culture is most important. Cigarette smoking has experienced a big drop without any change in the laws. It is the culture specifically that has changed.

Further, there is a more general point. Criminal law is not an effective way to reduce crime, claims Glasser. It is estimated that there are 34 million crimes per year and that 31 million of them go undetected. It is necessary to deal with underlying social problems, says Glasser.

Although the points Glasser raises are useful, they do not stand unchallenged. To say that laws cannot affect behavior is like saying that price does not affect quantity purchased. Both statements appeal to common sense, but neither one is true. What may be true is that the penalties required to make the laws bite are not acceptable to society. There is a structure of laws and penalties that affect behavior, however. Proponents of prohibition believe that the necessary penalties are not too great and that society should impose them. Whether those penalties can be effective is an unanswered question.

The major difficulty with the Glasser argument is that he wins it by setting up a straw man. Once the argument is made that society does not care about the health costs of drugs, but only about the crime costs, his case is won. Few serious proponents of prohibition would argue that violent crime will rise if drugs are decriminalized. They worry about increases in more subtle "crimes," such as causing highway fatalities, and creating a social environment that stifles productivity and creativity. To be sure, the prohibitionists have yet to show that the two necessary conditions to sustain their argument hold. It has yet to be documented that drug use will increase substantially with decriminalization; nor has it been shown that the differential impact of drugs is to impair judgment and affect productivity in a highly adverse fashion. Arguing the case on the basis of the presumed effect of drugs on violent crime alone begs many of the important questions, however.

Edwin Meese argues vigorously against decriminalization of drugs. He objects to the tendency (for example, by Glasser) to lump all social problems with drug problems. Social problems existed before crack cocaine was a problem, and there is no evidence that elimination of poverty would reduce the use of drugs. Indeed, expenditures on many (although not all) addictive goods rise with income.

Legalization involves a major change in social policy, and such a change has not been carefully articulated by proponents of decriminalization. Many questions come to mind; for example: Who will be permitted to sell drugs? Will sales be restricted to state stores or licensed stores? Will there be quantity limitations on the amounts purchased? Will there be restrictions on the way in which the drugs are packaged?

In thinking about decriminalization of drugs, Meese points out four key concerns: First, which problems would be alleviated by legalization? Second, what benefits would accrue by legalization? Third, what new problems would be created? Fourth, how high will taxes be? If the price is too high, then incentives are created for a black market and no problems are solved. If the price is allowed to be very low, then usage may be expected to be high. Cigarette and alcohol use are good examples. Nicotine and alcohol are far more detrimental to society in total because usage is so high. Legalization of drugs with a low price may be expected to follow similar patterns.

Meese points out the historical perspective. The drug problem is really one of the 1970s and 1980s. Further, there is currently a trend away from drug use, especially among the employed and those in school. The American public is overwhelmingly against drug decriminalization. There are factual reasons to support the widespread view.

Many individuals who are arrested are under the influence of drugs when arrested but their crimes are unrelated to drugs. This does not imply, however, that drugs induce these individuals to commit crimes. What is most likely is that those who are most likely to commit crimes of any kind are also most likely to use drugs.

Under any legalization scheme, minors are almost certain to be prohibited access to drugs. This means that youth will become the target of the black marketeers.

Meese concludes by reporting that a large proportion of individuals state that they do not use drugs because their illegality is a deterrent. Making drugs legal would substantially increase their usage, Meese believes.

James Ostrowski began his conference presentation with the provocative statement that the war on drugs should be renamed the war on blacks, since they are the main victims of drug-enforcement policy. Ostrowski presents arguments made by proponents of prohibition and then attacks them.

Ostrowski tells us that William Bennett argues that the black market will still supply drugs even if drugs are legalized. Again the point is made that no one expects children to be allowed access to drugs, so there will be a natural illegal demand by youth. Ostrowski suggests that the drugs will be legally produced drugs for adults and so their quality and purity should be higher. The gray market, he argues, is not as harmful as the black market.

Ostrowski attacks James Q. Wilson's boasts of success in containment of heroin. He points out that to claim success, it must be shown that individuals who quit using heroin do not switch to something equally bad or, in the cases of some drugs, perhaps worse. Additionally, it is important to determine how much of the decrease is due to the policy and how much is due to other factors—for example, the introduction to the market of "superior" products.

He goes on to argue that the prohibitionist view is an elitist one which ascribes no sense to typical U.S. citizens. He does not believe that the absence of prohibition would place them up to their necks in drugs. Ostrowski concludes by arguing that prohibition does much harm to third parties without much positive effect on drug use. Society should use self-restraint as the major limitation on drugs use, he concludes.

James Peterson takes the opposite view. He says that the rhetoric from the legalization group has been inflammatory, that "prohibitionist" is a propaganda term. Further, he says, it is important to speak carefully about what would happen to the black community under various legal regimes. The data are sketchy, but Peterson argues that some lessons can be learned from examining the increase in alcohol consumption associated with lowering the drinking age to 18.

Like Meese, Peterson presents some evidence on national sentiment against decriminalization of drugs. In 1978 there was a movement toward legalization which was killed off by the outcries of "mom and pop." There is hardly a groundswell of support for decriminalization, he points out.

Further, what evidence we do have on the effects of decriminalization on drug use is not encouraging. Alaska recently decriminalized the use of marijuana and Alaskan usage rates of that drug are now about twice those of the rest of the country.

Since there is only very little evidence on the effects of legalization on usage, and since these data go to the heart of the argument against legalization, it is important to examine that evidence closely. In particular, it would be useful to know whether the level of usage in Alaska went up significantly after the law was changed and whether this increase can be attributed to decriminalization. It also would be useful to establish whether the level of alcohol usage went down after the Alaskan marijuana law was changed. If increased use of marijuana reflected the substitution of marijuana for alcohol rather than for other legal goods, the consequences of the Alaskan law change would be put in a different light.

Other evidence comes from Spain, which had tough laws against drug usage. Their relaxation in 1983 was followed by a large influx of drugs, which has now created a backlash. European data are interesting, but it must be remembered that the possibility for intra-Europe migration may prevent those lessons from being applied directly to the United States.

Peterson points out that even if drug crime is eliminated, there may be a transfer by drug criminals toward other kinds of crime. Just as the end of alcohol prohibition resulted in the growth of organized crime's interest in gambling, making drugs legal may not reduce the overall crime rate very much, if at all. Indeed, Peterson claims, the evidence shows that robbery rates have fallen as crimes have been transferred to drugs.

There is also evidence that drug usage and highway accidents are linked. A recent study found that a significant proportion of truckers had marijuana in their blood at the time of an accident.

MEDICAL AND HEALTH IMPLICATIONS

Lester Grinspoon opened this session by discussing the medical value of marijuana. He documents its usage in treating nausea, especially in association with chemotherapy. It can also be used to retard damage to eyesight in certain conditions. It is the drug of choice in treating muscle spasms, and has been especially effective in treating patients with multiple sclerosis.

Grinspoon argues that the marijuana laws are irrational. Morphine can be used for medical purposes and marijuana cannot, even though the downside on morphine is much more pronounced. Perhaps. Rightly or wrongly, however, the illegality of marijuana is based on its popularity and usage in the nonmedical context, which is less pronounced for morphine and similar drugs.

Grinspoon concludes with a more controversial statement. He argues that there are nonmedical virtues to marijuana. Many individuals use it regularly and find it helpful in their work. This point begs for substantiation because others in the conference provide documentation that marijuana is harmful, not helpful, to productivity.

A discussion followed in which the general consensus, even among those opposed to drug legalization, was that marijuana should be permitted for legitimate medical purposes. The argument is over the definition of legitimate use.

Leong Way began with the point that the law is not based rationally on the legality of the drug. He explains that drugs affect biological processes for two reasons: Individuals like the drug and/or a physical dependence is created.

All drugs are not alike in their potential addictiveness. The most addictive are cocaine and amphetamines, followed by heroin and morphine. The least addictive are marijuana and LSD.

It is important to recognize that physical dependence is not the same as emotional dependence. It is relatively easy to cure the physical dependence to heroin, but the emotional dependence is much more difficult to cure.

Addiction is one dimension on which drugs can be ranked. The harm they do to the individual is another. Even though heroin and morphine are highly addictive, for example, they do not have major adverse consequences for motor activity or for the cardiovascular system.

With this in mind, Way provides a hierarchy of drugs, taking into account both addictiveness and harm. Way is clear that the weighting of addictiveness and harm are subjective. Even the measure of harm is not unambiguous, however, since it depends on the weights attached to the various kinds of health impediments. This having been said, his ranking is interesting. At the top, he places cocaine and alcohol; at the bottom, marijuana and tobacco.

Avram Goldstein says the key issue is finding the right balance. He makes a number of points.

First, the discussion should avoid hyperbole and instead should focus on which issues can be clarified with more data.

Second, drugs should not be thought of as an ordinary commodity. They have profound biological effects but most of the decriminalization debate has been uninformed as to toxicological aspects. All drugs are potentially hazardous, and the toxicity varies significantly across people.

Third, the libertarian position is naive. All of society is affected by drug addiction. We cannot ignore those who hurt themselves. If we bear the costs, then we have the right to regulate.

Fourth, total legalization would create new problems. Our experience with alcohol and tobacco shows that current regulation of those substances is hardly the ideal model to be followed. Alcohol and tobacco are by far our greatest problems.

Fifth, criminalizing use per se is probably counterproductive. Total victory over drugs is unattainable. The draw of drugs is simply too great. Evidence of animals self-administering drugs to the point of death is relevant and troublesome.

Sixth, interdiction is not a cost-effective policy. The ability to substitute on the supply side is too great. Little can be accomplished if we do not reduce demand.

John Morgan followed by telling the story of Jamaica ginger extract, which poisoned many Americans and paralyzed 50,000 people. This was a drug that rose to prominence during prohibition as an inferior substitute for high-quality alcohol products.

Morgan makes the important point that prohibition tends to generate more potent forms of the substance. If caffeine were illegal, it would likely come in little tablets that were easily smuggled, not in coffee. The more concentrated forms are more dangerous and may actually lead to greater total use.

Kildare Clarke brings to the debate his experience in an inner-city hospital. He argues that leaving drug policy as it is now is tantamount to genocide. Clarke provides data on the trends in violent crime in the New York City area. He finds that there has been a substitution of stab wounds for gunshot wounds. Although the killing and injury are found primarily in the poorer neighborhoods, the big drug hauls are in wealthy neighborhoods. Thus, the major trafficking in drugs cannot be thought to be a poor black man's problem.

Another key issue is that of treatment. Even if drugs remain illegal, treatment can be made more available. Then the results of drug abuse can be dealt with more effectively.

Robert Millman tells us that drug usage actually has declined from its peak in 1979, but the distribution of usage has changed dramatically. It has gone from an epidemic, which implies broad usage, to being endemic and attacking only those in high-risk groups.

Millman echoes the earlier point that drugs are very different and should be treated differently. The pharmacology is important here. Cocaine, for example, is not classically addicting, but it is strongly reinforcing. The drugs that tend to be most reinforcing are those with most rapid onset and rapid waning. This leads to hyperalertness and therefore paranoia. Heroin leads to ease and is followed by irritability. The important lesson is that since effects are different, the law should deal with them differently.

The dinner speaker was Melvyn Levitsky. He defended the federal government's position on drug policy. A strong opponent of legalization, Levitsky argued that the government's policies were working, both on the supply side and on the demand side. Drug usage in high schools is tapering off, he argued, reflecting decreases in demand that have resulted from antidrug campaigns. Further, he said that the price of drugs was rising in the cities, which he interpreted as evidence that supply interdiction was working.

The audience was skeptical. Most felt that the supply of drugs was quite elastic and that interruption of one country's supply generally shifted production to another country. Some voiced the concern that the United States did not have the right to do to countries what our drug policy has done to Colombia, for example.

Many voiced the view that this conference had the effect of changing views. Positions that started out somewhat polarized grew a bit closer. Virtually everyone agreed at the end that there were some absurd prohibitions, like the one against medical use of cannabis. Even strong proponents of decriminalization, however, accept the view that there must be some regulation of drugs—for example, use by children. Those against legalization made convincing the point that simple adoption of the most extreme libertarian position was not practical, nor supported by the public. Those in favor of legalization made convincing arguments that there are major flaws in current policy that could be remedied by some forms of decriminalization.

PART ONE

HISTORICAL OVERVIEW

THE WRONG QUESTION: CRITICAL NOTES ON THE DECRIMINALIZATION DEBATE

Franklin E. Zimring and Gordon Hawkins

I. INTRODUCTION

This chapter is both a summary and a critique of the current debate about decriminalization of drugs in the United States. Section II begins by rehearsing the argument in favor of decriminalization advanced in the mid-nineteenth century by John Stuart Mill in *On Liberty* and the late nineteenth-century critique of that argument advanced by James Fitzjames Stephen, "the most powerful and penetrating of the contemporary critics of John Stuart Mill" (Quinton, 1978:87). The Mill–Stephen exchange seems to us to be exhaustive of most of the ideas currently employed in what we called the "polar debate" about drug decriminalization in the United States, a debate in which both sides believe that the only significant question is whether drugs should be prohibited by criminal law.

Section III adds two important new wrinkles present in the late twentieth-century continuation of the Mill–Stephen exchange as it relates to drugs. These new points of emphasis, both prominent in the work of John Kaplan, are the significant role of the costs of maintaining a criminal prohibition in the calculus of policy and the likelihood that a separate cost-benefit analysis for each of a wide variety of drugs will produce differing conclusions for different drugs.

Section IV restates the decriminalization debate as a clash of presumptions in which those who favor decriminalization argue that when the facts are uncertain, government should presume that a policy that enhances liberty will best serve the public good, while those who support continuation of the criminal sanction argue that in uncertainty it is safest to presume that a continuation of current policy will maximize public welfare. This conservative presumption explains why those who favor continuing prohibition do not also support extension of prohibition to current licit substances. Preferring known to unknown evils is a legitimate technique of policy analysis in the drug area. There is value, too, in seeing the decriminalization debate as a competition of two presumptions, each with significant support in the American political tradition.

Section V outlines our critique of the polar debate, which we find unfortunate in two respects. First, it puts emphasis on the question of whether the criminal law should be used in drug control when almost always the more important questions concern *how* rather than *whether* criminal law will be used to control drugs. Second, the polar debate involves what we shall call "trickle-down" methods of policy determination. Both sides in the decriminalization debate think the details of correct policy can work themselves out once the broad strokes of criminal justice policy are in place. It is assumed that the details of effective drug control can be inferred once the right answers to broad policy questions have been determined. It is more plausible, we believe, to invest in a process of "trickle-up" policy analysis in which priority problems are identified and resources allocated in real-world settings to particular problems.

II. John Stuart Mill and James Fitzjames Stephen

"In discussing drug control and freedom," say Bakalar and Grinspoon, "it still makes sense to start with John Stuart Mill's essay *On Liberty*" (Bakalar and Grinspoon, 1984:1). It does make sense because Mill was particularly concerned about drug-control laws, and his statement of how they infringed on human liberty is a model of forceful argument. Writing in the 1850s at the time of America's first experiment with prohibition, he said, "Under the name of preventing intemperance the people of . . . nearly half of the United States, have been interdicted by law from making any use whatever of fermented drinks, except for medical purposes: for prohibition of their sale is in fact, as it is intended to be, prohibition of their use." He described this development as a "gross usurpation upon the liberty of private life" and an "important example of illegitimate interference with the rightful liberty of the individual" (Mill, 1859:143–45).

"No person," he wrote, "ought to be punished simply for being drunk" (Mill,

1859:138). He also objected to taxes designed to limit consumption: "To tax stimulants for the sole purpose of making them more difficult to be obtained is a measure differing only in degree from their entire prohibition" (Mill, 1859:156). He was opposed to laws requiring the certificate of a medical practitioner for the purchase of dangerous drugs for this, he said, "would make it sometimes impossible, always expensive" to obtain them. Although he did allow that "such a precaution, for example, as that of labelling a drug with some word expressive of its dangerous character, may be enforced without violation of liberty" because "the buyer cannot wish not to know that the thing he possesses has poisonous qualities" (Mill, 1859:152).

The basic principle underlying Mill's attitude to drug control was stated in an often-quoted passage which says:

> that the sole end for which mankind are warranted, individually or collectively, in interfering with the liberty of action of any of their members is self-protection. That the only purpose for which power can be rightfully exercised over any member of a civilized community against his will, is to prevent harm to others. His own good, either physical or moral, is not a sufficient warrant, he cannot rightfully be compelled to do or forbear because it would be better for him to do so, because it will make him happier, because, in the opinion of others, to do so would be wise or even right. (Mill, 1859:72–73)

Less often cited are Mill's four qualifications on this principle that may be regarded as significant in relation to drug control. The first of these concerns children and young persons. "It is, perhaps, hardly necessary to say," he wrote, "that this doctrine is meant to apply only to human beings in the maturity of their faculties. We are not speaking of children, or of young persons below the age which the law may fix as that of manhood or womanhood. Those who are still in a state to require being taken care of by others, must be protected against their own actions as well as against external injury" (Mill, 1859:73). Indeed, he thought that an important reason why society should *not* have "the power to issue commands and enforce obedience in the personal concerns of [adult] individuals" was that it "has had absolute power over them during all the early portion of their existence; it has had the whole period of childhood and nonage in which to try whether it could make them capable of rational conduct in life" (Mill, 1859:139).

With regard to this exception, one of Mill's more cogent critics, John Kaplan, has argued that "Mill's exception for the young is unpersuasive" in that making a drug "available to adults would render completely unenforceable any effort to prevent the young from having access to the drug." "The median age for first heroin use is currently less than nineteen," said Kaplan, "and it is quite likely that giving adults freer access to the drug would considerably increase the number of users younger than this. That at least would be the natural conclusion we might derive from our experience with alcohol and tobacco, where our laws attempting to keep these drugs from the young have been rendered notoriously ineffective by their complete availability to adults." He suggests that Mill might have "countenanced a law making the drug unavailable to all on the ground that this was the only way of protecting youth" (Kaplan, 1983:104).

This suggestion itself is unpersuasive, however, for two reasons. In the first place, Mill, who was adamantly opposed to the prohibition of alcohol and other drugs, cannot have been unaware that giving adults free access to them raised some problems for anyone attempting to keep them from the young. In the second place, acceptance of the principle that the protection of children justified restrictions of this nature on adults would in large measure reduce adults to the status of children and, to use Mill's own words, "there is no violation of liberty which it would not justify" (Mill, 1859:146).

As a matter of fact, Mill did not think that prohibition was a feasible policy even in relation to adults, and he noted that in America "the impracticability of executing the law has caused its repeal in several of the States which had adopted it" (Mill, 1859:145). His objection to it was based on the more fundamental ground that the prohibition movement represented acceptance of a "doctrine [that] ascribes to all mankind a vested interest in each other's moral, intellectual, and even physical perfection, to be defined by each claimant according to his own standard." He viewed this as "monstrous," particularly in view of the fact that "there are many who consider as an injury to themselves any conduct which they have a distaste for, and resent it as an outrage to their feelings" (Mill, 1859:140, 146).

The second exception to his principle related to "backward states of society in which the race itself may be considered as in its nonage." Despotism, Mill said, "is a legitimate mode of government in dealing with barbarians" (Mill, 1859:73). As we shall see, Mill's most notable contemporary critic, James Fitz-james Stephen, regarded this exception as constituting a fatal flaw in Mill's argument, for in Stephen's view even in advanced, civilized communities there was "an enormous mass" of people who in relevant respects were in effect barbarians (Stephen, 1873:72).

The third exception to Mill's principle relevant to drug control concerns what he called "the right inherent in society, to ward off crimes against itself by antecedent precautions." This he said implied "obvious limitations to the maxim, that purely self-regarding misconduct cannot properly be meddled with in the way of prevention or punishment." In particular, he said:

> Drunkenness, for example, in ordinary cases, is not a fit subject for legislative interference; . . . I should deem it perfectly legitimate that a person, who had once been convicted of any act of violence to others under the influence of drink, should be placed under a special legal restriction, personal to himself;

that if he were afterwards found drunk, he should be liable to a penalty, and that if when in that state he committed another offence, the punishment to which he would be liable for that other offence should be increased in severity. The making himself drunk, in a person whom drunkenness excites to do harm to others, is a crime against others. (Mill, 1859:153)

[*Note*: Over a century later, the British Committee on Mentally Abnormal Offenders proposed that there should be an offense of "dangerous intoxication" punishable by one year's imprisonment for a first offense and three years for a second or subsequent offense. The committee, however, did not go so far as Mill, who thought that intoxication alone should incur a penalty in the case of those previously convicted of violence while drunk. Their recommendation was intended to deal with people who, having become violent while intoxicated, might otherwise avoid conviction on the ground that they had lacked the intent necessary for the alleged offense. (Great Britain, Home Office, 1975:235–37)]

This third exception to Mill's principle might at first glance seem to be contrary to both his general commitment to individual liberty and his particular concern with the preventive function of government as "liable to be abused to the prejudice of liberty." For in that connection he observed that "there is hardly any part of the legitimate freedom of action of a human being which would not admit of being represented, and fairly too, as increasing the facilities for some form or other of delinquency" (Mill, 1859:151). In fact, however, there is no contradiction involved: Approval of the use of criminal law to deal coercively or punitively with persons who, under the influence of a drug, commit crimes that harm others in no way conflicts with the principles that it should *not* be used against those whose conduct does no direct harm to others.

The fourth and final exception to his principle related to the possibility of an individual's selling himself into slavery, which, according to Mill, the state had a right to prevent:

The ground for thus limiting [an individual's] power of voluntarily disposing of his own lot in life is apparent, and is very clearly seen in this extreme case. The reason for not interfering unless for the sake of others, with a person's voluntary acts, is consideration for his liberty. But by selling himself for a slave, he abdicates his liberty; he forgoes any future use of it, beyond that single act. He therefore defeats, in his own case, the very purpose which is the justification of allowing him to dispose of himself. He is no longer free; but is thenceforth in a position which has no longer the presumption in its favor, that would be afforded by his voluntarily remaining in it. The principle of freedom cannot require that he should be free not to be free. It is not freedom, to be allowed to alienate his freedom. These reasons, the force of which is so conspicuous in this peculiar case, are evidently of far wider application. (Mill, 1859:157–58)

John Kaplan has questioned whether this "far wider application" might permit the government to prohibit heroin on the ground that heroin addiction is a species of slavery to which the user is at risk (Kaplan, 1983:106). It seems unlikely that Mill would have accepted this. In first place, Mill had nothing to say about acts that might involve *some risk* of slavery; and the use of heroin merely involves some risk of addiction. In the second place, Mill cannot have been unaware of both alcohol and opiate addiction, yet he makes no mention of them in this context. De Quincey's widely acclaimed *Confessions of an English Opium Eater*, incidentally, first appeared in 1821, 38 years before the publication of *On Liberty*.

However one may interpret the various limits on the application of his central principle, there is no doubt either about Mill's essential position or the relevance of his ideas to America today. In fact, in contemporary America, as in nineteenth-century England, "there are many who consider as an injury to themselves any conduct which they have a distaste for, and resent it as an outrage to their feelings" (Mill, 1859:140). Nor is this peculiar to America. Indeed Mill himself said, "It is not difficult to show, by abundant instances, that to extend the bounds of what may be called moral police, until it encroaches on the most unquestionably legitimate liberty of the individual, is *one of the most universal of all human propensities*" (Mill, 1859:140–41; emphasis added). Mill went on to give numerous instances of the way in which the public in his own and other countries "improperly invests its own preferences with the character of moral laws"; prohibition in America is only one such example.

Mill regarded America as providing a singularly striking example of a country in which the government and the public upheld "the pretension that no person shall enjoy any pleasure which they think wrong." There was, he noted, "in the modern world" a strong tendency toward a democratic constitution of society accompanied by popular political institutions. Moreover, he said that "in the country where this tendency is most completely realised—where both society and the government are most democratic—the United States—the feeling of the majority, . . . operates as a tolerably effectual sumptuary law." Where public opinion did not provide sufficient sanction, it was accepted that there was "an unlimited right in the public . . . to prohibit by law everything which it thinks wrong" (Mill, 1859:143–44).

What Mill saw as characteristic of America in the early nineteenth century remains true in the late twentieth century. Mill's maxim that "the individual is not accountable to society for his actions, in so far as these concern the interests of no person but himself" (Mill, 1859:149) is no more generally accepted as a fundamental principle today than it was in 1859. Gore Vidal may have exaggerated when he said that the American people are "devoted to the idea of sin and its punishment" (Vidal, 1972:375). It is certainly true that "in this country we have a highly moralistic criminal law and a long tradition of using it as an instrument for coercing men toward virtue" (Morris and Hawkins, 1970:5). Now as then it is probable that a great many Americans would echo Thomas Carlyle's angry reaction to Mill's essay. "As if," he said, "it were a sin to control, or coerce into better methods, human swine in any way; . . . . Ach Gott im Himmel!" (Packe, 1954:405).

If it makes sense in discussing drug control and freedom to start with John Stuart Mill's essay *On Liberty*, it makes equally good sense to follow with his most formidable contemporary critic's *Liberty, Equality and Fraternity*. One of the things that makes Stephen's critique formidable is that he shared Mill's basic assumptions. As Anthony Quinton has put it, Stephen's assumptions "were simply a more firmly held version of Mill's own first principles. He criticized Mill's deductions from utilitarian principles from the inside." Like Mill, he did not regard as natural rights the ideals of the French revolutionary formula that he took for his title. He saw them as "valuable only to the extent that they contribute to the overriding end of the general happiness and, in Stephen's view, they did so only in a very qualified fashion" (Quinton, 1978:87–88).

Mill died only a few months after Stephen's book appeared, but he is on record as having said that Stephen "does not know what he is arguing against" (White, 1967:1). Stephen, however, was quite clear that he was arguing against what he called Mill's "religious dogma of liberty" (Stephen, 1873:54). In what has been called "the finest exposition of conservative thought in the latter half of the nineteenth century" (Barker, 1915:172), displaying that "certain brutal directness of mind" (Quinton, 1978:87) that characterized all his polemical writings, Stephen subjected that "dogma" to vigorous criticism.

In particular, he was sharply critical of Mill's statement that "as soon as mankind have attained the capacity for being guided to their own improvement by conviction or persuasion (a period long since reached in all nations with whom we need here concern ourselves), compulsion either in the direct form, or in that of pains and penalties for noncompliance, is no longer admissible as a means to their own good, and is justifiable only for the security of others" (Mill, 1859:73–74). This, said Stephen, represented an exception or qualification to Mill's libertarian principle and reduced his doctrine either to an empty commonplace that no one would dispute or to an unproved and incredible assertion about the state of human society. Said Stephen:

> Either then the exception means only that superior wisdom is not in every case a reason why one man should control another—which is a mere commonplace—or else it means that in all the countries which we are accustomed to call civilised the mass of adults are so well acquainted with their own interests and so much disposed to pursue them that no compulsion or restraint put upon any of them by any others for the purpose of promoting their interests can really promote them. No one can doubt the importance of this assertion, but where is the proof of it? (Stephen, 1873:67–68)

Stephen noted that Mill had allowed that compulsion was justified as a means of dealing with barbarians, "provided the end be their improvement, and the means justified by actually effecting that end" because "liberty as a principle has no application to any state of things anterior to the time when mankind have become capable of being improved by free and equal discussion" (Mill, 1859:73). He interpreted Mill as saying, however, that "there is a period now generally reached all over Europe and America, at which discussion takes the place of compulsion, and in which people when they know what is good for them generally do it. When this period is reached, compulsion may be laid aside" (Stephen, 1873:69).

> To this, I [Stephen] should say that no such period has as yet been reached anywhere, and that there is no prospect of its being reached anywhere within any assignable time. Where, in the very most advanced and civilised communities, will you find any class of persons whose views or whose conduct on subjects on which they are interested are regulated even in the main by the results of free discussion . . . of ten thousand people who get drunk is there one who could say with truth that he did so because he had been brought to think in full deliberation and after free discussion that it was wise to get drunk? (Stephen, 1873:69)

In Stephen's view, the idea that "in all nations with whom we need here concern ourselves" the period had long since been reached in which mankind have "attained the capacity of being guided to their own improvement by conviction or persuasion" was nonsensical.

Stephen not only saw no objection to people being coerced for their own good but regarded it as necessary. He said:

> Men are so constructed that whatever theory as to goodness and badness we choose to adopt, there are and always will be in the world an enormous mass of bad and indifferent people—people who deliberately do all sorts of things which they ought not to do, and leave undone all sorts of things which they ought to do. Estimate the proportion of men and women who are selfish, sensual, frivolous, idle, absolutely commonplace and wrapped up in the smallest of petty routines, and consider how far the freest of free discussion is likely to improve them. The only way by which it is practically possible to act upon them at all is by compulsion or restraint . . . the utmost conceivable liberty which could be bestowed upon them would not in the least degree tend to improve them. (Stephen, 1878:72–73)

It is somewhat ironic that Mill, who had attacked English judges for their "extraordinary want of knowledge of human nature and life, which continually astonishes us in English lawyers" (Mill, 1859:126), was here in effect being told by an English judge that his own knowledge of human nature and life was defective. Stephen took the view that, human nature being what it was, it was necessary for society to use criminal law to enforce society's moral code whether or not breaches of it caused harm to others.

"Criminal law in this country," he said, "is actually applied to the suppression of vice and so to the promotion of virtue to a very considerable extent; and I say this is right." In his view, the criminal law was "in the nature of a persecution of the grosser forms of vice" and he saw nothing wrong with that, because "the object of promoting virtue and preventing vice must be admitted to be a good one." It was therefore necessary "to put a restraint upon vice, not to such an extent merely as is necessary for definite self-protection, but generally on the ground that vice is a bad thing from which men ought by appropriate means to restrain each other" (Stephen, 1873:143, 150, 152); and amongst those appropriate means he included criminal law.

Stephen complains that in Mill's essay "there is hardly anything . . . which can properly be called proof as distinguished from enunciation or assertion" (Stephen, 1873:56; see also 67, 74). It is true that the principles enunciated by Mill are not supported by any proof; and in fact are not susceptible of proof or logical demonstration. When they have read all the arguments in the debate on law and morals initiated by Mill, some readers may feel, with Herbert Packer, that "there is, perhaps, not much further to be said about it" (Packer, 1968:251). Stephen's case against Mill was not directed at Mill's principles so much as at their application in the real world, however; and in this connection some modern commentators have, tacitly at least, supported Stephen.

In our own time, the notion that Mill's knowledge of human nature was deficient has been echoed by H. L. A. Hart, who says that:

> Underlying Mill's extreme fear of paternalism there perhaps is a conception of what a normal human being is like which now seems not to correspond to the facts. Mill, in fact, endows him with too much of the psychology of a middle-aged man whose desires are relatively fixed, not liable to be artificially stimulated by external influences; who knows what he wants and what gives him satisfaction or happiness; and who pursues these things when he can.

Hart maintains that Mill carried his protests against paternalism "to lengths that may now appear to us fantastic."

In particular, Hart cites Mill's criticism of restrictions on the sale of drugs as interferences with the liberty of the would-be purchaser, and says: "No doubt if we no longer sympathize with this criticism this is due, in part, to a general decline in the belief that individuals know their own interests best, and to an increased awareness of a great range of factors which diminish the significance to be attached to an apparently free choice or to consent." In this connection, Hart takes the view that "a modification in Mill's principles is required." Such a modification, he argues, need not abandon Mill's objection to the use of criminal law to enforce morality. It would "only have to provide that harming others is something we may still seek to prevent by the use of the criminal law, even when the victims consent to or assist in the acts which are harmful to them" (Hart, 1963:32–33). It is clear that acceptance of this modification of Mill's principle provides a rationale for a drug-prohibition policy directed at traffickers and purveyors if not consumers.

John Kaplan is another critic who appears to disagree with Mill's "conception of what a normal human being is like." He says, "It almost seems to be the nature of man to regard some types of predominantly self-harming conduct as, for one reason or another, the proper subject of official prohibition." He asserts that "the great majority of us do not agree with Mill's principle to begin with. Indeed, no modern state (or, so far as is known, any premodern state) has ever followed Mill's principle with respect to all activities."

Kaplan cites, as an example of "confrontation between Mill's principle and our nation's actions," the laws in about half of the American states requiring that motorcyclists wear protective helmets, although the helmetless cyclist does not pose any threat or cause any harm to others. In this case, the justification for the law is that the helmetless cyclists expose all of us to the risk that we as taxpayers may, in the case of an accident, have to pay for expensive hospital treatment and, if they have families, to provide public assistance for them (Kaplan, 1983:106–7).

As with Stephen, it is the application of Mill's doctrine to the real world that Kaplan questions. He prefaces his discussion of the likely costs of legalizing cocaine by noting that the question is one that cannot be decided by reference to John Stuart Mill's "simple principle." Mill's rule regarding self-harming conduct, he says, is "probably unworkable in a complex, industrial society—particularly one that is a welfare state" and, moreover, it "seems singularly inappropriate when it is applied to a habit-forming, psychoactive drug that alters the user's perspective as to postponement of gratification and his desire for the drug itself" (Kaplan, 1988:36).

III. Contemporary Polarity

The survey of current opinion that follows shows that the general terms of the decriminalization debate have not changed much at all. Most of the commentary we observe at the end of the twentieth century owes a great debt (most often unacknowledged) to the Mill–Stephen exchange. Sampling the current arguments of a wide variety of contemporary writers has value beyond making this basic point, however. Our canvas reveals a split among political conservatives between Stephen-style prohibitionism of the *National Drug Control Strategy* and anticriminal sentiments on Millian principles by Milton Friedman and William Buckley. The texture and style of these general sentiments can be contrasted with the cost-benefit rhetoric of specific policy analyses as practiced by John Kaplan.

For Legalization

Although many critics have said that "we will never return to the social and intellectual conditions that made possible Mill's opposition to all drug laws" (Bakalar and Grinspoon, 1984:69), today a number of intellectual descendants of Mill have reaffirmed his basic principle that adults should be free to live their lives in their own way as long as their conduct is not directly hurtful to others (though others may think it foolish, perverse, or wrong). Some also reinforce Mill's concern with the "mischief of the legal penalties" (Mill, 1859:92) by enumerating the excessive collateral social costs of endeavoring to preserve various prohibitions. These writers argue in effect that changing social conditions since Mill's day have not rendered his opposition to drug laws irrelevant but have provided powerful prudential reasons for supporting his principled objection to them.

Many, however, see the crucial question as being not so much a matter of the collateral disadvantage costs or harmful side effects of prohibitions but rather a question, in Mill's words, of "the proper limits of what may be called the functions of the police; how far liberty may be legitimately invaded" (Mill, 1859:152). Thomas Szasz, for example, like Mill himself, is primarily concerned with the moral or ethical aspects of drug control in a free society dedicated to individual liberty. Unlike Mill, who declared "I forgo any advantage which could be derived to my argument from the idea of abstract right" (Mill, 1859:74), Szasz maintains that we should regard "the freedom of choosing our diets and drugs as fundamental rights" (Szasz, 1987:342).

Economist Milton Friedman is another authority who argues that we have no right in respect of adults "to use the machinery of government to prevent an individual from becoming an alcoholic or a drug addict. . . . Reason with the potential addict, yes. Tell him the consequences, yes. Pray for and with him, yes. But I believe that we have no right to use force, directly or indirectly, to prevent a fellow man from committing suicide, let alone from drinking alcohol or taking drugs" (Friedman, 1987:135). The correspondence with Mill's words is so close as to be almost paraphrastic. In such cases, wrote Mill, there may be "good reasons for remonstrating with him, or reasoning with him, or persuading him, or entreating him, but not for compelling him, or visiting him with any evil in case he do otherwise" (Mill, 1859:73).

Another opponent of drug prohibition laws, Gore Vidal, sees Mill's admission that a precaution, such as "labeling the drug with some word expressive of its dangerous character may be enforced without violation of liberty" (Mill,

1859:152), might provide a solution to all the problems of drug addiction. "It is possible," says Vidal, "to stop most drug addiction in the United States within a very short time. Simply make all drugs available and sell them at cost. Label each drug with a precise description of what effect—good and bad—the drug will have on the taker . . . it seems most unlikely that any reasonably sane person will become a drug addict if he knows in advance what addiction is going to be like" (Vidal, 1972:373–74).

Not all the opponents of drug-prohibition laws, however, have placed their emphasis on questions of liberty. Ronald Hamowy has summarized some of the arguments offered in recent years "by a host of writers calling for repeal of our drug laws" as follows:

> Complete abandonment of all prohibitory laws . . . the decriminalization of marijuana, cocaine, and the opiates would halt the current massive drain of public funds and the substantial suffering brought about through attempts to enforce these unenforceable laws. Evidence indicates that legalization would do much to reduce the current crime rate and thus contribute to restoring the safety of our city streets. It would reduce the amount of government corruption, which is partly a function of the immense fortunes that are constantly made in the drug trade, and it would play a large part in decreasing the profits that flow to organized crime. (Hamowy, 1987:32)

Herbert Packer, who thought that "a clearer case of misapplication of the criminal sanction" than its use to enforce a policy of suppressing drug abuse "could not be imagined," noted a number of other socially harmful effects of this misapplication:

> A disturbingly large number of undesirable police practices—unconstitutional searches and seizures, entrapment, electronic surveillance—have become habitual because of the great difficulty that attends the detection of narcotics offenses. . . . The burden of enforcement has fallen primarily on the urban poor, especially Negroes and Mexican-Americans. . . . Research on the causes, effects and cures of drug use has been stultified. . . . A large and well entrenched enforcement bureaucracy has developed a vested interest in the status quo, and has effectively thwarted all but the most marginal reforms. (Packer, 1968:332–33)

Ernest van den Haag argues that from the history of the prohibition of alcohol in America "one may infer a general principle. In a democracy one can regulate, but one cannot effectively prohibit, sumptuary activities desired by a substantial segment of the population. Unenforceable attempts to prohibit certain substances will cause more harm than good." Van den Haag, who describes himself as, not a "libertarian ideologue," but rather as "a strong political conservative," says that his "argument for the legalization of marijuana, cocaine and heroin rests on the fact that their prohibition can be no more effective than the prohibition of alcohol." Those drugs, he says, "must be made as legal as alcohol is" (Van den Haag, 1985).

William Buckley is another conservative who, although a one-time opponent of legalization in regard to heroin, now says "the accumulated evidence draws me away from my own opposition on the purely empirical grounds that what we now have is a drug problem plus a crime problem plus a problem of a huge export of capital to the dope-producing countries." Buckley is also derisive about the possibility of making prohibition more effective. "Maybe we should breed 50 million drug-trained dogs to sniff at everyone getting off a boat or an airplane; what a great idea!" He advocates "legalization followed by a dramatic educational effort in which the services of all civic-minded, and some less than civic-minded, resources are mobilized" (Buckley, 1985).

Milton Friedman, whose opposition to drug prohibition we noted earlier, also supplemented his libertarian case against it by reference to the social costs of prohibition. He argued that, even if it were ethically justified, "considerations of expediency make that policy most unwise." Prohibition, he says, is "an attempted cure that makes matters worse—for both the addict and the rest of us." Not only are addicts driven to crime to finance their addiction but also "the harm to us from the addiction of others arises almost wholly from the fact that drugs are illegal" (Friedman, 1987:135–36).

Those who advocate legalization tend to emphasize the social and fiscal costs of prohibition and the benefits of legalization as though it were, if not a wholly costless policy, at least unlikely to involve any serious costs. Friedman, for example, says that "legalizing drugs might increase the number of addicts, but it is not clear that it would." He goes on to say that if controls were removed and drugs were made legally available, not only would they lose the attractiveness of "forbidden fruit," but also drug pushers would be put out of business because "any possible profit from such inhumane activity would disappear" (Friedman, 1987:136). The latter point was also made by another economist, Thomas Schelling, when serving as a consultant to the 1967 President's Commission on Law Enforcement and Administration of Justice: "If narcotics were not illegal, there could be no black market and no monopoly profits, and the interest in 'pushing' them would probably be not much greater than the pharmaceutical interest in pills to reduce the symptoms of common colds" (Schelling, 1967:124).

One advocate of legalization who has paid more than parenthetic attention to the probable costs of that policy is Ethan Nadelmann, who acknowledges that "all the benefits of legalization would be for naught, however, if millions more Americans were to become drug abusers" (Nadelmann, 1988:24). He maintains that there are "reasons to believe that none of the current illicit substances would become as popular as alcohol or tobacco, even if they were legalized." In particular, he asserts that "none of the illicit substances can compete with alcohol's special place in American culture and history."

"There is," he says, "good reason to doubt that many Americans would inject cocaine or heroin into their veins even if given the chance to do so legally . . . the drugs and methods of consumption that are most risky are unlikely to prove appealing to many people, precisely because they are so obviously dangerous." He does not deny that legalization might lead to increased consumption of the illicit drugs in their more benign forms. In his view, however, because in those forms they are less damaging to the human body than alcohol or tobacco and less strongly linked with violent behavior than alcohol, this does not invalidate "the logic of legalization" (Nadelmann, 1988:28–29).

For John Stuart Mill drug prohibition represented an intolerable infringement of the moral and political principles of a free society. In our time, opponents of prohibition place much greater emphasis on the social costs that policy is thought to entail. "Essentially," says Thomas Schelling, "the question is whether the goal of somewhat reducing the consumption of narcotics. . . . or anything else that is forced by law into the black market, is or is not outweighed by the costs to society of creating a criminal industry" (Schelling, 1967:125). Those who favor legalization are doubtful about the extent to which consumption of the proscribed substances is reduced by prohibition, and even argue that consumption of them in more harmful forms is frequently increased. They argue also that such reduction as may be achieved is always outweighed by its social costs, including the criminalization of consumers, the corruption of law enforcement, and the increase in organized crime.

For Prohibition

Section 6201 of the Anti-Drug Abuse Act of 1988 states categorically that "(1) proposals to combat sale and use of illicit drugs by legalization should be rejected; and (2) consideration should be given *only* to proposals to attack directly the supply of, and demand for, illicit drugs . . ." (*Criminal Law Reporter*, 1988:3011; emphasis added). This legislative interdiction of giving consideration to the repeal of drug-prohibition laws has had little effect on either those who favor legalization or those who oppose it. So far as those who oppose it are concerned, this is probably because those who favor the status quo—and prohibition in regard to drugs has been the status quo in America since 1914—rarely feel the need to defend it unless it happens to be threatened; and it has never been seriously threatened.

This is certainly true at the present time when the policy of prohibition is largely unqestioned and the "war on drugs" appears to enjoy wide public support. As Ethan Nadelmann puts it:

No "war" proclaimed by an American leader during the past forty years has garnered such sweeping bipartisan support; on this issue, liberals and conservatives are often indistinguishable. The fiercest disputes are not over objectives or even broad strategies, but over turf and tactics . . . on the fundamental issues of what this war is about, and what strategies are most likely to prove successful in the long run, no real debate—much less vocal dissent—can be heard.

As for legalization:

Politicians and public officials remain hesitant even to mention the word, except to dismiss it contemptuously as a capitulation to drug traffickers. Most Americans perceive drug legalization as an invitation to drug-infested anarchy. Even the civil liberties groups shy away from this issue. (Nadelmann, 1988:3–4).

It may be true, as Nadelmann asserts, that there is "a significant silent constituency in favor of repeal, found especially among criminal justice officials, intelligence analysts, military interdictors, and criminal justice scholars who have spent a considerable amount of time about the problem." It may also be true that for many individuals in those categories "job-security considerations, combined with an awareness that they can do little to change official policies, ensure that their views remain discreet and off the record" (Nadelmann, 1988:4–5). Insofar as those assertions are correct, they may explain why drug-prohibition laws are not seen to be in need of justification. Silent constituencies do not require audible responses and off-the-record views call for no on-the-record rebuttals.

An important exception to what might otherwise almost seem to be a conspiracy of silence can be found, however, in the writings of James Q. Wilson, who was in 1972 appointed chairman of the National Advisory Council for Drug Abuse Prevention by President Nixon, with "marching orders . . . to figure out how to win the war on heroin" (Wilson, 1990a:21). Wilson specifically takes issue with advocates of legalization such as Milton Friedman and Ethan Nadelmann and provides a rationale for drug prohibition and a defense of its political legitimacy.

Just as those who advocate legalization emphasize the costs of prohibition, those who favor prohibition tend to lay the emphasis on the costs of legalization. Wilson summarizes his views as follows: "I believe that the moral and welfare costs of heavy drug use are so large that society should bear the heavy burden of law enforcement, and its associated corruption and criminality, for the sake of keeping the number of people regularly using heroin and crack as small as possible" (Wilson, 1990b:527).

The distinction between moral costs and welfare costs reflects the distinction between those libertarians who are concerned primarily with the moral as opposed to those who are more concerned with the economic, social, and fiscal costs of prohibition. Wilson says that the costs of legalizing drugs are "difficult to measure, in part because they are to a large degree moral." His account of this aspect of drug use as a problem is in total accord with James Fitzjames Stephen's view of the proper role of criminal law in ensuring "the suppression of vice" and "the promotion of virtue" (Stephen, 1873:14, 150, 152).

"The moral reason for attempting to discourage drug use," Wilson says, "is that the heavy consumption of certain drugs is destructive of human character. These drugs—principally heroin, cocaine, and crack—are, for many people, powerfully reinforcing. The pleasure or oblivion they produce leads many users to devote their lives to seeking pleasure or oblivion and to do so almost regardless of the cost in ordinary human virtues, such as temperance, fidelity, duty, and sympathy" (Wilson, 1990b:523).

Society, according to Wilson, has an "obligation to form and sustain the character of its citizenry." As against "libertarians [who] would leave all adults free to choose their own habits and seek their own destiny so long as their behavior did not cause any direct or palpable harm to others," Wilson maintains that "government, as the agent for society, is responsible for helping instill certain qualities in its citizens" (Wilson, 1990b:524). The use of drugs can "destroy the user's essential humanity" and "corrode those natural sentiments of sympathy and duty that constitute our human nature and make possible our social life." In short, "dependency on certain mind-altering drugs is a moral issue and their illegality rests in part on their immorality . . . legalizing them undercuts, if it does not eliminate altogether, the moral message" (Wilson, 1990a:26).

One principal advantage "of making certain drugs illegal and enforcing the laws against their possession," according to Wilson, "is that these actions reinforce the social condemnation of drug use and the social praise accorded temperate behavior." They help "to alter the moral climate so that drug use is regarded as loathsome" and help also "in shaping the ethos within which standards of personal conduct are defined" (Wilson, 1990b:542–43).

Wilson is concerned not only with what he calls "the tangible but real moral costs" (Wilson, 1990b:527) of legalization but also with the social costs, which he believes are underrated by those he refers to as "academic essayists and cocktail-party pundits." If the legalizers prevail, he says, "then we will have consigned millions of people, hundreds of thousands of infants, and hundreds of neighbor-hoods to a life of oblivion and disease. To the lives and families destroyed by alcohol we will have added countless more destroyed by cocaine, heroin, PCP, and whatever else a basement scientist can invent" (Wilson, 1990a:28).

Even if we decided that government

> . . . should only regulate behavior that hurts other people, we would still have to decide what to do about drug-dependent people because such dependency does in fact hurt other people . . . these users are not likely to be healthy people,

productive workers, good parents, reliable neighbors, attentive students, or safe drivers. Moreover, some people are directly harmed by drugs that they have not freely chosen to use. The babies of drug-dependent women suffer because of their mothers' habits. We all pay for drug abuse in lowered productivity, more accidents, higher insurance premiums, bigger welfare costs, and less effective classrooms. (Wilson, 1990b:524)

Apart from Wilson's essay on the subject, the most emphatic defense of current drug-prohibition policies may be found in the Office of National Drug Control Policy's *National Drug Control Strategy*. Although possibly somewhat more strident in tone than Wilson's writing, the rationale for prohibition provided in the latter document is essentially the same as his and most of the differences are matters of emphasis.

The only substantial, apparent disagreement relates to the effectiveness of drug prohibition as presently administered. According to Wilson, "Though drugs are sold openly on the streets of some communities, for most people they are hard to find" (Wilson, 19909b:525). In the *National Drug Control Strategy* it is said that "[H]ere in the United States, in every state—in our cities, in our suburbs, in our rural communities . . . drugs are available to almost anyone who wants them" (Office of National Drug Control Policy, 1989:2). Despite the disagreement about the availability of drugs and by implication about the current effectiveness of drug law enforcement activities, there is no dispute about the need for drug prohibition or about the nature of its justification.

Like Wilson, the authors of the *National Drug Control Strategy* see drug use as primarily "a moral problem." Although "people take drugs for many complicated reasons that we do not yet fully understand," for "most drug users" their use is the result of "a human flaw" that leads them to pursue what is "a hollow, degrading and deceptive pleasure." It is necessary to take "a firm moral stand that using drugs is wrong and should be resisted." A person's "first line of defense against drugs is his own moral compass" (Office of National Drug Control Policy, 1989:9, 48, 50, 53).

Unfortunately, too many citizens appear to have defective moral compasses so that America faces "a crisis of national character." Although "this crisis is the product of individual choices" it is not a matter that can be left to individuals; for "a purposeful, self-governing society ignores its people's character at great peril." It is necessary therefore for the state, by such means as "tough and coherently punitive anti-drug measures," a "significantly expanded . . . criminal justice system," and "the creation of more prison space," to ensure that "the number of Americans who still use cocaine and other illegal drugs, to the entire nation's horrible disadvantage, is . . . dramatically reduced" (Office of National Drug Control Policy, 1989:2, 7, 9, 26).

It cannot be said that the current debate about drug decriminalization has produced any particularly novel or illuminating insights into the issues of political principle or practice at stake. On the one hand, there is the libertarian's almost ritual invocation of Mill's assertion of the individual's right to do what he likes with his own body providing he does no harm to others. On the other hand, Stephen's assertion of the legitimacy of using criminal law to regulate individual conduct whether or not breaches of it cause harm to others is re-echoed. On the conceptual level, the solution to "the drug problem" is viewed for the most part as a matter of choosing between diametrically opposed alternative expedients.

Specifism

A notable exception to such oversimplification may be found in the writings of John Kaplan, who recognized that whether or not John Stuart Mill's understanding of human nature was more or less accurate than that of Fitzjames Stephen or H. L. A. Hart, the fact is that the world he lived in, early nineteenth-century England, was very different from late twentieth-century America. Moreover, America in the 1990s bears little resemblance to America in the 1890s when today's illicit drugs were freely available. Thus, he made the point, in relation to the possibility of making heroin freely available, that we should hesitate "to extrapolate from our past experience in a predominantly rural, relatively crime-free, free-enterprise society to our present urban, crime-ridden, partially-welfare state."

There is, he said, "no turning back the clock. If we made heroin available today, it would be made available under very different conditions, with social variables such as the purpose and meaning of use and the availability of group support all very much changed. Even the drug would be different. Before the Harrison Act, the problem was opium or morphine drunk in tonics and medicines. Today it is injectable heroin" (Kaplan, 1983:112). Kaplan regarded the rehearsal of past pieties as largely irrelevant to present problems. Mill's principle regarding self-harming conduct might have been "correct for early Victorian England" but today it is best viewed "as a very wise admonition to restrain in an exceedingly complex and emotion-laden area" (Kaplan, 1983:106).

Two features distinguish Kaplan's approach to problems in the drug area from that of most other scholars. The first is his emphasis on what Herbert Packer called "the practical or 'social cost-accounting' aspects of the criminal process" (Packer, 1968:266). The Kaplan analysis places special emphasis on the costs related to administering a criminal prohibition. The premise of this kind of cost-accounting approach is that "every law that seeks to control human behavior entails social costs, as well as social benefits, and that laws should be chosen to maximize the excess of benefits over costs. The clear implication is that, at the least, we should choose controls that entail more benefits than costs—or we should have no controls at all" (Bartels, 1973:441). Kaplan, in the first chapter of his first book on drug policy, dealing with marijuana, which he saw then as "the key problem in the drug area," put it as follows: "The wisdom of a law should be determined in pragmatic terms by weighing the costs it imposes upon society against the benefits it brings. The purpose of this book is to apply this principle to the laws criminalizing marijuana" (Kaplan, 1970:x, 18).

This emphasis on cost-benefit analysis rather than the ideological or political aspects of drug policy is a feature of all Kaplan's writing on drugs. His book on heroin was, in his own description of it, "devoted to examination of the costs and benefits of different policies toward heroin" (Kaplan, 1983:237). In his last contribution to the debate about drug policy dealing with cocaine, he says once again that "the issue boils down to a careful weighing of the costs of criminalization of each drug against the public-health costs we could expect if that drug were to become legally available" (Kaplan, 1988:37).

The reference to "the criminalization of each drug" in that passage reflects the other feature of Kaplan's analysis of the problems involved in criminal-justice policy toward drugs: his rejection of the idea that psychoactive drugs represent a unitary social problem to which the solution must be either prohibition or decriminalization. "Criminalization and legalization," he said, "are not the only possibilities." More importantly, he added that "if the choice for each of the 'recreational' drugs is between criminalization and some kind of legalization, then *it must be made on a drug-by-drug basis*" (Kaplan, 1988:35, 36; emphasis added).

Kaplan's emphasis on the specificity of the problems presented by each of the psychoactive drugs and his close attention to such variables as the singular pharmacological makeup of each of them and the costs of attempting to suppress them is in sharp contrast to the approach of James Q. Wilson. Wilson sees all illicit drugs as representing an equal threat to "the moral climate" and as indistinguishable items in the total of "tangible but real moral costs" of drug use (Wilson, 1990b:527, 542).

Against that kind of tendentious oversimplification, Kaplan in his book on marijuana demonstrated that objective analysis led to a very different conclusion. Before becoming a professor of criminal law, he had as an assistant U.S. attorney prosecuted many violators of the federal drug laws. He says that "like many Americans of my generation, I cannot escape the feeling that drug use, aside from any harm it does, is somehow wrong." He found it "easy to understand how, under the historical and social conditions present in this country at the time, the emergence of a strange intoxicant such as marijuana might have been felt to justify the official and popular apprehension it received" (Kaplan, 1970:x, xi).

Nonetheless, in 1966, as one of the reporters to the Joint Legislative Committee to Revise the Penal Code of the State of California, Kaplan was assigned the drug laws as his first major item of concern. After reading everything available on the drug laws and the drugs themselves and discussing the relevant issues with law-enforcement officials and the natural and social scientists most concerned, he decided that the only way to achieve a rational solution to the problems involved in drug control was to subject each drug and the relevant legislation to separate analysis.

Alcohol prohibition, he maintained, had taught us that "a law is in essence society's purchase of a package of social effects." Whether the law was a wise one or not depended on the answers to two crucial questions: "(1) What are the total social and financial costs attributable to the law? (2) What are the benefits that flow from this outlay?" "The important thing to note," he said, "is that all laws have their costs" (Kaplan, 1970:1–2).

After a detailed analysis of all the factors entering into the costs and benefits of the marijuana laws, he concluded that in this case there was "an enormous disparity between the costs and benefits of the marijuana laws" and that "the social and financial costs directly and indirectly attributable to the criminalization of marijuana far outweigh the benefits of this policy." In the circumstances, he said, "the only responsible course of action . . . is a liberalization of the marijuana law so extensive as to constitute an abandonment of primary reliance on the criminal law in this area" (Kaplan, 1970:xi, 311, 374).

There are, of course, many difficulties involved in this kind of analysis. It is impossible to quantify with any precision the costs of criminalization, and it is no easier to predict the consequences of the removal of prohibitory laws respecting illicit drugs. As Robert J. Michaels has pointed out, "Anyone wishing to predict the consequences of legalized opiates must first invest in some facts . . . we clearly need numerical data about the present situation, summarized into relevant conceptual categories." He goes on to say that while all statistics are imperfect "those related to drug use are egregiously bad." In particular, he says "while they are frequently circulated and quoted with alarm, figures on the number of users and the volume of crime for which they are responsible are meaningless political constructs. They are highly sensitive to the use of arbitrary assumptions and are dependent on surveys or registers whose methodology is questionable and whose coverage is poor" (Michaels, 1987:289, 290, 324–25).

In short, it seems as though none of the conditions for plausible prediction are met; to offer quantitative forecasts regarding the future in the absence of reliable data about the present is to infer from the unknown to the unknown. Kaplan acknowledged that "it is hard to measure with precision the costs of laws, especially the human costs" and that "aside from more or less intelligent guesses, we are usually uncertain of the benefits of laws" (Kaplan, 1970:1–2). He did not agree, however, that because existing estimates are unable to provide reliable quantitative predictions of the consequences of legalization, therefore nothing could be said or that all conjecture must be futile.

Moreover, it is significant that when he applied the same mode of analysis to marijuana that he had used in relation to heroin and cocaine, he reached very different conclusions regarding the probable consequences of decriminalization. In respect to both heroin and cocaine, he demonstrated that it is possible to give some indication of some of the likely features of a world in which those drugs were legal and freely available and, in particular, what costs such a policy might entail.

Kaplan acknowledged that so far as the free availability of heroin is concerned, "the predictions are quite uncertain and difficult." He said that if we are to decide the wisdom of a free availability policy we must "attempt to predict what our society would look like if such a policy were adopted." Accordingly he considered "the two most relevant social variables." These, he said, were "how many people would use the drug in various use patterns, and how harmful would their use be for them and for society?" (Kaplan, 1983:111, 112).

In regard to the first of these variables, he argued that the "statement that opiate availability is a major determinant of use . . . means that within wide limits, the more available opiates are, the higher the rate of use—and of addiction." As examples of this, he cited our experience with American ground troops in Vietnam, where heroin was cheaply and easily available and some 14 percent became addicted to the drug, and considerably more became nonaddicted users. He also cited the fact that the medical profession, which has greater access to opiates than the rest of us, had an addiction rate estimated at about twenty times that of the general population. Moreover, he gave reasons for thinking that neither the Vietnam experience nor the extent of use among members of the medical profession "provide a ceiling on the use to be expected under free availability" (Kaplan, 1983:113–14).

He agreed with Ethan Nadelmann that there seemed to be a psychological barrier against the use of a hypodermic needle. He pointed out that heroin could be either smoked in cigarettes or snorted and that of users in Vietnam, who began by smoking or sniffing the drug, a good percentage went on to intravenous use. Moreover, he cited a study which suggested that many young people, "sustained apparently by peer encouragement and the promise of euphoria," took their first heroin intravenously; the psychological barrier might not be so formidable after all.

In addition, he argued that the act of making heroin legally accessible might change the message we convey about the dangers of the drug and could be taken to indicate that it was safe enough to try. In addition to this disadvantage inherent in the repeal of any drug prohibition, he noted another consequence of free availability, which is that it would accustom the population to moderate users and thus weaken the incorrect but "perhaps functional" belief that heroin use leads inevitably to addiction and serious social and health consequences.

As to the likelihood of increased addiction, he maintained that there was no reason for confidence that the availability of pure, cheap heroin would not lead to sizable increases in addiction. Certainly the little evidence that existed on the use of opiates under conditions of free availability (for example, the medical profession and the American soldiers in Vietnam) provided no support for any hope of low addiction rates. Moreover, apart from its effect in increasing addiction, free availability would be likely to make addiction longer-lasting and more difficult to cure, since the most important reasons why addicts give up heroin— the trouble and expense of maintaining the "habit," fear of legal sanctions, and inability to obtain good heroin—would be removed (Kaplan, 1983:112–26).

With regard to the second variable, the harmfulness of the increased use of heroin both for the users and for society, little is known about the consequences of addiction under conditions of easy access and, in particular, about the long-term health consequences of heroin use. In this connection, Kaplan noted that although tobacco use is recognized today as an important cause of sickness and death this was not recognized until investigations were carried out "far more probing than those to which chronic use of heroin has been subjected." The long-term health consequences of heroin use might well constitute a major public health problem.

In addition, there was the possibility that the free availability of heroin might produce widespread unwillingness or inability to work. If this were the case, it is possible that the lowering of productivity and increased welfare payments resulting from the use of heroin could impose even greater social costs than do our present efforts at suppression. There are, argued Kaplan, reasons to believe that for many people addiction would be incompatible with productive work and "one would have to be an incurable optimist to believe that heroin could be made freely available without a considerable degree of social dislocation" (Kaplan, 1983:126–46).

Kaplan's analysis of the anticipated costs of legalizing cocaine followed along the same lines as his calculation of the costs of heroin legalization. In the case of cocaine, however, he said that it was "far more prevalent than heroin [and] imposes greater social costs upon us—from the amount of money flowing into criminal syndicates to the number of users arrested for predatory crimes." In addition, he noted the widely held view at that time that cocaine was the more benign of the two drugs which, he said, was "probably mistaken."

He offered no estimate of how many more people would use the drug after it was legalized but pointed out that it was an extremely attractive drug with the highest "pleasure score" and greatest "reinforcing power" of any drug known to us. Although most of those who used the drug had not become dependent, this was because it was both expensive and difficult to procure. If the drug were made easily available and cheap, and the inconvenience and criminal danger to the user removed, we should anticipate a considerable increase in the damage brought by heavy cocaine use in terms of psychiatric symptoms and general debilitation.

There was, moreover, a considerable problem in relation to preventing teenagers from gaining access to the drug, for legalization would make it de facto available to the young, as with alcohol and tobacco. Being less bulky and more easily concealable than alcohol, and creating no aroma of smoke, it would be even more difficult to keep from minors. In addition, even if it were taxed as heavily as possible, the financial costs of cocaine would be greatly reduced by legalization. Kaplan calculated that, because of the cost including tax would have to be sufficiently low to make bootlegging unprofitable, the cost of one "hit" would be reduced to "only forty cents—a figure well within the budget of almost all grade-school children."

As for adults, Kaplan argued that the serious negative effects of heavy cocaine use on its users would render it extremely damaging in a complex, mechanized, and interdependent society such as ours. Further, there was no guarantee that legalization would not produce a situation in which there was a fiftyfold increase in the number of those dependent on cocaine. In the circumstances, he said "it is the height of irresponsibility to advocate risking the future of the nation." In an ideal world it might be that the best way to reduce the damage done by illegal drugs would be to persuade everyone not to use them, but in the real world we have to use coercion (Kaplan, 1988:36–44).

However one evaluates John Kaplan's drug-by-drug analysis and projections, the method he employed was quite different from the rhetoric on both sides of the decriminalization debate in two respects. First, the unit of analysis in Kaplan's policy universe is the single psychoactive substance. By contrast, the principal protagonists in the decriminalization debate seem to agree that the appropriate unit of analysis is the fortuitous assortment of drugs that happen to be currently prohibited.

The second distinction between the specific approach and the main part of the decriminalization debate concerns the basis for choice between policies. Kaplan's criteria for policy choice are exclusively pragmatic in a manner that can render those choices disconfirmable by subsequent experience. In arguing as a strict pragmatist that the prohibition of a particular drug generates more benefits than costs whereas the prohibition of another drug does not, the specifist holds to a standard that makes predictions about cost and benefit, in principle at least, testable against historical events.

Both sides of the decriminalization debate—and the tradition extends from Mill and Stephen on through to Nadelmann and Wilson—support their preferred policies for a mixture of moral and prudential reasons, making their proposals impossible to assess objectively and virtually incontestable. If the operative costs of either policy seem too steep, its proponents can always retreat to the moral high ground. At that level the claim that "adult Americans have the right to choose what substances they will consume and what risks they will take" (Nadelmann, 1988:11) is countered by the claim "that society has [an] obligation to form and sustain the character of its citizenry" (Wilson, 1990b:524). Nothing could count decisively against either claim.

Whether the imponderable element is the responsibility of the government for character formation or the freedom of adults to choose their own habits and seek their own destiny, the admixture of those elements with others that are at least in principle measurable renders the claims of both parties logically unassailable. In this respect the prohibitionist and the libertarian are closer to common ground with each other than either of them is to the specifist. It is thus possible to read the specifist analysis of drug policy as an implicit critique of both sides in the decriminalization debate, a critique we seek to extend in the next two sections.

IV. THE CLASH OF PRESUMPTIONS

Although the contending parties in the decriminalization debate disagree on a number of factual issues, the debate itself is not centered on factual matters. What divides the disputants fundamentally is the contrast between them in regard to assumptions about what kind of policy should be preferred when only incomplete information is available.

Those on John Stuart Mill's side in the debate hold to a presumption of liberty. They claim that in regard to drugs and drug control, where knowledge is limited and the outcomes of policy options cannot be predicted with any certainty, it is prudent to choose the course of conduct that maximizes individual liberty and freedom of choice. They assume that adults are capable of making up their own minds rationally and that rates of drug addiction are unlikely to soar if decriminalization is put into effect. They assume also that the interests of children are unlikely to be irredeemably compromised by the abandonment of drug prohibitions.

The contrary presumption associated with those who support drug prohibition is not so much a presumption in favor of authority or social control but more a presumption in favor of social continuity and adherence to established customs and institutions. As Edmund Burke put it, "It is a presumption in favour of any settled scheme of government against any untried project" (Burke, 1803:146). We know of no one who has argued that, in the absence of perfect knowledge, all psychoactive substances should be proscribed. Instead the prohibitionists discuss the risks of decriminalization in ways that suggest that, in the absence of definitive proof to the contrary, it is prudent to preserve and maintain governmental policies that have been developed, and not to subject it to innovative change and thereby disturb a settled, traditional scheme of things.

Adherence to the presumption of continuity involves opposition to the decriminalization of any currently prohibited substance. It does not afford support for initiatives directed at restricting the availability of drugs that are currently not prohibited. Since complete information is lacking, it is considered prudent to maintain, for instance, the prohibition of marijuana. The presumption in favor of social continuity, however, provides no reason for imposing restrictions on substances such as alcohol and tobacco, whose sale and consumption are currently permitted. Those who accuse prohibitionists of being inconsistent in their attitudes as between alcohol and other psychoactive drugs fail to recognize the underlying consistency implicit in a preference for the status quo, which is the fundamental basis of the prohibitionist position.

Recognition that the prohibitionist side of the decriminalization debate is grounded in a presumption in favor of continuity renders intelligible the limited scope of the prohibitionist case in regard to psychoactive drugs. Even as they recognize the damage done by alcohol, none of the prohibitionist spokespersons in the modern era see this as an argument for the prohibition of alcohol. Instead they argue that things would get even worse if yet more substances were added to the list of currently available psychoactive drugs. "If I am right and the legalizers prevail," says James Q. Wilson, "to the lives and families destroyed by alcohol we will have added countless more destroyed by cocaine, heroin, PCP, and whatever else a basement scientist can invent" (Wilson, 1990a:28).

Both the presumption in favor of liberty and the presumption in favor of continuity have deep roots in American culture. The sentimental enshrinement of personal liberty is reflected in all facets of American life from the Declaration of Independence to much popular music. The preference for preserving the status quo, and for known evils over those unknown, is reflected in such popular slogans as "If it ain't broke don't fix it" and "Why trade a headache for an upset stomach?"

The debate on drug decriminalization involves a tug of war between those two powerful sentimental forces, with the presumption in favor of liberty invoked in support of the removal of criminal sanctions on drugs and the preference for continuity providing support for the current categorization of licit and illicit substances. This clash of presumptions in relation to drug decriminalization differs from arguments about alcohol prohibition because in the case of that "noble experiment" (Fisher, 1930) the prohibition involved never achieved the tenure and consequent venerability that could have led people to see it as a stable and continuous feature of an historically evolved, established tradition.

The need to choose between the presumptions of liberty and continuity creates some strange crosscuts in customary political alignments in the United States. William Buckley and William Bennett are both identified as staunch political conservatives, yet in the current decriminalization debate they are diametrically opposed to one another. This contraposition, however, is readily intelligible in terms of a preference, on Buckley's part, for the presumption of liberty and, in the case of Bennett, for the presumption of continuity.

The conservative political tradition in the United States is unique in that it combines both libertarian and continuative principles or presumptions. These presumptions, however, are not invariably consonant; a potential for divisiveness in the conservative ranks is always present. Nor are political liberals immune to dissension in the drug-decriminalization debate. The mainstream liberal tradition in American politics incorporates both a reverence for established customs and institutions and a powerful attachment to libertarian principles.

In arguing that this clash of presumptions is the subtext in the decriminalization debate, we do not suggest that the combatants themselves would use this vocabulary to describe their differences or to explain what animates their disagreement. Nonetheless, it seems to us that explanation in these terms is consistent with the positions adopted by both parties to the debate. At the same time it renders intelligible the somewhat incongruous assortments of political bedfellows that have emerged as public spokespeople, both for decriminalization and for prohibition.

V. THE WRONG QUESTION

The debate about drug decriminalization is lively and educational, but threatens distraction when decriminalization becomes the focus of discussion of drug-control policy. As a policy centerpiece, decriminalization debates are flawed because they pose the wrong central question and because they use inappropriate methods to identify and resolve priority problems in drug-control policies.

From John Stuart Mill to the morning newspaper, the decriminalization debate is about whether or not criminal law should be a major element in governmental efforts to control drugs. A world in which the administration of criminal law and governmental efforts to control drugs inhabit totally different policy spheres, however, is not only unprecedented but also unimaginable. The key question is not whether criminal law should play a significant role in controlling drug behavior, but how such a criminal law should be constructed. In making this assertion, we do not take sides in the decriminalization debate: Criminal law for drug control would be substantial and multifaceted in the United States even if the decriminalization movement carried the day.

Even if the substantive goals of decriminalization can be achieved, the strong likelihood is that efforts at decriminalization would come by amending rather than repealing criminal laws and leaving the formal structure of prohibition intact. We need look no further than the more than a dozen experiments with marijuana in the United States and in Canada to discern a common pattern of reducing rather than abolishing penalties for possession of small quantities for personal use. This is the functional form of steps toward decriminalization for symbolic reasons, but also for practical ones. Retention of the criminal sanction not only pays lip service to the tradition of prohibition, but also allows some selective enforcement of the laws against suspected traffickers, and continued police presence for enforcement.

Further, the administrative burden of decriminalization tends to increase the number and complexity of criminal-law controls in drug markets. Reducing the criminal penalties for the use of drugs usually does not mean withdrawal of substantial penalties for drug trafficking in the same substances. Even when formal decriminalization occurs, the tax and administrative regulations that come with the change in the status of substances increase criminal-law controls. The most famous example of this was the aftermath of the repeal of alcohol prohibition in 1933. Within three years, the number of people in federal prisons, for violation of the tax laws and other administrative regulations produced in the post-prohibition period, was nearly equal to those serving sentences for violation of the prohibition regulations just prior to repeal. In his 1934–1935 report, the Director of the Federal Bureau of Prisons spoke of the failure of the repeal of prohibition to reduce the number of liquor violators and said that "penitentiary commitments for liquor are substantially the same as they were during Prohibition days" (U.S. Department of Justice, Bureau of Prisons, 1936:1–3).

The likelihood that criminal prohibition would stay for drugs historically treated by such prohibitions would mean that these drugs would generate even more business for criminal law even as reliance on prohibition was de-emphasized. In his statement of the case for "the repeal of drug prohibition laws," Ethan Nadelmann makes it clear that it is not "a call for the elimination of the criminal justice system from drug regulation." An "effective plan for legalization" would involve not only "consumption taxes" but also "restrictions on time and place of sale, prohibition on consumption in public places, packaging requirements, mandated adjustments in insurance policies, crackdowns on driving under the influence" (Nadelmann, 1988:30). In addition to taxes and administrative controls, any regime of decriminalization would involve prohibition of drug use for minors and significant criminal penalties for those who supply minors. Clearly, no matter how far toward an emphasis on regulatory and taxing controls the law might push, the residual role for criminal law would be substantial.

Further, if there are behavioral links between drug use and predatory criminal activity, these linkages must be addressed within the criminal law and the correctional system no matter what the formal status of the substances themselves. Whether and to what extent the number of drug users sent to our prisons would be reduced by various regimes of decriminalization is an empirical question that cannot yet be answered. If alcohol is a precedent, the link between serious drug abuse and the prison system would remain strong.

What kind of criminal law for drug control should we have? Where should drug control rank among the many other responsibilities of the criminal justice system? Which drugs and which strategies of enforcement of the law should receive priority? These are the questions that the decriminalization debate does not address. They are also among the most important issues policy planners must confront.

The "Trickle-Down" Fallacy

The broad strokes of the decriminalization debate are just as troublesome to us as the fact that the wrong central question is being addressed. Both sides in that debate assume the correctness of what we shall call "trickle-down" policy determinations—a process in which people assume that details such as strategies of law enforcement and levels of resource allocation get worked out as a matter of course once the large and general questions are settled. The propensity to avoid questions of detail is the major intellectual vice of the decriminalization debaters.

General conclusions about whether criminal prohibitions should be maintained provide very little guidance about how drug policy should be conducted. We live in a world where drug control competes with many other problems for public resources; where many different substances are subject to prohibition, and thus compete with each other for antidrug resources; where many different methods of combating drugs are alternative candidates for funds; and where the single-umbrella term of "prohibition" describes a range of public policies that vary from passive toleration of marijuana in many states to high-intensity police proactivity in anticrack and antiheroin campaigns elsewhere.

What we call the trickle-down fallacy has been the particular vice in recent years of those who maintain that criminal prohibitions should be continued for many drugs. Many prohibitionists simply ignore the detailed questions of enforcement priority and strategy. For these participants, inattention to particulars of policy is a sin of omission, regrettable because the general propositions of the debate on decriminalization are the only topics considered. There are also prohibitionists who seem to argue that the conclusion that drugs should be prohibited can translate to specific policy choices. For these actors, the trickle-down fallacy is a sin of commission.

Illustrations of why specific policy cannot be deduced from a prohibitionist stance are not hard to find. First, there are many claims on police, court, and prison resources, so that drug control must compete against other social problems that have also been deemed worthy of criminal prohibition. Should the marginal dollar or prison cell go to an antidrug campaign this year, or to child-sex abuse or convenience-store robbery?

Second, particular drugs must compete with other drugs for enforcement resources. Should the new task force emphasize marijuana or crack cocaine? To spread resources evenly across all prohibited drugs requires a conclusion that all drugs are *equally* deserving of criminal prohibition, and this no one has seriously suggested.

There is a third reason why drug-control policy cannot be deduced from a prohibitionist stance. Many different drug-control strategies compete with each other as alternative means to achieve the objectives of antidrug campaigns. Simply because heroin qualifies for the use of the criminal prohibition, that does not mean an extra police officer is the best method available for spending $50,000 in public funds to combat heroin dependence. Prohibition means that police and methadone maintenance can compete for antiheroin resources, but it does not mean that the police have a preferred position in that competition.

Those who propose decriminalization have also ignored issues of detail; their failure is somewhat more understandable in that they are advocating a radical structural change in the status quo. Still, as the history of alcohol control has shown, decriminalization does not make drugs a less compelling subject for government attention and resources. Further, the history of tobacco has shown us the importance of governmental choice and the complexity of the choice process even where criminal prohibition is absent. Decriminalization thus may be part of a drug-control policy, but it cannot be the whole of drug policy.

REFERENCES

Bakalar, James B., and Lester Grinspoon (1984). *Drug Control in a Free Society.* Cambridge, Eng.: Cambridge University Press.

Bartels, Robert (1973). "Better Living through Legislation: The Control of Mind-Altering Drugs." *Univ. Kansas Law Review* 21:439–92.

Buckley, William F. (1985). "Legalize Dope." *Washington Post*, April 1, 1985.

Burke, Edmund (1803). *Works*, Vol. VI. London: George Bell & Sons, 1890.

Fisher, Irving (1930). *The "Noble Experiment."* New York: Alcohol Information Committee.

Friedman, Milton (1987). *The Essence of Friedman*, ed. by Kurt R. Leube. Stanford, Calif.: Hoover Institution Press.

Great Britain, Home Office, Department of Health and Social Security (1975). *Report of the Committee on Mentally Abnormal Offenders.* London: Her Majesty's Stationery Office.

Hamowy, Ronald, ed. (1987). *Dealing with Drugs: Consequences of Government Control.* Lexington, Mass.: D. C. Heath & Co.

Hart, H. L. A. (1963). *Law, Liberty and Morality.* Stanford, Calif.: Stanford University Press.

Kaplan, John (1970). *Marijuana—The New Prohibition.* New York: World Publishing.

——— (1983). *The Hardest Drug: Heroin and Public Policy.* Chicago: University of Chicago Press.

——— (1988). "Taking Drugs Seriously." *The Public Interest* 92:32–50.

Michaels, Robert J. (1987). "The Market for Heroin Before and After Legalization," in Ronald Hamowy, ed., *Dealing with Drugs: Consequences of Government Control*, pp. 289–326. Lexington, Mass.: D. C. Heath & Co.

Mill, John Stuart (1859). "On Liberty," in *Utilitarianism, Liberty and Representative Government*, pp. 61–170. New York: Dutton, 1910.

Morris, Norval, and Gordon Hawkins (1970). *The Honest Politician's Guide to Crime Control*. Chicago: University of Chicago Press.

Nadelmann, Ethan A. (1988). "The Case for Legalization." *The Public Interest* 92:3–31.

Office of the National Drug Control Strategy (1989) *National Drug Control Strategy*. Washington, D.C.: U.S. Government Printing Office.

Packe, Michael St. John (1954). *The Life of John Stuart Mill*. London: Secker and Warburg.

Packer, Herbert L. (1968). *The Limits of the Criminal Sanction*. Stanford, Calif.: Stanford University Press.

Quinton, Anthony (1978). *The Politics of Imperfection*. London: Faber and Faber.

Schelling, Thomas (1967). "Economic Analysis of Organized Crime," in U.S. President's Commission on Law Enforcement and Administration of Justice, *Task Force Report: Organized Crime*, pp. 114–26. Washington, D.C.: U.S. Government Printing Office.

Stephen, James Fitzjames (1873). *Liberty, Equality and Fraternity*, ed. by R. J. White. Cambridge, Mass. Cambridge University Press, 1967.

Szasz, Thomas (1987). "The Morality of Drug Controls," in R. Hamowy, ed., *Dealing with Drugs: Consequences of Government Control*, pp. 327–51. Lexington, Mass.: D. C. Heath & Co.

U.S. Department of Justice, Bureau of Prisons (1936). *Federal Offenders 1934–1935*. Fort Leavenworth, Kans.: Federal Prison Industries Inc. Press.

van den Haag, Ernest (1985). "Legalize Those Drugs We Can't Control." *Wall Street Journal*, August 8, 1985.

Vidal, Gore (1972). *Homage to Daniel Shays: Collected Essays 1952–1972*. New York: Random House.

White, R. J. (1967). "Editor's Introduction," in James Fitzjames Stephen, *Liberty, Equality and Fraternity*. Cambridge, Eng.: Cambridge University Press.

Wilson, James Q. (1990a). "Against the Legalization of Drugs." *Commentary* 89:21–28.

——— (1990b). "Drugs and Crime," in Michael Tonry and James Q. Wilson, eds., *Drugs and Crime. Crime and Justice: A Review of Research*, vol. 13. Chicago: University of Chicago Press.

2

Drug Legalization and the "Goldilocks" Problem: Thinking about Costs and Control of Drugs

Stephen Mugford

The question of the control of drug use remains a vexing problem. On the one hand, we have those who espouse prohibition, often termed "drug warriors," who appear to believe that if we keep on keeping on with what we are now doing, things will be right in the long run. On the other hand, we have those who think that prohibition is a dreadful failure. The latter group often advocates the legalization of currently illicit drugs, so let us call them the "legalizers." They seem to think that all the ills currently associated with drugs arise from their illegal status. Drug warriors respond, with great vehemence, that legalizers must be crazy if they think that legalization would solve our problems. "Look at the problem with current legal drugs," say the smarter of the warriors. "Do you really want more of *that?*"

My starting point is that both groups are right—or, if you like, both are wrong. When it comes to drug laws, we have a version of the Goldilocks problem. In the fairy tale, when Goldilocks goes into the bears' house, she finds three beds. The first, Mama Bear's, is too soft. The second, Papa Bear's, is too hard. The third, Baby Bear's, is just right. In this paper I shall suggest that this is a useful metaphor for drug control. On the one hand, outright prohibition is too hard. On the other, legalization is too soft. Somewhere in between, we have to find a model that is just right.

The argument is predicated upon the pragmatic-utilitarian assumption that in policy we seek an outcome that is effective in minimizing harm and maximizing benefit. There are many in the drug-policy field who cannot accept that. They

have deep moral commitments either to one form of control or to the unacceptability of some drugs. This is not the place to enter such debates, though I have
done so elsewhere (Mugford, 1991a). For the moment, I presume the validity of
a utilitarian position and proceed.

If we are to aim for harm reduction, it is important that we achieve conceptual
clarity about what the phrase means, and some rigor in our arguments. Even
when we know from practice that some things work and others don't, we should
be trying to understand why that is the case in terms of a more far-reaching
analysis that orders not only what we know, but also tells us how to make
predictions about unknown states of affairs. This paper, then, starts with two key
assumptions. First, I assume that in all modern societies[1] there is at least some
desire on the part of some of the population to use some psychotropic drugs some
of the time. Which drugs, when, where, who uses and for what purpose, do not
matter for the central part of my argument, although those details become vital
if and when we move to practical policy discussion. Thus I take for granted that
there is, in economic terms, *demand for drugs* (O'Malley and Mugford, 1991).
The existence of demand raises other questions about the nature of that demand.
What is its source? How elastic is it? How substitutable are drugs, one for another,
and for other commodities (and vice versa)? I cannot answer these questions with
detailed argument—that would take another three papers, but here are a few key
points.

On the nature of demand, two arguments are frequently made. First, that
drug use is normal, because it is so widely documented historically and anthro-
pologically. If no drug-free society exists, one may say, then drug use is normal.
Second, it is argued, directly or implicitly, that drug demand is fueled by a desire
for escape. This model is implicitly a "deficit model"—that is, deficits in either
the user (such as poor coping skills) or the context (such as lack of jobs) motivate
use. These two arguments can, but do not generally, overlap. We assume here
that these are limiting case arguments. The social ubiquity of drug use tells us
little about the form it takes in modern societies and the deficit model is silent
about the fact that most users of most drugs have no noticeable deficit in their
lives (and use without major deleterious consequence). It goes on to assume that
a better understanding of drug demand is to see it as a demand for entertaining
and exciting commodities, part of a growth in modern society of a sector concerned with exciting and dangerous "pleasures." This argument is merely assumed
here, but I have argued it thoroughly elsewhere (O'Malley and Mugford, 1991).

Is demand elastic?[2] This question is rarely posed in drug debates. Those who
would argue for prohibition-type models, for example, don't address this, but
often they go on to import two completely contradictory elasticity models into
their arguments. On the one hand, when asked why certain drugs should be
banned, they argue that such drugs "enslave" or "addict" users. As a result, users
become desperate and "will pay any price for the drug." That is, they pose a model

of very low elasticity. On the other hand, they also suggest that legalizing such drugs would "open the flood gates to use." That suggests, rather, a model of high elasticity—as supply increases and total cost[3] decreases more use will occur. I suggest that apart from the obvious contradiction—they can't both be right—the evidence is probably for a model of moderate elasticity for many drugs. I can't demonstrate that here and my general argument neither stands nor falls by it, but concrete policy applications might hinge on having good elasticity data for any drug.

Finally, on the topic of demand, I assume that drugs are substitutable for one another to a considerable degree. I also assume that they can substitute for, and be substituted by, other goods and services. This assumption is the logical corollary of my model for demand in general. I suggest, in effect, that what is sought is not escape (at least not in the negative sense of deficit models) but rather excitement and intoxication. Since many drugs and other activities (hang gliding, driving fast cars, etc.; see Lyng, 1990) are also exciting, they may substitute for one another to a degree as well as being combined in all sorts of manners.[4]

My second principal assumption is that there is a *demand for the formal control of drugs*. (Note that the word "demand" is being punned on here to some degree. The first kind of demand is an economic demand, the second political.) Again, this should not be passed over lightly. Many people act as if the idea that some groups (such as the government) should seek to control the drug use of others through formal, bureaucratic means is "natural." In a more sophisticated version, the assumption is that in a world where there is a central, formal, bureaucratic state, control by government is the "natural" state of affairs to anticipate. The first version stands little scrutiny, precisely because of what the second acknowledges—namely, that the existence of centralized states is itself a historically specific development (Giddens, 1985).

The second version is more resilient, but my assumption is different. I see the control of drugs by the state as itself something that takes particular forms at particular times, forms that need to be studied and explained in detail. I would argue that the point made earlier about demand as a contingent feature of a modern market for exciting and dangerous commodities leads us to expect that in turn we need to see control as also contingent and specific. Again, I cannot argue the point here in detail, but we need to remember that attempts to control drugs are not simply and self-evidently driven by "natural" or even philanthropic desires (on the general issue, see Stallybrass and White, 1986; on drug laws, see, for example, Helmer, 1975; Morgan, 1978).

A third assumption, and the real starting point of my discussion, is that the key to harm reduction lies in specifying not only what "harm" and "reduction" are but also the nexus between use, control, and harm. That assumption will gradually be argued out as the paper unfolds.

In the rest of my presentation I set out to do three things. In Section 1, I propose a simple typology of harm, distinguishing intrinsic from extrinsic and direct from indirect. In Section 2, I discuss the three kinds of control—by the state, by the market, and by civil society in a very general context—attempting, both via historical evidence and theoretical argument, to produce an understanding of these matters that transcends common sense and gives us new purchase on the problem. In Section 3, I bring the types and levels of attempted control together with the issue of costs to try to develop an overall model of how patterns and levels of harm are distributed.

These three arguments are brought together in the conclusion, in which I make policy recommendations about harm reduction that flow from the arguments developed earlier.

1. An Outline of Types of Harm

If we are to talk of harm reduction, we need above all else a clear conception of what harm consists of and what the social and psychological roots of such harm might be[5]. Clearly, people are wont to use drugs for nonmedical reasons, especially leisure and pleasure. Equally clearly, such use has the potential to harm the user and society. There is no psychotropic substance known that does not have some possible deleterious effect when used to excess, and there is considerable merit, therefore, in having a clear picture of what kinds of harm can arise when such substances are used. My suggestion is that we can clearly delineate several types of harm as follows.[6]

First, we need to separate **intrinsic** from **extrinsic** harm.

Intrinsic harm from substance use I define as those negative economic, health, or social consequences that arise as a necessary result of the use of any drug (including tobacco and alcohol), even under "ideal" conditions. For example, the harm of tobacco smoking, even when smoking the best tobacco at a low price, includes decreased lung function plus a substantially increased chance of major disease (carcinoma of the lung, heart disease or the like).

Extrinsic harm I define as those negative economic, health, or social consequences that arise as a result of the use of any drug (including tobacco and alcohol) when substance use takes place under *less than* "ideal" conditions, or (a form of opportunity cost) when use has as its attendant consequence some other constraint that has negative impact. For example, the risk of heroin users' getting hepatitis B or AIDS because of dirty needles is extrinsic harm. Similarly, if the cost of heroin, and the time taken to "score" are both great, an extrinsic cost of heroin use may be the undermining of the individual's work or daily life.

A second distinction that needs to be made is between **direct** and **indirect** harm.

Direct harm I define as those negative economic, health, or social consequences that arise as a result of the use of any drug (including tobacco and
alcohol) and are *borne by the user*—such as ill health, expense, and so forth.

Indirect harm I define as those negative economic, health, or social consequences that arise as a result of the use of any drug (including tobacco and
alcohol) and are *borne by others* as a result of the use of psychotropic drugs by
another person. Indirect costs range from passive smoking or fetal alcohol syndrome through to more large-scale social costs such as lost production, accidents,
health-care costs, and so on.

It follows that we can now distinguish four kinds of harm—intrinsic direct,
intrinsic indirect, extrinsic direct, and extrinsic indirect. Complexities arise when
we realize that increase or decrease in one area has no automatic positive connection with another. For instance, an attempt to reduce the extrinsic direct
harm of heroin use through legalization could, some would argue, lead to an
increase in the intrinsic and extrinsic indirect cost component if a large increase
in use led to a sharp increase in such things as hospital admissions or drugged-
driver accidents. I will have more to say about harm and how it is distributed
later, but for the moment I want to turn to the issue of control.

2. CONTROL—CONCEPTS AND TYPES

In most drug discussions, control is seen covertly as downward
limitation. That is, if the issue is whether an individual has an alcoholic drink,
control is equated with either saying no, or saying no after a certain number of
drinks. This is a very truncated conception of control, however.

Consider rather Jack Gibbs' discussion of control:

> Attempted control is *overt* behavior by a human in the belief (1) that the behavior
> increases or decreases the probability of some subsequent condition *and* (2) that
> the increase or decrease is desirable. The *definiendum* is attempted control for
> two reasons: first, it forces recognition of a crucial distinction, that between
> successful and unsuccessful control; and second, it underscores the purposive
> quality of human behavior. (1990:4).

One could add to this Barry Hindess' argument for considering actors other
than individuals—such as corporations or governments—as worthy of the label
actor (Hindess, 1988:42–47). By substituting the word "actor" in Gibbs' definition
we come to the following definition:

Attempted control is *overt* behavior by any actor in the belief (1) that the behavior increases or decreases the probability of some subsequent condition *and* (2) that the increase or decrease is desirable.

With this definition in mind, we can see that each of the following is attempted control of drug use:

1. The person who says, "Don't be a wimp, one (or one more) won't do you any harm."
2. The corporation that advertises its beer under the slogan, "I feel good, oh so good!" with visuals showing the (ex-)world surfing champion drinking at a party (an ad for Toohey's beer in Australia).
3. The corporations that display their "messages" adjacent to the main scoreboard at the Superbowl (in 1991, Coca Cola and Marlboro).

In each of these three cases, the attempt at control is control in an upward direction. If "controlled" by the attempt, someone will take more of the drug in question or (with long-term effects in the same direction) the drug will be seen to be more socially acceptable, leading indirectly to greater use than might otherwise have occurred. Let us look at possible examples of control in this broad sense. We might best do this by looking at a series of typical reasons someone might offer for doing or not doing something, labeling each type and, where possible, linking each one to a particular social institution that might be thought relevant to attempted control of that area.

Reason	Control Label	Institution
I like/don't like doing X	Self	?
I ought/ought not do X	Moral	Religion, etc.
I'm legally allowed/not allowed to do X	Legal	Legal system
I can/can't afford to do X	Financial	Employment
X is safe/dangerous	Cognitive	Educational system
My friends like/don't like X	Network	Community
X does/doesn't fit my life-style	Consumer	Advertising

Self-control, emptied of such things as socially acquired tastes (which can be understood to result partly from consumer control and partly from network control; see Douglas and Isherwood, 1983; Bourdieu, 1987), I leave to one side. There is no need to assume that a sociological approach should want to model individual differences.

As for the others, I suggest that they can, without too much difficulty, be reduced to three pairs. Financial and consumer control are clearly related to the sphere of the economic; cognitive and legal control are aspects of the political sphere; and moral and network control are aspects of civil society. This tripartite division, which characterizes so much of the terrain of the social sciences, has recently been used by Alan Wolfe (1989) in a major overview of policy issues, and my discussion in the next few paragraphs benefits from that book. In simple terms, we may think of attempted control over drug use as being exercised by these three parts of a social order. The market, in aggregate effect, attempts to control drug use both through financial factors (which make it possible or impossible for a person to purchase the drug) and through consumer factors (which influence whether people desire the drug).

Consumer control is particularly interesting. Without launching a long exegesis on modern advertising, it is fairly clear that advertising has both specific and general effects. The specific effect is related to one's decision to purchase a given product, so if a beer company advertises its brand of beer, the effect is for someone exposed to that ad to buy the beer. More generally, however, such advertising has other effects. First, the same ads for the beer company may increase beer sales in general; second, such ads may increase alcohol sales in general; third and most important, such ads, couched as they most frequently are in images of excitement, achievement, sexuality, youth, and pleasure, help to build that broad ideological world of modern consumerism. This world exhibits qualities that are powerfully attractive, at very least to those of us raised in modern societies. The world is one of plenitude, of gratification without cost, of endless youth. But it is also a world of obligation. As Colin Campbell (1983:282) has argued, the modern consumer has an obligation to consume: If in response to the question "What do you want for Christmas (birthday, etc.)?" one replies "Nothing," the exasperated response comes back, "Well, you must want something!" The assumption of endless wants is itself not a natural feature of human life, but rather a product of socialization into a modern society (see Campbell, 1987.) *In this world of consumption, successful control does not limit consumption, but increases it.* The market functions to extend consumption. Drug use, powerfully valued in terms of the hedonism that consumer cultures espouse, is no exception.

From a public-health perspective that looks toward limitation of use in order to reduce harm, successful market controls are not successful policy control, but quite the reverse. Indeed, if we think of limitation as our goal and imagine for the purposes of argument that limitation might be excessive (overlimitation), optimal, or insufficient (underlimitation), then clearly the market will produce *underlimitation* insofar as it produces successful control.

Things are slightly more complex with the political sphere—the state. Although it is easy to see that increased consumption is in the interest of sellers and that to a great extent we may expect them to encourage sales, hence fueling the general notion of consumerism, there is no simple route into state control. Would a state seek to increase consumption, decrease it, or keep it steady? If we look at consumption in general, we may assume the former. That is, since the state, even in the most pluralist account, has a responsibility for the economy of the country, it is likely to seek limits to consumption only for two broad reasons. First, as a general instrument of economic policy there may be periods of restraint, driven by high interest rates, in an attempt to dampen inflation or rectify the balance of payments. Second, the state may seek to limit any area of consumption that is held either to imperil civil order or that causes costs to the state itself or to business. Clearly, drug use may fit into either of these types and as a consequence we might expect to see states, especially modern states, intervening in the area of drug consumption. What form would that intervention take?

Broadly, we might expect that any attempted control on the part of states will take the form of downward pressure, pressure toward limitation. The details can be complex. Some attempted control may intersect with market factors; taxes, licensing laws, age limits, and so forth are all examples of this. Some interventions will operate through attempted cognitive control—educational campaigns and so forth. Others will take the form of direct legal control through criminal law. These interventions range from more "procedural" matters, such as laws against drunk driving, to complete prohibitions on possession, sale, or use of substances. The latter are certainly the most visible types of attempted control, although careful examination would reveal them only to be a subset of all state interventions. Returning to our imagined dimension of degrees of limitation, it is easy to see that state control is likely to conform more to the condition of *overlimitation* than to underlimitation.

What of civil society? In ideal conditions, one might argue that civil society is more likely than either of the others to produce moderate, even optimum, levels of control, since the social ties of what Turner (1969) calls "communitas" lead neither to overlimitation nor underlimitation. This is because there is no vested interest that leads toward either under- or overlimitation. An excellent example of this is Pamela Watson's (1991) recent work on the economy and use of betel nuts in a Papua New Guinea community. Betel-nut chewing is well established in this community, and substantial consumption of the nuts leads to marked intoxication. The supply of nuts is excessive, since the number of trees one plants in this community is a sign of status, not need. Despite this oversupply, which one might imagine would fuel use, there is no evidence of excessive consumption, and betel-nut intoxication is not a problem. This turns out to be a result of community control. Betel-nut chewing is socially unacceptable in many settings, much as drinking in Western cultures is unacceptable during work hours. Such unacceptability is based not on law (although in the latter case, particular employers may have regulations) but upon custom. The key word here is "settings," recalling Zinberg's (1984) "drug, set, and setting" as well as his argument that setting is the principal agent that led to limitations on use—

limitations at both the higher and lower end of the range. This suggestion fits well with what we know of "recreational" use (or call it what you will) of illicit drugs. For example, in a study of cocaine users that I carried out in Australia, it was clear that the respondents limited their use, and did so because of the wider web of social ties into which they were embedded (Mugford and Cohen, 1989; for parallel findings in other countries see Erickson et al., 1987; Cohen, 1989; Scottish Cocaine Research Group, 1990). Indeed, careful review of such use might lead one to pose questions about illicit drug use in rather different ways. Rather than supposing that dependence and disorganization are the normal state of affairs with illicit users and that limitation and self-management of use are abnormal, we would do better to suppose the reverse.

In turn, we should account for this normal state by referring, in the case of those who use illicit drugs, to two principal factors that encourage control. First, let me examine some aspects of market control. In this case, the market is illicit and for this reason prices tend to be very high, a fact that itself reduces consumption. Second, and very significantly, the normal state is a result of those ties and relationships we call "civil society." Why, then, is our policy task not made simple? Surely, all we have to do is to strengthen civil society and it will provide all the answers to limiting drugs. Unfortunately, life is not that simple. We can identify three very general problems that restrict the capacity of civil society to limit successfully the use of drugs (and many other similar phenomena) at the optimal level.

First, modern societies are highly internally differentiated and stratified. As a consequence, individuals live in worlds that not only differ one from another but also contain internal contradictions. For example, the amount of alcohol that blue-collar workers think is reasonable to drink, the drinking patterns they follow, and the drinks consumed differ from those of white-collar workers, executives, and the rich. Similarly, the amount that a man's football club buddies think is reasonable to drink might differ sharply from what his workmates define as acceptable or from the standards of other friends, neighbors, or kin. There is no social consensus on these things, and in this mixed world, relying upon civil society to monitor use is optimistic, particularly if drugs are legal. (There is an irony here: Substances that are illicit can generate around them solidary groups, solidary precisely *because* of shared deviance, where social use is a central defining feature. If all use is use within the boundaries of that group and setting, then as Zinberg (1984) argued, it will be monitored and limited quite well.) This is linked to the second point. With the gradual spread of commodity relations and the cash economy on the one hand, and the powers and surveillance of the state on the other, into those areas that in the past were managed more by aspects of civil society, the latter shrinks and is weakened. This point is a familiar one to those who study sociology or social history.

The third point is a development of the first. We should consider that those who use illicit drugs in a manner that more or less conforms to the well-documented—if stereotyped—picture of "junkie" use, that is, heavy, destructive use associated with poverty, disorganization, unemployment, and crime, are, in a sense, those who have fallen out of the web of support (and hence control) that civil society provides in other contexts. Where this analysis differs from many more conventional analyses is that the latter presume that to use any illicit drug is to have left that web, whereas I argue that the web is powerful for most users who thereby manage their use successfully.

The conclusions that emerge from these three points are as follows. First, a proportion of those who use illicit drugs will, like those who use licit drugs, be at risk of excessive use with negative consequences for themselves and (very likely) others. Civil society cannot prevent those risks (although we might ask how it can be strengthened to do so more effectively), and therefore it follows that we should examine the market and state to see what resources, in combination, they can provide to overcome this problem. Second, we may be sure that this exercise will not be unproblematic, for in a morally plural society the standard we might set for optimal use will be too high to suit some, too low to suit others. What I want to do now is to try to combine the various separate strands to date.

3. An Overall Model of Types and Levels of Control

I have argued that there are three sources of control—market, state, and civil society. I have also argued that control does not equal (downward) limitation as is often assumed—that in the case of the market, the tendency is to underlimit, while for the state, at least in the case of drugs, the tendency is to overlimit. One could call this under- and overcontrol, but as I demonstrated earlier, this would be sloppy (albeit conventional) phrasing.

Here we must examine the relation between attempted limitation, use level, and costs. Let us start with limitation and use. It is probably reasonable to assume that this relation is more or less linear; that is, the more the attempted limitation, the less use will take place. This in turn can be linked to the distribution of intrinsic harm. In simple terms, the source of intrinsic harm is use and hence the greater the level of use then, *ceteris paribus*, the greater the level of harm. If we plot this on a graph, we may thus imagine that the graph would (in abstract) be a line rising from the origin away to the right.

What of extrinsic harm? Put simply, if the harm here *really* is extrinsic, then to borrow Zinberg's (1984) terminology, it is a result not of "drug" but of "set and setting." Significant among the questions of setting is limitation; that is, extrinsic costs will rise and fall in relation to limitation. When limitation is optimal, extrinsic costs will be low, and vice versa. Indeed, I think the evidence on limiting any social activity that many people desire to do can be understood as having an optimum level (at which the benefit to society and to individuals is at the attainable maximum) with two less optimal states on either side. These are, as discussed earlier, underlimitation and overlimitation. This concept (which is hardly new, and can be traced back at least as far as Aristotelian concepts of the Golden Mean) can be used to understand some of the complex issues surrounding drugs.

When drugs are underlimited, extrinsic harm tends to arise in the form of consumer exploitation, excessive pressure to buy, and so forth. Adulteration of alcohol with impurities like methanol is an example of underlimitation—a situation not where adulteration takes place intentionally to boost quantity, but rather where proper manufacturing standards are slighted to curtail production costs. It might well be argued that inadequate limits on alcohol or tobacco advertising and sales, which together produce underage drinking and smoking, are other examples of underlimitation. Note that the selection of examples here concentrates on licit substances. Some convinced drug warriors may believe that underlimitation relates to illicit drugs, but I shall argue the contrary and I believe that the evidence supports my view. That is, that insofar as underlimitation occurs in Western societies, it does so in respect to licit rather than illicit drugs.

Turning to overlimitation, extrinsic harm from drug use, especially illicit drug use, takes such forms as the deliberate "cutting" of drugs, purposeful adulteration for profit by apparent increase in quantity), the sharing of dirty equipment, secondary crime to support use when prices are high, and so forth. Such harm arises because limitation does not automatically produce its intended consequences. Indeed the "unintended consequences" of (overlimitation are the development of a black market, a growth in organized crime, the corruption of state officials (customs, police, judiciary), an increase in secondary crimes—including violent crime—and a sharp increase in extrinsic direct health costs for users. These relations can best be conceptualized by reference to Figure 2.1, which illustrates the relation that (in my view) arises between the legal availability (a measure of limitation) of a drug and the level of harm that use of that drug entails.

The overall relationship is, I contend, not linear (A1 to B) as prohibition-oriented arguments might lead one to believe. A linear relationship describes the distribution of intrinsic harm and the only real question here is whether the line starts up direct from the origin or (as with some drugs) low levels of use are possible without real harm, in which case the line would start somewhere to the right. On the other hand, the likely distribution of extrinsic costs is a U-curve (A2 to B). The argument underlying the U-curve relation is explained in greater detail in Mugford (1991b) but suffice to say here that it is logically connected to the underlimitation/optimum limitation/overlimitation model sketched above. That is, the two peaks of extrinsic cost/harm correspond to conditions of overlimitation and underlimitation in the drug field. In application, what the curve A2

FIGURE 2.1.   RELATIONSHIP BETWEEN LEVEL OF LEGAL AVAILABILITY
               AND LEVEL OF DRUG-RELATED HARM

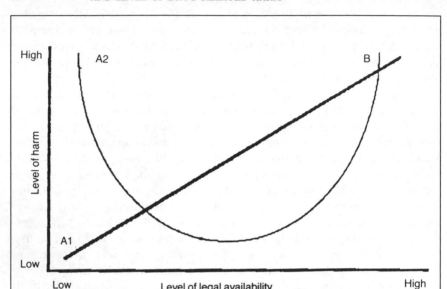

to B implies is that legal restriction is a limited policy, highly effective in limiting extrinsic costs in the right-hand part of the graph and ineffective and counter-productive in the left-hand part. Nonetheless, and despite the experience of alcohol prohibition in the United States (when, in terms of the graph, policy swung from the right-upper to the left-upper point), policies toward drugs today continue to be split between the tendency to overlimitation of the illicit drugs (through reliance on state control) and underlimitation of the licit drugs (through reliance on market control).[7]

If the distribution of intrinsic harm is linear (more or less) and of extrinsic harm U-shaped, it follows that the distribution of total harm must be their sum, which, as Figure 2.2 shows, is basically a J-curve.

4. CONCLUSIONS: POLICIES FOR HARM REDUCTION

Conflicts arise between reducing types of cost/harm. In addition to the general question of harm reduction as an aim, the harm-reduction approach has also to choose clearly between the kinds of harm that are to be reduced when

FIGURE 2.2. DISTRIBUTION OF TOTAL HARM

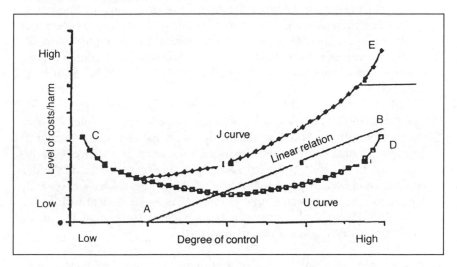

there is conflict between different types. A decision on these issues can be combined with the analysis above to guide policy. Ranking types of harm is an exercise in political and moral philosophy, and arguing out the full implications would take another separate presentation. Let me therefore offer one approach, acknowledging that this is merely a suggestion. In a society where a generally liberal approach to moral issues is the norm ("anyone can do what they want unless it harms others")—a stance to be found widely in my home country of Australia and in many other Western liberal democracies—the practical option is to concentrate on the reduction of harm in the following order of priority:

1. *Extrinsic indirect*. Such harm is unnecessary at best and is borne by other than the user. There is no sensible reason why a society should pay these costs. An excellent example is drunk-driving legislation, which aims to reduce the extrinsic costs (accident-related) particularly as they affect others (nondriving victims, taxpayers who pay the costs, including the perpetrator's health costs, and so on).

2. *Intrinsic indirect*. Such costs are borne by people who have no choice about the drug using but are affected by the intrinsic health (and associated) problems generated. Babies whose mothers use drugs in pregnancy and people who inhale sidestream smoke in workplaces or on public transport are cases in point here.

3. *Extrinsic direct*. Such harm is suffered by the user, but there is no intrinsic reason why it should be suffered at all. Alcohol and cocaine, for

example, all cause damage if ingested in appreciable quantity on a regular basis, but even greater damage is done if the drug contains impurities. (Thus careful monitoring is maintained on alcohol suppliers to ensure that methanol is not included as an impurity, since the consumption of methanol has severe effects.) Action to reduce these costs will also reduce extrinsic indirect harm (the suggested first priority) when the health bill for users is reduced.

4. *Intrinsic direct.* These costs should be the lowest priority if they conflict with others, in a version of *caveat emptor.* That an informed and responsible person should be allowed to take some risks in the pursuit of private ends that harm no one else seems a not unrealistic stance. Clearly, however, the rider of "informed and responsible" can only be met under certain conditions. In particular, "responsibility" should have at least an age barrier as an indicator, and "informed" is not consistent with heavy advertising pressure. No drug can be considered to be available under optimum conditions if it is heavily marketed.

Let me now combine the earlier argument on cost distribution with the philosophical point about the preferences of costs. The J-curve in Figure 2.2 shows the generalized distribution of all harm for drug use. Of course, the precise shape of the J depends upon knowing all sorts of things about a given drug. Where does the linear relation start? Does it have thresholds? How steep is the line? Are the extrinsic costs large or small in magnitude in comparison? And so on. Nonetheless, we can begin to make some conclusions. Minimum harm in total lies at the base of the J, that is, somewhere between optimal limitation (which minimizes extrinsic cost) and overlimitation, which tends to minimize intrinsic cost. It lies in a mix of some market controls with some state controls. For any one drug, the "magic formula" is that it should be available as a substance, but in a form that minimizes its standing as a commodity.

What does this look like on the ground? With some substances, such as cannabis, the answers that seem to be relevant range from home production without commercial sale through legal sale under government monopoly, without advertising. At minimum, "decriminalization" schemes are reasonable fits to this model. There are fine-grained issues to be thought out here. Do we want governments raising a cannabis tax? If so, does it go to the "drug area" or to consolidated revenue? What international treaty obligations does a government have that might make decriminalization more practical than legalization? With decriminalization, what is the best structure of enforcement and penalty that will optimize control in the direction of limitation? With cocaine or heroin, which cannot be grown in one's backyard and is unlikely to be the basis of a gift from a friend with the right plants, the system for supply has to undercut and vitiate the black market without becoming a dynamo for use. Registered/licensed users with moderate restrictions on access to user status are most likely to achieve this. Note also that the best possibility for heroin with its low intrinsic costs and high extrinsic costs may be different from cocaine with its more moderate extrinsic costs (at present, and excepting crack) but higher intrinsic costs. With synthetic chemicals (such as LSD) where the possibility for a severe extrinsic cost arises when the chemical is misproduced but where intrinsic costs may also be high, there may be yet another optimum mix of policies.

Turning to the licit drugs, it is clear that, in terms of the J-curve, we are high on the right and need to come down sharply toward the left. Current policies toward higher taxes, advertising bans, smoke-free workplaces, random breath testing of drivers for alcohol (and so on and so forth)—all are obviously useful steps in this direction. Whether political economy will permit us to reach the bottom of the curve is another question entirely.

In turn, the analysis I offer shows why, as many of its opponents have long claimed, prohibition does not work. Prohibition is state-based attempted control, with the purpose of sharp downward limitation of use and costs. To a great extent, it achieves partial success when properly implemented, because it does limit use (some are deterred; users who do so, do so covertly; and so on) and since limitation is linked with intrinsic cost, those costs are reduced. On the other hand, and especially in any society with a large market sector, the state cannot control the market completely. As the efficacy of the control reaches its boundary, so artificial shortage drives a new investment and distribution system (black market). In turn, this brings very high extrinsic costs, turning the J back up to the left. Some protagonists of prohibition argue that prohibition is better than an open market. They may be right. High on the left of the J curve may not be quite as bad as high on the right (depending upon the shape of the J) but both are worse than somewhere close to the bottom. Furthermore, the analysis offered above indicates that such an outcome cannot be produced merely by legislative/enforcement means. Attention has to be given to both regulation through these and through market means (manipulation of supply, price, and the like); and, which is even harder, to strengthening those aspects of civil society that might offer useful controls, too.

This brings me to my last concrete point. How can we do that? Clearly, if the effect of drug-using groups is to be drawn upon, those groups must not be weakened *as groups*. A very telling recent parallel looms. In the control of HIV transmission, the lesson we learned pretty quickly (at least in some countries) was that male homosexual transmission could not be combated by regulations, but needed the enlistment of the gay community. What is this if not the strengthening of the ties of civil society within a group previously (and to a degree still) socially stigmatized and legally disadvantaged? The moral is simple. Civil society offers some useful scope for limiting drug use and hence drug existence. Those benefits, however, can only be realized if we protect the ties upon which relevant parts of civil society are based. In the case of the legal drugs, the relevant ties (kin, neighbors, friends) are often undermined by market forces. The alcohol industry, for example, has so successfully domesticated the substance that rather than being constrained by civil society it has become a *part* of civil society. To this, we can only respond with state regulation (and state-based education) to turn the tide.

With the illegal drugs, however, we have to "bring them in from the cold" without going so far as to give them a warm spot on the hearth rug. That means creating conditions in which users will be accepted (if not praised) rather than condemned. In that way we may expect user groups to help the general regulation, and hence limitation, of use. It won't be easy and it won't produce a perfect outcome, since such things are not possible—but it should work a lot better than what we have now.

NOTES

1. By modern, I mean a society with a developed money economy, large markets for goods and services sold as commodities, a substantial part of its population living in cities, a substantial secondary and tertiary economic sector, and a centralized state. I do not presume that the polity is democratic, or that the government is of left or right.

2. That is, does the quantity a consumer purchases rise and fall with supply/price alterations?

3. Note that it is easy, from within a conventional economic perspective, to suggest that as well as cash price, risk of arrest also has a negative utility for users, such that mere legalization, even with constant cash prices, would "lower cost."

4. We know, for example, that much drug use, licit or illicit, is polydrug use. Commonly, the consumption of one drug (e.g., alcohol or cocaine) is accompanied by increase in use of other drugs (e.g., tobacco or cannabis).

5. I ignore the biomedical roots of harm here, because while it is vital to know these, and while such knowledge has policy relevance, biology is less amenable to alteration for policy purposes than social arrangements.

6. Note that in the passages that follow, I will occasionally refer to costs, because much of the harm is experienced as or measured in terms of cost. I have in mind, however, much more than just economic costs.

7. In turn, this raises the question as to how to explain these over- and underlimitation tendencies. Clearly, as is widely conceded by all but the most doctrinaire, it cannot be a rational result of the calculation of the relative dangers of the licit as opposed to the illicit drugs. (No illicit drug, for example, causes a fraction of the deaths that each year are provoked by tobacco smoking.) That is, we do not underlimit licit drugs because of their safety nor overlimit the illicit drugs because of their demonstrated dangers. There is, however, insufficient room to explore this here. It relates to the second assumption I make at the start of the paper (the demand for control) which needs separate study in itself.

References

Bourdieu, Pierre (1987). *Distinction: A Social Critique of the Judgement of Taste*, trans. Richard Nice. London: Routledge & Kegan Paul.

Campbell, Colin (1983). "Romanticism and the Consumer Ethic: Intimation of a Weber-Style Thesis." *Sociological Analysis* 44:279–96.

Campbell, Colin (1987). *The Romantic Ethic and the Spirit of Modern Consumerism.* Oxford: Basil Blackwell.

Cohen, Peter (1989). *Cocaine Use in Amsterdam in Non-Deviant Subcultures.* University of Amsterdam Report.

Douglas, Mary, and Baron Isherwood (1983). *The World of Goods: Towards an Anthropology of Consumption.* London: Allen Lane.

Erickson, Patricia, Edward Adlaf, Glenn Murray, and Reginald Smart (1987). *The Steel Drug: Cocaine in Perspective.* Lexington, Mass.: Lexington Books, D. C. Heath.

Gibbs, Jack P. (1990). "Control as Sociology's Central Notion." *Social Science Journal* 27(1):1–27.

Giddens, Anthony (1985). *The Nation-State and Violence.* Cambridge: Polity Press.

Helmer, John (1975). *Drugs and Minority Oppression.* New York: Seabury Press.

Hindess, Barry (1988). *Choice, Rationality and Social Theory.* London: Unwin-Hyman.

Lyng, Stephen (1990). "Edgework: A Social Psychological Analysis of Voluntary Risk Taking." *American Journal of Sociology* 95(4):851–86.

Morgan, Patricia (1978). "The Legislation of Drug Law: Economic Crisis and Social Control." *Journal of Drug Issues* 8(1):53–62.

Mugford, Stephen (1991a). "Least Worst Solutions to the Drug Problem." *Drug and Alcohol Review* (in press).

Mugford, Stephen (1991b). "Towards a Unified Policy for Legal and Illegal Drugs," in Terry Carney et al. (eds.), *An Unwinnable War against Drugs.* Sydney: Pluto Press, pp. 22–36.

Mugford, Stephen, and Phil Cohen (1989). "Drug Use, Social Relations and Commodity Consumption: A Study of Recreational Cocaine Users in Sydney, Canberra and Melbourne." Report to the Research into Drug Abuse Advisory Committee, National Campaign against Drug Abuse (Australia).

O'Malley, Pat, and Stephen Mugford (1991). "The Demand for Intoxicating Commodities: Implications for the War on Drugs." *Social Justice* (in press).

Scottish Cocaine Research Group (1990). "Scottish Cocaine Users: Yuppie Snorters or Ghetto Smokers?" Unpublished paper.

Stallybrass, Peter, and Allon White (1986). *The Politics and Poetics of Transgression.* London: Methuen.

Turner, Victor Witter (1969). *The Ritual Process: Structure and Anti-Structure*. Chicago: Aldine.

Watson, Pamela (1991). "Does Abundant Supply of Drugs Lead to Heavy Consumption?: A Papua New Guinea Case Study." *International Journal on Drug Policy* (in press).

Wolfe, Alan (1989). *Whose Keeper?: Social Science and Moral Obligation*. Berkeley: University of California Press.

Zinberg, Norman (1984). *Drug, Set and Setting: The Basis for Controlled Intoxicant Use*. New Haven: Yale University Press.

PART TWO

ECONOMIC IMPLICATIONS

3

THE WAR WE ARE LOSING

Milton Friedman

After everything that has been said on all sides of this issue, there is little new that is left to be said. I was going to say that one thing on which everybody has agreed is a need for more money for research—especially for the research we ourselves do—but I like to be contrary so I will express a disagreement with that. If on any subject whatsoever we waited until all the research we wanted to do was done, we would never do anything. If we are going to act, we have to act on the basis of the evidence that there is. I do not agree with those like my good friend, Ed Meese, who say that you need a detailed and well-reasoned alternative before you do anything about the present system, that the burden of proof is upon those who want to change the system. If the system is making a mess, it is a good thing to do something to change it even though you may not have a fully detailed alternative.

One thing that needs to be kept in mind is that we are fundamentally all on the same side. We all have the same objectives. We all recognize that drugs are currently doing a great deal of harm. What divides us is our judgment about the best means to minimize the harm done by drugs. We must not let ourselves get diverted from trying to reach reasonable, sensible conclusions by attributing bad motives to those who disagree with us. There is a famous statement, which I have used many times, made by Pierre S. du Pont almost precisely two centuries ago (September 25, 1790) to the National Assembly in revolutionary France in which he said, "Gentlemen, it is a disagreeable custom to which one is too easily led by the harshness of the discussions, to assume evil intentions. It is necessary to be gracious as to intentions; one should believe them good, and apparently they are; but we do not have to be gracious at all to inconsistent logic or to absurd reasoning. Bad logicians have committed more involuntary crimes than bad men have done intentionally."

I am obviously not going to add any arguments to the large number already presented. I want to use my limited time simply to try to bring a little order out of the discussion and to add a little evidence.

People tend to discuss the issue of drugs on two levels. One level was well described by one of the speakers as Plato versus John Stuart Mill: The philosophical disagreement between Plato's view that it is right for some of us ("philosopher kings") to tell others of us what they must do because it is good for them, and the doctrine of John Stuart Mill that the role of government is simply to prevent people from doing harm to others and that it is not right for government to try to force people to do anything simply for their own good. The philosopher-king perspective and the libertarian perspective, if you will. No doubt there is a wide disagreement on that level, and as many of you know my own sympathies are on the side of John Stuart Mill. That consideration is not decisive in this issue, however, as it is not in many. Nonetheless, it does affect people's attitudes and the way in which they look at things. I think that it is worth recognizing.

Why is it not decisive? Because even the libertarians justify interference to prevent harm to others. In my opinion, the most basic distinction that needs to be kept in mind in this discussion is between innocent victims and self-chosen victims. That has come out again and again in many discussions. As everyone recognizes, self-chosen victims may and do harm others as well. Even if there were no laws against drugs whatsoever, if they were completely legal, there would still be innocent victims. The most obvious, of course, are the crack babies. I don't know how many there are—that is for you medical people to decide—but insofar as there are any they are obviously innocent victims of their mothers. So legalizing drugs would not eliminate all innocent victims. Even a strict libertarian might argue for prohibiting certain drugs, or putting strict limits on them, on the ground that interference with individual behavior is more than offset by the prevention of harm to innocent victims.

That brings the real issue to the second level—the level of expediency. We now have a system to control drugs. Is it working? Is it doing more good or more harm? If it is doing more harm, let's stop doing that harm and let's not wait until we have a fully worked-out, detailed plan for exactly what we are going to put in its place. Let's eliminate those features of it that are clearly and obviously doing the most harm. Again, everybody agrees on this level that the present methods are doing a great deal of harm. Dr. Clarke movingly and effectively presents one of the most important components of that harm (in Chapter 25).

The attempt to enforce the prohibition of the use of drugs is destroying our poorer neighborhoods in city after city, creating a climate that is destructive to the people who live there. This phenomenon is perhaps the greatest disgrace in the United States at the moment. I say "perhaps" because an alternative is what we are doing to other countries—a subject discussed in Chapter 20. Can anybody tell me that the United States of America is justified in destroying Colombia because the United States cannot enforce its own laws? If we enforced our laws, there would be no problem.

I don't mean to say we could not enforce our laws. In principle, there is no doubt that we could completely eliminate drugs if we were willing to use the methods that Saudi Arabia is willing to use: If we were willing to cut off the hands of a drug offender; if we were willing to impose capital punishment on drug dealers. We are not, and all of us without exception are proud of the fact that we are not willing to use those methods. Those are cures that are clearly worse than the disease. Given that we cannot enforce our own laws, I believe that there is no way to justify behavior by the United States that leads to the destruction of other countries.

We are destroying the poorer neighborhoods in central cities, but at least we are doing that to ourselves. I don't justify it—don't misunderstand me—but I see even less justification for destroying other people's countries. I have asked this question of many people who are in favor of our present policies. I have never had what I regard as a halfway satisfactory answer.

In discussing the issue of drugs, I, like many others, have cited the prohibition of alcohol in the 1920s as an obvious example of the evil effects of prohibition, as does Dr. Morgan (Chapter 24). In response, I have received a good deal of correspondence. Those who object to my conclusions tend to make two arguments in response, and the little bit of data that I would like to add is in response to these arguments.

Everyone recognizes that the prohibition of drugs makes drugs into a profitable illegal activity and creates a class of criminals. However, the proponents of prohibition answer, if you legalized or decriminalized drugs, or in any other way changed the situation, these people would still be criminals; they would just go on to other crimes. Look, they say, what happened after prohibition. You had Al Capone and the gangs, and after prohibition ended they just shifted over to other sectors. Unquestionably, there is some truth in that. The building-up of a criminal class is going to leave a hangover, and the hangover is going to mean more criminality.

How serious is it? I have a graph (Figure 3.1). The series that goes all the way back to 1910 is the homicide rate. Its scale is on the left. It goes to 1987, which is as far as the data were readily available. From 1910 on, there is an almost explosive growth in the number of homicides. The first part of the explosion is during World War I, and one phenomenon you observe over and over is that wars tend to lead to a rise in crime. What happened after the end of the war? The homicide rate kept on going up very rapidly and reached a peak in

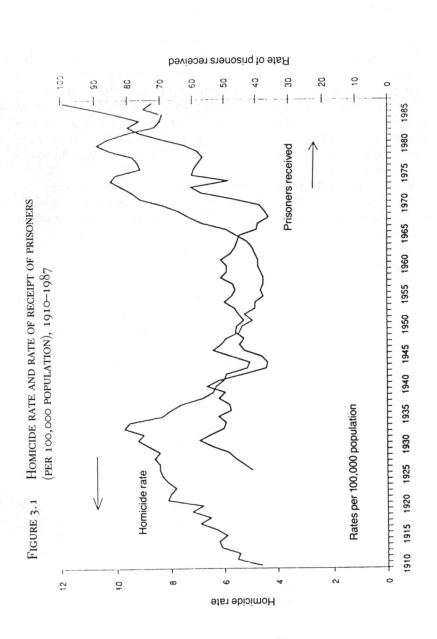

FIGURE 3.1   HOMICIDE RATE AND RATE OF RECEIPT OF PRISONERS
(PER 100,000 POPULATION), 1910–1987

precisely the year in which prohibition was ended, 1933. It then fell drastically, and it stayed down throughout the forties and the fifties, except for a rise during World War II. Since 1933 was also the end of the great contraction, it can be argued that the Great Depression was also a stimulus to crime and to homicide. Throughout the prosperous 1920s, however, homicides per hundred thousand persons were very much higher than throughout the prosperous forties and fifties, let alone in the late thirties which were not so prosperous. I believe that no one who looks at the evidence can doubt that ending prohibition had a significant and prompt effect on the homicide rate.

Homicides started to go up early in the 1960s and rose very rapidly after Nixon introduced his drug war. More recently, the rate has come down a little, but it is still at the same level as in 1933. I believe one can have great confidence that if drugs were decriminalized the homicide rate would fall sharply, most likely back to the level that it maintained throughout the fifties. That is no small matter: A reduction in the homicide rate from its average during the eighties to its average during the fifties would, with our current population, mean a saving in excess of 10,000 lives a year!

As another bit of evidence I have plotted the number of prisoners (per 100,000 population) received into all prisons—federal, state, and local—year by year. Those data, at least in the sources readily available to me, only went back to 1926. From then on, the number of prisoners received went up very sharply until 1931. It then went down, then rose again to 1940, went down sharply during the war, rose thereafter to a peak in 1961 and came down sharply to 1969. From 1970 on, the number of prisoners received rose dramatically, to a level in 1987 more than twice as high as in 1931. The increase in the number of prisoners received coincides with the beginning of Nixon's drug war, and received an additional boost when the Reagan drug war started.

To say the least, those are disheartening figures. Most discussions of innocent victims, including those I have heard here, leave out what I regard as one of the most important classes of innocent victims, those of us who are not protected by the police because the police are too busy trying to do something about drugs and are being corrupted by the drug industry. The destruction of the atmosphere of law enforcement, of the whole climate of law obedience, adds greatly to the list of innocent victims. Personally, I find it hard to see how anyone can deny the enormous importance of the innocent victims who have been produced by making possession of specified drugs and dealing in them a crime.

Few persons do deny the importance of such innocent victims. Those who nonetheless defend drug prohibition reply that decriminalizing drugs may well reduce the number of such innocent victims, but the price society pays for that gain will be a large increase in the number of addicts. Again they go back to alcohol and its prohibition for evidence. They claim that the end of alcohol prohibition was followed by a tremendous increase in the fraction of the population consuming alcohol and in the number of alcoholics.

The next two charts from my trusty computer are designed to answer that claim. The first (Figure 3.2) shows the fraction of total consumption expenditures spent on alcoholic beverages. It is available only for legal alcoholic beverages; that is why it starts in 1933. Unfortunately, all estimates of alcohol consumption during the prohibition era are necessarily highly indirect and uncertain, so I have chosen to stick only to the figures for legal beverages. Dr. Morgan refers to some data on consumption during prohibition, and it is clear that consumption did not disappear. Incidentally, among the innocent victims of prohibition are the addicts themselves, because of the factors that Dr. Morgan brings out. In an illegal market, there is bound to be adulteration and impure substances, which shows up in people dying. Indeed, it has always seemed to me that the greatest beneficiaries from the decriminalization of drugs would be the present addicts. They are made to become criminals. They can't ask for help without admitting that they are criminals. The argument in favor of the present method, thus, has to be that if drugs were decriminalized, you would have a vast increase in the number of addicts.

What does our experience after alcohol prohibition tell us? In the first three years, as legal beverages were being substituted for illegal beverages, it is not surprising that the reported percentage of all consumption expenditures spent on alcoholic beverages went up sharply. It peaked in 1937, then went down to 1940, then rose during the war until 1945. Thereafter it went down gradually but persistently.

I am old enough to be a veteran of that period myself. I remember a few months after prohibition had been repealed going to a Swedish restaurant in New York City with a Swedish friend of mine, a fellow graduate student at Columbia. It was a restaurant in which he had been able to buy Aquavit all during prohibition and he tried to get Aquavit for us. I had never tasted the stuff, and he thought that I ought to have that experience. They said, oh no, they couldn't serve it now because they hadn't received their license yet. He talked Swedish to them and finally was able to persuade them to take us back into the kitchen and give us a little taste of Aquavit. Anyone who believes that during prohibition there was any difficulty in getting alcohol in most of the United States should look at the evidence. I wasn't very old and was not much of a drinker but there was no difficulty in finding speakeasies.

To return to the chart, the skeptic may reply, and correctly, that it is a percentage. Total consumption is going up. Perhaps the smaller percentage of a larger total conceals a very large increase in the amount of alcohol consumed.

Figure 3.3 shows the expenditure on alcoholic beverages expressed in constant 1982 prices between the same dates. As you will see, absolute expenditures, like the percentage spent, went up to 1937 and then fell briefly. During the war,

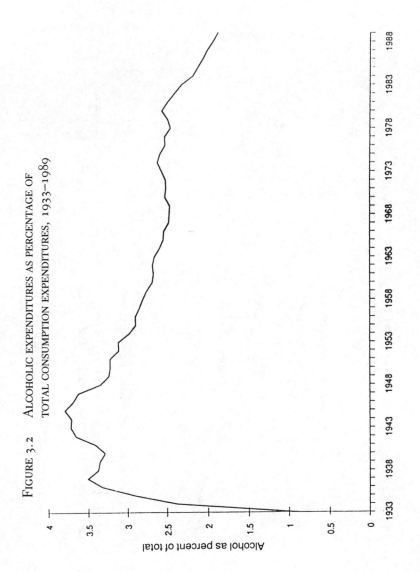

FIGURE 3.2   ALCOHOLIC EXPENDITURES AS PERCENTAGE OF
TOTAL CONSUMPTION EXPENDITURES, 1933–1989

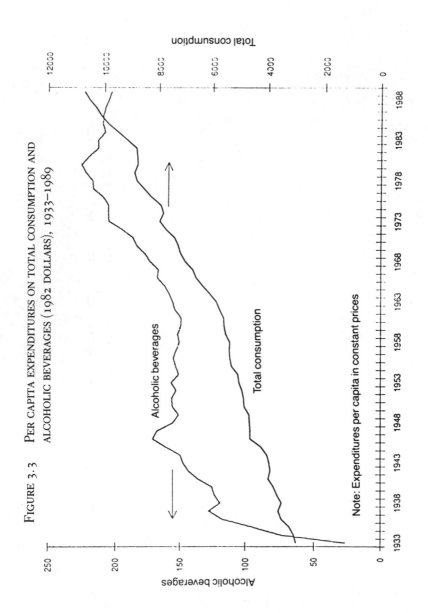

FIGURE 3:3   PER CAPITA EXPENDITURES ON TOTAL CONSUMPTION AND
ALCOHOLIC BEVERAGES (1982 DOLLARS), 1933–1989

Total consumption

Alcoholic beverages

Total consumption

Alcoholic beverages

Note: Expenditures per capita in constant prices

expenditures went up sharply, peaking this time in 1946. Expenditures then fell and remained fairly constant during the forties and fifties and then, beginning in 1961, there was a sharp increase in expenditures on alcoholic beverages. For our purposes, however, the important lesson from the chart is that the legalization of alcohol clearly did not stimulate alcoholism. The legalization of alcohol was followed by a plateau in the consumption of alcohol. The kinds of things that many people have talked about as occurring during the sixties produced the sharp increase in expenditures on alcoholic beverages from 1961 to 1980. Since then expenditures have been falling in absolute terms and not only as a percentage of total consumption.

The obvious implication is that if currently illicit drugs were decriminalized and handled exactly the way alcohol is now handled, there is no reason to suppose that there would be a vast increase in the number of addicts. That is by no means a certainty, but every statement that I have seen asserting the contrary is based on pure conjecture and hypothesis. I have seen no hard evidence. The closest to it that I have come across is reference to the opium craze in China. Given the evidence we have—not only from alcohol prohibition but also from Holland, Alaska, and others—the burden of proof, it seems to me, is on those who maintain that there would be a completely unacceptable increase in the number of addicts.

One thing we really do know for certain is that what we are now doing is not working. There is a wider measure of agreement on that proposition than appears on the surface. It is natural for people to exaggerate their differences. It is hard to impress people without overstating one's case. I suspect, for example, that on the issue of marijuana that Dr. Grinspoon addresses so movingly (Chapter 21), few people believe that dealing in marijuana ought to be a capital offense. I suspect that almost everybody would agree that there is no case whatsoever for treating marijuana the way we do.

It seems to me that we ought to recognize the harm that we are now doing, and not let the tyranny of the status quo prevent us from making some changes that can stop the killing in the slums and ghettos of our cities. We can stop destroying the possibility of a decent family life among the underprivileged in this country. I do not agree with many people who would agree with me on that point about the role that government ought to play in the treatment of addiction. I do not agree either with those who say that the tragedy of the slums is really a social problem, that the underprivileged do not have enough jobs and therefore government has to provide them with jobs. I want to tell those people that government performance is no better in creating jobs and solving other social problems than it is in drug prohibition. Just as a very large fraction of our crime is, in my opinion, caused by government measures, a very large fraction of our poverty is caused by government measures. If those of you who have studied the drug situation were to study as carefully the effects of government measures in the areas of welfare, social services, housing, and so on, you would not have any difficulty in recognizing that there is at least a little bit of sense in what I am saying. That is a different subject, however, and we ought to separate those subjects. Let's not draw ideological lines on this issue because, although there is no doubt an ideological element, the expediential considerations are so strong and so overwhelming that it seems to me they really dominate the situation.

Discussion

Q. I just wanted you to comment on some of the precedent that has been set by the fact that nicotine is legal and a great amount of education has gone into it recently and I believe nicotine consumption is going down on a per capita basis.

Friedman: I know nicotine consumption is going down on a per capita basis just as alcohol consumption is going down on a per capita basis.

Q. And the second part of that is what about the drug enforcement agencies. If we do legalize it, how do we respond to their losing their income or their financing from the government. If we legalize it we have to have something for the enforcement agencies . . .

Friedman: Nonsense. Why? The taxpayers are wasting their money now. Why should they continue to waste it?

Q. I am in 100 percent agreement, but how do we convince them not to? How do we turn the funds off?

Friedman: We can't convince them. We cannot get a change in procedure by convincing the people who have a strong interest in continuing the present methods. There is no area in our government in which we can do that. We cannot get rid of tariffs by trying to convince the people who are being protected by tariffs. We can't get rid of farm subsidies by persuading the farmers. It's the rest of us as citizens who have to be convinced. I don't believe that maintaining a full-employment policy for bureaucrats ought to deter us from taking the right measures.

Q. (Kildare Clarke) The question you state that it is more of a medical problem, which I do agree with because if we legalize or decriminalize drugs, even if we increased the number of addicts, it is a medical problem. Right now as a physician

I think God has given me the privilege to cure someone who is an addict, but he has not given me the power to raise Lazarus from the dead. When a man is dead with a gunshot wound to his head . . .

Friedman: I couldn't agree with you more.

Q. (Kildare Clarke) Therefore, based on that factor, would you comment a little about whether we should be looking at this as strictly a medical model as I state in my paper?

Friedman: I am not sure what that means and I don't think we want to draw hard and fast lines. For example, I believe that you would agree that we should make the sale of all drugs to youngsters under the age of 18 illegal, as we now do for cigarettes and alcohol. The question of advertising is a very difficult question. I must confess that my libertarian instincts lead me not to want to prohibit advertising, and yet I am repelled at the notion of seeing a pretty young lady on the television screen saying, smoke my brand of cocaine instead of his, or my brand of smack or crack. So I am very much torn on the question of advertising, but again we don't have to decide all those issues. We now prohibit much advertising of hard liquor, and that is why I tried to say let's treat drugs the way we treat alcohol now, which is a mixture of regarding it primarily as a medical problem, but on the margins, on the fringes, as a criminal problem.

Q. (Robert Millman) I would like you to belabor a point. I don't think that legalization of drugs will cure the problem of the inner city.

Friedman: It won't.

Q. (Robert Millman) And you act as if there is nothing that government can do, or that anyone can do, and I disagree. I think we can do enormous amounts to change the educational system. I think we have to start sooner, doing more along the way. My point is that there is a tendency to think that a technologic answer like legalization will alter suicides or alter crime or change the American dream in those areas, and that worries me.

Friedman: I don't call it a technological change. But whatever you call it, legalization of drugs will improve the conditions of the inner cities enormously, even if it does not completely cure the problem. In my opinion, the most important thing we can do to improve the inner city beyond that is to get the government out of doing most of what it is doing and into something else, which is privatizing the school system. The most destructive area of government inter-vention in the inner cities, other than the prohibition of drugs, is in the school system. What we have to do is to privatize the school system. This is something that I suggested doing thirty years ago through unlimited vouchers for schooling which could be used in any governmental or private school. In New York City it is also easy to see that you need to eliminate rent control, which has been a major factor in destroying housing in the inner cities.

Q. (Joseph McNamara)   Professor Friedman, what do you think realistically is the political potential for decriminalizing drugs, given what we have seen for seventy years?

Friedman: Unfortunately, very small, but you know that doesn't mean we shouldn't keep trying. For example, in education, I have been working on the voucher system for thirty years, even longer, and I have participated in one unsuccessful attempt to get one experiment started after another—in New Hampshire, in Connecticut, in Michigan, in Oregon—but that does not mean we should give up hope. I have also seen cases in which things that were said to be politically unfeasible became politically feasible almost overnight. They are not in this area, but I could cite you examples.

Q. (Joseph McNamara)   I have a personal example. I have been trying to get some reasonable firearms control for twenty years.

Friedman: I understand we're all in that position, and the one thing we must not do is to give up the fight. If we do, we are through.

Q.   Professor Friedman, you described it as mere conjecture that consumption of the currently illicit drugs would go up under legalization. If cocaine were made legally available and taxed at the same rate per dose as alcohol is now taxed, the price of cocaine would fall to approximately 10 percent of its current value. Do you think it is mere conjecture that the price elasticity for demand of cocaine is likely to be unity, more or less?

Friedman: No, no. Don't misunderstand me. I did not deny that consumption might go up. There is a high likelihood that it would. But there are offsetting forces that I will come to in a moment that might keep that from happening. What I designate as conjecture is the notion that there would be a manifold multiplication of the number of addicts, that the number of drug addicts would become comparable to the number of people consuming alcohol. That I believe is pure conjecture.

If you make something lower in price, it is likely that more will be purchased. There is price elasticity. But there are two offsetting forces. One is the effect of the forbidden-fruit kind of thing, especially on the young to whom doing something illegal has a certain value in and of itself. But, second . . .

Q. But under your proposal it would remain illegal. So the forbidden fruit wouldn't change.

Friedman: I beg your pardon. It would remain illegal for the children, but consuming drugs would not be doing something that in a sense was sneering at social values. That is what they want to do. Second, and more important, under present circumstances drug dealers have a financial incentive to create addicts. If they can create an addict, they have a captive customer. Under a legalized system, you don't see anybody on the street corners giving away bread. It doesn't pay you to give away bread because if you create somebody who loves bread he can buy it at the cheapest place. It would not pay anybody, for financial reasons, to create addicts.

Q. Unless people create brand-name drugs as, for example, R. J. Reynolds does hand out free examples of their cigarettes.

Friedman: They do hand out cigarettes, that is right. If there were brand-name drugs of that kind, the same thing would happen. But it would be on a much smaller scale. I am not questioning for a moment that the number of drug addicts is likely to go up. What I am saying is that the innocent victims created by even a much higher level of addiction would be vastly smaller than the number now created by drug prohibition. There have been cost-benefit analyses such as Rich Dennis published in the *Atlantic Monthly* in which he tried to estimate the financial costs and benefits from decriminalizing drugs. He establishes a highly persuasive case that the benefits are far greater than the costs.

However, I am inclined to rest the case much more on the human innocent-victim aspect than on the financial consequences. With respect to the notion that drugs should be taxed, I believe that we overtax alcohol now, in the sense that we tend to generate an illegal black market in alcohol. Very likely, the same thing would occur with drugs. We probably would end up overtaxing them. Everyone of us has a different law he would write, and no one of us is going to be able to write the law. What we can do is to agree that the present system is a mess and isn't working and that we should at least move to some extent in a direction that will reduce the major harm now being done.

On the political level, I want to cite one example that offers a bit more hope. Back in the 1940s and 1950s we had a military draft. And I may say, I was just as opposed to the military draft as I now am to the prohibition of drugs. It looked as if you couldn't get rid of it. It was politically unfeasible to get rid of the draft. We had a conference like this at the University of Chicago; I have forgotten the

exact date—sometime in the fifties or early sixties. It was one of the few conferences in which opinions were changed. I hope this will be another. We took a
poll at the beginning of the draft conference. We had, just as here, people in
favor of the draft, people opposed to the draft—a much wider group than here,
including politicians, academicians, and so on. At the beginning of that conference the vote was one-third in favor of the volunteer army and two-thirds in favor
of the draft. After three days of the conference, the vote was precisely reversed.
Two-thirds expressed themselves in favor of the volunteer army and one-third
still in favor of the draft. I believe that was a major factor in starting the ball
rolling, which ultimately got rid of the draft in 1973.

I believe that this is the same kind of an issue. The evidence is highly
persuasive to those who are willing to look at it from the point of view not of one
extreme or the other, but of the sensible middle that everybody is looking for.
We must change the present policy. I am not without hope that something will
happen. At least, the vigor of the attempt at enforcement will lessen.

Q.   The thing that concerns me, of course, is exactly the issue that you don't
say much about, except to say it is speculative, how much the user pool would
increase. But let me ask you this. Just make the assumption now that the use of
cocaine, particularly crack cocaine which is smoked, that is a socially acceptable
way to take things. Just suppose we ended up with as many crack smokers as we
have nicotine users today. So that the expansion would be that great. Would that
change your views at all about the issue of legalization?

Friedman: It probably would, not about the legalization of marijuana or some
other drugs, but about crack. However, I believe that the likelihood of that
happening is extremely small. I cannot claim to be an expert on this, but I have
looked at a great many studies. I find the evidence of anything like that explosion
in usage occurring very underwhelming.

Q.   But that is the central issue, isn't it?

Friedman: No, it is not the central . . .

Q.   Since you would change your position if that were true, then it is important
to get a better estimate of whether that is true.

Friedman: Yes, and let me ask you a question. In the meantime, should we allow the killing to go on in the ghettos? Perhaps 10,000 additional murders a year? In the meantime, should we continue to destroy Colombia? Let me ask you a question. Suppose we succeeded in legalizing drugs and the smoking of crack went up 5 percent. Would you change your position?

Q. Probably.

4

DRUG LEGALIZATION AND THE CONSUMPTION OF DRUGS: AN ECONOMIST'S PERSPECTIVE

Jeffrey A. Miron

As the nation's concern with drug policy has escalated in recent years, the question of whether to legalize drugs has received renewed attention. From the perspective of economic analysis, many of the arguments on both sides of the issue are incomplete. The proponents of legalization point out that it would have significant benefits to society, such as freeing for other uses the resources currently devoted to enforcing the drug laws. The opponents of legalization note that it would result in lower prices for drugs, implying increases in consumption and the associated costs. In fact, both sides make correct points but fail to provide a complete answer. The question is not whether there are costs or benefits of legalization but whether the costs outweigh the benefits. To answer this question one must enumerate all the possible costs and benefits and attempt to assign quantitative magnitudes to each in order to arrive at an overall calculation of the net gain or loss from legalization.

This paper contributes to such a cost-benefit calculation by discussing the effects of legalization on the consumption of drugs. The question of how much consumption would increase under legalization is clearly at the center of any rational analysis of this proposed policy. Since there is no serious disagreement that enforcement of the drug laws involves significant costs, it is clearly desirable to legalize drugs if their prohibition has little or no effect on consumption.

There are three main themes of my discussion of the effects of drug legalization on the consumption of drugs. The first is that increases in consumption are not a cost per se; in fact, increases in consumption are a benefit. There is only a cost associated with increases in consumption to the extent that consumption of drugs produces significant externalities. The second theme is that theoretical considerations suggest both that the increases in consumption may be modest and that one needs to gather evidence on this issue in a particular way. Finally, evidence from the United States experience with prohibition of alcohol suggests that legalization of drugs is not likely to lead to significant increases in consumption.

COSTS ASSOCIATED WITH
INCREASED CONSUMPTION OF DRUGS

The first point to make about any increase in consumption that occurs because of legalization is that this increase, in and of itself, is a benefit rather than a cost of legalization. The reasoning is simple. Prohibition of drugs keeps their price above their cost. If individuals are willing to pay more for a good than it costs to produce, then it is inefficient to prohibit the production and consumption of that good. This line of reasoning applies to consumption of illegal drugs as much as it does to the consumption of milk, cars, or televisions. It is an extremely simple point from the perspective of standard economic analysis, yet it is one often overlooked by both noneconomists and economists in the debate over legalization.

The statements made in the previous paragraph may strike many as absurd. In order to rebut the argument advanced there, however, it is necessary to argue that illegal drugs are not commodities just like toaster ovens or ice cream cones. That is, one must argue that illegal drugs are commodities with a significant characteristic that causes the standard economic reasoning to fail. The question then becomes, what exactly is the difference between illegal drugs and those commodities that society does not prohibit?

A common response to this question is that illegal drugs are addictive. From the perspective of economic analysis, however, addictiveness per se does not justify discouraging consumption of illegal drugs. To see this point, one must first ask what addiction means. The definition of addiction is potentially complicated and controversial from the perspective of sociology, pharmacology, or medicine, but it is quite simple from the perspective of standard economic analysis (Becker and Murphy, 1988). A good is addictive if consumption of the good this period raises the desirability of consuming that good in future periods.

When addiction is defined in this manner, it is immediately clear that a huge range of currently legal goods are addictive. Alcohol, gambling, caffeine, and nicotine are the most obvious examples, but the list goes far beyond these. If going to the opera for the first time teaches me an appreciation of opera, so that I enjoy the second opera more than the first, then going to the opera is addictive by the standard economic definition. Likewise, if practicing my back-hand makes me a better tennis player, and I enjoy the game more the greater my ability, then playing tennis is addictive. It is obvious that the list of potentially addictive items is enormous according to this definition. It is also obvious that, from this perspective, a particular good may be addictive for some individuals but not for others.

So long as individuals correctly anticipate the effects of their current con-sumption decisions on the desirability of future consumption choices, there is no reason for policy to interfere with individuals' decisions to consume addictive goods. When someone decides this period to begin going to the opera, under-standing that this will affect the set of consumption choices he wishes to make in the future, that individual can correctly trade off the benefits and costs of the initial consumption of the addictive good. Similarly, if an individual chooses to consume an addictive drug, with full understanding of the future effects on desired consumption, there is no economic rationale for interfering with that decision.

If the possibility of addiction does not provide a rationale for prohibition of drugs, then what does? The compelling line of argument, from an economic perspective, is that the consumption of drugs creates negative externalities. An externality is an effect on another person's consumption or production possibilities (other than an effect on price) that results from a given individual's actions. The consumption of illegal drugs may produce significant externalities in some in-stances. If the consumption of crack during pregnancy affects the health of the newborn infant, that is an externality. If the consumption of marijuana impairs one's ability to drive a car, thereby endangering other persons and property, that is an externality. In situations in which consumption produces negative exter-nalities, it is a standard result of economic analysis that individuals consume too much of the good.

It does not follow that the presence of negative externalities due to drug consumption necessarily provides a compelling case against legalization. The crucial point is that the consumption of many legal goods produces negative externalities. For example, consumption of alcohol during pregnancy is known to have serious negative effects on the health of newborns, similarly to cocaine, and consumption of alcohol impairs one's ability to drive and therefore endangers other persons and property, similarly to marijuana.

The fact that all sorts of activities create externalities does not by itself argue against the prohibition of drugs; if consumption of goods such as alcohol creates negative externalities, then it may be desirable government policy to discourage their consumption as well. The fact that consumption of many goods creates externalities, however, shows there is a broader question to be considered: Given that society has limited resources it can devote to discouraging consumption of externality-producing goods, which goods would it be most desirable to discourage? It is possible that the answer is drugs, but the answer might be speeding on the highway.

To justify prohibition of drugs, therefore, it is necessary to argue that consumption of drugs creates more externalities than would arise if consumption of drugs were reduced or eliminated. This need not be the case. Raising the price of marijuana relative to that of alcohol, for example, may result mainly in a substitution from marijuana to alcohol rather than a significant reduction in the total amount of both substances consumed. Since alcohol impairs one's ability to drive as much or more than marijuana, the total reduction in externalities arising from the decrease in marijuana consumption may be substantially offset by the externalities created by increased consumption of alcohol. There is not likely to be a large benefit from prohibiting marijuana under these conditions. More generally, prohibition of drugs may not significantly reduce externalities because it simply results in a substitution toward consumption of other goods that also create externalities.

There is one additional point to be considered in the discussion of externalities related to consumption of drugs. In a world in which health care is subsidized by government, consumption of many goods produces externalities simply because of the effect on one's health. For example, the excessive consumption of saturated fat may increase one's risk of heart attack, implying an increased demand for health resources that are partially funded by others. It does not follow, however, that such behavior should be discouraged. It is also necessary to argue that this behavior creates greater externalities than the alternative. In the case of health, everyone is going to die of something. If eating lots of chocolate ice cream causes me to die suddenly of a heart attack at age 60 instead of living for an extended period with Alzheimer's disease, then the total drain on the health care system may actually be less if I indulge in saturated fat. In this hypothetical world, given that the government subsidizes health care, it should also subsidize the consumption of Ben and Jerry's New York Super Fudge Chunk ice cream.

To state the argument in the paragraph above is to immediately make clear how complicated policy can be in a world where health care is subsidized. More important for the purposes here, it shows that there is not an obvious case for prohibiting drugs simply because they may lead to health problems. It is also necessary to argue that the demand for health care that results when drugs are illegal is less than would be the case under the alternative scenario where drugs are legal. There are at least a few reasons why just the reverse might occur. Under legalization, there would be fewer overdoses from drugs because they would be readily available in small, clearly designated dosages. Similarly, deaths and illness resulting from consumption of impure drugs would be essentially eliminated. It is also plausible that if consumption of drugs were legal, more pregnant mothers using drugs would seek medical attention early during pregnancy to obtain help in reducing their drug consumption.

How Much Would Consumption Increase under Legalization?

The arguments presented above should not be read as saying there is no economic case for reducing the consumption of illegal drugs. It is possible that, once correctly carried out, an analysis of the effects of legalization would indicate significant costs resulting from drug consumption. If so, the question for analysis then becomes, how much would consumption increase? If the answer to this question is that increases would be modest, there is potentially a strong case for legalization given the significant costs attached to the enforcement of drug prohibition. If, alternatively, the answer is that increases in consumption would be substantial, then a correct accounting of the costs and benefits might indicate a need to discourage consumption of illegal drugs, although not necessarily along the lines currently employed.

In this section, I discuss some theoretical issues that must be addressed in any attempt to measure the effects of legalization on consumption, and I suggest that, on a priori grounds, the increases in consumption may be expected to be modest. It is also useful to note that, even though consumption may increase, some of the increase would not lead to additional externalities. If an individual smokes marijuana occasionally in order to relax, but abstains from consuming it when driving or while pregnant, then the increased consumption does not create the externalities discussed above. Since those most likely to consume drugs when illegal are also those most likely to consume them in an irresponsible way, it is plausible that the increases in consumption, which are desirable per se, would not be accompanied by negative externalities in all cases.

The first key point is that there is likely to be substantial diversity in the population with respect to individuals' desire to consume currently illegal drugs. Specifically, many people may have no desire to consume any quantity of such goods no matter how low the price, in the same way that many currently have no desire to attend the opera and others have no desire to watch baseball. Some opponents of legalization appear to believe there is an enormous latent demand for drugs that would surface the instant such goods became legal. The people who make such arguments, however, do not find it the least implausible that millions do not watch the hours of free and legal television programming that are available, or that many who could easily afford to smoke or to drink alcohol and coffee choose not to do so. There is no reason why the same situation may not obtain with respect to drugs.

The second crucial point about the possible increases in consumption that might result from legalization follows directly from the first. If, at least in part, the world consists of individuals who have some demand for these goods at positive prices and others who do not, then it is likely that those who have the greatest desire to consume such goods are the ones already doing so. The important implication of this view is that extrapolation from elasticities estimated on the basis of existing consumers is likely to overstate the increases in consumption that would occur as the result of lower prices under legalization.

It *is* possible to obtain plausible estimates of the effect of legalization on the consumption of drugs, but this requires a methodology different from that often employed. The appropriate methodology is to compare the patterns of consumption across different countries or time periods that have substantial differences in the legal status of drugs. One might ask whether the consumption of heroin in the United States decreased substantially after it was criminalized in 1914, for example, or whether the consumption of marijuana decreased substantially after its criminalization in 1937. Alternatively, one might compare the level of drug consumption in countries such as the United States, which treats drug consumption as a criminal act, with countries such as the Netherlands, which treats drug addiction as a medical problem. Ideally, one would like to observe instances where the prohibition of drugs (or similar goods) has been significantly reduced or eliminated. This is the experiment that is most relevant to current discussions of drug legalization.

CONSUMPTION AFTER DRUG LEGALIZATION: THE EVIDENCE FROM PROHIBITION

Since any careful evaluation of the costs and benefits of drug legalization relies crucially on the effects of legalization on consumption, it is essential to examine evidence on the effects of prohibition of drugs on the amounts consumed. Unfortunately, there is an extreme scarcity of evidence on this subject. The obvious explanation is that since prohibition makes drugs illegal, accurate data are no longer collected. In addition, since most drugs have been illegal in the United States since before the government began effective collection of any kind of economic data, there are few episodes in our history for which one can compare consumption before and after prohibition, using any kind of data at all. As discussed above, it is potentially crucial to see what happens to consumption of drugs after the removal of legal penalties, since demand elasticities estimated on the basis of current consumption are potentially biased in the direction of showing excessive price sensitivity.

In this section I summarize briefly some evidence on the likely effects of legalization based on the United States experience with the prohibition of alcohol during the 1920s and early 1930s. For the period of alcohol prohibition itself, there are no official data on consumption of alcohol. For the periods before and after prohibition, however, accurate data are available. This allows us to determine whether certain other series that are closely related to the consumption of alcohol are good proxies for consumption.

The evidence that I summarize here is taken from work conducted jointly with Jeffrey Zweibel (Miron and Zwiebel, 1991). The estimates of alcohol consumption discussed are closely related to those reported by Warburton (1932) but improve on his in two ways. First, they are based on more reasonable functional forms, although this has only minor effects on the results. More important, the estimates discussed here indicate what happened to consumption when prohibition ended, while Warburton's do not because his analysis was conducted in the middle of prohibition. As discussed above, the most relevant question for current discussions of drug legalization is what happens to consumption when prohibition is removed.

The evidence in Miron and Zwiebel shows that a number of different series are all excellent proxies for the consumption of alcohol. The series considered are the death rate from cirrohsis of the liver, the death rate from alcoholism, the drunkenness arrest rate, and the number of first admittances to mental hospitals for alcoholic psychosis. In the periods before and/or after prohibition, each of these measures correlates extremely well with the consumption of alcohol per capita. Of course, no measure is perfectly correlated, and there are plausible reasons why the relation between each measure and the consumption of alcohol may have changed during prohibition. Prohibition may have encouraged enforcement of the drunkenness laws, for example, leading to a higher number of arrests per given amount of alcohol consumption. Alternatively, if deaths due to consumption of wood alcohol were reported as deaths due to alcoholism, this measure would overstate the amount of alcohol consumption during prohibition.

Note, however, that in many cases the biases introduced by prohibition cause the proxy series to understate true consumption. In the case of drunkenness, it may be that prohibition caused consumption to move out of bars and restaurants into the home, thereby lowering the arrest rate for a given level of consumption. Similarly, if there were stigma attached to being a heavy drinker or an alcoholic, some deaths from cirrhosis or alcoholism might have been classified as other diseases. It is therefore not obvious that the measures of alcohol consumption discussed here contain systematic biases in the direction of overestimating alcohol consumption during prohibition. In addition, reliance on a number of series reduces the likelihood of significant bias since any biases are unlikely to be highly correlated across series.

As it turns out, the four different measures of alcohol consumption tell a consistent story about the behavior of alcohol consumption during prohibition. At the beginning of prohibition, consumption declined significantly, to approximately 30 percent of its preprohibition level. Beginning in the early 1920s, however, alcohol consumption increased sharply, to about 60–70 percent of the preprohibition value. Most important, alcohol consumption immediately after the repeal of prohibition remained virtually the same as during the latter part of prohibition, although consumption increased to approximately its preprohibition level during the subsequent decade.

There are at least four reasons why prohibition of a good might discourage consumption. First, prohibition increases illegal supply costs, since these must include the cost of evading detection and the potential cost of punishment. This implies a higher equilibrium market price and less consumption. Second, prohibition may decrease consumer access to the good, leading to higher search costs and more uncertain quality. Third, prohibition may discourage consumption by creating a sentiment that a good is "bad" or "immoral." Finally, under prohibition some individuals may choose not to consume a good out of "respect for the law."

The results reported here on prohibition suggest that of these factors, the only ones that had a significant effect on alcohol consumption were the changes in price and availability, rather than the legal status per se or any effect of public sentiment. The reasoning is based on the observation, due to Warburton, that price increased approximately threefold from the preprohibition period to 1930. Since the fall in consumption between these two periods was only 20–30 percent, even a modest demand elasticity explains all the quantity variation. This means that there is essentially no change in consumption for other factors to explain.

There are, of course, important similarities and differences to keep in mind when trying to draw inferences from prohibition about how drug legalization might change consumption of drugs. First, the prices of illegal drugs appears to have been forced further above their production costs than that of alcohol during prohibition, presumably because of more stringent enforcement. This effect, however, may be countered by a more inelastic demand for illegal drugs than alcohol. Hence, the price for drugs is likely to fall more than that of alcohol after prohibition, but it is unclear whether consumption will rise more due to price effects. Second, there seems to be no reason why "respect for the law" or other social impediments are any more likely to have a significant impact on drug consumption than they did on alcohol consumption during prohibition. It is plausible that any increase in consumption from such sources following drug legalization would be small.

CONCLUSION

This paper has analyzed several issues related to the changes in consumption of illegal drugs that might occur if drugs were legalized. The main points are, first, that such increases in consumption are by themselves a benefit rather than a cost of legalization, and that calculating the costs of externalities related to drug consumption is subtle and may not imply a significant total cost. Second, there are theoretical reasons to anticipate small increases in consumption from legalization, and the evidence from alcohol prohibition confirms these expectations. Of course, any debate on drug legalization is incomplete if it solely considers changes in consumption. The point of the discussion here is to indicate that the primary costs to society, in terms of the increased social ills that may accompany drug consumption, are probably not as great as often claimed.

References

Becker, Gary S., and Kevin M. Murphy, "A Theory of Rational Addiction," *Journal of Political Economy*, 96 (August 1988), 675–700.

Miron, Jeffrey A., and Jeffrey Zwiebel, "Alcohol Consumption during Prohibition," *American Economic Review* 81, no. 2 (May 1991), 242–47.

Warburton, Clark, *The Economic Results of Prohibition* (New York: Columbia University Press, 1932).

5

RATIONAL ADDICTION AND THE EFFECT OF PRICE ON CONSUMPTION

Michael Grossman, Gary S. Becker, and Kevin M. Murphy

Legalization of such substances as marijuana, heroin, and cocaine surely will reduce the prices of these harmful addictive drugs. By the law of the downward sloping demand function, their consumption will rise. But by how much? According to conventional wisdom, the consumption of these illegal addictive substances is not responsive to price. Limited empirical evidence from the 1970s does not support this view. Nisbet and Vakil (1972) report a price elasticity of demand for marijuana ranging from -1.0 to -1.5 in an anonymous mail questionnaire of U.C.L.A. students. Silverman and Spruill (1977) estimate the price elasticity of demand for heroin in an indirect manner from the relationship between crime and the price of heroin in a monthly time series of 41 neighborhoods in Detroit. They obtain an elasticity of $-.3$

These empirical estimates are too unreliable to be given much weight. Conventional wisdom, however, is contradicted also by Becker and Murphy's (1988) theoretical model of rational addiction. Their analysis implies that addictive substances are likely to be quite responsive to price. Empirical applications of the model to the demand for such legal addictive substances as cigarettes (Becker, Grossman, and Murphy, 1990; Chaloupka, forthcoming) and gambling

Our research has been supported by the Lynde and Harry Bradley Foundation through the Center for the Study of the Economy and the State, University of Chicago, and by the Hoover Institution.

(Mobilia, 1990) support this prediction. In addition, related work on the demand for heavy consumption of alcohol by Cook and Tauchen (1982) is consistent with the notion that price elasticities of addictive goods are relatively large.

In this paper we summarize Becker and Murphy's model of rational addiction and the empirical evidence that supports it. We use the theory and evidence to draw highly tentative inferences concerning the effects of legalization of currently banned substances on consumption in the aggregate and for selected groups in the population.

Addictive behavior is usually assumed to involve both reinforcement and tolerance. "Reinforcement" means that greater past consumption of addictive goods, such as drugs or cigarettes, increases the desire for present consumption. "Tolerance" cautions that the utility from a given amount of consumption is lower when past consumption is greater.

These aspects of addictive behavior imply several restrictions on the instantaneous utility function.

$$u(t) = u[c(t), S(t), y(t)] \tag{1}$$

where $u(t)$ is utility at t, $c(t)$ is consumption of the addictive good, $y(t)$ is a nonaddictive good, and $S(t)$ is the stock of "addictive capital" that depends on past consumption of c and on life-cycle events. Tolerance is defined by $\frac{\partial u}{\partial S} = u_s$ < 0, which means that addictions are harmful in the sense that greater past consumption of addictive goods lowers current utility. Stated differently, higher $c(t)$ lowers future utility by raising future values of S.

Reinforcement $\left(\frac{dc}{dS} > 0\right)$ requires that an increase in past use raises the marginal utility of current consumption: $\left(\frac{\partial^2 u}{\partial c \partial S} = u_{cs} > 0\right)$. This is a sufficient condition for myopic utility maximizers who do not consider the future consequences of their current behavior. Rational utility maximizers also consider the future harmful consequences of their current behavior. Reinforcement for them requires that the positive effect of an increase in $S(t)$ on the marginal utility of $c(t)$ exceeds the negative effect of higher $S(t)$ on the future harm from greater $c(t)$.

Becker and Murphy (1988:680) show that a necessary and sufficient condition for reinforcement near a steady state (where $c = \delta S$) is

$$(\sigma + 2\delta) u_{cs} > -u_{ss} \tag{2}$$

where u_{cs} and u_{ss} are local approximations near the steady state, σ is the rate of time preference, and δ is the rate of depreciation on addictive capital. Reinforce-

FIGURE 5.1

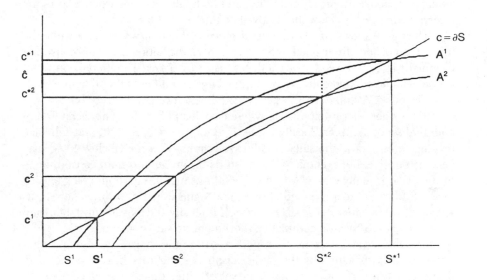

ment is stronger, the bigger the left-hand side is relative to the right-hand side. Clearly, $u_{cs} > 0$ is necessary if u is concave in $S(u_{ss} < 0)$; that is, if tolerance increases as S increases.

It is not surprising that addiction is more likely for people who discount the future heavily (a higher σ) since they pay less attention to the adverse consequences. Addiction to a good is also stronger when the effects of past consumption depreciate more rapidly (δ is larger), for then current consumption has smaller negative effects on future utility. The harmful effects of smoking, drinking, and much drug use do generally disappear within a few years after a person stops the addiction unless vital organs, such as the liver, become irreversibly damaged.

Reinforcement, as summarized in equation (2), has the important implication that the consumptions of an addictive good at different times are complements. Therefore, an increase in either past or expected future prices decreases current consumption. The relation between these effects of past and future prices depends on both time preference and the depreciation rate.

Figure 5.1 illustrates several implications of our approach to addiction, where S(t) is measured along the horizontal axis and c(t) along the vertical one. The line c = δS gives all possible steady states where c and S are constant over time. The positively sloped curves A^1 give the relation between c and S for an addicted consumer who has a particular utility function, faces given prices of c and y, and has a given wealth. The initial stock (S^0) depends on past consumption and past life-cycle experience. Both c and S grow over time when S^0 is in the interval where A^1 is above the steady-state line, and both fall over time when S^0 is in the intervals where A^1 is below the steady-state line.

The figure shows clearly why the degree of addiction is very sensitive to the initial level of addictive capital. If S^0 is below S' in the figure, a rational consumer eventually lays off the addictive good. If S_0 is above S^1, even a rational consumer becomes addicted, and ends up consuming large quantities of the addictive good.

The curve A^1 intersects the steady-state line at two points: $c^1 = \delta S^1$ and $c^{*1} = \delta S^{*1}$. Other relevant points are where $c = 0$ and $S \leqslant S^1$. The second point and third set of points are locally stable. If initially $c = 0$, $S \leqslant S^1$, and a divorce or other events raise the stock of addictive capital to a level below S^1, c may become positive, but eventually the consumer again refrains from consuming c. Similarly, if initially $c = c^{*1} = \delta S^{*1}$, c falls at first if, say, finding a good job lowers S from S^{*1} to a level $>S^1$; but c then begins to rise over time and returns toward c^{*1}. The other steady state $c^1 = \delta S^1$, is locally and globally unstable; even small changes in S cause cumulative movements toward $c = 0$ or $c = c^{*1}$.

Unstable steady states are an important part of the analysis of rational addictions, for they explain why the same person is sometimes heavily addicted to cigarettes, drugs, or other goods, and yet at other times lays off completely. Suppose the consumer starts out at $c^{*1} = \delta S^{*1}$, and experiences favorable events that lower his stock of addictive capital below S^{*1}, the unstable steady state with A^1. The consumer goes from being strongly addicted to eventually giving up c entirely. If A^1 is very steep when S is below the unstable steady state—if reinforcement is powerful in this interval—consumers would quit their addiction "cold turkey" (see the more extended analysis in Becker and Murphy, 1988).

To analyze a rational addict's responses to changes in the cost of addictive goods, suppose they are at $c^{*2} = \delta S^{*2}$ along A^2, and that a fall in the price of c raises the demand curve for c from A^2 to A^1. Consumption increases at first from c^{*2} to $\hat{c}$, and then c grows further over time since $\hat{c}$ is above the steady-state line. Consumption grows toward the new stable steady-state at $c^{*1} = \delta S^{*1}$. This shows that long-run responses to price changes exceed short-run responses because initial increases in consumption of addictive goods cause a subsequent growth in the stocks of addictive capital, which then stimulates further growth in consumption.

Since the degree of addiction is stronger when A is steeper, and since long-run responses to price changes are also greater when A is steeper, strong addictions do not imply weak price elasticities. Indeed, if anything, rational addicts respond more to price changes in the long run than do nonaddicts.[1] The short-run change is smaller than the long-run change because the stock of addictive capital is fixed. Even in the short run, however, rational addicts respond to the anticipated growth in future consumption since future and current consumption of addictive goods are complements for them. The *ratio* of short- to long-run responses does decline as the degree of addiction increases.[2]

The presence of unstable steady states for highly addictive goods means that the full effect of a price change on consumption could be much greater for these goods than the change between stable steady states given in note 1. Households with initial consumption capital between S^2 and S^1 in the figure would be to the left of the unstable steady state at S^2 when price equals p^2, but they would be to the right of the unstable steady state at S^1 when price equals p^1. A reduction in price from p^2 to p^1 greatly raises the long-run demand by these households because they move from low initial consumption to a stable steady state with a high level of consumption.

Temporary changes in prices of addictive goods have smaller effects on consumption than permanent changes—even when all changes are utility-compensated. The reason is that the complementarity between present and future consumption is less relevant with temporary price changes since future prices do not change.

The total cost of addictive goods to consumers equals the sum of the good's price and the money value of any future adverse effects, such as the negative effects on earnings and health of smoking, heavy drinking, or dependence on crack. Either a higher price of the good—due perhaps to a larger tax—or a higher future cost—due perhaps to greater information about health hazards—reduces consumption in both the short and long runs.

It is intuitively plausible that as price becomes a bigger share of total cost, long-run changes in demand induced by a given percentage change in the money price get larger *relative* to the long-run changes induced by an equal percentage change in future costs.[3] Money price tends to be relatively more important to poorer and younger consumers, partly because they generally place a smaller monetary value on health and other harmful future effects.

Poorer and younger persons also appear to discount the future more heavily (this is suggested by the theoretical analysis in Becker, 1990). It can be shown that addicts with higher discount rates respond more to changes in money prices of addictive goods, whereas addicts with lower rates of discount respond more to changes in the harmful future consequences.[4]

These implications of rational addiction can be tested with evidence on the demand for cigarettes, heavy consumption of alcohol, and gambling. Becker, Grossman, and Murphy (1990) fit models of rational addiction to cigarettes to a time series of state cross sections for the period from 1955 to 1985. We find a sizable long-run price elasticity of demand ranging between −.7 and −.8, while the elasticity of consumption with respect to price in the first year after a permanent price change (the short-run price elasticity) is about −.04. Smoking in different years appears to be complementary: Cigarette consumption in any year is lower when both future prices and past prices are higher.

Chaloupka (forthcoming) analyzes cigarette-smoking over time by a panel of individuals. He finds similar short-run and long-run price elasticities to those we estimate, and that future as well as past increases in cigarette prices reduce current smoking. He also finds that smoking by the less educated responds much more to changes in cigarette prices than does smoking by the more educated; a similar result has been obtained by Townsend (1987) with British data. Lewit, Coate, and Grossman (1981) and Lewit and Coate (1982) report that youths respond more than adults to changes in cigarette prices. By contrast, the information that began to emerge in the early 1960s about the harmful long-run effects of smoking has had a much greater effect on smoking by the rich and more educated than by the poor and less educated (Farrell and Fuchs, 1982, for the United States; Townsend, 1987, for Britain).

Cook and Tauchen (1982) examine variations in death rates from cirrhosis of the liver (a standard measure of heavy alcohol use), as well as variations in per capita consumption of distilled spirits, in a time series of state cross sections for the years 1962 through 1977. They find that state excise taxes on distilled spirits have a negative and statistically significant effect on the cirrhosis death rate. Moreover, a $1 increase in 1982 prices in a state's excise tax lowers death rates by a larger percentage than it lowers per capita consumption (10.8 percent versus 7.2 percent).

Mobilia (1990) applies the rational addiction framework to the demand for gambling at horse-racing tracks. Her data consist of a U.S. time series of racing-track cross sections for the period from 1950 through 1986 (tracks over time are the units of observation). She measures consumption by the real amount bet per person attending (handle per attendant), and price by the takeout rate (the fraction of the total amount bet that is retained by the track). Her findings are similar to those in the rational addictive studies of cigarettes. The long-run price elasticity of demand for gambling equals − .7 and is more than twice as large as the short-run elasticity of − .3. Moreover, an increase in the current takeout rate lowers the handle per attendant in both past and future years.

The evidence from smoking, heavy drinking, and gambling strongly supports our model of rational addiction. In particular, long-run price elasticities are sizable and much bigger than short-run elasticities, higher future as well as past prices reduce current consumption, lower-income persons respond more to changes in prices of addictive goods than do higher-income persons, whereas the latter respond more to changes in future harmful effects, and younger persons respond more to price changes than do older persons. It seems reasonable to us that what holds for smoking, heavy drinking, and gambling tends to hold also for drug use, although direct evidence is not yet available, and many experts on drugs would be skeptical. Lacking the evidence, we simply indicate what to expect from various kinds of price changes if responses of drug addicts are similar to those of persons addicted to other goods.

To fix these ideas, consider a large permanent reduction in the price of drugs—perhaps due to partial or complete legalization—combined with much greater efforts to educate the population about the harm from drug use. Our analysis predicts that much lower prices could significantly expand use even in the short run, and it would surely stimulate much greater addiction in the long run. Note, however, that the elasticity of response to very large price changes would be less than that to modest changes if the elasticity is smaller at lower prices.

The effects of a fall in drug prices on demand would be countered by the education program. Since drug use by the poor would be more sensitive to the price fall than to greater information about harmful longer-run effects, drug addiction among the poor is likely to become more important relative to addiction among the middle classes and rich. For similar reasons, addiction among the young may rise more than that among other segments of the population.

A misleading impression about the reaction to permanent price changes may have been created by the effects of temporary police crackdowns on drugs, or temporary federal "wars" on drugs. Since temporary policies raise current but not future prices—they would even lower future prices if drug inventories are built up during a crackdown period—there is no complementary fall in current use from a fall in future use. Consequently, even if drug addicts are rational, a temporary "war" that greatly raised street prices of drugs might well have only a small effect on drug use, whereas a permanent "war" could have much bigger effects, even in the short run.

Clearly, we have not provided enough evidence to evaluate whether or not the use of heroin, cocaine, and other drugs should be legalized. A cost-benefit analysis of many effects is needed to decide between a regime in which drugs are legal and one in which they are not. What this paper shows is that the permanent reduction in price caused by legalization is likely to have a substantial positive effect on use, particularly among the poor and the young.

NOTES

1. Becker and Murphy (1988) consider price effects in the context of a quadratic instantaneous utility function of the form

$$u(t) = \alpha_c c(t) + \alpha_s S(t) + \left(\frac{1}{2}\right)\alpha_{cc}[c(t)]^2 + \left(\frac{1}{2}\right)\alpha_{ss}[S(t)]^2 + \alpha_{cs}c(t)S(t)$$

where α_c and α_{cs} are positive, and all other parameters are negative. They show (1988:685, eq. 18) that the long-run change between stable steady states in response to a permanent change in p_c is

$$\frac{dc^*}{dp_c} = \frac{\mu}{\alpha_{cc}\beta'}$$

where μ is the marginal utility of wealth, and

$$\beta' = 1 + \frac{\alpha_{ss} + (\sigma + 2\delta)\,\alpha_{cs}}{\alpha_{cc}\delta\,(\sigma + \delta)}$$

The term β', which ranges between 0 and 1 for an addictive good, measures the degree of addiction. Since a decrease in β' means greater addiction—$\beta' = 1$ indicates no addiction—the long-run change in c is positively related to the strength of the addiction.

2. One can show that a rational addict's short-run response to a permanent change in p_c equals

$$\frac{dc_s}{dp_c} = -\frac{\lambda}{\delta}\frac{dc^*}{dp_c}$$

where $-\delta \le \lambda \le 0$, and λ is larger when the degree of addiction is stronger (see Becker and Murphy, 1988:679–80). Therefore, the ratio of the short- to long-term response gets larger as the degree of addiction (measured by λ) is larger. One can also show that $\frac{dC_s}{dp_c}$ itself gets larger as the degree of addiction increases.

3. With a quadratic utility function, the discounted value of future cost in steady states equals

$$\frac{-u_s}{\sigma + \delta} = \frac{-\alpha_s - \alpha_{ss}S - \alpha_{cs}c}{\sigma + \delta}$$

If these costs change because of a change in α_s, the induced change in steady-state consumption would be

$$\Pi_c\frac{dc}{d\Pi_c} = \frac{dc}{d\log\Pi_c} = \frac{-\alpha_s}{\alpha_{cc}\beta'\,(\sigma + \delta)\,\mu} = \frac{\Pi_c}{\alpha_{cc}\beta'}$$

where $\Pi_c = \frac{-\alpha_s}{(\sigma + \delta)\mu}$. Hence, from note 1, the ratio of the changes in c due to changes in $\log p_c$ and $\log \Pi_c$, respectively, are

$$\frac{\frac{dc}{d}\log p_c}{\frac{dc}{d}\log\Pi_c} = \frac{p_c}{\Pi_c}$$

This ratio depends only on the ratio of these prices.

In the text we claim that Π_c is larger for adults, and for the rich and more educated. One reason why this is so is that an increase in the addictive stock is likely to lower earnings as well as utility by reducing the time available for work. To include this effect, redefine

α_s to include a component $\mu\beta w$ that gives the effect of S on earnings, where w is the hourly wage rate and β is the negative effect of S on working time. An increase in the absolute value of β would have a larger effect on cost when w is greater.

4. An increase in the rate of time preference (σ) both raises the response to a change in money price (p_c) and lowers the response to a change in future costs (Π_c) if

$$\frac{-\alpha_{ss}}{\delta^2} > \frac{\alpha_{cs}}{\delta}$$

and

$$-\alpha_{cc} > \frac{\alpha_{cs}}{\delta}$$

An increase in c between steady states, c = δS, reduces the marginal utility of c, while the increase in S raises it. The second inequality states that the direct effect exceeds the cross effect. The first inequality assumes that the increase in S has a larger effect on its marginal utility than does the increase in c. If μ is concave, at least one of these inequalities must hold, for then

$$-\delta^2\alpha_{cc} - \alpha_{ss} > 2\delta\alpha_{cs}$$

We assume that both hold.

By differentiating with respect to σ the absolute value (n) of the long-run change in c induced by a change in p_c (given in note 1), we get

$$\frac{\partial n}{\partial \sigma} = \frac{-[\mu(\alpha_{ss} + \delta\alpha_{cs})]}{\alpha_{cc}^2 \delta(\sigma + \delta)^2 \beta'^2}$$

This equation is positive by the assumption $-\alpha_{ss} > \delta\alpha_{cs}$.

Differentiating the absolute value (m) of the long-run change in c with respect to log Π_c (given in note 3), we get

$$\frac{\partial m}{\partial \sigma} = \frac{(\sigma + \delta)\delta(\alpha_{cc}\delta + \alpha_{cs})(-\alpha_s)}{[\alpha_{cc}\delta(\sigma + \delta) + \alpha_{ss} + (\sigma + 2\delta)\alpha_{cs}]^2}$$

This equation is negative by the assumption $-\alpha_{cc}\delta > \alpha_{cs}$.

REFERENCES

Becker, Gary S., "Optimal Discounting of the Future." Department of Economics, University of Chicago, April 1990.

Becker, Gary S., Grossman, Michael, and Murphy, Kevin M., "An Empirical Analysis of Cigarette Addiction." National Bureau of Economic Research Working Paper No. 3322, April 1990.

Becker, Gary S., and Murphy, Kevin M., "A Theory of Rational Addiction." *Journal of Political Economy* 96, 4 (August 1988), 675–700.

Chaloupka, Frank J., "Rational Addictive Behavior and Cigarette Smoking. "*Journal of Political Economy*," forthcoming.

Cook, Philip J., and Tauchen, George, "The Effect of Liquor Taxes on Heavy Drinking." *Bell Journal of Economics* 13, 2 (Autumn 1982), 379–90.

Farrell, Phillip, and Fuchs, Victor R., "Schooling and Health: The Cigarette Connection." *Journal of Health Economics* 1, 3 (December 1982), 217–30.

Lewit, Eugene M., and Coate, Douglas, "The Potential for Using Excise Taxes to Reduce Smoking." *Journal of Health Economics* 1, 2 (August 1982), 121–45.

Lewit, Eugene M., Coate, Douglas, and Grossman, Michael, "The Effects of Government Regulation on Teenage Smoking." *Journal of Law and Economics* 24, 3 (December 1981), 545–69.

Mobilia, Pamela, "An Economic Analysis of Addictive Behavior: The Case of Gambling." Ph.D. diss., City University of New York, 1990.

Nisbet, Charles T., and Vakil, Firouz, "Some Estimates of Price and Expenditure Elasticities of Demand for Marijuana among U.C.L.A. Students." *Review of Economics and Statistics* 54, 4 (November 1972), 473–75.

Silverman, Lester P., and Spruill, Nancy L., "Urban Crime and the Price of Heroin." *Journal of Urban Economics* 4, 1 (January 1977), 80–103.

Townsend, Joy L., "Cigarette Tax, Economic Welfare and Social Class Patterns of Smoking." *Applied Economics* 19 (1987), 355–65.

COMMENT

Victor R. Fuchs

"Rational Addiction and the Effect of Price on Consumption," by Michael Grossman, Gary Becker, and Kevin Murphy, is a remarkable paper. Who would imagine that an economist, let alone three economists, could say so many interesting things about addiction in so few pages? This brief paper offers a fully developed theoretical model of demand for addictive commodities, several important empirical results, and a thoughtful discussion of the relevance of this research to the question of drug legalization.

I'd like to focus on a small portion of the paper—beginning with the paragraph that describes the evidence that "rather strongly supports our model of rational addiction." The authors offer us five empirical conclusions or stylized facts about the demand for addictive commodities; these conclusions are based mostly on research with legal commodities thought to be addictive, such as alcohol, cigarettes, and racetrack betting.

Conclusion 1 There is substantial price elasticity of demand. This finding will not surprise most economists, but it is a useful one because there are probably many drug experts who believe that demand is completely inelastic. The Rand health insurance experiment, costing over $100 million, was deemed necessary because there were so many health experts prepared to come to Washington to testify (incorrectly) that the demand for medical care was completely insensitive to price. Incidentally, the elasticities reported by Grossman and his colleagues for addictive commodities are substantially higher than those found for medical care. If the elasticity of demand for an addictive commodity is substantial, that must mean there is a good substitute for that commodity, or many fair substitutes. What are these substitutes? Could they be other addictive commodities? If, for instance, illegal drugs and alcohol are substitutes, the implications for public policy are different than if the substitution is between illegal drugs and bran muffins. We need to know more about the specifics of substitution that underlie these high elasticities.

Conclusion 2 The long-run price elasticity is greater than the short-run elasticity. This is hardly surprising. This is thought to be true for most commodities. When oil prices rose sharply in the 1970s, the quantity demanded did not change much at first, but when the high prices persisted there was a significant decrease in demand. To be sure, the rise in price was unanticipated. These authors seem to be saying that even when the change in price is anticipated, the long-run elasticity will be greater than the short-run. Moreover, they assert that the *ratio* of the long-run to the short-run response will be greater, the greater the degree of addiction. Indeed, this is a way of defining "addiction."

Conclusion 3 This deals with the difference between low-income and high-income consumers. We are told that either the price elasticity is greater for lower-income people, or that their responsiveness to changes in information about future harmful effects is smaller than for high-income people, or both. I am quite prepared to believe the latter part of the proposition, especially if income is standing as a proxy for education. One explanation would be different rates of time-discount across social classes. With respect to the first half of the proposition, namely price elasticities varying with income level, that's likely to be true if we are talking about changes in prices where the income effects are not compensated for. Otherwise it's not clear why low-income people would have more good substitutes available than high-income people.

Conclusion 4 Young people have higher price elasticities than older people. This might be simply another way of talking about the relationship between elasticity and income. Alternatively, it may reflect selectivity biases as people sort themselves into addicted or nonaddicted categories over the life cycle. If everything else were held constant, it's not clear to me why young people would have more good substitutes available. I wonder, too, whether the empirical results concerning income and age and elasticity reported for addictive commodities might not be characteristic of many other commodities as well. Are they stronger for addictive commodities? Is this another way of defining "addiction"?

Conclusion 5 This might be the most important of the empirical generalizations. Grossman and the others report that past and future prices of addictive commodities affect current consumption the same way that present prices do. In other words, past and future consumption are complements of present consumption. This is a very interesting result. I wonder how robust the result is, and how sensitive it is to alternative econometric specifications. I also wonder what would happen if the same econometric methods used to produce this result were applied to so-called normal commodities. If these other commodities did not show this relationship, this might prove to be a powerful way to identify an addictive commodity. Notice, however, that this "addictive" property might be present in commodities far different from alcohol, cigarettes, or heroin. For instance, the certain knowledge that future gasoline prices would be much higher (or lower) than they are this year would probably affect the quantity demanded this year through changes in the types of cars purchased and similar decisions. The finding of complementarity would confirm "addiction" in the economic sense, but not in the physiologic sense.

I hope these remarks indicate the wide range of interesting issues discussed in the paper and that they stimulate its authors to undertake further research.

6

EXTERNALITIES AND DECRIMINALIZATION OF DRUGS

Paul Taubman

Economists have a long intellectual history concerning the appropriateness of the intervention of governments in an individual's determination of the allocation of resources and activities. Adam Smith (1776), for example, argued that "the invisible hand" of the competitive marketplace would achieve what today would be called the "Pareto Optimum Allocation of Resources." With such an allocation, no one's welfare could be increased without decreasing someone else's welfare or utility. Although economists recognize that there can be different Pareto Optimum outcomes if tastes differ and income is redistributed, they generally do not examine the consequences of such a redistribution.

Smith does not contain a rigorous proof of his proposition that the invisible hand leads to a Pareto Optimum Allocation, but Arrow (1951) does, at least for a competitive, decentralized market in which production is subject to diminishing returns, and there are markets for all present and future goods. If the conditions necessary for his model (or more complicated models) exist, economists generally reach the conclusion that governments should not intervene in or influence individuals' and firms' choices. Musgrave's (1959) "merit goods" are an exception. In other words, the use of currently illegal drugs should be decriminalized.

I wish to thank Steve Nako and Geoff Taubman for obtaining much of the information used, and Geoff Taubman for suggesting and investigating several topics explored in this paper.

Economists, however, also understand that the proof of this welfare proposition and the resulting decriminalization of drugs requires a number of strong assumptions to guarantee that there is no "market failure." Market failure can arise for a number of reasons, some of which may involve high enough costs to society and its members that decriminalization may not lead to an overall improvement in welfare.

In this paper I will try to identify some of these problems. I warn the reader that there are gaps in the empirical research that may bias some of these estimates, especially since few of the studies are based on an experimental design or have adequate controls. Moreover, it is possible that I have not considered some of the market failures. Finally I note that in principle some (maybe all) of the market failures might be overcome with appropriate alternative policies or social arrangements, thereby making decriminalization possible. The costs of these rearrangements may also be large.

I will begin with some statistics on the extent of drug use and trends, and then I will consider measures of convictions and imprisonment for illegal drug activities and present some price elasticity estimates. Next I will jump back to the notion of market failure and its prevalence.

Some Facts

Whether or not decriminalization of drugs is a sensible policy depends on the costs and benefits to society of such a policy. We argue that in a decentralized economy with complete markets, rational individuals will make decisions that maximize their own utility, and firms will act to maximize their own profits. The markets are not complete—currently there is no futures market for heroin—but the only implication of decriminalization policy is that currently, resource allocation would not be Pareto Optimal. Of course, with decriminalization a futures market might be created. We argue that many of the costs and benefits should be judged by their impact on other people or firms, or what economists call "externalities." Enforcing the current law is costly, however, and it is possible that society would be better off with more addicts and less crime. We shall begin our discussion with some estimates on the current state of, cost of, and trends in drug use and related crimes.

Drug Use

The number of people who have ever used illegal drugs is fairly large, although newspaper accounts tend to be misleading. The best-known questionnaire is conducted annually by researchers at the University of Michigan, who survey high school seniors. A recent study shows that in 1987 "in the past 30 days" about 20 percent of those students had used marijuana, 4 percent had used cocaine, and less than 1 percent had used heroin. In comparison with earlier surveys of high school seniors, marijuana use has fallen sharply since 1980 while cocaine use has remained about constant until 1990, when it fell. (See L. Johnson, P. O'Malley, and J. Backman, 1988.)

A subsample of each high school sample is also followed annually as a panel. In 1987, the 19 to 22 and 23 to 26 age groups showed the same use of marijuana as when they were high school seniors. The same is true for cocaine for the first age group, but for the second group usage has fallen to less than 1 percent.[1] Trends for the various age groups are positive if we substitute an "ever used" measure; hence, some high school seniors have subsequently explored the use of these drugs even though continued use in the last 30 days drops off for previous users.

One problem with the high school senior sample is that high school drop-outs and truants, who may have heavier concentrations of drug users, are not included. The National Institute of Drug Abuse (NIDA), however, has been conducting surveys on a random (but smaller) sample of the noninstitutionalized population older than 12 about every other year since 1971. (See National Institute of Drug Abuse, 1988.) In 1985, of the population 12 and older, they estimated that in the past month about 10 percent used marijuana, 3 percent used cocaine, and less than 1 percent used heroin. The 1987 data is due about now. Data collected over time suggest that for 18- to 23-year-olds peak use of marijuana in the past 30 days occurred in 1979, and that use in 1985 was lower than in 1972. Cocaine use also peaked in 1979 but was still more than twice as high in 1985 as in 1974 (the first date data are available). However, it is generally believed that cocaine use (in the form of crack) has soared since 1985, at least through 1989. Habel and his associates (1988), for example, report that in New York City between 1986 and 1987 there was a 20 percent rise in the demand for admission to drug-treatment centers, mostly for "crack"-related problems.[2] There is a sharp decline in use of cocaine with age in a cross section in all years for which the NIDA data are available.

Another problem with the high school senior and the NIDA samples is that they only study the noninstitutionalized population. Drug use among the institutionalized is very large, although maybe not in the past month. For example, before imprisonment about 80 percent of prisoners in state prisons in the mid-1980s had used illegal drugs regularly—22 percent used cocaine, 17 percent used heroin, and 55 percent used marijuana. (See Innes, 1988.) Similar percentages hold for jails and for federal prisons. (See Bureau of Justice Statistics, 1988, p. 4.) Presumably those in drug rehabilitation clinics had also used drugs recently.

The above summary focuses on the use of drugs. What is also important for this piece are the costs of using drugs. These costs go beyond the purchase price

TABLE 6.1   DISPOSAL OF FEDERAL DRUG CASES,
OCTOBER 1, 1985 TO SEPTEMBER 31, 1986

	Suspects Referred to U.S. Attorney	Cases Filed in District Court	Prosecution Declined	Convicted	Interned	Length of Sentence (months)
All	19,646	80%	17%	84	77	51
Distributed/ manufactured	17,087	80%	17%	85	80	61

SOURCE: Bureau of Justice Statistics, *Federal Offenses and Offenders: Drug Law Violators, 1980–86,* June 1988.

and include property stolen, plus governmental and private expenditures on health, legal, and incarceration expenses. Looking at internees in state prisons, almost 50 percent of those imprisoned for property offenses had used drugs daily in the month before the offense for which they were jailed. Slightly more than 40 percent of all incarcerated state prisoners had used drugs in the month prior to the offense for which they were imprisoned. (See Bureau of Justice Statistics, 1988.) Similar percentages are found in other detention modes. (See Bureau of Justice Statistics, 1988, p. 20.)[3]

It is also of some interest to ask how important drug arrests and convictions are in our society. One answer is that about 20 percent of referrals to the relevant prosecuting office for federal crimes involve drug-law violations. As another way to examine this, we have collected some statistics from both the federal and the state legal systems. In Table 6.1 we see that during the period October 1, 1985, to September 31, 1986, in the federal system nearly 20,000 drug cases were forwarded to United States Attorneys for prosecution; nearly all the suspects were allegedly engaged in the distribution or manufacture of drugs. About 80 percent of them were incarcerated for an average term of 50 to 60 months. (See Bureau of Justice Statistics, 1988.)

Prisoners in state and local jails have somewhat different characteristics. In 1986, about 15 percent of convicted felons in state prisons were guilty of drug trafficking, of whom 76 percent were incarcerated and were sentenced an average of 63 months in prison or 13 months in jail. (See Bureau of Justice Statistics, 1988.)

The United States Attorneys and the Attorney General of the United States (1989) estimate that in 1990 the comprehensive costs to taxpayers for drug-related enforcement and crime activities exceeded $12 billion a year. If drugs were decriminalized, much of these costs would vanish, at least in the long run. All these costs will not disappear because some criminal types would switch to other illegal activities, just as crime did not vanish after the end of prohibition. More-over, if more prison space is available, judges could incarcerate more people and for longer terms for other crimes.

Drug users are also associated with other major social problems in the United States, although the available evidence is not strong enough to prove the causality of drug usage. For example, 44 percent of the recent growth in homelessness in the past few years has been among alcoholics and drug abusers, with the latter group contributing 13 percent. (See Whitman, Friedman, and Thomas, 1990.)

Breakey and his colleagues (1989) show that 22 percent of the male and 17 percent of the female homeless in Baltimore (in 1986 and 1987) suffered from drug-abuse problems. Wright and Weber (1987) examined the prevalence of various diseases and illness of the homeless by drug use. They found many categories of greater prevalence among drug users,[4] and only three categories[5] of acute disorders and four chronic categories with lower prevalence.[6] Moreover, the police and the courts are spending much time and effort on enforcing drug laws. (See Nadelmann, 1989.)

Drug users and the homeless also put a severe strain on medical facilities. Gelberg and Linn (1989) demonstrated that the homeless in New York City have more severe health problems than the poor in shelters. Their conclusions are, in part, based on physical examinations by doctors. Part of the expenses of the homeless are paid for by society and by individuals.

Moreover, Morrisey and Jensen (1988) showed that the percentage of large- and middle-size firms who had health-care coverage for treatment of drug abuse rose from 43 to 67 between 1983 and 1985. Following up on their sources, this percentage had jumped to 74 percent by 1988. The costs associated with this coverage are borne by society at large.

There are large costs associated with drugs over and above the consumption expenses of users. In the next section we will erect a formal framework to examine the implication of these costs for the policy of decriminalization, and then we will see the extent to which costs are important.

EXTERNALITIES AND MARKET FAILURES

An externality is defined by Lafont (1989, p. 6) as ". . . any indirect effect that either a production or consumption activity has on a utility function, a consumption set or a production set. By 'indirect' we mean both that the effect is created by an economic agent other than the one who is affected and the effect is not transmitted through prices." These are so-called nonpecuniary externalities, such as an upriver manufacturer polluting a river without being charged for the value of so disposing of waste products. Lafont, following Arrow (1951), also points out later that even when the pollution is charged for, pecuniary externalities only yield Pareto Optimal results when there is a complete set of current and future markets with no informational asymmetries.

Market failure, which arises in the case of externalities, can also occur if some markets are noncompetitive or if the government imposes taxes that distort decisions as all but randomly (ex post) imposed taxes will do in societies where there are substitutes.

In the rest of this paper, we will try to examine what is known about market failures and their costs as related to illegal drugs. We will consider the available evidence for individuals, firms, and society. We will consider effects on health, productivity, and crime, and how these effects may vary with decriminalization. We will first examine the scanty evidence on the price elasticity of demand, since decriminalization would lower the street price of drugs and raise their use, unless either the price elasticity of demand were zero or the price elasticity of supply were infinite. The latter elasticity has not been estimated, but is surely not infinite.

PRICES AND THE PRICE ELASTICITY
OF DEMAND FOR DRUGS

Reuter and Kleiman (1986) present some estimates of the price of heroin, cocaine, and marijuana at various stages of sale ranging from the farm through the retail markets. These are reproduced as Table 6.2. Cocaine that can be purchased in Colombia for $1500 may have a street value in New York of $650,000. The markup on other drugs is as big or bigger. Some of this difference represents costs of processing, transportation, bribery, and losses incurred by shipments seized by law-enforcement agencies. No one doubts, however, that billions of dollars in profit are made on the sale of drugs and that the price of drugs would fall sharply if drugs were decriminalized. What is not known is exactly by how much prices would fall, how much drug usage would increase, and how many new people would use drugs.

Even if we use the average of the import and the export price in Table 6.2 as an indicator of the price of the decriminalized drug, the price could fall to only 5 to 30 percent of the current levels. Moreover, we argue below the street price could fall even lower. Even small demand-price elasticities would have large quantity effects unless the supply-price elasticities are large, which seems unlikely since drugs that would have been previously stored in policy evidence rooms or destroyed to obliterate evidence would become available as an addition to the current supply.

There is a little bit of information on the price elasticity of demand. Brown and Silverman (1974) made use of monthly data on heroin prices and quantities

TABLE 6.2   STRUCTURE OF DRUG PRICES, 1980[a]
             (PER PURE KILOGRAM)

	Heroin	Cocaine	Marijuana[b]
Farmgate	$350–$1,000[c]	$1,300–$10,000	$7–$18
Processed	$6,000–$10,000	$3,000–$10,000	$55
Export	$95,000	$7,000–$20,000	$90–$180
Import[d]	$220,000–$240,000	$50,000	$365–$720
Retail	$1.6–$2.2 million	$650,000[e]	$1,250–$2,090

[a]No more recent data are available for source-country prices. It is not likely that there have been significant changes in the relationship of prices at different points in the distribution system.

[b]Prices are for Colombian-origin marijuana, estimated to account for 75 percent of total U.S. consumption in 1980.

[c]The price of the 10 kg of opium required to manufacture 1 kg of heroin.

[d]The import price refers to price at first transaction within the United States. Marijuana is purchased roughly in ton lots, cocaine in multikilo lots, and heroin in kilo lots.

[e]The original data source reported a retail price of $800,000. Other DEA data, such as those reported in Reuter and Kleiman (1986) consistently indicate prices in the range $600–$650,000 in 1980.

in various cities in the early 1970s to estimate price elasticities. Note that they did not control for income, which may not change much in a city during the short period studied. They used ordinary least squares to obtain an estimated price elasticity of about $-.2$ in most cities. Their estimates range from $+.14$ to $-.8$; 37 out of 46 of the elasticities are negative; and 35 of these 37 are statistically significant.

In a sample described in more detail below, Silverman and Spruill (1977) find a price elasticity for heroin of about $-.25$ using monthly data from Detroit for the period November 1970 through July 1973.

We recently have been provided with a quarterly time series on heroin prices by city for the period 1980–1989.[7] The NLS has matched this city data to that in the National Longitudinal Survey of Youth, which asks questions on recent drug use (by type of drug) and when the respondent started to use a drug.[8] The sample is a random-clustered sample. Unfortunately, we have not been able to begin our analysis at this date.

As shown in Table 6.2, the retail markup on heroin is many times the importers' price, which is already above the price that would obtain if drugs were decriminalized, since more efficient transport could be used and the cost of shipments seized by authorities and bribes would not be incurred. Even these small elasticities would be applied to large price changes and lead to much greater usage. At this time it is not possible to say how this increase would be split between more drugs per user and more users.

Nisbet and Vakil (1972) used data from the early 1970s on students from UCLA, who were asked to trace out their theoretical demand functions for marijuana. Data on actual price paid and on quantity used were also collected. Nisbet and Vakil estimated price elasticities for marijuana in the range of − .07 to − 1.0. In their subsequent analysis, they use elasticities around − 1.0. So far as I know, no one has estimated the demand function for cocaine, "crack," or other drugs, but it is commonly observed that in recent years as "crack" prices have fallen usage has increased.

EFFECTS ON OTHER INDIVIDUALS

In this section we will examine the effects on other individuals of the use of currently illegal drugs. The main groups to be considered are children, spouses and other adult partners, crime victims, other prisoners, and employers.

Fetuses, Infants, and Children

Fetuses, infants, and children can be affected by one or more parents' use of drugs. These impacts appear in the children's birth weight, which can affect survivability and functioning; the child's addiction to the drug; and child abuse.

The existing literature (see, for example, footnote 7 in Rosenzweig and Schultz, 1983) indicates that low birth weight translates into lower IQ and higher mortality, though either relation may be highly nonlinear. Recent studies, summarized in FitzGerald (1990), also indicate that low-birth-weight babies (less than 5.5 pounds) have lower IQs.

The Infant Health and Development Program (1990) studied low-birth-weight, prematurely born children at eight sites. They studied about 100 to 135 children per site and randomly assigned one-third at each place to the "intervention" group. Their study clearly shows that low-birth-weight, prematurely born children have lower IQs at age 3. In the two birth-weight categories of 2001 to 2500 grams and 2000 and fewer grams, average scores on the Stanford-Binet tests at age 3 are 84.8 and 84.4 for the heavier and lighter groups. (The nationwide average score is 100.)

This, of course, does not prove causation, but this program also assigned children randomly to an experimental group to see the effect on early IQ of dispensing parenting information at home on a weekly or biweekly basis. After the first year, the assisted children attended child development centers five days a week. In the intervention group, the average scores at the same age are 98.0 to 91.0 for the heavier and lighter groups. The assisted children also show a lower mortality rate. Thus, low-birth-weight effects can be at least partially overcome by special investments in human capital. Such investments are, however, costly. In Philadelphia, day care for a normal child runs about $110 a week, and this may not include the expenditures for improving instead of maintaining intellectual capacity.

Rosenzweig and Wolpin (1990) examined the effect of marijuana use on fetal growth. They used the National Longitudinal Youth Survey (NLSY) with self-reports of drug use, augmented with data on their children's characteristics, whose birth outcomes have been measured since 1983 in the NLSY.[9] They found that smoking marijuana every month during the first trimester of pregnancy leads to lower birth weight, which is associated with greater infant mortality and development problems. The lower-birth-weight estimates range from 3.3 to 6.7 ounces, or up to 5 percent, with their results depending on what other variables are controlled. Their most sophisticated analysis used siblings as controls and ended up with effects in the middle of the above range.[10]

Using the NLSY sample and controlling for maternal weight before and during pregnancy, birth order, and child's gender, maternal age, family fixed effects, and other variables, Rosenzweig and Wolpin (1989) found that the use of marijuana in all three months of the first trimester reduces birth weight by about 5 percent. Lesser use results in lower weight loss. They did not consider the impact of pre-pregnancy use of this narcotic or of other narcotics before or during pregnancy.

Grossman and Joyce (1988) used a large data set drawn from New York City's 1984 vital statistics to study the determinants of birth weight of non-Hispanic women 20 and older. Controlling for child's gender, mother's education, and other variables, they found that the use of narcotics that complicated pregnancy reduced birth weight by about 8 percent.[11] In their analysis they corrected for selectivity. They also studied the determinants of abortion but did not use narcotics usage as an independent variable here.

Cocaine's use has grown rapidly in the United States. Chasnoff (1987) reported that at Harlem Hospital 10 percent of babies "born recently" showed up positive for drugs (using urine analysis). He also presented the results of a survey mailed to some 600 doctor subscribers to *Contemporary Ob/Gyn*. Presumably the use of this readership list causes some selectivity if some cocaine users do not get prenatal care or if clinics cannot afford to subscribe to this journal. Nevertheless, he found that 24 percent of the doctors report that 5 percent of obstetric patients used cocaine and another 24 percent of doctors report a 1 percent cocaine usage rate. In another study reported in the same article, he compared pregnancy outcomes of users and nonusers of drugs. He found users more likely to have spontaneous abortions while the children that are born have other abnormalities, are shorter, and weigh less.

The Katzenbach (1990) report estimates that to provide adequate health to pregnant drug-using women and their offspring, New York would have to spend $10 million a year.

Zuckerman and his associates (1989) prospectively studied 1226 mothers attending a general prenatal clinic in the Boston City Hospital. These women overrepresented young, low-income, black, and Hispanic women. Basing drug use on both self-reports and on urine analysis, they found that nearly 30 percent of the women had used marijuana and almost 20 percent had used cocaine while pregnant. Women who used marijuana had newborns with a 79-gram decrease in weight (about 13 percent) and about a 10 percent decrease in length. The corresponding decreases for cocaine users were 15 and 14 percent. Some multiple-regression analyses indicate significant effects of marijuana and cocaine use even when controlling for ethnic background, sexually transmitted diseases, mother's weight, and number of prenatal visits. More statistically significant results are obtained using urine analysis than with self-reported drug use, even though the research protocol must have involved informed consent of the women.

Kline, Stein, and Hutzler (1987) used a sample of more than 3,000 New York City pregnant women recruited between 1975 to 1983 in both public clinics and in private care. Two different questionnaires were used. The first asked about drug use during the three months prior to the interview and the second asked about drug use since two months before the woman's last menstrual period. The first sample did not show significant drug effects on the infant's birth weight. In the second sample, marijuana use of 2 or 3 times per week, 4 to 6 times per week, and daily was associated with decreases in birth weight of the child of 127 grams, 143 grams, and 230 grams, respectively.

Linn and colleagues (1983) studied 12,000 Boston women to determine the impact of prior marijuana use as reported after delivery but during delivery care. The data indicate that the infants of the users have lower birth weight, shorter gestation periods, and more major malfunctions. These effects become insignificant, however, when controls for personal characteristics and medical care were included. Note that this early study did not employ urine analysis to determine drug usage.

In New York City the number of children born addicted to drugs doubled between a six-month period in 1985 and 1986, while the number of child-abuse cases increased nearly 50 percent in 1986. About two-thirds of the court cases involving child abuse were drug-related. (See *New York Times*, 1987.)

The same article reports that the government spends money caring for the drug-addicted infants both because they are often premature and of low weight and to wean them off their habit. The government may have to spend more funds to prepare them for school. There are also growing demands for foster care that appear to be drug-related.

Regan, Ehrlich, and Finnegan (1987) compared women in a methadone maintenance program with a matched group of drug-free women in the Philadelphia Family Center. They reported that infants suffer more abuse and receive poorer parenting when the mother was on drugs.

Black and Mayer (1981) reported that addicted mothers spend less time with children and use more violence, but their findings were not standardized against a control group.

The effect of IQ on earnings and the bias on the estimates of the returns to schooling have been subject to much controversy and discussion, in which I have participated. So far as I can tell, IQ does not matter much on earnings in the first year at work; it does matter after about half a dozen years of employment; it also matters later in the career, but the peak percentage effect may occur after about 8 to 10 years of work experience. (See Hauser and Daymont, 1977; Taubman, 1975; and Behrman et al., 1980.) The total effect of IQ—including its impact on schooling, which also affects earnings—may have an elasticity ranging up to 50 percent. The Taubman study, which has fewer selectivity problems and more statistical controls for family background and own characteristics, suggests a 20 percent difference in earnings around age 50 between those at the middle and top of the IQ distribution.

Drugs and Spouse and Parental Abuse

A few studies have studied the relationship of drug abuse on the welfare of the spouse or of the parent. None of these have been able to use randomly assigned control groups, but some have controlled for family background measures. Wolk and Diskind (1961) provided anecdotal evidence that mothers of addicts are severely abused. The effect on wives depends on whether they knew their husbands were addicts when they married. At least when heroin is involved, the women who know of spouse's addiction before marrying may wive to be the dominant member of the pair. If she does not know of heroin addiction when she marries, Taylor, Wilbur, and Osnos (1966) report some spousal violence in a small sample with no control groups. However, Gelles and Strauss (1988:47) report that heroin use is rarely associated with violence.

Heroin is a "downer." The same violence conclusion is apparently not true of cocaine, which is an "upper," or to large dosages of amphetamines. For example, New York City officials recently reported a tripling of child abuse and neglect cases (over the prior two years), and this was associated with increased drug use (*New York Times*, 1987). Presumably similar impacts would be found for spouses even if there are less record keeping and fewer court cases.

Drugs and Crime

Drug use can cause property crime and homicide because of—in Goldstein's (1985) terminology—psychopharmalogical, economic compulsive, and systemic reasons.[12] The first type occurs because of an individual's altered behavior, either when "stoned" or because of irritability when leaving the drugged state. The second reason is that money is needed to support the habit. The systemic reasons include drug dealers' territorial fights, elimination of informers, fights over drug paraphernalia, and the like. Decriminalization, which results in lower prices and greater usage, may eliminate or reduce crime committed by an individual for economic compulsive and systemic reasons, but may increase crime for the psychopharmalogical reason. Moreover, the greater number of people on drugs and the greater usage per person under decriminalization may also increase crime for the other two reasons, although one study discussed below suggests otherwise.

Many studies exist that examine the interrelationship of crime, and especially property crime and homicide, to drug use. These studies, which use a variety of techniques of various degrees of statistical sophistication, are summarized in Anglin and Speckart (1988). They point out that, although there is some controversy on the connection of drugs to crime, there is evidence that in those periods when an individual is using drugs more heavily, his or her property crime rate is sharply elevated. They also examine the temporal ordering of (self-reported) arrests for criminal activity and drug use. A majority of people in two samples— 370 Anglos and 301 Chicanos from seven California counties studied around 1980—were arrested before any narcotics use. About 20 percent were first arrested between the first use of narcotics and their becoming addicted. They study both the number of days and time spent in criminal activity—some of the latter based on official records and some self-reported. They show that the daily use of drugs is associated with a more than doubling of arrests. There is a quadrupling of the amount of time spent on (self-reported) property crime as you move from less than daily drug use to daily drug use.

This conclusion, of course, doesn't indicate what would happen if drugs were decriminalized and the prices fell substantially, perhaps to one-tenth of their current level. There are at least two competing forces at work. At lower prices, there will be more drug users and usage. Some people, however, will be able to support their new habit or increased use of an old habit out of legal earnings and not engage in crime, although the statistics earlier cited (footnote 3) on the share of income obtained from illegal activities and its increase with the greater involvement with drugs should cause some pause. Nonetheless, some—maybe more—people may need to be engaged in property crime, in welfare dependency, or in panhandling.

How does property crime respond to changes in drug prices? The few answers to this question are surveyed in Silverman and Spruill (1977). For example,

Brown and Silverman (1974) found a positive effect of heroin prices on property crime in New York City about 20 years ago.

Silverman and Spruill also reported long-run price elasticities for crime in several areas in Detroit for the period November 1970 through July 1973. The price data were taken from "buys" made by law-enforcement agencies in Detroit at that time. They estimated crime price elasticities (controlling for variables such as local law-enforcement activities but not for unemployment or income). The results varied from poor nonwhite to rich white communities. With few exceptions, the elasticities were positive. The elasticity for robbery was .5 to .6 in the two types of areas; for burglary, .6 and .1 with the latter not statistically significant; larceny, .25 and −.1 with the latter not statistically significant; and other crimes not having statistically significant elasticities except for the 1.0 for simple assault in rich white neighborhoods.

Since this study looked at crime in Detroit and not at crime per drug user, it incorporates the effect of both new and increased use of drugs as their prices fall. Since Detroit's enforcement activities are controlled in Silverman and Spruill's equation, this is mostly a demand-side effect. However, the supply of drugs to Detroit can be influenced by enforcement activities outside of Detroit and other factors such as heroin crop yields. Thus, some identification problems remain.

In judging these results, it should be recognized again that heroin is a downer whereas cocaine, which is more widely used today, is an upper and is more associated with violence. Unfortunately, I am not aware of comparable studies for the price of cocaine, though we are currently obtaining some data. The effect of property crime, then, seems important but has not been pinned down.

Illegal drugs may also influence homicide rates, reflecting the killing of rival dealers, informers, police, or innocent bystanders. The newspapers and television news reports are replete with examples of each category. Goldstein (1986) provides more systematic evidence for New York City and a survey of prior work. For example, in 1977 in New York City about 15 percent of people arrested for homicide had been previously arrested for drug offenses, and almost 20 percent of the victims had been arrested for prior drug offenses. In 1981, the police considered 24 percent of known New York City homicides drug-related.

Using medical-examiner autopsy conclusions, Goldstein also reports that 15 to 30 percent of homicides were drug-related in cities such as San Diego and Philadelphia during the same time period. My impression of Philadelphia is that the percentage of drug-related homicides is much higher in 1990 than in prior years, often involving children and other innocent bystanders. Such deaths would probably decrease if drugs were decriminalized.

AIDS

It is well known that drug use has contributed to the spread of AIDS. Kleiman and Mockler (1988), using Center for Disease Control data, reported that as of mid-1985 19 percent of AIDS cases involved heroin users who were not homo-sexuals. The percentages were much higher in New York City and Boston. Moreover, they indicate that many heroin user infect with AIDS sexual partners who do not use heroin.

Prisoners

Currently people sentenced to jail or prison for drug offensives comprise about 40 percent of the people in federal prisons and about 10 percent of those in state prisons for felony convictions. Forty states and the federal government report that their prisons are at 100 percent or more of their rated capacity. (See Bureau of Justice Statistics, 1989b.) A reduction in the number of prisoners would improve conditions for the remaining convicts and would mean less pressure or fewer court orders for the early release of prisoners. Of course, some people who currently engage in drug transactions might commit and be convicted of other crimes, and judges would probably commit other criminals to jail and for longer periods. Nonetheless, prison overcrowding would almost surely fall.

I will not weigh heavily the costs of the overcrowding of prisoners, but the costs of incarceration may be very large for society.[13] To obtain some idea of the cost of providing prison space, I note that until the end of July 1990, Philadelphia was under a federal court order to increase prison and jail facilities. Besides releasing prisoners early, the city was paying a fine of $5,000 per day for not complying with the court order. Since the court judged that the city was not acting because this daily fine was too low, in August the fine was increased to $20,000 per day. At the former price, the annual cost was more than $1.5 million dollars; at the new level the cost exceeds $6 million per year. This figure applies to one city that was still paying the fine as of late 1990.

Automobile Fatalities

As with alcohol, cocaine use may lead to more automobile accidents and fatalities, either because of impaired driving skills or increased aggressiveness. Passengers, drivers of their own and other cars, and pedestrians can all be harmed by these accidents. This issue has been examined for New York City by Marzuk and his colleagues (1990). They find that nearly 20 percent of fatalities caused by auto accidents in the period 1984–1987 tested positive for cocaine use within the 48 hours before the occurrence. Interestingly, they find no statistically sig-nificant difference in this percentage for deaths in 1984 and 1985 versus the next two years, when crack addiction is supposed to have spread rapidly as indicated in hospital emergency-room-use data. They note that this lack of a trend may mean that the people driving and using crack could have begun using it earlier than the general population. Alternatively, it is possible that those using crack could naturally be more aggressive and greater risk-takers and no causation is involved.

DRUGS AND THE EMPLOYER

Illegal drug usage by an individual may affect production costs and the profitability of the user's employer. If a worker is paid an amount equal to his marginal product in a spot market, any reduction in his skills associated with drug use would be paid for by the individual and there is no nonpecuniary externality.

Problems can occur, however, if there is asymmetric information, a nonspot-labor market, teamwork, legal liabilities incurred by the employer, or investment in nongeneral human capital. Asymmetric information in this case means the individual knows he is using drugs and that his productivity has decreased, but the employer only learns this after a lag. The employer may not recognize these conditions immediately because in most jobs a person's contribution to output is not measured directly. Instead, a team's or a plant's output is observed. A person using drugs may be hired because this is not known, although more employers use pre-employment drug tests, which are not completely accurate and which only reveal use within some time period that varies by drug.

A person previously not on drugs may work for some period of time before his drug-induced incompetence is recognized. Even then, an employer may have little recourse to adjust real wages to marginal product. Using illegal drugs is probably not grounds for dismissing a tenured professor unless he is sentenced to jail, for example. Decreased productivity of such a professor would not lead to decreased nominal wages, though perhaps to decreased real wages. Similar constraints may apply to unionized employees unless a person's performance is so bad that he is fired for cause.

Firms can be held liable for accidents and errors caused by their workers while employed. A drugged train driver can hurt or kill hundreds of people and expose the firm to many millions of dollars of damages. For these reasons, firms will subject potential employees to pre-employment drug tests and, sometimes, to random tests during employment. Drug sales and usage in nuclear plants have been reported in the press. Philadelphia's bus and train transportation firm has negotiated a post-employment testing arrangement with its drivers' union.

There is another reason for an employer to be affected. Earnings profiles generally rise with years of work experience. Economists have developed several models to explain this pattern. (See Becker, 1975; Mincer, 1974; and Lazear, 1984.)

The most relevant model for this purpose is the specific human capital model, as in Becker. He distinguishes general from specific human capital. In the first instance, the worker pays all the costs of the investment via reduced wages or tuition while being trained. The worker also gets all the benefits via increased wages and fringes. Thus, if he fries his brain and produces less, he suffers the consequences. In the specific human capital case, either the firm or the worker could bear the investment costs and receive the benefits. Becker argues that since the benefits to either party depend on the worker's continuing to be employed by this firm, and since both parties can help determine whether this condition holds, it makes sense for both the worker and the firm to share both the costs and benefits. If the firm pays for any of the investment, drug-taking by workers could depreciate the value of the firm's investment. How pervasive is specific human capital? Mincer (1990) presents a rough estimate, using 1979 data, of about $60 billion.

There is another set of information that suggests that firms have substantial specific investments in their managerial and nonmanagerial employees. Nearly all large firms will provide for drug-rehabilitation programs in the firm or at an outside center.[14] Treatment is usually voluntary, although supervisors who recognize a person as being heavily into drugs may strongly urge treatment. Drug-treatment expenses, as noted earlier, are covered by most middle-size and large firms' health insurance. The associated costs are paid by fellow workers, the firm's owners, and consumers.

SUBSIDIES, EDUCATION, AND TREATMENT

Many of the above studies are drawn from samples that are small and/or have inadequate controls, but it seems clear that decriminalization, per se, will lead to lower drug prices and more use of drugs, which will generate additional externalities. Some of these externalities may be positive, such as the possibility of less crime, and some will be negative, such as more premature, low-birth-weight babies.

Is it possible to offset the effect of lower drug prices? One approach is to equate social and private prices and costs via subsidies and taxes. Victims could be reimbursed for losses. Low-birth-weight, addicted children born prematurely could be given extra attention. Cocaine-addicted people could be given vouchers with each purchase of the drug. These vouchers could be used to provide medical care or tutors to others. These steps, however, do not sound very practical and may be costly. Alternatively, the government could decriminalize drug use while stepping up antidrug education. The rationale for such an apparently contradictory behavior is that the government wishes people to make free, but informed, choices, and the government could provide more information at a social cost less than the social costs arising from the use of drugs.

New education programs are started frequently, and some have generated good results, at least as reported in the press, but systematic studies on older education programs have not shown much, if any, impact. (See Glynn, Leukefield, and Ludford, 1983; and Goodstadt, no date.)

Anglin and Hser (1989) examined the impact on crime of legal coercion to enter drug-treatment programs. They discuss the California Civil Addict Program (CAP), the New York Civil Commitment Program (CCP), and the program of the Federal Narcotic Rehabilitation Act (NARA). In these programs people are moved from jail to in-patient drug-treatment facilities. Based on prior research, they found that those in CAP for long periods reduced their narcotic use by 22 percent and criminal activities by 19 percent. In comparison, a group originally enrolled in CAP but released shortly thereafter because of legal errors in the commitment process had corresponding reductions of 7 percent and 7 percent, respectively.

They also examined results for three groups in CAP—a maturing-out sample, a methadone maintenance group, and a chronic street-addict group. They reported that these three groups had relatively similar narcotics use prior to commitment. Over the next twelve years, daily drug use fell for the first group, with less than 10 percent using drugs at the end. The second and third groups initially had decreases in drug use but by year 12 they were using drugs more frequently than before joining CAP. Those in the methadone program showed slightly lower use than those in the street-addict group.

The CCP, which for a time was voluntary, seems to have little positive impact. For a variety of reasons, NARA seems not to have worked.

CONCLUSION

Although the quality and quantity of available research reported above could be improved, it seems likely that the price elasticity of demand is not zero. Since decriminalization would sharply lower prices, there would probably be a noticeable increase in use of drugs and new users and addicts. People other than the users would be affected, with children being one of the largely impacted groups. The costs to make these children "whole" would be large. There would probably be an increase in homelessness, imposing health and other costs on society and its members. An increase in child, spouse, and parental abuse is likely, especially if cocaine and crack are used more heavily. Putting a value on these changes is difficult.

All the externalities may not be bad. The little evidence based on studies more than a decade old, and thus derived primarily from a heroin culture, which may be much different from a cocaine culture, indicates that a fall in the price of drugs would reduce property crime and homicides. The savings from fewer crimes and lower enforcement costs may be as high as $12 billion, although a 90 percent reduction in price may only lead to a 45 to 50 percent reduction in burglary; hence, the savings may be substantially less.

Suppose it took $4,000 to make a child born to a drug-addicted mother whole. Then 300,000 children, about 10 percent of live births, would offset the $12 billion costs of crime if all such costs were eliminated. The $4,000 figure is arbitrary but related to the day-care costs discussed above, and some of these costs might be justifiable even if the mothers did not use drugs. Moreover, there are other negative externalities to include in the balance.

The estimate of all the effects of drug use need to be improved substantially before a firm judgment can be reached on whether the value of the benefits outweigh the costs of decriminalization.

NOTES

1. This is not fully explained by drug users dying early. See Desmond and Maddux (1980).

2. See also the material below on trends in child abuse and addicted newborns that are associated with drug use by mothers.

3. Johnson et al. (1985) report results around 1980 on the amount of income derived from crime—theft, burglary, drug sales, prostitution, etc.—from a sample of Harlem heroin users who were engaged in criminal activities. It is not obvious how to generalize from this sample, but they show (p. 99) that the total share of cash income obtained from illegal activities ranges from 50 percent for irregular users to 80 percent for daily users.

4. There are 3 acute and 16 chronic-illness groups with greater prevalence.

5. These are infestations, obesity, and serious respiratory infections.

6. These are endocrinological, hypertension, CVA, and arthritis.

7. The price data are taken from police buys as testified in court. To consummate a deal, the offer from an unknown person must be near the going rate. These data may not match well with the earlier price data.

8. Mensch and Kandel (1988) argue that drug use is underreported in the NLS, perhaps because respondents have a long-term relationship to interviewers to whom they don't want to reveal this aberrant behavior. However, the NLS found the same usage rates when mail-in questionnaires were substituted. When studying abortions, another "socially bad" behavior, the mailed-in questionnaires showed much higher rates than those obtained

from personal interviews. (Telephone conversation with R. Olsen, who directs the NLS, in spring 1990.)

    9. There may be a selectivity problem if birthrates in this age interval are affected by drug use. See also footnote 8. Random measurement error on drug usage will bias its coefficient toward zero.

    10. It should be noted, however, using within-pair differences of siblings does not automatically lead to the elimination or even a reduction in omitted variable bias. (See Griliches, 1979.)

    11. Since narcotic use that did not complicate pregnancy was not measured, the birth weight in the control group may be slightly understated although their correction for selectivity may have solved this problem.

    12. Goldstein presents some anecdotal evidence to illustrate his categories.

    13. In 1985 the estimated total justice expenditures were nearly $46 billion. About one-fifth of this goes to running the state and local prisons and jails. (See Department of Justice, 1989.)

    14. The Bureau of National Affairs (1987) estimates that drug use costs employers $500 to $1,000 a year per user. They also report that the percentage of companies with Employee Assistance Plans (EAP) in the Fortune 500 companies rose from 25 to nearly 60 percent from 1972 to 1979. As discussed above, Morrisey and Jensen (1988) show that firm-provided health insurance that covers drug treatment has risen over time.

REFERENCES

Anglin, M. D., and Hser, Y. I., "Legal Coercion and Drug Abuse Treatment: Research Findings and Social Policy Implications." Los Angeles, University of California, mimeo, 1989.

Anglin, M. D., and Speckart, G. "Narcotics Use and Crime: A Multisample, Multimethod Analysis." *Criminology* 26 (1988): 197–233.

Arrow, K. *Social Choice and Individual Values.* New York: John Wiley, 1951.

Attorney General of the United States. *Drug Trafficking: A Report to the President of the United States.* Washington, D.C., 1989.

Becker, G. *Human Capital*, 2d ed. New York: Columbia University Press, 1975.

Behrman, J. R., Hrubec, Z., Taubman, P., and Wales, T. J. *Socioeconomic Success: A Study of the Effects of Genetic Endowments, Family Environment and Schooling.* Amsterdam: North-Holland Publishing Company, 1980.

Black, R., and Mayer, J. "Parents with Special Problems: Alcoholism and Opiate Addiction," in H. Kempe and R. Helfer, eds., *The Battered Child.* Chicago: University of Chicago Press, 1981, pp. 104–13.

Breakey, W. R., Fischer, P. J., Kramer, M., Nestadt, G., Romanoski, A. J., Ross, A., Royall, R. M., and Stine, O. C. "Health and Mental Health Problems of Homeless

Men and Women in Baltimore." *Journal of the American Medical Association* 262 (1989): 1352–57.

Brown, G. F., and Silverman, L. P. "The Retail Price of Heroin: Estimation and Applications." *Journal of the American Statistical Association* 69 (1974): 595–606.

Bureau of Justice Statistics. *Federal Offenses and Offenders: Drug Law Violators, 1980–86*. Washington, D.C., U.S. Dept. of Justice, 1988.

————. *BJS Data Report 1988*. Washington, D.C., U.S. Dept. of Justice, 1989a.

————. *Prisoners in 1988 Bulletin*. Washington, D.C., U.S. Dept. of Justice, 1989b.

————. *Special Report: Felony Case Processing in State Courts, 1986*. Washington, D.C., U.S. Dept. of Justice, 1990.

Bureau of National Affairs. *Alcohol and Drugs in the Workplace: Costs, Controls and Controversies*. Bureau of National Affairs Special Report, 1987.

Chasnoff, I. J. "Perinatal Effects of Cocaine." *Contemporary OB/GYN* (1987): 163–79.

Desmond, D. P., and Maddux, J. F. "New Light on the Maturing-Out Hypothesis in Opiod Dependence." *Bulletin on Narcotics* 32 (1980): 15–25.

FitzGerald, S. "For Vulnerable Babies Plan Shows Success." *Philadelphia Inquirer*, June 13, 1990.

Gelberg, L., and Linn, L. S. "Assessing the Physical Health of Homeless Adults." *Journal of the American Medical Association*, 262 (1989): 1973–79.

Gelles, R., and Strauss, M. *Intimate Violence*. New York: Simon and Schuster, 1988.

Glynn, T. J., Leukefeld, C. G., and Ludford, J. P. *Preventing Adolescent Drug Abuse: Intervention Strategies*. National Institute on Drug Abuse, Research Monograph Series 47, Washington, D.C.: U.S. Dept. of Health and Human Services, 1983.

Goldstein, P. J., "The Drugs/Violence Nexus: A Tripartite Conceptual Framework." *Journal of Drug Issues* 15 (1985): 493–506.

————. "Homicide Related to Drug Traffic." *Bulletin of the New York Academy of Medicine* 62 (1986): 509–16.

Goodstadt, M. *Drug Education*. National Institute of Justice Crime File, no date.

Griliches, Z., "Estimating the Returns to Schooling: Some Econometric Problems." *Econometrica* 45 (1977): 1–22.

Grossman, M., and Joyce, T. "Unobservables, Pregnancy Resolutions and Birth Weight Production Functions." Cambridge, Mass.: National Bureau of Economic Research Working Paper 2746, 1988.

Habel, L., Kaye, K., and Grossi, M. T. "Trends in Reporting of Maternal Substance Abuse in New York City, 1978–1987." APHA Presentation, mimeo, 1988.

Hauser, R., and Daymont, T. "Schooling Ability and Earnings in Cross-Sectional Findings 8 to 14 Years after High School Graduation." *Sociology of Education* 50 (1977): 182–206.

Infant Health and Development Program. "Enhancing the Outcomes of Low-Birth-Weight, Premature Infants." *Journal of the American Medical Association* 263 (1990): 3035–42.

Innes, C. J. *Drug Use and Crime: State Prison Survey, 1986*. Washington, D.C.: Bureau of Justice Statistics Special Report, 1988.

Johnston, L., O'Malley, P., and Bachman, J. *Illicit Drug Use, Smoking, and Drinking by America's High School Students, College Students and Young Adults 1975–1987.* Washington, D.C.: National Institute on Drug Abuse, U.S. Dept. of Health and Human Services, 1988.

Katzenbach, N. de B. *Report and Recommendations to the Mayor on Drug Abuse in New York City.* Mimeo, 1990.

Kleiman, M.A.R., and Mockler, R. A. "AIDS and Heroin: Strategies for Control." Washington, D.C.: Urban Institute, mimeo, 1988.

Kline, J., Stein, Z., and Hutzler, M. "Cigarettes, Alcohol and Marijuana: Varying Associations with Birthweight." *International Journal of Epidemiology* 16 (1987): 44–51.

Lafont, J. *Fundamentals of Public Economics,* trans. by J. Bonin and H. Bonin. Cambridge, Mass.: MIT Press, 1989.

Lazear, E. "Why Is There Mandatory Retirement?" *Journal of Political Economy* 87 (1984): 1261–64.

Linn, S., Schoenbaum, S. C., Monson, R. R., Rosner, R., Stubblefield, P. C., and Ryan, K. J. "The Association of Marijuana Use with Outcome of Pregnancy." *American Journal of Public Health* 73 (1983): 1161–64.

Marzuk, P. M., Tardiff, K., Leon, A. C., Stajic, M., Morgan, E. B., and Mann, J. J. "Prevalence of Recent Cocaine Use among Motor Vehicle Fatalities in New York City." *Journal of the American Medical Association* 263 (1990): 250–56.

Mensch, B. S., and Kandel, D. B. "Do Job Conditions Influence the Use of Drugs?" *Journal of Health and Social Behavior* 29 (1988): 169–84.

Mincer, J. *Schooling, Experience, and Earnings.* National Bureau of Economic Research, 1974. Distributed by Columbia University Press, New York.

———. "Job Training: Costs, Returns and Wage Profits." National Bureau of Economic Research Working Paper No. 3208, 1990.

Morrisey, M., and Jensen, G. "Employee Sponsored Coverage for Alcoholics and Drug Abuse Treatments." *Journal on Studies on Alcohol* 49 (1988): 456–61.

Musgrave, R. *The Theory of Public Finance.* New York: McGraw-Hill, 1959.

Nadelmann, E. "Drug Prohibition in the United States: Costs, Consequences, and Alternatives." *Science* 245 (1989): 939–47.

National Institute of Drug Abuse. *National Household Survey on Drug Abuse: Main Findings 1985.* Washington, D.C.: U.S. Dept. of Health and Human Services, 1988.

New York Times. February 9, 1987, p. B1.

Nisbet, C. T., and Vakil, F. "Some Estimates of Price and Expenditure Elasticities of Demand for Marijuana among UCLA Students." *Review of Economics and Statistics* 54 (1972): 473–75.

Regan, D. O., Ehrlich, S. M., and Finnegan, L. P. "Infants of Drug Addicts: At Risk for Child Abuse, Neglect, and Placement in Foster Care." *Neurotoxicology and Teratology* 9 (1987): 315–19.

Rosenzweig, M. R., and Schultz, T. P. "Estimating a Household Production Function:

Heterogeneity, the Demand for Health Inputs, and their Effects on Birth Weight." *Journal of Political Economy* 80 (1983): 723–46.

Rosenzweig, M. R., and Wolpin, K. I. "The Effect of the Timing and Frequency of Marijuana Use on Fetal Growth Based on Sibling Birth Data." Minneapolis: University of Minnesota, mimeo, 1989.

———. "Inequality at Birth: The Scope for Policy Intervention." Minneapolis: University of Minnesota, mimeo, 1990.

Reuter, P., and Kleiman, M.A.R. "Risks and Prices: An Economic Analysis of Drug Enforcement," in M. Tonry and N. Morris, eds., *Crime and Justice*, 1986, pp. 289–340.

Silverman, L. P., and Spruill, N. L. "Urban Crime and the Price of Heroin." *Journal of Urban Economics* 4 (1977): 80–103.

Smith, A. *The Wealth of Nations*. London: Printed for W. Strahn and T. Cadell in The Strand, 1776.

Taubman, P. *Sources of Inequality of Earnings*. Amsterdam: North-Holland Publishing Company, 1975.

Taylor, S. D., Wilbur, M., and Osnos, R. "The Wives of Drug Addicts." *American Journal of Psychiatry* 123 (1966): 585–91.

U.S. Department of Justice, Bureau of Justice Statistics. *Justice Expenditure and Employment in the U.S. 1985*, Washington, D.C.: U.S. Government Printing Office, 1990.

Whitman, D., Friedman, D., and Thomas, L. "The Return of Skid Row." *U.S. News and World Report*, January 15, 1990.

Wolk, R. L., and Diskind, M. H. "Personality Dynamics of Mothers and Wives of Drug Addicts." *Crime and Delinquency* 7 (1961): 148–52.

Wright, J. D., and Weber, E. *Homelessness and Health*. Washington, D.C.: McGraw-Hill, 1987.

Zuckerman, B., et al. "Effects of Maternal Marijuana and Cocaine Use on Fetal Growth." *New England Journal of Medicine* 320 (1989): 762–68.

7

HOMICIDE AND CRACK
IN NEW YORK CITY

Hope Corman,
Theodore Joyce,
and Naci Mocan

According to many newspaper accounts, the widespread distribution of crack is a "plague" wreaking havoc on our society. This drug, a cocaine derivative ingested by smoking, is believed to be responsible for, among other things, an unprecedented surge in violence. Many policymakers believe that public policy must address itself to this "scourge" and that vast expenditures of public funds are necessary to make our country safe from further destruction. Although there is considerable debate about which policies will be most effective in reducing the devastating impact of this "epidemic," most people believe that there is great urgency in finding solutions.

Before addressing the policy issues, however, it is prudent to examine these claims in a more systematic and objective fashion. Decisions regarding the speed and intensity of public policy should follow an assessment of the severity of the problem. The purpose of this paper is to add to the public policy debate, by providing a statistical assessment of one of the most potentially serious consequences of crack—homicides. Toward this end, we focus on one of the geographic areas believed to be most severely affected by crack—New York City.

Specifically, we examine the claim that the crack epidemic is responsible for

We wish to thank Michael Grossman, Ed Bonfield, Bob Kaestner, Steve Klein, and Don Wise for helpful comments. Gordon Liu, Ahmet Kocagil, and Bill Underwood provided able research assistance.

an unprecedented surge in homicides in New York City. We use currently available data and statistical techniques to assess the magnitude and significance of the increase in homicides in New York City, following the introduction of crack. The importance of current increases in homicide rates can only be assessed through comparison with past levels and changes.

RELATIONSHIP BETWEEN CRACK AND HOMICIDE

There are several reasons why drugs, in general, and crack, in particular, are believed to be related to increased levels of violence. Users are often earners of low wages who can only support their habits through illegal means. Further, the stronger the addiction and the greater the immediate need for drugs, the more risk the user will be willing to take to obtain money. This means that users will be more likely to resort to violence to obtain needed funds. If users are temporarily under the influence of drugs, or are experiencing withdrawal when engaging in crime, their judgment will be impaired and they will be more likely to react violently to an unexpected situation.

Some claim that the addiction changes the individual's valuation of time and risk. The addict is depicted as present-oriented and either indifferent to or favorably inclined toward risk. Since the cost of committing crimes is possible future incarceration, present-oriented, risk-preferring individuals are most likely to commit crimes, and most likely to resort to violence. Those who claim that the crack "epidemic" is worse than prior periods of drug use claim that the drug, itself, is different. Crack produces an immediate, intense high followed by a sharp crash, with a compelling drive to get high again. Crack is thus believed to be far more addictive than cocaine powder. It is also cheaper to obtain, opening the door to potential addiction for those who couldn't afford to even try cocaine. Unlike both cocaine powder and heroin, crack is believed to cause greater aggression in users. Unlike the availability of methadone for treating heroin withdrawal, there is no treatment to alleviate symptoms of withdrawal from cocaine or its derivative, crack.

Many believe that violence associated with drugs is primarily due to the illegality of the market. Drug producers and sellers have no other recourse to settling disputes and force is a typical method in obtaining market power. Some claim that individuals involved in crack production and distribution are a younger, tougher breed of drug marketeers, more violent and more indifferent to human life than in prior generations. For all of these reasons, we would expect the crack "epidemic" to be related to significantly elevated levels of homicide.

All the above arguments have a common but potentially erroneous premise: that the close association between drug use and crime reflects causation. That is, the drugs "cause" all the negative outcomes, which implies that by eliminating the drugs, or their illegal status, all the negative outcomes associated with drug use will be eliminated. Consider, for example, the argument that drug users commit crimes to support their habits. The implication is that if these individuals were not using drugs, they would not commit crimes. Researchers, however, find that many drug-using criminals began their criminal activities before they began using drugs.[1] The same characteristics believed to lead individuals to commit crimes—low wages in the legal sector, high rate of preference for the present compared to the future, high tolerance for risk, willingness to participate in activities thought to be illegal by many citizens—may also lead the same individuals to use and become addicted to drugs. It may be that the same individuals who commit violent acts also use drugs, but by eliminating drugs, we may not have as much impact on crime as suggested by newspaper accounts that criminals were on drugs.

The same causality issue applies to the supply side of the drug market. Although it may be true that illegal markets tend to be violent, it may also be true that individuals with a high tolerance for risk and violence are attracted to these industries. If all drug markets were legalized, these individuals might find other illegal or legal industries where they could apply their skills.

It is possible, then, that illegal drugs do not cause otherwise peaceful, law-abiding citizens to become murderers. Rather, it is possible that some individuals who either use or sell drugs would be criminals and violent in the absence of such drugs. Introduction of a new, highly addictive drug such as crack may not, necessarily, cause soaring murder rates, even if a high fraction of murders is committed by crack sellers and users. It becomes an empirical question. Was the introduction of crack associated with statistically significant increases in murders in New York City? If the answer to this question is no, then policymakers need to reexamine the causes and potential solutions to crime and other problems believed to be caused by drug use.

EMPIRICAL IMPLEMENTATION

Data

The monthly data on murders from January 1967 through March 1990 were obtained from monthly statistical reports from the Crime Analysis Unit of the New York City Police Department. The monthly numbers represent complaints (offenses known to have occurred) in the categories of murder and nonnegligent manslaughter. These categories conform to the guidelines issued by the Uniform Crime Reporting Committee of the United States Federal Bureau of Investigation. Annual figures dating from 1930 were obtained from a special report of the Crime

Analysis Unit of the New York City Police Department. In both cases, we began with the data from the first available date. We excluded the March 1990 Bronx social club fire, which resulted in 87 deaths, from the analysis.

Monthly population figures pertain to New York City residents 16 years and older and are from the U.S. Bureau of Labor Statistics' Current Population Survey beginning in January 1970. Because of the small sample size, race, sex, and age breakdowns are unavailable. Moreover, due to budget cuts at the Bureau of Labor Statistics, the number of households surveyed in New York City was reduced from 2,200 to 1,300 between March 1988 and October 1989. The population series was discontinued during this time but resumed in November 1989. The missing population figures were estimated by applying the compounded monthly rate of growth between February 1988 and November 1989 to the months with missing data.

Annual population figures for New York City residents of all ages are based on the census. Intercensal years represent the annually compounded rate of growth between the census years. Annual population figures for 1981 through 1989 apply the annual rate of growth (from April to April) in the population 16 years and over from the Current Population Survey measured to the 1980 census.

There is considerable controversy about the growth or decline of the population of New York City between 1980 and 1990. It may take years to have an accurate assessment of New York City's 1990 population. Our methodology results in a modest increase in the city's population over the second decade of our study. To increase the validity of our results, however, we employ not only murder rates per 100,000 population aged 16 and above, but we also employ the actual number of murders. It should be noted that no matter whose population estimates are used, the city's population was relatively stable over the two decades of our analysis.

Figures 7.1a through 7.1c plot the annual number of murders, murder rates per 100,000 residents, and murder rates per 100,000 males aged 15 to 29 in New York City between 1930 and 1990. Several trends are apparent. First, murders increased approximately fourfold in the decade of the 1960s through the early 1970s. Second, there has been a sharp increase in murders and murder rates from approximately 1986, but this was preceded by a sharp decrease from 1982 to 1986. These trends are irrespective of whether murders or murder rates per resident or murder rates per young male are examined. Even though we cannot distinguish population subgroups in our monthly estimates, it is helpful to know that, on an annual basis, neither the large increase in the young male adult population in the 1960s nor the decline in the young male adult population in the 1980s can account for the trends in murders observed during these decades.

Figures 7.2a and 7.2b plot monthly murders and murder rates, respectively. The (latter part of the) upward trend from the early 1960s to the early 1979s is, again, apparent. The decline from 1981 to 1985, followed by the rise from 1985,

FIGURE 7.1A. NUMBER OF MURDERS, 1930–1989.

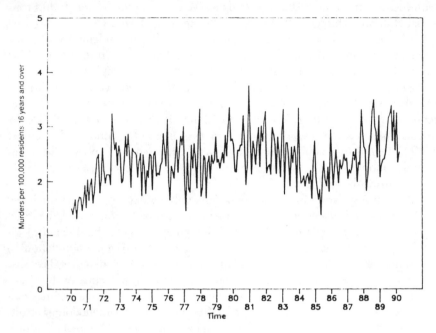

is also evident. It is also clear that there are large month-to-month variations in murders and murder rates in New York City. We need to examine the data in a more structured manner, specifically examining whether the rising murder rates of the late 1980s is a statistical reality.

Methodology

We address two questions: First, does the upturn in murders and in the murder rate in or about 1985 in New York City represent a statistically significant shift in the series given the previous 23 years? If yes, is it reasonable to link the rise to the introduction and spread of crack in New York City?

Given the seasonality in the murder series and its inherent variability, it is difficult to pinpoint a turning point. According to Figures 7.2a and 7.2b, a rough estimate would be mid-1985. Similarly, there is no exact date that defines the introduction of crack into the New York City drug market. The best guess is that crack became a factor sometime between 1984 and 1985; the Public Affairs Office of the U.S. Drug Enforcement Agency reports that crack was a "serious problem" in New York City by the beginning of 1986. Consequently, any attempt to establish a turning point in murders and to link it to the introduction of crack

FIGURE 7.1B. NUMBER OF MURDERS PER 100,000 RESIDENTS, 1930–1989

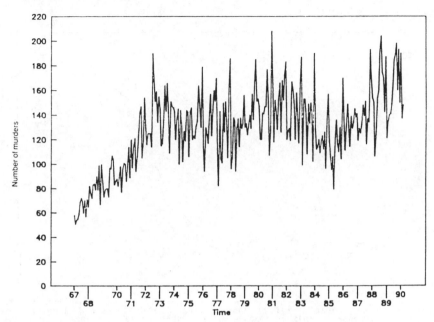

must be considered exploratory. As a result, we have approached the problem in several ways.

First, we fit univariate time-series models to murders and murder rates up until a hypothetical turning point.[2] We then project the series forward from that point and assess how well the actual data compare to the forecasts. If a true turning point occurred at the proposed date, then the forecasts should be poor compared with the actual data. One indicator of poor forecasts would be if the actual data were consistently above the 95-percent confidence interval for the forecasts. A second indicator would be whether the mean of the forecast errors is large in absolute value relative to the standard deviation. If we have specified the true underlying process correctly, and if there has been no important shift in the series, then the forecast errors T-periods ahead should be distributed symmetrically around zero. If the mean of the forecast errors divided by its standard deviation were positive and greater than 2, then this would be evidence that an unanticipated upturn in murders or murder rates may have occurred.

In the second approach we build an intervention model for the entire series by adding a dummy variable to the autoregressive integrated moving-average (ARIMA) specification. The dummy variable equals zero prior to the hypothesized turning point and one thereafter. A positive and statistically significant

FIGURE 7.1C. NUMBER OF MURDERS PER 100,000 MALES AGED 15 TO 29, 1930–1989

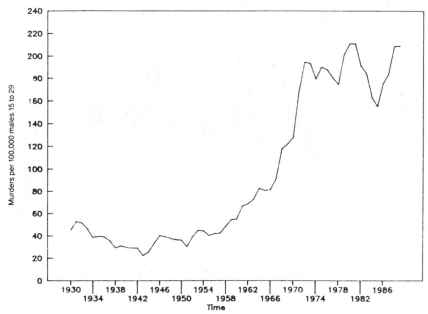

coefficient on the dummy variable would be evidence of a potentially important upward shift in murders.

The drawback to the intervention analysis is the uncertain timing of the introduction of crack into New York City. It would be possible to find one statistically significant intervention date in the 24-month span between 1984 and 1986 when in fact no true intervention occurred. The reverse is also possible. Multicollinearity among the parameters as well as a lack of sufficient postintervention data points could prevent us from finding a statistically meaningful change in the series.

Because of these drawbacks, we also employ a third approach to test whether there was a significant increase in murders coincident with the crack epidemic. Our third approach uses the intervention models from our second approach to forecast murders from January 1987 through March 1990. We compare these forecasts to the forecasts obtained in models that exclude the intervention components. If by modeling an intervention we can improve our forecasts over a period in which crack is well established, then we would accept such a result as evidence that a potentially meaningful upward shift in murders took place at or around the hypothesized date.

The most convincing evidence of a significant upturn in murders coincident

FIGURE 7.2A. NUMBER OF MURDERS 1967–1990 (MONTHLY)

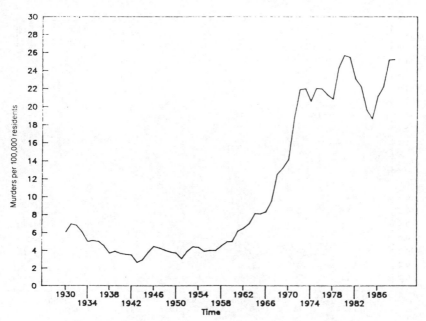

with the introduction of crack in New York City would be agreement across the three approaches for at least one of the hypothesized intervention dates between January 1984 and January 1986. Similarly, forecast errors that were no different from zero, forecasts that were within the confidence intervals, intervention components that were statistically insignificant, and forecasts that were not improved by modeling the intervention would suggest that although murders have risen since 1985, the shift is not inconsistent with past movements in the series.

RESULTS

Figures 7.3 through 7.7 compare the projected number of murders to the actual number over a 24-month horizon. The forecasts are based on data up until the hypothesized introduction of crack to the New York City market. We use January 1984, July 1984, January 1985, July 1985, and January 1986 as possible dates associated with the introduction of crack. Figures 7.8 and 7.12 make the same comparisons for murder rates per 100,000 residents aged 16 and above. We include only the upper 95-percent confidence interval because we are most interested in whether actual murders exceed predicted murders. Table 7.1

FIGURE 7.2B.   MURDER RATES 1970–1990 (MONTHLY)

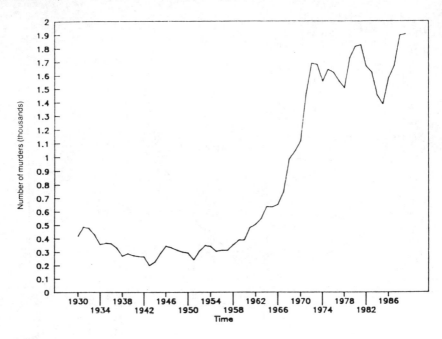

TABLE 7.1.   THE MEAN AND THE STANDARD DEVIATION OF THE MEAN
               (IN PARENTHESES) FOR FORECAST ERRORS OVER
               A 24-MONTH HORIZON

January 1984	July 1984	January 1985	July 1985	January 1986
		Murders		
−20.2	−5.0	4.9	23.0	21.7
(2.9)	(3.3)	(3.4)	(3.1)	(3.6)
		Murder rates		
−3.3	.3	3.0	5.9	4.9
(.6)	(.7)	(.8)	(.7)	(.8)

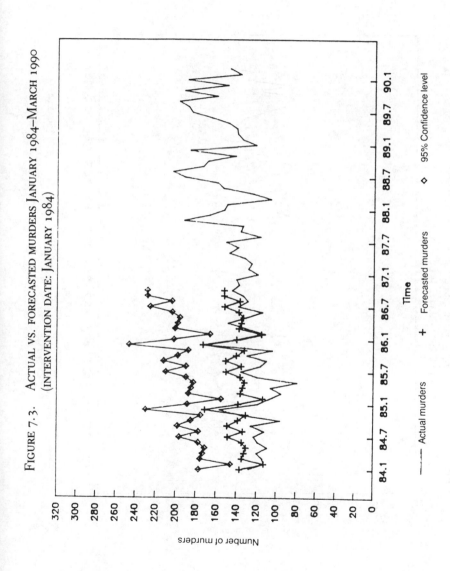

FIGURE 7.3.   ACTUAL VS. FORECASTED MURDERS JANUARY 1984–MARCH 1990
(INTERVENTION DATE: JANUARY 1984)

FIGURE 7.4.   ACTUAL VS. FORECASTED MURDERS JANUARY 1984–MARCH 1990
(INTERVENTION DATE: JULY 1984)

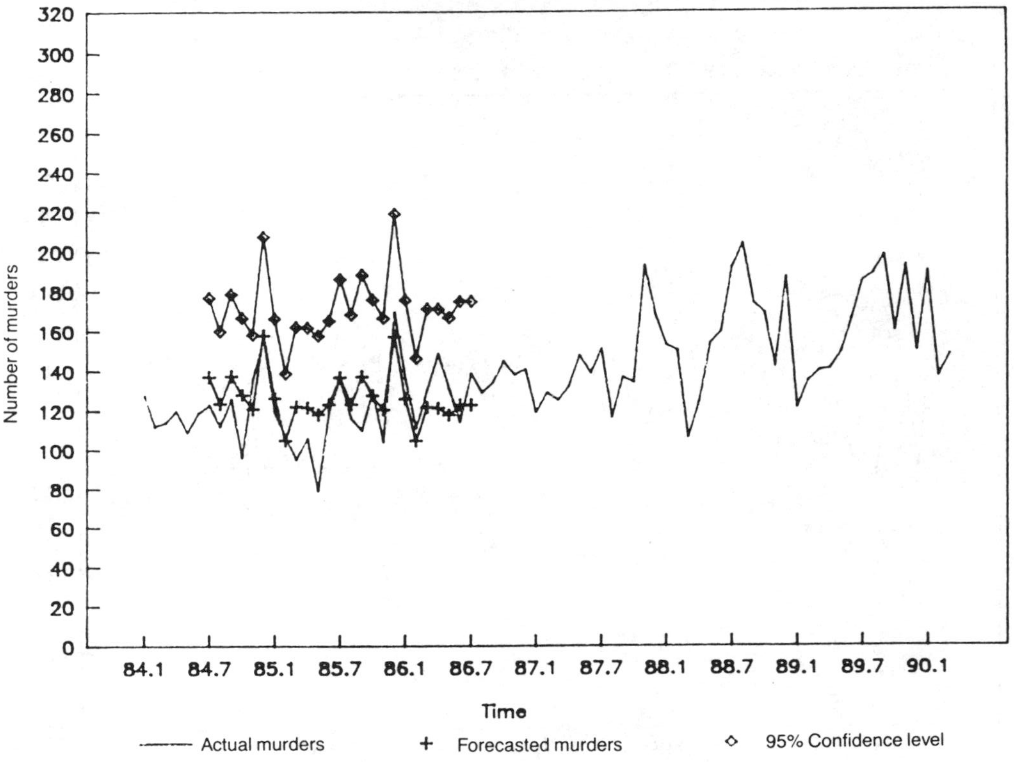

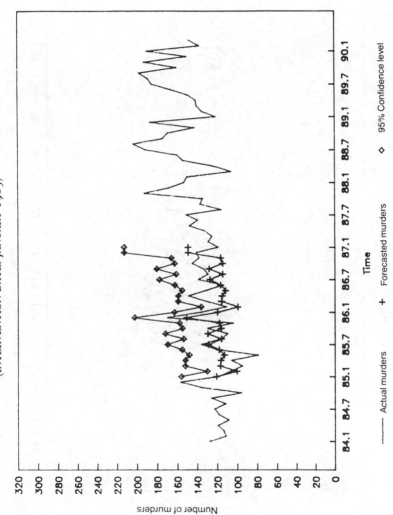

FIGURE 7.5. ACTUAL VS. FORECASTED MURDERS JANUARY 1984–MARCH 1990 (INTERVENTION DATE: JANUARY 1985)

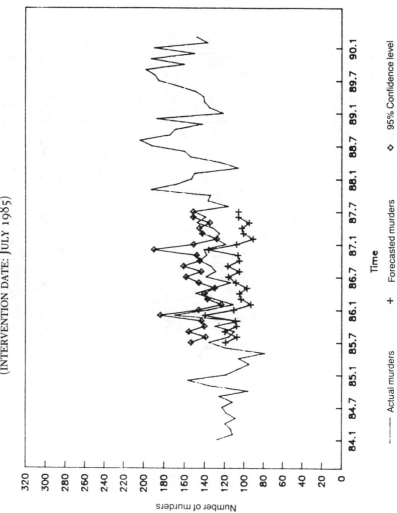

FIGURE 7.6. ACTUAL VS. FORECASTED MURDERS JANUARY 1984–MARCH 1990 (INTERVENTION DATE: JULY 1985)

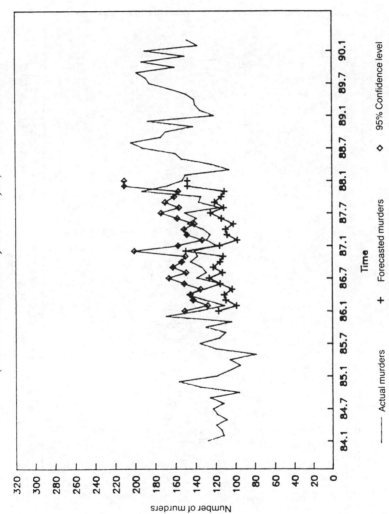

FIGURE 7.7. ACTUAL VS. FORECASTED MURDERS JANUARY 1984–MARCH 1990
(INTERVENTION DATE: JANUARY 1986)

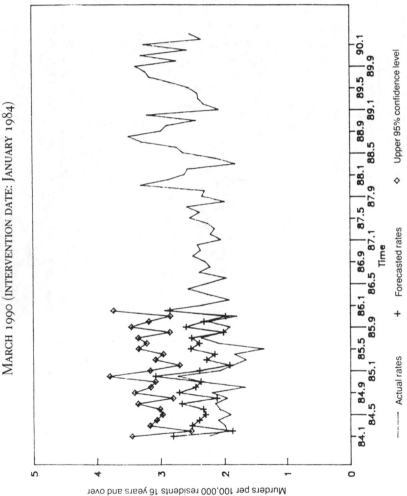

FIGURE 7.8. ACTUAL VS. FORECASTED MURDER RATES JANUARY 1984–MARCH 1990 (INTERVENTION DATE: JANUARY 1984)

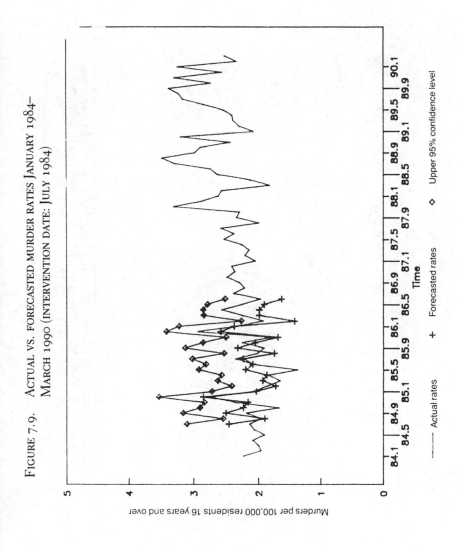

FIGURE 7.9. ACTUAL VS. FORECASTED MURDER RATES JANUARY 1984–MARCH 1990 (INTERVENTION DATE: JULY 1984)

Murders per 100,000 residents 16 years and over

Time

——— Actual rates   + Forecasted rates   ◇ Upper 95% confidence level

FIGURE 7.10. ACTUAL VS. FORECASTED MURDER RATES JANUARY 1984–MARCH 1990 (INTERVENTION DATE: JANUARY 1985)

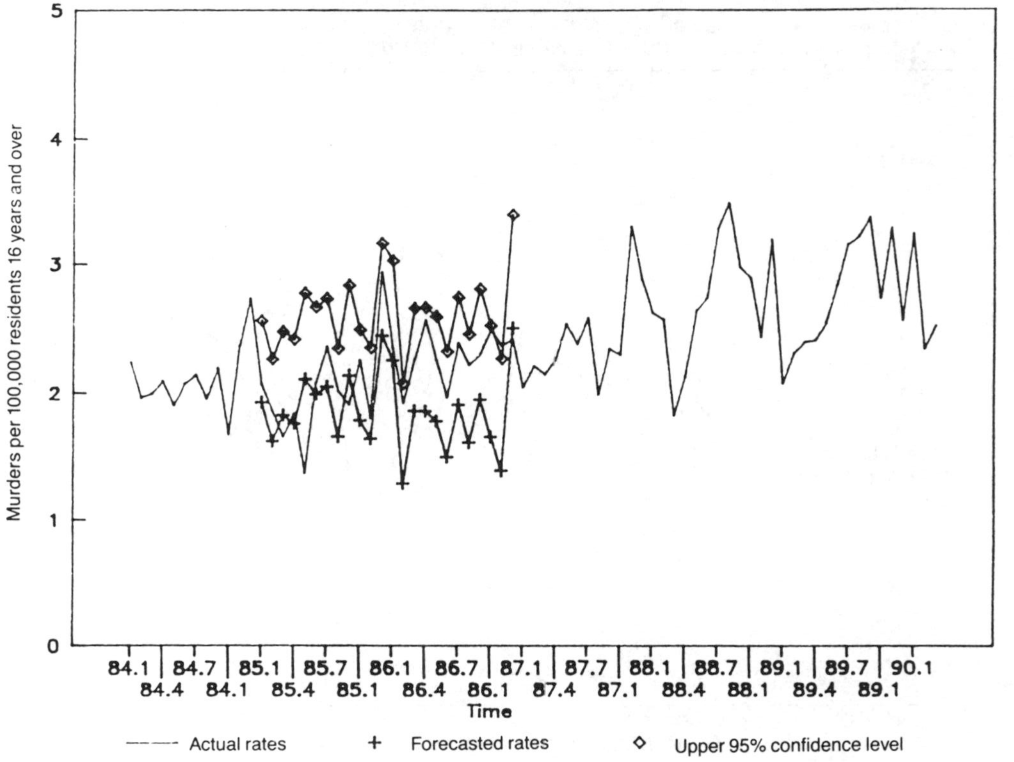

FIGURE 7.11. ACTUAL VS. FORECASTED MURDER RATES JANUARY 1984–MARCH 1990 (INTERVENTION DATE: JULY 1985)

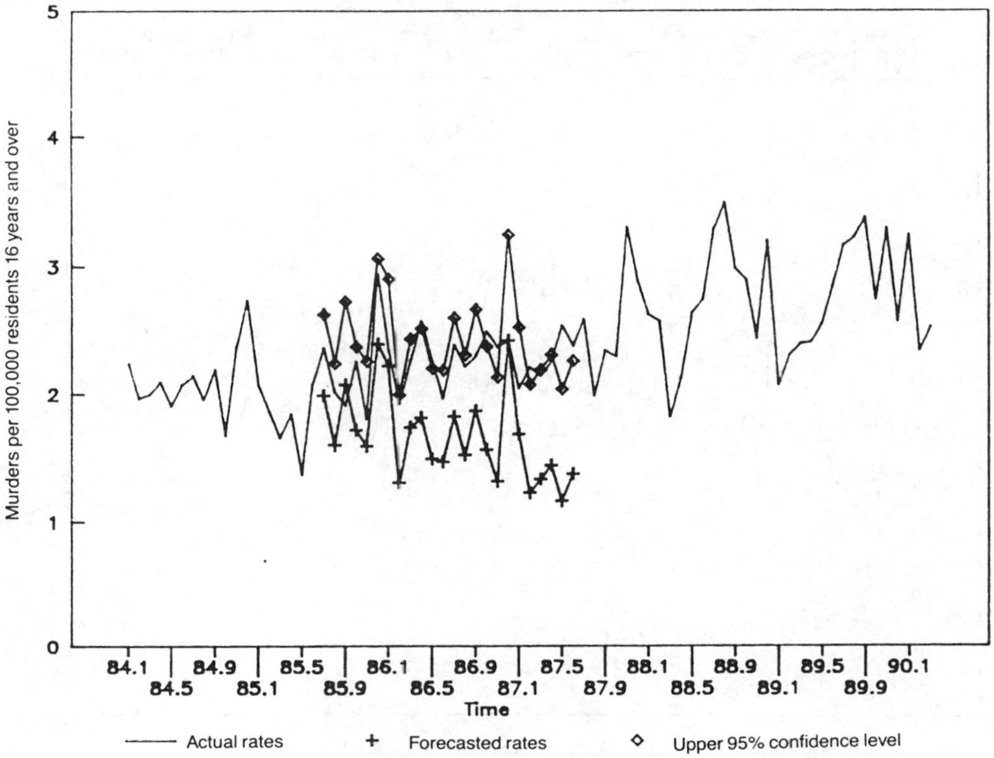

FIGURE 7.12. ACTUAL VS. FORECASTED MURDER RATES JANUARY 1984–MARCH 1990 (INTERVENTION DATE: JANUARY 1986)

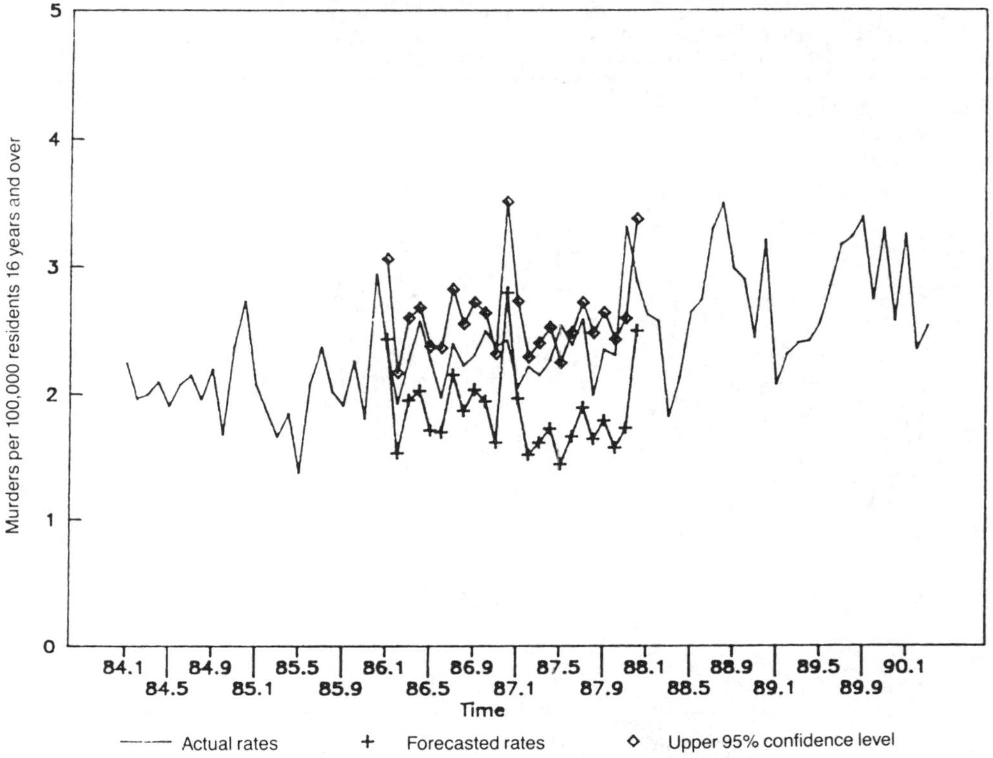

presents the mean forecast errors for the 24-month horizon and the respective standard deviations.

Figures 7.3 through 7.12 indicate that the model's ability to forecast murders is rather poor. As shown in Figures 7.3 through 7.7, and Table 7.1, predicted murders at first exceed actual murders based on forecasts in January and July of 1984, but then the mean of the errors becomes positive and large relative to the standard deviation of the mean after July 1985. The same pattern occurs with murder rates, except that the mean of the errors becomes positive beginning with forecasts in July 1984. As can be seen from Figures 7.1 and 7.2, the steep decline in murders after 1981, coupled with an equally steep upturn in 1985, make this an especially difficult series to forecast.

Nevertheless, actual murders never exceed the 95-percent confidence interval for forecasts made in January 1985; they exceed it only four times for forecasts made in July 1985 and only three times for forecasts made in January 1986. The results for murder rates are the same except for forecasts made in July 1985 in which the actual exceeds the 95-percent confidence interval seven times. In short, the results are mixed. The nonsymmetrical errors imply weak forecasts, but the forecasts are not consistently outside their expected bounds.

The results from the intervention analysis are also ambiguous (Tables 7.2 and 7.3). We again specified January 1984, July 1984, January 1985, July 1985, and January 1986 as possible intervention dates and estimated a separate model for each date. We constructed an intervention component that allowed the data to dictate the rate at which the series reached a new level.[3] In none of the cases was the month-to-month change as measured by the numerator of the intervention component statistically significant. The denominators in the intervention components are large in absolute value, however, and often outside the bounds of stability.

In the case of murders with a January 1985 intervention date, the coefficient on the denominator is equal to one, which means the change in murders is nonstationary—in other words, it fails to level off. The same is true for murder rates with a July 1984 intervention date. The intervention models simply confirm what can be seen from Figures 7.1 and 7.2: The upturn in murders has failed to reach a new level. Taken at face value, the lack of statistical significance of the month-to-month change in murders and murder rates implies that even if the series had reached a new level, we would still reject the null hypothesis that an important intervention had occurred. One is cautioned from such an interpretation, given the instability of the parameters and the lack of precision; without more postintervention data, we cannot eliminate the possibility that a statistically significant intervention might have occurred. With the second approach, as with the first, we are left with uncertain results.[5]

The third approach used the intervention models to project murders and murder rates from January 1987 through March 1990. The projections were compared to similar ones made by models that excluded any intervention terms. In other words, we asked whether forecasts improve when the forecasting equation explicitly models a shift in the series.[6] The answer is yes. As displayed in Table 7.4, the mean squared error and the mean absolute percent error fall for interventions specified at January 1985 for murders and July 1984 for murder rates, relative to their respective naive models. Are the improvements substantial? Again, the answer is yes. For murders the mean absolute percentage error falls 3.9 points or 25 percent; in the case of murder rates, it falls 7.5 points or 38 percent. A comparison of mean squared error reveals similar improvements. Clearly, the intervention models yield gains that should not be ignored if one were attempting to forecast beyond March 1990.

As a final exercise, we use the "best" model for murders and murder rates to forecast each of the series through 1991. For murders, this is the intervention

TABLE 7.2.   ARIMA INTERVENTION MODELS FOR MURDERS (IN LOGS) IN NEW YORK CITY: JANUARY 1970–MARCH 1990

Intervention dates and coefficients	84:1	84:7	85:1	85:7	86:1
θ_1	−.835	−.828	−.822	−.817	−.823
	(−24.3)	(−23.30)	(−23.29)	(−22.76)	(−23.12)
Θ_{12}	−.863	−.861	−.850	−.836	−.856
	(−26.4)	(−26.30)	(−23.75)	(−26.38)	(−35.47)
ω	−.055	−.144	−.007	−.007	−.176
	(−1.19)	(−.97)	(.82)	(.07)	(1.43)
δ	.769	−.095	.998	.938	−.468
	(3.49)	(−.09)	(−29.78)	(−.59)	(−.62)
Q-statistic	51.86	50.5	52.83	51.07	50.93
	(.32)	(.37)	(.29)	(.35)	(.36.3)

NOTE: The estimated model can be specified as follows:

$$LM_t = \frac{\omega}{1 - \delta B} I_t + \frac{(1 - \theta_1)(1 - \Theta)}{(1 - B)(1 - B_{12})} a_t$$

where LM_t is the natural log of murders, I_t is the intervention component that equals zero prior to the intervention date and 1 thereafter, and a_t is the residual. B is the backshift operator. Estimated t-statistics are in parentheses except for the Q-statistic, in which the marginal significance level is in parentheses. Note that the nonintervention ARIMA model is comprised of the second right-hand term.

TABLE 7.3.   ARIMA INTERVENTION MODELS FOR MURDER RATES
IN NEW YORK CITY: JANUARY 1970–MARCH 1990

Intervention dates and coefficients	84:1	84:7	85:1	85:7	86:1
θ_1	−.859	−.846	−.378	−.825	−.823
	(−22.94)	(−21.69)	(−4.91)	(−20.31)	(−24.15)
Θ_{12}	−.714	−.715	−.686	−.713	−.706
	(−11.39)	(−11.39)	(−11.17)	(−11.36)	(−11.36)
Θ_{24}	−.497	−.496	−.503	−.499	−.495
	(−7.61)	(−7.60)	(−7.97)	(−7.62)	(−7.66)
ω	−1.684	−.217	−.000	−.663	−.001
	(−1.27)	(−1.43)	(00)	(.32)	(1.11)
δ	.683	1.009	−1.155	.953	−1.221
	(2.52)	(76.63)	(−.02)	(−2.75)	(−5.45)
Q-statistic	36.69	36.27	67.10	38.00	40.46
	(.70)	(.72)	(.08)	(.65)	(.54)

NOTE: The estimated model can be specified as follows:

$$MR_t = \frac{\omega}{1 - \delta B} I_t + \frac{(1 - \theta_1)}{(1 - \Theta_{12} - \Theta_{24})(1 - B)(1 - B_{12})} a_t$$

where MR_t is the murder rate, I_t is the intervention component that equals zero prior to the intervention date and 1 thereafter, and a_t is the residual. B is the backshift operator. Estimated t-statistics are in parentheses except for the Q-statistic, in which the marginal significance level is in parentheses. Note that the nonintervention ARIMA model is comprised of the second right-hand term.

model with January 1985 as the intervention date. For the murder rate, it is the model with July 1984 as the intervention date. Figures 7.13 and 7.14 present the two projections. Although the forecasts rise, they begin to level off. The average monthly number of murders was 161 in 1989 and we estimate that it will be 169 in 1990 and 172 in 1991.[7] The same is true for murder rates. The average monthly rate was 27.5 in 1989, and is projected to be 29.8 in 1990, and 30.47 in 1991.

TABLE 7.4.   SUMMARY STATISTICS OF WITHIN-SAMPLE FORECASTS OF
              MURDERS AND MURDER RATES FOR INTERVENTION MODELS
              AND A NAIVE MODEL

Interventions	84:1	84:7	85:1	85:7	86:1	
	Murder intervention models					Naive
Mean error	13.9	17.5	5.01	21.1	24.9	21.2
Mean squared error	708.0	832.1	535.9	1002.6	1211.7	1007.9
Mean absolute percent error	12.8	14.1	11.6	15.4	16.9	15.5
	Murder rate intervention models					Naive
Mean error	1.9	2.0	4.6	5.2	5.3	5.4
Mean squared error	18.1	18.4	36.8	43.7	44.4	46.3
Mean absolute percent error	11.8	12.1	16.4	19.1	19.1	19.6

NOTE: The forecast period is January 1987–March 1990. The summary statistics are based on projections made from the estimated intervention models in Tables 7.2 and 7.3. The naive model has the same ARIMA specification as the intervention models less the intervention term.

DISCUSSION

We began this analysis by stating that public-policy response should be commensurate with the importance and severity of the problem. Since many claim that crack is responsible for a surge in murders, and that this is an extremely important problem, we examined the increase in murder rates since the introduction of crack into New York City. We found only weak evidence of any significant upturn in murders and murder rates. Murders increased from 151 per month in 1980 to 161 per month in 1989, a 6 percent increase in 9 years. We estimate that murders will increase another 6.8 percent to 172 per month, between 1989 and 1991, with the rate of increase slowing substantially between 1990 and 1991. The magnitude of the increase in murders is thus far from the "tidal wave" effect depicted in the media. Further, if our population estimates underrepresent the true New York City counts, then we have overstated the rise in murder rates. Moreover, it is the steep drop in murders from 1981 to 1985 that has made the subsequent rise so alarming. One would have had little reason to suspect an intervention in 1985 without the decline after 1981. Perhaps the introduction of crack caused an upturn in murders that otherwise would have continued on its downward path. If the decline in 1981 is part of the inherent variability in murders, however, then crack is a convenient confounder of more fundamental causes.

FIGURE 7.13. ACTUAL AND FORECASTED MURDERS
JANUARY 1980–DECEMBER 1991

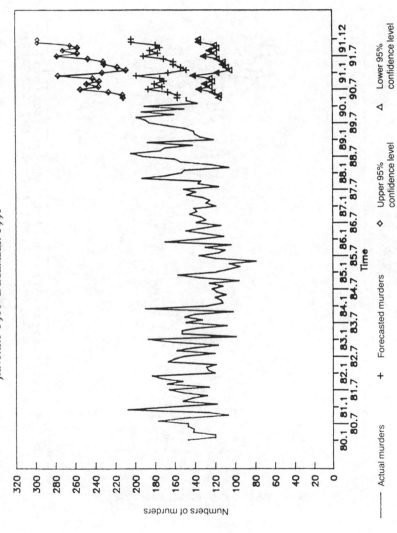

FIGURE 7.14. ACTUAL AND FORECASTED MURDER RATES
JANUARY 1980–DECEMBER 1991

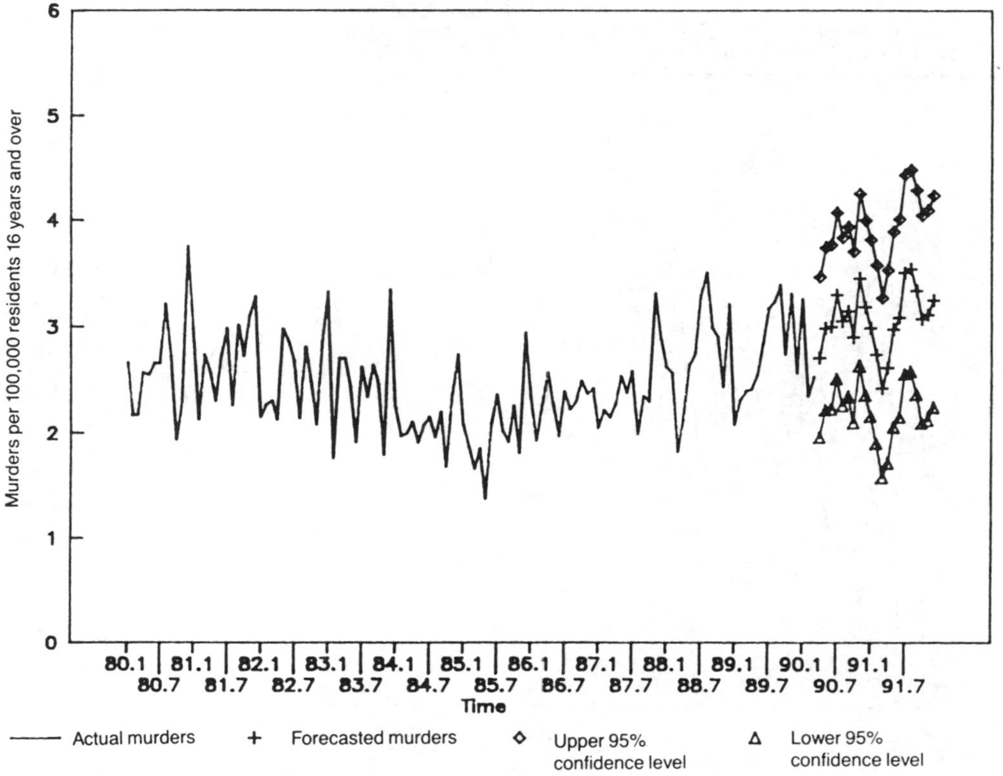

NOTES

1. For example, see Anglin and Speckart (1988), in the Bibliography.

2. See notes to Tables 7.2 and 7.3 for a description of the (nonintervention) ARIMA model.

3. More technically, we used a first-order transfer function for the intervention component. The notes to Tables 7.2 and 7.3 give the detailed specification.

4. See McCleary and Hay (1980), in the Bibliography.

5. In results not shown we tested other intervention dates around January 1985 for murders and July 1984 for murder rates. The results were also inconclusive.

6. Note the estimated model that generated the forecasts used the entire series on murders and murder rates.

7. Note the averages for 1990 include the three actual figures for January, February, and March.

BIBLIOGRAPHY

Anglin, M. Douglas, and Speckart, George. "Narcotics Use and Crime: A Multisample, Multimethod Analysis," *Criminology* 26, no. 2 (1988), pp. 197–233.

Bachman, James E., and Witte, Ann D. "The Effectiveness of Legal Sanctions on Individuals Addicted to Alcohol or Drugs," in Leveson, Irving, ed., *Quantitative Explorations in Drug Abuse Policy* (New York: Spectrum Publications, 1980), pp. 111–27.

Becker, Gary S. "Crime and Punishment: An Economic Approach," *Journal of Political Economy,* 76 (1968), pp. 169–217.

Becker, Gary S., and Murphy, Kevin M. "A Theory of Rational Addiction," *Journal of Political Economy* 96, no. 4 (August 1988), pp. 675–80.

Goldstein, Paul J. "Drugs/Violence Nexus: A Tripartite Conceptual Framework," *Journal of Drug Issues* 15, pp. 493–506.

Johnson, Bruce D., et al. "Drug Abuse in the Inner City: Impact on Hard-Drug Users and the Community," in Tonry, Michael, and Wilson, James Q., eds. *Drugs and Crime,* Vol. 13 (Chicago: University of Chicago Press, 1990), pp. 9–67.

McClearr, R., and Hay, R. A. *Applied Time Series Analysis for the Social Sciences* (Beverly Hills: Sage, 1980).

8

ON THE CONSEQUENCES
OF TOUGHNESS

Peter Reuter

Drug policy has generated two debates in recent years. The more entertaining
one concerns the retention of our current prohibitions—the legalization debate.
For better or for worse, this remains largely a parlor sport for intellectuals, divorced
from the policy-decision process. The more serious debate (and the one addressed
in this paper) is the narrower one between the hawks and doves of drug policy,
otherwise usually known as the supply-side advocates and the demand-side advocates. The hawks, while denying that they are slighting demand-side considerations, advocate continued expansion of the nation's effort to imprison drug
sellers and detect and punish (in various ways) drug users. The doves (whose
leaders include Senator Joseph Biden and Congressman Charles Rangel), while
generally accepting the need for "vigorous enforcement," argue that current
resource commitments to programs directly aimed at demand (prevention and
treatment) are grossly underfunded and should be massively increased, even if
this be at the expense of enforcement.[1]

The debate has been conducted largely in terms of images. The supply-side
advocates point to the immediacy of the problems in the streets (such as the
carnage surrounding drug distribution) and reasonably (though in intemperate

Support for this work was provided by Rand's Drug Policy Research Center, which is
funded by the Ford and Weingart Foundations. Joel Feinleib provided valuable research
assistance and Mark Kleiman made helpful suggestions on a late draft.

tones) ask whether drug prevention in particular offers any reasonable hope for controlling those markets and associated violence in the near future. They point to the low success rates of drug-treatment programs. Finally, they argue that effective prevention and treatment require a high level of enforcement, both to make drugs difficult to obtain and to make drug use appear legally risky.[2]

The doves are less eloquent, or at least their eloquence is less clear. They argue that drug enforcement has proven a failure. The intensification of enforcement throughout the 1980s failed to stem a massive growth in the nation's drug problems. Enforcement does not go to the root of the problem; with a loss of faith in source-country control programs (such as crop eradication and crop substitution), the root of the problem is now seen to be a recruitment of new users in the United States. Prevention and treatment receive a derisory share of what the nation spends to control its drug problems.[3] Public treatment programs, faced with the most difficult clients, have far fewer resources to spend on those clients that do private treatment programs (Institute of Medicine, 1990). *Sotto voce* they also suggest that drug enforcement increases crime and may exacerbate health problems related to drug use.

All of these are plausible statements. Indeed, I suspect that they are all true. None of them provide much help in working out what our drug policy should look like. No one can describe, even very roughly, the consequences of doubling the number of treatment slots available for addicts without insurance coverage for such treatment, or what would happen if we were to increase the number of drug arrests by 25 percent. Over (say) five years, would these result in declines of 20 percent in prevalence or in drug-related homicides? What else (positive or negative) might occur as a consequence of these actions?

The discussion is characterized by a rather casual interpretation of the recent past. Doves look at the increasing length of sentences for drug offenses[4] and the rapidly rising number of prison inmates serving time for drug offenses and assert that the criminal justice system has become much tougher about drugs. The hawks note the numerous incidents of drug dealers getting probation for their first three convictions and the overcrowding of prisons, which require early release of so many offenders,[5] and say that the criminal justice system is failing to be punitive at all.

The American discussion of society's alternatives, both in the legalization and the mainstream policy debate, focuses on the extent of drug use. That is, when comparing alternative policies, emphasis (often exclusive attention) seems to be given to which policy will result in the lower prevalence of drug use. I adopt instead what has come in Europe to be called a "harms minimization" criterion.[6] The question that policymakers (and their entourages of analysts) ought to be addressing is what choices minimize the harms resulting from drug use and drug control.[7] The value of this approach is that it takes account of the fact that many, though not all, of the adverse consequences of drug use are a function of the policies used to restrain that behavior. Here I give consideration to at least some of the negative effects of stringent drug enforcement, though I do not attempt to draw any conclusions about the optimal policy mix. Note that, as discussed in the final section, arguments against stringent enforcement are not necessarily arguments for the elimination of prohibitions.

The next section of the paper presents some conclusions on the changing intensity of enforcement during the 1980s; it summarizes highly uncertain calculations, more details of which are given in the Appendix. The remainder of the paper moves from speculative use of numbers to the realm of pure speculation. It considers certain consequences of toughness, in particular whether more intense enforcement does not have important negative effects that ought to be considered in the discussion of drug policy. The final section then considers the implications of these matters for the choices that are available to the nation.

THE CHANGING STRINGENCY OF ENFORCEMENT

Interpretation of the recent past is important to the policy debate, since it helps form the images of the contending parties. The disagreement between the hawks and doves about the punitiveness of drug control during the 1980s has two components. The first is whether the system now imposes greater risk of legal sanctions on users and sellers than it did ten years earlier. The second is whether the risk is, even now, substantial enough to be a credible deterrent.

The second component involves a difficult judgment about perceptions and responses to legal risks, but the first seems a relatively straightforward matter. Any appeal to the facts, any responsible attempt to test empirically the contending assertions, however, reveals the difficulty of measuring the stringency of enforcement. What follows is possibly tedious, probably inconclusive, and certainly very rough; the reader uninterested in methodological issues or squeamish about approximations may wish to skip to the last page of this section.

Conceptual Issues

The problems are both conceptual and empirical. It is not clear what one should choose as the unit against which risk is measured. For the user, is the relevant measure expected penalties per use episode, purchase transaction, or user year? Arguments can be made for each of them. Most use episodes expose the individual to risk, either because others are present (any one of whom is a potential informant) or because the use itself can be revealing (involving paraphernalia or distinctive odors, or generating conspicuous behavior). The purchase is a plausible alternative because most arrests seem to be associated with purchase transactions. The final candidate is the user year because the individual's choice may be less how often to use in a year than whether to be a user at all; this is probably consistent with the notion of dependency related to drug use.[8]

One weakness of each of these units is that averages will mask enormous variation across user groups. Purchase risk depends very much on location, for example; those who buy in street markets, whether because of ignorance, impatience, or lack of alternatives, are at much higher risk than those who are able to make their purchases in private settings. If the user year is the unit, then it masks variation associated with the intensity of use.

An added complication is that risks for sellers and buyers may have changed in different directions. If the police launch a campaign against the buyers in open-air drug markets, then buyer risk will rise relative to seller risk. Both risks are relevant for policy analysis but have different consequences; one operates directly on demand, the other only indirectly. We shall consider risks for the two groups separately in the following discussion.

The measurement of penalty presents its own problems. The criminal justice system imposes a variety of penalties on dealers; arrest, seizure of drugs and other assets, time incarcerated. These may not be highly correlated; a crackdown may produce a large increase in arrests but little change in total incarceration. Data are collected systematically (at some levels) on arrests and imprisonments; little is available on the value of assets seized. The following calculations ignore the asset seizures.

No matter which units are chosen, it turns out to be extremely difficult to gather the necessary data to develop a plausible estimate. What relevant evidence does exist produces somewhat ambiguous results. We provide here only a summary; more details are provided in the Appendix.

Penalty Levels

Let us start with the numerator of the calculation, namely, the volume of punishment. We seek to estimate the number of persons arrested for simple possession of marijuana and of cocaine and the total number of cell-years imposed on marijuana dealers and on cocaine dealers. This reflects my assumption that few possession arrests result in serious penalties beyond the arrest itself, whereas the primary punishment for distribution arrests is in the incarceration. The calculations will be done for 1979 and 1988, two years for which prevalence data and most of the relevant enforcement data are available. Results are presented in Table 8.1.

For users the calculations are relatively straightforward; the only problem is the allocation of heroin/cocaine arrests between the two drugs. The cell-year calculations are much more uncertain. With data described briefly below and in more detail in this chapter's Appendix, and with more than perhaps even a

TABLE 8.1.   PUNISHMENTS FOR DRUG BUYERS AND SELLERS, 1979, 1988
               (IN THOUSANDS)

	Marijuana		Cocaine	
	1979	1988	1979	1988
Arrests[a]				
Buyers	342	326	24	301
Sellers	50	65	11	147
Cell years				
Prison	12	28	3	70
Jail	8	3	2	8
Federal	2	10	3	30
Total	21	41	7	108

[a]Excludes federal arrests.
SOURCES: See Appendix.

"heroic" number of assumptions (also described at length in the Appendix), we can make crude estimates of total punishment for various drug-offense categories in 1979 and 1988.

The number of state and local arrests for drug offenses has increased rapidly, from 560,000 in 1979 to 1,150,000 in 1988. The composition of these arrests changed in an important way over the same period. Whereas the 1979 total was dominated by arrests for marijuana (70 percent) and possession (82 percent) offenses, in 1988 heroin/cocaine[9] arrests had come to exceed the number for marijuana (600,000 versus 391,000), and distribution arrests now accounted for a much larger share than in 1979 (27 percent versus 18 percent). In effect, the average seriousness of arrest offense has increased sharply; this points again to the importance of distinguishing among drugs and roles in analyzing risks.

Arrest is only the first step in the criminal justice process, but at the national level we cannot systematically trace through the disposition of these arrests.[10] Data from California (see Appendix Table 8.A.4) show that sentencing has become very much tougher in that state, at least for the more serious distribution offenses; whereas only 5 percent of those convicted on a felony drug charge in 1979 went to prison (that is, received a sentence of more than 12 months), that figure had risen to 17 percent in 1988. However, this might also have been accompanied by a decline in the severity of sentences for drug-possession cases as dockets became more crowded. For a group of five states tracked over the period 1983–1986, the percent of felony drug convictions resulting in some incarceration (prison or jail) rose from 71 percent in 1983 to 83 percent in 1986 (Bureau of Justice Statistics, 1989b).

At the national level, we have only data on the sentencing for felony drug convictions in 1986 and 1988 (Bureau of Justice Statistics, 1988 and 1990). In that two-year period there was a very sharp increase (from 135,000 to 225,000, approximately a 70 percent rise) in the number of persons convicted of felony drug trafficking or possession charges[11] and a modest decline in the expected time served for those who were convicted of drug trafficking (from 22 months to 20 months). In 1988 drug offenses accounted for approximately one third of all felony convictions in state courts. [12]

The available data permit rough estimates of prison and jail years meted out for drug felonies by state courts in 1988. About 90,000 persons were sentenced to prison, and another 65,000 were sentenced to local jails. Allocating across drugs in proportion to their share of distribution arrests nationally, I estimate the total cell-years for marijuana sellers from these sentences to be about 31,000, and for cocaine sellers, about 78,000.

The federal court system also imposes punishment on drug dealers. Though federal drug convictions constitute a small share of the total, the average time served for those incarcerated is much higher than for state-sentenced offenders. The federal courts simplify our estimation task by separating sentences according to the drug involved.

In 1988 these courts generated an estimated 50,000 years of expected prison time for drug dealers, compared to only one-tenth that amount in 1979. That reflected increasing numbers of convictions, rising sentence length and, most significantly, a rise in the share of sentence that the inmate expected to serve; this last was the result of the imposition of sentencing guidelines and the abolition of federal parole.

Estimating the 1979 cell-year totals is an even more speculative venture. For 1979 we have only national data on how many persons were in state prison for drug offenses (Bureau of Justice Statistics, 1988), a slender basis for developing dispositional data. Between 1979 and 1986 the number of persons in state prison on drug charges rose substantially, from 18,000 to 39,000, approximately in line with the increase in the number of sale/manufacture arrests.

To avoid taxing the data unreasonably, I adopt some very simple assumptions that bias the exercise against finding increasing severity of punishment. I assign all the drug-dealing inmates in 1979 to that year and assume that they are serving sentences as long as those served in 1986, the first year for which national time-served data are available. The number of persons receiving jail sentences is calculated on the basis of the share of sentences of incarceration going to jail in five states in 1983.

With those assumptions, the final estimates of cell-years give much more weight to marijuana, reflecting marijuana's dominance of distribution arrests at the state level. Marijuana cell-years were three times that given to cocaine dealers, though at the federal level more cocaine dealers received prison sentences, which averaged more months.

One surprising feature of the final numbers in Table 8.1 is the high cell-year estimate for marijuana, particularly in 1988. The estimated federal punishment level has a reasonably sound empirical base. Mark Kleiman (personal communication) suggests that the large number of marijuana cases still being brought in the federal system might be a function of federal prosecutors in primarily rural districts not having other drug-dealing cases available to them; with rising pressure to appear tough on drugs, they may choose to bring a lot of marijuana cases.

The state-prison calculations assume that marijuana-dealer convictions are as likely to result in prison sentences as convictions for distribution of other drugs, and that sentences will have the same time served. It is possible that marijuana dealers are given systematically lighter sentences; nonetheless, the total cell-years for marijuana dealers is very likely to have increased between 1979 and 1988.

Number of Transactions

The difficulty of estimating the numerator in the calculation of punitiveness pales beside that of estimating the denominator. Put aside the many conceptual problems discussed earlier and assume for the moment that the denominator is the number of purchases. That is a function of the number of users, their average consumption, and the amount they purchase at each transaction. As cocaine prices have fallen and the mode of ingestion has changed (from intranasal to smoking), the number of transactions per user may have risen very sharply. For marijuana, increased potency and price may have had the opposite effect.

The National Household Survey (NHS) estimate of the number of regular users (monthly) of the two drugs is sharply lower for 1988 than for 1979, contradicting other indicators and the general impression. Even if 1988 cocaine consumers made ten times as many purchases as 1979 consumers, the number of arrests per transaction (either for possession or distribution) would have risen. For marijuana, where transactions per user are likely to have fallen, the data also suggest that arrest risk per transaction has risen.

The NHS estimates are unconvincing, however. Wish (1990–1991) points out that data from the Drug Use Forecasting (DUF) system[13] point to more regular cocaine users just among the arrested population than are found in the whole household survey by the NHS.

An equally plausible (and weak) alternative measure of the increase in the number of transactions is the change in the number of mentions of cocaine in the DAWN Emergency Room (ER) data. That shows a 21-fold increase in the same nine-year period.[14]

For marijuana the DAWN system provides little relevant information, since marijuana rarely shows up except with another more dangerous drug. The High School Senior Survey (Johnston, O'Malley, and Bachman, 1989), a higher quality annual survey of twelfth-graders, also reports substantial declines in all measures of prevalence over the period 1979–1988; the percentage of respondents reporting daily use of marijuana fell from about 10 percent to about 4 percent.

Conclusions: Punishment per Transaction

The above figures provide some pleasingly unexpected results. Though the focus of drug enforcement in the late 1980s has been on cocaine, we cannot be certain that punishment stringency for that drug has gone up. If the DAWN data provide a reasonable measure of changes in the number of cocaine purchases and sales, arrest risk per purchase may have declined, even if users did not buy smaller numbers of doses per transaction. Even cell-time per transaction would have declined for cocaine sellers. The NHS data, of course, tell a very different story, since they point to a declining number of active regular users.

For marijuana the results are very clear-cut. Marijuana in 1988 got a much smaller share of punishment resources than it did in 1979, but the number of selling arrests rose and the number of possession arrests went down only slightly. With a rapidly declining user base, it is almost certain that the severity of punishment per transaction increased between 1979 and 1988.

It is of interest to calculate roughly the 1988 absolute risks per user-year for the two drugs. If there were 20 million marijuana users, as suggested by the survey data, then they faced an average risk of 2 percent of arrest in that year; though this seems low, note that in steady state that amounted to a 1 in 5 chance of being arrested in a ten-year using career. For cocaine, with a much smaller user base (no more than perhaps 5 million, ignoring those who use less than once per month), the annual arrest risk was 6 percent.

For sellers, the arrest risks differed even more substantially for the two drugs. Using the same assumptions as Reuter and Kleiman (1986) concerning the ratio of buyers to sellers for each drug, marijuana sellers may have faced not much more than a 10 percent probability of being arrested, compared to perhaps 40 percent for a cocaine seller. The cell-year calculations are of course more speculative, but 108,000 cell-years for a population of perhaps 350,000 cocaine dealers suggests that by 1988 that activity had indeed become risky.

Finally, let me comment on the price consequences of punishment. Over the period 1979 to 1988, marijuana prices, even adjusted for purity and inflation, have risen; see Moore (1990) for the data. Over the same period, cocaine prices have fallen substantially in nominal terms, let alone real terms. Given the potential importance of experience in determining the efficiency of high-level smuggling and distribution (Cave and Reuter, 1988) and of addiction for the supply curve of retail labor, not too much should be made of the relationship of

punishment stringency and price. It is, however, comforting to see that for
marijuana, where the addiction effect is minimal, price increased as punishment
rose.

ADVERSE CONSEQUENCES OF TOUGHNESS

At least three adverse consequences of intensified enforcement
need to be considered: increased violence and corruption on the part of drug
sellers, higher revenues for sellers, more crime and health-endangering behaviors
by both users and sellers.[16]

Increased Violence by Sellers

Most violence in the drug-distribution business appears to be directed against
other participants, not police. A business involving large sums of cash and
valuable commodities, staffed by young, poorly educated males, operating outside
the law, is one in which violence is likely to be an important method for settling
the numerous disputes that inevitably arise. That the commodity now most
frequently involved is a stimulant no doubt adds to the level of violence.

The caveat about the impact of the drug itself is important. The heroin
markets of the early 1970s were accompanied by little of the violence that has
characterized drug distribution in the late 1980s. Heroin distributors were of no
more general background than their cocaine-distributing contemporaries; the life
circumstances of the heroin user were no less desperate. The estimated number
of heavy heroin users are certainly smaller—at its height, probably no more than
one million, compared to a figure maybe three times that for cocaine in the late
1980s (Johnson et al., 1990). Impressionistically though, the level of violence
was far less than would be accounted for by this difference in scale.[17]

Little deadly violence is directed against the police. Though police are
occasionally shot in the course of drug enforcement, the numbers pale in comparison with the numbers of dealers killed by other participants. In Washington,
D.C., admittedly an extreme case, perhaps as many as 200 persons were killed
annually in homicides related to the drug business.[18] Only one police officer was
feloniously killed in the course of duty in 1987, and none in 1988. Tougher
enforcement will not increase violence much by raising the number of times that
dealers defend themselves against police in order to avoid prison sentences or loss
of property.[19]

With less certainty, we also reject the hypothesis that tougher enforcement
raises violence by increasing the frequency with which participants are suspected
to be informants or the severity with which suspected informants are punished.[20]

The disputes in the drug trades seem to be primarily over details of transactions or market territory.

There are yet other probable connections between enforcement and violence. The most troubling possibility is that some of the killings are the indirect consequence of intense police enforcement against street markets. This is not an argument against doing such enforcement; it is merely a sober reminder of the difficulty of achieving large social goals through law enforcement without causing harm to some group.

Competitive violence is an effort to increase market share or, defensively, to prevent a loss of market share. Over time, without outside disturbances, a group of drug sellers operating in the same area is likely to work out some set of arrangements that allow them to do their business peaceably. It may be the result of little more than becoming familiar with particular people on a corner or it may represent explicit arrangements about who can sell particular drugs at specific times and in specific places. Some level of harmony is useful to the dealers as a group, because violence will deter some customers, attract police attention, and increase their own physical risks.

Consider what happens when the police move in on one of these thriving markets. They arrest some dealers, create disturbance for customers, and drive some sellers to other locations. If sellers moved to corners that were currently not drug markets, there would be no marked incentive for violence. In a market with an excess supply of dealers, however, they are likely to move to locations that are already markets—places at which there is already a steady flow of customers and an established set of sellers. That may generate a particularly savage struggle between those sellers and the newcomers. In a legal market, competition for desirable locations is carried out via the rental mechanism; for drug markets the allocation is often by violence. Good policing, responsive to community concerns about concentrations of disorder and violence, may have the unintended consequence of increasing the overall level of violence.

To some extent we are dealing with a historical consequence of the blossoming of the drug trade as much as anything else. Drug-dealing has generated large revenues, permitting the purchase of more expensive and powerful weapons. The guns are now out there in the underworld; even if the drug trade declines in profitability, those guns will have a market in the U.S. underworld.[21] Disagreements may be no more likely to lead to violence than in the past; it is simply that the means for violence are so much more lethal.[22]

Increased Corruption Incentives[23]

The incentive to bribe criminal justice officials is positively related to the intensity of enforcement. The greater the probability of long prison terms and loss of other assets, the more aggressively a dealer will seek out officials who can mitigate those risks, and the more money he will be willing to offer for such mitigation.

One of the potential costs of more intense enforcement is thus raised corruption potential, particularly among the front-line enforcement agencies. At the risk of appearing naive, I suggest that these risks are modest in contemporary America, notwithstanding some large-scale and troubling cases, such as that involving allegations of theft of drug-dealer assets by officers of the Los Angeles County Sheriff's Department.

The structure of drug-law enforcement has become highly fractionated. Federal, state, and local agencies have overlapping jurisdictions and often mount operations that interfere with each other.[24] These unintended interactions are frequently cited as evidence of "lack of coordination," the bugbear of so many General Accounting Office reports, but they also point to the risks facing corrupt police (using that term generically to cover enforcement agents). No agency can grant a franchise for operating an illicit enterprise, as was the case in the first half of this century when local police departments had essentially exclusive criminal-enforcement responsibilities (see Schelling, 1967 for an analysis of this phenomenon). Moreover, taking money from dealers has become risky in an environment in which the individual paying the bribe has a reasonably high probability of being arrested by another agency; offering the name of the corrupt official may be the offender's best method for dealing with the second agency.

Drug enforcement certainly induces corruption, but I suggest that intensified enforcement within the plausible range will do little to exacerbate that evil.

Increased Dealer Revenues

It is generally believed that the demand for habit-forming drugs is inelastic— that a 1 percent increase in price will lead to less than a 1 percent reduction in consumption. This implies that higher prices will lead to higher revenues for dealers, at least in the short run.[25] If tougher enforcement raises prices, then it will also increase dealer revenues.

Much depends on the kind of enforcement. As Moore (1973) pointed out, a buyer of drugs incurs two kinds of costs. One is the conventional money cost, the other is the nonmoney cost associated with finding a willing seller. This second cost includes the risks associated with entering unsavory parts of town, transacting with dangerous and dishonest distributors, purchasing drugs that may have been diluted with toxic substances, and incurring the risk of being arrested. Any enforcement actions that raise these latter costs unambiguously lower demand; that is the peculiar allure of street-level enforcement for analysts such as Kleiman (1988).

Enforcement aimed exclusively at the seller has no direct-demand side effects; if it reduces drug consumption, it does so through raising the risks and other costs of dealers and hence the price charged in retail markets. It does not necessarily raise the *utility* of sellers, even if it raises their earnings; they are after all being compensated for incurring higher risks and they may prefer (but be unable to attain) lower risks and lower income.[26]

Even if dealers are worse off as the result of more intense enforcement, they now receive higher total revenues. These revenues are untaxed and provide an important component of the underground economy. Higher earnings may also be more salient than the increased risks in providing temptations for the young and poorly educated to join a trade that provides the path to such wealth (Taylor, 1990). Of course, if the enforcement can be triggered to making conspicuous consumption a risky behavior, then the latter concern is mitigated. That may be possible in more dour societies, but lavish and conspicuous consumption patterns are so much a part of the culture that such an enforcement pattern would either target too many of the (criminally) innocent or run the risk of being highly discriminatory in terms of age and, possibly, race.[27]

Health

Marijuana provides the clearest example of the adverse health consequences of intensified enforcement. It is frequently though not universally asserted that more potent marijuana poses higher health risks (Jacobs, 1987). Assume *arguendo* that the statement is true.[28] The potency of marijuana seized by police has risen very substantially over the past fifteen years. It is likely that more intense interdiction is the cause of that potency increase.

Interdiction has made Colombia a high-cost source of marijuana, even though the interior price ($3 per pound in 1989) is very much lower than that prevailing in Mexico ($100 per pound). The explanation for that is found in the high risks associated with maritime transportation from Colombia.[29] One means for minimizing smuggling risks is to increase the value per unit smuggled; higher potency strains achieve that.

The other major source of marijuana currently is domestic production, again probably the result of intense enforcement. The principal cost for domestic producers is seizure and arrest risk that is a function of the area required per dollar revenue. Their optimal strategy is to shift to higher-potency strains of marijuana.

It is also worth noting the consequence of bans on "head shops," outlets for water pipes and other equipment. The carcinogens in marijuana turn out to be water-soluble (Kleiman, 1989). By reducing the availability of water pipes, enforcement has increased the health risk associated with marijuana use.[30] Marijuana users now are constrained to use the drug in a particularly dangerous manner.

In the current regime, many (perhaps even most) of the health risks associated

with heroin are a function of the conditions surrounding its distribution—uncertain purity, sometimes toxic diluents, the use of dirty needles. The question
is whether these are a function of the intensity of enforcement or simply of
prohibition per se; put aside for the moment such innovations as "needle packs,"
à la Zurich.

I know of no study that has examined the relationship between the intensity
of enforcement and any of the above dimensions. Once again we can resort to
speculation untrammeled by inconveniently complicated empirical findings.

From a public-health perspective, it is desirable to encourage long-term
relationships between individual dealers and users. The prospect of repeat purchases gives the seller an incentive to minimize the risk of the customer's suffering
adverse effects from a particular purchase. Intensified street-level enforcement
has (at least) two effects, one in each direction. On the one hand, by raising
dealers' concern about whether a customer is an undercover policeman, it encourages them to cultivate known addicts as customers and to avoid novice buyers.
On the other hand, it causes turnover in the dealer and user populations (through
incarceration) and thus reduces their ability to maintain long-term relationships.

Summary Remarks

The above is by no means a complete list of all the harms resulting from
enforcement. Given limited prison capacity, the focus on incarceration of drug
offenders may have made the "price" of other, perhaps socially more damaging,
crimes lower, a factor rarely figured in to the discussion of drug-policy choices.

Note that the examples covered adverse effects of a variety of enforcement
tactics. Though most of them seem to be a function of street -level enforcement,
the increase in marijuana potency is a function of interdiction efforts and the
domestic eradication campaign. The analysis of enforcement effects must be
instrument-specific.

All of the above discussion is highly conjectural. None of the effects have
been measured and their sizes are impossible to determine with the available
data. All these effects (except corruption) are plausible and, to my mind, quite
troubling.

CONCLUSION

This paper was motivated by a curiosity about the punitive approach to drug control. Toughness has been discredited in part on supposedly
empirical grounds. "We tried it in the 1980s and it didn't work," summarizes the
(broadly) liberal critique. The admittedly crude calculations presented earlier

argue that it is uncertain whether the late 1980s did see intensified enforcement, as compared to the late 1970s, but that the weight of the evidence is that punishment risks probably did rise for both cocaine and marijuana users.

Judging whether the risks were adequate or appropriate is an even more difficult task, which I do not assay here. Even if they are low for some categories of drug offenders (such as marijuana users), this is not to say that current enforcement has no consequences for the use of drugs. The price of cocaine in illegal markets is approximately ten times that charged by pharmacists selling the drug for use as a local anasthetic. For many persons it may be difficult to find a source for the drug without a lengthy and difficult search. How much of that is accounted for by enforcement intensity as opposed to prohibition with something more than ritual enforcement is impossible to say.

The analysis might also be interpreted as a call for re-examination of how enforcement is executed. Some forms of enforcement have more serious negative consequences than do others. It may be that we should search for the "harm-minimizing" mix of enforcement.

Moreover, the High School Senior Survey data on marijuana use suggest that it was changed perceptions of health dangers rather than enforcement risks that reduced cocaine and marijuana use in that population (Bachman, Johnston, and O'Malley, 1989). In short, this nation has not been particularly tough in recent years and the evidence about the effects of toughness on drug use are decidedly mixed. The obligatory call for further research is taken as given.

There is a second argument against the highly punitive approach to drug control, namely the possibility that, whatever its effect on drug use, it makes society worse off by increasing (1) violence by sellers and users, (2) the incomes of sellers and the income needs of buyers, and (3) the crime, morbidity, and mortality associated with drug use. Lacking data on local variation in all these dimensions that would enable the sorting out of these effects, I have simply identified how some of these effects might be generated and suggested which ones are likely to be important.

None of this is, alas, dispositive; but it does suggest that the debate about drug policy requires a better specification of the goals of that policy. Enforcement has costs, even putting aside (as economists are wont to do) the infringement on civil liberties associated with heavy enforcement. Treatment and prevention, though the latter can be somewhat intrusive, have none of these undesired effects.

Moreover, the range of policy options available to society is also broader than is usually suggested. Retaining the current prohibitions does not require massive enforcement efforts. Prostitution is prohibited everywhere in this country, except for certain counties of Nevada, and yet enforcement of that prohibition is (at most) modest. The same holds for bookmaking and privately operated numbers games; though prohibited everywhere (again with the exception of Nevada), little effort is made to enforce those prohibitions. Such light enforcement is nowadays but rarely a source of concern (though historically it was the very focus of systemic corruption of the criminal justice and political systems). Prostitution is usually targeted by police only to the extent that it becomes conspicuous and/or aggressive, an assault on the safety or sensibility of noncustomers. Gambling is not even controlled to that extent. Symbolic raids on large bookmaking operations on Super Bowl Sunday, particularly those with Mafia connections, is about the extent of enforcement. There seems little concern that the nation is facing a crisis with respect to either illegal gambling or prostitution.

I mention these not to advocate that drug enforcement be relegated to quite such a marginal role but to suggest that the retention of prohibitions is not equivalent to the current "war on drugs." Even the "vigorous enforcement" generally accepted by Congressional doves may go too far. The prevailing (weak) evidence supports the following assertions, which in turn have policy implications:

1. General user sanctions have little deterrent effect.

2. Vigorous enforcement against high-level dealers, smugglers, and refiners does little to raise the retail price but may engender instability in producer countries, corruption in transit nations, and select out the more suspicious and paranoid distribution organizations in the United States.

3. Saturated enforcement against dealers in street markets increases the level of violence associated with such trafficking.

This suggests that we should examine the possibility of enforcement moving to the fringes of drug policy, aiming at getting dependent users into treatment and making drug dealing less conspicuous, and thus drugs less available to novice users. The case is far from proven but the truth is that we are far from knowing either whether toughness has been tried or whether its potential gains are worth the potential costs, given the other means available to us for achieving comparable reductions in drug use.

APPENDIX:
CALCULATING ENFORCEMENT STRINGENCY

There is no perfect measure of how punitive our drug-control system has been.[31] The best single measure of the stringency of drug enforcement is probably the expected time of incarceration per transaction, but even that has its ambiguities.[32] Is the relevant transaction for a user a purchase or a use-episode? Purchases are higher-risk activities than consumption episodes but, taking account

TABLE 8.A.1. ESTIMATED NUMBER OF USERS OF COCAINE AND MARIJUANA: HOUSEHOLD POPULATION, 1979 AND 1988

Drug/Frequency	1979[a]	1988
Cocaine		
Weekly	1,163	767
Monthly	4,090	2,698
Marijuana		
Weekly	10,616	5,840
Monthly	18,760	10,320

[a]Assumes ratio of weekly users to monthly users same in 1979 as in 1988.
SOURCE: National Institute on Drug Abuse (1980, 1990).

of the total number of each kind of transaction, it may well be that consumption episodes account for more of the total legal risk faced by users than do purchases. For sellers there is less ambiguity; sales are the risky transactions, though the size of the sale has an effect on the risk, and the passive holding of inventory also generates risk.

Transaction Trends

On a periodic basis, the National Institute on Drug Abuse (NIDA) performs a National Household Survey (NHS). These surveys provide the starting point for our estimates of the total number of transactions. In particular, we use the 1979 and 1988 surveys. Both surveys need considerable adjustment if the purpose is estimating the absolute number of transactions. Our goal, however, is simply to determine whether enforcement in 1988 was more or less severe than in 1979; thus all we need to know is the ratio of the two figures.

Table 8.A.1 presents data on the estimated total number of users of cocaine and marijuana in the household population for 1979 and 1988. To turn these figures into estimates of the number of transactions, we need to make assumptions about the intensity of use with respect to each category of drug and use-frequency. These intensities may have changed over time. For example, marijuana has become more expensive,[33] perhaps reducing the intensity of use; on the other hand, cocaine has become very much cheaper, presumably increasing the intensity of use.

Data from the High School Senior Surveys (Johnston, Bachman, and O'Malley, 1989) show that daily marijuana users are indeed very frequent users; they may average as many as three joints per day (Reuter, 1984a). They account

TABLE 8.A.2. DAWN COCAINE-RELATED EMERGENCY ROOM EPISODES

	1979	1988
All cocaine episodes	2,558	54,756
Cocaine w/heroin only	407	6,827
Cocaine only	1,092	26,228

SOURCE: Based on NIDA, Drug Abuse Warning Network data. See text for adjustment method.

for a very large share of all consumption. We have no similarly rich data on frequency of use by heavy cocaine users, and it is difficult to extrapolate from the marijuana. Cocaine is more likely to create dependency among those who use it regularly than is marijuana; that suggests use will be more evenly distributed among those who use cocaine regularly as compared to marijuana. One finds the same when fitting Gini curves for tobacco (highly addictive) and alcohol (addictive only for some groups).

All manner of adjustments could be made to these data. If, as shown by the general population surveys, drug use has become increasingly stigmatized, willingness to report drug use is likely to have declined. Our estimate of the number of drug users in the household population in 1988 is probably proportionately a smaller share of the true figure than is the 1979 figure. The rapid growth of the prison population, and the rising prevalence of drug offenders in that population, also may have an impact on the extent of underestimation of the total number of users.

The prison population represents a difficult element for this calculation. Remember that we are not attempting to estimate the number of *users* in 1979 and 1988 but the number of *transactions*. If prison inmates are unable to obtain drugs while imprisoned, then they may still be counted as drug users, in the sense that they wish to consume drugs and are being artificially constrained from doing so. In reality, it is widely believed that many are able to obtain some drugs even in prison. The quantities consumed are likely to be very small, however, since the distribution systems are constricted and expensive and the inmates have little earning capacity while confined. The larger the prison population, for these purposes, the better the household survey captures the currently active user population.

The alternative base for the change in the number of cocaine transactions is the number of mentions among those admitted to hospital emergency rooms (ER) in the NIDA DAWN (Drug Abuse Warning Network) system. DAWN contains a nonrandom sample of ERs in about 22 metropolitan areas. Table 8.A.2 presents DAWN figures for 1979 and 1988 in a quasi-consistent panel of

TABLE 8.A.3. DRUG ARRESTS BY STATE AND LOCAL AUTHORITIES

	1979	1988
Total state/local arrests	558,601	1,154,046
Sale/Manufacture	101,107	316,525
Heroin/cocaine	20,688	196,384
Marijuana	49,715	64,691
Other	30,164	55,450
Possession	457,494	837,521
Heroin/cocaine	47,481	403,165
Marijuana	341,305	326,922
Other	68,708	107,434
Federal arrests[a]	6,343	15,750
Marijuana	1,690	4,890
Heroin/cocaine and other	5,653	10,850

[a]Defendants charged with violations of Drug Abuse Prevention and Control Act in U.S. District Court; not necessarily arrested in that year.
SOURCE: FBI, Uniform Crime Reports, and Administrative Office of the U.S. Court.

ERs. In addition to the total number of cocaine mentions, it also lists those cocaine mentions that involve heroin as well as cocaine and the number that are cocaine only. Note that cocaine only accounted for less than half of the cocaine mentions in 1988; multiple drug use is increasingly the common pattern, making the punitiveness calculations even more questionable.

Estimating National "Punishment" Levels

Table 8.A.3 presents data on the estimated number of drug arrests by state and local authorities, broken down by drug type and by possession/distribution, for 1979 and 1988. The table also presents data on the closest equivalent federal enforcement figure, the number of defendants appearing in district court on drug charges.

No national arrest-disposition data are available for 1979. Only for California do we have details of the disposition of felony drug arrests in both years; these data are presented for 1979 and 1988 in Table 8.A.4.

Some other relevant data are available for five states from 1983 to 1986 (Bureau of Justice Statistics, 1989b); the states are California, Minnesota, New York, Pennsylvania, and Virginia. In 1986, these states reported 103,000 drug felony arrests, an increase of 52 percent from 1983. The states also showed

TABLE 8.A.4. DISPOSITION OF CALIFORNIA FELONY DRUG ARRESTS

	1979		1988	
Felony arrests	57,682		158,510	
Convictions	18,789		49,446	
Prison (% of convictions)	991	(5%)	8,393	(17%)
Jail	9,944	(53%)	36,001	(73%)
Probation only	5,273	(28%)	4,329	(9%)
Other	2,581	(14%)	723	(1%)

SOURCE: California Bureau of Criminal Statistics.

TABLE 8.A.5. SENTENCES FOR FELONY DRUG OFFENDERS IN FIVE STATES, 1983–1986

Year	Number Convicted	Percent Incarcerated		
		Total	Jail	Prison
1983	29,968	71	54	16
1984	35,070	74	58	16
1985	44,839	78	62	17
1986	53,942	83	63	20

SOURCE: Criminal Cases in Five States, 1983–1986.

increasing severity in the sentencing of drug felonies, over the four-year period shown in Table 8.A.5.

The figures in Table 8.1 (in the main text) are cobbled together from the sources mentioned there with a variety of assumptions. The following subsection lays out those assumptions.

Arrests

To estimate cocaine arrests, it was necessary to make an assumption about the share of heroin/cocaine arrests that were for cocaine only. In 1979, DAWN and expert opinion suggested that heroin was at least as prevalent as cocaine in the drug markets susceptible to police intervention. I assumed that 50 percent of all heroin/cocaine arrests (both possession and distribution) in 1979 were for cocaine.

By 1988 cocaine was much more widely used and marketed in open retail

TABLE 8.A.6. TOTAL PUNISHMENT CALCULATION: STATE COURTS

	1979	1988
Felony drug convictions	80,000	225,000
Prison	18,000	90,000
Jail	61,000	65,000
Sentence[a]	20 months	20 months

[a]Expected time served in state prison in 1988; 1979 assumed to be same.
SOURCE: 1988, Bureau of Justice Statistics, 1979; see text.

markets, whether in crack houses or on the street. I assumed that cocaine accounted for three-fourths of 1988 heroin/cocaine arrests. These assumptions possibly understate the increase in cocaine arrests, which may have been less than one-half of the 1979 figure and more than three-fourths of the 1988 figure.

Cell-Years

To estimate the rise in prison years assigned to drug distributors, it is necessary to splice together three sets of numbers: drug-distribution arrests, the size of the state prison population serving time for drug offenses in 1979 and 1986, and the number and disposition of felony convictions on drug offenses in state courts in 1986 and 1988. The fact that, for the years available, distribution arrests rose (very) approximately at the same rate as the number of felony drug convictions and the number of prisoners serving time for drug distribution, makes this splicing plausible.

In 1979, 18,000 persons were in prison on drug offenses; the average sentence length is unknown. In 1986, the number was 39,000 (Bureau of Justice Statistics, 1988). Using the increase in drug-distribution arrests as the multiplier, the estimated total population of drug offenders in state prisons in 1988 would have been approximately 60,000.

An alternative estimate can be derived from the figures on felony convictions in state courts, as shown in Table 8.A.6. Forty-one percent of the 112,000 convicted of drug trafficking were sentenced to state prisons; this gives 50,000 commitments to state prisons. Another 30 percent were sentenced to jail for this offense. We do not have sentencing data on the 113,000 drug-possession felony convictions but for the broader residual category in which they fall (accounting for nearly half the category), 35 percent received prison sentences. This would suggest an additional 40,000 commitments, for a total of 90,000 drug commitments. Given expected time served for the two classes of drug offenders, this also produces a total of approximately 140,000 cell-years in state prisons.

For punishment-risk calculations, total cell-years meted out in the year (commitments times expected time served[34]) is more useful than the number in prison at the end of the year. Thus we need to work backward and try to estimate commitments and time served in 1979.

Two other figures remain: sentences to jail and sentences to federal correctional institutions. Jail sentences are less than one year; I assumed that time served is three months. For 1988, approximately 65,000 persons were sentenced to jail on drug charges, adding approximately 16,000 cell years to the total. I used the same formula as before for allocating those years between marijuana, cocaine, and other drugs.

For state courts no source gives drug-specific sentences. The easiest assumption would be to allocate the total number of sentences for each drug in accord with its share of total sales/manufacture arrests and assume that sentence length is equal for each drug. Impression suggests that marijuana distribution is less heavily penalized than distribution of other drugs; that is certainly true for federal sentences. The difference may have increased as society's concern about the damages associated with cocaine have risen; whereas in 1970 federal marijuana sentences were 80 percent as long as those for heroin/cocaine, that figure had fallen to 70 percent by 1988. Given the small share of distribution arrests now accounted for by marijuana, however, such adjustments make little difference.

Marijuana accounted for approximately half of distribution arrests in 1979 and only 20 percent in 1988. Allocating cocaine arrests within heroin/cocaine arrests as before, I estimated that cocaine distribution arrests were 10 percent of distribution arrests in 1979 and almost half in 1988. This leads to the allocation of cell-years to drug given in Table 8.1.

The federal courts, though accounting for a relatively small number of

TABLE 8.A.7. FEDERAL COURT DRUG-SENTENCING DATA

	Marijuana		Cocaine/Heroin	
	1979	1988	1979	1988
Number convicted	1121	4018	2541	7829
Imprisoned	754	2414	1945	6575
Length of sentence (months)	47	57	61	83
Expected time served (months)	28	51	37	75

SOURCE: Administrative Office of the U.S. Courts, *Annual Report of the Director*.

defendants, add a surprising amount to the total because of the relatively long sentences imposed. For this level of court, drug-specific sentence data are available, though once again heroin and cocaine are not separated. The basic data are presented in Table 8.A.7.

Sentence length increased only moderately between 1979 and 1988. The shift to sentencing guidelines and the elimination of parole status, however, means that those incarcerated will serve a much larger share of the sentence imposed. Expected time served for those sentenced on marijuana offenses may have risen from about 28 months in 1979 (60 percent of average sentence length) to 51 months (90 percent of average sentence length).

Using these figures, I estimated that marijuana dealers received a sentence total of nearly 10,000 years in 1988, compared to 1,800 years in 1979. For cocaine dealers, using the same assumptions about the division of heroin/cocaine cases that are actually cocaine cases, I estimated prison years in the federal system assigned to cocaine dealers to have risen from 3,000 to 30,000.

NOTES

1. This question was given its most explicit formulation in the debate on the 1988 Omnibus Drug Control Act.

2. The argument is made most explicitly in the reports of the Office of National Drug Control Policy (1989, 1990a, 1990b).

3. The federal drug-control budget in FY 1990 allocated 26 percent of total expenditures to treatment and prevention (Office of National Drug Control Policy, 1990a). It is likely that state and local governments spend more in total than the federal government but allocate even less to treatment and prevention programs. It is hard to assemble a national drug-control budget, however, since most state and local drug enforcement is carried out by nonspecialized law enforcement agencies and the allocation of their budgets to drug control has a very judgmental element.

4. See, for example, the remarks of U.S. District Court Judge Stanley Sporkin on giving a ten-year sentence to a nineteen-year-old convicted of selling three vials of crack. The defendant had no prior conviction but Sporkin stated that this extraordinarily harsh sentence was mandatory. He advised the defendant to seek clemency from President Bush. (*Washington Post*, November 1, 1990.)

5. In Florida, the rapid increase in the number of drug offenders sentenced to prison, along with federally imposed limits on the prison population, have resulted in many felons serving extremely short sentences.

6. See Pearson (1991) for a discussion of the role this has played in recent British drug-policy decisions.

7. I ignore here James Q. Wilson's eloquent plea (Wilson, 1990) that we take into

account the moral costs of different policies. Policy choices should take such into account; policy analysis is unlikely to be persuasive on the matter.

8. Mark Kleiman (personal communication) argues for measuring the risk per gram. Even putting aside the problem created by varying potency (should it be per unit THC for marijuana), this puts too much strain on the available data. Estimates of total consumption begin with estimates of total numbers of consumers and/or use sessions; they cannot be developed from the production side, subtracting out seizures and other losses (Haaga and Reuter, 1991). Thus quantity estimation requires layering on yet another very speculative set of parameter estimates.

9. The Uniform Crime Reports system of the FBI combines heroin and cocaine arrests into a single category. It is generally believed that the increase in the category throughout the 1980s was dominated by an increase in cocaine-related arrests.

10. The Bureau of Justice Statistics (1989b) has collected such data for five states.

11. Since these possession charges were prosecuted as felonies, they are presumably possession with intent to distribute rather than simple possession offenses, which in most states are misdemeanors only.

12. All these dispositional data, both national and Californian, bear on felonies, primarily related to distribution and/or manufacture. There are literally no published data concerning the sentences received by those arrested on simple possession charges.

13. DUF is a monitoring program being carried out in twenty cities. Each quarter a sample of arrestees, mostly those arrested for nondrug felonies, is asked to submit a urine specimen for drug testing. The results are not made available to the courts or prosecutors.

14. This estimate is based on "splicing" a succession of consistently reporting panels to create a synthetic panel for the nine-year period.

15. As so often, many of my ideas here come from discussion with Mark Kleiman. In this case he has actually published some of his own thoughts on the topic; see in particular Kleiman (1987), considering the trade-off between the goals of drug control and organized crime control.

16. Some critics would also include unreasonably long sentences as a cost of toughness at the court level. For example, Michigan imposes life in prison without parole for those found in possession of more than 650 gm of cocaine (*Washington Post*, November 5, 1990). Federal sentencing guidelines impose mandatory lengthy sentences for distribution of large quantities of cocaine. Only cooperation with the government can mitigate the sentence. That produces apparently unfair results; principals in smuggling operations are able to provide the government with useful information and mitigate their sentence, but less culpable "mules" have no such information and receive the full sentence. That can be treated as an element of design of the toughness program, however. It is not inherent in stringent enforcement regimes. Moreover, less tough enforcement, by permitting more sellers to avoid punishment at all, creates its own unfairness.

17. Cocaine sellers appear to earn higher incomes than heroin dealers; compare, for example, the figures on heroin earnings provided by Anglin and Speckart (1986) and those on a predominantly cocaine-selling population provided by Reuter, MacCoun, and Murply (1990). The difference may reflect the fact that fewer of the cocaine dealers are drug-dependent and the existence of a larger middle-class market for cocaine. The fact that

heroin sellers take so much of their earnings in the form of heroin does not reduce their incentive to violence, however.

18. Reuter, MacCoun, and Murphy (1988, Section VI) estimate that in 1988 a drug dealer operating regularly (two days a week or more often) in the open-air markets of the city faced a 1 in 70 annual probability of being killed, and a 1 in 14 chance of being seriously injured.

19. In this respect, it is interesting to note that interdiction agencies, such as the Coast Guard and Customs Service, report very little violent resistance to their efforts.

20. Toughness in this case refers both to arrest frequency and expected severity of punishment following arrest. The willingness to take aggressive actions against collaborators and/or friends may be affected by either. On the economic sources of violence in illegal markets see Reuter (1983, Chapter 6).

21. Nor are they likely to leave for other markets even if the income and wealth of domestic U.S. offenders declines. Though there is an international market for arms of this kind, I suggest that few international buyers will purchase guns that may have been used in specific crimes here. The price of these guns may simply decline below that prevailing in other markets and no new guns will enter. Mark Kleiman (personal communication) suggests that the notion of a stock of guns is misleading; a gun may have a very short transactional lifetime, being used for only a few crimes and then being discarded so as to prevent tracing.

22. Data on Chicago robberies in the early 1980s (Zimring and Zuehl, 1986) showed a ratio of 14 to 1 nonfatal to fatal injuries. In the District of Columbia in 1988 there were 269 gunshot deaths and an estimated 1148 nonfatal gunshot wounds, a ratio of less than 5 to 1. In addition, guns are increasingly weapons of choice: Firearms accounted for 55 percent of all D.C. homicides in 1986, by 1988 that had increased to 72 percent, and to 77 percent by 1989.

23. This section adapts arguments found in Reuter (1984b).

24. Some examples can be found in Warner (1986).

25. The long-run elasticity may be substantially greater than the short-run elasticity, because prices have a greater impact on recruitment rates than on consumption levels of current users. This has been the finding from a number of studies of the elasticity of demand for cigarettes (e.g., Lewit and Coate, 1982). The only recent attempt to estimate the elasticity of demand for illicit drugs suffers from serious technical deficiencies (Godshaw, Pancoast, and Koppel, 1987).

26. This issue is examined exhaustively by Spence (1978), who finds that the utility effects depend on a large number of parameters.

27. One method for targeting conspicuous consumption is to check the tax records of those who purchase luxury goods, such as Mercedes, fur coats, and gold chains. Those purchasers whose declared income seems inconsistent would then find themselves subject to a tax audit and possible criminal investigation. This would, of course, affect more than just drug dealers and requires a very considerable increase in the cooperation among tax authorities at different levels of government. Unless the IRS were authorized and willing to provide state agencies with federal tax returns, those wishing to evade detection could simply make luxury purchases out of state.

28. The claim is most often made by hawks; hence, if it is incorrect, they are at least hoist on their own canard.

29. It might also be argued that the high price of Mexican marijuana is a function of the relatively intense enforcement in Mexico. In a world undisturbed by enforcement, either in the producer country or at the border, Mexico would have a transportation advantage but might nonetheless be the high-cost producer because of higher wage levels. But the export price, absent enforcement, would be a great deal lower.

30. As always, there is a countervailing factor. By forcing users to a less attractive mode of ingestion, head-shop bans may reduce total consumption. The net effect on population cancer risk is indeterminable; one can only say that the bans do raise the cancer risks of current marijuana users.

31. It might be argued that an adequate surrogate for the riskiness of drug selling can be found in the price. Enforcement risk, however, is only one of the factors determining the supply curve for illicit drugs. There are also physical risks associated with participation in an illegal market, which may influence price. Experience curves, diffusion of marketing innovations (most notably the introduction of crack), and consumption by dealers all complicate interpretation of historical price trends.

32. Reuter and Kleiman (1986) present some figures for severity against sellers, using "seller year" as the base and distinguishing among three drugs (cocaine, heroin, and marijuana).

33. Moore (1990) presents price data for marijuana, showing a sixfold percent increase from 1976 to 1988; however, he does not take account of increases in the potency of the drug over the same period or of inflation. After adjusting for these two figures, the price rise (real dollars per unit THC) is only 11 percent.

34. Ignoring the fact that some of the arrests were made in previous years.

REFERENCES

Administrative Office of the U.S. Courts, *Annual Report of the Director.* Washington, D.C., annual.

Anglin, M. Douglas, and Speckart, George, "Narcotics Use, Property Crime and Dealing: Structural Dynamics across the Addiction Career," *Journal of Quantitative Criminology* 2, 1986.

Bachman, Jerald G.; Johnston, Lloyd D.; and O'Malley, Patrick M., "Explaining the Recent Decline in Cocaine Use among Young Adults: Further Evidence that Perceived Risks and Disapproval Lead to Reduced Drug Use," *Journal of Health and Social Behavior* 31, June 1990.

Bureau of Justice Statistics, *Profile of State Prison Inmates, 1986.* Washington, D.C., 1988.

Bureau of Justice Statistics, *Felony Sentences in State Courts.* Washington, D.C., 1989a, 1990.

Bureau of Justice Statistics, *Criminal Cases in Five States, 1983–1986.* Washington, D.C., 1989b.

Cave, Jonathan, and Reuter, Peter, *The Interdictor's Lot: A Dynamic Model of the Market for Drug Smuggling Services.* Santa Monica: Rand Corporation, 1988.

Federal Bureau of Investigation, *Uniform Crime Reports*, Washington, D.C. (annual).

Godshaw, Gerald; Pancoast, Ross; and Koppel, Russell, *Anti-Drug Law Enforcement Efforts and Their Impact.* Bala Cynwyd, Pa.: Wharton Econometrics, 1987.

Haaga, John, and Reuter, Peter (eds.), *Improving the Quality of Data for Federal Drug Policy Decisions.* Santa Monica: Rand Corporation, 1991.

Jacobs, Michael (ed.), *Drugs and Drug Abuse.* Toronto: Addiction Research Foundation, 1987.

Johnson, Bruce; Williams, Terry; Dei, Kojo; Sanabria, Harry, "Drug Abuse in the Inner City: Impact on the Hard-Drug Users and the Community," in Tonry, Michael, and Wilson, James Q. (eds.), *Drugs and Crime.* Chicago: University of Chicago Press, 1990.

Johnston, Lloyd; Bachman, Gerald; O'Malley, Patrick, *Illicit Drug Use, Smoking, and Drinking by America's High School Students, College Students and Young Adults.* Rockville, Md.: National Institute on Drug Abuse, 1989.

Kleiman, Mark, "Organized Crime and Drug Abuse Control," in Edelhertz, Herbert (ed.), *Major Issues in Organized Crime Control.* Washington, D.C.: National Institute of Justice, 1987.

Kleiman, Mark, "Crackdowns: The Effects of Intensive Enforcement on Retail Heroin Dealing," in Chaiken, Marcia (ed.), *Street Level Drug Enforcement: Examining the Issues.* Washington, D.C.: National Institute of Justice, 1988.

Kleiman, Mark, *Marijuana: Costs of Abuse, Costs of Control.* Boulder, Colo.: Westwood Press, 1989.

Lewit, Eugene, and Coate, Douglas, "The Potential for Using Excise Taxes to Reduce Smoking," *J. of Health Economics* 1, 1982.

Moore, Mark, "Achieving Discrimination in the Effective Price of Heroin," *American Economic Review* 63, May 1973.

Moore, Mark, "Supply Reduction and Drug Law Enforcement," in Tonry and Wilson, *Drugs and Crime.*

National Institute on Drug Abuse, *National Household Survey of Drug Abuse: Population Estimates.* Rockville, Md., 1980, 1990.

Office of National Drug Control Policy, *National Drug Strategy.* Washington, D.C., 1989, 1990a.

Office of National Drug Control Policy, *White Paper on Drug Treatment.* Washington, D.C., 1990b.

Pearson, Geoffrey, "Drug Policy and Problems in Britain: Continuity and Change," in Morris, Norval, and Tonry, Michael (eds.), *Crime and Justice: A Review of Research.* Chicago: University of Chicago Press, 1991.

Reuter, Peter, *Disorganized Crime: The Economics of the Visible Hand.* Cambridge, Mass.: MIT Press, 1983.

Reuter, Peter, "The Economic Significance of Illegal Markets in the United States: Some Observations," in Archambault, Edith, and Greffe, Xavier (eds.), *L'Economies Non-Officielle*. Paris: Maspero, 1984a.

Reuter, Peter, "Police Regulation of Illegal Gambling: Frustrations of Symbolic Enforcement," *Annals of the American Association of Political Science* 474, July 1984b.

Reuter, Peter, and Kleiman, Mark, "Risks and Prices: An Economic Analysis of Drug Enforcement," in Morris, Norval, and Tonry, Michael (eds.), *Crime and Justice: A Review of Research*. Chicago: University of Chicago Press, 1986.

Reuter, Peter; MacCoun, Robert; Murphy, Patrick, *Money from Crime: An Economic Study of Drug Dealing in Washington, D.C.*. Santa Monica: Rand Corporation, 1990.

Schelling, Thomas, "Economic Analysis of Organized Crime," in President's Commission on Law Enforcement and the Administration of Justice, *Task Force Report: Organized Crime*. Washington, D.C. 1967.

Spence, A. Michael, "A Note on the Effects of Pressure in the Heroin Market." Discussion Paper 588, Harvard Institute of Economic Research, Cambridge, Mass., 1978.

Taylor, Carl, *Dangerous Society*. East Lansing: Michigan State University Press, 1990.

Warner, Roger, *The Invisible Hand: The Marijuana Business*. New York: Beech Tree Books, 1986.

Wilson, James Q., "Against Legalization," *Commentary*, January 1990.

Wish, Eric, "Drug Policy in the 1990s: Insights from New Data from Arrestees," *International Journal of the Addictions* 25 (3A), 1990–1991.

Zimring, Franklin, and Zuehl, James, "Victim Injury and Death in Urban Robbery: A Chicago Study," *Journal of Legal Studies* 15, no. 1, 1986.

COMMENT

Victor R. Fuchs

"On the Consequences of Toughness," by Peter Reuter, illustrates three important insights that the economic perspective brings to a complex technical and social problem such as drug addiction.

First, we are reminded that society has many diverse and conflicting goals. This is an important reminder because it may be overlooked by technical experts whose knowledge about a particular field is considerable but whose focus is likely to be exclusively on that field. If minimizing drug use and associated crime were the only goals of our society, no doubt our friends in Saudi Arabia could give us some valuable advice on how to achieve them. Americans would probably be reluctant to adopt the Saudis' methods, however, because improvement on the drug front would entail too much sacrifice with respect to other goals.

The second insight concerns the diversity of policy options. The drug question is often posed as if there were only two possibilities: Do we legalize, or don't we? Reuter offers a third possibility: Don't legalize, but don't enforce except in a token or symbolic manner, and use the drug funds for treatment and prevention. I will return to his discussion of adverse consequences of vigorous enforcement in a moment.

The third insight concerns the diversity of effects. If you change one element in a system, you must be prepared to trace out the consequences in many different directions, not simply the one that prompted or motivated the change. Indeed, economists are of one mind with ecologists on this point. The latter have a wonderful saying: "You can't change one thing."

My principal reservations about the Reuter paper are that he doesn't go far enough in making explicit these three insights or in discussing all their major ramifications. What are the implications of alternative drug policies for other major social goals such as personal autonomy and distribution of justice? What are some other policy options? For example, couldn't we have legalization with strict controls, such as those governing the sale of alcohol in Sweden? Further, just as Reuter has speculated about the possible adverse consequences of intensified enforcement, might not one speculate about possible adverse consequences of lax enforcement coupled with big expenditures for treatment and prevention? For example, as the markets for drugs shrink as a result of the treatment and prevention efforts, might not the drug suppliers be driven to increased violence and might they not increase their efforts to sell to ever-younger users? Might there not be increased corruption because enforcement is lax and arbitrary and you don't have the possibility of different enforcement agencies from different levels catching one another? You could create a situation in which everybody gets paid off regularly, as I believe was the custom with prostitution and gambling. The payoff is just a business expense and no one worries much about it.

Finally, would not such a policy lead to increased disrespect for the law in general? This is something that we might consider. I don't say that any of these things *would* happen. Indeed, Reuter may have thought about them and decided that they would not. I am simply asking for a more rounded treatment of this highly complex subject. What I would like to see Reuter do in a couple of tables is set down all the goals, all the policy options, and then speculate about how each of these policy options might relate to the specified goals.

PART THREE

LESSONS FROM ABROAD

9

DRUG POLICY IN THE NETHERLANDS FROM A PUBLIC HEALTH PERSPECTIVE

Eddy L. Engelsman

"Hey, drug user, try to imagine yourself in the position of other users of the neighborhood, such as the elderly, kids, and shopkeepers. Because, if you take other people's concerns seriously in what you do, they will take you seriously in their reaction." This is neither the text of a pamphlet in an annoyed neighborhood, nor the text from a local government, but the text of a leaflet circulated by one of the local unions of drug takers, the so-called junkie unions. Junkies also counsel their fellow junkies about health risks and teach them to be responsible for their own drug taking. The information is written and disseminated by the junkies themselves and financed by the Ministry of Health.

This practice of involving drug addicts in prevention activities exemplifies the pragmatism in Dutch drug policy. Drug use is neither favored nor encouraged, but if people take drugs the least we can do is to limit the hazardous effects. Addicts, it is felt, must be given the responsibility and the opportunity to protect their own health.

Each citizen is primarily responsible for safeguarding his or her own health. Personal freedom is therefore a key concept in our culture. People are allowed to drink alcohol and to smoke tobacco as much as they want, and patients suffering from alcohol- and tobacco-related diseases get appropriate treatment. As regards alcohol and tobacco, morbidity and mortality are high. Crime is highly correlated with alcohol misuse. User accountability is not applied here. We try to reduce the demand by means of public health strategies and public health laws, such as alcohol licensing acts, advertising bans, health warnings, and taxation, but there is no question of prohibition as regards production, manufacture, and distribution of alcohol and tobacco. We also try to reduce consumption by health education aimed at increasing the individual's responsibility for making choices. Self-control and social control are thus given equal emphasis. The state only creates good conditions for making individual choices, but does not take over responsibility. Criminal law alone does not succeed in controlling or eliminating undesired behavior or in solving public health and social problems.

As to drugs, we have introduced prohibitive penal legislation. Criminal law and its enforcement, however, are meant to reduce the supply of drugs, not to criminalize their use. The Dutch do not rely heavily on criminal law and law enforcement in general. They prefer a policy of social control, adaptation, and integration to a policy of social exclusion through criminalization, punishment, and stigmatization. Dutch criminal law functions as an instrument of social control rather than an instrument for expressing moral values. Therefore, we make a strict distinction between policies aimed at drug users on the one hand and at drug traffickers on the other.

Our primary aim is to protect health and social well-being and to reduce the harm and risks associated with drug use. We hold the view that drug use is not primarily a problem for police and the courts, but rather a matter of public health and social well-being. Therefore we have opted for a realistic and pragmatic approach to the drug problem. Of course, drug use is a habit that involves certain health risks, but the extent to which detrimental effects, in fact, occur, and in which manifestations, is largely dependent on the following factors.

EFFECTS OF PROHIBITION

First of all, the Dutch government recognizes openly that in drug policy, objectives may be conflicting. This recognition itself has created wide acceptance of our drug policy. In our efforts to reduce the supply of drugs because of their harmful—primary—effects, we see drug users and society afflicted by additional physical and social problems partly induced by the illegal character of the use of drugs. These are the negative side effects of drug policy. I refer, for instance, to problems of highly priced drugs causing drug-related crimes, of prostitution and social ostracism, and of increased health risks such as AIDS. The effects of heroin and cocaine use are too often confused with the effects of their illegality. This confusion has made the fight against international drug traffickers seem the main focus of drug policy. It is neither justified nor useful to hold drug users accountable for all these effects. On the other hand, drug use is no excuse for committing crimes. Since drug users are held responsible for their own criminal activities, like all other citizens, they are prosecuted.

PROCESS OF DEVIANCE

There is a second factor that influences the extent of the risks. The pharmacology of drugs is of course important, but we also acknowledge that the socio-cultural circumstances in which the drugs are taken, users' expectations regarding the drug, and the reasons why people take drugs are the major conditions that determine the nature and the extent to which drug use may, in fact, produce a problem. Here we encounter an often-underestimated process. By pursuing drug-abuse policies in the way currently favored by many countries, drug users are seen as making a "statement," which has an attraction to some (sociologists would say a "meaning" has been attached to the drug phenomenon, which generates a "meaning" to certain people). My view is that the less drugs are seen as making a "statement" to the rest of society, the less attraction there will be to some, particularly the young. The rejection of drug users and addicts by society may be counterproductive and encourage or reinforce deviant life-styles. Repression toward experimenters or casual users may have the same effect. They should neither be seen primarily as accomplices to drug traffickers nor as dependent patients or criminals, but as normal citizens, responsible for the risks they are taking.

SOCIAL PROBLEMS AS A CAUSAL FACTOR

There is a third factor when it comes to the risks. We believe that when we aim at demand reduction, we should not exclusively pay attention to substance abuse as such, as drug use does not stand alone. Poverty, discrimination of ethnic minorities, tensions between the rich and the poor, lack of access to social and health services, and dilapidated neighborhoods are all factors that could lead to substance abuse. In the Netherlands demand-reduction programs are therefore being integrated with the social security system, which guarantees a minimum income to every citizen, and with an accessible general health care system. Key notions here are social responsibility and solidarity. We believe that, if these multifactorial socioeconomic aspects are not taken into account, efforts to reduce demand will have little chance of success. They would only deal with the symptoms. Instead of a "war on drugs," we prefer to wage "a war against underdevelopment, deprivation, and lack of socioeconomic status."

Since the present drug-abuse situation is the result of an extremely complex social process of action and reaction of both the individual and society, individual responsibility cannot be disconnected from the responsibility of society as a whole.

DUTCH EXPERIENCES

What are the experiences in the Netherlands?

Possession of and trafficking in all drugs are prohibited by law. Criminal law enables the administration, by means of the so-called prosecutorial discretion, to pursue a pragmatic drug policy toward the possession and sale of small quantities of drugs. Criminal proceedings against consumers would not solve the problem but would aggravate it. People who use cannabis products can therefore do so openly. This policy prevents users from going underground and sliding into the fringes of society where we cannot reach them and where the risks may increase. This is a well-considered and very practical policy. We do not want to hide the problems of our society, and we do not want them to get out of control. Much attention to all drugs is paid in school education programs, as a part of an integrated approach aimed at the promotion of healthy life-styles. We are teaching kids to cope with the risks of life, drugs being one of them. There are no mass media campaigns in my country, because they are untargeted. Scare tactics, which do not work, are likewise rejected.

Youngsters do take the responsibility offered to them, since the vast majority is not interested in drugs. In the age group up to nineteen years, only 2.7 percent used cannabis during the past month. For heroin and for cocaine, this use was less than half a percent.[1] Apart from the group of poly-drug users, cocaine use in Amsterdam is embedded in nonmarginalized social settings where confrontation with the police is rare. Consequently, since no additional risks are introduced to nonproblematic users, which enables open communication about drug-use experiences, some kinds of informal use-control rules could be developed. There is very little violence.[2] We have seen waves of free-base cocaine use in 1983 and 1984, mainly in a regularly heroin-using group. This has not given any problems, after their first learning how to use this way. Crack use is still very low.

A second fact is that the number of drug addicts has stabilized and in some cities even decreased. Today, approximately 0.15 percent of the national population are drug addicts. That is approximately twenty thousand addicts out of fifteen million inhabitants. Their state of health is reasonably good. This may be regarded as a result of our harm-reduction approach, by which both users and addicts are taught to diminish the risks of drug use. It is not so much a "don't do it" message, but rather "it's better not do it, but if you do, these are the things you should know." The result is more health-consciousness and the majority of the heroin- and cocaine-using population not injecting drugs. In Amsterdam this is less than 40 percent.[3] In some smaller cities injecting is an absolute taboo among users.[4] Another indication is the number of Dutch drug-related deaths, which is rather stable; in 1988, 42 cases.[5] In Amsterdam in 1989 the figure was only eleven of the estimated five to six thousand drug addicts.[6]

Third, one of the most striking features is the wide range of treatment and counseling services, which is capable of reaching the major part of the population of addicts. This is a success in itself. One can only succeed by adopting realistic treatment approaches, primarily directed at improving addicts' physical and social functioning, without requiring abstinence immediately. Low-threshold methadone maintenance is one of the modalities. This is called the "harm-reduction" approach. Addicts are encouraged to try to retain relations with normal society as long as possible. The existence of "harm-reduction" facilities does not prevent an increasing number of addicts who do want to kick their habit from making use of drug-free facilities, which are also available. The care system has no waiting lists, it is easily accessible, free of charge, and treats addicts respectfully as fellow-citizens. Field studies among methadone clients and street addicts have shown that this approach has proved to be successful and that the typical addict is in no way an antisocial junkie. It shows the importance of harm-prevention strategies as primary mobilizers of health and harm-reduction.[7]

Fourth, keeping close contact with drug addicts is also a prerequisite for an effective AIDS-prevention policy. I stress that action to contain the overall drug problem should go hand in hand with realistic, appropriate measures to stop the spread of AIDS. Our policy aims at changing the risky behavior of addicts so far as feasible. The supply and use of sterile needles and syringes in exchange for used ones and the supply of condoms are two ways of dealing with the problem, but they are not a panacea. Solutions must be embedded in a broader care system. Persuasive face-to-face counseling, to change addicts' behavior in favor of safer practices, is essential. Syringe programs do not lead to more drug use or to more injecting, but to fewer people sharing syringes.[8,9,10] You may be surprised, but addicts are apparently able to act responsibly if the government allows them to do so. Addicts are indeed willing and able to change their behavior. The percentage of intravenous drug users among the total group of AIDS patients (1313 in July 1990) in the Netherlands is still relative low, namely 9.2 percent (N = 120).[11]

Fifth, the rather low homicide rate may serve as one of the indicators of criminality in the Netherlands. In 1989 our largest city, Amsterdam, with 700,000 inhabitants, counted 46 murder cases.[12] Nationally we had 175 cases.[13]

The problem of drug abuse is with us. I see no realistic prospect for its total eradication. It can be successfully contained, however, within the boundaries of drug prohibition. This is an important fact, as it demonstrates that there is a feasible middle course between the extreme options of militarization and total legalization. Policy changes are to be sought in this direction. Our thinking is that if demand-reduction and realistic and feasible treatment approaches are given substantial attention, a more positive perspective will be created with regard to the future of drug policies.

NOTES

1. H. N. Plomp, H. Kuipers, and M. L. van Oers, *Smoking, Alcohol and Drug Use among School Students from the Age of 10: Results of the Fourth Survey Conducted by the Youth Health Survey Centres 1988/1989*. (Amsterdam: University of Amsterdam; Utrecht: Netherlands Institute on Alcohol and Drugs, 1990).

2. P. Cohen, *Cocaine Use in Amsterdam in Non-Deviant Subcultures*. (Amsterdam: University of Amsterdam, Institute for Social Geography, 1989).

3. E. C. Buning, *De GG & GD en het drugprobleem in cijfers deel IV* [The Municipal Health Service and the Drug Problem: Facts and Figures]. (Amsterdam: Gemeentelijke Geneeskundige en Gezondheidsdienst, 1990).

4. D. J. Korf, R. Mann, and H. van Aalderen, *Drugs op het platteland* [Drug Use on the Country Side]. (Amsterdam: Universiteit van Amsterdam; Maastricht: Rijksuniversiteit Limburg, 1989).

5. *Jaarstatistieken: doodsoorzaken* [Annual Statistics: Causes of Death]. (Voorburg: Centraal Bureau voor de Statistiek, 1990).

6. E. C. Buning, *De GG & GD en het drugprobleem in cijfers, deel IV* [The Municipal Health Service and the Drug Problem in Data, Part IV]. (Amsterdam, 1990).

7. Ch. D. Kaplan and M. de Vries, *Protecting Factors*. (Rotterdam: Erasmus University, Addiction Research Institute, 1988).

8. H. J. A. van Haastrecht, J. A. R. van den Hoek, and R. A. Couthinho, *No Trend in Yearly I.V. Sero Prevalence Rate among I.V. Drug Users in Amsterdam: 1986–1988*. (Paper delivered at the International AIDS Conference, Montreal, 1989).

9. J. A. R. van den Hoek, H. J. A. van Haastrecht, A. W. van Zadelhoff, J. Goudsmit, and R. A. Coutinho, "HIV-infectie onder drug-gebruikers in Amsterdam; prevalentie en risicofactoren" [HIV-Infection among Drug Misusers in Amsterdam; Prevalence and Risk Factors]. *Nederlands Tijdschrift voor Geneeskunde* [Dutch Medical Journal] 16 (1988): pp. 723–28.

10. Th. Paulussen, G. J. Kok, R. Knibbe, and A. Cramer, *Aids en intraveneus druggebruik* [AIDS and Intravenous Drug Use in the City of Heerlen]. (Maastricht: Rijksuniversiteit Limburg, 1989).

11. *Kwartaalstatistieken AIDS* [Quarterly AIDS Statistics]. (Rijswijk: National Health Inspectorate, 1990).

12. Personal communication, Crime Analysis Office, Municipal Police, Amsterdam, 1990.

13. Wetenschappelijk Onderzoeks—en Documentatiecentrum, Ministerie van Justitie [Research and Information Centre, Ministry of Justice], 1990.

10

Pragmatic Incoherence: The Changing Face of British Drug Policy

David Turner

Background

The first thing I need do is sketch briefly the social framework in which our services have developed. This is important because there is often misunderstanding about the arrangements in Britain, yet the framework is the determinant of how services are delivered.

Since the late 1940s, Britain has had a National Health Service and an income and social support system available to the whole of the population. In parallel, there have been private health and social care systems, most commonly used by those who had the personal resources to pay for them. The state systems are funded through national and local taxation.

In practice, this has meant that health care deemed necessary for an individual has been available free at the point of delivery, with the cost met through taxation. The income and social support systems operate through many different routes, including, for instance, direct cash payment to an individual with inadequate means to afford even a basic living standard, specific financial support to families with low incomes, subsidized housing, free legal aid, cash payments for those who are sick or disabled, and direct care for children, handicapped people, and the elderly. Although how these services are delivered and who is entitled to them is subject to change and, at present, to some considerable political argument, the basic principle remains. The state has responsibility for the welfare of all its citizens, citizens have a responsibility for each other, and this responsibility is best delivered through a charge on citizens according to their means.

One other feature worth noting is that the development of all these provisions has been initially through the efforts of nongovernmental organizations and voluntary associations. Income support developed from charities established to give financial support to people from particular types of work or particular localities. The social care system developed from organizations such as Dr. Barnado's, the Salvation Army, and other church-based social care organizations that initiated child care, the probation service, and so forth. The National Health Service developed from a network of private and voluntary health care services. It was the community who demanded that evident need for the whole community was translated into state provision and inspired and sustained political action to achieve this.

This background is inevitably brief, but it provides a context for the way in which drug problems have been perceived and the responses that have been made in Britain.

DRUG USE—THE EARLY RESPONSES

During the nineteenth century, the use of opium and its derivatives and of cannabis was common as a means of both self-medication and medication prescribed by medical practitioners. A number of renowned figures of the time were drug users, such as De Quincey, Coleridge, Wilberforce and, in literature, Sherlock Holmes. Although the use of opiates was disapproved of, there was no great stigma attached to their use. It was a normal part of life and there can be no doubt that the extent of use, and the quantities used, vastly exceeded the extent of use and quantities used now in Britain.[1] Of course, it must also be noted that with the development of the pharmaceutical industry and the introduction of an enormous range of synthetic psychoactive drugs, the total consumption of drugs has risen and the need for self-medication with powerful analgesics has been reduced. The important point of this background is that opiate use was at a high level at the same time as Britain held the status of a major world power, was a leading industrial nation, and ruled a vast empire. Even in 1894, the Royal Commission on Opium[2] argued that controlled and regular use was not harmful and that the Indo-Chinese trade in opium should be maintained, while the Indian Hemp Commission found no harmful consequences from the use of hemp (cannabis).[3]

It was not until the second half of the twentieth century that drug addiction became a matter of serious domestic concern, although the United Kingdom had been party to international discussions and conventions concerned with the misuse of opiates. In 1916, during the First World War, it had passed the Defence of the Realm Act, aimed at deterring drug use among seamen and prostitutes, and in 1920 it passed the Dangerous Drugs Act. This latter act was largely designed to implement the International Opium Convention agreed on at The Hague in 1912. This was the first international accord that sought to regulate the trade in opium; it came into force in February 1915.

The first significant power battle occurred in 1923, with the passing of the Dangerous Drugs Amendment Act. This was inspired to some extent by the Harrison Act in the United States, and was an attempt to shift policy from a medical to a penal response. Medical practitioners, who had developed a model of sickness in responding to addiction, strongly opposed this shift in policy and the Ministry of Health, which had only recently been established, entered into battle with the Home Office on the side of the doctors. This battle for policy control, and hence for political control, has continued throughout the remainder of this century.

The key element in the response to addiction was the doctors' control of the prescribing of dangerous drugs. The Department of Health clearly expressed the view that when a drug user was willing to enter into a proper doctor/patient relationship, then the doctor should have the right to use his clinical judgment in determining appropriate treatment. When, however, the drug user was merely seeking drugs, he should be refused a prescription.[4]

This position was legitimized by the Interdepartmental Committee on Morphine and Heroin Addiction (the Rolleston Committee), which was established in 1924 to consider what measures should be taken to deal with those patients who became addicted to opiates prescribed legitimately in the course of medical treatment. It should be noted that the number of people involved was small, around 600, and that the source of opiates was almost exclusively from legitimate prescribing. The committee concluded that addiction was an illness and not a "mere form of vicious indulgence," and that the proper course of treatment was to seek to withdraw the patient from the drug of addiction by a gradual reduction in the prescription or, where this proved to be unsatisfactory, maintenance of the patient on a nonincreasing dose of the drug of addiction.[5] It is perhaps equally important to note that the primary concern was with middle-class addicts, over half of whom were women, and that the doctors involved in the committee were private doctors in the days before the National Health Service. Prison medical officers, who gave evidence and who were concerned with working-class addicts, took a significantly harsher view and favored abrupt withdrawal and a much greater punitive approach.

The recommendations of the committee were accepted and the philosophy and treatment guidance contained in the report formed the basis of the British response to drug addiction for almost 50 years. It is this which is commonly referred to as the British Treatment System. I was inclined to title this paper "The

British Treatment System—It's Neither Treatment, nor a System, but It's Certainly British."

The recommendations of the Rolleston Committee were confirmed in 1961 when an Interdepartmental Committee on Drug Addiction under the Chairmanship of Sir Russell Brain reported.[6] Although the new committee noted that there had been some changes since 1926, these were not sufficient to warrant any change in policies.

A Newly Defined Epidemic

In 1964 the Interdepartmental Committee on Drug Addiction (the Brain Committee) was hastily reconvened. The number of drug addicts had risen significantly. Moreover, most of this increase was due to the use of heroin by young people who had obtained the drug from legitimate medical sources but not for treatment of a medical condition. The use of heroin was the major change. The majority of drug users prior to this had been using morphine or pethidine and the like, were employed and, in the majority, were middle-aged and middle-class. The new drug users were young, often unemployed, working-class and, as importantly, enjoyed their drug use and showed their enjoyment in drug use to others.

The committee concluded that the rise in addiction was due to the over-prescribing of heroin by a small number of doctors, and its recommendations sought to cut off this source of supply and to provide a means of monitoring the extent of drug addiction. A system of licensing was proposed whereby only a doctor specifically licensed by the Home Office could prescribe heroin or cocaine for the treatment of addiction. These doctors would be attached to special treatment centers at hospitals. Additionally, any doctor who attended someone whom he considered or reasonably suspected of being addicted to one or more of fourteen named drugs, all narcotics, should be required to notify the Chief Medical Officer at the Home Office of certain details about the individual. The committee favored treating an addict as a "sick" person, maintaining the position won in the battles between the Department of Health and the Home Office in the 1920s. It also favored the medical orthodoxy that emerged in the early part of the twentieth century, which favored compulsory treatment, in line with attitudes to treatment of insanity and inebriety. Although medical opinion had changed to a large extent on treatment of mental illness and alcoholism, no such development had occurred in the treatment of addiction, and the committee recommended the introduction of compulsory treatment.[7]

Effectively, no suggestions were made for changing the recommendations of the Rolleston Committee about the form treatment might take. What was offered was increased control of supply and checks on the prescription of narcotics. The committee did, however, recognize the need for a balance between inadequate control of the supply of drugs and too rigid control. "If there is insufficient control it may lead to the spread of addiction—as is happening at present. If, on the other hand, the restrictions are so severe as to seriously discourage the addict from obtaining any supplies from legitimate sources it may lead to the development of an organized illicit traffic."[8] Thus, in addition to appropriate medical treatment, prescribing heroin or cocaine was seen as a means of preventing the development of illicit trafficking.

The recommendations of the Brain Committee, with the exception of compulsory treatment, were accepted by the government and were incorporated in a law that came into force in 1968. What was not done was to review the use of all drugs; the focus was on narcotics and the multiple drug use of many people largely went unremarked, although there was increasing evidence of the widespread use of amphetamines, barbiturates, cannabis, LSD, and the like.[9] The consequence of this narrowly focused approach was to leave responses to the use of other drugs either to the discretion of individual doctors or to legal sanctions. The other element in the recommendations was to retain the authority of the doctor to prescribe any drug that, in his clinical judgment, was necessary for the treatment of a medical condition, The National Health Service had been born through agreement between the doctors and the government that general practitioners would individually contract to provide medical services and that they should have clinical freedom to prescribe drugs as they considered appropriate. In effect, doctors had a general license to prescribe any drug. The Brain Committee maintained this position and, to the present day, a doctor may prescribe any drug for the treatment of organic illness. The sole restriction is on the prescription of heroin, cocaine, or dipipanone as a specific treatment for addiction—and even this restriction aroused considerable opposition from doctors.

The hospital treatment centers that opened their doors in 1968 were in the majority out-patient services. Most doctors and many hospitals were reluctant to provide facilities for drug treatment. The services were only established because the Department of Health paid directly for them. Initially, they prescribed heroin and cocaine, but they rapidly changed to the use of methadone. With typical British compromise, however, methadone was given in ampoule form for self-injection, not in linctus form for oral consumption. Concomitant with this was the provision of sterile disposable needles and syringes, a subject now of some international controversy but normal practice in the 1960s and first half of the 1970s. What was most significant, perhaps, in the changes introduced was that treatment of addiction was moved from the general practitioner to the psychiatrist. The "sickness" model of addiction was retained but was now defined as mental sickness and moved into a specialty.

Parallel with the development of official responses to drug problems, there was the growth of voluntary organizations concerned with the same subject. It will not surprise you to know, given the context of social action in Britain, that their approach was radically different. Essentially, two types of service were established, day care and drug-free rehabilitation, with two competing philosophies. The day care services saw drug use as a personal and social problem in which individuals were the victims of social conditions that prevented them from realizing their potential. Their response was to provide basic social facilities, shelter, food, assistance with practical problems, representation in court, and hygienic facilities in which individuals might self-inject their prescribed drugs. They were advocates for their clients, whom they saw as disenfranchised. Residential services saw drug use as a pathological condition that could only be dealt with through total abstinence and a major restructuring of the personality of the individual, either through intense group-work and strictly enforced discipline or through religious conversion to evangelical Christianity. Although there were these major differences, there was also common cause in the direct challenge to medical domination and a medically determined response to drug problems.

Although there were, therefore, major conflicts of approach to work with drug users, in practice the growth of addiction appeared to be contained for a number of years. During the 1970s, the misuse of drugs continued and the number of addicts reported to the Chief Medical Officer at the Home Office increased each year. The annual rise was relatively small, however, and the belief was that the United Kingdom had controlled the spread of addiction. This was not entirely true because information was only collected on the use of opioids. No information was available about the misuse of barbiturates or amphetamines, although the experience of those working with addicts was that misuse of these drugs was a serious problem. [10]

A second problem was that many doctors were unaware of their duty to notify opioid addicts and did not do so, with the result that the number of known addicts was almost certainly less than the actual number of addicts. Despite this, as a political issue that required attention and policy guidance, drug use was virtually off the agenda. The changes that occurred in practice, the move from long-term prescribing of injectable methadone to contract-based, short-term prescribing of oral methadone, the closure of day centers in favor of counseling services attended by appointment, the enforcement of abstinence through court-imposed rehabilitation orders—all these were subject to little debate.

A RENEWED PROBLEM

At the end of the 1970s, there was a sudden and unexpected increase in the number of new addicts, particularly those addicted to heroin and dipipanone, and a substantial increase in the amount of seized heroin destined for the United Kingdom.

This new phase of the drug problem in the United Kingdom has been linked with political changes in Iran and southwest Asia, particularly northwest Pakistan and Afghanistan. In Pakistan, after much pressure from the United States, the government agreed to close the licensed opium shops. These shops had operated for many years and provided a licit outlet for traditional production and use of opium. Their closure, without any alternative offered to the producers, left a surplus of opium with no legitimate market. The combination of political upheaval in Afghanistan and Iran with a surplus of opium and the skills to produce and market heroin produced a new source of supply, with Britain one of its natural markets.

Within the United Kingdom, the changes were seen most significantly through the spread of drug use throughout the country, not just concentrated in the centers of large urban areas. It is now the case that virtually every part of the country has people with serious drug problems, with some areas having particularly noticeable concentrations of addicts. In the first half of the 1980s, known addiction was rising at a rate of 30 percent each year, while local epidemiological studies showed that the actual level of drug use was between 5 and 20 times greater than the level of notified drug use. This, then, is the background to the rapidly changing policies of the 1980s and 1990s.

I have titled this paper "Pragmatic Incoherence." This is deliberate because the development of policy has essentially been based on a national framework, a form of broad guidance about the range of responses and the goals of intervention, without any desire or capacity to enforce particular actions at a local or regional level. At the local and regional level, policy and practice has largely been determined by individuals with particular views about the correct approach to drug problems, often with competing approaches between different individuals and professional groups. It is no more a treatment system than the arrangements before 1968, referred to as the British Treatment System. The difference is that the number of individuals pursuing their own "clinical judgments" within a broadly permissive framework has increased substantially as drug use has risen. I want, therefore, to concentrate on policy themes rather than attempt to analyze the diversity of practice in Britain.

POLICY CHANGES AND CONFLICTS

The first major change in policy occurred in 1982, when the Advisory Council on the Misuse of Drugs completed its report on "Treatment and Rehabilitation."[11] At the center of its recommendations was the view that the focus of work with drug users should be on problems arising from their drug use rather than on diagnosis and restricting availability to those thought to be addicted.

This was a direct challenge to the central role of specialist drug services, centered around the work of hospital-based treatment services. It signaled a shift back to a greater involvement of generic services, general practitioners, youth services, housing services, education, training, social services, and so on. The role of specialist services was to act as advisory and support services to generic services and to provide specialist treatment for those individuals whose drug problems could not be managed in the community. To enable these changes, it was argued that more specialist services were needed to support generic services. Drug advisory committees, involving all relevant agencies, should be established to coordinate and develop all responses to drug problems.

Two years later, a further report from the Advisory Council was published, this time on "Prevention." Its central recommendation was that prevention should have two basic criteria:

1. Reducing the risk of an individual engaging in drug misuse
2. Reducing the harm associated with drug misuse

Earlier concepts of prevention that centered on a classical medical model of primary, secondary, and tertiary prevention were rejected as too narrow and inappropriate. Prevention was thus not an absolute but a balance between competing options, weighing the advantages against the disadvantages of particular courses of action. Increased repressive measures, for instance, might have some impact on supply of drugs and the introduction of people to drug use. It might also result in drug use becoming more hidden, increased criminal activity, and greater social problems.

Further reports followed, with the House of Commons Social Services Committee on Social Services publishing a report in 1985[13] and the House of Commons Home Affairs Committee publishing a report in 1986.[14] These reports most clearly presented the policy conflict between social and penal responses to drug problems. The former built on the reports of the Advisory Council, advocating a community services response to drug problems, supported by specialist services, and guided and funded by the central government. The latter focused on penal sanctions, on increased international cooperation to reduce production and supply, increased penalties, better policing, and improved coordination and cooperation between law-enforcement agencies. There was no cross-reference between these reports; they were parallel and competing strategies, not complementary approaches to a common problem.

Government response was a reflection of this confusion. At a political level, the government was determined to reduce the role of the state, to place greater responsibility on individuals and on local decisions rather than on central intervention. At the same time, it was subject to considerable national and international pressure to take action on drugs. To maintain this position, it developed an approach in which prevention, treatment, and rehabilitation were the responsibilities of local and regional authorities, with additional funds provided by the central government, while the direct role of government was in strengthening international activity and attacking the supply of drugs through, for instance, introducing additional penalties for drug offenses. The inevitable consequence was that the language of the government and its actions became increasingly separated from the reality of practice at local and regional levels.

One means of presenting government concern was through a national anti-drug campaign. Initially this was directed at heroin and involved television commercials, advertisement in the youth press, and billboard advertising. The message was, "Heroin screws you up." There were many criticisms of this campaign, which continued over a number of years. The main ones I wish to concentrate on are the conflicts this campaign created. Although heroin was the major drug problem in many parts of the country, it was also the case that other forms of drug use were more important in various parts of the country. A national campaign could not take account of the reality of drug use at local levels. The thrust of policy through the Advisory Council on the Misuse of Drugs had been toward a much greater role for generic services in responding to drug problems. The ads presented an image of drug use that maintained a stereotype of the drug user, and this did not encourage generic staff to work with this client group. Drug education at the local level was designed to be integrated into a broader framework of health and social education, assisting in the development of decisionmaking skills and the promotion of healthy options. National advertising emphasized one drug alone, one that in most areas was the least likely to be encountered by young people. One ironic consequence of using an advertising company for the campaign was that the young man depicted in the advertisements and on billboards was good-looking and epitomized the emerging "look" for young people. The ads became pin-ups for many, rather than warnings against heroin!

Conflict also existed in the introduction of more repressive legislation. In 1985, penalties for drug offenses were raised to make the maximum penalty for trafficking in opiates, cocaine, and the like, life imprisonment. Sentencing practice at courts has been to establish penalties in line with the maximum penalty for the offense. In effect, the "tariff" for drugs offenses rose for all these offenses as the maximum penalty rose for the most serious offenses.[15] At the same time, local policy was to attract drug users into services, to bring them into treatment. Identification as a drug user, however, meant increased likelihood of arrest and imprisonment, with a reduced inclination to seek treatment. Increasingly, police officers used formal cautions, which did not require the drug user to attend court, and referral to treatment services, thus countermanding national policy toward greater repression.[16]

New Policy Challenges

The contradictions have become even stronger in recent years, following publication of the Advisory Council's two reports on "AIDS and Drug Misuse."[17] The central theme of these reports was that "the spread of HIV is a greater danger to individual and public health than drug misuse. Accordingly, services which aim to minimise HIV-risk behaviour by all available means should take precedence in development plans." The first report argued that services should aim to attract as many drug users as possible to them and should work with people who were not ready to stop drug use but who might be assisted away from the most risky behaviors. It also argued that attitudes and policies that encouraged drug users to remain hidden needed to change if the continuing increase in drug use and in HIV infection among drug users was to be effectively tackled.

The long-established framework of the central government, devolving responsibility for service provision to local and regional health authorities, within a broad framework established by the government, was maintained. Additional funds were made available for the development of services intended to curb the spread of HIV infection among drug users. There was a difference, however. For the first time, recommendations were concerned with services that were the specific responsibility of and under the direct control of the central government, notably the way in which drug laws were enforced and the treatment of prisoners. In essence, those recommendations that were the responsibility of local and regional authorities were accepted, while those that were the responsibility of the central government were rejected. That pragmatic incoherence, which is at the center of British drug policy, was retained.

Parallel Policies

In effect, in Britain two policies operate side by side. Both are official policies. Both are funded through government money. Intellectually they are barely compatible, but in practice they work together.

On the one hand, there is the political policy. This is to a large extent led by the Home Office, which coordinates government drug policy. Its focus is on supply reduction and penal policies, in a belief that elimination of drug use is possible. On the other hand, there is the services policy, largely led by the Department of Health. Its focus is on local prevention campaigns, on providing a variety of local services including detached work, needle and syringe exchange schemes, advice and counseling services, diversion from custody, a variety of prescribing options ranging from short-term out-patient detoxification to long-term prescribing and rehabilitation. At the heart of this approach is the view that drug use cannot be eliminated, but its most harmful consequences for the individual, society, and public health can be moderated.

During the 1980s, there was undoubtedly a battle for supremacy between these two policies. The political policy was the most publicly obvious and popular. It involved increased staffing for the Customs service; the stationing of liaison officers abroad; the establishment of a Central Drugs Intelligence Unit based at Scotland Yard; bringing additional drugs under the control of the Misuse of Drugs Act to enable Britain to become a party to the Psychotropic Drugs Convention; legislation to increase penalties for drug trafficking, to seize the assets of anyone involved in drug trafficking (including the reversal of the legal maxim that someone was innocent until proved guilty), to control the sale of solvents and volatile substances, to enact the Drug Trafficking Convention; the establishment of drug squads in every police force; the establishment of drug squads as part of regional crime squads; a substantial increase in the use of imprisonment for all drug offenses; the removal of the right of parole for people receiving a sentence of over five years imprisonment for drug trafficking; a national antidrug campaign on television, in the youth press, and on billboards; a leaflet drop to every household in Britain about drugs. The cost of such a program was substantial, but it is almost impossible to provide an accurate statement of the actual cost.

The service policy was a quieter affair. Initially, it had been at the forefront in calling for action as the number of new drug users approaching services started to rise rapidly. It was the stimulus to public concern but was overwhelmed by the initial reaction, which was to stop the polluters of our young people. It has been a feature of much reaction to developing drug problems that the outsider, the foreigner, is the corrupter. Xenophobia and racism are part of the protective armory, and it was no different in Britain. Harsher legislation, action abroad, and international cooperation took the limelight in the battle against drugs.

The service policy was designed to develop local responses to drug problems, under the guidance of local drug advisory committees drawn from a range of professions and interests. The dilemma was that these committees were advisory—they had no executive capacity and no resources at their disposal. Implementation of whatever actions they proposed was reliant on the goodwill of the participant agencies and their willingness to divert resources to specific actions. Initially they developed an assessment of the local problem and a strategic plan to deal with it. Without resources or executive capacity, however, a strategic plan was useless. Local services were developed, but these were uncoordinated and essentially depended on the availability of a nongovernmental organization or a health authority willing to take the initiative to make a proposal and bid for limited national funds. For most of the 1980s, the service policy was implemented randomly, based on the tenacity of local agencies and hopefully linked to local need.[19] In such circumstances, political policy had an open field for action.

CHANGING PRIORITIES, CHANGING POLICIES

The change began in the second half of the 1980s. The largest number of new services were locally based advice, counseling, and advocacy services. Many employed staff from a variety of disciplines in a single team and developed links with local doctors, housing associations, youth organizations, and the like. They presented drugs as a social problem with a medical dimension rather than a medical problem engendered by personal pathology. This approach was strengthened by research which began to be published at that time identifying drug problems as being most acute in areas with the highest level of deprivation.[20] The Advisory Council on the Misuse of Drugs, in its report on prevention, had noted that broad social and economic policies had an indirect effect on the use of drugs and prevention policies.[21] By the late 1980s, this cautious observation was becoming hardened into acknowledged fact.

Awareness of the spread of HIV infection among drug users acted as a catalyst to this process of change. Drug use was widespread, ranging from experimental use of a variety of drugs through casual and occasional use to both controlled and uncontrolled regular use. Curbing the spread of HIV infection among drug users required increased efforts to contact drug users and to limit increases in drug use. This was a serious change because, prior to this, the focus of services had been on limiting scarce resources to those who had the motivation to change, a focus on detoxification and abstinence. Although these goals were not abandoned, they were now a desirable end and other goals were equally acceptable, depending on the situation of the individual drug user.

With additional resources made available by the Department of Health,[22] detached work, needle and syringe exchange schemes, regular health checks, open access services, free contraception, substitute drug therapy including the use of cocaine and amphetamines,[23] heroin, injectable and oral drugs, and teaching safer injecting practices were introduced in different parts of the country. The central theme of responses to drug problems became harm-minimization for the individual and society; this has influenced every aspect of policy from prevention aimed at reducing the likelihood of someone trying drugs to assisting the injecting drug user not to share equipment and to inject in a way least likely to cause major physical damage.

By the 1990s, the division between political policy and service policy has been reduced, although it remains. Most recently, proposals have been made to reduce the use of imprisonment as a punishment for people with drug problems.

The intention is that alternatives to custody should be used more widely, and legislation is expected shortly.[24] Many local police forces have already introduced a policy of cautioning those found in possession of controlled drugs. Although this policy is largely used for possession of cannabis, a number of police forces use it for possession of any controlled drug and some use it for dealing with small scale user/dealers. Increasingly, police forces refer drug users they meet to drug services rather than arrest them and process them through the courts.[25] Legislation recently passed has, for the first time, placed a responsibility for drug services with local authorities.[26] This is important because local authorities are the agents for government in the implementation of social policy. They are responsible for social services, housing, education, youth work, leisure services, and environmental services. It is a recognition that drug problems are more than just matters of health.

The Home Office itself, the guardian of political policy, has funded the establishment of a number of local drug-prevention teams. These teams are to be guided by local advisory committees but, more importantly, examples of the tasks they might help to finance are social and environmental improvements that might reduce the likelihood of people using drugs and/or developing drug problems. These include social facilities, improvements to housing estates to make drug use and dealing more difficult, and the introduction of alternative activities that make drug use less attractive. Although their resources are inadequate for the tasks they have been given, they are a symbol of a changed awareness—that at the root of drug problems are the social, economic, and environmental policies that make drug use an attractive alternative.

FUTURE OPTIONS

The pragmatic incoherence of British drug policy remains at the heart of our responses. On the one hand, there is the bellicose language of the political policy; on the other hand, there is the service policy that directly contradicts it. What is essential in understanding British drug policy is to recognize that political policy is for public consumption. It is the means of presenting a strong image that can camouflage service policy. Such an arrangement has both benefits and disadvantages. It has allowed the development of responses to drug problems relevant to local needs, which recognize both the social and medical dimensions, and are responsive to the needs of the individual drug user rather than seeking to slot the drug user into a system. On the other hand, by the public image the policy has created, it has maintained stereotypical images of drug use, it has promoted misunderstanding rather than created understanding, and it has raised expectations that cannot be realized.

We have now reached the point where political policy and service policy are equals. The battle for supremacy of the 1980s has led to this, but it has also led to service policy now directly challenging political policy. It is a battle between those who hold the view that the elimination of drug use is possible and those who believe that this goal is unrealistic and the objective must be to reduce the harm arising from drug use to the individual, society, and public health. How this battle will be resolved cannot readily be predicted. My own suspicion is that service policy will eventually be victorious, but this will be a slow process and one that occurs through gradual evolution, not through frontal confrontation. Political policy has been too public and too successful in convincing the uncommitted and uninvolved to change suddenly. It has in practice been changing but at a pace that does not create embarrassment for those who have been at times its keenest proponents. The political declaration adopted at the end of the World Ministerial Summit on Demand Reduction is one overt signal of this change. Its first draft was prepared by a British Home Office official. Although modified in the drafting committee, it was still a major advance over earlier declarations and over the Comprehensive Multidisciplinary Outline, the handbook adopted in 1987 by the United Nations International Conference on Drug Abuse and Illicit Trafficking.

In the 1980s, governments slowly recognized that putting enormous resources into supply reduction had not actually reduced supply; in fact, supply and use continued to rise. They have now adopted demand reduction as the new focus for action on drugs. Demand reduction, however, is in danger of being created in the image of supply reduction, where penal sanctions, refusal of or loss of employment, eviction from housing, education, and the like are seen as key components of demand reduction. If such interpretations are allowed to go unchallenged, then we are in danger of exacerbating rather than mitigating the harm to the individual, to society, and to public health. British drug policy is at present balanced between political and service policy. The next few years will determine where the new balance will lie. In this instance at least, I hope that the "special relationship" between Britain and America will be broken and that we will adopt the policies relevant to *our* needs and *our* experience.

NOTES

1. Virginia Berridge and Griffith Edwards, *Opium and the People: Opiate Use in Nineteenth-Century England* (London: Allen Lane and Yale University, 1981 and 1987).

2. Royal Commission on Opium, *First Report* (London: Parliamentary Papers, 1894).

3. *Indian Hemp Drugs Commission, Report* (Simla: Government Printing Office, 1894).

4. Ministry of Health papers, *MH 58/275/Memorandum by Dr. E. W. Adams* (London, 1923).

5. *Report of the Departmental Committee on Morphine and Heroin Addiction* (London: Her Majesty's Stationery Office (HMSO), 1926).

6. *Drug Addiction: Report of the Interdepartmental Committee* (London: HMSO, 1961).

7. *Drug Addiction: The Second Report of the Interdepartmental Committee* (London: HMSO, 1965).

8. Ibid., para. 15, p. 7.

9. See, for instance: T. H. Bewley, "Heroin and Cocaine Addiction," *The Lancet* 1 (1965): 808–10; T. H. Bewley, "Recent Changes in the Incidence in All Types of Drug Dependence," *Proceedings of the Royal Society of Medicine* 61 (1968): 175–77; M. Mitcheson, J. Davidson, D. Hawks, L. Hitchins, and S. Malone, "Sedative Abuse by Heroin Addicts," *Journal of Psychedelic Drugs* 4, no. 2 (1971): 123–31; I. P. James. *British Journal of Criminology* 9 (1969): 108.

10. H. A. Ghodse, "Drug Dependent Individuals Dealt with by London Casualty Departments" *British Journal of Psychiatry* 131 (1977): 273–80; *Barbiturate and Similar Drug Misuse* (London: Standing Conference on Drug Abuse (SCODA), 1973). It should also be noted that the first study of the Advisory Council on the Misuse of Drugs, when it was appointed in 1973, was on the misuse of barbiturates. Its slowness in acting was largely because of the general level of prescribing these drugs in ordinary medical practice.

11. *Treatment and Rehabilitation: Report of the Advisory Council on the Misuse of Drugs* (London: HMSO, 1982).

12. *Prevention: Report of the Advisory Council on the Misuse of Drugs* (London: HMSO, 1984).

13. House of Commons Social Services Committee, *Fourth Report of the Social Services Committee: Misuse of Drugs with Special Reference to the Treatment and Rehabilitation of Misusers of Hard Drugs* (London: HMSO, 1985).

14. House of Commons Home Affairs Committee, *First Report from the Home Affairs Committee, Session 1985–86: Misuse of Hard Drugs* (London: HMSO, 1986).

15. In 1985, 11.2 percent of all those charged with unlawful possession of a controlled drug received a prison sentence, compared to 7 percent in 1981 and 1983. By 1989, this had fallen to 5.5 percent. In 1985, 80.1 percent of possession offenses were for cannabis; however, by 1989 this had risen to 90.5 percent.

16. In 1989, 13,443 people were cautioned for drug offenses, representing 35 percent of all drug offenders.

17. *AIDS and Drug Misuse, Part 1: Report by the Advisory Council on the Misuse of Drugs* (London: HMSO, 1988); *AIDS and Drug Misuse, Part 2: Report by the Advisory Council on the Misuse of Drugs* (London: HMSO, 1989).

18. *Government Response to the Report* (London: Department of Health, 1988), Annex to Circular HC(88) 26/LAC(88) 7.

19. *Drug Misuse Prevalence and Service Provision: A Report on Surveys and Plans in English National Health Service Regions* (London: Department of Social Health and

Social Security (DHSS), 1985); *Social Services Inspectorate Project on Drug Misuse* (London: Social Services Inspectorate, DHSS, 1986).

20. See, for instance: S. Haw, *Drug Problems in Greater Glasgow* (London: SCODA, 1985); S. Haw and O. Liddell, *Drug Problems in Edinburgh* (London: SCODA, 1988); H. Parker, R. Newcombe, and K. Bakx, "The New Heroin Users: Prevalence and Characteristics in Wirral, Merseyside," *British Journal of Addiction* 82 (1987): 147–58; G. Pearson, *The New Heroin Users* (Oxford: Basil Blackwell, 1987).

21. *Prevention: Report of the Advisory Council on the Misuse of Drugs* (London: HMSO, 1984), pp. 13–14 and pp. 30–31.

22. Between 1983 and 1989, the Department of Health issued a number of circulars announcing arrangements for the provision of funds to develop drug services. These included: *Treatment and Rehabilitation: Report of the Advisory Council on the Misuse of Drugs (ACMD): Central Funding Initiative,* HN(83)13/LASSL(83)1; *Services for Drug Misusers—Curbing the Spread of AIDS and HIV Infection,* HC(88)26/LAC(88)7; *Preventing the Spread of HIV Infection among and from Injecting Drug Misusers,* HC(88)53/LAC(88)18; *HIV and AIDS: Resource Allocations 1989/90,* EL(89)P/36.

23. *Working with Stimulant Users* (London: SCODA, 1989).

24. *Crime, Justice and Protecting the Public: The Government's Proposals for Legislation.* By the command of Her Majesty, 965 (London: HMSO, 1990), para. 4.14.

25. N. Dorn, K. Murji, and N. South, "Drug Referral Schemes," *Policing* 6(2) (1990): 482–92.

26. *National Health Service and Community Care Act 1990: Chapter 19* (London: HMSO, 1990).

PART FOUR

SOCIAL COSTS OF DRUG USE

11

THE OPTIMAL DESIGN OF DRUG-CONTROL LAWS

Mark A. R. Kleiman

My topic is the justification and design of drug-control laws. Being at the Hoover Institution and talking on this topic reminds me of a conversation I had some years ago with one of the Institution's most distinguished scholars, when he and I were both teaching at the University of Rochester. When I introduced myself as a student of drug policy, my colleague, a good, solid libertarian, immediately shot back, "But there shouldn't be any such policy!"

That instant response is as clear an expression as one could wish for the core of the libertarian case against drug laws—the case for what is loosely called drug legalization or drug decriminalization. As I hope to demonstrate, neither "drug" nor "legalization" is a sufficiently well-defined term to permit a sensible answer to the question, "Should we legalize drugs?" Nonetheless I take that impulse very seriously.

One of the central motives behind this conference and behind the legalization movement is the belief that drug laws are either just plain silly, a subspecies of sumptuary laws or, worse, ill-intentioned (or at least small-minded) attempts on the part of some to interfere with the innocent pleasures of others, or to impose the preference of the majority or the powerful on an oppressed minority. It is to those who feel that impulse, who share that belief, that I wish to address myself.

In brief, I want to try to explain why someone who has read and understood *Capitalism and Freedom* and *On Liberty* might still be in favor of having drug laws. I want to use that question to explore how, and to what extent, legal restrictions on drug use can be justified, given the assumption that the only proper role of government is to help individuals achieve their own welfare as they perceive it, rather than to impose some external idea of well-being on them or to achieve some collective end independent of the wishes of the citizens.

Although I will start with that individualist assumption, it is important to note that it is not the only assumption on which we could proceed. One could believe instead, with Plato and Calvin, that human beings are systematically bad guardians of their own welfare, that they are systematically deceived about what is good for them because of flaws in their character or because of their ignorance about what constitutes a truly good life. Alternatively, one could believe with Burke and Rousseau that an organically collective life outranks in dignity the mere seeking after individual benefit, and that it is the role of the state to protect the general will (for Rousseau) or the compact among the living, the dead, and those not yet born (for Burke) against individual selfishness. On those assumptions, one could obviously justify very vigorous drug-control laws. On the same basis, however, one could also justify many other things that would ill fit either the Constitution or the native genius of the people of the United States. I will restrict myself to those drug laws that can be justified as protecting the interests of individuals.

The clearest case arises when drug consumption leads some drug users to behave in ways that damage other people: what Stephen Mugford (see Chapter 2) calls "indirect" (an economist would say "external") costs. Your smoking is of concern to me if we are sharing the same elevator. Your drinking is of concern to me if we are sharing the same highway. Drug laws to this extent are like pollution-control laws: They are required to correct an imperfection in the market that fails to include in the price of some commodity all the costs of its production and use. I take that to be relatively unproblematic as a reason to have drug laws, or at least drug taxes.

You will notice that my first two examples involve substances—alcohol and tobacco—that are not "controlled substances" under our current laws. That is, their nonmedical use is not now forbidden. As both Franklin Zimring (Chapter 1) and Stephen Mugford have pointed out, it would be silly to have a conversation about drugs that excluded those drugs which are not forbidden. The world contains a wide variety of psychoactives—substances that if ingested change mood, thought, sensation, and behavior, other than providing nutrition. If we are going to discuss policy toward these substances, we ought to discuss all of them at once and on a level playing field. That some drugs should be forbidden and some permitted ought to be among the conclusions of our discourse and not among its assumptions. This is not to disparage Zimring's point that there is an argument for avoiding change, particularly in light of the fact that inherited social customs are important drug-control mechanisms. Still, it seems to me we should not assume that molecules come into the world legal or illegal; rather we should think about whether and why they should be put into those statuses.

It will not follow from anything I am going to say that all psychoactives ought to be forbidden; indeed, I believe no such thing. What policy we ought to have toward each drug and toward all drugs together is an interesting and complicated question, but it should be considered only once one has provided a satisfactory answer to the prior question of why to have such policies at all.

Mentioning alcohol serves another purpose as well. Most people in this room, as has been pointed out, drink. Everyone here knows people who drink, and who drink without suffering visible damage themselves or doing visible damage to other people. That usefully constrains what we say here about drinking and about drinkers. Just because some people get drunk and beat their children, we do not say, "Alcohol users are child-beaters." That would obviously be an overgeneralization and its inaccuracy would be obvious to all of us because we know alcohol users who are not child-beaters. We say, more carefully, "Alcohol is linked to child-beating among some users."

Few, if any, people in this room use cocaine. Few people here even know people who use cocaine. I do not (so far as I am aware) know anyone who is a current user of cocaine. This leaves us freer to generalize about cocaine users and to imagine that they are all alike in important ways: In particular that any cocaine use inevitably leads to disaster, if not now, then later. This is in fact the explicit message of the National Drug Control Strategy and of the Media Partnership for a Drug-Free America. It is not supported by data, however, and is in fact almost certainly false. The proposition that drug X damages person A obviously does not conflict in any way with the proposition that drug X does not damage person B.

To say that—to acknowledge that there is innocuous drug use, and even innocuous use by some people of drugs that cause great damage to and by others— is sometimes taken as treason in the war on drugs. If this be treason, the fanatics can make the most of it. None of my argument will rest on the proposition that a given class of effects is inevitable for all users of a given drug, or even a majority of them.

Still less do I want to pretend that all currently illicit drugs are the same and that one can therefore generalize about drug use or drug users in a way that treats people who routinely binge on crack and people who occasionally puff a joint of marijuana as being identical. None of that is true.

Insofar as a given psychoactive substance tends, only tends, to produce user behavior that damages other people, a government that seeks to improve the welfare of its citizens may want to have laws about that substance different from the laws that regulate ordinary commerce. Joel Hay (Chapter 12) discusses the actual extent of drug-caused harm to nonusers. For the moment let me just list some categories: crimes, accidents, and public nuisances.

This last is an underconsidered category. There are myriad ways in which intoxicated persons in public can cause nuisances to others. Although nuisance does not sound as serious as crime, if you ask people why they leave cities for suburbs you will find that most of the things that really drove them out are nuisances that do not rise to the level of criminal conduct.

With respect to these three categories, all involving observable damage to others, one might ask, "Why do we need drug laws? If someone gets drunk and hits someone else, we should punish assault. If someone gets drunk and falls down in public, we should punish him for being disorderly in public. If someone gets drunk and drives his car into mine, we have a tort-law system that allows me to sue." The answer to that argument is that all those systems are very costly, very inefficient, and have limited capacity. It is not the case that we can use either the criminal law or the civil tort law in an unlimited way to control each other's behavior. Those systems only work if most people stay out of them. Particularly if one has the liberal impulse in favor of relatively loose forms of social control— a preference, for example, for not having lots of police around—then one must ask what characteristics of the residents of an area would be consistent with *both* loose formal controls *and* acceptable levels of crime, disorder, and accidents.

For loose control and social order to coexist. it is necessary to have citizens who for the most part do not need police watching them in order to behave well. That is to say, the looseness we value depends on a certain distribution of dispositions among the citizens. For example, if you are in charge of maintaining order in a football stadium you may want to concern yourself with the availability of beer inside the stadium. If you do not concern yourself with the supply of beer, you will need to hire a large security force or accept a large number of fights breaking out. The terms of the trade-off between security and order will be much worse if there is lots of beer around.

Why is it not equally obvious that the persons responsible for maintaining public order downtown on Saturday night ought to concern themselves with the supply of beer to the people downtown on Saturday night? It seems to me to be the same problem. The difference, of course, is that the stadium can try to control the amount of beer allowed into the stadium, in effect making private drug laws, whereas if you are responsible for patrolling the streets, the only drug laws you have are the public drug laws of the country where you are. If, then, drugs cause some people to have dispositions to damage other people, that turns out to be a nontrivial problem for liberal society.

Crimes, accidents, and nuisances do not exhaust the catalog of direct damage to others. Involuntary exposure to drugs is a problem, both as passive drug-taking by proximity and as *in utero* exposure. The spread of communicable disease is also a problem: People who wind up on skid row as a result of their drug use and are chronically malnourished and exposed are likely to be carriers of such diseases as tuberculosis. Again, a general level of ill health in the society at large is of concern to others, for reasons beyond mere empathy.

Drugs can also induce failures to carry out voluntarily assumed responsibility: for example, the responsibility of parents. If people fail their responsibilities as parents, that is not a small problem for the rest of us. If you think of the upbringing of new citizens as a fundamental piece of public work to be done, then it is an important fact about liberal society that child-raising is assigned largely to private parties. Insofar as they fail, we fall back on extremely expensive, and not very good, public systems. If it turns out that some drug tends to reduce its users' effort or competence as parents, that is not of minor concern to the rest of us. Again, it is not essential to this argument that the effect be universal among drug users, only that it happen in a noticeable number of instances.

Drug use can also create drains on common resources—on the health care system, on the system of income maintenance, and on all the other risk-spreading mechanisms on which we rely. Both privately funded insurance and public insurance systems are attempts to spread the risks of loss by providing resources to those in need. If more people wind up in need because of their drug use, all of us wind up worse off.

One could say—and a strong libertarian would say—let't get rid of those undesirable social insurance systems. That of course does not get rid of all the private insurance systems, for which drug use will multiply underwriting problems. More to the point, we have those social insurance systems because I think people are (in my view, rationally) risk-averse. In many instances it is easier and cheaper to reduce risk by spreading it than by eliminating it at its source. If drug use causes such drains on risk-spreading devices, then we have to reduce our level of social insurance, a reduction that imposes real welfare costs for nondrug users.

One could also point out the risk of decreased contributions to common resources: not only taxes paid and charitable contributions, but citizenship and voluntary activism such as neighborhood associations, PTAs, and volunteer fire departments. We do not require these things to be done; we cannot require them to be done if they are to remain voluntary, but neither can we easily manage a society where no one wants to vote or campaign for office or give to the Red Cross or join the block watch. Here again, the regime of liberty is not indifferent to the distribution of dispositions among its citizens.

One disposition particularly inimical to ordered liberty is impulsiveness, the inability to defer gratification. Not only is it harmful in itself, but it also disables all of our social-control mechanisms. Criminal law relies on people being afraid of being arrested and going to prison. If you spread some substance in the society which makes people less sensitive to that threat, you either have more crime or more prisons or both. All the intoxicants—alcohol, cocaine (at least in the smoked form), marijuana, heroin—appear to increase impulsiveness on average. (Note that nicotine and caffeine are not intoxicants in this sense, and this is one good reason to treat them differently from other drugs.)

One noteworthy thing about impulsiveness is that it makes people less good stewards of their own welfare. That is to say, it makes them less like the rational decisionmaker from which economic theory derives all those lovely theorems about the optimality of market equilibria. The law therefore regards intoxicated consent as inadequate for a large list of purposes, from the validity of a contract to the voluntariness of a sexual relationship. There are a lot of assumptions about people built into a liberal society which some drugs will tend to falsify for some of their users. That is not a small problem.

This analysis leads to the second major set of reasons to have drug laws: the protection of drug users. One can, I think, identify various ways in which drugs fool individual decisionmaking mechanisms so that people who are perfectly good stewards of their own welfare about the consumption of cornflakes or clothes are not good stewards of their own welfare about the consumption of cocaine. If that is true, and if you support individual liberty for John Stuart Mill's reason, that it in fact leads to better outcomes, rather than Robert Nozick's reason that people have an absolute right to mess up their own lives, then you will be less libertarian about cocaine than you are about cornflakes.

If my argument so far establishes that we need some drug laws, the question is "what kind of drug laws?" The answer in general must be some mix of taxes and regulations. Prohibition is the extreme form of either of those.

Enforceability is always an issue, as much with respect to regulations as with respect to prohibition. The question "Should we legalize?" thus reduces itself to the question, "What is the optimal set of control policies, and for which, if any, of the currently illicit drugs can we find a set of policies that will leave us better off than we are now?" Thinking about that question, and contemplating the unsatisfactory results of alcohol and tobacco legalization, suggests the importance of finding currently unused or underused control measures that might be applied to the currently illicit drugs in place of single prohibition (or to the currently licit drugs in place of virtually unrestricted availability). Taxation is an obvious instance: at current tax rates, legal drugs are too cheap.

Among the regulations we are currently underusing are quantity limitations and limitations about who can use drugs. We distinguish between legitimate and illegitimate users of alcohol on the basis of age only. We do not, for example, take away the drinking license of a drunken driver; that is unfortunate. It is also, I think, unfortunate that we do not limit the quantity of alcohol any one user can buy and consume.

The more broadly we think about possible regimes for regulating user licenses and quantity limits, the more we can reduce the damage done by currently licit drugs and the more likely we are to find means short of prohibition for controlling some of the currently illicit drugs. For others, particularly smokable cocaine, I think that the optimal regulation will turn out to be prohibition.

My conclusion, then, is that the question, "Should we legalize drugs?" has no answer as framed, and that we should work on the less simple questions, "What laws best fit which drugs?" and "How should we enforce the drug laws we have?"

12

THE HARM THEY DO TO OTHERS: A PRIMER ON THE EXTERNAL COSTS OF DRUG ABUSE

Joel W. Hay

> *November, 1990: A woman is brought to the emergency department of a New York City hospital. She is strung out on crack, and would not even be there except that someone at the crack house phoned her in to city emergency services because she was bleeding badly. The woman gives birth to a 1,000-gram baby, about the size of an average New York City rat. The infant is placed into one of the most advanced neonatal intensive care units in the world. A couple of days later, the woman slips away from her hospital bed, having given the medical staff false identification. Seven months and $150,000 later, the baby is dead, and the same woman is readmitted to the same hospital for another premature delivery.*
>
> *Each year, the damage wrought on innocent victims in the United States by crack alone exceeds the death and destruction at Pearl Harbor in December 1941.*

The most enthusiastic recreational drug users are usually too stoned or burned out to provide a coherent intellectual rationalization for this ultimate self-indulgency beyond "turn on, tune in, and drop out." It has been left to the sober libertarians, usually with little or no personal interest in consuming opiates, cocaine, or other psychoactive drugs, to rush to the defense of drug use on the general principle that anything a person does is his or her own business unless and until it harms someone else. As J. S. Mill [1859] put it:

> . . . the only purpose for which power can be rightfully exercised over any member of a civilized community against his will, is to prevent harm to others. . . . The only part of the conduct of any one, for which he is amenable to society, is that which concerns others. In the part which merely concerns himself, his independence is, of right, absolute.

This fine sentiment should be and has been taken very seriously in public policy and the law. Although laudable in the abstract, the principle of government noninterference in activities undertaken by mutually consenting individuals can clash with other individual and societal objectives. It is often troubling and not always possible to reconcile the conflicting desires of individuals living in close interaction, or even to reconcile those wishes of a single individual across different points in time, particularly for activities with a large potential for regret. Schelling [1968] provided the example of an expectant mother who, prior to labor, insisted on a natural childbirth without use of painkilling medication, but during labor screams for an anesthetic injection. Which of the woman's contrary requests is the physician obliged to honor?

There are many socially proscribed activities that, it might be argued, do not harm anyone but the willfully consenting participants. It would take a very hardy libertarian, however, to advocate the decriminalization of each or all of the following activities: voluntary contracts of slavery, incest, prostitution, public nudity or lewdness, private sales of nuclear, chemical, or biological weapons, eating human flesh, and the production of snuff movies. For this sort of activity, and for drug use as well, society is fully justified in establishing legal restrictions and prohibitions when, in comparing the unrestricted regime relative to the restricted one, the costs of the activities imposed by the consumers on others are unacceptably high.

A tragic blindness to the external costs of drug abuse has warped the perspective of the libertarian drug legalizers. Prolegalization physicians such as Lester Grinspoon and James Bakalar [1985] attempt to reassure us that "there is little evidence that [cocaine] is likely to become as serious a social problem as alcohol . . . or as serious a medical problem as tobacco," as if that were good news. And libertarian physician Thomas Szasz [1987] states that "no one has to ingest any drug he does not want, just as no one has to read a book he does not want," while thousands of infants die and millions of infants suffer other tragic but nonfatal consequences of maternal drug abuse—with alcohol and tobacco the leading culprits.

Milton Friedman [1972, 1989] and Ethan Nadelmann [1988] have argued that there is an inconsistency in allowing legalized alcohol and tobacco consumption, when each of these drugs kills many more people than heroin, cocaine, or all other illicit drugs. They are correct; but alcohol and tobacco are the larger social tragedies, precisely because of their easy accessibility. Even with the well-criticized current problems of drug-related crime and poor drug-law enforcement, illegal drugs cause less damage to society than tobacco and alcohol, precisely because of the relative difficulty and cost of obtaining them. The inconsistency should be resolved by making it more difficult to abuse alcohol and tobacco, rather than making it easier to abuse cocaine, heroin, marijuana, PCP, or other psychoactive drugs.

In advocating drug legalization, a consistent libertarian should also argue against the drunk-driving laws. A drunk behind the steering wheel harms absolutely no one. It is only when he crashes into someone or something else that he becomes a problem. By libertarian standards, the legal system should only focus on punishing those who harm others, irrespective of their state of mind or health at the time.

The arguments on both sides here should be quite familiar to readers of the drug-legalization literature. Enforcement of drunk-driving laws costs money, criminalizes an activity that is not harmful in itself, causes large-scale lawbreaking and flaunting of the legal system, creates a potential for bribery and corruption of law-enforcement officials, and could never prevent all vehicle accidents in any case. Why should drunk drivers be singled out for legal punishment, when sleepy or suicidal drivers remain legal until they violate a specific traffic ordinance?

As most libertarians are willing to admit, the benefits of drunk-driving laws derive from the empirical observation that drivers who have consumed illegal levels of alcohol are at unacceptably higher risk for causing traffic accidents than those who are sober. This is policy based on mere statistical relationship! There is a clear infringement of individual freedoms and a crude justice in basing traffic statutes on simplistic empirical regularities.

Drunk-driving laws suffer problems of sensitivity—not all drunk drivers will (instantly) have an accident—and specificity—not all traffic accidents are caused by drunk drivers. Nevertheless, they reduce the rate of traffic accidents at an acceptable social cost. The fact that some (possibly tiny) fraction of drunks would never have a driving accident in the absence of drunk-driving laws, and that others will continue to drink and drive in the face of stiff legal restrictions, are acceptable prices to pay to rid the roads of a large part of the drunk-driving menace.

AN ECONOMIC FRAMEWORK FOR
DRUG POLICY COST-BENEFIT ANALYSIS

Illegal drugs are not harmless to those who do not choose to consume them. The abuse of licit and illicit drugs imposes enormous external costs on others. These costs exceed the external costs of maintaining the current drug-law regime and they would rise substantially if illicit drugs were legalized.

Adapting Wagstaff's [1987] categorization, the external costs of drug use are those costs that befall third parties who do not choose to consume drugs themselves. The social cost of drug use is the sum of the private and external costs. The external costs of drug use include: (a) drug-addiction treatment and additional health-care costs caused by drug abuse that are borne by the taxpayer or the nondrug-using health insurance beneficiary; (b) the damage done by drug-abusing parents to their offspring; (c) the accidental deaths, injuries, and property losses imposed by drug abusers on third parties due to drug-induced violence, incapacity, misjudgment, irresponsibility, neglect, and other behavioral impairments; (d) the excess damage done by drug abusers to themselves, but only to the extent that the consequences of drug use were not fully anticipated a priori; and (e) the pain, suffering, distress, and anxiety imposed by drug abusers on their friends and relatives.

There are also external costs of drug-abuse control. When drug consumption is legally restricted, people engage in criminal activity to supply and use drugs. There are costs of law enforcement, incarceration, and criminal activity specific to the procurement of illicit drugs. These costs would disappear in a free and unrestricted competitive drug market. They would, however, continue to some degree under any legalization scheme imposing drug-use restrictions on minors or other population subgroups, or under a system of drug-use taxation, licensure, or rationing (see, for example, Kleiman and Saiger [1989]). In the short run, the greater the level of government restriction, taxation, or law-enforcement activities, the greater the external costs of drug-use control. If, however, government discouragement of drug use through public education and legal restrictions shifts demand downward sufficiently, the long-run external costs of stiffer drug penalties could actually fall.

Certain external costs of drug abuse will occur under any socioeconomic arrangement—for example, the destruction or injury of infants in the womb by drug-abusing mothers, or the motor-vehicle and other accidental deaths and injuries to third parties caused by impaired drug abusers. The extent of external costs will depend to some degree on societal arrangements for finance and delivery of health care, pensions, sickness and disability leave, and the like. In the United States, with government health programs for the poor and disabled, the additional health-care costs of drug abusers fall directly on taxpayers. Drug-addiction treatment services, sick leave, disability and other welfare entitlements that are paid to or for drug abusers are also external costs of drug use in societies where these costs are government-financed.

Libertarians may argue that in addition to legalizing drugs, what they really have in mind is a total dismantling of the welfare state. If drug abusers were still found rotting in the streets, it would be no one's problem but their own. This argument is specious, however, since there is little likelihood that social welfare programs will ever be fully abolished in any country. The reality for the forseeable future is that drug abusers will continue to impose substantial external costs, in no small part specifically because many drug abusers and their offspring are the net beneficiaries of social welfare programs (Ooms and Herendeen [1990]; Kusserow [1990]).

External Costs 1:
The Perinatal Consequence of Maternal Drug Abuse

In a path-breaking evaluation of the medical costs of smoking, Leu and Schaub [1983] obtained the startling result that Swiss smokers actually averaged lower lifetime medical costs than nonsmokers. Because of their shorter life expectancies and the resulting reduction in pension payouts, smokers were argued to be substantial net contributors to social health and pension schemes, rather than burdens on nonsmokers. This result, which has remained troubling to the public health research community, was essentially reconfirmed in a recent U.S. analysis by Manning et al. [1989a], who calculated the external costs of smoking to be the equivalent of $0.15 per pack of cigarettes. They argued that at the existing average state and federal excise tax of $0.37 per pack, smokers' subsidies of pensions and nursing-home payments for nonsmokers substantially exceed nonsmokers' subsidies of medical care and life insurance for smokers.

As Rufleth [1989] pointed out, however, Manning and his colleagues vastly underestimated the external costs through their failure to consider the impacts of maternal smoking on the health, birth outcomes, and long-term growth of infants damaged in utero by maternal smoking during pregnancy. Manning et al. [1989b] uncharacteristically admitted their omission and provided a revised estimate that the external costs of smoking, once one considers the maternity costs, are not $0.15 per pack of cigarettes, but rather $0.31 to $0.52 per pack—or two to three times higher! The public health community was correct to be troubled by economic estimates of the external costs of smoking that were off by several magnitudes.

In making this correction, the Manning group ignored Rufleth's important point about the costs of long-term intellectual and physical developmental consequences from smoking-induced fetal pathology. They calculated that one-fourth of the 1986 $2.9 billion ($3.5 billion current estimates) cost of neonatal intensive care should be attributed to care for smoking-induced low birth weight. This added $0.02 external costs per pack. Manning and the others then further stated that the 2,500 annual infant deaths due to smoking during pregnancy should be counted at the full value of an adult life or, by their estimate, $1.66 million per infant. This added $0.14 per pack to the external cost estimate, as much as all their other external costs combined.

I agree with Manning that infant lives should be fully valued. I also believe that fetal lives have value. Without getting into a lengthy discussion of maternal versus fetal rights, I will state the obvious. Any positive valuation of fetal lives places the health economist squarely in the midst of the political storm over abortion rights. It is not possible, without some intellectual contortions, to place significant positive economic value on fetal lives while maintaining simultaneously that these lives have no value beyond what the mother chooses for them. Aside from this, it is not appropriate in any case to ascribe the same maternal motivation toward the fetus in the case of spontaneous abortion as for a willful termination of pregnancy.

It would be most convenient to ignore this vexing issue, particularly as it may seem tangential to a discussion of the external costs of drug abuse. It is not. As Manning discovered, the value placed on lost infant lives can swamp all other external costs of smoking combined. Furthermore, the chosen estimate of the economic value of life is probably too low by a factor of two to three (see Hay [1989]).

We now consider the external costs of maternal drug abuse to the infant. Although data on the impacts of illicit drugs on fetal and infant development are incomplete and subject to research design flaws and biases, the results obtained thus far concerning the medical impacts of maternal drug abuse are quite troubling.

There are nearly 60 million women of childbearing age (15–44) in the United States. In 1985, 30 percent of these women were current smokers and 58 percent were current drinkers, with 4 percent reporting two or more drinks per day (National Center for Health Statistics [1988]). According to the National Institute on Drug Abuse (NIDA), 15 percent (8 million) of women age 15–44 reported current uses of illicit substances in 1985, with 5.6 million women over age 17 reporting current use of marijuana (JAMA [1989]). According to NIDA, in 1988 one million women age 15–44 reported using cocaine during the previous month (State University of New York [1990]). It has been estimated that 150,000 to 200,000 women in the United States are addicted to narcotics, and that there are 5,000–10,000 infants born to these women each year (Edelin et al. [1988]). Each year 70,000 tobacco-affected infants and 50,000 alcohol-affected infants are born with an additional 5,000 annual cases of fetal alcohol syndrome (*Medical Benefits* [1990]).

Based on a sample of 8,974 cocaine-positive infants in eight cities in 1989, the U.S. Department of Health and Human Services estimated that 100,000 babies exposed to cocaine are born each year in the United States (Kusserow [1990]). This estimate (2.5 percent of all live births) coincides with the results of a 1988 survey of 36 U.S. hospitals by Dr. Ira Chasnoff (National Association for Perinatal Addiction Research and Education) showing that 11 percent of live births were exposed to some type of illicit drugs, and with an estimate by Prof. Richard Barth (UC Berkeley School of Social Work) that 1–4 percent of all babies are crack-exposed (Gieringer [1990]).

In 1989 there were 4.02 million live births in the United States, and 38,900 infant deaths (National Center for Health Statistics [1990b]). These statistics place the United States 22nd in world infant-mortality rankings, well behind a number of countries with substantially lower per capita incomes, including Hong Kong, Singapore, and the United Kingdom (Poullier [1989]; Yeun [1990]). In 1989 there were an additional 940,000 spontaneous (unplanned) abortions (personal communication, Alan Gutmacher Institute, November 1990). In 1988, 270,681 (7 percent) of all U.S. live births were low birth weight—less than 2,500 gm. (National Center for Health Statistics [1990a]). Of these, 48,580 (18 percent) were less than 1,500 gm. In 1988, 13 percent of U.S. black live births were low birth weight.

There is little question that maternal drug abuse plays a leading role in these poor U.S. infant vital statistics. Table 12.1 lists several of the major infant health outcomes that have been associated with maternal abuse of five drug classes: cocaine/crack, heroin and/or other opiates, amphetamines, alcohol, and tobacco. Less is known about the fetal or infant health effects of marijuana, hallucinogens, and other illicit drugs. It is known, however, that fetal development is highly sensitive to many biochemical influences. Many drugs that are safe and effective for adults can also be teratogenic (see, for example Hawkins [1987]). It should be pointed out that causation has not been definitely established for use of any of these drugs for each of the associated health outcomes. Particularly in the United States, maternal drug abuse is correlated with low socioeconomic status, low education, poor access to prenatal and perinatal medical care, dysfunctional family structure, and nonwhite race/ethnicity. All these factors are also correlated with poor infant health outcomes. This is not the case for maternal drug abuse studies from other, particularly western European, countries (see, for example, Verloove-Vanhorick et al. [1988]).

As in the case of the "smoking-causes-lung-cancer" debate between the tobacco industry and everyone else, it is not ethical to undertake a randomized experimental trial of the health effects of each of these drugs to establish definitive causation, but the evidence from animal model studies, epidemiological case-control studies, clinical observations, and laboratory experiments is highly suggestive of causation in all these associations. Relative to more epidemiological issues, the evidence on perinatal health outcomes is quite sharply focused, since many infant health outcomes are directly observable in the first year following concep-

TABLE 12.1. PERINATAL HEALTH OUTCOMES OF THE DEVELOPING INFANT ASSOCIATED WITH MATERNAL DRUG ABUSE

Pregnancy Outcomes	Longer-Term Clinical Problems	Behavioral or Developmental Problems
Cocaine and Crack		
spontaneous abortion	sudden infant death	slow development
precipitous delivery	syndrome	hemiplegia
abruption of the placenta	maternally transmitted	irritability
low birth weight	infections	tremors
perinatal cerebral	respiratory distress	lagging motor development
infarctions	apnea	impaired orientation and
genitourinary	seizures	state regulation
malformation	EEG abnormalities	sleep dysfunction
cardiac defects	secondary withdrawal	poor feeding
CNS defects		hypertonia
hypoxia		abnormal visual potentials
		auditory system defects
		spastic quadriparesis
		parenting dysfunction
		lagging visual motor
		coordination
Heroin and Methadone		
spontaneous abortion	aspiration syndrome	permanent head-
premature delivery	intravenously acquired,	circumference
low birth weight	maternally transmitted	retardation
neonatal meconium	infections	irritability
opiate addiction	sudden infant death	tremors
withdrawal syndrome	syndrome	difficult to comfort
Amphetamines		
premature delivery	clinical seizures	slow development
low birth weight		poor feeding
placental abruption		poor visual tracking
microcephaly		tremors
fetal distress		sleep dysfunction
		lethargy
Alcohol		
prenatal growth deficiency		mild to moderate mental
microcephaly		retardation
low birth weight		facial dysmorphia
cardiac abnormalities		irritability
neurologic defects		sleep dysfunction

(table continues on next page)

TABLE 12.1.   PERINATAL HEALTH OUTCOMES OF THE DEVELOPING INFANT
                ASSOCIATED WITH MATERNAL DRUG ABUSE (continued)

Pregnancy Outcomes	Longer-Term Clinical Problems	Behavioral or Developmental Problems
Tobacco		
spontaneous abortion	sudden infant death	reading and math
neural tube defects	syndrome	development delay at
premature delivery	reduced risk of respiratory	age 10
low birth weight	distress syndrome	growth retardation
placental defects		

SOURCE: See "References for Table 12.1."

tion. The longer term developmental effects are less well studied and more
uncertain. In the case of the newest and most damaging form of cocaine—
crack—the initial exposed U.S. crack-baby cohort is only five to six years old at
present.

The U.S. Department of Health and Human Services has estimated the
average costs for delivery, perinatal care, and foster care services at $33,430 per
cocaine-exposed baby (Kusserow [1990]). They estimated that the additional
developmental, educational, and health-services costs through age 5 (borne almost completely by taxpayers) at $169,033 per cocaine-exposed babies. With
around 100,000 babies each year exposed to cocaine prenatally, this works out
to slightly more than $20 billion annually for supplemental care of new cocaine-
exposed babies. This figure substantially understates the external costs of maternal
cocaine abuse, because it ignores the value of lives lost through cocaine-induced
infant mortality and spontaneous abortion.

Using consistent costing methodology across each drug category, I will now
present external cost estimates for the four most important classes of maternal
drug abuse: heroin/opiates, cocaine/crack, tobacco, and alcohol. Although I
believe these calculations to be conservative, I acknowledge that the parameters
used in them are not known with much precision. During the past three years,
however, there has been a rapid increase in clinical knowledge regarding the
infant risks and outcomes of maternal drug exposure, particularly regarding the
effects of cocaine/crack, characterized by Dr. Suzanne Dixon [1989] of U.C.
San Diego as ". . . this horrible human experiment."

As shown in Table 12.1, each of these four drug categories is associated with
low birth weight (LBW), a potentially life-threatening neonatal condition. Table
12.2 summarizes calculations of the numbers of infants experiencing death or
serious permanent handicap (such as severe mental retardation, cerebral palsy,

TABLE 12.2. ESTIMATED ANNUAL U.S. INCIDENCE OF FETAL/INFANT HEALTH OUTCOMES AS RELATED TO FOUR MAJOR DRUG CLASSES

Drug Category	Cocaine	Heroin	Tobacco	Alcohol (more than two drinks/day)
Relative risk for				
Low birth weight (<2,499 gm)	5.0	3.0	2.0	17
Drug exposure	2.50%	0.19%	35.00%	4.20%
Attributable risk for				
Low birth weight (< 2,499 gm)	9.09%	0.37%	25.93%	2.86%
Birth weight (<1,500 gm)				
Infant mortality	2,208	91	3,778	694
Permanent handicap	297	38	504	291
Birth weight (<1,500–1,999 gm)				
Infant mortality	234	10	668	74
Permanent handicap	836	34	454	263
Birth weight (<2,000–2,499 gm)				
Infant mortality	775	32	2,211	244
Permanent handicap	684	28	371	215
All low birth weight				
Infant mortality	3,218	132	6,658	1,011
Permanent handicap	2,448	101	1,330	769
Spontaneous abortion	4,222	317	59,103	7,092

SOURCE: See text.

incapacitating seizures, traumatic injury, and the like) or spontaneous abortion as a result of maternal drug exposure. The LBW relative risk for cocaine is synthesized from Petitti and Coleman [1990] (RR 4.0, 95% CI 1.8, 8.9) and Chasnof et al. [1989] (LBW with cocaine use 25%, matched controls 5%, p < .003). This is probably a very conservative estimate, since Petitti and Coleman found that the LBW relative risk for crack used exclusively throughout pregnancy is 10.1, and the current cocaine epidemic is primarily one of crack usage.

Koren et al. [1989] have suggested that there has been a bias against the presentation and dissemination of scientific studies failing to observe reproductive hazards associated with cocaine use. Astonishingly, Koren and his associates failed to report power calculations (probability of Type Two errors) for those negative studies they identified. Taking just six well-designed and controlled studies published in peer-reviewed scientific journals (Petitti and Coleman [1990]; Chasnoff et al. [1989]; Cherukuri et al. [1988]; Burkett et al. [1990]; Dixon [1989]; Chouteau et al. [1988]; and Little et al. [1989]) the Type One (Alpha) error probability that all could be mistaken on the independent positive association between cocaine use by pregnant women and low birth weight is much less than one in one trillion.

The LBW relative risk for heroin is extrapolated from Edelin et al. [1988] (LBW in heroin/methadone users 30 percent, matched controls 11 percent—highly significant). The LBW relative risk for tobacco is taken from the U.S. Department of Health, Education, and Welfare [1979]. It falls between the Petitti and Coleman estimates for tobacco used but stopped during pregnancy (RR 1.3, 95% CI 0.6,2.6) and for tobacco used throughout pregnancy (RR 3.1, 95% CI 2.1, 4.5). The LBW relative risk for alcohol (three or more drinks per day) is taken from Petitti and Coleman (RR 1.7, 95% CI 0.7, 4.1).

The relative risk of spontaneous abortion (1.24) for maternal drug abusers is estimated by comparing the Gutmacher Institute's national estimate of 14.7 percent to Brukett et al.'s report that 18.6 percent of pregnancies for drug-abusing females resulting in spontaneous abortion. This relative risk rate matches that found for maternal smokers and is conservative for those consuming three or more alcoholic beverages per day (Harlap and Shiono [1980]).

The estimated percent of U.S. births exposed to each drug category is as reported above. I note that the alcohol prevalence figures for U.S. women of childbearing age is for those that report drinking two or more alcoholic beverages per day, while the Petitti and Coleman relative risk estimate is for those consuming three or more drinks per day. Self-reported drinking habits have been found to be unreliable. Manning et al. [1990a] state that two or more reported drinks per day translates into five or more actual drinks per day.

The percentage of LBW births resulting in death or permanent handicap is taken from Verloove-Vanhorick et al.'s [1988] survey of the Dutch population. They report a 50 percent infant mortality rate for very low birth weight (<1500 gm) live infants born to maternal drug abusers (excluding tobacco abusers) compared to 30 percent in the total Dutch population (including tobacco abusers), with a corresponding permanent handicap rate of 21 percent compared to 4 percent. These rates probably understate the United States experience, since the Netherlands has substantially less socioeconomic variation than the United States and better perinatal-care access, particularly for their drug-abusing populations. I applied these outcome rates to all drug-exposed very-low-birth-weight babies. The mortality rate for LBWs above 1,499 gm is assumed to be 5 percent (Resnick et al. [1989]). The permanent severe handicap rate is estimated by applying the

TABLE 12.3.   ANNUAL EXTERNAL COSTS OF MATERNAL DRUG ABUSE
(PARTIAL LIST): UNITED STATES, 1990 ($ BILLIONS)

Drug	NICU	Social Hospital and Short-Term Foster Care	Permanent Neurological Handicap	Infant Mortality	Other Developmental Disabilities	Total
Cocaine	$0.36	$2.99	$2.14	$10.06	$6.25	$21.79
Heroin	$0.01	$0.22	$0.09	$0.41	$0.47	$1.21
Tobacco	$1.02	$0.00	$1.16	$20.80	$87.50	$110.48
Alcohol	$0.11	$0.50	$0.67	$3.16	$10.50	$14.94

SOURCE: See text.

Verloove-Vanhorick et al. rates to NICU admissions probability estimates for the >1500 gm LBW categories reported by Oster et al. [1988].

The total estimated drug-related infant deaths matches independent information that infants born to substance-abusing mothers (excluding tobacco abusers) are 2.5 times more likely to die than other infants (Chavkin et al. [1989]; Rosen and Johnson [1988]), and that 3 to 7 percent of neonates born to drug-abusing mothers die (Martin et al. [1988]). The rates of tobacco-related infant fatalities match previous estimates. For example, the 1980 Surgeon General's report on Smoking and Women (U.S. Department of Health and Human Services [1980]) describes the relative infant mortality risk for maternal smokers as ranging between 1.01 and 2.45. It describes a particularly large and well-designed Finnish study showing an infant-child mortality relative risk of 1.5. This would translate into 5,764 U.S. infant deaths attributable to maternal smoking in 1989.

The data in Table 12.2, Table 12.3, and Figure 12.1 provide a summary of the U.S. annual maternal drug abuse-related external costs. It is only a partial list because it excludes many drugs of abuse, it excludes AFDC and other welfare benefits that are provided to the drug-incapacitated mother and her household, it excludes the costs of pain and suffering to the infants and those around them, and it excludes longer-term health consequences, many of which are not yet observable. The NICU cost estimates are derived using Oster's [1988] admission rate and cost estimates, updated to 1990 price levels. For the tobacco category, they match Manning's [1990b] estimates, after correcting for price-level change.

There is substantial evidence that infants born to drug-abusing mothers, particularly cocaine-exposed infants, remain substantially longer in the hospital after birth, both because of additional medical complications and under social holds because of dysfunctional or nonexistent family support structures (Hurt et al. [1990]; Noble [1990]; Chavkin et al. [1989]; State University of New York [1990]; Kusserow [1990]). Many of these infants are ultimately placed in foster

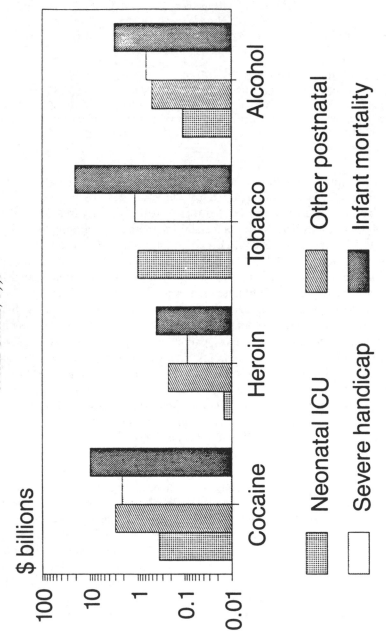

FIGURE 12.1. POSTNATAL COSTS OF MATERNAL DRUG ABUSE: UNITED STATES, 1990

care. I have applied Kusserow's [1990] estimate of these costs (roughly $30,000 per drug-exposed infant) to the number of infants exposed prenatally to cocaine and heroin, and to those born with fetal alcohol syndrome. The level of such costs associated with maternal tobacco abuse was conservatively assumed to be negligible. Costs of managing permanent neurological handicaps were taken as the present discounted value of lifetime institutional care services valued at $30,000 per year over the infants' expected lifetime (Hay and Daum [1987], [1990]).

Using a willingness-to-pay formulation, the present discounted average economic value of life was taken to be $3.25 million per infant fatality (Hay [1989]; Hay and Daum [1987], [1990]). Because of the controversy surrounding the value of fetal lives, beyond estimating the numbers of spontaneous abortions in Table 12.2, I do not include an explicit economic calculation of the losses due to drug-related spontaneous abortions.

I estimate the longer-term behavioral and developmental disability associated with prenatal drug exposure at roughly 2 percent of total economic life value among those exposed. Although somewhat arbitrary, this level is motivated by examining the potential long-term impacts of maternal drug abuse on mental development and future earnings potential. There is evidence that prenatal tobacco exposure results in significant long-term developmental delay. Butler and Goldstein [1973] reported that children of smoking mothers averaged four months retardation on reading, mathematics, and general ability tests when compared to children of nonsmokers, after adjusting for associated social and biological factors. Using Hay's [1980] estimate that the earnings rate of return to years of education is 6 percent per year of schooling, a reduction in schooling performance equal to four months of education would translate into a 2 percent reduction in lifetime earnings and in the lifetime opportunity cost of leisure. No information is available on the impacts of maternal abuse of the other drug categories (heroin, alcohol, or cocaine) on long-term ability and earnings outcomes, but I presume that the tobacco-based estimates are conservative for these other drugs.

The choice of a 2 percent reduction in lifetime economic value can also be motivated, subjectively, on a willingness-to-pay basis by considering the formidable list of fetal developmental abnormalities (see Table 12.1) associated with maternal drug use, and considering under a fully unrestricted and legalized drug regime, beyond the infant deaths and severe handicaps associated with low birth weight, what sort of insurance premium an average individual would be willing to pay to ensure that their own mothers would have abstained from drug use during pregnancy. If this hypothetical insurance premium were spread across the entire birth cohort, the cost would be less than 1 percent of lifetime earnings.

External Costs 2:
Accidents and Injuries

Little is known regarding the rates of homicide, aggravated assault, injury, property loss, and accidental damage imposed on others by illicit drug abusers. There is, however, substantial information on the costs of the two legal drugs, alcohol and tobacco. The Centers for Disease Control [1990] estimate that in 1987, 1.5 million years of potential life were lost before age 65, and 2.7 million years of potential life were lost due to alcohol consumption. Rice et al. [1986] calculated that in 1980, 3.9 million years of life were lost due to smoking. These figures translate into enormous economic costs. Using my willingness-to-pay estimate for an average life year of $64,250 ($11 per hour × 16 hours per day × 365 days per year), the cost for alcohol-lost years of life is at least $173 billion annually, and the cost for tobacco-lost years of life is more than $251 billion.

A large part of these and the other costs of these drugs is borne directly by the abusers of tobacco and alcohol—but far from all of them. After updating to 1990 prices, translating the rather obtuse reporting of external costs in terms of packs of cigarettes and ounces of alcohol consumed, and once more noting that their calculations excluded the impacts of prenatal drug exposure, the Manning group's [1990a] annual external cost estimate is $5.71 billion for tobacco and $37.30 billion for alcohol. For tobacco, this includes the external costs of medical care, sick leave, group life insurance, nursing home care, and fire damage. For alcohol, this includes all of these plus the lives of nondrinkers and the property damage caused by alcohol-related motor-vehicle accidents and costs of criminal justice.

There is much literature on the costs of smoking (for example, Rice et al. [1986]; Kronebusch [1989]), but there does not appear to be other external cost estimates in the literature beyond those of Manning [1990a]. Adrian [1988] estimated the social costs of alcohol consumption in Canada at $5.7 billion ($ Canadian); $1.3 billion of this was for reduced labor productivity and $1.4 billion was for social welfare services, neither of which corresponds to calculations made by Manning, partly because the set of government welfare programs differ between the United States and Canada. Adrian fails to cite the year used to reference prices (if any). Under the assumption that costs were measured in 1981 Canadian dollars, and translating this to 1990 U.S. dollars and the U.S. population, her estimate would be on the order of $60 billion. This matches the Parker et al. [1987] social-cost estimate for Minnesota in 1983, which, when extrapolated to the entire United States, is about $62 billion. The Parker social cost figure does include costs for treatment of fetal alcohol syndrome and child abuse, which are excluded from the Adrian and Manning estimates.

DISCUSSION AND CONCLUSION

Table 12.4 and Figure 12.2 summarize my partial list of the annual external costs of drug abuse in the United States. Little is known about the accident and injury rates for cocaine and heroin (or marijuana, PCP, or other illicit drugs), but they are probably substantially lower than those for alcohol, precisely because of the relative success in restricting population access to these drugs. By my estimate, tobacco and alcohol, the two legal drugs, impose by far the largest total external costs on society. The external costs of illicit drugs, particularly cocaine and crack, are also substantial.

Ostrowski [1989] suggests that drug criminals obtain $80 billion annually in illegal gains from the supply of illicit drugs. Most of this revenue, however, is not really the economic cost of drug supply (real productive resources actually used in the production and distribution of illegal drugs) but rather transfer payments from consumers of illegal drugs to those willing to provide them in an extremely risky environment. As is apparent from any big-city murder statistics, the illegal drug market satisfies none of the prerequisites for perfect competition.

Modified from a Research Triangle Institute report, Ostrowski [1989] provides a more appropriate calculation for the external costs caused by drug-prohibition laws (mortality, crime, and interdiction) of $21.37 billion annually. Although I dispute his methods and estimates, this amount is only about equal to my estimate of the external costs inflicted only on infants, by mothers abusing cocaine or crack. There is a fundamental, qualitative difference between the costs that Ostrowski is worried about and those I am discussing.

TABLE 12.4.   ANNUAL EXTERNAL COSTS OF DRUG ABUSE (PARTIAL LIST): UNITED STATES, 1990 ($ BILLIONS)

Drug	Prenatal Maternal Drug Exposure	Property Damage, Accidents, and Injuries to Others	Total
Cocaine	$21.79	?	$21.79
Heroin	$1.21	?	$1.21
Tobacco	$110.48	$5.71	$116.19
Alcohol	$14.94	$37.30	$52.24

SOURCE: See text.

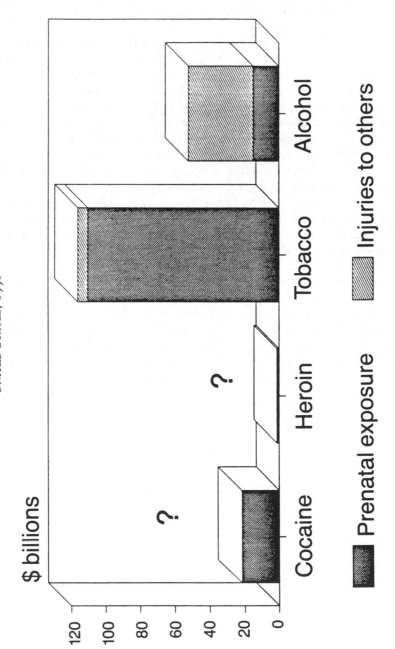

FIGURE 12.2. ANNUAL EXTERNAL COSTS OF DRUG ABUSE:
UNITED STATES, 1990

It is indeed tragic when a drug abuser dies from overdose of bad heroin or from AIDS by using unsterile needles; maybe less so when a drug dealer dies in a gun battle over street turf. Some of these costs would probably disappear in a fully legalized drug regime; they would clearly not disappear in a regime that maintains taxes, licensures, or other restrictions on drug use. The users themselves have some say over the vast majority of these "costs," however. The libertarian in particular should be sensitive to the fact that someone who engages in drug dealing or drug abuse under the current set of legal prohibitions is at least partially responsible for the consequences of his or her own actions. Under any set of drug laws, however, the infant who dies in the neonatal intensive care unit because his mother smoked crack could never be anything but an innocent victim of drug abuse.

If drugs are legalized, there will be more of these dead infants. I agree that the crack epidemic, like the cocaine, heroin, and LSD epidemics that preceded it, probably has its own natural cyclical momentum, with a rapid initial increase in abuse followed at some point by a slowing in usage and an ultimate decline (Musto [1987]). Where we are in that cycle now, and who should take credit for the recent welcome slowing in cocaine abuse, is difficult if not impossible to pin down. Given the long-term dynamics, however, drug abuse can only rise at every point of the historic cycle under a legalized or less restrictive drug-law regime than under a more restrictive one. As government restrictions on drug sales and consumption ease, the demand curve shifts up at every price and the supply curve shifts out. A loosening in government restrictions will almost certainly lead to a substantial increase in the utilization of currently illicit drugs (Becker et al. [1990]). The attendant increase in external costs, particularly to the infant and child victims of parental drug abuse, is not worth the dubious benefits of more people getting stoned more often and more easily.

Some might argue that the solution to the external costs of maternal drug abuse would be to crack down hard not on all women who use drugs, but on those who use drugs and get pregnant. This appears to me to open an even nastier can of worms. At least since Roe vs. Wade, the legal rights of fetuses in the United States have been rather weak. To put it mildly, it is problematic to enforce laws saying that a woman cannot expose the fetus to drugs during pregnancy, but she can abort it during the first two trimesters.

Regardless of one's position on the abortion laws, allowing legal access to drugs while at the same time applying criminal sanctions to women who carry drug-damaged fetuses to term appears to be fundamentally unfair and unworkable. For many people, drugs and sex go together. With legal adult drug use and illegal fetal drug exposure, a man could wake up in the morning after an intimate night none the worse while, unbeknownst to her, his female partner could become an overnight felon. Such laws would place the drug-abusing mother in an untenable adversarial position via-à-vis the medical profession and the law. Is there anyone foolish enough to argue that men should be granted legal access to drugs but not fertile women? Or that any such restrictions could ever be enforced?

As I mentioned above, the appropriate analogy for justification of the drug laws, all the more ironic because of the enormous damage caused by alcohol abuse itself, is to the drunk-driving laws. A drunk driver is not guaranteed to cause a traffic accident any more than a crack-addicted woman is guaranteed to spontaneously abort—although the risks may be lower for the drunk driver. We outlaw drunk driving rather than merely outlawing the accidents that it causes because the activity of drunk driving is unacceptably risky to others, and because this sends an unambiguous warning that drinking and driving is dangerous and lacks societal approval.

Some have advocated a balanced rational approach where, on a drug-by-drug basis, the external costs are tallied and a set of taxes or licenses for controlled and permitted use are established for those drugs with sufficiently low thresholds of external cost. I see two problems with this.

First, using the estimates in Table 12.4 and for the alcohol abuse category considering just those who report two or more alcoholic beverages per day, the external costs for each of these drug categories work out to more than $1,000 per drug user per year. For cocaine, the external costs would exceed $20,000 per female drug user per year. Such a high tax or licensure fee levied per dose or per person is guaranteed to generate a flourishing black market with most or all of the attendant drug-law enforcement problems that are so roundly criticized today. We could well end up with both a greater external cost burden and a greater drug-law enforcement problem.

Second, one of the biggest impediments to educating the public and to slowing the demand for the licit drugs, tobacco and alcohol, is precisely the fact that they are legal. When drugs are legal to produce and consume, the producers become respectable and very powerful legitimate economic special interests. It is quite natural for a U.S. senator from a tobacco-producing state to filibuster against the reduction in government tobacco-price supports or against antismoking-education campaigns, and for political parties to realize that they have to go along with him to carry the South. It is respectable for California wine producers to give large contributions to libertarian think tanks because alcohol is safe as long as the battle lines are drawn at marijuana, heroin, and cocaine.

Once heroin and cocaine are legalized, regardless of how fair, rational, and balanced are the paper legal restrictions on their use, a vast political and economic industrial force will surface as a legitimate and respectable pillar of the local community. Once respectable, the drug lords, who currently find harassment by U.S. Customs, Drug Enforcement Agency, and FBI officials to be a relatively minor irritant, will have no problem locating and getting their message to the state houses or the congressional office buildings, if and when their newly virtuous industry falls under attack.

I do not have the answer to the drug-policy dilemma other than to keep moving ahead pretty much as we have been. I would focus substantially more effort, using both carrots and sticks, on discouraging demand (Goldstein and Kalant [1990]). I agree with the critics that supply interdiction, by itself, is extremely expensive and ultimately futile. If we are going to make policy for this difficult and tragic problem with simplistic solutions that can be fit into 30-second TV sound bytes, then I would definitely prefer a real drug war, with swift and certain punishment of casual drug users, to a drug-legalization surrender.

REFERENCES

Adrian, M. [1988], "Social Costs of Alcohol," *Canadian Journal of Public Health* 79 (September/October 1988), pp. 316–22.

Amaro, H., Zuckerman, B., Cabral, H. [1989], "Drug Use among Adolescent Mothers: Profile of Risk," *Pediatrics* 84, no. 1 (July 1989).

Becker, G., Grossman, M., Murphy, K. [1990], "Rational Addiction and the Effect of Price on Consumption," paper presented at the the Hoover Institution Conference on U.S. Drug Policy, Stanford, Calif., November 1990.

Burkett, G., Yasin, S., Palow, D. [1990], "Perinatal Implications of Cocaine Exposure," *Journal of Reproductive Medicine* 35, no. 1, pp. 35–42.

Butler G., and Goldstein, H. [1973], "Smoking in Pregnancy and Subsequent Child Development," *British Journal of Medicine* 4, pp. 573–75.

Centers for Disease Control [1990], "Alcohol-Related Mortality and Years of Potential Life Lost—United States, 1987," *MMWR* 39, no. 11 (March 23, 1990), pp. 174–87.

Chasnoff, I. J., Griffith, D. R., MacGregor, S., Dirkes, K., Burns, K. A. [1989], "Temporal Patterns of Cocaine Use in Pregnancy," *JAMA* 261, no. 12 (March 24/31, 1989), pp. 1741–44.

Chavkin, W., Driver, C. R., Forman, P. [1989], "The Crisis in New York City's Perinatal Services," *New York State Journal of Medicine*, December 1989, pp. 658–63.

Cherukuri, R., Minkoff, H., Feldman, J., Parekh, A., Glass, L. [1988], "A Cohort Study of Alkaloidal Cocaine ("Crack") in Pregnancy," *Obstetrics and Gynecology* 72, no. 2 (August 1988) p. 147.

Chouteau, M., Namerow, P. B., Leppert, P. [1988], "The Effect of Cocaine Abuse on Birth Weight and Gestational Age," *Obstetrics and Gynecology* 72, no. 3, part 1 (September 1988), pp. 351–54.

Dixon, S. D. [1989], "Effects of Transplacental Exposure to Cocaine and Methamphetamine on the Neonate," Speciality Conference, *The Western Journal of Medicine* 150, no. 4 (April 1989), pp. 436–42.

Edelin, E., Gurganious, L., Golar, K., et al. [1988], "Methadone Maintenance in Pregnancy: Consequences to Care and Outcome," *Obstetrics and Gynecology* 71, no. 3, part 1 (March), pp. 399–404.

Friedman, M. [1972], *Newsweek* column for May 2, 1972, as reprinted in *New Dimensions*, June 1990, p. 56.

Friedman, M. [1989], "An Open Letter to Bill Bennett," *Wall Street Journal*, Sept. 7, 1989, p. A16.

Gieringer, D. [1990], "How Many Crack Babies?" *Drug Policy Letter* II, no. 2 (April), p. 4–6.

Goldstein A., and Kalant, H. [1990], "Drug Policy: Striking the Right Balance," *Science* 249, pp. 1513–21.

Gorsky, R. D., Schwartz, E., Dennis, D. [1988], "The Mortality, Morbidity, and Economic Costs of Alcohol Abuse in New Hampshire," *Preventive Medicine* 17 (1988), pp. 736–45.

Grinspoon, L., and Bakalar, J., [1985], *Cocaine: A Drug and Its Social Evolution*, rev. ed., New York: Basic Books.

Harlap, S., Shiono, P. H. [1980], "Alcohol, Smoking, and Incidence of Spontaneous Abortions in the First and Second Trimester," *The Lancet*, July 26, 1980, p. 73.

Hawkins, D., ed. [1987], *Drugs and Pregnancy: Human Teratogenesis and Related Problems*, 2nd ed., Edinburgh: Churchill Livingstone.

Hay, J. [1980], *Occupational Choice and Occupational Earnings: Selectivity Bias in a Simultaneous Logit-OLS Model*, Ph.D. diss., Yale University, published by National Technical Information Service, Rockville, Maryland.

Hay, J. [1989], "Econometric Issues in Modeling the Costs of AIDS," *Health Policy* 11, no. 2 (April 1989), pp. 125–45.

Hay, J., and Daum R., [1987], "Cost-Benefit Analysis of Two Strategies for Prevention of Haemophilus Influenzae Type B Infection," *Pediatrics* 80, no. 3 (September 1987), p. 319–29.

Hay, J., and Daum, R., [1990], "Cost-Benefit Analysis of Haemophilus Influenzae Type B Prevention: Conjugate Vaccination at Eighteen Months of Age," *Pediatric Infectious Disease Journal* 9 (April 1990), pp. 246–52.

Hospital & Community Psychiatry [19889], "National Study of Drug Abuse Treatment Finds Benefits Include Less Drug Use, Fewer Crimers," News & Notes 40, no. 12 (December 1989), pp. 1309–10.

Hurt, H., Porat, R., Gedon, D. E., Sheffer, E. C., Brodsky, N. L. [1989], "Nursery Length of Stay (LOS) Is Increased in Infants of Cocaine-Abusing Mothers," *Pediatric Res.* (1989), p. 254A.

JAMA [1989], "Scope, Specifics of Maternal Drug Use, Effects on Fetus Are Beginning to Emcrgc from Studies," *Journal of the American Medical Association* 261, no. 12 (March 24/31, 1989), pp. 1688–89.

Kleiman, M., and Saiger, A. [1989], "Drug Legalization: The Importance of Asking the Right Question," Working Paper #89-01-16, Program in Criminal Justice Policy and Management, John F. Kennedy School of Government, Harvard University.

Koren, G., Graham, K., Shear, H., and Einarson, T. [1989], "Bias against the Null

Hypothesis: The Reproductive Hazards of Cocaine," *The Lancet* (December 16, 1989), pp. 1440–42.

Kronebusch, K. [1989], "Smoking and Economic Costs," *Cancer Investigation* 7(5), pp. 463–77 (1989), U.S. Congress, Office of Technology Assessment, Washington, D.C.

Kusserow, R. [1990], *Crack Babies*, A Report of the Office of the Inspector General, Department of Health and Human Services, Washington D.C. (February, 1990).

Leu, R., and Schaub, T. [1983], "Does Smoking Increase Medical Care Expenditure?" *Social Science and Medicine* 17, pp. 1907–14.

Little, B. B., Snell, J. M., Klein, V. R., Gilstrap, L. C. [1989], "Cocaine Abuse during Pregnancy: Maternal and Fatal Implications," *Obstetrics and Gynecology* 73, no. 2 (February 1989), pp. 157–60.

Manning, W., Keler, E., Newhouse, J., Sloss, E., and Wasserman, J. [1989a], "The Taxes of Sin: Do Smokers and Drinkers Pay Their Way?" *Journal of the American Medical Association* 261, pp. 1604–9.

Manning, W., Keeler, E., Newhouse, J., Sloss, E., and Wasserman, J. [1989b], "The Taxes of Sin: Do Smokers and Drinkers Pay Their Way?" (Reply) *Journal of the American Medical Association* 262, p. 901.

Martin, J. N., Martin, R. W., Hess, L. W., McColgin, S. W., McCall, J. F., and Morrison, J. C. [1988], "Pregnancy-Associated Substance Abuse and Addiction: Current Concepts and Management," *Journal Mississippi State Medical Association* (December 1988), pp. 369–74.

McCormick, M. C. [1989], "Long-Term Follow-up of Infants Discharged from Neonatal Intensive Care Units," *JAMA* 261, no. 12 (March 24/31, 1989), pp. 1767–72.

Medical Benefits [1990], "Troubling Trends: The Health of America's Next Generation," 7, no. 8 (April), p. 6.

Mill, J. S. [1859], "On Liberty," in *Utilitarianism, Liberty and Representative Government*, New York: Dutton, 1910, pp. 61–170.

Musto, D. [1987], "The History of Legislative Control over Opium, Cocaine, and Their Derivatives," in R. Hamowy, ed. *Dealing with Drugs: Consequence of Government Control*, San Francisco: Pacific Research Institute for Public Policy Research, pp. 37–72.

Nadelmann, E. [1988], "The Case for Legalization," *The Public Interest*, no. 92 (Summer), pp. 3–31.

National Center for Health Statistics [1988], "Adult Health Practices in the United States and Canada," *Vital and Health Statistics*, series 5, no. 3, DHHS pub. no. (PHS) 88-1479, Public Health Service, Washington, D.C.

National Center for Health Statistics [1990a], "Advance Report of Final Natality Statistics, 1988," *Monthly Vital Statistics Report* 39, no. 4, suppl. (August), Public Health Service, Hyattsville, Md.

National Center for Health Statistics [1990b], "Annual Summary of Births, Marriages, Divorces, and Deaths: United States, 1989," *Monthly Vital Statistics Report* 38, no. 13, suppl. (August), Public Health Service, Hyattsville, Md.

Noble, L. M., Kim, M., Checola, R. T., Hand, I. L., Yoon, J. J. (spon. by G. Nathenson)

[1989], "Cost of Maternal Drug Use on Neonatal Care in the South Bronx," *Pediatric Res.* (1989), p. 225A.

Ooms, T., and Herendeen, L. [1990], "Drugs, Mothers, Kids and Ways to Cope," Background Briefing Report and Meeting Highlights, Family Impact Seminar, American Association for Marriage and Family Therapy, Research and Education Foundation, Washington, D.C. (April 1990).

Oster, G., Delea, T. E., Colditz, G. A. [1988], "Maternal Smoking during Pregnancy and Expenditures on Neonatal Health Care," *American Journal of Preventive Medicine* 4, no. 4 (1988) pp. 216–19.

Ostrowski, J. [1989], "Thinking about Drug Legalization," *Policy Analysis*, Cato Institute, no. 121 (May 25, 1989).

Parker, D. L., Shultz, J. A., Gertz, L., Berkelman, R., Remington, P. L. [1987], "The Social and Economic Costs of Alcohol Abuse in Minnesota," *American Journal of Public Health* (1987), pp. 982–86.

Petitti, D. B., Coleman, C. [1990], "Cocaine and the Risk of Low Birth Weight," *American Journal of Public Health* 80, no. 1 (January 1990), pp. 25–28.

Poullier, J. P. [1989], "Compendium; Health Care Expenditure and Other Data," *Health Care Financing Review*, Annual Supplement (December).

Resnick, M. B., Carter, R. L., Ariet, M., Bucciarelli, R. L., Evans, J. H., Furlough, R. R., Ausbon, W. W., Curran, J. S. [1989], "Effect of Birth Weight, Race, and Sex on Survival of Low-Birth-Weight Infants in Neonatal Intensive Care," *American Journal of Obstetrics and Gynecology* 161, no. 1 (1989), pp. 184–87.

Rice, D. P., Hodgson, T. A., Sinsheimer, P., Browner, W., Kopstein, A. N. [1986], "The Economic Costs of the Health Effects of Smoking, 1984," *Milbank Quarterly* 64, no. 4, pp. 489–547.

Rosen, T. S., Johnson, J. H. [1988], "Drug-Addicted Mothers, Their Infants, and SIDS," *Annals of the New York Academy of Sciences*, pp. 89–95.

Rufleth, P. [1989], "The Taxes of Sin: Do Smokers Pay Their Way?" (letter) *Journal of the American Medical Association* 262, p. 901.

Schelling, T. C. [1968], "The Life You Save May Be Your Own," in *Problems in Public Expenditure Analysis*, Washington, D.C.: Brookings Institution.

State University of New York [1990], *Research* 10, no. 2, p. 20.

Szasz, T. [1987], "The Morality of Drug Controls," in R. Hamowy, ed., *Dealing with Drugs: Consequence of Government Control*, San Francisco: Pacific Research Institute for Public Policy Research, pp. 327–51.

U.S. Department of Health, Education, and Welfare [1979], *Smoking and Health: A Report of the Surgeon General*, Washington, D.C., DHEW Pub. (PHS) 79–50066.

U.S. Department of Health and Human Services [1980], *The Health Consequences of Smoking for Women: A Report of the Surgeon General*, Public Health Service, Washington, D.C., pp. 215–25.

U.S. Department of Health and Human Services [1989], *Reducing the Health Consequences of Smoking: A Report of the Surgeon General*, DHHS Pub. (PHS) 89–8411.

Valentine, P. H., Jackson, J. C., Kalina, R. E., Woodrum, D. E. [1989], "Increased Survival of Low Birth Weight Infants: Impact on the Incidence of Retinopathy of Prematurity," *Pediatrics* 84, no. 3 (September 1989), pp. 442–44.

van Zeben-van der Aa, T. E., Verloove-Vanhorick, S. P., Brand, R., Ruys, J. H. [1989], "Morbidity of Very Low Birthweight Infants at Corrected Age of Two Years in a Geographically Defined Population," *The Lancet* (February 4, 1989), pp. 253–54.

Verloove-Vanhorick, S., van Zeben-van der Aa, T. E., Verwey, R. [1988], "Addicted Mothers and Preterm Babies: A Disastrous Outcome," *The Lancet* (February), pp. 421–22.

Wagner, L. [1990], "Caring for Babies Exposed to Crack Could Cost $20 Billion—Government Officials," *Modern Healthcare* (March 12, 1990).

Wagstaff, A. [1987], "Government Prevention Policy and the Relevance of Social Cost Estimates," *British Journal of Addiction* 82, pp. 461–67.

Yeun, P. P. [1990], "A Critique of the Proposed Hospital Authority," Paper presented at the Conference of the Management Society for Health Care Professionals, Hong Kong (June).

REFERENCES FOR TABLE 12.1

Amaro, H., Fried, L., Cabral, H., Zuckerman, B [1990], "Violence during Pregnancy and Substance Use," *American Journal of Public Health* 80, no. 5 (May 1990), pp. 575–79.

Aduana, S., Pyati, S., Tsui, P., Gokhale, R., Pyati, A., Wilks, A., Pildes, R. S. [1989], "Perinatal Morbidity in Intravenous (IV) vs. Other Routes (NIV) of Drug Abuse," *Epidemiology and Preventive Pediatrics*, Division of Neonatal and Blood Bank, Cook County Hospital, Chicago, p. 95A.

Chasnoff, I. J. [1989], "Cocaine Abuse in Pregnancy," *JAMA* 262, no. 6 (August 11, 1989), p. 771.

Chasnoff, I. J., and MacGregor, S. N. [1989], "Cocaine in Pregnancy: Trimester Abuse Pattern and Perinatal Outcome," *Pediatric Research* 23, no. 4, part 2, p. 403A.

Chasnoff, I. J., and Griffith, D. R. [1989], "Cocaine: Clinical Studies of Pregnancy and the Newborn," *Annals New York Academy of Sciences* 562 (1989), pp. 260–66.

Chasnoff, I. J., and Lewis;, D. E. [1988], "Cocaine Metabolism during Pregnancy," *Developmental Pharmacology* 23, no. 4, part 2, p. 257A.

Chasnoff, I. J. [1988], "Cocaine Use in Pregnancy," *Abstracts of Neurotoxicology Conference* 9, no. 4, p. 669.

Chasnoff, I. J. [1989], "Drug Use in Pregnancy," *New York State Journal of Medicine*, May 1989, p. 255.

Chasnoff, I. J. [1988], "Drug Use in Pregnancy: Parameters of Risk," *Pediatric Clinics of North America* 35, no. 6 (December 1988), pp. 1403–12.

Chasnoff, I. J. [1988], "Newborn Infants with Drug-Withdrawal Symptoms," *Pediatrics in Review* 9, no. 9 (March 1988), pp. 273–77.

Chasnoff, I. J., Chisum, G. M., Kaplan, W. E. [1988], "Maternal Cocaine Use and Genitourinary Tract Malformations," *Teratology* 37, no. 3 (March 1988), pp. 201–4.

Chasnoff, I. J., Griffith, D. R., MacGregor, S., Dirkes, K., Burns, K. A. [1989], "Temporal Patterns of Cocaine Use in Pregnancy Perinatal Outcome," *JAMA* 261, no. 12 (March 24/31, 1989), pp. 1741–44.

Chavez, G. F., Mulinare, J., Cordero, J. F. [1989], "Maternal Cocaine Use during Early Pregnancy as a Risk Factor for Congenital Urogenital Anomalies," *JAMA* 262, no. 6 (August 11, 1989), pp. 795–98.

Chavez, G. F., Mulinare, J., Cordero, J. F. [1988], "Maternal Cocaine Use and the Risk for Genitourinary Tract Defects: An Epidemiologic Approach," *American Journal of Human Genetics* 43, no. 12 (September 1988, supplement), p. A43.

Chen, C., Neto, G. S., Tan, S., Bandstra, E., Dura, S., Gerhardt, T., Hurwitz, B., Bacalari, E. [1989], "Respiratory Stability in Neonates with Prenatal Exposure to Cocaine," Part 2, *Pediatric Research* 25, no. 4 (April 1989, supplement), p. 48A.

Chokshi, S. K., Whelton, J. A., Isner, J. M. [1989], "Evidence that Fetal Distress in Newborns of Cocaine Users Is Due to Vascular Spasm and May Be Attenuated by Pre-Treatment with Biltiazem," *Circulation* 80, no. 4, suppl. 2 (Abstracts of the 62nd Scientific Sessions, 1989).

Centers for Disease Control [1989], "Congenital Syphilis—New York City—1986–1988," *MMWR* 38, no. 48 (December 8, 1989), pp. 825–29.

Cohen, M. E., Anday, E. K., Leitner, D. S. [1989], "Effects of In-Utero Cocaine Exposure on Sensorineural Reactivity," *Annals of the New York Academy of Sciences*, June 1989, pp. 344–46.

Deisher, R. W., Farrow, J. A., Hope, K., Litchfield, C. [1989], "The Pregnant Adolescent Prostitute," *AJDC* 143 (October 1989), pp. 1162–65.

Doberczak, T. M., Bouzouki, M., Upal, V., Kandall, S. R. [1989], "Cranial Sonograms of Cocaine-Exposed Newborns," *Pediatric Research* 25, no. 4, p. 355.

Doberczak, T. M., Shanzer, S., Senie, R. T., Kandall, S. R. [1988], "Neonatal Neurologic and Electroencephalographic Effects on Intrauterine Cocaine Exposure," *Journal of Pediatrics* 113, no. 2, pp. 354–58.

Doberczak, T. M., Rongkapan, O., Davis, L., Kandall, S. R. [1989], "Peripheral Nerve Conduction Studies in Cocaine-Exposed Neonates," *Pediatric Reserach* 25, no. 4, pt. 2, p. 355A.

Donvito, M. T. [1988], "Cocaine Use during Pregnancy: Adverse Perinatal Outcome," Correspondence, *American Journal of Obstetrics and Gynecology* 159, no. 3 (September), pp. 785–86.

Ferriero, D. M., Wong, D. F., Townsend, R., Simon, R. P. [1985], "Neurologic Complications in Infants of Cocaine-Abusing Mothers," *Neurology* 38, Suppl. 1 (March 1985), p. 163.

Frank, D. A., Zuckerman, B. S., Amaro, H., Aboagye, K., Bauchner, H., Cabral, H., Fried, L., Hingson, R., Kayne, H., Levenson, S. M., Parker, S., Reece, H., Vinci, R.

[1988], "Cocaine Use during Pregnancy: Prevalence and Correlates," *Pediatrics* 82, no. 6 (December 1988), pp. 888–95.

Goldin, K. [1989], "Cocaine Abuse in Pregnancy," Letters, *JAMA* 262, no. 6 (August 11, 1989), p. 771.

Krug, S. E. [1989], "Cocaine Abuse: Historical, Epidemiologic, and Clinical Perspectives for Pediatricians," *Adv. Pediatr.* 36, pp. 369–406.

Livesay, S., Ehrlich, S., Ryan, L., Finnegan, L. P. [1989], "Cocaine and Pregnancy: Maternal and Infant Outcome," *Annals of the New York Academy of Sciences*, pp. 358–59.

Naeye, R. L., Tafari, N. [1983], *Risk Factors in Pregnancy and Diseases of the Fetus and Newborn*, New York: Williams and Wilkins.

National Library of Medicine [1990], "Cocaine, Pregnancy and the Newborn," *Current Bibliographies in Medicine*, no. 90-7, National Institutes of Health, Bethesda, Md.

Pediatrics in Review [1988], Commentary—"Alcohol and Psychoactive Drug Use during Pregnancy," vol. 9, no. 9 (March 1988), p. 271.

Rossett, H. L., Weiner, L. [1984], *Alcohol and the Fetus: A Clinical Perspective*, Oxford, Eng.: Oxford University Press.

Sulaimin, N. D. (and others) [1988], "Drug and Alcohol Misuse in Pregnancy," *British Medical Journal* 297 (July 2, 1988), pp. 68–69.

Valanis, B., Waage, G., Dworkin, L., Romig, K. [1988], "Prevalence of Drug Use during Pregnancy by Source of Data Used," *Society for Epidemiologic Research: Abstracts*, p. 944.

Vanderveen, E. [1989], "Public Health Policy: Maternal Substance Use and Child Health," *Annals of the New York Academy of Sciences*, pp. 255–59.

13

THE LOGIC OF LEGALIZATION: A MATTER OF PERSPECTIVE

Mitchell S. Rosenthal

Legalization of many, most, or all presently illicit drugs is now being proposed as an appropriate response to drug abuse. At the heart of the debate sparked by this latest revival of the antiprohibition proposition is the question of just what legalization will remedy, for there is no single, universally acknowledged "drug-abuse problem."

Drug abuse is a complex of interconnected issues, and what we identify as *the* drug-abuse problem is largely determined by what aspect of this complex is most apparent to us.

My drug-abuse problem, or the issues I identify as central, seem obvious from my vantage point, which is the treatment center. The same problem is not nearly so apparent when drug abuse is viewed from the workplace, the courtroom, or city hall, and it is substantially different from what can be seen from the university campus, available economic data, or the company of seemingly sensible drug-using friends. To a large extent, our perspective determines the drug problem as each of us defines it and dictates what (if anything) we believe should be done about it.

To proponents of legalization, levels of drug-related crime and the cost of enforcing drug laws are the issues that most clearly define the drug-abuse problem. Ethan Nadelmann finds law-enforcement efforts "highly costly and counterproductive," and further maintains that "many of the drug-related evils that most people identify as part and parcel of the drug problem are in fact the costs of prohibition policies."[1]

Legalization, Nadelmann holds, would curb these evils. Not only would doing away with drug laws eliminate drug-law offenses but, according to him and other legalization advocates, the subsequent availability of legal and affordable drugs would further reduce crime by eliminating the need for addicts to steal, mug, or burgle to pay inflated "street" prices. Moreover, they contend that drug gangs, with no profits to protect, would cease battling to hold or expand their share of the illicit drug market, and spare inner-city communities the carnage of intergang conflict. From the legalization point of view, it is the enforcement of drug laws—far more than the abuse of drugs—that is the root cause of the "drug-abuse problem" as they define it.

Drug prohibition and the enforcement of drug laws appear considerably less malign when seen from the treatment center, for treatment professionals address the full range of drug-abusing behavior. We deal with personality disturbance, social dysfunction, educational and vocational deficits, and *all* manifestations of drug-related disordered behavior. We therefore are not concerned about crime to the exclusion of the other forms of social disorder caused or exacerbated by drug abuse.

DRUG-DISORDERED BEHAVIOR

Treatment professionals are hardly indifferent to crime. We have observed, however, that the criminal involvement of most drug abusers is less the result of drug laws or drug prices than a common manifestation of their disordered behavior. Drug abusers do not commit crimes *in order to* use drugs so much as they commit crimes *because* they use drugs.

This perception of crime causes us to look more closely at criminality than at crime rates, and we have observed how rising levels of criminal involvement among young Americans paralleled increasing drug involvement of this age group during the past several decades. This increased criminality is evident in a study by the Criminal Justice Targeted Research Program of California's Bureau of Criminal Statistics.

The California researchers challenged the assumption that a relatively small number of criminals were responsible for the large number of crimes committed in the state. To do this, they set out to discover the prevalence of arrests—how many people were arrested in a given period of time. They looked at all California men born in 1956, and (adjusting for migration) determined how many members of this group had been arrested between 1974 and 1985 (from the time they turned 18 until they were 29).[2]

Results showed that 35 percent of these men (more than one out of three) had been arrested—and nearly half of them, more than once. Eleven percent of the group had been arrested three or more times. Moreover, 16.5 percent (or one out of six) had been arrested for serious felony offenses (FBI index crimes)—murder, manslaughter, rape, robbery, burglary, felony assault, felony theft or larceny, and motor vehicle theft—none of which are drug offenses. Treatment professionals, looking at the astonishing prevalence of arrests in this group, see a strong connection to levels of drug use among this age group, which peaked during the very years studied by the California researchers.

While crime rates—as measured by victimization surveys of the Census Bureau—have declined in recent years,[3] the criminality of drug abusers does not appear to have been reduced at all. In 1988, the National Institute of Justice's Drug Use Forecasting Program estimated that 75 percent of felony arrestees nationwide were drug abusers. Only recently—in April 1990—have Forecasting Program studies revealed any weakening of the linkage between criminal behavior and drug use.[4,5]

Although criminality of drug abusers clearly remains a major societal concern, it is being overshadowed now by the recent and rapid spread of other drug-related disordered behavior. Indeed, the fastest-rising costs of drug abuse today are associated, not with crime, but with homelessness and chronic mental illness, with adolescent suicide and runaways, with the spread of AIDS, domestic violence, child neglect and child abuse, with drug-damaged children, and with the number of new drug-impaired, addicted, and abandoned infants.

Drug abuse among the homeless appears to be substantially higher than even the earlier estimates of 13 to 25 percent.[6] It is prevalent not only among the single homeless but also among homeless mothers with children. At a New York City shelter for these women, where Phoenix House operates a small and separate treatment unit, our counselors estimate that approximately 60 percent of all mothers in residence abuse drugs—most often crack. According to one New York City deputy mayor, the overall incidence of drug abuse among the city's homeless may now be as great as 70 percent.

There were between 1.2 and 1.5 million teenage runaways on the streets in 1988[7]—about three times the number reported in 1984. Street workers estimate 75 to 80 percent are substance abusers.[8]

Teen suicide has increased dramatically during the past few years to become the third leading cause of death for 15- to 24-year-olds. According to a recent multistate study, drug-using adolescents are three times as likely as their non-drug-using peers to attempt suicide.[9]

Chronic mental illness in the United States today is inextricably linked with drug abuse. In New York State, between 30 and 50 percent of hospitalized mental patients fit the MICAA designation—as mentally ill, chemical abusing, and addicted.[10] Department of Mental Health officials estimate that between 50 and 60 percent of patients now presenting for care are substance abusers—particularly abusers of stimulants such as cocaine and crack.[11] Moreover, there is strong evidence that drug abuse may be the most potent determinant of readmission for schizophrenic patients.[12]

Drug abuse is to blame for rising levels of violence, and not only murder, rape, robbery, and assault. The incidence of domestic violence has increased sharply,[13] while complaints of child abuse, throughout the United States, rose 82 percent after 1981, to reach 2.2 million late in the decade.[14]

Child abuse and neglect have raised the number of U.S. children in foster care to nearly half a million, and authorities estimate an increase to 840,000 by 1995.[15] A study by the American Welfare Association notes a nearly 30 percent rise between 1987 and 1990, with the most substantial increases in states hit hardest by drug abuse (California and New York together account for 55 percent of the increase).[16]

We are seeing a fearsome fallout from the present drug-abuser baby boom. An estimated 11 percent of new mothers were using drugs during pregnancy in 1988, suggesting that as many as 375,000 newborns had prenatal exposure[17]—a 300 percent increase from 1985.[18] It is likely that 100,000 of those infants were exposed to crack.[19]

Although these estimates are disputed (Besharov puts the total of "drug-related births" no higher than 80,000 in 1989),[20] there is no disputing the tragic number of impaired, addicted, and abandoned infants born today. In New York City, drug-related admission of infants to neonatal intensive care rose by close to 40 percent *each year* between 1983 and 1987, and the New York State Department of Health projects as many as 5 percent of all New York City–born infants (and 10 percent of all nonwhite infants) will require such care by 1995.[21]

Crack babies are not only likely to suffer severe birth defects; it now appears that they may have major developmental disabilities as well. Neurological damage is suspected as the reason why so many appear disorganized and unresponsive, why they are slow to learn and relate so poorly to others.[22]

Crack babies are not unique. Dr. Judy Howard at UCLA, working with children of mothers who had been chronic users of cocaine, amphetamines, and PCP—as well as crack—has found that more than 30 percent share what she describes as "a new kind of disability." Pilot classes have been set up by the Los Angeles school system to learn how to deal with the impulsive and uncontrollable behavior of these children.[23]

There seems little that the children of drug abusers are spared. Infants are now also the victims of addict-born AIDS, for the rate of transmission of HIV infection from mothers to their newborn children is approximately 40 to 50 percent.[24]

No one discounts the increasingly menacing role played by drug abuse in the spread of AIDS. Most treatment professionals, however, regard this not as a separate phenomenon that can somehow be independently addressed (by clean needles or free condoms) but as another manifestation of the irresponsibility and disorder that characterizes so much drug-abusing behavior.

Recognizing all the ramifications of drug-abusing disordered behavior—and its destabilizing impact on communities that suffer most from drug abuse—it is difficult to accept the analysis of legalization advocates that tends to discount the social consequences of almost all forms of drug-related disorder other than crime. Treatment professionals find the economic arguments for legalization flawed by the failure to give more than minimal consideration to current and future economic costs of *noncriminal* disordered behavior that derives, in whole or in part, from drug abuse.

Disordered drug abusers and their children are enormous consumers of public services. They now place inordinate burdens on welfare, education, and child-protective services, and thus contribute substantially to the escalating costs of health care. Moreover, it is impossible to estimate the future costs of medical care, public assistance and foster care, education, and subsequent support for today's drug-impaired infants and older children.

PHYSICAL VERSUS BEHAVIORAL DANGERS

The apparent indifference of legalization advocates to drug-disordered behavior and its impact would seem to result from their failure to acknowledge that the primary dangers of drug abuse are behavioral rather than physical. This is a mind-set with which treatment professionals are all too familiar, for what parents of youngsters first ask about drugs is, "Will it do them any harm"? By harm, they mean *physical* harm, as though they might somehow overlook their children's infantilism, hostility, lack of goals, loss of ambition, dishonesty, anger, self-loathing if only their lungs and liver were not imperiled.

There is a different focus of concern, however, once a youngster actually becomes involved with drugs. As Marvin Snyder of the National Institute on Drug Abuse explains, "The mother who cannot talk to her son because he is stoned is not worried about cancer. She is worried about the son she once knew. The husband who can't reach his drunk wife on the phone is not concerned about cirrhosis of the liver. He's worried about where the kids are."[25]

The perception of drug abuse—as altering pathologically the nature and character of abusers—is hard for proponents of legalization to accept, since it vitiates the assumption, inherent in their arguments, that drug abusers are otherwise normal people who happen to use drugs. On that point is pinned the presumption that drug prohibitions exist only to protect individuals from the consequences of their own actions or to impose moral restraints on their freedom of choice.

The Practical Basis for Drug Prohibitions

Although James Q. Wilson and James J. DiIulio acknowledge "an obvious moral reason for attempting to discourage drug use" in the threat it poses to "the dignity, autonomy, and productivity of users,"[26] drug prohibitions are actually based on far more practical concerns. They are not meant to protect otherwise normal folks from themselves, but to protect society from folks who can easily lose the ability to function normally.

The treatment community does not contend that society is at risk from the behavior of *all* drug users, or even from the great majority of them. Although sustained use soon diminishes the capacity to perform normally—to hold a job, keep up with schoolwork, or maintain responsible social, sexual, or family relationships—it would be hard to justify prohibition on this basis alone.

The case for prohibition rests instead on the substantial number of abusers who cross the line from permissible self-destruction to become "driven," out of control people who place others in danger because of their irresponsibility, risk-taking, violence, abuse, or HIV infection. As much a part of the drug-abuse syndrome as chemical dependency are changes in attitudes and values that lower self-esteem, erode character, and prompt behavior that is antisocial, often violent, frequently criminal, and manifests an almost absolute indifference to the welfare of others.

Tobacco and Alcohol Parallels

The physical damage done by illicit drugs, although significant, is simply not in the same league with the behavioral consequences. Nor does it threaten others. Therefore it does not—for the very reasons put forth by legalization advocates—provide a basis for prohibition.

The argument that tobacco, which is certainly as addicting and at least as physically harmful as most illicit drugs, should *also* be banned—for consistency's sake if none other—does not hold. "Tobacco shortens one's life," says Wilson, "cocaine debases it."[27] It is perhaps more significant, however, that tobacco makes you your own worst enemy, whereas cocaine can make you everyone else's.

A drug-alcohol parallel is also raised by legalization advocates, and this one cannot be so easily dismissed—nor should it be. Alcohol is no less a mind-altering substance than marijuana. It is our society's primary drug of abuse. Although consumed with relative impunity by the overwhelming majority of users, it is, nevertheless, responsible for more crime and social disorder than any other single substance[28] and is (because of the sheer volume required to achieve disinhibiting effects) the most physically harmful of psychoactive chemicals.

Although there are reasons why drug treatment professionals consider alcohol a less threatening substance than marijuana (including the ways in which marijuana is used, its function as a "gateway" drug, and its effects on the intellectual development of adolescents), these reasons are not—by themselves—sufficient to justify the inclusion of marijuana and the exclusion of alcohol from present drug prohibitions. The exclusion of alcohol derives not from any assessment of relative risk but from the rejection of prohibition by the American public in 1933.

Although it is right to note the gains of prohibition in reducing alcohol-related mortality and disordered behavior, it would be naive to contend that the experiment "succeeded." Only a bare majority of Americans ever supported prohibition, and it was never possible, as David Musto points out, "to achieve the popular consensus necessary for success of the laws."[29] Such a consensus, however, does exist for present drug laws, which enjoy overwhelming public support,[30] and this makes rejection of prohibition a most unconvincing argument for legalization.

An Example from Abroad

Proponents of legalization marshall many arguments to support their case for doing away with drug prohibitions, including liberal drug policies of other countries. They note, for example, that the prescription of heroin for the maintenance of addicts is permitted in Britain. If we are to draw any lessons from the British experience, however, it is probably most important to understand why—while they were free to prescribe injectable heroin—treatment-clinic physicians turned overwhelmingly to oral methadone.

Professor Griffith Edwards, of the Addiction Research Unit at London University's Institute of Psychiatry, who was a clinic physician, maintains that the changeover occurred because heroin proved to be such a bad drug for social functioning, leaving addicts high much of the time and still, as he notes, "intermittently drug-hungry."

Moreover, he explains, "It is quite impossible to find the right dose"—one that will indeed "maintain" a patient. Although the clinics were prescribing huge doses (20 to 30 times what New York street addicts consume), patients always wanted more, and a good number were selling their heroin on the black market or trading it for other drugs. "You are not being a good doctor, prescribing a good drug, by giving people heroin," says Edwards.[31]

PERCEPTIONS OF TREATMENT

If it is difficult and inappropriate to use heroin as a maintenance drug, it is impossible to use cocaine. Nonetheless, that is what several legalization scenarios propose. Not only are there greater physical dangers, but cocaine is metabolized in a matter of minutes—not hours—and causes extreme mood swings. The nature of the drug makes it impossible to stabilize patients, which is, after all, the purported goal of maintenance. At no dosage can sustained comfort be achieved. Cocaine abusers will always crave more—and the more they receive, the more agitated and disordered they will become.

Suggestions such as cocaine maintenance make it evident that many positions taken by legalization advocates reflect considerable ignorance of both the nature of drugs and the capabilities of drug-abuse treatment today. Indeed, the failure to appreciate what treatment can achieve allows such advocates to assume that "everything else has failed" and to advance what they agree is a proposal of last resort.

Treatment professionals have a considerably more sanguine point of view. We see drug abuse as behavior that can be altered, a disorder for which proven and predictably effective therapeutic regimes exist, enabling former abusers not only to overcome chemical dependency but also to change attitudes and values that prompt self-destructive and antisocial behaviors of all kinds.

Successful treatment, it should be noted, does not depend on the development of new medications, although these might prove valuable. Whether it is chemically assisted or not, treatment for drug abuse is essentially behavioral and psychological and requires the active participation of the patient, for it is the patient who must confront and resolve underlying emotional problems, anxieties, and fears.

The efficiency of drug-abuse treatment is no longer in question. The issue was resolved long before the National Academy of Science's Institute of Medicine issued its report in September 1990, endorsing—as both beneficial and cost-effective—the treatment methods we have developed over the past quarter century.[32] The institute based its evaluation on a series of large-scale, long-term outcome studies that documented the impact of treatment on post-treatment behavior—specifically on drug use, criminality, and employment.[33,34] These studies, and our own research at Phoenix House,[35] make it clear that a major factor in determining successful outcome is prolonged involvement in the treatment process.

Requirements of active patient participation and prolonged involvement make drug abuse a difficult disorder to treat, for few abusers are able to perceive a need for treatment. Because drugs of abuse have such powerfully reinforcing properties, drug-taking often becomes compulsive behavior, and a unique characteristic of drug abuse is the ways its symptoms are masked from the victims themselves. Most abusers experience few physical effects and do not recognize behavioral and psychological effects. They do not realize when they are out of control. For this reason, drug abusers are rarely prompted to cease drug use for any but the most compelling reasons, and they generally will not seek treatment unless confronted by far less desirable alternatives. Although motivation is needed to overcome drug dependency, few abusers bring much of it with them to the treatment setting. Indeed, generating motivation is the first goal of the treatment process.

It is external pressure that generally brings drug abusers into treatment—and keeps them there long enough to recognize and accept the need to modify their behavior. These pressures reflect societal attitudes toward drug use. When there is widespread tolerance for drug use, the level of community or social pressure on drug abusers to quit, or to get the help they need in order to quit, is low. When tolerance declines, pressures rise.

Families, friends, and employers often exert the pressure that moves drug abusers to treatment. For a good many abusers in treatment today, however, pressure has come from the criminal justice system. Drug abusers placed in treatment as an alternative to incarceration generally fare as well as those who enter under less formal pressure. Indeed, the demonstrated effectiveness of treatment programs operating within a prison system make it clear that compulsion is no barrier to successful treatment outcome.[36]

It is understandable, therefore, for drug-abuse professionals to oppose vigorously the notion of legalization. Recognizing how today's treatment methods enable us to intervene successfully in drug abuse of even the most profound and disordering kinds, we are prompted to seek from society whatever will most effectively move drug abusers to accept the help we can provide. We encourage intolerance for drug use and view disincentives—including the enforcement of drug laws—as potent adjuncts to treatment.

Our view appears to be shared by an overwhelming majority of former abusers who entered treatment via the criminal justice system. Indeed, I have never heard one of these former abusers—or one parent whose child came to treatment after arrest (often after imprisonment)—respond to the prospect of legalization with anything other than horror.

IMPACT ON CRIME

Although treatment professionals dread what we believe would be the impact of legalization on treatment, we are not convinced that there would be *any* compensating benefits—not even a reduction in crime.

It is hard to deny that legalization would shrink the market for illicit drugs. It is equally hard, however, to envision elimination of all illicit sales, for no legalization formulation anticipates legal sales to minors and few postlegalization scenarios would make available *all* presently illegal substances including crack, ice, PCP, and the latest in designer drugs. Although we might anticipate that some youngsters would get drugs through diversion from the legal adult market, we should also expect others to secure drugs as they do now. It would be surprising if both youthful and adult consumers did not turn to street dealers for whatever substances were legally unavailable.

The persistence of an illicit market would be further ensured, as Musto explains, were legalization to involve "anything less than open access to cocaine." As evidence, he points out that, prior to passage of the Harrison Act, when New York State law made a physician's prescription necessary for the legal purchase of cocaine, an illicit market was created with prices that were much higher (in terms of the average hourly industrial wage) than street prices are today.[37]

Even were there "open access" to almost all drugs, we cannot assume that drug-abusing criminals would cease robbing and stealing simply because low-cost drugs had been made available to them. No experienced treatment professional would make such an assumption, for we recognize that long-term drug abusers do not commit crimes *only* to buy drugs. It is generally a significant source of income. Indeed, a year-long study of patients being provided with prescription heroin at a British clinic during 1975 and 1976 found that fully half were convicted of a crime during that period.[38] Lowering drug prices may reduce the level of criminality among drug abusers, or it may increase their disposable income, or it may simply permit them to buy and use greater quantities of drugs.

What treatment professionals do expect to see sharply increase is the amount of drug-related crime that is not committed for gain (homicide, assault, rape, and child abuse). This, we believe, will result from a higher incidence of drug-related disorder, due to both higher levels of consumption and a greater number of abusers. To a great extent, then, how legalization will affect crime rates (along with all other forms of disordered behavior) turns on the question of how it will affect drug use.

IMPACT ON USE

It is difficult to imagine that making drug use affordable and legal will not produce significantly higher levels of use. By increasing access, removing disincentives—and, in effect, sanctioning or "normalizing" use—we would be eliminating all the impediments that, no matter how imperfectly, now limit its spread.

Lowering drug prices and *increasing* access plainly influence drug use. As

Wilson points out, heroin consumption was rising sharply at the start of the 1970s, when supplies were plentiful. This "epidemic" ended between 1973 and 1975 as supplies tightened, prices climbed steeply, and purity declined. The number of new heroin users fell, and consumption rates flattened out.[39]

Price and supply, Wilson suggests, also help to explain why so many heroin-abusing Vietnam veterans left their drug habits overseas. Heroin use was widespread among soldiers in Vietnam, where the drug was cheap, potent, and easily acquired. Lee Robins's study of Vietnam veterans three years after their return found that only 43 percent of the veterans addicted in Vietnam used any heroin after their return, and just 12 percent became readdicted.[40] Heroin was much harder to come by in the United States and sanctions against its use were much more severe.

The treatment community would not only anticipate an enormous increase in drug use to follow legalization, but we would also expect a greater proportion of drug use to be heavy and high-risk. In the absence of disincentives and high prices, it is extraordinarily difficult for regular users to control the amounts they consume; cocaine abusers in treatment almost uniformly report that cost alone limited their intake.

In recent years, as overall drug use has declined, the heavy and high-risk use of the most potent and reinforcing substances has persisted,[41] and it is heavy, high-risk users who most often become disordered. Moreover, this most destructive form of drug abuse hits hardest at the most vulnerable segments of the population—the poor, the unemployed, the emotionally disturbed, and the troubled young.

Nowhere will the impact of increased drug use, high-risk use, crime, and other drug-related disorders be more severe than in those neighborhoods that are now the bloodiest battlefields of the "other drug war," the conflict for control of illicit drug markets. And it is in these communities—generally poor, minority, and urban—that intolerance for drug use and approval of drug laws runs highest.

What seems most evident from the treatment perspective, and apparently not quite so evident from the legalization camp, is that there are no easy answers to drug abuse. Legalization will only exacerbate the drug-abuse problem *we* perceive, and I cannot believe it will do much to alter the problem *they* perceive.

NOTES

1. Nadelmann, E. A. "Drug Prohibition in the United States: Costs, Consequences, and Alternatives." *Science* 245 (September 1, 1989), pp. 939–47.

2. Tillman, R. *The Prevalence and Incidence of Arrest among Adult Males in California.* Sacramento: State of California, Department of Justice, 1987.

3. Wilson, J. Q., and J. J. DiIulio, Jr. "Crackdown." *New Republic*, July 10, 1989.

4. "Study: Drugs Linked to Most Felony Arrests." *Newsday*, March 28, 1990.

5. Hemphill, C. "Turning a Corner on Crack." *Newsday*, October 11, 1990.

6. "Shattering Myth about the Homeless." *U.S. News & World Report*, March 20, 1989.

7. *Annual Runaway and Homeless Youth Report to Congress*, Washington, D.C.: U.S. Department of Health and Human Services, 1988.

8. Shaffer, D., and C. L. M. Caton. "Runaways and Homelessness in New York City." Report to the Ittleson Foundation, 1984.

9. Berman, A. L., and R. H. Schwartz. "Suicide Attempts among Adolescent Drug Users." *American Journal of Diseases of Children* 144 (March 1990), pp. 310–14.

10. Galanter, M. *Year End Report of the Task Force on the Mentally Ill, Chemically Abusing and Addicted—Summary Statement*. Albany: New York State Office of Mental Health, 1987.

11. New York State Office of Mental Health, Albany.

12. Craig, T. J., S. P. Lin, M. H. El-Defrawi, and A. B. Goodman. "Clinical Correlates of Readmission in a Schizophrenic Cohort," *Psychiatric Quarterly* 57 (1985), pp. 5–10.

13. National Coalition against Domestic Violence (NCADC). "Statistics from 1987 NCADC Domestic Violence Statistical Survey."

14. Leefeldt, E. "Reforming the Delinquent Foster-Care System." *Wall Street Journal*, October 16, 1990.

15. "No Place to Call Home, Discarded Children in America." *Report of the Select Committee on Children, Youth, and Families*. Washington, D.C.: U.S. House of Representatives, November 1989.

16. Besharov, J. D. "Crack Children in Foster Care," *Children Today*, July–August 1990.

17. Ring, J. J., et al. "Drug Abuse in the United States: The Next Generation." *Report of the Board of Trustees to the American Medical Association House of Delegates*. Honolulu, 1989.

18. "The Crack Children." *Newsweek*, February 12, 1990.

19. Leefeldt, "Reforming."

20. Besharov, "Crack Children in Foster Care."

21. French, H. W. "Rise in Babies Hurt by Drugs Predicted." *New York Times*, October 18, 1989.

22. *Newsweek*. "The Crack Children."

23. Howard, Judy. School of Medicine, UCLA. Personal communication.

24. Ring, et al. "Drug Abuse."

25. Snyder, Marvin. National Institute on Drug Abuse. Personal communication.

26. Wilson and DiIulio. "Crackdown."

27. Wilson, J. Q. "Against the Legalization of Drugs." *Commentary*, February 1990.

28. Seventh Special Report to the U.S. Congress on Alcohol and Health. U.S. Department of Health and Human Services. 1990.

29. Musto, David. Yale School of Medicine. Personal communication.

30. "Poll Finds 90% Favor Keeping Drugs Illicit." New York Times, September 15, 1988.

31. Edwards, G. Addiction Research Unit, Institute of Psychiatry, University of London. Personal communication.

32. Gerstein, D. P. and H. Howard (eds.). Treating Drug Problems. Washington, D.C.: National Academy Press, 1990.

33. Simpson, D. D., and S. B. Sells. Highlights of the DARE Followup Research on the Evaluation of Drug Abuse Treatment Effectiveness. NIDA Monograph Series, Washington, D.C., 1981.

34. Hubbard, R. L., et al. Drug Abuse Treatment: A National Study of Effectiveness. Chapel Hill: University of North Carolina Press, 1989.

35. DeLeon, G. The Therapeutic Community: Studies of Effectiveness. Treatment Research Monograph Series, DDMS Pub. No. (ADM) 84-1226, National Institute on Drug Abuse, Rockville, Md., 1984.

36. Wexler, H. K., D. S. Lipton, F. Foster. "Outcome of a Prison Therapeutic Community for Substance Abusers: Preliminary Results Presented at the American Criminological Association, San Diego, November 1985.

37. Musto, D. F. "Illicit Price of Cocaine in Two Eras: 1908–14 and 1982–89." Connecticut Medicine 54, no. 6 (June 1990), pp. 321–26.

38. Mitcheson, M., and R. Hartnoll. "Prescribing Heroin: Does it Work?" in D. J. West (ed.), Problems of Drug Abuse in Britain. Cambridge, Eng.: Cambridge University Press, 1978.

39. Wilson. "Against the Legalization."

40. Robins, L. N., et al. "Veterans Three Years after Vietnam," in L. Brill and L. C. Winnick (eds.), Yearbook of Substance Use and Abuse. New York: Human Sciences Press, 1980.

41. Leading Drug Indicators. Office of National Drug Control Policy, Washington, D.C., September, 1990.

COMMENT

Barbara R. Williams

The speakers that we have just heard [Kleiman, Rosenthal] have talked to us from different perspectives, to use Mitchell's word—Mark is an economist talking about crime control, and Mitchell is a doctor talking about drug treatment. They both are advocating essentially the same position, however, that in fact it will be too expensive to decriminalize or to legalize drugs, because the social costs will go beyond what could be gained by reducing the crime costs associated with our current legal policies.

I have had the advantage of reading several papers by Kleiman, so I know more than you heard this morning about what he actually thinks; let me just sketch what I think the argument is. Today's laws governing drugs are imperfect and often perverse. Legal sanctions are probably too light and lenient for alcohol, too stringent for marijuana and maybe even heroin, relative to the damage those drugs do to society and to individuals.

Mark [Kleiman] would control these latter drugs with a range of sanctions— more taxation, more regulation—essentially using our civil justice system in addition to our criminal justice system to exert more direct control over different kinds of drugs. Although his arguments are thoughtfully set out and economically sound, I would be more compelled by them if we were initiating them de novo since inevitably there would be a rockier transition than Mark suggests when people with preexisting views and behaviors toward currently illegal drugs are asked to change those views and behaviors in response to new taxes and regulations. For that reason, I would call for more systematic empirical estimates before I could recommend changing our current control strategy. Regard, for a moment, Mark's suggestion that we consider making alcohol more difficult for people to get and marijuana easier for people to get. On the one hand, it is possible that we could, in fact, improve the health of people in the United States by reducing the number of addicts. (Alcohol is addictive for some people and marijuana seems not to be.) On the other hand, that might produce a different mix of substance users and abusers. Will, for example, drivers who have smoked two joints be more or less dangerous than drivers who have had two beers? I am not convinced that we can answer those questions today. Overall, I think that it would be irresponsible to change our laws until we can better evaluate both safety and health outcomes.

Like most who practice drug treatment and prevention, Mitchell [Rosenthal] is against legalizing currently illegal drugs. His experience suggests that in order for people to abandon addictive behaviors, they need help from the environment they will enter after treatment. No treatment program alone can cause a person to abstain from addictive drugs. Social settings in which access to the preferred drug is low, in which more unpleasant than pleasant associations with drugs occur, and in which social disapproval from people one respects is felt all help extend periods of abstinence for addicted people. I speak with some authority; as a former cigarette smoker, I understand addiction. To stop smoking, I have found most useful the tremendously negative social pressure that has been brought to bear on cigarette smoking in the past decade. What Mitchell obviously anticipates, should more drugs be legalized, is an environment that would be even more supportive of continued addiction than the current one.

Let me end my comments by suggesting that we consider the lessons that we might take from the cigarette-desistance experience in the United States. With cigarettes, we have a drug that is legal and highly addictive, but which millions of people have ceased using. I challenge this audience to address the question "Is the relative success in smoking desistance due to its legal status?" My answer is no. It is not clear to me that the legal status of drugs is the critical quality about them that will precede behavioral change.

14

BEYOND DRUG PROHIBITION: EVALUATING THE ALTERNATIVES

Ethan A. Nadelmann

During the past two years, political and public interest in considering alternatives to drug prohibition has risen substantially. Mayors Kurt Schmoke and Carrie Saxon Perry, federal judges Robert Sweet, Warren Egington and James Churchill, Congressman George Crockett, former Secretary of State George Shultz, economists Milton Friedman and Gary Becker, columnists William Buckley and Mike Royko—these represent merely the most prominent and outspoken of those who have criticized the current emphasis on criminal justice approaches to the drug problem and called for examination of the alternatives. There is no question any longer that this chorus of voices will grow more numerous and more powerful in coming years, with the potential for instigating significant changes in U.S. and international drug-control policy.

The rising interest in drug legalization stems not from any belief that it represents a solution to the drug problem but rather from the growing sense that drug-prohibition policies are proving fairly ineffective, increasingly costly, and highly counterproductive. Most drug-legalization strategies, by contrast, present numerous advantages: substantial reductions in drug-related crime and violence; diminished opportunities for organized and unorganized criminals; substantial savings in criminal justice costs; reduced risks of overdoses, hepatitis, AIDS, and other medical illnesses that derive from adulterated drugs and dangerous means of drug consumption; reduced threats to privacy and other civil liberties; greater opportunities to pursue drug prevention and treatment strategies without interference from the criminal justice system; substantial opportunities for tax revenue from legal sales of psychoactive drugs; and so on. Legalization strategies do, however, present one substantial disadvantage: the risk of substantial increases in drug abuse.

THE NEED FOR RESEARCH

To date, most discussion of drug legalization has been confined to increasingly detailed critiques of current drug-prohibition policies; relatively little sustained attention has been devoted to considering the range of alternatives to current policies and their relative risks, costs, and benefits. In this respect, the growing debate over drug prohibition and legalization resembles the debate in the United States over alcohol prohibition. During the mid-1920s, the cost and benefits of prohibition were vigorously debated by scholars, journalists, and others; the Wickersham Commission appointed by President Hoover in 1931 provided perhaps the most thorough analysis of what prohibition had and had not accomplished. During the early 1930s, increasing attention was devoted not just to evaluating prohibition but also to considering alternative alcohol-control strategies. The leading study of this sort was commissioned by the Rockefeller Foundation and directed by Raymond Fosdick. It examined Canadian and European approaches to alcohol control, focusing on the roles of taxation, licensing, and education, and distinguishing among the various approaches to light wines, beer, and spirits. Its recommendations helped shape the thinking of those charged with devising new alcohol-control measures in the United States.

Today, studies similar to that of the Wickesham Commission and the Rockefeller Foundation report are necessary to any systematic evaluation of drug prohibition and its alternatives. Replicating the Wickersham study is a relatively straightforward process; my articles on drug prohibition provided much of the initial groundwork and now I and others are in the process of elaborating on the analysis. Even more important to the future of drug policy, however, is a contemporary analysis of the alternatives to drug prohibition comparable to the Rockefeller Foundation study. To date, most attempts to consider the implications of drug legalization, by both advocates and opponents of the notion, have been lacking in research, infused by ideological assumptions, and reliant on somewhat simplistic caricatures of what legalization means. A more scholarly, research-oriented, and sophisticated approach is sorely needed. This paper suggests how such an approach might be pursued.

IDENTIFYING THE OBJECTIVES

There is, of course, no one legalization option. Just as the array of prohibition policies ranges from the very harsh Malaysian and Singaporean models to the more tolerant approaches found in the Netherlands and other parts of Europe, so "drug legalization" incorporates a wide range of policies reaching from libertarian approaches to the more restrictive "medical models" directed only at the addicted population of illicit drug users. Indeed, any drug policy inevitably incorporates both prohibition and legalization aspects. Although we consider alcohol a legal drug, for instance, it is illegal to sell it to minors, illegal to drive while under its influence and, in many states and localities, illegal to buy it except from government-controlled or government-licensed outlets. Conversely, although cocaine and various opiates are considered illegal drugs, both cocaine and methadone are legally prescribed by doctors, the former for nasal and dental surgery as well as treatment of pain, the latter as an addictive alternative to illicit heroin. The distinction between prohibition and legalization is thus less one of government control of drug distribution than one of emphasis: The drug-prohibition approach is one that relies primarily on criminal sanctions to control drug abuse; the legalization approach, one that relies primarily on public health approaches, nongovernmental controls, and the private decisions of citizens.

Any analysis of "drug legalization" must attempt to assess the relative costs, benefits, risks, and advantages of the many alternatives to drug prohibition. Just as we know that different prohibition strategies—international drug control, air and sea interdiction, street-level enforcement, targeting of drug trafficking organizations, drug testing, focusing enforcement efforts on particular drugs, and so on—vary in their potential costs and consequences, so different legalization strategies present different risks and potential benefits. The risks of legalizing only marijuana, for instance, are much less than the risks of legalizing crack cocaine; but so are the potential benefits. The risks and potential benefits of any legalization strategy will vary greatly depending on how it is designed, implemented, and maintained, as well as on the impact of policies toward other drugs.

Consider, for instance, marijuana. It is safe to assume that making marijuana legally available would yield many positive consequences: dramatic reductions in marijuana arrests and government expenditures on marijuana interdiction and domestic enforcement of marijuana laws; tax revenues amounting to billions of dollars annually; reduced risks from adulterated marijuana ; elimination of the violence associated with illicit marijuana trade; easy availability of marijuana for medical purposes; and so on. It is also reasonable to assume, particularly if we rely on traditional economic models, that marijuana consumption would rise from current levels as a consequence of its greater availability, lower price, more reliable quality, and the removal of the criminal sanction—although actual evidence from the Netherlands as well as from those U.S. states that decriminalized marijuana during the 1970s casts doubts on these assumptions. The impact of marijuana legalization would vary, of course, depending on the way in which the strategy was designed, implemented, and maintained. Just as variations in the control of alcohol and tobacco availability and use affect consumption, so we can expect marijuana consumption to be affected by the level of taxation, zoning restrictions on sale, time and place restrictions on use, controls on the potency of legally available marijuana, advertising campaigns for and against marijuana use, and so on. It is also reasonable to assume that the legalization of marijuana would create some substitution effect; that is, users of other drugs, both legal and illegal, might substitute marijuana for their use or abuse of alcohol, tobacco, cocaine, or other drugs. Most difficult to assess is the impact on marijuana consumption of changing fads and fashions, as well as other developments in the economic well-being, cultural identity, religiosity, and spirituality of Americans.

Similar types of questions arise in evaluating the impact of more far-reaching legalization strategies that include some degree of legal availability of cocaine, heroin, and other drugs that present greater risks of addiction and other forms of abuse. The libertarian model, for instance, offers both the greater advantages in reducing the many costs and negative consequences of drug prohibition as well as the greatest risks in terms of increased use and abuse. It thus provides a valuable starting point for critically examining decades-old assumptions about the need for criminal justice measures and other government involvement in drug control as well as the potential role of social controls other than government over the availability, use, and abuse of drugs. The libertarian model also raises fundamental questions regarding the policy distinction between over-the-counter and prescription drugs, the rationale for distinguishing between psychoactive and nonpsychoactive drugs, the nature of the moral issues implicated in drug policy and the impact of information concerning the relative risks and benefits of different drugs and means of consumption on patterns of use and abuse. Perhaps most importantly, it raises the basic questions of which drugs people would use, and how they would use them, in a "free market" of drugs. (Opponents of legalization tend to point to the current legal market for alcohol and tobacco and the illicit market for drugs such as crack and assume the worst. Proponents argue that current policies bias drug use toward two drugs that are in many respects more dangerous than many illicit drugs; they also point out that current trends toward less potent legal drugs and more potent illicit drugs are more a function of the legal status of the respective drugs than of their pharmacology.)

The central question in designing an optimal drug-control policy can be posed from two alternative perspectives: How do we best maximize the benefits of the libertarian model and minimize the risks? Alternatively: How do we best retain the advantages of drug prohibition but minimize its direct and indirect costs? This question is best addressed by considering two sorts of subsidiary questions—those that inquire into why people use, abuse, and abstain from, drugs; and those that examine the impact of drug-control policies on drug consumption and other behavior. These two sets of questions are, of course, intricately intertwined, but it is important to keep in mind that in the final analysis public policies are only one among many determinants of drug-use patterns. Equally important is the recognition that although we must distinguish among drugs, and among different forms, potencies, and means of administration of the same drug, in considering these two sets of questions, the most important answers to these questions involve the overall impact of a person's aggregate drug use on his or her well-being.

The first set of questions includes the following: Why do some people abstain from using most drugs? Why, for instance, do most Americans refrain not just from illicit drug use but also from tobacco use? Why do tens of millions of Americans abstain even from using alcohol? Why do some people use drugs? How do some people learn to control their drug consumption? Why do some people abuse themselves with drugs? What role do factors such as the pharmacology of a drug, its potency, and its means of administration play in determining the likelihood of abuse? How important are factors such as the "set and setting" of drug use? What is the psychological and physical impact of different drugs, and different patterns of use, on human beings? What role do genetic features play in influencing susceptibility to drug abuse? To what extent can people who have abused a drug return to safe patterns of drug consumption? How can we think most productively about the nature of addiction? Many of these questions remain both controversial and unresolved; but it is impossible to construct an effective drug-control policy without addressing them as competently as possible.

The second set of questions includes the following: To what degree can drug-consumption patterns be manipulated in safer directions by legalization policies that make some drugs more available than others, or that only legalize drugs at lower potency levels? What is the impact of variations in pricing and availability of different drugs on drug-consumer preferences? What policies are more or less effective in curtailing black market activity in a particular drug? What is the impact of various drug-treatment approaches, drug-education programs, and non-drug-specific prevention programs such as pre- and postnatal care, Head Start, and other educational initiatives on levels of drug abuse? To what degree is it possible to construct and implement a two-track policy—a low-cost, or subsidized, easy availability policy for addicts and a more restrictive, high-tax policy for all other users? To what extent is it possible to prevent leakage from the former system into the latter?

The answers to these questions provide us with the means of constructing two models that can be used to evaluate the effectiveness and impact of any drug-control policy. Model A is the more comprehensive: It distinguishes among those who are the intended beneficiaries of a public policy, those who are the unintended beneficiaries, those who are the intended victims, and those who are the unintended victims. Model B focuses more narrowly on the issue of consumption: It distinguishes first between those who will or will not use a drug, given a particular drug policy, and then between those drug users who will or will not cause harm to themselves and others as a consequence of their drug use. The advantage of Model A is that it captures all the consequences of drug policies; the advantage of Model B is that it focuses on the central risk of all legalization strategies—the potential for increased levels of drug abuse. Each of these models can be applied either to a particular drug and the policy toward it or, more valuably, to the impact of public policies on overall levels of drug use and abuse. These models are, most certainly, both somewhat crude and limited, particularly in their failure to distinguish adequately among types and degrees of drug abuse; but they are useful in providing a relatively objective means by which to identify the populations at risk from different drug-control policies as well as the overall consequences of different policies.

EVALUATIVE METHODS AND PERSPECTIVES

Unlike the Rockefeller Foundation study, which addressed many of the questions noted above with respect to alcohol, scholars today can draw on neither a recent domestic history of legalization nor contemporary examples abroad of drug-control regimes that are not primarily dependent on criminal sanctions. Nor is it possible, given legal, political, and even practical limitations, to carry out experimental legalization programs. Economic models offer important insights, but are limited in their predictive power by the powerful influences of fad and fashion, by cultural traditions and moral values, and by the very irrationality of much drug abuse. As a consequence, we are obliged to evaluate alternatives to drug prohibition more indirectly, relying on (1) contemporaneous experiences with limited forms of legalization, (2) more distant historical experiences with legal drug-control regimes, (3) the lessons of U.S. and foreign alcohol- and tobacco-control policies, (4) our understanding of nondrug-related forms of compulsive and self-abusive behavior, and (5) projections from current patterns of illicit drug use, abuse, and nonuse. Only in this way can we devise satisfactory models by which to evaluate the alternatives to current drug-control policies.

Contemporaneous Experiences with Limited Forms of Legalization

During the 1970s, eleven states decriminalized possession of marijuana (that is, reduced the criminal sanction for possession of small amounts of marijuana from a felony to a misdemeanor), and Alaska legalized it. In 1976, the Netherlands decriminalized cannabis to the point that police no longer arrest cannabis dealers or users. Comparable policies also are in force in parts of Spain, India, and some other countries. Some states in India are also reported to provide opium to registered addicts. In many countries, addicts are provided with methadone. In Britain addicts can also be provided with maintenance doses of injectable methadone, heroin, and cocaine. Over a dozen countries as well as a growing number of U.S. cities have now instituted needle-exchange programs to attempt to stem the spread of AIDS by illicit intravenous drug users. The city of Zurich, Switzerland, has implemented an experimental program in which drug dealers are permitted to sell their wares extralegally in a designated park in which needle-exchange and other drug-treatment and harm-reduction strategies are also available. Other European cities and states are considering similar strategies. Although none of these approaches provide for legal, government-regulated, over-the-counter sales of drugs, they do provide the closest contemporary examples of limited forms of legalization. They therefore provide insights into the nature and extent of drug use and abuse in the relative absence of criminal sanctions; and they are invaluable in assessing the potential effectiveness and consequences of drug-control programs addressed specifically to the needs of addicts as opposed to those of recreational users.

Drug Legalization in Historical Perspective

Most illicit drugs (that is, drugs that either cannot be purchased at all or that require a doctor's prescription) were legally available in the United States and elsewhere in earlier decades. Use of opium, coca, cannabis, and assorted hallucinogens all date back thousands of years. Morphine, heroin, and cocaine were all synthesized during the nineteenth century, and legally available in various forms throughout much of the world until the end of that century or the early decades of this century. Much can be learned from examining both patterns of use and abuse of these drugs in the absence of any governmental controls and the impact of noncriminal drug controls, such as labelling requirements and public diffusion of information, on patterns of drug use and abuse. Particularly important is research into the nature of cocaine use in Europe and the United States before the distribution of the drug was restricted—a subject about which virtually nothing has been written. The Asian experience with government-run opium monopolies, many of which remained in force until recent decades, also provides insights, as do patterns of drug use among traditional cultures, some of which have proven successful in inculcating notions of safe drug use even with highly potent psychoactive drugs.

Historical perspectives also remind us of the great impact that technological developments can have on the nature of drug use and abuse. The synthesis of morphine, cocaine, and heroin, as well as the invention of the hypodermic needle, all during the nineteenth century, exerted a powerful impact on drug-consumption patterns that few foresaw before the fact. Just ten years ago, it is worth recalling, no one had ever heard of crack cocaine, a drug that today is seen as the scourge of many inner cities. It is equally possible that ten years hence millions of Americans will be using and abusing drugs that remain little known or even unknown today, and that many of these drugs may be easily synthesized from readily available materials by untrained chemists. Indeed, technological advances may make widely available not just new psychoactive drugs as well as new forms of existing drugs and new forms of drug administration, but even new ways of altering one's state of consciousness without ingesting psychoactive drugs.

Lessons of Alcohol- and Tobacco-Control Policies

The study of policies designed to reduce alcohol consumption, and particularly the ills associated with alcohol abuse, date back hundreds of years. Much systematic study was performed during the first three decades of this century, when the United States and a few European countries experimented with alcohol prohibition and many other governments attempted more modest alcohol-control measures. Britain, for instance, proved highly successful in reducing alcohol-related ills during the 1920s and 1930s without resorting to alcohol prohibition. There is an abundance of studies today on the impact of changing drinking ages, taxation, DWI laws, zoning controls, restrictions on advertising, and so on. Similar studies of tobacco-control policies have also emerged in abundance during the past two decades. This extensive literature should prove valuable in attempting to assess the potential to control the availability, use, and abuse of other psychoactive drugs by public policy measures short of criminal sanctions. There is also something to be learned from examining patterns of caffeine consumption in the United States.

Nondrug-related Forms of Compulsive and Self-abusive Behavior

Using psychoactive drugs is only one way of altering one's state of consciousness; abusing oneself with drugs is only one way of doing harm to one's mind and body. Some scholars have examined gambling behavior and attempted to identify the explanations for "compulsive" and other self-destructive forms of gambling as well as the impact of different public policies. Studies of obesity and other eating disorders also examine the fundamental question of why people engage in self-destructive behavior despite awareness of the risks. A growing body of literature is involved in identifying a steadily increasing variety of "diseases" and "addictions." This literature has been harshly criticized for its loose use of terminology and its eager advocacy of "treatment" for a growing array of ills. Both authors and critics agree, however, that the causes of addictive and other self-destructive behavior may be similar for very different types of such behavior.

Understanding why people do or do not engage in "bad habits" and other self-destructive behaviors that have nothing to do with drug consumption can provide insights into drug-related behavior as well.

Projections from Current Patterns of Illicit Drug Use and Abuse

The National Institute on Drug Abuse collects aggregate figures on illicit drug use. Sociologists, criminologists, and other scholars have been studying drug-use patterns among illicit drug users for decades. Portions of this literature examine not just the impact of different public policies on patterns of use and abuse but also the impact of changing fashions and fads, evolving cultural mores, the shifting economics of the illicit drug trade, trends in drug availability, and broader changes in economic, social, and educational opportunities. Because the drug-prohibition regime exerts such a powerful impact on patterns of use and abuse, any attempt to estimate drug-consumption patterns under a legal-drug regime by projecting from recent and current patterns is highly speculative. Yet because the population of drug users, abusers, and nonusers under the current regime comes closer to resembling the population of users, abusers, and nonusers under a future regime than do any of the populations involved in historical and comparative perspectives, it is essential to examine current patterns of illicit drug use for insights into drug-use patterns under a legal-drug regime.

It is also important to recognize that any legalization regime will invariably incorporate components of current prohibition policies. It is possible, for instance, that drug testing, or performance testing, may play an even broader role under a drug-legalization system. It is safe to assume that laws against driving, flying, and operating other potentially dangerous machinery under the influence of powerful psychoactive drugs will persist. The problem of drug consumption by pregnant women is also one that is not clearly resolved by legalization assumptions; indeed, it raises the broader question of whether criminal penalties should apply to any drug use or other activity that potentially endangers a fetus. To the extent that a legalization strategy retains criminal sanctions on the sale and possession of certain drugs, analysis of current prohibition policies suggests what the potential market for such drugs will be and which control policies will be more or less effective.

CONCLUSION

It is, in the final analysis, unreasonable to expect all advocates of what has been called "legalization" to unite on a single plan. Like the "drug prohibitionists," they are split among themselves on moral, ideological, and political questions and vary greatly with respect to both their assessments of the costs and benefits of alternative policies and their recommendations of which policies should be implemented. Moreover, the very notion of distinguishing two camps of drug legalizers and prohibitionists is, as I have suggested above, somewhat foolish given the broad and somewhat bumpy spectrum along which drug policies can be arrayed and classified. The distinction does make some sense at the respective extremes, and it is useful in categorizing the respective mixes of policy preferences that can be identified on either side of the spectrum, but it tells us relatively little about the broad range of noncriminal justice and relatively noncoercive measures in the middle of the spectrum.

There also can be no escape from the bare fact that analyses of costs and benefits, particularly in the domain of psychoactive drug policy, are powerfully shaped by the ideological and moral values of the analysts. Those who highly value notions of individual privacy and tolerance for diversity inevitably will diverge in their assessments of costs and benefits from those who emphasize communitarian notions of consensus and homogeneity as well as absention from all psychoactive substances. One would think, and hope, that the notion of minimizing loss of life as well as physical pain would represent a common middle ground on which all segments of the drug-policy spectrum would unite; but that has not, unfortunately, been the case to date. The result is that the debate over the future of drug policy will, and must, continue on two levels: the objective *identification* of the costs and benefits of alternative drug policies, in which the more value-based *evaluations* of their relative merits and weightiness are left to the side, and the more broadly based debate among both experts and the public over which values must be given precedence in evaluating drug policies and shaping the optimal alternative.

15

DRUG WAR FOREVER?

Kevin B. Zeese

When a government chooses drug war as its method of controlling drug abuse, it is choosing a war that will never end. There will be a perpetual state of war because there is a natural human desire for altered states of consciousness, there are many and varied sources for drugs, and because even the most repressive government cannot control the most private acts of its citizens. The evidence of the ultimate failure of drug war is the fact that even the tightly controlled atmosphere of a prison is rarely drug-free.

It is important to recognize that a war on drugs cannot be won, because then the choice between decriminalization and prohibition becomes easier. Under neither policy will drug use stop entirely. The goal must be to reduce the harms caused by the use of drugs and to prevent the policy from causing greater damage in other areas of our lives. When these goals are accepted, then any rational balance between drug war and drug peace comes out in favor of peace.

One of the great costs of the war-on-drugs approach is that it creates war zones. Our borders become war zones for battles between the government and the smugglers. Our neighborhoods become war zones for the battle between rival drug dealers as well as with the police. Foreign governments become war zones between the United States, allied governments, and drug lords. The war on drugs, if it has any impact at all, merely moves the war zone from one place to another, spreading violence, instability, and misery.

To some extent the *National Drug-Control Strategy* of the Bush administration recognizes that it cannot ever win the war on drugs. Even the title of the report with its focus on "control" acknowledges that drug use will always be with us. The rhetoric speaks of a "drug-free" society, but the reality speaks of harsh enforcement efforts with the goal of marginally reducing drug abuse. As a result the Bush administration policy is an admission that drug war will be with us indefinitely.

A Drug War History

A brief review of the war on drugs demonstrates that the Bush administration strategy is a mere repeat of previous drug-war efforts. The drug-prohibition policy dates back to the Harrison Narcotics Act of 1914. The modern war on drugs dates back to September 1969 when the Nixon administration announced "Operation Intercept." The war on drugs is now old enough that all the policies of the present are merely repeats of the failures of the past. A review of history will demonstrate that these "new" strategies of the Bush administration have in the past been counterproductive, making the drug problem a more destructive one.

Destruction at its Source Has Been a Failure

The centerpiece of the current drug was is the so-called "Andean Strategy." The administration touts this as a new strategy to destroy the cocaine crop at its source. In fact the policy of destroying drugs at their source began with the appointment of Harry J. Anslinger as the head of the Bureau of Narcotics in 1930. Prior to serving in that capacity, Anslinger served as the chief of the Division of Foreign Control, Prohibition Unit, of the Treasury Department. Getting the crop at its source was one of Anslinger's prime strategies. Indeed as early as 1933 the League of Nations ratified a treaty limiting the manufacture of narcotic drugs.

Drug warriors point to two great successes in the "destroy it at its source" strategy. The first was the eradication of the Turkish opium crop in the early 1970s. Yet where did that leave us? Has the heroin problem disappeared? No, in fact it was after the great Turkish success that there was an explosion of heroin use throughout the world. The Mexican opium market quickly made up the difference within two years; by 1974, its share of the illicit American heroin market jumped from 38 percent to 77 percent.

Today the opium crop is virtually untouchable as it has moved to the jungles of Southeast Asia. I recently attended a meeting with one of former drug czar William Bennett's top international policy planners who admitted that the opium crop was untouchable since it was controlled by generals with more powerful armies than the local governments of the Golden Triangle in Southeast Asia. In addition, more potent forms of manmade heroin substitutes such as China White have come on the scene. As a result of these realities, there is nothing in the Bush administration plan discussing getting opium at its source. It is likely that the Andean Strategy of the Bush administration will force some future president, a decade or two from now, to acknowledge that cocaine cannot be eradicated at its source. Not only that, but at a recent conference in Greece I learned that Turkey is flooding the European market with heroin.

The other great eradication "success" was the destruction of the opium and marijuana crops by spraying the herbicide paraquat in Mexico in the late 1970s. Three administrations played a role in paraquat spraying. It was the creation of G. Gordon Liddy during the Nixon administration, developed during the Ford administration, and implemented during the Carter administration. The spraying program's impact on the opium trade was to solidify the generals of the Golden Triangle. In addition, the opium trade of Mexico has not been eradicated. During the 1980s a resurgence has caused significant new heroin problems, particularly in the northwestern part of the United States with the spread of black tar opium.

The effect of the paraquat program on the marijuana market was even more dramatic. As a result of paraquat spraying in Mexico the slowly developing U.S. marijuana market exploded. Within a few years marijuana became the top cash crop in many states in the United States. Now marijuana has been reported under cultivation in all of the fifty states. Indeed the Bush-Bennett report indicates that the United States produces the finest marijuana in the world, accounts for 25 percent of the U.S. market, and has even become an exporter of marijuana.

In addition to creating the U.S. marijuana market, the paraquat-spraying program in Mexico encouraged an already rapidly growing Latin American marijuana market. The State Department reports that marijuana is being culti-vated in a dozen South and Central American countries. Of particular note was the rapid expansion of the marijuana market in Colombia. In addition, Mexico continued to be a major supplier of marijuana to the United States. The Drug Enforcement Administration reports that Mexico was the second largest exporter of marijuana to the United States in 1989.

The initial impact of eradication programs has been to spread the source of drugs out to new markets. This makes law enforcement's job more difficult and less cost-effective. It was much easier to limit the marijuana supply when it was all coming from Mexico than it is to limit the marijuana supply coming from fifty U.S. states, Latin America, and Southeast Asia. Paraquat spraying was not a success.

If the initial impact of past eradication programs demonstrated the failure of the "destroy it at the source" strategy, the long-term impacts are even more devastating. The Colombian marijuana smugglers who were helped in their success by the eradication of their competitors in Mexico became the cocaine lords of the 1980s. In reaction to the spread of the market to Colombia, the

Reagan administration focused on drug interdiction. They brought in high-tech military surveillance, AWACs and U.S. Customs balloons. These strategies were effective at catching marijuana mother ships. As a result Colombian smugglers switched to cocaine, an already developing market, and became wealthier and more powerful. This switch from marijuana to a more dangerous drug also made the drug scene in the United States more dangerous. In the past ten years cocaine use has exploded, cocaine has become more pure, and we have added crack to the drug marketplace. All these evils can be traced to paraquat spraying in Mexico.

The secondary effects in the United States were equally discouraging. The United States quickly developed into a popular source of nonpoisoned marijuana. United States farmers put their agricultural creativity to the task and developed sinsemilla marijuana, which the United States government now complains is more potent than the pre-paraquat marijuana. In response the United States mounted an attack on the home front. Aerial surveillance and eradication programs were developed throughout the country. These programs added to the rapid erosion of the right to be free from unreasonable searches. In the name of suppressing the U.S. crop the Supreme Court has upheld warrantless aerial searches, in *California v. Ciraolo*, 476 U.S. 435 (1986), low-level aerial searches of greenhouses, in *Florida v. Riley*, No. 87-764 (1989), the warrantless searches of barns adjacent to houses, in *United States v. Dunn*, 107 S.Ct. 1134 (1987), and allowing the police to trespass on private property without a warrant, in *Oliver v. United States*, 466 U.S. 170 (1984). National Guard troops have participated in eradication programs in dozens of states and in 1990 the U.S. Army was even used against U.S. citizens. This use of some of the same troops that invaded Panama is being challenged in *Drug Policy Foundation v. Bennett*, No. 4-90-2278 (N.D. Cal.).

The result of this home-front war zone has been predictable. The marijuana market reacted and began to grow smaller, more dispersed crops. Growers even hired their own airplanes to ensure that their crops could not be seen from the air. Indoor marijuana cultivation also became increasingly popular. In Oregon, one of the largest marijuana-growing states in the United States, more marijuana is grown in the city of Portland than in the rest of the state combined. The indoor marijuana market is making up an increasing share of the marijuana supply throughout the United States. Once again, law enforcement has made its job more difficult. Now they have to find a way to get into the basements and closets of millions of Americans.

Clearly, the "destroy it at its source" strategy has had many negative repercussions. It created new markets for the drugs under attack, created new and more powerful drug lords, encouraged more potent and dangerous drugs, eroded privacy and civil liberties, and made it more difficult to control the supply of drugs. In short, it created a less healthy, less stable, and more dangerous world.

Interdiction at the Borders Has Not Been Successful

Closely related to the "destroy it at its source" strategy is the "interdict it at the border" strategy. The results of this policy approach have been similarly ineffective. In addition it has been very costly and would not survive any reasonable cost-benefit analysis.

The effectiveness of interdiction programs is perhaps best demonstrated by the first large effort—Operation Intercept. This program was pursued by the Nixon administration in late 1969. The goal was to stop the marijuana traffic from coming across the border between the United States and Mexico. Commerce between the two countries was brought to a halt when the United States virtually militarized the borders and searched one out of every three cars that crossed the border.

The short-term effect was a reduced supply of marijuana. As a result, marijuana users switched to whatever other drugs were available. Most notable was an increase in amphetamine use. In the long run, marijuana smugglers switched from smuggling by land to smuggling by land, sea, and air. As a result, in a few months there was a marijuana glut.

Operation Intercept is a microcosm of the effectiveness of interdiction. In the short run, users switch to other drugs, usually more dangerous ones; in the long run, the smugglers find new routes for the old drug. As a result, a new drug is introduced, the old drug remains available, and interdiction becomes more difficult as smuggling routes become more diverse.

This same series of events repeated itself in the 1980s when the Reagan administration focused its resources on the South Florida Task Force in an effort to interdict drugs flowing into Florida. This task force, headed by then Vice President George Bush, created two new problems. First, they spread the smuggling routes from South Florida to the Gulf coast, the west coast, and the east coast. With the spread of smuggling routes came newly organized crime syndicates. These syndicates spread the murders that made South Florida's cocaine cowboys the center of attention in the early 1980s to murders occurring at record rates throughout the United States.

In addition to spreading the cocaine and violence problems to all coasts, the Reagan interdiction effort encouraged smugglers to switch to less bulky drugs. Smugglers switched from marijuana to cocaine. As a result cocaine prices dropped, potency and purity increased, and crack came on the drug scene. History repeated itself—interdiction caused diversified smuggling routes and created more dangerous drugs.

These results were not the only negatives of the Reagan interdiction program. Another cost was the destruction of a time-honored doctrine in American law. The *Posse Comitatus Act* of 1878, 18 U.S.C. Section 1385, was amended in 1981 to allow the military to become involved in the enforcement of civil laws.

The Constitution nowhere authorizes the military to be used to execute the laws; indeed the American Revolution was fought in part because of King George's misuse of his army in enforcing laws in the colonies. Perhaps the traditional view of the use of troops to enforce civil law was best expressed by Representative John D. Atkins (D-Tenn.) during the debates on the passage of the *Posse Comitatus Act*, when he said: "American soldiers policemen! Insult if true, and slander if pretended to cover up the tyrannical and unconstitutional use of the Army" [5 Cong. Rec. 2112, 44th Cong. 2d Sess., pt. 1 (Mar. 2, 1877)]. With the breach of that tradition in the name of the war on drugs, the military has become a lead player in the enforcement of drug laws, spending tens of millions of dollars annually on interdiction efforts.

Interdiction has become less and less cost-effective. In 1988 the Navy and Coast Guard spent a combined $40 million and seized a grand total of 17 ships—an average cost of $2.4 million per ship. The Air Force spent $8 million on AWAC surveillance planes in 1987 and 1988, to arrest a suspected 26 smugglers—an average cost of over $300,000 per arrest. These are obviously not effective ways of spending money to control drug supplies.

Unfortunately the interdictors have not given up. Now there are proposals to shoot down suspected smuggling planes, to build ditches and fences across the Mexican border, and to have the National Guard strip-search passengers flying into U.S. airports. The effects of these policies no doubt will be the same as Operation Intercept and the South Florida Task Force; more dangerous drugs, more drug abuse, and less civil liberties.

Going After the User Has Not Succeeded

Once again a brief look at history will demonstrate that we have gone after the user before, have made the user into the scapegoat—and have failed to improve the drug situation. Indeed the recent rhetoric comparing the user to a co-conspirator to murder is reminiscent of drug-war rhetoric of long ago. As Mr. Anslinger said: "Heroin smugglers and peddlers are selling murder, robbery, and rape, and should be dealt with accordingly. Their offense is human destruction as surely as that of a murderer. In truth and in fact, it is 'murder on the installment plan,' leading not only to the final loss of one's life but to [that of] others who acquire this contagious infection through association with the original victim."

This extreme rhetoric resulted not only in the aggressive prosecution of big-time drug dealers but also of small-time dealers and users. At the very beginning of the enforcement of the Harrison Narcotics Act of 1914, addicts became a major focus of drug enforcement. Within a few years of the act's passage 30 percent of federal prisoners were drug offenders and approximately 70 percent of these were addicts.

In the 1960s it was a felony to possess any amount of marijuana anywhere in the United States. People received long prison terms for possession of small amounts of marijuana. Throughout the 1970s hundreds of thousands of drug-possession arrests were made each year. Indeed, possession cases have consistently made up over 40 percent of all drug cases.

During these years of going after the user, drug use became widespread in the United States; from 1968 to 1978 marijuana use tripled. As a result, the strategy switched from going after the user to going after larger-scale dealers. In 1972 a national commission appointed by Richard Nixon recognized the failures of going after the user and unanimously recommended that possession and casual distribution of marijuana no longer be a criminal offense. Unfortunately the Bush administration has not learned the lessons of drug-war history and is returning to the original failed strategy of going after the user.

The thought of going after the user at this stage of the drug war must be considered ridiculous. The idea of going after the tens of millions of Americans, whether it is by placing them in "shock confinement," denying them jobs, taking away their cars, or denying them federal benefits, demonstrates abuse of power. It is also impossible. If it has any impact at all on drug users it will be to create an underclass, thereby causing new, more complex social problems.

In addition to being unfair to drug users, the policy is also unfair to nonusers. When government attempts to persecute tens of millions of its citizens, many innocent citizens will be abused. An example of this is drug testing. Drug testing has become commonplace. The vast majority of people test negative. They are innocent, yet they are forced to degrade themselves by urinating on demand.

The only good thing that can be said about the "going after the user" approach is that in the past it has been one of the last steps before decriminalization. One example noted above is the case of marijuana in the 1970s. Not only did the commission appointed by President Nixon recommend marijuana decriminalization, eleven states encompassing one-third the population enacted decriminalization and over thirty other states enacted laws that allowed first offenders to be placed on probation and to have no criminal record. Similarly, alcohol prohibition was in its last years when the prohibitionists attempted to go after the user.

Mandatory Minimum Sentences Have Not Worked

Another strategy that has made its way back into the drug war is mandatory minimum sentences. Until recently the most repressive federal drug laws and penalties in American history were the mandatory minimum sentences imposed in the 1950s. In 1951 the Boggs Act amended the Harrison Act to impose mandatory minimum penalties—two to five years for the first offense, five to ten for the second, and ten to twenty for the third, with no possibility for a suspended sentence or probation after the first conviction (P.L. 81-255, 65 Stat. 767, 1951).

The Boggs Act of 1956 was even harsher, increasing penalties for many drug-law offenses, including a sentence of five to twenty years for any first-offense sale or smuggling conviction and the death penalty for sale of narcotics by an adult to a minor under eighteen years of age (P.L. 84-728, 70 Stat. 767, 1956).

The other harsh mandatory sentencing law was the famed Rockefeller drug law enacted in 1973. It provided extremely harsh sanctions; for example, a person who possessed over two ounces of heroin or who sold one ounce was subject to a mandatory minimum sentence of fifteen years to life, with no chance for plea bargaining. A 1977 study by the New York City Bar Association found that heroin use was as widespread in 1976 as in 1973 when the law first took effect.

These laws only created problems and did not prevent the spread of drug use. They resulted in prison overcrowding, difficult-to-manage inmates, and juries and judges who refused to convict people because they realized people were facing lengthy mandatory minimum sentences. Interestingly, they were enacted just before the advent of the 1960s, the decade in which drug use became widespread in the United States. I am not saying that the mandatory minimum sentences caused the drug use explosion of the 1960s, but they also did not stop it from occurring. The high costs and failures of these laws became evident and, as part of the 1970 Controlled Substances Act, the mandatory minimum sentences were for the most part repealed.

Unfortunately in the 1980s mandatory minimum sentences have made a comeback. Their effects have been as they were before—the overcrowding of federal prisons with no reduction in drug abuse or crime. Currently drug offenders make up nearly half of the federal prison population. We have once again returned to the harsh failures of the past. Even conservative, heavy sentencing judges are finding great discomfort in handing down mandatory minimum sentences.

Harsher Policies Will Not Work

Two examples of perhaps the harshest punishments available indicate that no matter how extreme we get on the law-enforcement side it will never be effective in limiting drug use. The death penalty and civil commitment of addicts, two policies the Bush administration is encouraging, demonstrate that the drug-war approach will never be effective no matter how harsh it becomes.

Although the death penalty for drug offenses has been enacted into law in the United States, it has never been seriously enforced. Other countries, however, have attempted to use the death penalty as a real enforcement tool. The Malaysian model is a popular example. The Dangerous Drugs Act of 1975 in Malaysia demands a death sentence for drug trafficking. Mere possession of small amounts of drugs results in a presumption of trafficking—15 grams of heroin, 200 grams of marijuana. From 1975 through September 1988, 73 people were executed for violation of the drug laws. (In the United States on an equivalent population basis that would be 1,100 executions).

The effectiveness of the death penalty, and other harsh policies in Malaysia, demonstrates that even this extreme will not work. In the early 1970s there was no significant drug problem; by the early 1980s there were 300,000 regular drug users and 61,000 addicts. By 1988 the number of addicts jumped to between 90,000 and 250,000, depending on which reports you believe. Widespread executions did not prevent a rapid increase in drug addiction.

The other policy the Bush administration is encouraging, civil commitment, has also been tried and been unsuccessful. Civil commitment is the involuntary placement of a drug user into an in-patient treatment program without being convicted of a criminal offense. This results in the user's long-term confinement without the protections of the criminal process. Civil commitment has been tried before in U.S. history. Indeed, in one form or another the confinement of addicts in institutions has been the predominant mode of treatment during this century.

The most noted program was the U.S. Public Health Service program at Lexington, Kentucky, which opened its doors in 1935. Reviews of the success of the program have found that less than 10 percent, in most studies less than 5 percent, of addicts released from the program did not relapse into drug abuse. Similarly, programs in California and New York during the 1960s had single-digit success rates.

THE HIGH COSTS OF THE WAR ON DRUGS

No matter how extreme we become, drug-war policies will not succeed. A review of history demonstrates that the maxim of Andrew Weil from *The Natural Mind* is correct: "Drugs are with us to stay. Fight them and they will grow ever more destructive." Indeed, as indicated above, the cycle of the war on drugs has been the harder we fight the war, the more dangerous drugs become and the more destructive their effects are on society. In addition to not reducing the drug problem, the drug war has many other costs that must be considered in choosing appropriate drug policies. These costs are more directly caused by the policy than by the effects of the drugs.

Some of the costs of prohibition policies have already been discussed. Following is a brief review of some of the other costs of the drug-war strategy.

Criminal Justice Overcrowding

The criminal justice system is overburdened at every stage. The cause of this logjam can almost always be traced back to the war on drugs. Last year 1.3 million people were arrested for drug offenses, according to the FBI. That is two drug arrests every minute of every day, and half of them are for possession, not sale, of drugs.

Nationwide, drug offenses account for nearly one-fourth of all felony convictions. The impact is also felt in the prison population; nearly one-half of all prisoners are drug offenders. In 1990, for the first time in U.S. history over one million Americans were behind bars. The next time someone complains about unsolved murders, rapes or robberies, or complains about the inefficiency of our court system or about prisons being overcrowded, you will know the culprit— overzealous enforcement of drug laws.

Prohibition Creates Crime

Prohibition adds to a variety of forms of crime. Turf battles between rival drug gangs have caused homicide rates to soar through the United States—1990 produced a record 20,000 homicides. Drug lords have created new organized-crime entities, whether it is the cartels of Colombia, the Jamaican drug gangs, or the street gangs of Los Angeles and other cities. In addition, addicts who crave illegal drugs and who pay black market prices often have to steal to get enough money for their habit. Many of those that do not steal sell drugs, thereby expanding the problems caused by drugs. As Milton Friedman said seventeen years ago, the quickest way to reduce crime in the streets is to end drug prohibition.

The Drug War Creates Corruption

Throughout the United States, in every agency involved in the war on drugs, there have been reports of corruption. Hundreds of local police, prosecutors, judges, and federal agents have all been convicted of various drug charges. One single case can have a dramatic impact on the success of drug enforcement. For example, during October of this year four ex-customs agents were indicted on drug charges. Allegedly they were informing drug smugglers when it was safe to bring their goods into the United States. These four agents alone cleared the way for over four tons of cocaine and 35 tons of marijuana. The combination of immense profits and the frustration of failed drug enforcement make it impossible to prevent future cases of corruption.

Civil Liberties Are Undermined in the Name of Drug Enforcement

Drug prohibition violates privacy because the government in essence tells individuals what they can put into their bodies and how to alter their consciousness. As the war on drugs fails and becomes more intense, courts and legislatures are weakening the civil liberties of all Americans. Above I have reviewed some of the Supreme Court decisions and legislation related to the eradication and interdiction efforts that demonstrate some of these trends. There are many other examples: allowing search warrants to be issued based on an anonymous tip in *Illinois v. Gates*, 462 U.S. 579 (1983); allowing warrantless searches based on drug-courier profiles, in *U.S. v. Montoya de Hernandez*, 473 U.S 531 (1985); allowing widespread automobile searches without a search warrant, in *U.S. v. Ross*, 456 U.S. 798 (1982); allowing the searching of bodily fluids without any suspicion of drug use, in *NTEU v. Von Raab*, 109 S. Ct. 1384 (1989); allowing dogs to search luggage without a warrant or probable cause, in *U.S. v. Place*, 426 U.S.606 (1983); and allowing searches of trash left on the sidewalk for disposal, in *California v. Greenwood*, 108 S. Ct. 1625 (1988). It is clear that when it comes to drug enforcement the criminal justice system is no longer a system of justice but a weapon of war.

The Drug War Warps Foreign Policy

The immense profits of the drug trade have made some drug lords more powerful than the governments of the countries in which they operate. Indeed, some countries seem to have been taken over by traffickers or are at least working with them. Drug money has been used to create instability in foreign countries. Our relationships with foreign governments have been strained by the drug war. We force countries to allow us to prosecute their citizens, we bring our troops to foreign soil, we threaten to cut off financial assistance to desperately poor countries if they do not follow our drug-war policy, we spray environmentally dangerous herbicides on foreign lands, we indict officials of foreign governments, and we kidnap citizens of foreign governments to prosecute them in the United States.

The Drug War Threatens Health

Perhaps the best example of the war on drugs creating an unhealthy situation is the spread of the AIDS virus among IV drug users. The prohibition of needles and the refusal to adopt addict-friendly needle-exchange programs is causing the AIDS virus to spread throughout the United States. The largest source of new AIDS cases is intravenous drug users. In New York City alone over 100,000 addicts are infected with the HIV virus. Drug warriors are willing to risk an epidemic of death rather to compromise in any way in the war on drugs.

There are just a few of the other costs of prohibition policies. There are many more, indeed even the billions of dollars spent on ineffective drug-law enforcement could be better spent on treatment, prevention, or dealing with the underlying social problems that lead to abuse.

The Benefits of Decriminalization

Before discussing whether decriminalization would succeed in controlling drug abuse better than prohibition, I will examine the side benefits of decriminalization, because another way to look at the costs of prohibition is to look at the benefits of reform. Among the benefits of decriminalization are the following.

Billions of Dollars in New Tax Revenue Could Be Raised

Decriminalization *could* include taxes on illicit drugs for three reasons. First, like any product it should pay its share of the costs of government. Second, this money could be earmarked for treatment, prevention, and research in the drug field. Finally, taxes should be used as a discouragement tool. The harmfulness-tax concept espoused by Lester Grinspoon makes obvious sense. By taxing more dangerous drugs more heavily we would discourage their use. We must recognize that overtaxing these products is not appropriate, however. Taxes must be designed in a way related to the costs of the product to society. Overtaxing the product could be as counterproductive as prohibiting it.

Decriminalization Would Allow the Regulation of Drugs

Decriminalization allows society to implement other forms of controls over drugs. Basic regulations for any legal product often include restrictions or requirements for proper packaging, labeling, and advertising. This could include health warnings and potency labeling. Drugs can also be regulated to ensure their purity. This alone would make drug use safer. Restrictions can also be placed on where and when drugs can be used. For example, driving under the influence should be prohibited, as should consumption in public areas. In addition, age restrictions should be placed on drug use, as well as restrictions on the use of drugs by pregnant women.

Decriminalization Would Result in Safer Drug Use

By decriminalizing drugs they are brought from the underground to above ground. In this way, drug addicts will be able to have contact with doctors or other professionals. They will be able to learn the difference between safe and unsafe use of drugs. Social controls will be allowed to be developed so that drug abuse will be prevented. Those who need treatment will not be afraid to get it.

Friends, families, or employers of drug abusers will be able to talk with the abuser without the criminal law blocking communication. Addicts will be more likely to come forward when treatment is user-friendly and where there is no threat of criminal prosecution.

Decriminalization Will Allow Greater Medical Use and Research

Currently many drugs are prohibited not only for recreational use but also for medical use. This situation prevents drugs with known medical value from being used to treat a wide variety of serious illnesses. It also prevents research on drugs with potential medical value. Allowing doctors to make decisions with their patients will create a healthier society. Similarly, treatment options will be broadened. Not only will drug-free treatment be available, but addicts will be able to switch to less dangerous drugs; heroin addicts could be allowed to smoke opium, for example. In addition, in cases where the doctor and patient decide it is appropriate, maintenance on the drug can be used as a treatment option.

Decriminalization Will Encourage People to Move to Safer Drugs

Many of the most potent drugs available exist because of the pressures of the black market: Since the first goal of black market trafficking is not to get caught, and since more potent and purer drugs are easier to smuggle and easier to hide from authorities, they are more popular under black market conditions. When prohibition policies are ended, the consumer will control the market. Just as the cigarette market has moved to low tar and low nicotine cigarettes and the alcohol market has moved toward wine coolers nonalcoholic beers, drug use generally will move toward safer drugs. This natural movement can be encouraged by government regulatory and tax policies.

In addition to all these advantages, all the disadvantages of prohibition described above will be removed. Crime will be reduced, organized criminal enterprises will be weakened, the criminal justice system will become more efficient, and the erosion of civil liberties will slow or perhaps even be reversed.

CAN DECRIMINALIZATION WORK?

When considering the alternative to prohibition one must recognize a variety of possible forms of decriminalization. Just look at some of the substances that are currently legal; there are tomatoes, over-the-counter drugs, alcohol, tobacco, and prescription drugs. All these substances are legal but all are controlled differently. When one talks of decriminalization versus prohibition, it is necessary to recognize that this is not a black and white choice. Surely, the decriminalization model that is chosen will be more sophisticated than the tomato model. It will give society control over the drugs, indeed more control than there is currently with the black market approach to illegal drugs.

In addition, since legalization offers a variety of options, each drug will be treated differently based on the various risks involved with its use. Even within a class of drugs there could be differences. For example, coca leaves and opium could be less restricted than crack and heroin. Unlike prohibition policy, decriminalization is complex and sophisticated.

The critical question is whether decriminalization would result in a massive increase in drug use. A knee-jerk reaction to this question is that decriminalization would of course lead to massive increased use, but there is good evidence that decriminalization would not result in any significant additional use of illegal drugs and that any increase that did occur would be short-term. In the long run other social controls—family, religion, peer pressure, school, and employment— would be powerful tools to discourage drug use.

A good example of how these controls can be effective is the treatment of alcohol and tobacco. It has only been during the past two decades that society has attempted to develop discouragement policies for these drugs. It is evident that these policies have been effective. Two decades ago, half the population was addicted to tobacco, now less than one-third is. That is very significant because nicotine is perhaps the most addictive drug available (yes, even more addictive than cocaine) and because it is still controlled very loosely—that is, it is available over the counter and in vending machines, it is advertised, and it is subsidized by the government. No doubt under present political realities even marijuana, the safest currently illegal drug, would be controlled more stringently than tobacco. In addition to seeing reductions in the use of both alcohol and tobacco, we have also seen movement to safer, less potent forms of the drugs, nonalcoholic beers, wine coolers, low-tar and low-nicotine cigarettes.

Another example of the relaxation of laws not causing increased use is the decriminalization of marijuana. By 1978 eleven states encompassing one-third of the population had decriminalized marijuana. In addition, over 30 other states had enacted conditional discharge laws which allowed first offenders to be placed on a brief period of probation and, when that was completed, to have no criminal record. This relaxation of laws did not result in increased use. Indeed, since 1978 there has been a dramatic decline in marijuana use among all age groups, particularly adolescents. I am not claiming the change in laws caused the decline, but relaxation of the laws did not prevent a decline in use.

This case is similar to, although not as dramatic as, the success of marijuana law reform in Holland. The Dutch went further than we did. They actually allowed marijuana and hashish to be sold in stores. They saw an even more dramatic decline and, in fact, only .5 percent of Dutch adolescents now use marijuana on a regular basis; in the United States approximately 5 percent do so. The Dutch claim the change in law actually caused the decline. Normalization of the law made marijuana boring.

Another example of successful drug-law reform is the medical heroin model of Britain. The British continue to allow heroin to be prescribed. Prohibitionists attempt to describe the British experience as a failure, yet a look at the statistics will demonstrate that in fact heroin-use rates in Britain are much lower than in the United States and drug-related violent crime is virtually nonexistent. Clearly, if we could rid our society of drug-related violent crime and reduce our drug-use rates to those of Britain, we would consider the policy a dramatic improvement over today's rates.

There are two reasons prohibition actually encourages the use of illegal drugs. The first is the "forbidden fruit" glamorization of illegality. This is particularly powerful among youth going through their rebellious teenage years. The second affects adults as well as youth—black market profits. This is especially true in our ghettos where there is little hope or opportunity for success. Decriminalization does away with both these causes and thus we should not be surprised that reform might actually result in a decline in drug use.

The only evidence prohibitionists offer to demonstrate that repeal would cause increased use is our experience with repeal of alcohol prohibition, but this is very deceptive. Although there was an increase in use it is impossible to tell how large it was since we can only guess at alcohol-use rates during prohibition. In addition, if one looks at alcohol use throughout U.S. history, one will see massive swings in use rates. The laws do not cause those changes. Much broader and more powerful societal trends cause use to go up and down. In fact even during prohibition, use of hard alcohol increased.

Arguably alcohol use is higher now than during alcohol prohibition, yet no one advocates return to alcohol prohibition. We as a society recognize that the costs of such prohibition policy are higher than any marginal reduction in alcohol use that might occur. In reality, the same cost-benefit analysis holds true for drug prohibition as well.

We can learn from the repeal of alcohol prohibition, however. Repeal of drug prohibition should not be entered into with a partying frenzy. It should be entered into with great caution. There should be strong antidrug messages while repeal of drug prohibition takes place. We should spend money to develop the social controls needed to prevent drug use. If we take precautions and develop decriminalization, with some regulation and taxation, we can prevent any significant increase in drug use.

Repeal of drug prohibition respects the decision-making ability of each individual. The individual is responsible for his or her own health and well-being, rather than the government. When presented with the true risks of drug use most individuals will make sensible choices. We are a health-conscious society. One need only look at our concern with cholesterol, or eating oat bran, or sales of workout tapes to recognize that most people do not want to hurt themselves. Decriminalization, entered into with caution, will not inevitably result in massive increases in drug use.

How Would Decriminalization Work?

Each drug would be controlled differently, but the basic scheme for decriminalization would include the following.

Free Market Controls

The most powerful control would come from the tendencies of the free market. Just as tobacco products have gotten safer—low-tar and low-nicotine cigarettes, and alcohol has gotten safer—nonalcoholic beers and wine coolers, currently illegal drugs would move to safer forms. This would occur because consumers prefer the products and because producers prefer healthy customers. This is just one example of how the free market would positively affect the drug trade.

Age Limitations

Only adults should be allowed to purchase any drug. The same age for legal purchase of alcohol should apply to all drugs. Although this could continue a black market in drugs it would be small, something similar to the black market for alcohol, which goes virtually unnoticed. As a parent I am more afraid of the black market in illegal drugs than I am of the black market in alcohol. With alcohol, I feel relatively confident that the dealers are known and regulated by the government.

Purity Controls

Drugs would be regulated to ensure that they were pure and did not contain contaminants, like bacteria and fungus, or adulterants, like other drugs or chemicals. This would significantly reduce the hazards of drug use.

Marketing Controls

Marketing controls would include regulation of advertising, labeling, packaging, and any other promotion. Advertising could be banned, or at least severely restricted. It could also be heavily taxed to allow prevention advertising to be funded as well. Labeling and packaging would include health warnings, potency information, and dosage information. In this way drug users would be told the risks they are taking and also told how to use a drug properly to limit the risk of its use.

Drugs Would Be Taxed

Taxation is an effective tool for controlling use. By taxing more-dangerous drugs more heavily, we could use tax policy to encourage the use of safer drugs. In addition, tax levels should be consistent with the costs of the drug to society and should include money for research on addiction, health hazards, and prevention of drug abuse.

Time and Place Restrictions

Restrictions would include where drugs could be used—perhaps only at home for some drugs, for others maybe a clinic or government-regulated recreational center. These restrictions would also include prohibiting being under the influence of drugs while driving.

Insurance Regulations

Insurance carriers could be required to treat drug users differently from non-drug users. In this way the health risks of drug use would be borne by those taking the risks. This could also be an effective discouragement tool by making drug use more expensive.

These are the *options* for a controlled decriminalization plan. As I noted at the outset of this section, restrictions would vary from drug to drug. For the most dangerous drugs, some or all of these restrictions could be included. In short, decriminalization offers society an array of controls. Indeed, there seems to be strong evidence that we could reduce drug abuse at the same time that we reduce all the adverse effects of drug prohibition.

THE WORLD AFTER REPEAL

What would the world look like if drug peace broke out? The world would be healthier, safer, and more humane. Drug use would not disappear, but that cannot be promised under any policy option. Drug use would be more controlled and safer.

We would be able to walk virtually any street at night as crime would be significantly reduced. Our criminal justice system would no longer be in gridlock. Our police could spend their time becoming members of the community rather than being at odds with a large percentage of it. Police would be able to focus their resources on more violent criminals. Courts would not be forced to plea-bargain in virtually every case to keep up with their workload, and prisons would have reduced populations and provide a greater opportunity for rehabilitation.

Doctors and patients would not have their relationship interfered with by the government's desire to prevent even the medical use of banned drugs. Researchers would be able to conduct research with currently banned drugs so that the secrets of their healing powers could be discovered. Addicts would have a wider variety of treatment options available to them. Doctors would be able to treat addicts as human beings rather than as criminals. They could help prevent the dangers of drug abuse by telling their patients how to use drugs safely and by teaching them the importance of using clean needles.

Social controls would be allowed to develop. Parents and children would be able to talk to each other about drug use. Employers would not have to play the role of police; instead, they would become partners with their employees in helping to prevent drug abuse and in helping those with drug problems. Schools would not have to compete with "forbidden fruit" glamorization and the entice-ment of black market profits.

The constitutional foundations of American society could be restored. No longer would police be wiretapping, entrapping, and invasively searching tens of millions of Americans. We can stop the erosion of our individual rights and perhaps return to a society that recognizes individual rights and the limits our constitution places on the powers of government.

Substituting prohibition with controlled legalization will not make a perfect America, but it will make a better one.

REFERENCES

Brecher, Edward, *Licit and Illicit Drugs* (1972)

King, Rufus, *The Drug Hang-up* (1972)

Musto, David, *The American Disease* (1972)

National Commission on Marihuana and Drug Abuse, *Drug Use in America: Problem in Perspective* (1973)

National Research Council of the National Academy of Sciences, *An Analysis of Mari-juana Policy* (1982)

Trebach, Arnold, *The Heroin Solution* (1982)

Weil, Andrew, *The Natural Mind* (1972)

Trebach, Arnold, and Zeese, Kevin, *Drug Prohibition and the Conscience of Nations*, Drug Policy Foundation (1990)

PART FIVE
LEGAL IMPLICATIONS

16

DRUG PROHIBITION:
AN ENGINE FOR CRIME

Ira Glasser

For the past seventy-five years, the United States has pursued a policy of criminal prohibition with respect to certain, but not all, mind-altering drugs. Despite its all too apparent failures, a succession of administrations from both political parties, both locally and nationally and with virtually no exceptions, has persuaded the American public that a prohibitionist policy is the best, indeed the only, way to control drugs and the crime associated with them.

Curiously, although this policy has historically failed to curb the drug market or reduce the associated crime, our policymakers have never seriously reconsidered its underlying premises. Instead, they have called for more of the same. This has led to a cycle of more vigorous enforcement of stronger and stronger laws, despite the persistent failure of such laws to achieve lasting remedial results. Wide public acceptance of this approach has enabled the state to remain largely above criticism and at the same time to accumulate tremendous and sometimes unconstitutional powers.

The unvarnished truth is that far from controlling the drug market and the crime related to it, prohibition is an engine for crime and violence of an increasingly virulent nature. The analogy between the alcohol prohibition of the 1920s and current drug prohibition is far from exact, but just as alcohol prohibition produced an increase in violent crime in the 1920s,[1] drug prohibition, and especially the current war on drugs, has produced an increase in violent crime in the 1980s. If current policies continue, we will see more of the same in the

1990s. When the American public finally understands this paradox, drug-policy reform will be not only possible, but also inevitable.

WHICH DRUG PROBLEM?

In 1989, a staggering 64 percent of the American public named drugs as the nation's most serious domestic problem in a *New York Times*-CBS poll. This was the highest percentage ever received by a single issue in any public-opinion poll.[2] Although recently drug policy has been eclipsed by the Persian Gulf war and the economy, the public's concern still remains very high. Indeed, Americans are so concerned about drugs that many say they are willing to give up fundamental Constitutional rights in return for a solution to the drug problem.[3]

When you probe beneath the superficialities of public-opinion polls and talk with people one-on-one or in focus groups, you immediately run into a definitional problem: Which "drug problem" are people so intensely concerned about? Are they concerned about the health consequences of drug addiction? After all, the underlying rationale for drug prohibition is that the state has a moral and legal obligation to protect its citizens from the ravages of substance abuse. The drug laws exist to dissuade otherwise law-abiding Americans from using taboo substances. Those substances are taboo because, according to the United States Supreme Court, "to be a confirmed drug addict is to be one of the walking dead. . . . the teeth have rotted out; the appetite is lost and the stomach and intestines don't function properly. . . . Often times, too, death comes—much too early in life. . . . Such is the torment of being a drug addict; such is the plague of being one of the walking dead."[4]

The fact is that, for the vast majority of Americans, the adverse medical and social consequences of the use of illicit drugs is not the "drug problem" they are talking and worrying about. If the public were really concerned about the physical and emotional health of drug users, then the chief objects of their concern would not be the 9.5 million Americans who use illegal drugs on a regular basis;[5] they would be concerned about the 94 million who abuse our two most lethal (but legal) drugs, cigarettes and alcohol.[6] When measured by the number of users, the number of addicts, the number of deaths, the costs to our health and insurance systems, and the costs to employers, then clearly cigarettes and alcohol exact a far greater toll on the nation's medical and social well-being than do all the illicit drugs combined.[7] Even though the public knows that cigarettes and alcohol exact a terrible toll, we do not see newspaper headlines announcing that 64 percent of the American people think of them as our number-one problem.

When people talk about the "drug problem," they are really talking about the pervasive violence and crime that they have come to associate with illegal drugs—

the guns, the automatic weapons, the bullets flying, the degradation of their quality of life. The internecine violence we are witnessing today brings to mind the opening scene of the movie, "The Untouchables," which depicts the determined efforts of Elliot Ness to put Al Capone behind bars. A ten-year-old girl is shown, lunch pail in hand, entering a store on an errand for her mother. Unbeknownst to her and to the proprietor of the store, but known to the movie audience, a revengeful bootlegger has placed a valise full of dynamite inside the store. The little girl makes her purchase and, as she turns to leave, the camera pans back and the store is blown to smithereens. It is a shocking and deeply disturbing scene, and the viewing audience invariably groans in unison.

Today, in real life, innocent bystanders are being similarly slaughtered by the bullets of our modern-day bootleggers—the drug dealers. On December 2, 1990, Maria Rodriguez, a fifty-three-year-old mother of seven, was gunned down in front of her Brooklyn, New York, apartment building.[8] Two weeks later, Randall Wade, a 42-year-old man, was shot and killed while chatting with a friend on a Harlem, New York, street corner.[9] Randall Wade was the 26th innocent bystander killed in New York in 1990 by the stray bullets of drug dealers settling their commercial disputes with guns.[10]

Violence is the predictable outcome when the government defines a highly profitable economic transaction as illegal and places it outside the rule of law. When Schenley's and Seagram's have a price war, they sue each other in court. If a liquor store owner is in debt to a liquor manufacturer, the creditor can turn to the courts for help in collecting the debt. Merchants involved in black-market commercial disputes do not have that luxury; they must settle their differences in the streets where innocent bystanders may get in harm's way.

DRUG-RELATED VIOLENCE IS INCREASING

The public perception of mounting out-of-control violence is accurate. Despite the fact that drug use is actually on the decline,[11] homicide and robbery rates in many urban areas are soaring.[12] Although the rising crime rate cannot be entirely attributed to drug-related crime, much of it can.[13] Certainly police chiefs around the country believe that the increases in homicides are largely caused by drug-related violence. New York City police commissioner Lee Brown estimates that more than 30 percent of all homicides in that city are drug-related, and that a still larger percentage of innocent-bystander homicides are drug-related.[14] "Drug-related crime" is an extraordinarily imprecise term that has been used by the media and others to describe many very different scenarios. What does it mean? One thing it usually does not mean is people killing other people because they are high on drugs. Just as Al Capone did not order the

LEGAL IMPLICATIONS

executions of rival bootleggers because he was drunk, drug dealers are not killing their rivals in the streets of New York, Chicago, Detroit, or Washington, D.C. because they are high on cocaine. At the height of Washington, D.C.'s outbreak of murderous violence in 1989, then Police Chief Maurice Turner knowingly observed: "Eventually the turf will be divided. They will go out and sell their drugs. People will pay their bills on time. And we're not going to have all of these shootings we have now."[15]

That drug-related violence is primarily a consequence of the illegality of those drugs was borne out by the rather dramatic findings of a 1989 government-funded study by Narcotic and Drug Research, Inc.[16] The researchers scrutinized the circumstances surrounding all 218 "drug-related" homicides in four of New York City's high-crime Police Department "zones" over an eight-month period in 1988. They discovered that the great majority of these homicides were cocaine-related (166, or 84 percent). Of those 166 murders, 87 percent were classified as "systemic"; that is, "arising from the exigencies of working or doing business in a black market."[17] In only one case was the perpetrator of the murder actually under the influence of cocaine. In almost all the "psychopharmacological" homicides (in which a specific substance caused the perpetrator to behave in a violent manner), the culprit was not an illegal drug at all; it was alcohol. In fact, 21 out of a total of 31 psychopharmacological homicides were alcohol-related (and in another four of those 31, alcohol was present along with one or more other drugs). The "drug problem," by which most people mean the drug-related crime and violence problem, is almost entirely a function of our bankrupt drug policy— prohibition.

THE LIMITS OF THE CRIMINAL SANCTION

For many years the criminal sanction has been the government's preferred tool for dealing with the use of drugs other than cigarettes and alcohol. Various law-enforcement stratagems have been employed in an attempt to control the drug problem, based on the definition of it as a criminal rather than a medical or social problem. During the early 1980s, the Reagan administration favored a "supply-side" strategy and spent billions of dollars trying to keep illicit drugs from entering the country. This strategy's greatest accomplishment may have been the successful interdiction of the relatively benign marijuana, whose bulk and odor made it easy to detect. Drug smugglers soon discovered that powdered cocaine was far easier to conceal, and during this period the quantity of cocaine entering the United States rose astronomically.[18] Many experts now believe that the successful interdiction of marijuana was a significant contributing factor not only in nurturing the domestic cultivation of marijuana but also in creating the cocaine epidemic of the middle and late 1980s.[19] By the time George Bush came into office, the supply-side strategy had been largely discredited and replaced by "demand reduction." In his inaugural speech, President Bush made the new strategy official: "The answer to the problem of drugs lies more in solving the demand side of the equation than it does on the supply side, than it does on interdiction or sealing the borders.[20]

There are many ways for the government to reduce the public's demand for a potentially harmful product. There is, for example, the extraordinarily successful government public-education campaign to curtail cigarette smoking. The percentage of Americans using this highly addictive drug has dropped dramatically in the past two decades, from 43 percent in 1964 to 30 percent in 1980.[21] This reduction was accomplished without resort to urine tests, without reliance upon criminal law, and without bombing tobacco fields in North Carolina. (Indeed, it was accomplished at the same time the government was paradoxically subsidizing the nation's tobacco crop!)

The campaign to reduce cigarette-smoking has been primarily founded on considerations of public health. Through persistent and pervasive public education, we have changed the way our culture views cigarette-smoking. We did use some laws, but sparingly. We said you could no longer smoke in circumstances where your habit would irritate innocent bystanders. People can no longer smoke in elevators, in subways, on airplanes, or in certain parts of restaurants. These laws focused on innocent bystanders and did not attempt to criminalize smokers who smoked privately or in a way that did not impose the habit on other unwilling people. Moreover, even those laws were passed *after* a significant change had taken place in the public's attitude toward smoking and those laws, in turn, fostered a deepening of those attitudes.[22] The breaking of a dangerous national drug habit (nicotine) that was far more institutionalized and widespread than all the illegal drugs combined was achieved without bludgeoning our citizenry with a heavy dose of the criminal sanction and without causing violent crime.

For reasons of history and cultural bias (but not for reasons of science or public health), we have chosen a different path in our efforts to reduce the demand for the currently illegal drugs. For cocaine, marijuana, and heroin, we have used criminal law as our primary instrument. Law-enforcement officials, however, are often the first to admit that our criminal-justice approach to drug control has enormous limitations. Police chiefs, district attorneys, and corrections officials throughout the country have repeatedly warned us that our over-reliance on criminal sanctions will lead only to the strangulation of our criminal-justice system, not to a resolution of the drug problem.[23]

When asked what we should be doing to reduce the demand for drugs, those same law-enforcement officials suggest that we should be dealing with the underlying social problems that lead so many of our youth to seek escape through intoxication: poverty, unemployment, lack of educational and vocational opportunities. This approach has often been derided as an old-fashioned, liberal view. By late 1990, however, this theme *among police chiefs* had become so persistent that then federal drug czar William Bennett felt compelled to criticize them for departing from official dogma. According to the *Los Angeles Times*, in private meetings with police chiefs around the country, Bennett "chided them for emphasizing the role of others, including schools and families, in combating the drug problem." He urged them to "stress their own role in battling narcotics" instead.[24]

Bennett's hostility to the proposition that criminal sanctions might not be the best way to reduce this country's huge appetite for drugs shows the extent to which our drug policy has been guided by ideology rather than facts. The truth is that the government is far more interested in law enforcement, no matter how counterproductive, than it is in figuring out how to bring drug use *under control*. Although we may experience periods of relatively low drug use (we appear to be heading into such a period now that the cocaine epidemic of the 1980s is abating), our drug problem (crime and violence) will remain out of control so long as we pursue the illusory goal of achieving a "drug-free America" by means of criminal prohibition.

NEGATIVE CONSEQUENCE OF CRIMINAL PROHIBITION

Prohibition has not only caused escalating levels of violence; it has produced other negative social consequences as well:

• Prohibition-driven laws criminalizing the possession of hypodermic syringes have led to an explosion of AIDS cases among intravenous drug users. Against all common sense and in the face of mounting scientific proof that these laws encourage unsafe injection practices, those states with the highest rates of contagion, including New York and New Jersey, have refused to decriminalize needle possession, much less initiate publicly funded needle-exchange programs.
• Functionally, our drug laws are protective legislation for criminal drug cartels. They protect the cartels against competition, against taxation, against regulation, and against quality control. Because there is a demand that cannot be extinguished and that remains large enough even when it is repressed to support a flourishing market, prohibition operates to create and sustain a violent criminal market entirely beyond the reach of government regulation and the rule of law. Empowered by their immense wealth, the drug barons corrupt our legal system, and shoot our citizens and our police.
• In our single-minded prosecution of the war on drugs, we have diverted funds from social programs, including economic opportunity programs, that even

law-enforcement officials say are the best crime-prevention tools we have. The only economic opportunity program we have for inner-city youth today is drug-dealing. For the teenager or pre-teenager living in the ghettos of this country, often with an unemployed mother and a father he has never met or rarely sees, who has no legitimate job options and exists in the midst of an economy that is not likely to accommodate him, drug-peddling is a lure, a magnet, and a high even more than the drug itself. Asking such a child to "just say no" to $300 a day is a cruel joke. These young people, raised in a violent crime subculture, will grow into adults who have nothing but contempt for the law and who operate outside it.

• Our hyperactive enforcement of criminal drug laws is destroying our criminal justice system. The sheer volume of drug arrests is overwhelming our police, our prosecutors, our defense bar, our courts, and our jails and prisons. The focus on primarily nonviolent drug offenders has meant inattention to other far more serious crimes, including violent crimes such as rape and murder.

These negative consequences of prohibition have produced a sense of crisis and the growing public perception that law enforcement has not ended the "drug plague" because we have not been tough enough. The public has been led to believe that we have not been tough enough because of the ACLU, because of lenient judges, because of the cultural residue of the sixties, and because of the constitutional handcuffs placed on the police. None of this is true. People want results, and they want them right away: If they are told that more prisons are the answer, they will support more prisons. If they are told more street sweeps and more arrests are the answer, they will say, "fine." If they are told that constitutional rights, even their own, are getting in the way of the war on drugs, they will give them up. Our politicians, ever mindful of the public's mood, have responded by building more prisons and passing an astonishing array of repressive laws that strike at many of our most fundamental rights.

The United States now has the dubious distinction of having the world's highest known rate of incarceration. According to a new study by The Sentencing Project, we have surpassed even the incarceration rates of the Soviet Union and South Africa with our curent 426 prisoners per 100,000 population.[25] Our incarcerated population has doubled during the past decade to its present, unprecedented level of one million. The study names the war on drugs as the "largest single factor behind the rise in prison population during the past decade."[26]

The public has been willing to pay dearly for this dubious distinction. It now costs $16 billion per year to incarcerate one million people in our jails and prisons.[27] They have been willing to pay because they believe that putting drug offenders behind bars will make the streets safer. The truth is that our bulging jails and prisons have not given us safe streets. Even with the highest incarceration rate in the world, we only arrest and convict a tiny percentage of those who buy and sell illegal drugs. In 1988, approximately 28 million Americans used illicit drugs,[28] and billions of illegal drug transactions took place but only one million of those offenders were arrested, and two-thirds of them were arrested for possession, not sale.[29] Those dealers who did get caught were quickly replaced by other willing recruits. Indeed, at the same time our prison population was growing by leaps and bounds, so was our rate of violent, drug-related crime.

The public has also accepted and supported the steady erosion of civil liberties. Individual rights are always among the first casualties in any war, and the war on drugs is no exception. A fearful public is most vulnerable to false claims that constitutional "technicalities" shackle the police and prevent them from doing their job.[30] High crime rates always spell trouble for civil liberties.

Over the past decade we have seen the evolution of what some legal experts have called "the drug exception to the Constitution." Random, suspicionless drug-testing has become so widespread that Supreme Court justice Antonin Scalia has railed against this "immolation of privacy and human dignity in symbolic opposition to drug use."[31] For the first time since the Civil War, and in a radical departure from American tradition and the Posse Comitatus Act, the military has participated in domestic law enforcement. During the summer of 1990, soldiers were deployed in rural counties in California and Oregon to eradicate marijuana cultivation. "Drug-courier profiles," which circumvent the requirements of the Fourth Amendment, are being used in airports, train stations, bus depots, and on highways. If you are black and well-dressed and pay for your ticket in cash, you are in real danger of being interrogated by the police. People are losing their homes through streamlined forfeiture proceedings because they were caught growing a few marijuana plants in their basements. We are prosecuting impoverished, pregnant women for using drugs while at the same time denying them access to prenatal care and drug treatment. The war on drugs has altered our constitutional landscape much to the detriment of civil liberties. These tough-sounding measures have not brought the relief from the drug problem that the politicians promised. The crime rate is still climbing. Innocent bystanders are still dying.

Clearly prohibition has failed. The criminalization of a social problem—drug use—leads only to escalating levels of violence, which leads to a fearful public clamoring for more prisons, tougher laws, and fewer rights. In the end, everybody loses except for the drug dealers.

DECRIMINALIZATION WILL LEAD TO A HEALTHIER, LESS CRIME-RIDDEN COUNTRY

The strongest argument prohibitionists have against decriminalization is that it would almost certainly lead to an unacceptable increase in drug use and drug abuse. This is an article of faith among prohibitionists and has gained credence through repetition. The actual evidence is far from clear. There is even some evidence that drug use actually remains constant or may even decline after decriminalization.[32] This is a very complex issue that requires further research and study.[33]

Merely focusing on the possible increase in drug use begs the many more important questions that need to be asked and debated. Even if more people use drugs under a regime of decriminalization:

- Will drug-related violence decrease?
- Will the health of drug users be enhanced through quality control of drugs, regulated potency, and the legal availability of sterile needles?
- Will civil liberties and the rule of law be strengthened?
- Will the criminal justice system be released from the impossible burden of adjudicating more than one million drug arrests a year?
- Will the criminal drug cartels be to a large extent defunded?
- Will the corruption of public officials decrease?
- Might we focus on the real social and economic problems faced by our inner-city residents instead of on one of the symptoms?

Decriminalizing drugs will make it possible to recognize drug abuse as a health problem and a social symptom, not a crime problem. By shifting the responsibility for drug control from the criminal justice system to the health system where it properly belongs, those who use drugs need no longer be consigned to a life of criminality. Liverpool, England, which embraces a medical approach to drug misuse, boasts "the healthiest addicts in the world." It is a boast worthy of emulation. Decriminalizing drugs will also lead to an enormous reduction in violent crime. Reducing the harm to drug users is a worthy goal; reducing the harm to the rest of the population is even more worthy.

NOTES

1. During prohibition, violence was commonplace in establishing exclusive sales territories, in obtaining liquor, or in defending a supply. Between 1923 and 1926, the peak period of struggle for control of the Chicago market, an estimated 215 bootleggers died in that city at the hands of rivals. In New York, over 1,000 gangland murders occurred during prohibition. See David E. Kyvig, *Repealing National Prohibition* (University of Chicago Press, 1979), p. 27.

2. *New York Times*, September 12, 1989, p. B8.

3. According to a *Washington Post*-ABC News poll taken just after President Bush's September 1989 national address on drugs, 62 percent of those interviewed said they would be willing to give up "a few of the freedoms we have in this country" to reduce illegal drug use. Eighty-two percent said they favored the use of the military in domestic

drug-law enforcement; 52 percent said they would agree to let police search homes of suspected drug dealers without a court order, even if the houses "of people like you were sometimes searched by mistake"; 67 percent favored allowing the police to stop cars at random to search for drugs, "even if it means that the cars of people like you are sometimes stopped and searched"; and 83 percent favored encouraging people to report drug users to the police, "even if it means telling police about a family member who uses drugs." See Richard Morin, "Many in Poll Say Bush Plan Is Not Stringent Enough," *Washington Post*, September 8, 1989, p. A1.

4. *Robinson v. California*, 370 U.S. 660 (1962), concurring opinion of Justice William O. Douglas. The adverse physical consequences of drug addiction are grossly exaggerated in this passage and ignore both the differences among drugs and different patterns of usage, but this gruesome description is still deeply embedded in the public's consciousness as the singular image of all users of all drugs.

5. National Institute on Drug Abuse, *National Household Survey on Drug Abuse: Population Estimates* (1988).

6. Surgeon General's Office (1989); *National Household Survey* (1988).

7. According to the National Council on Alcoholism, Inc., 97,500 Americans per year die from alcohol abuse. (Marsha Rosenbaum, *Just Say What?* (National Council on Crime and Delinquency, 1990) p. 6.) In 1990 there were 434,000 smoking-related deaths in the United States, an 11 percent increase over 1989. (S. Okie, "Smoking-Related Deaths Up 11% to 434,000 Yearly, CDC Reports," *Washington Post*, February 1, 1991, p. 1.)

8. Donatella Lorch, "Mother of Seven Killed on Street by Stray Bullet," *New York Times*, December 4, 1990, p. B3.

9. James McKinley, Jr., "Man Killed on Corner, Apparently by a Stray Bullet," *New York Times*, December 16, 1990.

10. Lorch, "Mother of Seven," p. B3

11. The results of the National Institute on Drug Abuse's ninth periodic National Household Survey on Drug Abuse, issued in July 1989, showed that the estimated number of Americans using any illegal drug on a "current" basis (once per month) had dropped 37 percent—from 23 million in 1985 to 14.5 million in 1988. Current use of marijuana and cocaine were down 36 and 48 percent, respectively. (*National Drug-Control Strategy* (The White House, September 1989), p. 1.)

12. An August 1990 report issued by the FBI showed significant increases in the rates for murder, robbery, and aggravated assault between 1875 and 1990. During that period murder rose by 13 percent; aggravated assaults rose by 32 percent; robberies rose by 16 percent; forcible rapes increased by 7 percent. ("F.B.I. Report Confirms Sharp Rise in Violent Crime," *New York Times*, August 6, 1990.) In 1990 homicide records were broken in eight of the country's largest cities. New records were set in New York City, Washington, D.C., Dallas, Phoenix, San Antonio, Memphis, Milwaukee, and Boston. ("Many Cities Setting Records for Homicides in Year," *New York Times*, December 9, 1990, p. 41.) According to the Federal Centers for Disease Control, homicide is ravaging the community of young black men. The homicide rate among black men between the ages of 15 and 24 rose by two-thirds in the five years through 1988. In 1987, homicides accounted for 42

percent of deaths among men in this group. (Seth Mydans, "Homicide Rate Up for Young Blacks," *New York Times*, December 7, 1990, p. A26.)

13. In 1990 drugs were the leading cause of killings in Washington, D.C., accounting for 39 percent of all homicides. ("Again in Capital, a Homicide Record," *New York Times*, November 25, 1990.) The Federal Centers for Disease Control also named drug trafficking as a major contributing factor to the rising homicide rate among young blacks. (Mydens, "Homicide Rate Up.")

14. Jonathan Greenberg, "All About Crime," *New York Magazine*, September 3, 1990, p. 27.

15. "Capital Official Sees Crime Drop Once Pushers Divide Markets," *New York Times*, March 26, 1989, p. 20.

16. Paul Goldstein, Henry Brownstein, Patrick Ryan, and Patricia Bellucci, "Crack and Homicide in New York City, 1988: A Conceptually-Based Event Analysis," *Contemporary Drug Problems*, Winter 1989, pp. 651–87.

17. The researchers classified as "systemic homicides" those killings that resulted from territorial disputes, robbery of a drug dealer, assault to collect a debt, punishment of a drug worker, dispute over a drug theft, retribution because a dealer sold bad drugs. (Goldstein, "Crack and Homicide," p. 14.)

18. See Peter Reuter, "Can the Borders Be Sealed?" *The Public Interest*, Summer 1988, p. 53; Arnold Trebach, *The Great Drug War* (Macmillan Publishing Co., 1987), pp. 177–78.

19. See Ethan A. Nadelmann, "Drug Prohibition in the United States: Costs, Consequences, and Alternatives," *Science*, September 1, 1989, p. 940; Mark A. R. Kleiman, *Marijuana: Costs of Abuse, Costs of Control* (Greenwood Press, 1989); Richard C. Cowan, "How the Narcs Created Crack," *National Review*, December 5, 1986, p. 26; Daniel Lazare, "How the Drug War Created Crack," *The Village Voice*, January 23, 1990, p. 22.

20. Gerald M. Boyd, "Bush, Citing Costs, Says Drug War Will Focus Largely on Education," *New York Times*, January 26, 1989, p. 1.

21. That cigarette smoking is highly addictive is no longer a matter of controversy. According to the Surgeon General's 1988 report on nicotine addiction: "The pharmacologic and behavioral processes that determine tobacco addiction are similar to those that determine addiction to drugs such as heroin and cocaine." ("The Health Consequences of Smoking," *Surgeon General's Report*, 1988, p. 9.)

22. In his classic book, *Drugs, Set, and Setting*, Dr. Norman Zinberg describes this interaction between informal social controls (social sanctions and rituals) and formal social controls (laws and institutional rules). Zinberg's research supported his theory that conditions for controlled, nonaddictive drug use are optimal when informal and formal social controls are in harmony, as has been the case in the government's campaign to reduce cigarette-smoking. (Norman E. Zinberg, *Drugs, Set, and Setting* [Yale University Press, 1984], p. 5–18.)

23. See Robert Reinhold, "Police, Hard Pressed in Drug War, Are Turning to Preventive Efforts," *New York Times*, December 28, 1989, p. 1, quoting various law-enforcement officials to the effect that police, on their own, cannot solve the drug problem.

24. Ronald Ostrow, "Briefing/Law Enforcement," *Los Angeles Times*, October 15, 1990, p. A5.

25. Mark Mauer, "Americans Behind Bars: A Comparison of International Rates of Incarceration," The Sentencing Project, January 1991.

26. Ibid, p. 9. The Sentencing Project also documents the radically disproportionate representation of black men in U.S. prisons compared to their representation in the general population. The United States now incarcerates black men at a rate of four times that of black men in South Africa.

27. "Justice Expenditure and Employment, 1988," Bureau of Justice Statistics, United States Department of Justice, July 1990.

28. National Institute on Drug Abuse Household Survey, 1988.

29. "Sourcebook of Criminal Justice Statistics, 1989," Bureau of Justice Statistics, United States Department of Justice, 1990.

30. Police and prosecutors, on the other hand, know that constitutional protections do not impede them in their efforts to enforce the law. In its November 1988 report, the American Bar Association's Special Committee on Criminal Justice announced the results of its national telephone survey of over 800 defense lawyers, judges, prosecutors, and high-ranking police administrators. The committee found that, "Taken as a whole, the testimony and the survey results demonstrate that constitutional limitations are not seen as a relatively significant problem by the people who must work within those limitations." ("Criminal Justice in Crisis,") American Bar Association, November 1988, p. 14.)

31. *National Treasury Employees Union v. Von Raab*, 109 S. Ct. 1384 (1989).

32. Following decriminalization of possession of small amounts of marijuana in a number of states in the early 1970s, follow-up studies in several of them indicated that marijuana use had not increased at a significantly greater rate since decriminalization and that some law-enforcement resources had been freed to deal with more serious crimes. (Oregon: "Marijuana Survey—State of Oregon," 1977. California: "Impact Study of S. B. 95, 1976." Maine: "An Evaluation of the Decriminalization of Marijuana in Maine," 1978; "A Time/Cost Analysis of the Decriminalizaiton of Marijuana in Maine," 1979, cited in Zinberg, *Drugs, Set, and Setting*, p. 196.) In the Netherlands, where possession and sale of marijuana were decriminalized in 1976, the number of new users has decreased in the intervening years. Before 1976, 10 percent of Dutch 17- and 18-year-olds used marijuana; by 1985 the rate had dropped to 6.5 percent. (Dr. Frits Ruter, "The Pragmatic Dutch Approach to Drug Control: Does It Work?" *Drug Policy Forum*, May 25, 1988, p. 15.)

33. Zinberg argues persuasively that prohibition causes more, rather than less, drug abuse because repressive criminal laws prevent users from developing more effective informal social controls that promote moderate, controlled use. (See *Drugs, Set, and Setting*, pp. 196–97.)

17

Drugs, Change, and Realism: A Critical Evaluation of Proposed Legalization

Edwin Meese III

Recent proposals to legalize the importation, distribution, and sale of illicit drugs, including such substances as marijuana, cocaine, and heroin, would mark a sweeping change in United States public policy, dramatically reversing laws that have existed since the early part of this century. Despite increasing evidence of the health hazards and public safety dangers of illegal drugs, advocacy for their legalization has been pressed in some circles of opinion despite the fact that such ideas conflict with public opinion, historical experience, the current status of antidrug-abuse efforts, and common sense.

Because proponents of legalization seldom provide a detailed prescription for how such a scheme would be implemented, usually making only vague references to taxing and regulating drug sales, there is much uncertainty about how such a system would work in practice. This makes it difficult to calculate with any degree of specificity the exact danger to health, the public safety risks, and the societal damage that would be caused by legalizing the traffic in drugs.

Since the burden of proof is on the proponents of such change in drug policies, it is incumbent upon them to provide the answers to several critical questions:

1. How would a plan for the legalized sale and distribution of illicit drugs be structured? (The types of issues raised by this requirement are discussed below.)

2. What problems encountered under current laws would be alleviated by legalization?

3. What other benefits to society, if any, would be provided by legalization?

4. What new problems would be created by the legal sale of illicit drugs?

5. On the basis of the factors set forth above, how would the people of our nation be better served by changing to a scheme for the legalized sale of illicit drugs?

It would take a clear and certain demonstration of significant beneficial effects for the United States to abandon its current policies and to embark on a radically new course of drug legalization. This paper will discuss the reasons why this burden has not been met by legalization proponents and why the available evidence points toward the opposite conclusion.

ORIGIN AND STATUS OF THE CURRENT DRUG PROBLEM

Advocates of legalization usually base their arguments on the premises that drug abuse is an inescapable fact of modern life, that current policies and practices are failing to reduce drug use, and that legal penalties against drug trafficking and drug abuse cannot succeed. Analysis of the origin and history of the nation's current "drug epidemic" presents a contrary view.

Although in the 1950s and early 1960s there was concern in many parts of the country about the use of illicit drugs—primarily heroin and the increasing experimentation with marijuana—only a relatively small and isolated segment of society was involved in such conduct. Most citizens of all ages were not involved in or affected by drug abuse, except for those who were victims of the crimes, such as burglary and theft, that drug users committed to support their habits.

During the "days of rebellion" and social unrest of the 1960s and early 1970s, however, the illegal use of drugs spread to virtually every segment of society. As Dr. Mark S. Gold, a New York psychiatrist and leading authority on drug abuse, has described it:

First, young college students began to experiment with drugs they redefined, calling them "recreational drugs"—primarily marijuana and psychedelic substances like LSD. The counterculture movement, which sprang up as part of this era . . ., embraced mind-altering drugs and their use spread across the country. Adults imitated students and young people, who were the trend-setters in the 1960s.

As these drug users grew older, the use of cocaine became more frequent, particularly among young professionals. According to the National Institute of Drug Abuse, by 1985 an estimated 36.8 million people in the United States had at some time in their lives been involved in the use of illegal drugs and some 23 million were current users—current use being defined as having used illicit drugs at least once in the previous 30-day period.

During the 1960s and 1970s, supposed experts on drugs were giving conflicting advice, and society's prevailing attitudes on this subject were, to be charitable, ambivalent. Some high federal officials were dismissing the "recreational use" of cocaine as harmless and there was discussion, even in the White House, of decriminalization of certain drug use. As one analyst of the drug scene has written, "The explosion of drug use during the 1960s and 1970s was the result of a misguided acceptance of drugs and the *de facto* legalization policies of the time."

In 1981 and 1982 the situation changed. Medical research increasingly pointed up the health dangers inherent in the use of marijuana and cocaine (heroin already being recognized for its hazardous nature). A new federal strategy was established, combining strong law enforcement and international efforts to restrict the supply of drugs with a major domestic campaign to reduce the demand for these substances through prevention, education, treatment, and rehabilitation.

By the end of the 1980s, a new trend toward decreased use of illicit drugs was clearly identifiable. The 1988 National Household Survey on Drug Abuse, conducted by the National Institute on Drug Abuse (NIDA), showed that between 1985 and 1988 the number of people using any illicit drug in the 30-day period preceding the survey dropped 37 percent, from 23 million to 14.5 million regular users.

This finding has been confirmed by virtually every other drug indicator. The National High School Senior Drug Abuse Survey, conducted annually by the University of Michigan's Institute for Social Research, is the leading indicator of both drug use and attitudes toward drugs among that age group. The 1988 survey showed that during the three-year period, 1985 to 1988, use of any illicit drug by high school seniors during the 30 days prior to the survey dropped from nearly 30 percent to 21.3 percent. The most recent survey, taken in 1989, showed that this downward trend in current use continued to a low of 19.7 percent. This contrasts sharply with the peak drug-abuse years of 1978 and 1979, when 38.9 percent of high school seniors reported current drug use.

Particularly significant is the change in attitudes toward drug abuse among high school students. Seniors who disapprove of even occasional marijuana use increased from 74 percent in 1988 to 77.2 in 1989, while the number disapproving of occasional cocaine use rose from 89.1 percent to 90.5 percent during the same period. A similar pattern was found in students' perception of the harmfulness of drug use.

Although the problem of drug abuse is yet far from solved, these data do reveal that widespread indulgence in these illicit substances is neither inevitable nor uncontrollable.

LEGALIZATION AND PUBLIC OPINION

A corollary to the trend in both attitude and behavior is the overwhelming public opinion against the legalization of illicit drugs. Numerous polls over the past several years have reflected this viewpoint, with antilegalization sentiments prevailing by margins of three or four to one. One of the most extensive recent opinion surveys, a Gallup Poll taken in January 1990, indicates that 80 percent of those questioned think drug legalization is a bad idea, and only 14 percent think it is a good idea. Furthermore, 75 percent of those who oppose legalization feel very strongly about their position but less than half of those who think it is a good idea are strong in this feeling.

Anecdotal evidence of the public's trend away from drug abuse is shown by a news account of early November 1990 that *Sinsemilla Tips*, a magazine for marijuana growers, is going out of business after ten years. Its publisher blames the nation's "antidrug climate," which has reduced his publication's circulation by 80 percent, for the demise of his magazine.

A further indication of public attitudes is the action of Alaska voters at the November 1990 election, where marijuana-decriminalization laws were repealed and that substance once again was made illegal.

THE ANALOGY BETWEEN DRUGS AND ALCOHOL

Proponents of legalization often claim that alcohol and illicit drugs are comparable substances and that therefore, because one category is legal, the other should be also. They contend that because the legal prohibition against alcohol was repealed, the illegal status of dangerous drugs is doomed to failure also. It is therefore important to point out the differences in kind between these two types of substances.

Initially, it should be noted that alcohol can be used responsibly and that only a small percentage of those who drink liquor become intoxicated. By contrast, the only purpose of using illicit drugs is to "get high," and the inevitable intoxicating effect of such drugs provides the essential difference from alcohol. This should not be taken as minimalization or approval of the inebriation that does occur among some drinkers, nor as an underestimation of the devastation wreaked upon society by those who abuse alcohol. The exponential expansion of that devastation, however, by legalizing substances that are much more likely to lead to more dangerous and irresponsible conduct is hardly the answer to the alcohol problem that does exist.

A second difference is that alcohol has an extensive social and cultural history, has normally been regarded as a legal commodity in most civilizations, and enjoys public support for its availability to adults who use it responsibly. That is why a lack of moral consensus for its prohibition caused the repeal of that ban after the "Great Experiment," between 1918 and 1933. By contrast, illicit drugs have been banned from general legal use in most societies, do not have a history of responsible use, and face an overwhelmingly negative public response to the concept of legalization.

Another difference is the experience with the addicting qualities of the two substances. With approximately one millions users of alcohol in the United States, about 10 million, or 10 percent, are acknowledged alcoholics—addicted persons. With illicit drugs, the addiction rate can go as high as 50 to 60 percent, with even higher rates for substances such as crack.

Finally, it should be noted that the experience with alcohol prohibition is instructive in analyzing the proposals to legalize illicit drugs. During its nearly fifteen years of existence, prohibition was successful in terms of its own objectives as a public health measure. Alcohol consumption was reduced by 50 percent. Deaths for men due to cirrhosis of the liver decreased by over 60 percent. The numbers of admissions to mental institutions declined by over 40 percent. The suicide rate and other alcohol-related medical problems were reduced by over 50 percent.

CRIME AND DRUGS

It is argued by prolegalization advocates that the legal availability of illicit drugs at lower prices will reduce crime because it will eliminate drug trafficking, with its associated violence, and will make it unnecessary for drug users to steal and rob to obtain the money to buy drugs and maintain their habits. Whether or not legalization will eliminate the black market in drugs—and thus traffickers and drug-oriented organized crime—is discussed later, as is the impact on demand caused by lower prices and greater availability through legal outlets. The likelihood of a decrease in drug-related crime is extremely questionable.

The Drug Use Forecasting program (DUF), initiated during the 1980s by the National Institute of Justice, provided for urinalysis testing of persons arrested for nondrug crimes in several cities throughout the United States. This testing revealed that these people, charged with a variety of crimes from murder to violent assault to sex offenses and child abuse, tested positive for drugs in their system at rates up to 80 percent. Studies by the National Institute of Justice also show that drug abusers are at least as violent as, and perhaps more violent than, criminals who have not used drugs. These findings, a change from law-enforcement experience during the era when opiates and marijuana were the most frequently used drugs, correlate with the violence-inducing propensities of cocaine and its counterpart, crack.

A 1986 State Prison Inmate Survey, conducted by the Bureau of Justice Statistics in the U.S. Department of Justice, provides further evidence that the low-cost availability of drugs will increase serious crime. The study showed that many inmates began to use drugs only after their criminal careers had already started. Half of the inmates who had ever used a major drug and 60 percent of those who had ever used a major drug regularly did not do so until after their first arrest. Only 13 percent of inmates, the survey found, seemed to fit the pattern of drug addicts who committed crimes for gain. In crimes unrelated to stealing for drug money, 32 percent of those convicted of rape, 24.9 percent of those convicted of sexual assault, and 37.2 percent convicted of kidnappping were under the influence of a drug at the time of the offense. Violent and dangerous criminal behavior results from the influence of mind-altering drugs and such crimes will only increase if substances such as cocaine are readily available at low cost.

LEGALIZATION, DEMAND, AND THE BLACK MARKET

The most frequent claim of legalization proponents is that it would eliminate the black market by making drugs legally available and would "take the profit out of drugs" by lowering the price. This, it is contended, would put the drug trafficking syndicates out of business, thus stopping the violence and deaths resulting from the turf wars, drug and money thefts, and narcotic-debt collections. The low price, it is said, would make it unnecessary for users to rob and steal to gain the money for their drugs. For several reasons, these arguments are fallacious, as will be subsequently discussed.

Even if these optimistic predictions were to occur, society would still lose because the lower price, legal status, and ready availability of drugs would most certainly lead to an increased demand, both in terms of the numbers of people using and the frequency of use. Cocaine, in powder form and when crystallized as crack, creates in most people an intense desire for gratification through increasingly frequent use of the drug. The easy access to inexpensive cocaine would result in more intensive use (an assumption already validated during periods of low street prices and by the appearance of crack at an "affordable price" over the past several years).

Some libertarians may argue that people ought to be able to destroy themselves through massive drug abuse if that is their choice, but the price—in both financial and human terms—is usually paid by society. Emergency medical treatment and extensive hospital costs are usually a public charge since many drug users are indigent, a proportion that will increase as intensive drug abuse makes them unemployable. Likewise, the higher involvement in traffic fatalities (already 10–15 percent) and workplace accidents, as well as family abuse and the birth of over 100,000 cocaine-damaged babies each year, produce costs that are borne by the entire citizenry. It is clear that drug abuse is not a "victimless" endeavor.

REGULATION, PRICE, AND DRUG USE

Some advocates of legalization have suggested that a relatively high price be placed on the newly legal substances to provide an economic disincentive to overly intensive use. Others recommend a special tax on drug sales, both to limit use and to provide additional funds for prevention and treatment of addiction (presumably to counteract the flood of new users that might well be expected if drugs become legal). Still other ideas involve extensive regulation to attempt to contain the potential societal damage that might emerge from changes in drug policy.

All these proposals, intended to offset the negative effects of a legalized regime, might be desirable under those circumstances. But each measure that makes it more difficult to obtain the legalized drugs makes it more likely that a black market will continue to operate. If, for example, the price remains high, then a black market will flourish by undercutting the legally established price. In this regard, it should be noted that crack became popular as an alternative to powder cocaine because the quantity involved in each sale was designed to be affordable to the less affluent purchaser.

Similarly, if certain types of drugs are excluded from the menu of legal sales, the potential for a black market in those commodities continues. It is highly unlikely, therefore, that legalization would totally eliminate the opportunity for illegal drug trafficking, and that the attendant public safety problems would not exist as they do today. This should not be surprising. Just as bootlegging syndicates did not turn to legitimate enterprise when prohibition was repealed, but turned to other forms of organized crime such as gambling, prostitution, or loansharking, it is highly probable that if illicit drugs were legalized, today's trafficking rings would continue in illegal activity and seek every possible way to develop a market for those substances that remain outside of legitimate commerce.

It is possible that the black market activity might take an even more sinister turn, with illegal purveyors of illicit drugs concentrating on youths and seeking to expand use among those who are too young to purchase drugs legally. Whereas the 1988 National Household Survey showed 75 percent of young people aged 12 to 17 had never used illicit drugs of any type, that situation could change drastically if this age group became the prime target for economically displaced drug pushers.

ILLEGALITY AND ATTITUDES TOWARD DRUGS

Proponents of legalization charge that current antidrug statutes make criminals out of otherwise law-abiding citizens, whose only offense is the desire to use illicit drugs for their own private enjoyment. Although this is the plight of any individual who seeks his or her personal pleasure in ways that are legally prohibited by society, the fact of illegality itself has a positive benefit in discouraging the use of illicit drugs in the first place. Among high school age young people, as many as 70 percent of respondents in New Jersey and 60 percent in California said that fear of getting in trouble with the law constituted a major reason not to use drugs. Among mature adults similar views prevail, which accounts for the relatively small proportion of people who do indulge in illicit drug use.

Dr. Robert DuPont has made the same point by comparing trends in legal versus illegal substances, where both have been the subjects of major health campaigns. In 1988 users of the legal products—alcohol and cigarettes—numbered 106 million and 57 million, respectively. Among users of the illegal products, there were only 12 million marijuana users and 3 million users of cocaine. Between 1985 and 1988, extensive educational efforts were conducted to inform the public of the health hazards of all four items (including warnings on cigarette packages, notices at liquor sales outlets, and extensive television advertising). During this period marijuana use declined 35 percent and cocaine use was 50 percent lower, while alcohol and tobacco use dropped only 6 percent and 5 percent, respectively. The fact that dangerous drugs are illegal is one of the most powerful deterrents to their use. On the other hand, abruptly changing a basic public policy—saying in effect that what was wrong yesterday is all right today—would send exactly the wrong message to young people who are currently choosing not to use drugs.

DRUG POLICY AND INTERNATIONAL RELATIONS

The United States is a signatory to the Single Convention on Narcotic Drugs of 1961 and the Convention on Psychotropic Substances of 1971. Both agreements obligate us to control and reduce the use of illicit drugs. This country also took an active part in the United Nations Conference on Drug Abuse and Illicit Trafficking in 1987, which involved 138 nations, including all the major industrial and commercial powers. The United States joined in signing the agreement to combat illegal drugs that resulted from that conference. For this nation now to legalize drugs such as cocaine, heroin, and marijuana would be to abandon the obligations under these treaties and to destroy our credibility on this subject in the eyes of other countries.

CONCLUSION

While uncertainty prevails about exactly how a drug legalization scheme would work, what is known provides little promise that problems that currently exist in the present system—crime, black markets, and so on—would be alleviated, let alone that a net benefit to society would result. Certainly an example of the historical success of such an endeavor remains to be demonstrated. To prevent an increase in the number of users of illicit drugs, with the attendant personal and societal costs, to keep faith with international obligations, and to avoid changing course just when current efforts are beginning to show significant progress, proposals for the legalization of illicit drugs should be soundly rejected.

COMMENT

Joseph D. McNamara

It is a wonderful opportunity to be at the Hoover Institution and talk about a war on drugs. We have already had consensus here—which I certainly share—that "war on drugs" is a very poor term. I have to risk my career once again by agreeing with the ACLU and Ira Glasser—many of the things he said were quite true. The connotation of war and the methods that one uses in a war have unfortunately created problems in policing. I have to hasten to add that, before I get fired for agreeing with the ACLU, I have to say—and I'm sorry about this, Ira—that I do not agree with some of your other ideas.

The fact is that we have a very complex situation on our hands. A thought came to me earlier, when Frank Zimring answered a question; it seems to me that we already are in the midst of de facto decriminalization of drugs despite an announced public policy of war. We certainly are moving away substantially from the past policy of 70 or 80 years of more and more draconian penalties and stricter law enforcement.

What Frank mentioned was that we can have public policies that we call wars or whatever, or talk about building consensus, and the bureaucracies will go on doing what they like to do anyway. Anyone who thinks that because Bill Bennett speaks about a war on drugs means cops out on the street are not going to be motivated by how much overtime they get on a drug arrest or other things that really influence police decisions is ignoring reality. Similarly, the courts and correctional systems are not going to respond more to a message from Washington than to their own needs. The fact is that in our large cities there are not enough police to make drug arrests consistent with this policy of a war on drugs. From the most conservative judge to the most liberal judge, they agree that the courts are already clogged by drug cases. You can see there is a lot of unhappiness about that. There is no room in the jails for more people. We as a nation do not want to build more prisons and we certainly do not want a tax increase according to last Tuesday's elections.

There has been, then, a de facto decriminalization. We in San Jose, and in some other cities, are still making a lot of the arrests for casual drug use and drug possession that are called for under the law—but that's about where it ends. People are being cited. There is no capacity for them to go through trial and they are diverted, before trial, into a treatment program. Unfortunately, there aren't enough treatment programs either, and we just go through this kind of mass self-delusion that we're somehow really seriously trying to use criminal law to wage war against drug abuse.

I have to agree with Ira Glasser that we do not really know what drug abuse is. No one has defined that. For example, I think the price rise of drugs gets a lot of debate. I have been personally outraged by the enormous increase in the price of Chardonnay and the question of public policy on wine prices set by the California legislature. On the other hand, police departments and public officials on a local level do feel a tremendous amount of pressure. Ed Meese was correct when he said that the "public opinion polls are still very strong." People are demanding that there be more law enforcement against drugs.

The last time I spoke on this kind of issue I got into an awful lot of trouble. I made what I thought was a rather reasonable statement, that there is need for a blue-ribbon presidential panel to research and analyze the extremely complex and important issues involved in United States drug-control policy. Two weeks later the National Rifle Association took out ads with my picture in uniform in *Time* magazine, *Newsweek* magazine, and *USA Today*, falsely saying that I wanted to legalize crack cocaine. The other side of that story is that had I said it, maybe I would still be here today but I probably would not be here as the police chief of San Jose, because there is a tremendous concern about drug abuse and people do view law enforcement as the answer to it.

I have to say that my experience goes back to Harlem, where I started more than 30 years ago walking a beat, and had the very unpleasant duty of carrying out youngsters with powerful muscles—dead. Some of them with the needle still stuck in their arm. When I first got to Harlem, the heroin epidemic had not yet hit. I do not think it started in the 60s here in Berkeley. I think that was a different kind of movement, but the things that I saw in Harlem are very troublesome and at that time we thought this was the most deadly drug that ever came along. What days of innocence! We now are concerned about ice and crack cocaine. In my midcareer, I suddenly got sent to Harvard Law School as a Criminal Justice Fellow. I stayed on and did my doctoral dissertation in the Kennedy School of Government on drug-enforcement strategies, and in 1972, when I finished it, I was very pessimistic. I did not think what I saw law enforcement doing in the future was going to work. I wish that I had not been so correct.

The police chiefs of this country, who just met last week in Tulsa, disagree with Bill Bennett and the federal government. We think there is just as much drug abuse out there as there ever was. I think what we have heard here in these sessions is true. We are talking of values, and society wants to limit some behavior that is very negative. When youngsters get stoned on drugs and drop out of school it does have an impact on democracy. Clearly, drug abuse also puts many people in danger of violence. The question is, are the solutions that we are suggesting, with more and more criminal laws, worse than the problem? I think one solution is worse than the problem, and that is the increasing use of the military. I happen to believe personally that that is far more dangerous to the future of the democracy than the drug problem, and use of the military is growing as politicians expand the rhetoric of a war on drugs. Wars are fought against an identifiable group of people. Who are the enemies in the war on drugs?

I think inevitably we will move toward policies that place much greater emphasis on drug-prevention education and on treatment, even though we do not really know very much about either. My own feeling is that this will be an improvement. It is a much more humane approach than strip searching and jailing users, of whom many are minorities. We are reaching the combustion point in many of our cities. That is one of the costs of drug enforcement that we ought to talk about. The police in this country are becoming increasingly militant. I think one partial solution is to immediately prohibit the sale of military-type assault rifles so that police do not have to do military raids every time they hit a drug pad, but I have not been successful in convincing legislators about that argument.

In the end, drug-control policies are value judgments, and we should consider them very carefully. To just say, "legalize," and possibly throw away generations of people, most of whom will be minorities, seems to me something that we cannot afford to do. It is also clear that our past and present efforts are unacceptably costly failures on many levels. This conference has raised many questions about a possible "middle ground." It is important to pursue this concept.

I remember Professor Ed Banfield speaking at Harvard to a group of us mid-career bureaucrats, and it was a rather hostile audience. He had just published *The Unheavenly City*, which was a rather articulate description of how poverty programs failed and were actually counterproductive, and many people in the room had dedicated their careers to those programs. The first very angry question to Professor Banfield was, if you were president and you had to do away with these programs, which one would be the first that you would eliminate: Head Start, Social Security, and so on. And he gave an answer that has stuck in my mind all of these years. He said, "I'm not sure that I'd eliminate any of them, even though I don't think they achieve what they set out to do, because maybe the price that we have to pay for a democracy is to show that government cares about people."

I suggest that as we search for alternatives we are going to have to take into consideration much more than what I have heard today about what impact changed policies will have on the large minority populations of our cities. We will not build walls around those cities. The people there are just as American as we are.

18

ANSWERING THE CRITICS OF DRUG LEGALIZATION

James Ostrowski

Since the spring of 1988, the proposal to legalize drugs has received widespread public attention. Prominent proponents of legalization include columnist William F. Buckley, Jr., economist Milton Friedman, Professor Ethan A. Nadelmann, Baltimore mayor Kurt L. Schmoke, and federal judge Robert W. Sweet. This paper will analyze and critique many of the arguments made against the legalization of drugs by five of its leading critics.[1] Two of these critics are politicians—[former] National Drug Policy director William Bennett and New York governor Mario Cuomo. Three are academics—James Q. Wilson, James A. Inciardi, and Duane C. McBride. Many politicians have attacked the legalization concept, but Bennett and Cuomo stand out. Bennett was the first "drug czar." Cuomo is a potential presidential candidate in 1992 and has been dubbed "America's best political speaker" by William Safire. Additionally, both are considered intellectuals as well as politicians. Wilson, Inciardi, and McBride are among the few academics who have taken direct aim at drug legalization in published articles.

GENERAL COMMENTS ON THE CRITICS

Cost-Analysis Lacking

All the critics of legalization have plunged into the debate without the benefit of a comprehensive cost-benefit analysis of drug prohibition that supports their case.[2] I do not mean the prohibitionists have not thought about legalization in cost-benefit terms—almost everyone does so. What I mean is that no prohibitionist has systematically analyzed all the costs of prohibition, and then all the benefits of prohibition, put the various factors into numerical terms wherever possible, "weighed" the costs against the benefits to the extent possible, and found that the benefits exceed the costs.

The lack of solid data supporting prohibition has helped shape the nature of the critique of legalization. Some claim that we cannot legalize because we are not certain what would happen.[3] Some suggest that the legalizers will not be able to get the details right.[4] Some try to escape the cost-benefit argument entirely by arguing that legalization would have no benefits whatsoever.[5] Each response avoids the critical fact that prohibitionists have no positive case to offer for prohibition's beneficial effects. For the most part, they are merely sniping at proposals for legalization.

Methodological Problems

Not only have prohibitionists presented no systematic cost-benefit analysis of prohibition, but also their critiques of legalization have generally been methodologically unsound. Prohibitionist arguments often follow the simple non sequitur—"Drugs are bad; therefore, they should be illegal." Leaving aside that many of the "bad" aspects of drugs result from their illegality, this is not a good argument. A utilitarian would argue that drugs may be bad, but a war on drugs is worse.[6] A libertarian would argue that drugs may be bad, but decisions whether to engage in (noncoercive) bad activities should be made by the individual.[7] The crucial question in a cost-benefit analysis of prohibition is: Do drug laws cause more harm than good? To prevail in a cost-benefit analysis, prohibitionists must demonstrate that *all* the following are true:

1. Drug use would increase substantially after legalization.
2. The harm caused by any increased drug use would not be offset by the increased safety of legal drug use.
3. The harm caused by any increased use would not be offset by a reduction in the use of dangerous drugs that are already legal (such as alcohol and tobacco).
4. The harm caused by any increased drug use not offset by items 2 or 3 would exceed the harm now caused by the side effects of prohibition (such as crime and corruption).

In the absence of data supporting these propositions, neither the theoretical danger of illegal drugs nor their actual harmful effects is a sufficient basis for prohibition. Neither is the bare fact, if proven, that illegal drug use would rise under legalization. Prohibitionists face a daunting task—one that no one has yet accomplished or, apparently, even attempted.[8]

Any cost-benefit analysis of prohibition must separate the four categories of harm related to illegal drug use. The distinctions between theses categories have been blurred in the legalization debate so far. These categories are:

1. Harm caused by prohibition
2. Harm prevented by prohibition
3. Harm not prevented by prohibition
4. Harm related to, but not caused by, drug use

Harm caused by prohibition. This category includes all the problems caused by the law-enforcement approach to the drug problem. Obvious examples include: drug-enforcement costs, law-enforcement officers killed in drug enforcement, and police corruption related to drugs. Less obvious examples include: crime committed by people as a result of the diversion of resources away from violent crime enforcement and toward drug enforcement, drug-related AIDS, black market violence, and drug-related street crime.

Harm prevented by prohibition. This category includes all the harm that people *do not* do to themselves or others because drugs are illegal and thus less available. By and large, these are people who (a) are not currently abusing a serious legal[9] or illegal drug, and (c) would, in spite of warning labels, quality controls, and objective education, recklessly cause harm to themselves after legalization. It is for the benefit of such people that the war on drugs is fought.

That a great deal of such harm is prevented is the main (only?) practical argument for prohibition. Strictly speaking, this category is unknowable, since accurate quantitative predictions of future human behavior are impossible. One reason for this is that predictions themselves can affect future behavior.[10] For example, dire predictions of high drug use after prohibition could well stimulate antidrug educational, cultural, and treatment efforts that, if successful, might actually lead to a reduction in drug use after prohibition.

It is generally believed that the uncertainty argument favors the status quo. In fact, the notion that we should not legalize drugs because we are not certain what would happen has become the last refuge of many a prohibitionist. Lacking cost-benefit evidence in support of their policy, prohibitionists latch onto the uncertainty argument in the same way that criminal defense lawyers whose clients are clearly guilty latch onto the presumption of innocence. They use the uncertainty argument as a substitute for evidence they do not possess, secure in the knowledge that no one predicting the future can ever be refuted in the present.

Does the uncertainty argument really favor the status quo? As previously discussed, the main practical benefit of prohibition is its alleged harm-prevention value; that is, that without prohibition, harmful drug use would increase. The inability of prohibitionists to prove that harmful drug use would increase after repeal of prohibition, however, means that they are at the same time unable to prove that prohibition provides any practical benefit. The lack of evidence in favor of prohibition, combined with the major problem undeniably caused by prohibition, make a persuasive argument for repeal.

It must be insisted that the prevention of mere drug use, without evidence of actual harm, does not qualify as harm prevented by prohibition. Although mere drug use may violate norms of morality that prohibitionists believe the state must enforce, such drug use cannot be considered in a cost-benefit approach because such an approach considers only harmful consequences of drug use. Prohibitionist literature is filled with references to levels of mere drug use in certain places and times of legal availability, but without any effort to demonstrate any actual harm this level of use caused. [11]

Another methodological hurdle for prohibitionists is the drug-switching/ addiction-switching problem. It is not controversial to argue that people use drugs either to make themselves feel better than they already do, or to take away bad feelings that they have. Prohibition at best reduces the availability of certain types of drugs, but does nothing to make people feel better or take away bad feelings. Presumably, many people who are deprived of certain drugs by prohibition will seek out legal drugs as a substitute (drug-switching) and/or will engage in addictive forms of behavior not involving drugs (addiction-switching), such as gambling or overeating. To prove that some level of harm has been prevented by prohibition, it also has to be shown that harmful illegal drug-taking behavior has not been replaced by harmful legal drug-taking behavior or by harmful nondrug addictive behaviors.

Harm not prevented by prohibition.   This category includes all the harmful consequences of illegal drug use today, excluding those consequences traceable to the impact of prohibition as opposed to drug use per se; that is, we must conclude that prohibition has failed to prevent all acts of illegal drug use occurring today in spite of prohibition. We must be extremely careful, however, to separate, to the fullest extent possible, the harm caused by drug use per se from the harm caused by the fact that drug use is illegal. If a person smokes marijuana today, for example, any harmful consequences of marijuana smoking (which would occur even if marijuana were legal and quality-controlled) would fall into the category of harm not prevented by prohibition. If the person is arrested and put through criminal court proceedings, all the financial and other costs of this proceeding fall into the category of harm caused by prohibition. If, unknown to the smoker, the marijuana was laced with herbicide sprayed on it by law-enforcement agents with resulting injury to the smoker, this again would amount to harm caused by prohibition.

We can thus conclude that any harm resulting from the use of illegal drugs falls into the category of either harm caused by prohibition or harm not prevented by prohibition. From this fact, we can further conclude that no evidence of the harm caused by current illegal drug use, without more, can be utilized as evidence in support of prohibition. Without additional data showing that the repeal or prohibition would increase the level of harmful drug use, evidence of current harm from illegal drug use—even excluding harm caused by prohibition—is of no use to the prohibitionist argument. What prohibitionists must do is (a) demonstrate that legalization would lead to some level of increased use; then (b) use evidence of harm from existing use to show the extent of the harm that would be caused by legalization. To engage in step (b) without step (a) is meaningless.

Harm related to, but caused by, drug use. Prohibitionists often fall into the trap of scapegoatism. They blame a seemingly endless list of human problems—most of which have been around for thousands of years—on the use of illegal drugs: violence, child abuse, prostitution, spouse abuse, laziness, joblessness, irresponsible pregnant women, and so on.[12] Prohibitionists have presented very little evidence that drug use per se is the cause of these problems. It is more likely that drug use is a mere correlative of these problems and that both drug use and the other problems have a separate cause—the personality, character, and values of the drug user, or perhaps adverse social conditions.[13]

We can illustrate this point by a thought experiment. Ask yourself, if a hundred nuns and a hundred congressmen smoked crack, how many would become violent and murder someone? Most reasonable people would likely answer zero. In fact, I am not aware of any wealthy person, physician, or pharmacist who became violent after using cocaine, although many thousands of them have used the drug. This suggests that too often the blame for antisocial conduct is placed on the drug and not the person. As Stanton Peele writes, "It is the mark of naivete—not science—to mistake the behavior of some drug users with the pharmacological effects of the drug, as though addictive loss of control and crime were somehow chemical properties of [the] substance."[14]

Consider the following passage:

> The desire for crack runs wild and takes madness into its service; any opinions or desires with a decent reputation and any feelings of shame still left are killed or thrown out, until all discipline is swept away, and madness usurps its place. . . . When crack has absolute control of a man's mind . . . life is a round of orgies and sex and so on. . . . So that whatever income he has will soon be expended . . . and next of course he'll start borrowing and drawing upon capital. . . . When he comes to the end of his father's and mother's resources . . . he'll

start by burgling a house or holding someone up at night, or go to clean out a church. Meanwhile the older beliefs about honor and dishonor, which he was brought up to accept as right, will be overcome by others, once held in restraint but now freed to become the bodyguard of his desire for crack. . . . Under the tyranny of his desire for crack he becomes in his waking life what he was once only occasionally in his dreams, and there's nothing, no taboo, no murder, however terrible, from which he will shrink. His desire tyrannizes over him, a despot without restraint or law.

This sad story sounds so familiar and could easily have been lifted from the latest magazine piece on crack—but it has been edited to substitute "desire for crack" for the author's term "master passion." The author was Plato, writing more than two thousand years before the invention of crack.[15]

Overview

The cost-benefit argument hinges on whether prohibition causes more harm than it prevents, but prohibitionists have rarely, if ever, sought to supply evidence that meets this criterion. Rather, prohibitionists have mainly focused on the harm that prohibition has failed to prevent, and have also been guilty of smuggling into their argument various types of harm caused by prohibition and harm related to, but not caused by, drug use.

THE POLITICIANS

William Bennett

William Bennett's discussion of legalization appeared in the March 1990 issue of *Reader's Digest*. Bennett puts forth four main arguments against legalization:

1. Legalization will not take the profit out of drugs.
2. Legalization will not eliminate the black market.
3. Legalization will not dramatically reduce crime.
4. Drug use is not a victimless crime.

Bennett's approach to the issue is understandable given the lack of cost-benefit evidence for prohibition. He simply denies that legalization would have any benefit at all. This allows him to avoid the difficult task of showing how the benefits of prohibition outweigh the benefits of legalization. Since Bennett "finds no merit in the legalizers' case," he feels no obligation to defend prohibition on cost-benefit grounds.

Bennett argues that since legal drugs would have to be taxed heavily, the black market could undercut the legal price and still make money.[16] At best, this is intellectually dishonest. There is no admission that the bulk of profits would dry up. For example, if legal cocaine were sold for $10 a gram with $5 going for taxes, it is possible that the black market might be able to sell cocaine for $8 and still make a profit. That would mean, however, a loss in gross revenue of $92, since the black market price of cocaine has been about $100 per gram for several years.

The argument is also self-serving since the prohibitionist can always conjure up some hypothetical level of taxation that would allow a substantial level of black market activity to exist. Carrying the taxation argument to extremes begs the question. To assume very heavy taxation is to negate the assumption that drugs have been legalized. Prohibitionists may not believe that what we have in mind is legalization at close to free market prices, but that is exactly what many of us have in mind.

Serious questions can be raised about whether a black market would continue to exist merely to compete with the legal market for marginal profits. These marginal profits will probably be too small to compensate drug dealers for the risk of selling drugs illegally. The black and gray markets in alcohol and tobacco today are quite small and are not a major social problem.[17] Besides, the black market would have to compete with the legal market not only on the basis of price, but also on the basis of quality and safety. Since legal drugs would be subject to product-liability law, an incentive to sell safer drugs would exist in the legal market. This incentive is lacking in the black market.

Bennett makes another question-begging argument—because not all drugs will be legalized, the black market will still supply drugs.[18] He wins a cheap victory by simply assuming as true what is in fact hotly disputed. The logic of the legalization argument runs as follows: For any drug X, the social costs of making that drug illegal exceed the social costs of making that drug legal. The prohibition of any mind-altering drug should have the same impact as the prohibition of alcohol and cocaine have had—loss of quality control, generation of crime and violence, creation of a criminal subculture, police corruption, clogged courts and prisons, diversion of time, energy, and money away from private sector solutions to drug abuse and toward law-enforcement efforts.

We cringe at making some drugs legal, but these are the very same drugs that the public would cringe at using if they were legalized. The drugs that we feel more comfortable legalizing would for the very same reason be more widely used, and are already more widely used. There is reason to believe that the most pernicious drugs would lose out to relatively safer drugs in free market competition. In the legal market, more people use caffeine than alcohol because caffeine is safer than alcohol. More people use alcohol than tobacco because alcohol is less harmful than tobacco. In the illegal market, more people use marijuana than cocaine because marijuana is less harmful than cocaine. More people use cocaine than crack cocaine because they realize that crack is worse. It is likely that more people use cocaine than heroin because they perceive that cocaine is less dangerous than heroin.[19] The fact that a particular drug is pernicious does not suggest that it should remain illegal because its illegality will make it even more pernicious and socially costly, and its very perniciousness will dissuade large numbers of people from using it, particularly when other less pernicious drugs are available for those who want them.

Let's assume that Bennett is right—not all drugs will be legalized. Let's just say we legalize marijuana, heroin, and cocaine and nothing else. Since these drugs constitute the bulk of current black market sales, their legalization would dry up the bulk of the black market. All the problems attributed to these drugs' share of the black market would thus be solved. Naturally, a black market would still exist to supply people with PCP or whatever, but this is not a problem for the legalizers. It would only mean that we were able to persuade the public to solve the bulk of the illegal drug problem, but not the *entire* illegal drug problem. The problems that would continue to be caused by the small remaining black market could be solved when public opinion was ready to do so by legalizing the remaining illegal drugs.

As for crack, Bennett correctly points out that it could be made easily from legal cocaine even if crack itself is not legalized.[20] He fails, however, to acknowledge the benefits of such a scheme. The price of crack made from legal cocaine would not be much greater than the legal price of cocaine. Therefore, since the profits to be made would be quite modest, crime caused by crack users to pay for the drug would decline and violence between drug dealers fighting for the "right" to sell crack would also decline.

Bennett argues that a black market would still exist to serve children.[21] Even if true, this would still mean that the bulk of the black market would be eliminated since those under 18 years old comprise only about 7 percent of the cocaine market, while those 18–20 years old comprise another 16 percent of that market.[22] Bennett's argument is misleading. If drug production is legalized and drug sales for adults are legalized, then any leakage of drugs to minors would constitute a gray market. From a social-cost perspective, a gray market is far preferable to a black market. A gray market generally sells quality-controlled drugs—since it illegally sells legally produced drugs. Profit margins on the gray market are much lower than profit margins on the black market. All the consequences of high black market profits, such as violence between dealers and street crime by addicts, would thus be reduced.

In today's black market, a 12-year-old can buy crack for five or ten dollars from a drug dealer who doesn't care who he sells to. A 12-year-old can also risk his life selling cocaine to make thousands of dollars. No 12-year-old can buy bathtub gin or wood alcohol, however, and there are no 12-year-olds risking their lives to make thousands of dollars selling booze on the black market. Some legal alcohol does reach minors, but at least those who sell it to them are legally accountable, and at least the alcohol they consume is not instantly poisonous as it often was during prohibition. Children would on balance benefit from legalization insofar as it directly affects them, particularly those in inner cities who now live in a violent criminal subculture. Additionally, children would benefit from legalization since they would grow up and live in a freer, safer, and more harmonious society.

Bennett argues that legalization would not reduce crime because "many drug-related felonies are committed by people involved in crime *before* they started takings drugs."[23] A comprehensive analysis of the drug-crime connection contradicts Bennett:

> Heroin addiction can be shown to dramatically increase property crime levels.
> . . . A high proportion of addicts' preaddiction criminality consists of minor and drug offenses, while post-addiction criminality is characterized much more by property crime.[24]

This study suggests that many of those who Bennett asserts were criminals before they started *using* drugs were criminals in that they were *selling* drugs; that is, the illegality of drugs encouraged them to adopt a criminal life-style in the first place. The argument of Bennett and others[25]—that drug prohibition does not stimulate enormous property crime—turns out to be somewhat circular. The fact that so many among the poor and minorities are involved in crime is in large part due to the fact that prohibition has created a criminal subculture in inner-city neighborhoods.[26]

The analytical error here is the failure to realize that prohibition stimulates crime in many ways. First, prohibition creates an entire class of criminals—drug users and sellers—simply by making their activities illegal. The mere illegality of drug use has two main effects: It forces drug users into a criminal subculture to obtain their drugs and it provides many drug users with criminal records—or worse, prison—making it more difficult to secure legitimate employment (and thus avoid crime). Second, prohibition raises drug prices, forcing poorer users into street crime to support their habits. Third, by making illegal that which millions of people believe is acceptable behavior, prohibition breeds disrespect for law. Fourth, prohibition encourages people to become drug dealers by creating an extremely lucrative black market in drugs. Fifth, prohibition destroys, through drug crime, the economic viability of low-income neighborhoods, leaving young people fewer alternatives to working in the black market. Sixth, prohibition removes the settling of drug-related disputes from the legal process, creating a context of violence for the buying and selling of drugs. Seventh, prohibition diverts enforcement resources away from the prevention of coercive crimes like robbery and rape, thereby increasing the incidence of such crimes. Eighth, prohibition supplies enormous profits that subsidize organized criminal enterprises whose activities unfortunately extend beyond the realm of noncoercive crimes. Finally, prohibition corrupts many law-enforcement officials, thereby decreasing their ability to fight coercive crimes.

Although Bennett suggests that prohibition-related street crime is rare, he contradicts himself by citing the case of a "nun who worked in a homeless shelter and was stabbed to death by a crack addict enraged that she would not stake him to a fix."[27] Then he cites another example of an addict who would do anything to get high, including stealing from relatives.[28] Bennett's assertion, based on mere anecdote, that "crime rates are highest where crack is cheapest,"[29] is contradicted by evidence that in 1990 crime was up nationwide while cocaine prices were also up significantly.[30]

Bennett makes the irresistible argument that drug use is not a "victimless crime."[31] But this is sheer word play. Such an argument involves changing the definition of "victim" without telling the audience. Drug use certainly is a victimless crime if "victim" is defined in the traditional sense as one who has been subjected to force or fraud by a criminal. Drug offenses are also victimless crimes because one can be convicted of violating them even though no actual harm has been done to anyone.

Bennett, however, uses the term "victimless crime" in a totally different sense. Drug use is a "victimful" crime because some of the people who use drugs do bad things to others allegedly *because* of their drug-taking.[32] There are numerous problems with this argument. First, it assumes that drug use, as opposed to personality and other factors, is a major cause of harmful conduct. It is very difficult, however, to prove this causal relationship. Nevertheless, under legalization, any actual harm a drug user might cause to person or property would be punishable and/or compensable under existing law. Furthermore, greater resources would be available to deal with actual third-party harm from drug use once these resources were no longer devoted to preventing and punishing drug use per se. This is a far better solution to the problem than punishing all drug users to prevent *some* from *possibly* harming others. The rights of all drug users should not be infringed solely because prohibition *might* prevent *some* drug users from causing harm to third parties, when such harm is already unlawful. Besides, outlawing drug use because *some* users might harm others is self-contradictory since it necessitates harming *many* drug users who themselves have harmed no one.[33] Finally, any third-party harm caused by illegal drug use today is dwarfed by the third-party harm caused by illegal drug *laws*.[34] Ironically, while drug users under legalization would be legally responsible for the harm they cause to third parties, prohibitionists today are not at all responsible for the harm they cause to others. The moral argument from third-party consequences thus actually runs in favor of legalization, not against it.

Mario Cuomo

In his 1989 State of the State speech, New York governor Mario Cuomo was sharply critical of drug legalization.[35] A skilled lawyer before he went into politics, Cuomo knows how to marshall evidence in support of a case. He also knows the various rhetorical ploys that can be used when hard evidence is lacking. In September 1989, *The Economist* noted that "two senior politicians, Mr. William Bennett (President Bush's drugs tsar) and Mr. Douglas Hurd (Britain's home secretary), have been stirred to join the [drug-legalization] debate," but that "neither Mr. Bennett nor Mr. Hurd offers any positive evidence that prohibition works."[36] We can now add Governor Cuomo to this distinguished list for his failure to justify the war on drugs with anything but rhetoric.

In addition to failing to prove his own case, the governor far from rebutted the argument for legalization. The argument for repealing prohibition—that prohibition fails to stop millions of Americans from using illegal drugs, but does succeed in causing black market violence and street crime, while providing drug users with such extras as AIDS and criminal records—is conveniently ignored by Governor Cuomo. Rather than confronting the legalization challenge head-on, the governor side-steps it with standard rhetorical ploys.

First, the strawman: "The legalizers are saying this: you've lost the war; you've tried everything you could, and you've lost. So why should we spend any more money in the combat?" There's only one small problem here—no serious proponent of legalization has made this argument. The out-of-pocket costs of the war on drugs are almost trivial compared to its human costs.[37]

Second, the ad hominem attack: "Let's legalize it and hope that if some kid or somebody else gets addicted, they are not in our family; they are in someone else's family." Translation: Legalizers are callous and indifferent. Only advocates of drug war have compassion; advocates of drug peace apparently have none. When compassion really counted, though, when compassionate drug warriors in Albany could have saved thousands of lives by allowing clean hypodermic needles to be sold, compassion lost out to the absolutism a war mentality requires.[38]

Third, the red herring: Legalization equals "surrender."[39] Legalization is clearly not surrender, any more than the Chinese students were surrendering in 1989 when they called for the repeal of another failed policy—communism. It is prohibition that surrenders drug production and sales to the black market where extremely dangerous drugs are made by vicious criminals and where artificially high profits stimulate violent battles between dealers. Legalization would in fact be victory over drug dealers who would be out of a job, victory over drug-related violence and crime, victory over drug-related AIDS, victory over police corruption and the social and economic decay caused by the illegal drug business.

Finally, the emotional appeal: "I believe this state must reject this idea as the abandonment of a whole generation of children and adults now caught in addiction and of generations to come who would be caught in addiction. I would not do it to my children. We ought not let this state do it to our children." Legalization, however, is not abandonment of drug abusers any more than legalization of alcohol is an abandonment of alcohol abusers. Rather, it is a recognition that such people need to be helped, not hurt. Troubled people need police, guns, handcuffs, courts, criminal records, and jails—about as much as quarterbacks need interceptions.

It is odd that prohibitionists believe their concern for the welfare of drug users is proven by their willingness to put them in prison next to murderers and rapists, and the callousness of legalizers is proven by their abhorrence of such methods. It is ironic that in the same speech in which the governor boasts of his concern for "our children," he brags of nearly doubling prison cells. Who is going to occupy those cells but "our children," particularly our minority children, seduced by the quick highs and fast bucks of illegal drugs? Then, "our children" who have the misfortune to get mixed up in illegal drugs could well end up as mere statistics in next year's State of the State speech, showing that the governor can be as tough on drugs as Rockefeller, Nixon, and Reagan were before him.

The streets of New York are filled with violent crime and murder. The jails are crammed with drug offenders. The courts are clogged with drug cases. The hospitals are loaded with drug-related AIDS patients. The schools look more like prisons each day, with students searched for weapons and beepers. Children are risking life and limb selling a potent, unregulated drug—crack—to other children. Anywhere you look, the evidence of the failure of drug prohibition is patent— everywhere, that is, but in the governor's State of the State address. Last year was the seventy-fifth anniversary of the war on drugs.[40] What Governor Cuomo is really saying is let's have another seventy-five years of failure.

THE ACADEMICS

James Q. Wilson

James Q. Wilson, probably the most influential criminologist in America, had his go at legalization in *Commentary* earlier this year.[41] He begins his argument by boasting of one of the alleged successes of prohibition—the containment of heroin.[42] He asserts that intensified law-enforcement efforts under President Nixon were responsible for halting a trend toward increasing heroin use. The claim is that the number of heroin users has not increased significantly since 1972 as a result of these efforts.

Even if true, this is not the type of argument that is sufficient to justify prohibition. First, the war against heroin did and does produce enormous social costs such as increased crime, corruption, and drug-related AIDS.[43] Wilson's efforts to explain why some marginal decrease in heroin use was worth the price paid are paltry at best. Prohibition's impact on drug-use levels is just the beginning of the inquiry, but Wilson effectively ends there. It is no excuse that the "micro" statistics pertaining to drug-use levels are more available than the "macro" statistics pertaining to social cost, although this is no doubt the case. That we are quite ignorant about the exact consequences of massive interventions into the social fabric, such as the war on drugs, is a strong argument against such interventions.[44]

Furthermore, even if one could somehow prove that the social costs of heroin prohibition were outweighed by a reduction in the number of heroin users, this fact alone would not be sufficient to vindicate prohibition. We would further have to know whether those deprived of heroin simply switched to some other illegal drug,[45] or some other legal drug, or to gambling, or to overeating, or to rape, or to other *consciousness-altering* activity, and what the social costs of these activities were compared to the social costs of the deterred heroin use.[46] We hear nothing of these matters from Wilson. Most likely, no one, including Wilson, has accurate knowledge of these matters, which only means that neither Wilson nor anyone else is able to put forth an argument for prohibition that can withstand methodological scrutiny. We can thus dismiss Wilson's heroin argument as incomplete.

(There is an important lesson here for how we can fairly evaluate the efficacy of legalization once it is enacted. It is extremely difficult to trace the precise effects of prohibition. We have seen that although it is possible to argue that prohibition caused a reduction in drug use at a certain time, it is difficult to know which consciousness-altering activities those potential drug users engaged in after being deprived of, say, cocaine. Their options were many, but our means of determining this are few or nonexistent. Therefore, it would seem that the real impact of legalization should be measured, not by micro-statistics, but by macro-statistics. That is, legalization should be evaluated negatively only if it seems to produce a substantial increase in social trauma of all types. The measures of social trauma that should be evaluated include murder rates, rates of robbery, rape, larceny, and assault, death rates among the young and middle-aged, child-abuse cases, accidents, unemployment and other measures of economic progress in cities, and so on. If legalization correlates with an improvement in these figures or stability in them, it should be judged a success, regardless of what the micro-statistics show. Focusing mainly on the micro-statistics—such as usage rates or overdose rates—will tend to produce a biased view of the impact of legalization since the *costs* of legalization are easily measurable, whereas the *benefits* of legalization will tend to be hidden in the macro-statistics of general social trauma.)

Granted that Wilson's heroin argument is incomplete, is it valid so far as it goes? Not necessarily. The problem with evaluating any reduction in the use of an illegal drug is that we do not know how much the reduction is attributable to enforcement effects and how much is attributable to dissatisfaction with the product or changing social fashions or self-restraint. Here again is a critical factual element of Wilson's argument on which he supplies very little data.

There is common sense and data contradicting Wilson's argument. Common sense suggests that since heroin is a painkilling depressant, its main appeal lies with those at life's bottoms whose normal state of mind is pain, such as "young blacks in Harlem," or soldiers in Vietnam. To paraphrase Stanton Peele, most people have better things to do than to be drug addicts. Historical data suggests that with legal availability, opiate consumption peaks at a small percentage of the population and then may actually decline. [47]

The notion of free people acting rationally seems to be foreign to Wilson and his colleagues. [48] Rather, he believe, "Society is not and could never be a collection of autonomous individuals." Since an autonomous individual is one whose actions are guided by his own judgment, and such an individual could be called "free," Wilson's statement could be translated: "Society is not and never could be a collection of *free* individuals." The problem here is that society never could be a collection of nonautonomous individuals—our actions must be guided by *someone's* judgment. The only question is, will it be our own or will it be another's? Will we be autonomous or will someone be "autonomous" for us? [49] If we lack the intellectual and moral abilities to run our own lives, how can we possess the seemingly greater intellectual and moral abilities needed to run other people's lives? This is the great dilemma facing all paternalistic political theories.

The obvious answer to this dilemma, of course, is that "we" do not possess this ability; "they" do. "We" being the general public; "they" being the small number of people who generate public-policy ideas and guide them into legislation. [50] What the prohibitionist policy elite wants to do is to be "autonomous" over the general public when it comes to drugs. They wish to substitute their own judgment and will for what they perceive as the inadequate judgment and will of the public. This is arrogance of the worst kind. Are William Bennett, Mario Cuomo, James Wilson, and James Inciardi any more qualified to dictate the details of our personal lives than Leonid Brezhnev or Mao Tse-tung were able to dictate the details of our economic lives?

Wilson argues that "we all have a stake in ensuring that each of us displays a minimal level of dignity, responsibility, and empathy." [51] The problem is that these moral qualities are each the function of the individual's exercise of moral *choice*. It is precisely the goal of prohibition to eliminate choice. The elimination of choice, however, at the same time eliminates genuine morality. As Henry Veatch writes:

> No human being ever attains his natural end or perfection save by his own personal effort and exertion. No one other than the human individual—no agency of society, of family, of friends, or of whatever—can make or determine or program an individual to be a good man, or program him to live the life that a human being ought to live. Instead, attaining one's natural end as a human person is nothing if not a "do-it-yourself" job.[52]

Wilson's coercive paternalism must fail in its mission to make people better. It merely restricts "the opportunity for vice which simultaneously restricts the opportunity for virtue. In the end such efforts promote not moral excellence, but a drab form of moral mediocrity and conformity."[53]

Wilson has every right to argue that chronic cocaine use "debases" life,[54] but he should accept the fact that others share with him the same faculty of reason that allowed him to reach that conclusion in the first place. Wilson, Cuomo, Bennett, and other advocates of drug abstinence should therefore aim arguments, not guns, at other people.

Wilson argues against any experimentation in legalization: "If cocaine is legalized and the rate of its abuse increases dramatically, there is no way to put the genie back into the bottle, and it is not a kindly genie." This point overlooks the fact that the genie is already out of the bottle. Millions of Americans are using cocaine and there is apparently nothing the government can do to stop them. The likely effect of legalization would be to make black market production and distribution systems obsolete. Pharmaceutical companies and drugstores would take the place of the black market. If legalization turned out to be a failure, then the supplies of cocaine could be fairly easily confiscated. No doubt, clever speculators would stockpile cocaine, betting that it would be re-prohibited. The impact of stockpiling in making cocaine available after re-prohibition, however, would be balanced against the major disruption of previous black market arrangements. Each new drug prohibition benefits from a one-time reduction in drug supplies, due to the time it takes for a functional black market to develop.

Wilson believes the British experience with heroin maintenance argues against legalization. The British system worked only until it was challenged by a serious drug problem in the 1960s, he argues. What he fails to mention is that the enforcement approach also cracks under the pressure of an increased demand for drugs. The classic British system was scaled back in the late 1960s, but drug use still increased. Much of this increased use was fueled not by medically dispensed heroin, but by "cheap, high-quality heroin, first from Iran and then from Southeast Asia,"[55] as Wilson himself admits. Both heroin maintenance and enforcement thus failed to deter heroin use when there was a demand for such use. The difference is that as the British moved toward the criminal model of drug control, heroin users were forced to turn to the ever-waiting black market, leading to an "explosion of heroin importation" in the 1980s:[56]

> The evidence suggests that the illicit market in heroin and the involvement of criminal syndicates, increased in direct relationship to the policy of the clinics in rapidly cutting heroin prescribing.[57]

Even the British government now acknowledges a "growing incidence of serious crime associated with the illegal supply of controlled drugs" and describes the drug problem as "the most serious peacetime threat to our national well-being."[58]

Wilson and other prohibitionists argue that drugs such as cocaine are far too addictive to legalize. Legalizers respond that the data suggest that only a small percentage of those who currently use cocaine became addicted. Wilson responds: "The percentage of occasional users who become binge users *when the drug is illegal* (and thus expensive and hard to find) tells us nothing about the percentage who will become dependent when the drug is legal (and thus cheap and abundant)."[59] Of course, legalizers have no choice but to use data on illegal cocaine use since cocaine is illegal. One of the costs of prohibition is that it makes reliable data very difficult to obtain.

Nevertheless, this data does have value. It shows that the vast majority of those who have tried cocaine did not, for a variety of possible reasons, become chronic users. These reasons could include: risk of arrest, price of the drug, fear of overdose, fear of addiction, inconvenience of obtaining the drug, fear of using a potent drug, or dissatisfaction with the effects of the drug. We do know that cocaine is not so addictive that most people will continue to use it in spite of the risks and costs mentioned—but that is exactly the impression one gets from reading prohibitionist literature. The fact that the vast majority of those *who have tried cocaine* have made a rational cost-benefit judgment not to use it, suggests that the prohibitionist portrait of addictive illegal drugs is overdrawn.

Furthermore, the unique value of data showing low incidence of cocaine addiction among those who have illegally tried it, is that these people are arguably the least cautious and least risk-averse people in the population, and most likely to be prone to drug problems initially. The fact that no more than 10 percent of impetuous people who try cocaine become addicted suggests an even lower rate of potential addiction among the more cautious general population. Inciardi and McBride's point that "most people in the general population have never had a chance to use cocaine"[60] is circular. They may not have had a chance to use cocaine because, being more cautious and less interested in drug experimentation than their drug-using fellows, they have chosen not to place themselves in situations where cocaine would be available.

The conclusions reached from examination of data on illegal drug use are

consistent with data from times and places where drugs are either legal or decriminalized. Data on cocaine use in the Netherlands suggests that liberalizing drug
laws does not necessarily result in greater use.[61] The data available from the time
cocaine was legally available suggest that cocaine use was not a major problem
back then. Prior to the first national prohibition of cocaine, less than one percent
of Americans regularly used the drug.[62] Furthermore, as a *legal* drug, cocaine
did not cause anything like the social trauma now associated with it. A search
through the *New York Times Index* for 1895 to 1904—years of peak drug use and
minimum legal control—for articles about the negative effects of cocaine use
found none.[63] In contrast, there were 1,657 articles about the cocaine problem
during the peak years of the drug war—1979 to 1988.[64]

The basic error that prohibitionists make in projecting large increases in drug
use under legalization is to separate the seductiveness of drugs from the perniciousness of drugs. When arguing that increased use would occur, the "short-
lived euphoria"[65] is emphasized. Then, when arguing why increased use should
not be allowed to occur, the "severe depression"[66] is emphasized. The ups and
downs of drug use, however, are part of one package for the user. To gain the
pleasure, one must endure the pain. Both factors must be considered when
projecting future rates of drug use. In sum, drug tolerance and withdrawal serve
as a natural check on drug use.

James A. Inciardi and Duane C. McBride

In 1989 Inciardi and McBride published the first detailed critique of legalization.[67] Their primary criticism of the concept of legalization is a strange one:
"Current legalization proposals are not proposals at all."[68] That is, legalization
proposals do not address all the detailed regulatory issues that prohibitionists
would like them to address. It is difficult to think of other major policy debates
that focused, not on broad questions of morality, cost, and benefit, but on
regulatory details. Here again, we see prohibitionists adopting a rhetorical strategy
in the absence of reliable data in support of prohibition. Since the prohibitionists
apparently have no cost-benefit data to support their policy, they have developed
the red herring of "how will it work?" questions. Although the prohibitionists
claim not to know what legalization would mean, that does not stop them from
positing a huge increase in drug use under legalization, apparently assuming a
free market model in the process.[69] Conversely, it does not stop them from
arguing that, due to various regulatory restrictions, legalization will not eliminate
the black market.[70]

The entire subject of implementing legalization should be guided by the
insight that *any* system of legalization would be better than the current drug war
or any escalation of that war. That point settled on cost-benefit grounds,[71] we
can move on to the issue of how far legalization should go. That in turn is a

question, not of minute detail, but of several major issues that need to be resolved. A legalization proposal is "complete" when its author has stated a clear position on those issues—bill drafters can do the rest. Those issues are as follows:

1. Which drugs should be legalized?
2. Should there be potency restrictions?
3. Should there be age restrictions?
4. Should sales be restricted to "addicts"?
5. Where should drugs be sold?
6. Should there be a free market as to
   (a) price?
   (b) advertising?

Other questions along these lines could also be asked. All such issues can be merged into one large question: Which legalization regime is appropriate given legalization's risk-benefit ratio? A complete free market would present the greatest risk of increased drug use, but would eliminate the greatest cost because it would eliminate the black market. On the other hand, the legalization of hypodermic needles would be the least risky, but would also eliminate the fewest costs. A middle-ground proposal, such as maintaining addicts while in treatment, would be less risky than a free market, but not nearly as effective in eliminating the black market and its attendant evils. Deciding which legalization model is best involves the following steps:

1. Evaluate the costs of prohibition (the elimination of which being the potential benefits of legalization).
2. Evaluate the risks of full legalization.
3. Make a judgment as to which element has more weight.
4. Choose a legal regime that is appropriate given step 3.

Broadly speaking, there will be three responses to step 4. First, prohibitionists will assert that in *no* legal regime will the benefits of legalization outweigh the risks (costs). Second, those who believe that the benefits of legalization greatly outweigh the risks of ready access to drugs will tend to favor a (relatively) free market model of legalization, usually dubbed "the alcohol model." Finally, those who concede that the evils of prohibition must be reduced, but who are greatly concerned with ready public access to drugs, will tend to favor regimes of heavy regulation, featuring high taxes, a total ban on advertising, and the like. It is ironic that prohibitionists, who would oppose legalization even if they were allowed to choose the details, have the greatest concern over the details of legalization. The debate over the details should be between those legalizers who favor a free market model and those legalizers who favor a regulatory model.

This writer, believing that the benefits of legalization *far* outweigh its risks,[72] favors the alcohol model. This model was outlined by David Boaz:

> When we legalize drugs, we will in all likelihood apply the alcohol model. That is, marijuana, cocaine, and heroin would be sold only in specially licensed stores—perhaps in liquor stores, perhaps in a new kind of drugstore. Warning labels would be posted in the stores and on the packages. It would be illegal to sell drugs to minors, now defined as anyone under 21. It would be illegal to advertise drugs on television and possibly in print. Driving under the influence of drugs would be illegal, and there would be added penalties for committing crimes under their influence.[73]

The question of how to legalize is more a question of politics than of policy. The task is to construct a proposal that meets the goal of ardent legalizers— elimination of the black market and its numerous traumas—while at the same time addressing the concerns of the sympathetic public that drugs be kept from children and kept off television. Boaz's alcohol model achieves this compromise.

Returning to the major questions facing proponents of legalization, my answers would be as follows: Which drugs should be legalized? All consciousness-altering drugs.[74] Should there be potency restrictions? No, because this would encourage gray market production with a loss in quality control. Should there be age restrictions? Yes, the age of consent in each state. Should sales be restricted to "addicts"? No, this scheme would not substantially eliminate the black market. Where should drugs be sold? In specially licensed stores. Should there be a free market as to price? Yes. Advertising? Advertising on television should be banned. Private social pressure should be relied upon to restrain other methods of advertising.[75]

Inciardi and McBride concede that legalization would reduce the systematic violence associated with the illegal drug trade, but assert that "in all likelihood *any declines in systematic violence would be accompanied by corresponding increase in psychopharmacologic violence.*"[76] The problem here is that, although systematic drug violence is estimated to annually cause about 825 murders, and murders incident to drug-related street crime cause an additional 1,200 murders each year,[77] there is no reliable estimate of murders allegedly caused by the chemical effects of illegal drugs. When the New York City Police Department announced that 38 percent of murders in the city in 1987 were "drug-related," Deputy Raymond W. Kelly explained:

> When we say drug-related, we're essentially talking about territorial disputes or disputes over possession. . . . We're not talking about where somebody is deranged because they're on a drug. It's very difficult to measure that.[78]

Thus there is no basis to argue that an increase in chemically induced murders would negate the reduction in drug-related murders that legalization would certainly cause. When the drug most associated with chemically induced violence—alcohol—was legalized, the murder rate dropped dramatically.[79]

Inciardi and McBride's paper is marred by the following rhetorical tirade: "The legalization of drugs would be an elitist and racist policy supporting the neocolonialist views of underclass population control."[80] The notion that legalization is "neocolonialist underclass population control" is gibberish. More intelligible is the now-common charge that legalization is a racist proposal.

The charge of racism is of mostly psychological significance. First, it is the type of red herring that is thrown out by those who are devoid of both methodology and data to support their position. Second, the charge of racism is interesting because it requires as a premise the notion that blacks are less capable of acting responsibly under conditions of freedom than are whites. This comes quite close to being a racist belief itself. It is belied by the facts. In the most vulnerable age group—12- to 17-year-olds—whites are more likely than blacks to use alcohol (27.4 to 15.9 percent), cigarettes (13.9 to 5.1 percent), marijuana (6.8 to 4.4 percent), cocaine (1.3 to less than 1 percent[81]), and psychotherapeutics (2.9 percent to 1.1 percent).[82] In the other age groups, illegal drug use among whites was higher than among blacks in each group except those over 35.[83]

Since no prohibitionist has produced evidence of intentional racism among legalizers, what they must mean is that legalization would be racist in effect. Actually, the reverse is true—it is prohibition that is racist in effect. In general, a greater portion of prohibition's costs are borne by those in minority communities than by those in white communities. Even Wilson admits this.[84] In general, the benefits of prohibition, if any, are disproportionately felt in white areas. The reasons for this are fairly simple. Low-income people are more likely to sell drugs than are high-income people. Therefore, drug markets and the violence they stimulate tend to be located in low-income neighborhoods. Since drug suppliers and retailers operate there, drugs are more readily available in low-income areas than in high-income areas. Furthermore, it is low-income users, naturally residing in low-income areas, who tend to commit the street crime due to the high price of illegal drugs. Higher-income users are more likely to dip into their savings accounts, take out a second mortgage, or embezzle at work. Finally, although many whites sell drugs, blacks are easier targets for arrest and imprisonment. Blacks are arrested on drug charges out of proportion to their level of drug use.[85] In summary, the notion that legalization is a racist policy is absurd.

Wilson's claim that "people are not calling for legalization" in low-income neighborhoods[86] is misleading. Two recent polls show that blacks are supporting legalization somewhat more than the national average.[87] The claim by many whites that legalization is a racist policy apparently has not been accepted even by blacks themselves.

ELITISM AS THE UNIFYING THEME
OF THE PROHIBITIONISTS

In 1990, a Senate Judiciary Committee report[88] concluded that the nation's homicide toll will break a decade-old record that year, largely because drug dealers are fighting over "scarce" supplies of cocaine, using assault rifles as their weapon of choice. It appears that the government—perhaps unwittingly—has finally conceded that drug prohibition causes violent crime and murder. For what else can cause allegedly "scarce" supplies of cocaine but antidrug-law enforcement? Perhaps the next admission will be that drug prohibition—by making clean needles scarce—caused the drug-related AIDS catastrophe. Other admissions could follow in rapid succession: Drug prohibition—by raising the price of addictive drugs—stimulates a massive amount of street crime. Prohibition clogs the courts and prisons, corrupts policemen, fosters a criminal subculture in poor neighborhoods, makes drug dealers rich, and so on.

What is the point of a policy that causes such a mess? Stripped to its essence, drug prohibition is based on the undemocratic[89] belief of an elite,[90] that while *they* are intelligent enough and responsible enough to see the wisdom of avoiding harmful drug use, the vast bulk of the American people are not. "[Americans] would be up to their necks [in drugs] under legalization," warns William Bennett.[91] Only the threat of jail time will deter Americans from destroying themselves with drugs, the prohibitionists believe. Prohibition is therefore premised on a denial of the intelligence and responsibility, and thus the rights and freedoms, of the American people to run their own lives.

In short, because the drug warriors don't trust the American people to act responsibly, they are supporting a policy they now admit causes violence and murder across America. When all the ugly consequences of prohibition are laid bare, serious questions arise, not about the intelligence and responsibility of the American people, but about the intelligence and responsibility of the prohibitionists. Is it intelligent to support a policy that creates a criminal black market worth more than many large industries combined? Is it intelligent to remove potent drugs from any sort of legal regulation or quality control? Is it responsible to support a policy that causes so much pain and suffering for so many people: drug-murder victims, residents of high-crime areas, drug-related AIDS victims, and residents of countries such as Colombia where drug terrorism is a fact of daily life?

Prohibitionists—whose touchstone is preventing harm to innocent third parties caused by drug users—have rather unintelligently and irresponsibly supported a policy that produces a massive amount of harm to innocent third parties.

In their defense, it can be said that prohibitionists did not necessarily intend to create all these negative side effects. They simply did not know in advance that they would occur. True enough. No one knows or can know, however, all the consequences of grand social experiments such as the war on drugs. We're just too stupid. We just don't have the brains required to run other peoples' lives.

Since we lack the skill to foresee all the negative consequences of telling others how to live, we should restrain that powerful impulse in the first place. Prohibitionists—who believed they were an elite group who could micro-manage other people's personal affairs—need to learn self-restraint and humility. They need to realize that far from being superior to the American people in running their lives they are in fact inferior. With all our imperfections and limitations, we individual Americans are better able to manage our own lives than politicians and bureaucrats and policemen and drug czars.

APPENDIX: A NOTE ON THE ECONOMIC COST OF PROHIBITION

A question was raised at the Hoover Conference about my estimate of the economic cost of drug prohibition. This estimate was contained in a study published by the Cato Institute in May of 1989.[92] My estimate of the *calculable* costs of prohibition ($80 billion) contained two components—the out-of-pocket costs of enforcement ($10 billion) plus the lost purchasing power of drug users who must pay artificially inflated black market prices for drugs ($70 billion). Specifically, it was alleged that the lost purchasing power of drug users represents a transfer payment to drug dealers and is therefore not a social cost. This argument was explicitly addressed in my prior study and I believe it is erroneous. It is no more valid when applied to the illegal drug market than it would be if applied to the (hypothetical) illegal car market.

The argument that drug sales are transfer payments assumes that drug production, distribution, and sales are cost-free activities. Obviously, this is not the case. If it were, then anyone could sell drugs and make huge profits without cost or risk. Like any good or service, illegal drugs must be produced, distributed, and sold. Each of these steps involves costs. The fact that drugs are illegal increases the amounts and prices of land, labor, and capital needed to sell drugs. (Likewise, illegalization would increase the costs of *any* industry.) Labor in particular becomes more expensive, since labor faces the risks of prosecution and imprisonment, and even death at the hands of rival dealers. What is the monetary measure of the cost of selling drugs? There is no better measure than the price of sale.

Dealers charge enough to compensate them for the total cost and provide them with a profit over and above their cost.

The claim that the economic loss to drug buyers is countervailed by the economic gain to drug sellers is false. Although drug buyers have suffered a complete economic loss to the extent black market prices exceed free market prices, the drug seller's profit is measured, not by gross revenue, but by net profit. Furthermore, the drug seller's net profit is not measured by monetary profit (which can be as little as 30 percent for a street-level dealer[93]) since much the monetary profit in a drug transaction is compensation for risk. That subjective risk is a real economic cost is undeniable and is the basis for multibillion-dollar insurance industry. Nor can the "psychic" profits of drug sellers be deducted from the economic loss to drug buyers. If drugs were legalized and sold at free market prices, the drug buyer would have extra funds to purchase other legal goods and services. This would benefit the sellers of those goods and services to the extent their prices exceed their production costs. In sum, drug prohibition causes an economic loss to illegal drug buyers to the extent that illegal drug prices exceed free market prices. The net profit of illegal drug sellers is canceled by the lost net profit of legal businesses the drug buyer would patronize if drugs were legalized.

Since economic analysis is value-free, it is quite legitimate for prohibitionists, who would prefer that there be no drug profits at all, to attempt to argue that drug profits have economic value. Conversely, they cannot deny that the economic harm to drug users is quite real, even though they may view such harm as beneficial to deterring drug use. Such deterrence value would enter the cost-benefit analysis, not in the present context of determining the cost of prohibition, but on the issue of the benefits of prohibition.

Where prohibitionists generally violate the value-free principle is in their failure to admit and calculate the *benefits* of drug use.[94] An accurate cost-benefit analysis should include, in addition to the costs of drug use, the value of drug use that has been deterred by prohibition. The components of lost value would include recreational value, medical value, and utilitarian value. By utilitarian value I mean, for example, the ability of certain drugs such as caffeine to stimulate physical and mental labor and reduce the risk of errors and accidents. Naturally, when measuring the cost of depriving people of illegal drugs, the standard would be the marginal loss of utility given the availability of legal substitutes.

It should not be thought that $80 billion is the limit of prohibitions costs. Rather, it is simply the amount of the readily ascertainable costs. The actual economic costs of prohibition are enormous and extremely difficult to calculate. A complete analysis would have to consider, in addition to those already discussed, the following costs:

1. Lost productivity of those who die as a result of prohibition (8,000)[95]

2. Lost productivity of those in prison on drug convictions and of drug users who must "hustle" all day to pay for their drugs

3. Costs imposed by organized crime activities funded by drug profits

4. Government and private funds spent on prohibition-caused illnesses such as AIDS, hepatitis, and accidental overdose

5. Funds spent on private security to fight drug-related crime

6. Medical costs of treating prohibition-caused injuries resulting from drug-related violence

Another difficult-to-measure economic cost of prohibition merits special mention: the negative impact of prohibition on the economic viability of inner cities and their inhabitants. Prohibition-related violence and property crime raise costs, make loans and insurance difficult or impossible to secure, and make it difficult to attract skilled workers. Prohibition lures some workers away from legitimate businesses and into the black market, where salaries are astronomically higher. So long as a black market in illegal drugs thrives in the inner cities, it is difficult to see how they can ever become economically viable.

NOTES

1. For a comprehensive defense of legalization on moral and cost-benefit grounds, see James Ostrowski, "The Moral and Practical Case for Drug Legalizaiton," 18 *Hofstra Law Review* (Winter 1990), pp. 607–702. See also Ethan Nadelmann, "Drug Prohibition in the United States: Costs, Consequences, and Alternatives," 245 *Science*, p. 939.

2. Ostrowski, pp. 642–43. For a defense of legalization purely on cost-benefit grounds, see Ostrowski, "Thinking about Drug Legalization," Cato Institute Policy Analysis No. 121 (May 25, 1989).

3. James Q. Wilson, "Against the Legalization of Drugs," *Commentary* February 1990, pp. 21, 28.

4. James. A. Inciardi and Duane C. McBride, "Legalization: A High-Risk Alternative in the War on Drugs," 32 *American Behavioral Scientist*, pp. 259, 261 (1989).

5. "I find no merit in the legalizers' case." William Bennett, "Should Drugs Be Legalized?" *Reader's Digest*, March 1990, pp. 90, 94.

6. Ostrowski, "Moral and Practical Case," p. 641 et seq.

7. Ostrowski, "Moral and Practical Case," p. 625 et seq. A libertine might argue that drugs are good!

8. For a more detailed discussion of the methodology of drug-policy analysis, see Ostrowski, "Moral and Practical Case," p. 609 et seq. It might be noted, parenthetically, that a 1984 study by the Research Triangle Institute on the economic costs of drug abuse (Harwood, H. J., Napolitano, D. M., Kristiansen, P. L., and Collins, J. J., *Economic*

Costs to Society of Alcohol and Drug Abuse and Mental Illness. Research Triangle Park, N.C.: Research Triangle Institute, 1984) has been erroneously cited in support of drug prohibition (*New York Times*, May 15, 1988, pp. 1, 24; Morton Kondracke, "Don't Legalize Drugs," *The New Republic*, June 27, 1988, p. 16; see also *Time Magazine*, May 30, 1988, pp. 14–15). This report, which estimates the cost of drug abuse at $60 billion for 1983, is not, and was not intended to be, an evaluation of the efficacy of prohibition or the wisdom of legalization. It does not mention the terms "legalization" or "decriminalization" and makes no attempt to separate the costs attributable to drug use per se from the costs attributable to the illegality of drug use. In fact, the study seems to include some costs of *legal* drugs in its estimates (Harwood et al., pp. 49–50). Many of the costs cited are clearly the result of prohibition—for example, interdiction costs ($677 million). Furthermore, the report considers only costs that prohibition has failed to prevent, making no attempt to measure the costs prevented—or caused—by prohibition. The study is therefore almost entirely irrelevant to the issue of legalizing drugs.

9. See Ostrowski, "Moral and Practical Case," p. 669 et seq.

10. See Murray N. Rothbard, *Individualism and the Philosophy of the Social Sciences* 33 (Washington, D.C.: Cato Institute, 1979).

11. For example, see William J. Bennett, "A Response to Milton Friedman," *Wall Street Journal*, September 19, 1989.

12. See Bennett, p. 93 (sexual abuse, child abuse); Wilson, p. 24 (crack babies).

13. Stanton Peele, "A Moral Vision of Addiction: How People's Values Determine Whether They Become and Remain Addicts," *Journal of Drug Issues* 17 (1987), p. 187.

14. "Does Drug Addiction Excuse Thieves and Killers from Criminal Responsibility?" *Drug Policy 1989–1990: A Reformer's Catalogue* (Washington, D.C.: Drug Policy Foundation, 1989), p. 204.

15. Passage from *The Republic*, Book Nine (Middlesex ed., 1955); some archaic terms were deleted from the passage.

16. Bennett, p. 92.

17. Most noticeable is the gray market in cigarettes, due to ever-increasing taxes on them. A gray market sells legally produced goods illegally (to children, for example) with taxes being paid.

18. Bennett, p. 92.

19. That the evidence on this is mixed does not affect my point.

20. Bennett, p. 92.

21. Ibid.

22. See *National Household Survey on Drug Abuse: Population Estimates 1988* (National Institute on Drug Abuse), p 29. Actually, it is likely that these younger groups comprise an even smaller percentage of the cocaine market since the NIDA survey does not take account of the greater purchasing power of older people.

23. Bennett, p. 93; see also Inciardi and McBride, pp. 267, 269; Wilson, p. 25.

24. George Speckart and M. Douglas Anglin, "Narcotics and Crime: An Analysis of

Existing Evidence for a Causal Relationship, 3 *Behavioral Science and the Law* (1985), p. 259.

25. Inciardi and McBride, pp. 268–69.

26. Almost one out of every four young black men in New York State is under the control of the criminal justice system. (*New York Times*, October 4, 1990, p. B6.)

27. Bennett, p. 93.

28. Bennett, pp. 93–94.

29. Bennett, p. 93.

30. Associated Press, August 1, 1990 (1990 murders to exceed 1989 total by 2,000); Associated Press, October 8, 1990 (wholesale price of cocaine up about 35 percent; retail prices up 19 percent).

31. Wilson also makes this argument (p. 24). A better term for a "crime" that involves neither violence nor property theft is "noncoercive crime."

32. By the same reasoning, alcohol use would be a victimful noncrime.

33. The notion that *all* illegal drug users today cause harm by subsidizing dangerous drug gangs, a flawed argument on its own terms, can by no means be considered an argument against legalization, since legalization would put a stop to this transfer of wealth.

34. Ostrowski, "Moral and Practical Case," p. 641 et seq.

35. January 3, 1990, Albany, N.Y.

36. September 16, 1989, p. 13.

37. The out-of-pocket cost of the war on drugs is no more than 5 percent of its total social cost. See Ostrowski, "Moral and Practical Case," passim.

38. Ostrowski, "Moral and Practical Case," pp. 637–39.

39. See also Bennett: "I never realized surrender was so fashionable until I assumed this post" (p. 90); Wilson: "[Our goal was] not to run up the white flag of surrender" (p. 21).

40. The Harrison Narcotics Act took effect in 1915.

41. Wilson, p. 21.

42. Wilson, pp. 21–23.

43. Ostrowski, "Moral and Practical Case," p. 641 et seq.

44. See Randy Barnett, "Curing the Drug-Law Addiction: The Harmful Side Effects of Legal Prohibition," in *Dealing with Drugs*, R. Hamowy, ed. (Lexington, Mass.: Lexington Books, 1987), p. 99; Ostrowski, "Moral and Practical Case," pp. 636–38; see also F. Hayek, "The Use of Knowledge in Society," 35 *American Economic Review* 519 (1945); Thomas Sowell, *Knowledge and Decisions* (New York: Basic Books, 1980).

45. The leveling-off in heroin use does correlate with increasing use of cocaine. More recently, with more enforcement resources directed at cocaine, heroin use appears to be rising (Associated Press, October 8, 1990; heroin use up in several cities including New York, Dallas, and Denver).

46. The problem being that the coercive mechanism of prohibition does nothing to improve the human being or the human condition in general, and thus does nothing to

eliminate the urgent need in some people to alter their consciousness (Ostrowski, "Moral and Practical Case," pp. 619–20).

47. D. Musto, *The American Disease: Origins of Narcotic Control* (New Haven: Yale University Press, 1987), pp. 41–42.

48. Bennett (pp. 92–93) and Wilson (p. 26) both disparage drug education, i.e., rational persuasion.

49. This discussion was stimulated by Hans-Hermann Hoppe's analysis of the universalization principle of ethics in A *Theory of Socialism and Capitalism* (Boston: Kluwer Academic Publishers, 1989), pp. 127–44.

50. Thomas R. Dye estimates that no more than 3,000 people comprise the public-policy elite in the United States; see *Who's Running America? The Reagan Years*, 3rd ed. (Englewood Cliffs, N.J.: Prentice-Hall, 1983), p. 14.

51. Wilson, p. 24.

52. Henry B. Veatch, *Human Rights: Fact or Fancy?* (Baton Rouge and London: Louisiana State University Press, 1985), p. 84.

53. Douglas J. Den Uyl, "Freedom and Virtue Revisited," in W. Block and L. Rockwell, Jr., eds. *Man, Economy, and Liberty: Essays in Honor of Murray N. Rothbard* (Auburn, Ala.: Ludwig von Mises Institute, 1988), p. 202.

54. Wilson, p. 26.

55. Wilson, p. 23.

56. 82 *British Journal of Addiction* (editorial) 457 (1987).

57. K. Leach, "Leaving It to the Market," *New Statesman*, Jan. 4, 1985, p. 9.

58. "The Prevention and Treatment of Drug Misuse in Britain," British Information Services (1985), p. 1.

59. Wilson, p. 24.

60. Inciardi and McBride, p. 271.

61. E. Engelsman, "The Dutch Model," *New Perspectives Quarterly* (Summer 1989) pp. 44, 48.

62. Laurence Kolb and A. G. Du Mez, "The Prevalence and Trend of Drug Addiction in the United States and the Factors Influencing It," 39 *U.S. Public Health Reports* 1181 (1924).

63. However, one article suggested that firemen not use cocaine in their eyes to fight the effects of smoke because it might become habit-forming (*New York Times*, June 25, 1897).

64. See *New York Times Index* 1979–1988.

65. Wilson, p. 23.

66. Inciardi and McBride, p. 266.

67. Inciardi and McBride, "Legalization: A High-Risk Alternative in the War on Drugs," 32 *American Behavioral Scientist* 259 (Jan./Feb. 1989).

68. Inciardi and McBride, p. 261.

69. Bennett, p. 91.

70. Bennett, p. 92.

71. See Ostrowski, "Moral and Practical Case," p. 641 et seq.

72. See Ostrowski, "Moral and Practical Case," passim.

73. D. Boaz, "The Consequences of Prohibition," in *The Crisis in Drug Prohibition*, D. Boaz, ed. (Washington, D.C.: Cato Institute, 1990), p. 6.

74. See the earlier discussion, in the section on William Bennett.

75. For example, many newspapers do not carry advertisements for sexually explicit movies, Nazi party rallies, and the like.

76. Inciardi and McBride, p. 273 (emphasis in original). See also Wilson, p. 25.

77. Ostrowski, "Moral and Practical Case," pp. 647–51.

78. *New York Times*, March 23, 1988, p. B1.

79. Ostrowski, "Moral and Practical Case," p. 641.

80. Inciardi and McBride, p. 279.

81. Author's estimate based on 1988 NIDA study.

82. See, generally, 1988 NIDA survey.

83. 1988 NIDA survey, p. 18.

84. Wilson, p. 25.

85. See *New York Times*, Oct. 4, 1990, p. B6.

86. Wilson, p. 25.

87. *Los Angeles Times*, Dec. 12, 1989; Targeting Systems, Inc., Feb. 4, 1990.

88. "Summary of Findings of a Majority Staff Study Prepared for the Use of the Committee on the Judiciary, United States Senate," 101st Congress, Second Session, July 31, 1990.

89. "Democracy" is here defined as a social system in which, in addition to being given an equal voice in choosing their rulers, individuals for the very same reason are given a large measure of control over the details of their personal lives.

90. "Elite" here means a group that is able to dictate coercive behavioral controls to the general public, based on their belief that the public is unable to decide certain matters for themselves due to their moral and intellectual inferiority. For example, Wilson writes "great personal commitment" is "in short supply among . . . young people, disadvantaged people . . ." (p. 27).

91. Bennett, p. 91.

92. Ostrowski, "Thinking about Drug Legalization," Cato Institute Policy Analysis No. 121 (May 25, 1989).

93. "The Cocaine Business: Big Risks and Profits, High Labor Turnover," *Wall Street Journal*, June 30, 1986, p. 16.

94. See, for example, Joel W. Hay, "The Harm They Do to Others: A Primer on the External Costs of of Drug Abuse," Hoover Institution Conference on U.S. Drug Policy, November 15, 1990 (Chapter 12 in this volume).

95. Ostrowski, "Moral and Practical Case," pp. 647–55.

19

LEGALIZATION:
THE MYTH EXPOSED

Robert E. Peterson

It is intriguing to see how national debates get started in our society. One U.S. mayor, in disagreement with the overwhelming majority of his colleagues, suggests returning to a failed approach to the drug problem and it is front-page news in the *New York Times*.[1] A university professor and the director of a twenty-year-old marijuana consumers' lobby form a new group, and it is declared proof of a growing national movement.[2] Two leading conservatives with libertarian leanings are cited as recent converts to the cause, although they were for it fifteen years earlier.[3] The media had an instant sensation, and columnists, editors, television producers, and readers cranked out letters, columns, programs, and articles on the issue. The lecture-debate circuit became a profitable enterprise for prolegalization proponents. Funding to scholars and special interest organizations flourished, including a single donor's $2-million commitment to the nation's most active pro-drug-legalization group, the Drug Policy Foundation.[4] With such promotion, a position held by about 10 to 14 percent of the people of the United States became a fixture in the popular drug debate.[5]

A few new public figures have joined the call to legalize drugs, but most of the proponents have supported the concept for years. There is no groundswell of ranks to legalize drugs, the concept is opposed by a six-to-one margin, politically it is a dead issue, and the nation's recognized leaders in drug prevention, education, treatment, and law enforcement adamantly oppose it.[6] The drug legalization discussion is more a pseudo-academic and entertainment exercise than a policy debate. The president and Congress do not find the position meriting serious consideration and refuse to divert energy from the national strategy they adopted.[7] *Why* we are again talking about relegalizing drugs is as significant as *what* we say about the topic.

The peculiar history of the drug-legalization "debate" must be taken into account in any intelligent review of the issue. The last time this debate raged was in 1977, when the president and his "drug czar" asked Congress to decriminalize marijuana and indicated that laws against cocaine were also undergoing review. The intellectual community, social psychologists, and media editors were generally supportive. Then, as now, this vocal group was out of step with the people and oblivious to the interests of children and parents. A spontaneous movement of outraged parents arose to defeat the organized marijuana lobby and beat back the multi-million-dollar drug-paraphernalia industry.[8] In 1977, one in ten high school students was stoned on marijuana every day of the week and student cocaine use was above today's levels. Prolegalization drug permissiveness was blamed for these phenomena and many experts now attribute the less tolerant attitudes of today with success in cutting the likelihood of teen drug use in half since 1980.

With the public and elected officials opposed to abolishing drug laws and drug use dropping, the question arises: Why the renewed call for legalization?

There are three rationales for drug legalization, with overlap among adherents to each. First, there are theorists who apply a form of economic, legal, political, or health-policy analysis to the issue and conclude that drug laws do not pass a cost-benefit test. Legalizers have offered little new in the way of facts or objective analysis since the 1970s. They have instead played on public frustration arising from the crack epidemic to bolster the "drug-laws-do-not-work" position, although crack use is now declining. This paper examines the various theories and data proposed, and exposes their logical deficiencies.

A second group of legalization advocates holds to a political and personal ideology that drug use is an individual right that should not be intruded upon by the government. This group includes both conservative libertarians and left-of-center civil libertarians. Timothy Leary was perhaps the first to propose adding to the Bill of Rights: "Congress shall not infringe on one's right to alter one's consciousness." In its purest form, this right to use drugs is absolute and the outcome of a cost-benefit analysis or the degree of harm imposed to society at large from drug legalization does not matter. Others would allow government curtailment of the right to alter one's consciousness if private use causes a sufficient amount of harm to others. This ideology fails to balance the interests and rights of children and society at large with that of personal intoxication, but it has gained in intensity as youth of the 1960s and early 1970s age into positions of responsibility in the 1990s.

Richard Dennis, $2-million donor to the prolegalization Drug Policy Foundation, perceives the nation's drug strategy as "about sort of repealing the 60s."[9]

When high school students expressed opposition to marijuana legalization to Loren Siegel of the ACLU, her reaction was one of alarm, not relief.[10] To many in the 30-to-40 age bracket, marijuana and drug use was a symbol of youth, rebelliousness, and personal freedom.[11] Although the dangers and damage of these chemicals are apparent, and fear of use by children is real, it is hard to look at drugs from an objective perspective when the "just-say-no" philosophy is considered more a personal threat than a healthy life-style for youth. Drug-legalization proponents often mix an emotional appeal of guilt and hypocrisy with selective facts and rationales to support legalization. Today's drug intolerance is blamed on "big brother," and the loving and concerned parents who fought the government to end the age of drug permissiveness are accused of irrational drug hysteria.[12] Only through awareness of this bias and the resultant cognitive dissonance can rational review of implications of legalization on youth and nonusers take place.

The third and perhaps the largest numerical group for legalization are those that use illicit drugs. It would be naive to ignore the strong self-interest of drug users in seeking legalization. Drug users come from all walks of life. It is not surprising that former Mayor Marion Barry seconded the call for legalization at the conference of mayors that launched the public debate. Ironically, of the population that has tried an illicit drug, only about a third support drug legalization. It is not coincidental that the legalization movement became more vocal after enactment of laws holding drug users accountable. A renewed cry for legalization is for some an act of desperation, in an age when drug use is increasingly viewed as selfish, unhealthy, and harmful to society. Marijuana promoters in particular grasp at straws with campaigns like "Hemp for America" that declare hemp rope and cloth is a miracle cure for the economy and that the highly carcinogenic drug is good for the environment.[13] Current drug users, although accounting for only 7 percent of the population, are not all politically disenfranchised. The National Organization to Reform Marijuana Laws (NORML) is the oldest drug-user-rights organization and has strong ties to both the Libertarian party and the Cato Institute, the Drug Policy Foundation, and the ACLU.[14]

Treatment experts note that as drug use progresses the drug becomes a focal point of the user's life.[15] Drug magazines, such as *High Times*, have centerfolds of marijuana buds and articles that raise the drug to the level of a religious sacrament. Drug users, even occasional marijuana smokers, have a personal bias built in to their analysis of drug policy. Although policy analysis is alluded to, rational review is not likely to have an impact over the strong emotional and chemical attachments that bind users to psychoactive drugs.[16]

Although drug legalization is not widely popular nor an official part of the national policy debate, the public discussion on it is having an effect and may portend future developments as the United States grapples with the drug problem in the 1990s. A return to social acceptance of drug use could bring about a reversal in dropping drug-use trends, especially among youth. It is important to understand not only the various theoretical arguments made for drug legalization, but also to assess the practical impact of the debate itself.

DRUG LEGALIZATION: FAULTY ASSUMPTIONS

There is an old joke about three professors on a deserted island trying to open a can of food without any utensils. The physics professor suggests dropping a rock onto the can and estimates the weight, height, and velocity needed to do the job—but the contents would be scattered, so that solution is rejected. The chemist says to apply heat to expand the contents to the bursting point, but again the contents would be lost. The economist has a better solution, "Let's suppose that we have a can opener," and from there his theory is successful. Legalization proponents often begin their argument with assumptions that do not reflect reality.

Is the War on Drugs "Hopeless"?

Major articles and editorials for drug legalization begin with the premise that the drug war is unwinnable and the problem only grows worse the more we fight it. This assumption derives its validity not from data and accepted methods of policy analysis, but rather from public frustration with the complex social problem of drug abuse. Due to the emotion of the issue, it is often accepted without critical analysis. Nearly all the available data and the historical experience of the United States and other nations contradicts this assumption.

Frustration and media accentuation on the negative have led many to despair over the drug issue. Legalization proponents use propagandistic analogies to Vietnam or alcohol prohibition, although these events did not have the support of three-fourths of the public, as President Bush's drug strategy does.[17] That may be why drug abuse is actually declining. Legalization advocates say it is time to call off the war and gracefully withdraw from efforts to stop drug abuse.[18] As former Pennsylvania Attorney General LeRoy Zimmerman stated regarding the Vietnam withdrawal analogy, however, this is a war for the hearts, minds, and souls of our children. There is no place to which we can withdraw.[19] We can run, but we can never hide.

The Data on Drug Use

Today, a high school child is half as likely to try an illicit drug as was his or her counterpart a decade ago.[20] In 1979 there were 23 million illicit drug users, in 1988 there were 14.3 million, a 40 percent drop, with monthly cocaine use falling 50 percent from 1985 to 1988.[21] Nearly seven of ten children in New Jersey and California who do not use drugs said that fear of getting in trouble with the law was a major deterrent to drug use.[22] Cocaine use skyrocketed in 1985 and a combination of education, prevention, and tough laws was put in place. Regular high school use of cocaine has dipped to 2.8 percent.[23] Crack use in the inner city is now showing signs of decline.[24]

Daily teenage marijuana use has plummeted 75 percent since 1978, when the president and his top drug advisor sought to decriminalize the drug.[25] It is still dropping, except in Alaska. In that state, when marijuana was legalized for adults, high school students are twice as likely to smoke pot as those in the lower forty eight.[26] As a result, Alaskan citizens voted in 1990 to recriminalize the drug. Drug users are considered the out-crowd and student drug-free groups have grown nationwide. Citizens in the inner cities have teamed up with policy to oust neighborhood drug dealers. Most of those in the field of education, prevention, and treatment believe progress is being made. Why, then, the frustration and fear and emergence of the "war-is-hopeless" sloganeering?

The emergence of the drug crack, the fact that drug abuse is still too high, and peak addiction levels following record cocaine drug use in 1985 have been sources of irritation. Use among the poor, especially the young poor, has increased disproportionately to the rest of the population.[27] In addition, fewer drug buyers increased competition and violence among dealers. Drug-legalization proponents note that after all these years of fighting drug abuse the problem still persists. The problem is still severe. It is a long leap in logic, however, to the conclusion that such laws will never work, are not working, and that they should be abandoned. Ironically, the leading legalization proponents admit that legalization is no panacea and that drug use will increase as a result of legalization.[28]

The facts are that today drug use is down, way down, for almost every sector of the population, and the public is more united against drug abuse than ever. There is still a long way to go, priorities may have to be shifted, and care must be taken not to leave anyone behind—but advances have been made as a result of a combination of drug awareness, education, prevention, treatment, and law enforcement.

The Role of Drug Laws

The case built against drug laws is in part dependent on the artificial extractions of drug laws from the more comprehensive and complex social context in which the law operates. Legalizers assume that in order to handle the multifaceted problem of drug abuse a choice is required between law enforcement or education, treatment, and prevention.[29] There may be honest disagreement about whether funding is adequately distributed among health, legal, and educational approaches to counter drug abuse, but trying to find a federal or state drug strategy that pursues law enforcement as the sole solution is like trying to find the economist's hypothetical can opener. Such a strategy simply does not exist.

Although a systemwide approach is now being implemented and most states have comprehensive drug plans, many drug-legalization proponents continue to view law enforcement in isolation. A poll sponsored by the legalization activist group, the Drug Policy Foundation, polarized options offered respondents, and forced an unrealistic choice between treatment, education, and prevention *or* imprisonment. Pollsters were instructed *not* to provide the option of choosing both approaches.[30]

The national drug strategy clearly notes that dividing the drug problem into supply and demand side tactics is "a bad idea" and that ". . . the reality of the drug problem cannot be met through an exclusive 'law enforcement' strategy on the one hand, or a 'prevention and treatment' strategy on the other. Most Americans recognize by now that we require both approaches."[31] Americans do know this and recent polls, reflecting record support for drug laws, also reveal that the top strategy endorsed is drug education.[32] The national strategy notes that drug education cannot work if law enforcement does not clear school zones of drug traffickers, and that law enforcement has a part in drug education. Drug laws drive people to receive treatment, both voluntarily and as justice-system referrals. The strategy concludes, "Most leaders of prevention and treatment programs recognize this; their task is made easier when drug enforcement works."[33]

To reach the conclusion that the drug war cannot succeed, legalization advocates narrowly define the war and ask, can drug laws alone defeat the problem of drug abuse? It is a safe question because even the staunchest advocates for drug laws, including the president and the attorney general, agree that the law cannot work in isolation. The drug czar says that millions of users should *not* be locked up and that reliance on law enforcement alone is a delusion.[34] The question for legalizers is, how would drug education, prevention, and treatment efforts improve, if repeal of drug laws increased drug use, reduced prices, and increased availability? No agreed-upon answer, or detailed alternative plan, has yet been offered.[35]

A *False Dichotomy*

Legalization proponents compare drug effects and costs with lack of comprehension of the polydrug-abuse concept and adherence to a mistaken model of drug substitution. Medical experts find a strong link between frequent cocaine use, alcohol abuse, and marijuana use. As cocaine use climbs, so does the use of these other substances.[36] Those who have smoked marijuana a hundred times or more are 75 percent more likely to use cocaine than those who abstain from marijuana smoking, a correlation that is estimated to be ten times stronger than the link between cigarette smoking and lung cancer.[37] Legalization would compound societal costs by increasing not only harm due to new illicit drug use, but also costs from upswings in other drug use, including alcohol. Drug abusers seldom chose a single drug to abuse; they use active combinations of substances. Legalizers often attribute the rise in cocaine use to the decline in marijuana availability. The data actually indicate that cocaine use has declined 50 percent since 1985, as marijuana use also fell. Today, with marijuana use at a low, use of cocaine is below the level in 1977 when marijuana smoking was near an all-time high.[38]

Measuring Drug-Use Risk

In an article for drug legalization in *Foreign Policy* magazine, Ethan Nadelmann makes this erroneous assumption: "Clearly there is no valid basis for distinguishing between alcohol and tobacco, on the one hand, and most of the illicit substances, on the other, as far as their relative dangers are concerned."[39] Before making this point he compares alcohol and illicit-drug statistics and attempts to extrapolate drug-addictiveness indicators from drug-use surveys. In measuring dangerousness, emphasis is put on dangers to the user, not to society at large. Marijuana safety is "proven" because there are no documented overdose deaths. The impact of marijuana use on others, such as the sixteen deaths and $51-million cost imposed by a Conrail engineer on pot, is largely disregarded.[40]

The Risk to Nonusers. The reason illicit drugs pose a high risk to nonusers is that these substances significantly impair the judgment and though processes of users *every* time they are shot, smoked, snorted, or swallowed. Tobacco has minimal disruptive psychoactive impact and its primary risk is chronic disease for the user. Alcohol can be used as a beverage without significant mental impairment. The greatest risk of alcohol use to others is when it is used to a point of intoxication or impairment; the leading alcohol-related cause of death is injuries, not overdoses—chiefly from drunken driving.[41] Because illicit drugs are always used for their intoxicating effect, any analogy to alcohol use should be to getting drunk, not to having a drink. One ounce of alcohol is incapable of intoxicating the average adult, but one ounce of marijuana could impair over 100 people.[42]

Opposition to drug intoxication is based on more than "puritan" distrust of altered consciousness; it involves public safety. An intoxicated person not only has motor and behavioral impairment, but the very capacity to make safe and sound choices regarding driving, future drug use, child care, and other matters also is diminished. There is evidence that illicit drug users are more likely to be involved in accident fatalities and serious injuries than are alcohol users. Although there are nine times as many current drinkers as there are marijuana smokers, a Maryland study found recent marijuana use as prevalent as alcohol use (35 percent for each) for those treated at a hospital for serious injuries. Another 16.5 percent had both drugs in their systems.[43] A study of national truck-driver fatalities shows that the proportion who died with marijuana in their systems (13 percent) equaled the percentage with alcohol in their systems[44] Cocaine is used by 1.5 percent of the U.S. population, but was implicated in 8.5 percent of the truck fatalities. In a New York study, the drug had been used within 48 hours by 20 percent of drivers fatally injured.[45] In most cases, use of illicit drug goes undetected.

The argument is made that under drug legalization dangerous behavior such as drugged driving would still be illegal. Drugged driving is already illegal and with the data above indicating that on a per user basis, drug users are five to ten times as likely to be involved in fatal accidents as those who use alcohol, there is little rationale for making drugs legal and increasing the risk imposed by drug use. Why kill more innocent drivers? Dr. Schultz of the University of Miami School of Medicine summarized his study on alcohol deaths by stating that if everyone who drank did so very occasionally, at levels not likely to produce injury-prone behavior, there would be few alcohol-related deaths.[46] Many alcohol drinkers do drink at safe levels, but every user of illicit drugs uses to get intoxicated. Every one else is put at risk from their mental impairment.

The Risk to Users. The addictiveness of various substances cannot be determined by the ratio or the number of people who have tried a drug to the number who are "hooked." Medical scientists disagree with political scientists and social psychologists advocating legalization because illicit drugs are not dangerous or addictive as commonly believed. Dr. Gabriel Nahas, a scientific researcher and expert on marijuana and cocaine, has extensively reviewed these issues in his writings and provides a chemical basis for his findings, centering on biological disruption in the brain.[47] Dr. Robert Gilkeson clearly states the issue: "The toxicity of intoxicants is not determined by debate. . . . We cannot vote for or against the 'toxicity' of a drug."[48]

Health risks of illicit drug use have now been clearly established.[49] These drugs induce biochemical changes in areas of the brain that regulate memory and coherent behavior, thereby affecting personality and survival. Such changes are in many cases irreversible. It is the very exercise of freedom that is abridged by these drugs. In addition, illicit drugs impair the genetic code: They are genotoxic, and may affect germ cells, sperm, and ova, threatening future generations before they are even conceived. Cannabis, cocaine, and the opiates also are fetotoxic, damaging the growing fetus.

While demanding a health approach to the drug problem, legalization arguments often imply that addicts are a few individuals who simply cannot hold their drugs, "a minority without self-restraint."[50] One legalization proponent suggests that more sophisticated individuals are more immune to addiction.[51] Treatment specialists believe that addiction is not a respecter of race, religion, or social status and that anyone can fall prey to this disease and the resultant degradations.[52] Drug harm is not limited to addiction; as Len Bias tragically discovered, the effects of even casual use are not predictable. The fact that not everyone who uses drugs becomes an addict does not mean that all users are not at risk of addiction. Like Russian roulette, the more you play, the greater the risk.

Furthermore, prodrug-legalization advocates often refer to treatment of addiction as a cornerstone of their policy alternative. They cannot ignore that there is no cure for drug addiction. No foolproof specific psychiatric or psychological treatment is available. The addict knows it and is often reluctant to accept his only chance for drug-free recovery—a protracted and difficult period of drug-free rehabilitation. Drug laws save thousands of lives each year by insisting on such treatment as conditions of parole or probation or pretrial release. Even so, at best, only half the addicts in the typical treatment program are rehabilitated.

Even marijuana would not pass FDA approval standards if application were made by a pharmaceutical company to market this substance for the general public. Many of those favoring legalization are opposed to other, nonintoxicating environmental pollutants that cause far less biochemical damage. The risk of smoking a weed that combusts to release over 2,000 crude chemicals, with more carcinogens in stronger concentration than tobacco, and a fat-soluble neurotoxin with a half-life of five to seven days, is minimized for political, not health, reasons. Ironically, members of the marijuana consumer's lobby claim that the drug fight should be led by the "surgeon general, not the attorney general," yet many fail to heed the surgeon general's warning regarding marijuana use.

The Forgotten History of Civilizations and Drug Control

In spring 1990, the world's first international drug summit of leaders from 112 supplier and consumer nations convened and strongly rejected the drug-legalization option. Instead, a broad range of strategies, including treatment, prevention, education, eradication, and law enforcement, was adopted.[53] The European Parliament had reached a similar conclusion two years earlier. The United States would be in violation of international treaty if it legalized drugs.[54] The historical experience of various countries with drug abuse provides useful observations generally ignored in the legalization debate.

The United States. This country once had legal cocaine, heroin, and marijuana. At the turn of the century these substances were widely used and promoted, largely through medical and drugstore outlets. Home remedies touting cures for nearly every ailment often included one or more now-illicit drugs.[55] The outrageous claims made by drug and snake-oil salesmen for these substances rivaled those made by Timothy Leary for LSD, NORML for marijuana, or recent reports underwritten by the National Institute on Drug Abuse extolling the hallucinogen MDMA.[56] The result of this "honeymoon period" of drug acceptance was record addiction levels, crime, and associated social disruption. The murder rate jumped 300 percent from 1907 to 1917.[57]

Drug laws were the result of a public outcry by people victimized by the impact of these chemicals on themselves, their families and neighbors.[58] In the early 1900s, the cocaine and opium addiction rate rivaled that of today. In 1914, these substances were made illegal and by 1940 the number of addicts dropped from over a quarter million to 50,000. The availability of cheap, pure cocaine and other drugs led to their widespread use. When druggists stopped selling cocaine, neighborhood disorder declined. A medical model of drug distribution failed to curb the drug epidemic of the 1900s or to effectively limit availability. Law enforcement also has been credited by a leading criminologist with helping to contain a rising tide of heroin addiction in the 1970s.[59] Legal narcotics in the United States brought about the predecessor of current drug laws.

In 1988, the White House Conference for a Drug-Free America issued a final report that drew "on the innate wisdom and good sense of the American people." The bipartisan group of 127 conferees, made up of the nation's top leaders from diverse fields, heard from thousands of citizens on the front lines of drug treatment, education, and enforcement. The report reflected their recommendation that drug legalization be "vigorously opposed."[60]

Sweden. After attempting to soften drug laws to destroy the criminal element and remove the profit motive, Sweden's drug laws were stiffened in response to high abuse rates, especially of amphetamines in the late 1970s. The number of teenagers who had tried drugs was cut in half by 1987. Law enforcement was part of a broad approach that included mandatory treatment and selective drug testing of students.[61]

Japan. Our major global business competitor has one of the lowest drug-abuse rates and crime rates of any industrial nation. It also has some of the stiffest drug laws. Japan faced an epidemic of highly addictive amphetamine use, a central nervous system stimulant like cocaine, after World War II and a heroin use problem in the early 1960s. Both epidemics were successfully routed through a combination of strong law enforcement in conjunction with drug user stigmatization and rehabilitation.[62]

China. China overcame a severe national opium-addiction problem through public education, rehabilitation, and strict law enforcement.[63]

Spain. Spain provides a good example of what to expect when tough drug laws are liberalized. When the Socialists took over in 1983, Spain went from having some of the strictest laws in Western Europe to having some of the most lenient. A spurt in cocaine, heroin, and other drug use and trafficking, and the accompanying problems of crime and social disruption, plague that nation today. Spain has become a major transhipment point for drug kingpins. Outraged parents presented a drug report that shamed the government into action and antidrug laws were enacted and are being strengthened.[64]

Italy.   Italy has rescinded soft laws on the possession and use of heroin because of record addiction rates and overdose deaths.[65]

Germany.   Germany, America's major European business competitor, is taking a strong stance against drug abuse and has enacted tighter drug controls.[66]

Switzerland.   In 1987, the Zurich City Council approved a program allowing drug addicts to buy and use drugs freely, and providing clean needles and condoms in one city park. Overdose deaths dropped, but crime in the area rose 30 percent and Switzerland has the highest drug-abuse and AIDs rate in Europe. Half the addicts in Zurich test HIV-positive. In *Mother Jones* magazine, a publication that has printed prodrug-legalization articles, the scene is described as follows: "Platzpromenade Park is littered with hundreds of people thrusting needles into their arms and necks. Blood falls to the grass. Bodies overload the park's benches, heads dangle at impossible angles, eyes roll back."[67] Is this a model for America to follow on a national level?

Netherlands.   The Dutch drug experience is used as a model for U.S. drug policy. It is difficult to see how this example squares with most legalization propositions. Dutch drug laws reflect a liberal moral philosophy and a traditional toleration of more radical viewpoints. For instance, pornography legislation in 1986 included a provision (later rejected) to lower the age of consent from sixteen to twelve years of age.[68] Marijuana and other drugs are not legal in the Netherlands, but certain laws are simply ignored. The Dutch do not raise one dollar in tax revenue from drug sales because the junkies union, a political lobbying force for junkie rights, successfully sued to stifle tax provisions on the basis that, as a signatory to the United Nations drug convention, drugs were illegal and illegal substances could not be taxed.

The Dutch retain a narcotics police force and have hardened drug-trafficking laws, cracking down on border and customs patrols. Drug violators account for 50 percent of the Dutch prison population, a higher proportion than in the United States.[69] The Netherlands is the most crime-prone nation in Europe.[70] Most drug addicts live on state welfare payments and by committing crimes. Thievery and vandalism have skyrocketed. Unemployment is at 15 percent and minorities are overrepresented among the addict population.[71]

Legalization advocates boast that marijuana use has dipped since laws were liberalized, but this is based on a questionable survey. Other data suggests that Amsterdam marijuana use is not much lower than use in the United States.[72] The number of Amsterdam drug cafes rose from under 30 to over 300 in one decade. Legalizers fail to note that daily marijuana use by U.S. youth declined 75 percent following blockage of the decriminalization movement. The Dutch tried licensed legal heroin distribution but quickly scrapped the notion after a spurt in crime and overdose deaths. A recent Dutch report concluded that legal heroin distribution would not reduce drug-related crime.[73] A Dutch businessman quoted in *Forbes* magazine lamented, "If they had made jails instead of organizations to help the junkies, things would be much better."[74]

Britain. England discovered that allowing doctors to prescribe heroin led to a huge black market and an increase in drug problems.[75] The drug problem is of serious concern there and the British Prime Minister opposes efforts to legalize or liberalize drug laws. Britain's experience with liberal drug regulation and legislation led to stricter control and tougher drug laws.

Alcohol Prohibition: Propaganda or Useful Analogy?

Historically, "prohibition" describes the period (1919–1933) in which the Volstead Act was in effect banning alcohol sales and transport. Use of the word to describe current drug policies and laws is based on clever public relations, not careful policy analysis. Murder and child-abuse laws are not referred to as forms of prohibition. Although primarily a moral appeal, the term is interspersed throughout an often-cited article on legalization in the prestigious *Science* magazine.[76] Prohibition purportedly demonstrates lessons applicable to current drug law, most prominently its alleged failure as a social policy.

Is the Prohibition Analogy Appropriate? A useful historical analogy must exhibit facts and circumstances that made comparison meaningful. Important distinctions between current drug policy and alcohol prohibition must be noted before any "lessons" of prohibition are applied. Prohibition attempted to use the law to create a strong moral consensus against use of a popular drug and beverage that had over 2,000 years of cultural acceptance. Drug legalization attempts to use legal repeal to bring about cultural acceptance for the use of substances that are widely feared and traditionally rejected by the vast majority of the population. In a democratic government, it is essential that the law reflect the will of a substantial proportion of the general public. Alcohol prohibition never garnered the widespread backing given to current drug laws. Three years after prohibition, only 38 percent favored it, and in 1981 that figure dropped to a low of 17 percent. In contrast, today 80 percent of Americans want drugs kept illegal. Prohibition did demonstrate the difficulty of putting the drug "genie" back into the bottle and making a substance illegal, once legal status is granted.[77]

The use and purchase of alcohol was never outlawed by prohibition. Alcohol use was attacked almost solely through regulation of manufacturers and suppliers. The lesson, if any, is that current user-accountability statutes may be an essential improvement over drug-control efforts that allow drug use, but not manufacture and sale. Under alcohol prohibition, doctors could prescribe alcohol and the medical profession was a major source of alcohol products, "for medicinal purposes."[78] If there is any lesson here, it is that legalization through medical distribution is fraught with dangers and loopholes. Alcohol prohibition was not part of a comprehensive education, prevention, and treatment strategy as today's drug laws are.

Did Prohibition Fail?   Surprisingly, from a health and economic perspective, prohibition accomplished its goal, saving the nation both money and lives. The direct costs of prohibition and loss of tax revenues were more than recouped through fines and penalties assessed on violators.[79] Even though alcohol use was not illegal, prohibition significantly lowered alcohol consumption. On a public health basis, cirrhosis deaths were cut over a third, alcohol psychosis cases fell dramatically, in Massachusetts child neglect cases declined by over 50 percent, juvenile delinquency and alcohol-related divorces dropped by half.[80] Even with gangster killings, the overall murder rate declined. From 1905 to 1919 the murder rate rose 300 percent; during the prohibition period, 1918 to 1929, the overall rate rose 30 percent.[81] Arguments against prohibition are based more on public opinion and social consensus than economic or health data.

Since the repeal of prohibition, alcohol consumption has tripled. It is estimated alcohol abuse costs the nation $100 billion per year and over 300 lives per day, an amount that the $18 billion in state and federal excise tax revenues does not begin to cover.[82] Alcohol is also strongly linked (together with illicit drugs) to violent and property crimes. Ironically, legalization advocates somehow believe that the tremendous costs and dangers of alcohol abuse justify adding new, dangerous mind-altering substances to the public pharmacopoeia.

What Is the Real Lesson of Prohibition?   The choice is not whether society will absorb the heavy cost of legal alcohol or legal cocaine or legal marijuana or legal heroin; the choice is whether to multiply the cost incurred from legal alcohol *plus* legal cocaine, *plus* marijuana, *plus* heroin.[83] From an economic, health, or legal perspective no justification can be made.

To demonstrate that alcohol is the more dangerous and more costly substance, legalizers note that fewer deaths and lower costs (estimated at $60 billion per year) are currently attributed to illegal drugs, and therefore these substances are more worthy of legal status than alcohol. What is not acknowledged is that it is the drug laws that keep use, and its associated costs to the economy and human life, below that of alcohol. Because drug laws help keep use at such low levels, relative to alcohol use, the dangers of illicit drugs are grossly underestimated. What the analogy to alcohol dangers and costs indicates is that drug laws save the nation billions of dollars and thousands of lives each year.

Drug Laws: Costs and Benefits

Legalization theorists contend that drug laws cause problems more serious than the tragedies related to drug use. The "seriousness" of problems attributed to drug laws is defined and weighed in a highly subjective manner. Dangers of illicit drug use, for both users and those around them, are intentionally downplayed, while the impact of drug laws on creating new crime and criminals is exaggerated. The drug problem, as experienced by the majority of U.S. citizens, is redefined into the drug-law problem, as viewed through the eyes of intellectual theorists, drug users, and drug-use-rights civil libertarians.

What Is "the Drug Problem"?

In answering this inquiry, one must ask, the problem for whom? In this case, where you stand very definitely depends on where you sit.

From Conception to Birth. At this stage the drug problem is solely related to drug use by the mother. Illicit drugs pass in utero to developing infants, and cocaine-addicted mothers have higher miscarriage rates and increased risk of developmental damage and organ defects.[84] The offspring of mothers who smoke marijuana showed a tenfold increased risk of having a form of leukemia in a preliminary study.[85] Demands on health-care services, with an estimated cost of $90,000 per crack baby, have a public carryover cost.[86] Any drug-policy change that would increase drug availability and decrease price would have a damaging impact.

From Birth to One Year of Age. The number-one cause of death for this age group is homicide, mostly from abuse and neglect of caregivers. Parental cocaine use and child neglect are highly correlated.[87] Psychologists believe cocaine can override the mothering instinct. Babies of addicted mothers are difficult to care for and infants have been fed fatal drug overdoses to quiet them. In Washington, D.C., infant mortality rose 50 percent in the first half of 1989, and up to 15 percent of addicted babies died of sudden death syndrome.[88] The drug problem for this group is drug use by parents, and legal, cheaper drugs pose a severe threat.

Children from One to Twelve.   Accidents are the leading cause of death for this group and many of them are drug-related.[89] Child abuse and neglect are aggravated by drug use. Even if a child is not beaten, drugs steal the love and affection of parents that children are entitled to have. Peer pressure is a powerful factor in decisions to use drugs; parental drug use is the leading predictor of use by youth. Reducing drug demand among older students and siblings could reduce that risk. A Pennsylvania teenager, active in drug-prevention efforts with elementary children, noted that legalization would "destroy everything we have worked for."[90] First drug use is likely to be of alcohol, because of its legal status and wide acceptance. Children cannot separate the message that it is legal from the message it is all right to use it.[91] The greatest drug problem is drug use.

Teenagers.   The leading teen killer is not drug-gang shootings, lung cancer, or cirrhosis of the liver; it is automobile and other accidents largely attributed to alcohol and marijuana use; next comes suicides and homicides, also linked to use of illicit substances.[92] Even libertarians generally agree that children must be protected under the law and that not all choices available to adults should be available to children.

Adolescent drug use would rise dramatically if drugs were legalized for adults. This is amply demonstrated by alcohol-use patterns. Over 90 percent of high school seniors have experimented with alcohol, and two-thirds are current drinkers. In contrast, only 10 percent have tried cocaine, and only 1.5 percent use it regularly.[93] Marijuana use is less than half that of alcohol use, except in Alaska where use was legal for adults. In that state, most used both drugs and student marijuana use is twice the national average.[94] Drug legalizers should reduce student alcohol-use levels to those of illicit drugs before legitimating adult role modeling with other deadly substances.

Murder is the only major source of teen fatalities that is related to both drug use and the illicit drug trade. The drug crack causes unpredictable, violent behavior unrelated to the drug trade. Crack studies show a high degree of violence related to drug use, not just to drug laws.[95] Children are murdering others for leather coats, designer sneakers, and gold chains. Teens are more likely to engage in high-risk sexual behavior under the influence of drugs, not just to obtain more drugs. Drug use impairs mental judgment and restraint.[96] Psychological problems from teen drug use can be lifelong.

Parents.   For parents of nondrug users, the drug problem is primarily the risk that their child will succumb to the temptation to try drugs and end up with serious life problems. The chief concern is that there are too many drugs and too many drug users. Parents do not want a government crack store on their block any more than they want an illicit crack house. Increasing drug availability through legalization is not an answer to their problem; reducing drug use and drug demand is.

For parents of children involved with drugs, the primary problem is the impact these substances have on their child and family. Drug use changes the very personality of a child, never for the better, and puts their entire future at risk. Families become dysfunctional. The greatest fear is that drug use will lead to premature death. A *Wall Street Journal* reporter wrote of the drug-use tragedy of his son, "Because of drugs he is dead, and every day my heart breaks a little more."[97] There are deaths due to the drug trade, but there are thousands more broken hearts due to drug use, and its destructive power on children and adults.

The Nonusing Public. For those nonusers, the drug problem hits home hardest when a family member or friend has a substance-abuse problem. Drug users in the neighborhood and on the job constitute a second concern.[98] Crime related to drug abuse and the drug trade is another fear. The odds of being injured in an accident are twenty times those of being criminally assaulted, and the odds of being killed in an accident are over twice those of being murdered.[99] The impact of drug abuse on the national economy and tax rate also causes problems for the nonuser.

Recovering Addicts. To the recovering addict the problem is totally one of drug use. The vast majority of those in recovery do not see any merit in making illicit drugs any cheaper or more available. In 60 hours of drug hearings held by the governor and attorney general of Pennsylvania, drug addicts told how essential it was in recovery to get away from a drug-ridden environment. Some reported how law enforcement played an important role in their seeking treatment.[100]

People of Color. Leaders have been quick to call drug legalization "chemical apartheid," creation of a "bio-underclass," and Washington, D.C., Councilman Ray terms "state-sponsored addiction" a form of racism.[101] Peter Bell, former director of the Black Chemical Abuse Institute, wrote that he cannot think of one serious problem faced by the black community, be it teen pregnancy, unemployment, or educational opportunity, that would not be negatively impacted by drug legalization.[102] Homelessness is highly correlated with substance abuse, with 44 percent of the homeless identified as drug abusers.[103] Attacking drug demand, not creating a cheap legal market, is the only solution to both problems.

The Economist's Drug Problem

From a theoretical viewpoint the drug problem looks quite different. Drug problems arise from the economics of the drug market, not the impact of these chemicals on the brain's pleasure center. Subjective items, such as the pain felt by the *Wall Street Journal* reporter for his son, are difficult to calculate and therefore deemphasized. The drug problem is solely one of crime associated with the black market in drugs. Drug laws artificially raise drug prices and bring about criminal organizations that profit from this trade and fight off competitors with violence. High prices force addicts to commit more crime to feed their habits. Deaths from drug overdoses and drug-trade-related murder are given disproportionate weight over accident fatalities. The tremendous impact of drug use on children and youth is discounted in the cost-benefit calculation.

Two Solutions to End the Illicit Drug Traffic.   The national drug strategy puts top emphasis on taking away customers and reducing demand to put drug dealers out of business. Tactics include drug education and prevention to stop first use, drug treatment to break the cycle of abuse, and law enforcement to make drug use difficult, risky, and expensive.[104]

Drug legalization would end illegal drug trafficking by making drug trafficking legal. A legitimate drug market would wipe out the current drug trade through price-slashing competition. If necessary, a government monopoly would be created. It is estimated that the price for a dose of cocaine would drop to about forty cents, low enough for a child to purchase two hits with lunch money.[105]

How Legalization Would Work.   There are many variations and schemes for drug legalization, but if the goal is to significantly reduce the most dangerous forms of drug trafficking, only one method could possibly work and that is outright legalization of all drugs, of all potencies, to all users, at convenient twenty-four-hour locations with bargain-basement prices. Again, cocaine would go for about forty cents per dose.[106] Any new street drugs developed would be immediately manufactured and made legally available. Economists are wrong to assume that the black market is responsible for creating the crack form of cocaine. Crack became popular because drug users naturally crave more powerful highs. Crack is easier to market, but drug users do not select their drug of choice for the convenience of dealers. Wealthy cocaine users created freebase coke on their own, prior to the advent of crack. Hallucinogens increased in potency while they were legal (for example, peyote to mescaline, or LSD development). If new designer drugs were not instantly legal, the incentive to create stronger drugs illicitly would increase under legalization. The first drug deserving legal marketing would be crack, currently having the most violent black market. The last drug to legalize would be marijuana, since that market is already somewhat dry.

The government would most likely hold a monopoly because of the potential legal liability for private industry. No reputable law firm would advise a client to get into this business, nor would an insurance company issue policy protection. In some neighborhoods, there would have to be as many crack stores and smoking dens as there are liquor stores and bars. An illicit drug user would be no more willing to snort and puff and shoot in a sanitized medical setting that a beer drinker would. It would have to work like alcohol distribution to be successful.

Underage use could be prohibited, but if heavy penalties were put on illicit sales to children that would raise the risk and attendant profit margin for the youth market and a specialized trafficking network would prosper from this trade. Therefore, sales to youth would not be treated any more seriously than alcohol sales to children. If all of the above conditions were met, the black market would probably diminish, but would that really decrease the drug problem as experienced by the majority of citizens?

Drug-Law versus Drug-Use Problems

Former Secretary of State George Shultz indicates that legalization would take the "criminality" out of the drug business—and the incentives for criminality.[107] Most legalization arguments mistakenly assume that a legal drug market would reduce crime committed by drug traffickers, street dealers, and drug users. Recent research casts doubts on the legalizers' assumption that drug laws and the crack black market are the primary drive behind the burgeoning murder rate in the inner cities.[108] These murders appear to have more to do with a general disregard for life accompanied by family and community disintegration, factors highly correlated with drug use, not drug laws. In one survey, one-third of drug-hotline callers reported "uncontrollable violence" as an effect of their drug use.[109]

Organized Street Drug Gangs. Gangs would temporarily lose ground under an open, legal drug-market scheme. These individuals, however, will not stop selling drugs without a fight, and government crack centers had better be well fortified with armed guards. Government does not have a good track record of running competitive enterprises. If government competition with murderous drug thugs is successful, gangsters are not going to go out and get jobs. They are going to shift their emphasis to other crimes. Street gangs in Los Angeles and other cities existed long before the crack epidemic. With the advent of crack, dealer competition increased for a diminished demand, fueling open violence. The effect of the drug itself on human behavior plays an underrated role in the violence. Other drugs had been sold, but crack brought mayhem. Gangs that derived income from armed robberies, burglaries, and other crimes have higher income expectations through drug sales.

What will happen when gangs can no longer make money selling drugs?

First, they will sell whatever drugs the law still bans, to whomever still cannot get them. This means intensive marketing to younger children. Once that market is saturated, an upswing in armed robbery, burglary, and larceny against nondrug users can be anticipated. A detective in Washington, D.C., believes that a dip in burglary and robbery statistics is the result of criminals' either selling drugs instead of robbing, or robbing drug dealers instead of other citizens.[110] Nationwide, from 1984 to 1988, robbery arrests of those under 18 declined 11 percent and burglaries dropped 12 percent. Then, with the ebbing of the crack epidemic in 1988, arrests of minors for robbery rose 18 percent and the decline in burglaries slowed to a mere 1 percent in the 1988–1989 period.[111] The murder rate is high, due more to drug use and social factors than the drug trade. In fact, the legal drug alcohol has a prominent role in most murders.

Drug dealers who are not addicted sell drugs to make money. The criminal incentive and profit motive would not be destroyed by drug legalization; criminal activity would simply be transferred. Currently 50 to 80 percent of felony offenders have illicit drugs in their systems.[112] The increased availability of cheaper lethal drugs that impair judgment and self-control, together with the loss of drug-related income, would bring a wave of violent crime directed at those outside the drug trade.

The above should not lead one to conclude that there is any public interest in perpetuating the drug trade. By drying up demand to put dealers out of business, a more gradual transition will take place. Drug use often runs parallel to criminal involvement, and decreasing the number of drug users will also decrease potential criminal ranks. Incarcerated drug dealers are those with the most serious records, and keeping these individuals locked up deters redirected crime. Alternative sentencing, like boot camps and halfway houses, is being developed to teach work and life skills. Treatment in prison and in conjunction with parole also is increasing, albeit too slowly.[113]

Crimes Committed by Drug Users.   Contrary to popular belief, overall crimes by drug users would increase, not decrease, under a drug-legalization system. Just as alcohol-related crime has not declined since prohibition was repealed, neither would drug-related crime. Legal drugs would sell for 20 percent of the current cost, and thus cash requirements to feed a habit would be reduced, with an offset in this reduction caused by increased drug use. The number of users, especially addicted users, would skyrocket.[114] Heavy drug users are not likely to obtain gainful employment; they will hustle and steal. There would be an increased incentive to steal cash because the government crack store would not be likely to trade doses for "hot" goods. Users who sold drugs for a living would have to victimize outsiders. Neighborhoods where crack is widely available and sells for as low as $3 a hit have high, not low, crime rates. Even if drugs were free, users would need money to eat, pay rent, and buy clothing. As was noted earlier, the Dutch, with their "enlightened" drug policy, concluded that legal heroin would not reduce crime.

In Philadelphia, cocaine is implicated in half the cases in which parents beat their children to death, and in 80 percent of all abuse cases.[115] In the District of Columbia, 90 percent of those reported for child abuse were substance abusers.[116] Cheaper, purer, legal cocaine, used by more mothers, is only going to kill more babies. The number of children wounded and killed by stray bullets in tragic drive-by drug shootings pales in comparison to the impact of cocaine in the over 1,200 child-abuse murders in 1989. Add to that a significant increase in the 375,000 infants born to drug-dependent mothers and their 15 percent sudden-death-syndrome fatality rate.[117] Some children are abandoned at birth,[118] and many of the children who survive will have lifelong medical and psychological problems. Ethan Nadelmann candidly admits that the child-abuse problem would not improve, but he fails to acknowledge that it would dramatically escalate. Arnold Trebach, head of the Drug Policy Foundation, says that even with a doubling of the addicts, legalization would probably pay off with a "net increase in the health and safety of all Americans."[119] The prospect of 750,000 suffering babies with doubtful futures hardly seems to be a net benefit.

Drug users are more likely to commit rape, assault, and murder unrelated to obtaining drugs. It is stunning that illicit drugs, used regularly by only 7.3 percent of the population, were used by 60 to 80 percent of those arrested for violent felonies.[120] The reason is that illicit drugs are always used to get high, and getting high entails impairment of the mind. Marijuana, a drug often unassociated with criminal behavior, is frequently found in felony offenders. Intoxication lowers inhibitions, making crime-prone individuals more likely to act.

International Drug Trafficking The criminal element involved in international trafficking would be greatly aided by drug legalization in the United States. The number-one fear of cocaine kingpins in Colombia is fear of extradition to face U.S. laws. This fear has led drug terrorists to declare war on their own government. If cocaine were completely legal and inexpensive, the cartel would fill the void and lower prices due to lower risk resulting from the lapse of U.S. drug enforcement. If the cocaine market were totally licit, the drug cartels would control the legal market.

The United States would become the major safehouse and transhipment point for the European and Canadian markets. Drug kingpins choose nations with weak drug laws as distribution centers, such as Spain and the Netherlands in Europe.[121] European nations currently make up 30 percent of the cocaine market. A legal U.S. market would free billions of dollars in hidden drug proceeds amassed in foreign accounts that could be spent to establish new legitimate and illegitimate bases in the United States. Just as the end of prohibition, or the establishment of legal gambling and prostitution in Nevada did not destroy the mafia, legalization would only strengthen the drug cartels' hand. In the 1970s a conglomeration of marijuana growers and dealers donated a substantial sum of cash to NORML, the marijuana lobby. Drug traffickers long to see the United States establish a legal drug market. In a videotaped message to 7,000 antidrug volunteers in Florida, Colombia's former president pleaded with the people of the United States not to legalize drugs—to stop the demand.[122]

The Cost to Civil Liberties

Legalization advocates argue that the current drug war has led to "repressive" measures and has resulted in the loss of precious constitutional freedoms.[123] They note that a disproportionate number of drug felons are minorities, and that the courts have been upholding legal tactics such as asset forfeiture and drug testing. More disturbing are recent polls showing that U.S. citizens are willing to sacrifice certain "rights" to fight drug abuse; 97 percent support forms of drug testing and 78 percent of college freshmen agree employers have a right to test for drugs.[124]

The legalizers usually focus on the rights of drug users and their lawyers, not those of the general public. The rights of law-abiding citizens to be free to walk down the street safely, or to have peaceful neighborhoods, or to send children to secure schools, are seldom discussed. The right to a safe, drug-free work environment, or public transport system, is not weighed against the individual "indignity" of a drug test. In New York City, one of three bus-driver applicants tested positive for drugs.[125] The more the rights of drug criminals take precedence over the rights of law-abiding citizens, the more the civil liberties of all are lost. It is self-defeating to work for the right to use illegal drugs and at the same time oppose drug testing, sobriety checkpoints, drug-control efforts in the schools, jail reimbursement from drug offenders, and forfeiture of illegal drug assets.[126]

Giving drug users a legal right to use mind-altering drugs is not going to enhance civil liberties. Law enforcement may lose the power to act and fed-up citizens will act on their own. In some areas citizens have already taken the law into their own hands and burned down crackhouses.[127] In Europe, similar responses have taken place.[128] The loss of basic security and order that would result from legalization would bring a dangerous backlash. Plato once noted, "Far too great liberty seems to change into nothing else than too great slavery."[129]

THE MORAL DILEMMA

The Moral Question: Costs to Whom?

The moral appeal of the prohibition analogy, with its implicit hint at hypocrisy toward everyone who has ever had a drink or smoked a cigarette of tobacco or marijuana, has, on the surface, a more rational basis than any economic or health justification for combining the harm of legal alcohol with legalized dangerous drugs. Not only does the argument of "you have your poison, I have mine" grip alcohol and tobacco users with a tinge of guilt, but it also reaches the sentiments of civil libertarians and conservatives who want to keep government out of private affairs. When the biochemical nature of these substances and the risk users impose on children and nonusers are rationally assessed, however, the case for legalization self-destructs. The public health and welfare interest, and the future of generations to come, far outweigh the self-interest in using and having access to dangerous intoxicating chemicals.

The emphasis on harm to the user reflects another faulty assumption made regarding the primary justification for making drugs illegal. Legalization advocates, especially those of the libertarian bent, often contend that drug laws are designed to keep people from hurting themselves. Chicago columnist Mike Royko, supporting legalization, says that if someone wants to shoot, snort, or smoke his way into oblivion, that is his problem and "it's a lot easier to sweep up the gutters than to fight a hopeless war."[130] In reality it is also the problem of the user's family, neighbors, employer, coworkers, and all who share the same highways. It is the problem of all taxpayers, who carry the welfare, insurance, and health costs to "sweep up the gutter." That is why drug laws focus not only on harm to users, but also on the risks and costs that users impose on the rest of society, especially children.[131]

Libertarian theory contends that a man has a right to freely stretch out his arms until they strike someone else in the face. If this logic were truly followed, libertarians would seek to abolish drunk-driving laws. Why punish a drunk driver until he actually hits someone? After all, many drunks do make it home without incident. The fact is that no one has the right to intimidate and put others at unreasonable risk of harm. The degree of risk allowed is related to the extent of harm threatened. An additional problem is that society refuses to let individual rights be accompanied by individual responsibility. It is inconsistent for libertarians to use British and Dutch drug policy to bolster legalization arguments, and then be opposed to the socialized medicine and guaranteed income policies that support those systems. Under legalization, a person would have the right to become enslaved to drugs, but nonusers would pick up the health, social, and economic costs.

Whose Interests Will Prevail?

Most of the credit for the downturn of drug abuse has been attributed to an attitude of the American people of concern and intolerance.[132] Legalization proponents call for a return to the failed drug-tolerance policies of 1978.[133] They seek a return to "marijuana gladness" drug education that deemphasized drug harms and focused on how drugs made one feel. Drug education would again teach "safe" drug use. A 1979 book instructed students who chose to smoke pot to smoke with friends, clean out seeds, and use a waterpipe.[134] Internationally renowned scientist Gabriel Nahas has brilliantly traced how the dangers of cocaine were intentionally downplayed in public drug education by psychologists in his book Cocaine—The Great White Plague.[135] Scientific evidence on negative bio-chemical effects of marijuana has been even more censured and politicized.[136] Many drug-prevention specialists were trained with information written by those with a tolerant drug view and who were political activists in the prodrug-legalization issue.[137]

One result of the renewed debate over drug legalization is a resurgence of these older views on teaching children safe drug use.[138] Once again, divisions are developing just when public unity is beginning to make a difference. Although voices for alternative drug policies should not be censured, neither should precious resources be squandered. On a cost-benefit basis, is it wise to spend time and resources pursuing this discussion? The Congress and the president's top drug adviser do not think so. The media apparently do. The Alaskan people recently voiced their opinion in a statewide referendum to recriminalize marijuana. The vast majority of those on the front line, treating drug abusers, teaching children how and why to avoid drug use, and enforcing drug laws, oppose legalization. Despite intensive lobbying and public relations by leading drug-legalization organizations, no new facts or evidence are offered. The best they say is that it is "impossible to predict" what would happen if drugs were made legal.[139]

At its core, the legalization debate raises critical questions of who we are as a people. What values do we stand for, where are we headed, and to what extent will national policy reflect the needs of children?[140] Like racism, poverty, and environmental pollution, we have had to coexist with rampant drug-abuse problems and find it difficult to eradicate these tragedies. We have never formally thrown up our hands and resigned ourselves to passively accepting the chemical enslavement of a proportion of our people. It is my hope that we never will. The real issue is, perhaps, essentially a moral one. The question is, whose interests will prevail? The answer depends not on an abstract policy analysis, but rather on the spirit and will of the people of the United States.

NOTES

1. *New York Times*, May 15, 1988, p. 1.

2. *Chicago Tribune*, December 6, 1989, Sec. 1A, p. 29. The Drug Policy Foundation was founded by Arnold Trebach, who since 1983 spoke at National Organization to Reform Marijuana Laws' (NORML) conferences, and Kevin Zeese, former national director of NORML.

3. William F. Buckley and Milton Friedman have advocated forms of drug legalization since the early 1970s.

4. *Chicago Tribune*, May 24, 1990, Sec. 5, p. 2.

5. Diane Colasanto, "Widespread Opposition to Drug Legalization," *Gallup News Service Poll*, v. 54, no. 35, January 17, 1990.

6. Ibid. For compilations of leading views, see National Drug Information Center of Families in Action and the Scott Newman Center, "Arguments against Legalizing Drugs," *Drug Abuse Update* 26, Atlanta, Georgia, September, 1988; Committees of Correspondence, "Reasons Not to Legalize Drugs—A Compilation of Articles," *Drug Prevention Newsletter*, Danvers, Massachusetts, 1989.

7. *Washington Times*, December 15, 1989, p. F5. See also *Chronicle of Higher Education*, January 3, 1990, p. 1; *Harper's*, March, 1986, p. 4.

8. Marsha Manatt, *Parents, Peers, and Pot II*, National Institute on Drug Abuse, Washington, D.C., 1983.

9. *Baltimore Evening Sun*, November 2, 1989, p. A-14.

10. Ms. Siegel's comments to the National Organization for the Reform of Marijuana Laws (NORML), Twentieth Anniversary Conference, August–September 1990 (audiotape available through NORML, Washington, D.C.).

11. The difficult situation that parents from the 1960s now confront in warning their children about drugs is reported in *Wall Street Journal*, January 23, 1990, pp. A-1, 8.

12. Arnold S. Trebach, *The Great Drug War* (Macmillan Publishing Company, New York), 1987, pp. 120–21, 125–26. Healthy drug-free youth and caring parents involved in volunteer antidrug efforts are labeled "zealots" and personal attacks against its leaders are launched in this book. The author goes so far as to "guess" that drugs "prevent as many youth suicides as they cause" and that conceivably "the number of young people helped through school by the responsible use of alcohol and drugs may be roughly equal to the number hindered in attaining their educational goals because of the irresponsible use of such chemicals" (pp. 74–75).

13. *Pittsburgh Press*, September 16, 1990. The Hemp movement is backed by NORML, *High Times* magazine, and several promarijuana groups.

14. For an example of interaction see National Organization for the Reform of

Marijuana Laws, "NORML on the Front Lines," *The Leaflet* (Washington, D.C.), Fall, 1989, p. 1.

15. Robert L. DuPont, Jr., *Getting Tough on Gateway Drugs* (American Psychiatric Press, Inc., Washington, D.C.), 1984; Richard A. Hawley, *The Purposes of Pleasure—A Reflection on Youth and Drugs* (Independent School Press, Wellesley Hills, Massachusetts), 1983.

16. Gabriel Nahas and Henry Clay Frick, II, eds., *Drug Abuse in the Modern World* (Pergamon Press, Elmsford, New York), 1981.

17. Colasanto, *Gallup News Service Poll*, January 1990.

18. *Rolling Stone Magazine*, July 12–26, 1990, p. 11.

19. *New York Times*, March 31, 1988, p. A-26.

20. National Institute on Drug Abuse (NIDA), *National Household Survey on Drug Abuse: Population Estimates, 1988*, U.S. Department of Health and Human Services (DHHS Pub. No. (ADM) 89–1636), 1989.

21. Ibid.

22. Rodney Skagen, Dennis Fisher, and Ebrahim Maddahain, *A Statewide Survey of Drug and Alcohol Use among California Students in Grades 7, 9, and 11*, Office of Attorney General, May 1986; Wayne S. Fisher, et al., *Drug and Alcohol Use among New Jersey High School Students*, New Jersey Department of Law and Public Safety, 1990 (consistent with 1987 survey).

23. National Institute on Drug Abuse (NIDA), *National Trends in Drug Use and Related Factors among American High School Students and Young Adults 1975–1986*, U.S. Department of Health and Human Services (DHHS Pub. No. (ADM) 87–1535), 1987.

24. *Washington Post*, October 14, 1990, pp. A-1, 12. Article notes falling cocaine use with rising violence.

25. NIDA, *National Trends in Drug Use, 1975–1986*; NIDA, *National Household Survey: 1988*.

26. Department of Health and Social Services, *The State of Adolescent Health in Alaska*, Office of the Commissioner, Juneau, Alaska, May 1990; Bernard Segal, *Drug Taking among Alaskan Youth, 1988: A Follow-Up Study*, University of Alaska, Anchorage, November 1988.

27. White House, *National Drug Control Strategy*, Office of National Drug Control Policy (ONDCP), September 1989, p. 4; *New York Times*, August 30, 1987, p. 1.

28. Ethan A. Nadelmann, "Drug Prohibition in the United States: Costs, Consequences, and Alternatives," *Science*, September 1, 1989, p. 939.

29. Ethan A. Nadelmann, "The Case for Legalization," *Public Interest*, no. 92, pp. 3–65, Summer 1988.

30. Drug Policy Foundation, Washington, D.C.. The poll was conducted by Targeting Systems, Inc. for Richard Dennis and the Drug Policy Foundation on January 24, 1990, and February 4, 1990. Question 83 forces a choice between social problems *or* drug use as the sole cause of the drug problem; question 84 lectures on the costs of law

enforcement and the growing jail population before dividing options between imprisoning all drug users (an option no one is pursuing) *or* "less expensive" treatment options; question 85 plays on the prohibition analogy. Pollsters are told not to offer the option of combining approaches. The final question is a two-paragraph argument against law enforcement before polarizing options between laws *or* legalization and increased treatment and education lumped as one.

31. White House, *National Drug Control Strategy*, Office of National Drug Control Policy (ONDCP), January , 1990, p. 2.

32. *Gallup Poll News Service*, January 17, 1990.

33. ONDCP, *National Drug Control Strategy*, January 1990.

34. ONDCP, *National Drug Control Strategy*, September 1989, pp. 5–7.

35. Congressman Charles Rangel of New York City has repeatedly drilled legalizers on their agreed-upon plan and still awaits an intelligible response; see *New York Times*, May 17, 1988, p. A-25.

36. *Washington Post*, January 30, 1990, *Health Weekly*, p. 7; DuPont, *Getting Tough on Gateway Drugs*, 1984. See also Mark S. Gold, *800-Cocaine* (Bantam Books, New York), 1984; and NIDA, *National Household Survey: 1988*.

37. R. Clayton and H. Voss, *U.S. Journal of Alcohol and Drug Dependence*, January 1982; and Gabriel G. Nahas, *Cocaine—The Great White Plague* (Paul S. Errikson, Publisher, Middlebury, Vermont), 1989, p. 104.

38. NIDA, *National Trends in Drug Use, 1975–1986*.

39. Ethan A. Nadelmann, "U.S. Drug Policy: A Bad Export," *Foreign Policy*, Spring 1988, p. 96.

40. *New York Times*, January 15, 1987, p. A-1. A GAO report found that one in five rail workers involved in accidents tested positive for drugs and alcohol; see January 21, 1988, p. B-9. Drug testing has dropped this figure dramatically.

41. For a report on the National Centers for Disease Control study, see *New York Times*, March 27, 1990, p. C-10. Problems with underreporting are noted in *New York Times*, July 21, 1987, p. C-10.

42. An ounce of marijuana can be rolled into a minimum of 40 cigarettes, each capable at today's THC levels of intoxicating at least four average adults.

43. Carl A. Soderstrom, et al., "Marijuana and Alcohol Use among 1023 Trauma Patients," *Archives of Surgery*, vol. 123, June 1988, pp. 733–37; reported in *Washington Post*, June 2, 1988, p. D-4. The study was conducted by the Maryland Institute for Emergency Medical Services by Dr. Carl A. Soderstrom. It noted numerous other studies linking marijuana use and accidents (p. 736) and a high correlation of alcohol and marijuana use. Dr. Edward Cone of Johns Hopkins Addiction Research Center noted the incidence of marijuana use was "phenomenally high" and put a new slant on marijuana-use safety.

44. National Transportation Safety Board, *Fatigue, Alcohol, Drugs and Other Medical Factors Fatal to Drivers in Heavy Truck Crashes*, Washington, D.C., February 5, 1990; reported in *Washington Post*, February 6, 1990, p. A-1. An exposé on drugs and truckers was reported in *Chicago Tribune*, March 4, 1990, Sec. C, pp. 1, 6.

45. *Philadelphia Inquirer,* January 12, 1990, p. 21-A.

46. *New York Times,* March 27, 1990, p. C-10.

47. G. Nahas, *Cocaine—The Great White Plague;* see also Sabeh S. Tumeh et al., "Cerebral Abnormalities in Cocaine Abusers: Demonstration by SPECT Perfusion Brain Scintigraphy," *Radiology,* 1990, pp. 821–24; *Washington Post,* March 19, 1990, p. A-3.

48. Robert C. Gilkeson, "The Toxicity of Intoxicants Is Not Determined by Debate," *Drug Prevention Newsletter,* Committees of Correspondence, Danvers, Massachusetts, August 1990.

49. G. G. Nahas and C. Latour, eds., *Physiopathology of Cannabis, Opiates and Cocaine,* Pergamon Press, New York and Oxford, 1991.

50. Ethan A. Nadelmann, "The Case for Legalization," Summer 1988, p. 23.

51. James Ostrowski, "Answering the Critics of Legalization," paper delivered at Hoover Institution Conference on U.S. Drug Policy, Stanford, California, November 15–16, 1990 (Chapter 18 in this volume).

52. Avram Goldstein and Harold Kalant, "Drug Policy: Striking the Right Balance," *Science,* vol. 249, September 28, 1990, p. 1514. While the authors oppose legalization at present, they apparently would reconsider if a magic bullet is found to control addiction. They conclude more funds should go to such research, which, not surprisingly, they and their colleagues would carry out.

53. *Wall Street Journal,* April 10, 1990, p. A-1.

54. In addition to the Single Convention of 1961, several international agreements have been made regarding the illicit drug trade, such as a United Nations declaration in 1989 reported in *Washington Times,* January 11, 1990, and one in 1988 reported in *New York Times,* December 21, 1988, p. A-14.

55. David F. Musto, *The American Disease—Origins of Narcotic Control* (Oxford University Press, New York), 1987, pp. 7, 70–73.

56. Timothy Leary, known as the high priest of LSD, made many claims for LSD, including its ability to produce "hundreds" of orgasms in women. NORML distributes Jack Herer's book *The Emperor Wears No Clothes,* a work that portrays marijuana as a miracle cure for the economy, environment, and health. A recent report to NIDA—Marsha Rosenbaum, Patricia A. Morgan, and Jerome Beck, "Exploring Ecstasy: A Description of MDMA Users," *Final Report to the National Institute on Drug Abuse,* Washington, D.C., September 15, 1989—contains many glowing accounts from MDMA users.

57. U.S. Bureau of the Census, *Historical Statistics of the United States, Colonial Times to 1970,* Part One, Washington, D.C., 1975, p. 414.

58. Musto, *The American Disease,* especially pp. 91, 115; see also *Wall Street Journal,* June 11, 1986, p. 30; *Parade,* July 31, 1988.

59. James Q. Wilson, "Against the Legalization of Drugs," *Commentary,* February, 1990; pp. 21–28; Musto, *The American Disease.*

60. White House Conference for a Drug-Free America, *The White House Conference for a Drug-Free America Final Report,* U.S. Government Printing Office, Washington, D.C., June 1988.

61. *New York Times*, June 10, 1987, p. A-13; see also EURAD—Europe against Drugs, "Four Steps in the Development of a Narcotics Epidemic," *EURAD News* (Lomma, Sweden), no. 2, February, 1990.

62. Ministry of Health and Welfare of Japan, *A Brief Account of Drug Abuse and Countermeasures in Japan*, Pharmaceutical Affairs Bureau, Ministry of Health and Welfare, Japan, 1972; Masaaki Kato, "An Epidemiological Analysis of the Fluctuation of Drug Dependence in Japan," *International Journal of Addictions*, 4(4), December 1969.

63. *Wall Street Journal*, July 11, 1988, p. 18; *New York Times*, November 18, 1989, p. A-18.

64. *New York Times*, July 27, 1989, p. A-7; *New York Times*, April 29, 1989, p. A-1; *Economist*, April 18, 1987, pp. 45–46.

65. *Wall Street Journal*, January 22, 1990, p. A-10.

66. Ibid.

67. Lonny Shavelson, "Sunday in the Park," *Mother Jones*, February–March, 1990, pp. 36–38; see also *Washington Post*, May 29, 1989, p. A-18.

68. *Time*, August 31, 1987, pp. 28–29.

69. Jeffrey Eisenach and Andrew Cowin, "Fighting Drugs in Four Countries: Lessons for America?" *Heritage Foundation Backgrounder*, Heritage Foundation, Washington, D.C., September 24, 1990, p. 13.

70. *Wall Street Journal*, April 2, 1990, p. A-10 (report on study published by the Dutch Justice Ministry).

71. van de Wijngaart, G. F.,"Heroin Use in the Netherlands," *American Journal of Drug and Alcohol Abuse*, vol. 14, 1988, pp. 126–36.

72. Peter Cohen, *Cocaine Use in Amsterdam in Nondeviant Subcultures*, Instituut voor Sociale Geografie, Universiteit van Amsterdam, Amsterdam, Nederlands, 1989, p. 17.

73. Stichting INTRAVAL, *Hardrugs & Criminaliteit in Rotterdam* (Hard Drugs and Criminality in Rotterdam), Groningen, Stichting INTRAVAL, 1989.

74. *Forbes*, February 27, 1984, p. 46.

75. J. Wilson, "Against the Legalization of Drugs," pp. 22–23; see also Heritage Foundation, *Fighting Drugs in Four Countries*, pp. 2–4; *Wall Street Journal*, January 22, 1990, p. A-10.

76. Nadelmann, "Drug Prohibition in the U.S."

77. J. Wilson, "Against the Legalization of Drugs," p. 24.

78. W. B. McClure, "President's Address," *Kentucky Medical Journal*, 2:8, 1930, pp. 594–96; see Richard H. Schwartz, *Prohibition, 1920–1933: The Good, the Bad, and the Ugly*, unpublished manuscript, Vienna, Virginia, 1990.

79. Clark Warburton, *The Economic Results of Prohibition*, Columbia University Press, New York, 1932.

80. H. Emerson, "Prohibition and Public Health," *Survey*, vol. 2, 1928, pp. 289–400; L. I. Dublin, "Has Prohibition Improved the Public Health?" *American Journal of*

Public Health, vol. 18, pp. 1–14, 1928; H. Emerson, "Has Prohibition Promoted the Public Health?" *American Journal of Public Health*, vol. 17, 1927, pp. 1230–34.

81. U.S. Bureau of the Census, *Historical Statistics to 1970*, 1975, p. 414.

82. U.S. Bureau of the Census, *Statistical Abstract of the United States: 1989* (109th ed.), Washington, D.C., 1989, p. 268; *New York Times*, March 27, 1990, p. C-10.

83. *Washington Post*, May 20, 1988, p. A-21.

84. *Washington Post*, February 22, 1989, p. B-1; *USA Today*, June 8, 1989; *Philadelphia Daily News*, May 16, 1989.

85. Leslie Robison et al., "Maternal Drug Use and Risk of Childhood Nonlymphoblastic Leukemia among Offspring," *Cancer*, May 15, 1989, pp. 1904–10. This study investigated the impact of pesticides on fetal development and childhood leukemia and the marijuana correlation was unexpected (p. 1908).

86. *New York Times*, May 28, 1989, p. D-14; *Washington Post*, November 29, 1989, p. F-11.

87. *Philadelphia Inquirer*, December 27, 1987, pp. A–1, 6; *Philadelphia Daily News*, March 2, 1989 (report on John Hopkins University study).

88. *Washington Post*, September 30, 1989, p. A-1.

89. National Center for Health Statistics, *Health, United States, 1987*, Public Health Service (DDHS Pub. No. (PHS) 88–1232), Washington, D.C., March 1988; R. DuPont, *Gateway Drugs*, pp. 4–7.

90. Statement of Colin True, age 14, at news conference, Harrisburg, Pennsylvania, March 29, 1990; see *Pittsburgh Post-Gazette*, March 30, 1990.

91. For student's view, see Jennifer R. Steel, *We Didn't Start the Fire*, Campuses without Drugs, Pittsburgh, Pennsylvania, 1990; former NIDA director Robert DuPont withdrew support for marijuana decriminalization because of the impact on children; see R.DuPont, *Gateway Drugs*, pp. 62–65; for Alaska's experience, see Families in Action, *Drug Abuse Update*, September 1988, p. 16.

92. National Center for Health Statistics, *Health*, 1987.

93. NIDA, *National Household Survey*, 1988.

94. Alaska Department of Health and Human Services, *The State of Adolescent Health*; Bernard Segal, "Drug-Taking Behavior among Alaskan Youth," *Ketchikan Daily News*, May 23, 1988.

95. Users cite "uncontrollable violence" as drug effect in *Washington Post*, March 24, 1989, p. A-11; Hope Corman, Theodore Joyce, and Naci Mocan, "Homicide and Crack in New York City," paper delivered at Hoover Institution Conference on U.S. Drug Policy, Stanford, California, November 15–16, 1990 (Chapter 7 in this volume); *New York Times*, November 24, 1990, p. L-31.

96. *New York Times*, June 1988, p. B-1; *Philadelphia Inquirer*, February 10,1990, p. A-2.

97. *Wall Street Journal*, July 31, 1989, p. A-1.

98. *USA Today*, December 13, 1989, p. 1-A; over a third of the respondents said they knew of drug users on the job.

99. National Center for Health Statistics, *Health: 1987*, p. 58; Bureau of Justice Statistics, *Report to the Nation on Crime and Justice* (2nd ed., NCJ-105506), U.S. Department of Justice, Washington, D.C., March 1988, p. 24.

100. Statewide Penn-Free Drug Hearings, May–April, 1989 (see especially Williamsport, Pennsylvania session). Transcript available through Office of the Governor, Harrisburg, Pennsylvania.

101. Ray's article is in *Washington Post*, January 2, 1990, *Health Weekly*, p. 14; see also drugs as conspiracy against blacks, *Washington Post*, December 29, 1989, p. A-16; A. M. Rossenthal, "The Case for Slavery," *New York Times*, September 26, 1989, p. A-31; crack babies as "bio-underclass" in Krauthammer's column, *Washington Post*, July 30, 1989, p. C-7; and David R. Gergen, "Drugs and White America," *U.S. News & World Report*, September 18, 1989, p. 79.

102. Families in Action, *Drug Abuse Update* 1988, pp. 19, 22.

103. *Washington Post*, December 21, 1989, p. A-6; a report on U.S. Conference of Mayors study showing 44 percent of homeless are substance abusers, up 10 percent from previous year.

104. ONDCP, *National Drug Control Strategy*, 1989 and 1990 editions; a Rand study on the crack trade revealed how risky and unprofitable drug dealing is. See Scott Minerbrook, "Crack Dealers' Rotten Lives," *U.S. News & World Report*, November 12, 1990, pp. 36, 38.

105. John Kaplan, "Taking Drugs Seriously," *Public Interest*, no. 92, Summer 1988, p. 41. The late John Kaplan once served on NORML's board. His previous work underestimated the social and health costs of marijuana, but his assessment of the danger of legalizing other drugs is sound, as is his call for drug testing.

106. Ibid. ONDCP, *National Drug Control Strategy*, January 1990, pp. 6–7.

107. *Wall Street Journal*, October 27, 1989, p. A-16.

108. Hope Corman, "Homicide and Crack," 1990; *New York Times*, November 24, 1990, p. L-31.

109. *Washington Post*, March 24, 1990, p. A-11.

110. *Washington Post*, January 19, 1990, pp. E-1, 2.

111. Federal Bureau of Investigation, *Uniform Crime Reports for the United States*, U.S. Department of Justice, Washington, D.C., 1989; see also 1988 and 1987 editions.

112. Bureau of Justice Statistics, *Report to the Nation on Crime and Justice*, 1988, p. 51.

113. ONDCP, *National Drug Control Strategy*, 1990, pp. 23–26, 35–36.

114. Murray E. Jarvik, "The Drug Dilemma: Manipulating the Demand," *Science*, October 19, 1990, pp. 387–392; J. Wilson, "Against the Legalization of Drugs," p. 21. Ironically, legalizers argue that illicit drugs are not as harmful as alcohol and seek to teach safe drug use, while saying drug use would not climb significantly.

115. *Philadelphia Inquirer*, December 27, 1987, p. 1-A; this article includes an in-depth look into this tragedy and the drug-child abuse relationship.

116. *Philadelphia Daily News*, March 31, 1989, p. 19.

117. *New York Times*, March 17, 1990, p. 8.

118. *USA Today*, March 22, 1990, p. 11-A.

119. Arnold S. Trebach, "The Worst Case," *Reason*, October 1988, p. 29.

120. National Institute of Justice, *Drug Use Forecasting Program, 1989*, U.S. Department of Justice, Washington, D.C., 1989.

121. *New York Times*, April 29, 1989, p. A-1; Heritage Foundation, *Fighting Drugs in Four Countries*, pp. 14–15; *Wall Street Journal*, January 22, 1990, p. A-10.

122. Video message to International PRIDE conference held in Orlando, Florida, March 1990; available through PRIDE, Atlanta, Georgia.

123. E. Nadelmann, "U.S. Drug Policy: A Bad Export," p. 1; *Washington Times*, September 7, 1989, p. A-5; Drug Policy Foundation, *Drug Policy Newsletter*, vol. 1, no. 2, Washington, D.C., May/June 1989; cf. *Wall Street Journal*, October 3, 1988, p. A-22.

124. *USA Today*, December 13, 1989, p. 1-A; *USA Today*, January 25, 1990. The college survey also showed continued decline of support for marijuana legalization (16.7 percent).

125. *New York Times*, September 21, 1987, p. B-1.

126. *Wall Street Journal*, October 3, 1988, p. A-22; on sobriety checkpoints see *Wall Street Journal*, December 29, 1989, p. A-6; on school policy see *Wall Street Journal*, January 5, 1990, p. A-6; on jail reimbursement see *New York Times*, April 8, 1990, p. A-25.

127. *New York Times*, May 28, 1989, p. D-14. The article asks "How can citizens respect a government that can't even provide basic security?"

128. In the Netherlands 150 citizens stormed the homes of alleged drug dealers; *Boston Globe*, September 26, 1989, p. 11. In Spain, a drug bar and disco was blown up; *Economist*, April 18, 1987, p. 45.

129. Plato, *Republic*, Book VIII, W.H.D. Rouse translation (Mentor Books, New York, 1956).

130. Mike Royko, "Drug Wars Over: Guess Who Won?" *Playboy—The Playboy Forum*, November 1990, p. 46.

131. The social costs of legalization under liberal and libertarian schemes are compared by Charles Krauthammer in *Washington Post*, April 13, 1990, p. A-25.

132. Total drug-abuse costs to the nation are estimated at over $60 billion per year; *New York Times*, December 5, 1989, p. D-1.

133. In response to Milton Friedman's melodramatic "open letter," William Bennett notes there was nothing new in the legalization argument; see *Wall Street Journal*, September 19, 1989, p. A-30. For a review of 1978, see David Martin, "We Can Win the Drug War," *Human Events*, August 30, 1986, p. 12.

134. Ruth C. Engs, *Responsible Drug and Alcohol Use* (Macmillan Publishing Co., Inc., New York, 1979), p. 211.

135. G. Nahas, *Cocaine—The Great White Plague*, pp. 84–138.

136. Senate hearings on marijuana and health with Nobel prize–winning and inter-

nationally renowned scientists have been virtually ignored; see U.S. Congress, Senate, Committee on the Judiciary, *Health Consequences of Marijuana Use; Hearings before Subcommittee on Criminal Justice*, 96th Cong., 2d sess., January 16–17, 1980. Instead, outdated studies from the early 1970s, such as *Licit and Illicit Drugs* (1972) by E. Brecher, are repeatedly cited in prolegalization literature. Even the prestigious Merck Manual's marijuana information was written by a Drug Policy Foundation board member. The marijuana THC content could not be measured and standardized for scientific research until 1972. See also Frick and Nahas, eds., *Drug Abuse in the Modern World*, pp. 164–73; Peggy Mann, *Marijuana Alert* (McGraw-Hill Book Co., New York, 1985).

137. Frick and Nahas, eds., *Drug Abuse in the Modern World*, pp. 181–86.

138. William F. Jasper, "Some Kids Are Taught to Just Say Yes," *New American*, November 7, 1988, p. 47; Richard A. Hawley, "School Children and Drugs: The Fancy That Has Not Passed," *Phi Delta Kappan*, May 1987, pp. K1–K8. Articles advocating teaching "responsible" drug use include Ruth C. Engs and Stuart W. Fors, *Journal of School Health*, vol. 58, no. 1, January 1988, p. 26; Patricia A. Morgan, Lawrence Wallack, David Buchanan, *Waging Drug Wars: Prevention Strategy or Politics as Usual*, paper in introduction of briefing packet for Illinois Assembly on the Prevention of Alcohol and Other Drug Use, Department of Alcoholism and Substance Abuse, Springfield, Illinois, March 23–24, 1990; Marsha Rosenbaum, *Just Say What? An Alternative View on Solving America's Drug Problem*, National Council on Crime and Delinquency, San Francisco, California, 1989, p. 16. The council and research by Ms. Rosenbaum have received significant federal funds.

139. E. Nadelmann, *Science*, 1989, p. 943.

140. Excellent commentary on America's "schism of soul" over the drug issue includes Pat Buchanan's syndicated column, "Legalizing Drugs Leads to Crime," 1988; Max Lerner's "Our Schism of Soul over Drugs," *Washington Times*, January 15, 1990; Cal Thomas's "Don't Give Up on Drug Users," *Los Angeles Times*, May 19, 1988, p. B-7; and William Bennett's "Mopping Up after the Legalizers—What the Intellectual Chorus Forgets to Tell You," *Washington Times*, December 15, 1989, p. F-5.

COMMENT

Robert Sweet

Ladies and gentlemen, first the indulgence of a personal note. This is an extraordinary conference. It has been organized and peopled by extraordinary things—by experts who've wrestled long and hard over the institutional, societal, and personal anguish created by drug use and the current legal framework. The strongly differing views we have heard have been held in good faith, and they demonstrate that these issues are deep, intractable, and strike at the heart of our society, our life together indeed. Perhaps something as commonplace and vital as our ability to walk down the streets of our cities in safety. I am very privileged to be in this company and to be a discussant, whatever that is. I hope there will be more discussion.

Let me also say that I am evidence of the superb planning that has gone into this conference. You will recall just a few moments ago that Ed Lazear noted it was necessary to maintain a sufficient level of boredom and that, of course, is why I am the last speaker tonight. The problem I have been assigned, to be the last on this program, of course, is absolutely impossible—Sisyphus should have such a problem—to come up with a new idea and a new approach after those people that you have already heard.

My contribution, if I have one, I think must come as a result of my experience as a trial judge, although some of my days as deputy mayor might be relevant. The problem that was facing me in this present job is the sentencing of an eighteen-year-old with no criminal record to a mandatory ten years because he sought to make $200 working as a security guard in a drugstore. Of course, it was the wrong kind of drugstore, and it was in the South Bronx, and there was a bust. That problem made me really focus on our present policy. It is right morally, and is it successful pragmatically?

For me certain facts establish that the policy we have is a failure: An unregulated industry estimated to be at 150 billion dollars. Profit margins up to 5000 percent, federal expenditures of 11 billion dollars, an addict population of 5 to 6 million, and the greatest jail population in our history. Looking at those facts persuaded me that money is the root of this particular evil and that the elimination of illegality would eliminate the money and the crime and that the money spent on balloons and interdiction would be better spent on treatment and education. I guess, expressing this view, I attracted some attention and that, as a result, has forced me to join all of you today and to consider the consequences of positions such as the one that I've just described for you.

As a judge I daily hear opposing views and render opinions, profound or otherwise—so this is a marvelous busman's holiday for me. I'm sure you're not going to be surprised that I agree basically with Jim Ostrowski's view and his analysis of the problem. It can be considered as a reduction-of-harm position, and I'm for it. I think it was cool, careful, and a rational analysis that was, for me, compelling. There is an element in it that I found missing, however—and perhaps deliberately so. There is a resistance to this kind of an approach, and I think it comes from an emotional view that a magical quality can be attributed to drugs—a devil-drug concept. Drugs are not only evil, but they also have a magic, transforming quality. They turn good people into evil. It's the drug that's at fault, not the taker, not the society. Prohibition of evil by prohibiting drugs is therefore good, moral, and appropriate. It's that magic quality, the magic drug concept that I found missing in the analysis. I think maybe drugs are today's Wizard of Oz, distracting us from the real issues being presented.

Robert Peterson's submission to you, I think, was appropriate, and yet I found in his presentation some internal conflicts. He would have us, he says, do something about alcohol as a dangerous drug—without prohibiting it. That, it seems to me, you can flip over very quickly into the position Ostrowski and I support. He said, "Nobody's happy with what's going on." That may be the central and most important statement of the day. If we're not happy with what's going on, then we do have to consider alternatives. He discussed 112 nations and their getting together, but we cannot overlook, first of all, that there was treatment and education in that; second, that the United States swings a big bat. There is no question about what our national policy is in this regard, so I'm not sure that I take it as proof as to what our policy should be. I would also say, as far as the recital of national problems, with the United States and on down the list, I think that the realities of what is going on in at least two areas abroad, in the Netherlands and in England, is very exciting. I think those hands-on experiences are going to be more valuable to you than some of the assumptions that I think were made with respect to other nations.

Having heard the discussion, I feel I must as a matter of conscience tell you my own view. First, the question Ed Meese asks, which is in my view a fair one, is what program is being proposed? It is by the way difficult for the so-called legalizers—I would rather have them abolitionists and I was thinking the other day, maybe they should be liberators, but then I thought liberators have sort of a bombing image to me that didn't seem right—but whatever they are called they are those that seek change. I think it's fair to put them to their task and say, all right, what would you do? Well, first of all I think we should have reform, and I'll take anything I can get. I would take, for example, a shift from enforcement and incarceration to treatment and education. Second, medicalization of marijuana use. We're going to hear more about that later in this meeting. I'm sure it will be compelling, and there really can be no rational argument against it. Third, the prohibition against marijuana itself. I don't think any case has been made in the past or even today that any societal harm results from the use of marijuana. The hard question, of course, comes with cocaine, crack, and heroin. Medicalization and the elimination of criminal distribution seem to me to be achievable and acceptable and, on a cost-benefit basis, irresistible. The denial of needle exchange today is inhuman and cruel. Medicalization would shift the enforcement to the medical profession, to the doctors and would, in my view, evade the principal moral and, if you want, legal issue we have to confront. How far does the federal government go, and I say *federal*, in criminalizing and regulating mind alterations by individuals? I think that's an issue we should face. I would treat drugs as drugs: Sell, label, and control them as drugs.

You have heard the argument against these proposals and it would be an imposition on you, I think, to have my rebuttal on those questions, given the time-frame and given the fact that I am the only thing standing between you and the psychoactive substance you are looking forward to, which I take it is a baked potato tonight.

Let me just sum up today's evidence for you, as I heard it. John W. Davis, who was a marvelous lawyer in New York, some years ago, talking about argument, said, "You know, you have got to go for the jugular." What is the jugular that we heard today? Frank Zimring told us about the clash of presumptions, liberty, and continuity. He told us to look and think about the middle ground. Stephen Mugford gave us Goldilocks, and of course Goldilocks was looking for the comfy chair and that is the middle ground, if you will. He noted for us that there are elements in reaching this compromise, this middle ground—the state being a player, the market being a player, and society being a player. Mark Kleiman talked to us about loose social control and the optimal set of control policies. Mitchell Rosenthal, an old friend and a notable warrior in this field, discussed with us the manifestation of the disorder that he had seen and experienced arising out of drug use. A questioner said, in effect, who is setting the controls? Ethan Nadelmann, in his characteristic ebullient fashion, outlined the public debate and where it stands. Joel Hay pointed out to us the tragic blindness of ignoring the positions taken by Mitch Rosenthal. Kevin Zeese pointed out to us the necessity of finding the compromise, the center. Ira Glasser, in his dramatic and forceful way, talked about the engines that are producing crime. Ed Meese is really standing for the status quo, some change but the status quo. If you listened carefully, it seemed to me, one heard a willingness to change if persuaded. Joseph McNamara talked about our capacity for mass self-delusion and the interplay between drugs, democracy, and our value judgments.

After all that, what is the jugular, what is it that John W. Davis would have us draw from all this? I would say it is that change is the law of life, that we have to search for this middle ground between the extremes, and that we have to try to seize, define, and grasp the center. If that is correct, then have we really asked the right questions? We have this drug issue before us. Perhaps the really underlying question, the real issue, is why would somebody living in this country today want to alter their mind in a destructive way? What about their life requires them to artificially enhance a sense of satisfaction? Is it powerlessness and inability to obtain satisfaction by achievement or accomplishment? Has our society become slack and materialistic and self-absorbed? I think if you answer any of those questions yes, or even partially yes, then we are permitting a devil-drug ideology and a misuse of the criminal law to mask the need, the overwhelming need in our society, to educate, to enhance responsibility for oneself and the entire society. We have to enforce the values that Dr. Clarke points out to us in the discussion that were in his family: discipline, an ethic, a national ethic that stresses freedom along with responsibility. We should return to an American dream that talks about justice and responsibility for justice and responsibility for reaching a center, a supportable position that will enhance those goals.

20

U.S. Efforts in the International Drug War

Melvyn Levitsky

Thanks very much to the Hoover Institution for inviting me here this evening to talk to you about our international efforts. I hesitate to say the "war on drugs" since virtually everyone at this conference has said it is bad terminology. I feel, however, that we are mobilized and engaging in a real war effort so I am going to call it that anyway, if you don't mind.

In the past few years, we have seen enormous changes in the world. New, more representative governments have taken the place of oligarchies and dictatorships that ruled according to their own agendas. People all over the world have embraced democracy and have seized control of their own destinies. Global issues—the environment, nuclear nonproliferation, collective security, human rights, free trade and, yes, the flow of illegal drugs—have increasingly dominated the international agenda and the United States foreign policy. We are faced with new challenges, new opportunities and, with them, new threats to our national security. More and more, our bilateral relationships are called upon to serve our broader global interests. The problems we confront transcend national boundaries and affect all nations: developed or developing, rich or poor, without regard to geography, culture, religion, or form of government.

Thus it is, too, with the international spread of drug abuse, production, and trafficking. This epidemic has affected the economies, social fabric, stability, and political systems of virtually every country in the world.

Just as drug traffickers prey upon fragile governments and weak institutions in South America, Asia, and Africa, drug abusers and traffickers undermine the bases of stronger, more established democratic societies. If the underpinning of democracy is an alert, enlightened populace, able to choose its representatives freely and make rational choices on issues of public policy, then drugs are the mortal enemy of democracy. As Secretary of State Baker has said, "The drug pirates and profiteers attack the central nervous system and vital organs of democracy—the administration of justice, the integrity of government, the right of free speech." Even so-called casual users of drugs contribute to this decay; they help line the pockets of vicious criminals who murder public officials and who align themselves with equally vicious terrorist groups seeking to destroy representative government in so many countries around the world.

For domestic and foreign policy reasons, therefore, the war on drugs must be a central element of governmental concern. Let's be clear, however: the main front in this war is here at home. For many years a debate raged as to where we should focus our efforts—on supply or on demand. I can tell you that there is no doubt in the minds of policymakers in Washington on this score. If we do not diminish our appetite for illegal drugs, if we do not denormalize and erect intolerance against drug abuse here in this country, even our most strenuous efforts against the production and supply of drugs will, at best, be marginally useful.

At the same time, we learned lessons in the eighties about the demand/supply equation. It has become clear that the more drugs there are around, the cheaper they are, the purer they are, the greater the availability of them—the more people will try them.

Crack cocaine is the best example of this. In one sense, the development of crack can be seen as a clever marketing device. The traffickers found a highly powerful, highly seductive, and highly addictive product which could be produced and sold cheaply and which stimulated and spread demand for that product. The results in social disruption, crime, and violence can be seen every day on our streets.

The situation in Pakistan is another example. A country that ten years ago considered itself only a producer of opium and heroin and had only a minuscule addiction rate, now has over a million addicts, adding to its already formidable array of social, economic, and political problems. Overproduction and oversupply and the need on the part of the traffickers to create new markets for the heroin glut brought this burden to Pakistan and to other countries that formerly claimed drug abuse was strictly an American problem.

It is now widely acknowledged that trafficking and drug abuse are international problems. It is tragic that the problem had to get worse before it got better. Its identification as a worldwide problem, however, has opened the opportunity for us to work with other countries to control it and diminish its effects.

What are we doing internationally to combat the drug problem?

President Bush has elevated the war on drugs into a central issue of his administration. He has made it a top priority on our national agenda. The president's first national drug strategy of September 1989 and his implementing strategy of January 1990, which was made to coincide with the budget cycle, emphasized the need to attack all aspects of the drug chain. The strategies went beyond words to a substantial increase in resources devoted to antidrug efforts at home and abroad, against demand and supply.

I will not go into the broad array of domestic programs of drug prevention, education, treatment, and law enforcement except to say that the 10 billion dollars the president has devoted to the drug war is only part of the solution. As the drug strategy points out, our fight against illegal drug use and trafficking cannot be won on any single front alone. It must be waged everywhere at every level of federal, state, and local government and, most important, by private citizens and organizations in every part of the country. It is also a problem that transcends international frontiers.

Our domestic programs against drugs are really not my beat, but our international efforts certainly are. Let me tell you how we are using our foreign policy to deal with our counter-narcotics interests.

First, we have turned the drug issue into a priority in our international activities. When I took my job, I wrote Secretary Baker that I felt we needed to weave the antidrug thread into the fabric of our foreign policy. In the same way that support for human rights and democracy have become integral to the expression of our national interests, I felt we had to make action against drugs an important test of friendly relations with other countries.

Looking back over the past year and a half or so, I think we have come a long way toward doing just that. The drug issue is raised in virtually all our high-level contacts—trips, visits, international meetings. Quite frankly, I don't have to fight anymore to get the issue on the agenda—increasingly it *is* the agenda. The president's trip to Cartagena, where we worked out an antidrug cartel with the presidents of the Andean countries, is the best example of this.

We have strengthened the State Department's resolve and ability to deal with our drug interests. I sought and received nearly a 50 percent boost in our counter-narcotics personnel complement. In 1991, in my bureau—which is only a part of our international effort—we will spend about 150 million dollars on our narcotics assistance programs, again 50 percent greater than in 1989. We are trying and we are making the drug issue intrinsic to, rather than an afterthought in, our foreign policy.

As part of the State Department's approach to this, we have a dual method of working on this problem. Part of the work my bureau engages in is traditional diplomacy—that is, we try to convince other countries to support our position and do what we think is right. We also have a second element—a funded programmatic element—that is quite unusual for State Department activities.

Our diplomatic initiatives include strong efforts to promote money-laundering legislation worldwide, as well as the freezing, seizure, and redistribution of illegal drug assets, and stricter controls on essential and precursor chemicals. The last two economic summits—in Paris and in Houston—established multinational task forces for these purposes, and we are beginning to see good results around the world. We have established a consultative mechanism with the European Community, Canada, Japan, Sweden, and Australia to promote coordination and enhance resources aligned against drug abuse and trafficking. Through our support for multilateral counter-narcotics efforts—for example, via the new UN Convention against Drug Trafficking and vigorous efforts in other multilateral bodies—we are witnessing the formation of an international coalition against illegal drugs.

The program I described, of 150 million dollars in assistance, supports a number of activities. We support counter-narcotics police; drug crop-control, eradication, and income-substitution programs; judicial reforms; demand-reduction efforts; training programs; and UN counter-narcotics activities in such regions as the Andes, the Caribbean, Mexico, Central America, South and Southeast Asia, and West Africa.

We provide helicopters, cargo planes, and fixed-wing aircraft, as well as communications equipment, field gear, and vehicles to Colombia, Bolivia, and Peru to help them in their fight against the cocaine traffickers. We also provide seed and irrigation projects, farm-to-market roads, and general infrastructure development in countries such as Pakistan and Thailand to help persuade farmers to switch from opium growing to legitimate business.

Part of the new strategy is to add resources in military, intelligence, and economic assistance to our traditional programs. Our programs in the Andean region are illustrative of our comprehensive approach.

As you know, virtually all the cocaine that comes to the United States—and to other countries for that matter—originates and is produced in the three Andean countries of Colombia, Peru, and Bolivia. The problem involved here is classic. The primary growing areas in Bolivia and Peru are isolated, often not subject to civil authority. They are connected by clandestine air flights to the production and distribution centers in Colombia where traffickers have had greater control— in fact nearly sovereign—than the central government. One valley in Amazonian Peru—the Upper Huallaga Valley—alone produces about 60 percent of the coca leaves that end up as cocaine.

In devising our strategy, we felt we first had to help these countries gain control over the primary and final production areas where narcotraffickers and insurgents often work together against the government. To do this, the links between the traffickers and the primary producers needed to be harassed and disrupted, as did the routes for chemicals coming in, drugs going out, and money flowing both ways. We proposed and are implementing a five-year program of over two billion dollars to assist in this effort in these three countries. We have law-enforcement assistance programs to strengthen the police and judicial systems; we have military assistance to enhance antidrug efforts of armed forces where host governments have decided to employ them and give them a role; and we have intelligence assistance and information-sharing programs to provide basic targeting information to make counter-narcotics efforts more operational and more effective.

Finally, and this is a new element to begin in 1991, we have economic assistance, drug-related economic assistance that has been appropriated by the Congress for drug purposes for the first time. This assistance is primarily in the form of balance-of-payment support, but also includes developmental assistance for specific projects in drug areas. This assistance is designed to help these countries cope with success. We understand that if the program is successful and as control of the drug industry is gained and drug money begins to diminish in these economies, our economic assistance will be needed to help attract poor campesinos who are now involved in growing coca to turn to legitimate activities. It will also help strengthen economies that we hope will begin to rid themselves of drugs and pay for law-enforcement efforts, demand-reduction efforts, and provide a long-term boost to counter-narcotics programs. In addition, as part of this strategy, the president proposed the Andean and the Enterprise for the Americas initiatives, which are focused on providing markets and business and investment opportunities to these countries so their economies can be strengthened and sustained. The growers of drug crops thus will have legal alternatives to their current sources of income.

You may have read that we are trying to "militarize" the drug war. This is an oversimplified characterization that does not do justice to the comprehensive kind of program we have. Of course, military assistance is part of the program, but it is only one part of the program. We have made very clear in our dealings with other countries that military assistance is not a prerequisite to receiving the other kinds of assistance we are offering. In those areas, such as the Upper Huallaga Valley of Peru, where there is both insurgency and narcotrafficking, we believe there is a role for the military. We believe the police cannot provide all the resources necessary to deal with this very complicated problem and we have offered military assistance for drug purposes in countries such as Peru, Bolivia, and Colombia.

Let's look at how we are doing. As usual, in all these things there is good news and bad news. Let me give you the bad news first.

The bad news is that the traffickers are still strong. Drug production and trafficking are still increasing in some areas. Although we have made considerable progress in the Andes in harassing the drug industry, *heroin* production, especially in Southeast Asia, continues to expand. One country alone—Burma, which ignores international pressure—produces enough heroin for the entire world market. In fact, from 1988 to the present time the production of opium in Burma has almost doubled.

Corruption, inefficiency, and lack of political will to deal with the problem plague our efforts in a number of countries.

Although the United States has put into place a very strong chemical regime over the export of essential chemicals, the traffickers are obtaining more of these substances from European and other countries with less effective systems than ours.

More bad news: The trafficking organizations have shown great resiliency. As we become more successful in the Caribbean, working with other countries to stem drug trafficking, the traffickers switched more of their effort to our porous Mexican border. We are now seeing more than half the cocaine for the U.S. market coming to us across the Mexican border.

In addition, while we have worked on money laundering, bank secrecy laws in a number of countries stand in the way of international efforts to separate the traffickers from their profits.

Unfortunately, demand for drugs has been on the increase in many countries, in contrast to the United States, where the trend is the other way.

There is also good news, however.

First and, I think, the best news is that we are becoming more resistant to drugs. I do not think this is a subjective opinion. All the indicators—polls, surveys, the drug-warning network, hospital emergency admittances, statistics, drug-related crimes, and the general sense of things—support this trend toward the denormalization of drug usage in our country. This has been going on for several years.

In addition, we believe our cooperative assistance programs, of the kind I described in the Andean countries, are beginning to have an effect. Cocaine has gotten more expensive, less available, and less pure in most major markets in the United States in recent months. We are cautious about what we are seeing, but we believe we are beginning to get results from the assistance and the efforts we have put into some of these countries.

In the Andean countries themselves—primarily as a result of Colombia's strong efforts—the traffickers are on the run. They are finding it harder to operate and increasingly they are in jail. This is in contrast to the situation of only a few years ago when they were openly out on the streets having schools named after them, owning soccer clubs and private zoos of the kind you have seen described in the newspapers. They are now being increasingly harassed. Today we have in our country 24 major drug criminals Colombia has extradited to the United States in the past year and a half. The bad part of this is that the Colombian justice system cannot cope with these people itself because judges are bribed or threatened into letting them go or letting them off lightly. We have been working on a program with the Colombians to help them put into place a system that will allow these criminals to be tried in their own country.

More of the good news: We have seen in the past year increasing political will in the countries of South America and in Mexico where the results have gotten much better. Larger seizures of cocaine and increasing destruction of laboratories and airstrips have begun to sever the ties between the traffickers and the growers. This has brought the price of coca leaf at the farm gate in the Andes down to, and often below, the cost of production. This trend has been sustained over the past six months. If this continues—that is, if the coca growers continue to lose drug income and perceive that their future is not in coca growing—we can use our economic assistance and our general support to help get them out of the drug business and into legitimate enterprises.

We also have an invigorated program with the Salinas government in Mexico. I think it deserves special mention. The Mexican effort, which we assist, has resulted in scores of traffickers being jailed, seizures of cocaine amounting in one year to more than the previous six years, and, despite a number of continuing problems, an atmosphere much more conducive to cooperation on drugs than in the past.

Although we have a substantial problem of heroin production, as I mentioned, in Burma, we have seen that some of our crop-substitution projects in Pakistan, Thailand, and Laos have resulted in a net reduction of opium cultivation in those three countries over the past several years.

We are also coordinating and working better with our allies. We don't have to push hard on doors anymore because they are already open. Money-laundering, asset-seizure, and chemical-control legislation is beginning to spread to other countries. We are beginning to develop an antidrug international coalition.

The short answer to the question of how are we doing is, pretty well, but we still have a long struggle ahead of us.

This is an appropriate place for me to say a few words about the issue of legalization, which has been at the heart of your discussion here. I'm not going to attempt to address all the domestic angles of this question. I think the experts should look at that. I think the American people seem to have made up their minds. They have expressed themselves by very large margins against the legalization of drugs. Let me point out some of the international consequences of legalizing drugs. You should at least consider, I believe, what effect legalization would have on our foreign policy.

The first question you have to ask is what do we do about the fact that we are signatories to a number of antidrug treaties and conventions and that we have pressed strongly to influence other countries to ratify them. These treaties, the Convention and Protocol of 1961 and 1972 and the 1988 Antitrafficking Convention, outlaw narcotic drugs. They say drugs should be criminalized and that countries should attempt to stem drug abuse, production, and trafficking. So what do we say about that? Do we say we were wrong? Do we say that international law is wrong? To avoid being branded as violators of international law, are we now to lobby in favor of worldwide legalization? What kind of message would that impart and what would it say about U.S. leadership in the world, particularly moral leadership?

What do we say to other countries such as the Colombias, Bolivias, Thailands, and Turkeys of the world where we have been supporting counter-narcotics efforts over a long period of time? What do we tell them? Stop? We're not going to support you anymore? Let the criminals out of jail? Accept those people who have violated our laws, killed your officials, as legitimate businessmen?

Then there is the question of trade. If we are going to legalize drugs here, then why import them? Why not let our own companies produce cocaine, crack cocaine, or why not allow them to export it in the same way? It just doesn't make sense internationally. Legalizing drugs would be devastating to our international position in the world.

Besides, giving up now when we are witnessing a sea change away from drug abuse in this country would simply not be smart public policy in my view. So far as I am concerned, we have got to stick with our strategy of keeping up the pressure on all elements of the drug chain from field to street. It is beginning to work. It has the support of the American people and it has strong international support. Fighting drugs is a tough business and tough business demands hard work, determination, patience, and persistence.

This decade began amidst change and turmoil. A common theme running through the momentous events of the late eighties is that people and governments can make a difference, that they can make things better. So it is with drugs. With strong law enforcement, prevention, education, and treatment programs and citizen involvement at home, and with increasing support and cooperative efforts abroad, we can contain, diminish, and ultimately defeat the scourge of drugs in this country and internationally. We owe this to ourselves, to our children, and to the future of our nation.

Thank you very much for inviting me, and I would be glad to take any questions from the audience.

DISCUSSION

Q. (Tom Mark) You emphasize that in the United States we have many variations on the selling of legitimate products. It seems like the State Department has not learned anything from 25 years of drug war. In the late 60s Turkey was the major source of heroin. We moved to stamp out heroin in Turkey, they moved to Mexico. We moved to stamp out the heroin in Mexico, they moved to Burma, and they are still in Burma and also back in Mexico. I don't think your success in the Andean region means a success for the drug war. It means that new drugs have been created. The China Whites for cocaine will be created and more dangerous drugs will be created and will actually make the drug problem worse.

Levitsky: You assume that we move the drug problem around. In effect, what we are doing is helping other countries to deal with their own drug problems. After all, the fact that drugs are grown in Turkey is not a big benefit for Turkey. Nor is it for Mexico. Particularly with heroin, where we have much bigger markets in countries other than the United States. If you believe the experts, our heroin population has remained basically stable. Where are the growing markets? The growing markets are now in the producing countries. The countries that used to say, look, it's your problem. You stop the demand and we won't have a problem. They have developed demand problems of their own. We have an obligation to help them diminish both the supply, and the damage that does, and the demand within their countries.

Q. All it seems to accomplish is to spread the drug problem around rather than reduce it. And make the drug problem more dangerous. In the 1980s the success of our heroin policy created China White, which is much more deadly than heroin. In the 1980s the success of our cocaine policy created crack, which is more deadly than cocaine. The problem gets worse and worse as you try harder and harder to fight your drug war.

Levitsky: Well, that is an opinion. I don't believe it.

Q. That is correct.

Levitsky: It is an incorrect opinion in my view, but you have the right to it.

Q. (Ken Scott) You began by talking about the fact that policymakers in Washington have decided that the primary attention ought to be given to demand reduction as opposed to . . .

Levitsky: Not as opposed to but certainly as a primary emphasis, yes.

Q. But then 99 percent of what you had to say thereafter was all demand disruption.

Levitsky: That is right, supply disruption.

Q. Is that a reflection of your role or the allocation of the government?

Levitsky: I am not responsible for the domestic program, so my role here is to describe to you what we are doing on the supply side and I tried to describe the kind of comprehensive strategy we have. We believe we need to work on both sides of the equation. While the focus is on demand because it is like a magnet that attracts supply, there is a certain sense of supply creating its own demand. We have seen this with the production of drugs like crack cocaine. We believe you have to work on both sides. International programs I am describing basically are focused on the production in other countries and trying to disrupt that production and the supply lines that go between those countries and the United States. While we have a certain amount of our program devoted to helping stem demand in other countries, it is not something that we devote a lot of resources to. It is mostly on the supply side.

Q. (Tom Mark) You have been emphasizing the supply from other countries, but in the United States we have got all sorts of barriers to them selling us other legitimate products. Like Peru is a major—could be a major—supplier of flowers and other products, and yet we have strict quotas on them; what in the world are we doing about that?

Q. Providing some opportunities for these poor peasants to make a living outside of cocaine.

Levitsky: First let me correct the term "poor peasants," because when we use that description we think of idyllic tillers of the soil. In some of the places where drugs are produced, these were not traditional farmers who just decided to farm something else. They came from other places and other types of employment because the economies, particularly in countries like Peru, gave them no other way to make money.

So what are we doing? We do have programs in this regard. For example, you mentioned flowers. As part of the Cartagena process, we reduced the tariff on cut flowers from Colombia, which is a big exporter to the U.S. market. In fact, I think they have about 70 or 80 percent of our export market. That was part of the bargain that we made in Cartagena. They would take strong action and we would find ways of trying to find markets for their legitimate products, in addition to giving some of them economic assistance. Colombia, for example, really does not need a large amount of American economic assistance. They have a pretty viable economy even without the coca trade, which perhaps amounts to 5 percent or so of their total gross domestic product. So we agree. You need to have a component that will boost the legitimate part of the economy and give it some preference in terms of trade. We have proposed, as part of the present Andean initiative, a Caribbean Basin–like preference regime for those countries that would give them an advantage in the products they could sell here. Unfortunately, if you look at a country like Peru, there isn't much that we could probably import from Peru. The economy has been so devastated in the past few years, there is not much that Peru can produce besides coca that is attractive in the United States. But there are some things we can do to help generally to invigorate the economy.

We have to be frank about this. We have found obstacles. We wanted to increase Bolivia's soybean quota, which is a very, very small fraction of what we use in soybeans, and we ran into the traditional problem. The soybean lobby sees any inroad as an opening of the floodgates. We have tried to find other products we can give preferences to. What I am saying is, we haven't gotten there yet. The president's proposals on the Andean trade initiative have just gone up to the Congress and there will be a debate on this. I want to emphasize that the strategy is not, as it is sometimes described, to go kill the coca—that is, spray it, or chop it down. The strategy is a comprehensive strategy which includes a variety of assistance, including economic assistance, to deal with the end result.

Q.   Two questions. The indigenous people of the three countries that you have mentioned have been using coca leaves for many centuries.

Levitsky: That is right.

Q.   They use it as a medicine.

Levitsky: A small portion of the indigenous people chew coca leaves.

Q.   That is correct, they actually suck the coca leaves. They use it as a medicine, and use it also in the same way we use coffee. What is that policy of destroying coca doing to these people? Secondly, erythroxylon coca is a bush which grows anywhere where there is a mean temperature of 65 degrees, a lot of humidity, well-drained soil, which incidentally won't generally support other kinds of things. Let's suppose the Andean strategy works and all the coca erythroxylon bushes in that area are destroyed. They are going to . . . What are you going to do about the fact that it will grow in many other places in the world, that it has in the past? It is like pushing a balloon in here and it is going to pop out somewhere else.

Levitsky: Well, that is always a problem, but if you look at things like the alkaloid content in the leaf, for example, you find that Brazilian coca, which they call epadu in Brazil, has about half the alkaloid content as the Peruvian or

Bolivian leaf. While it will grow in some areas—we have grown it experimentally in Hawaii to see what will kill it as part of an experiment—it seems not to grow as well in other areas than the areas it now grows in. So it isn't a matter of growing it. They have tried to grow it in the Bekaa Valley in Lebanon and it did not take hold. So I can't tell you what the agricultural . . .

Q.   But it has grown in the past in like Java, like Borneo, and furthermore, that's a different coca bush. And it is true, it has less of the chemical mythylben-zoecna [sic], but it has a full complement of the other alkaloids and it is simply a matter of using . . .

Levitsky: It also takes a year and a half or so for a coca bush to produce and, if governments are vigilant about it, they can wipe it out. It is not a matter of transferring the crop. There was a second part of your question, though, that I haven't answered.

Q.   Well, the indigenous.

Levitsky: What do you do with the places like the Upper Huallaga Valley if it doesn't grow coca? I have flown over the Upper Huallaga Valley. I have heard the arguments from environmentalists against the spraying with herbicides of the coca bush and how it would destroy the valley. I would say to them, let them fly over that valley. What you see in the Upper Huallaga Valley is destruction of the Amazon. Huge areas, hills, completely deforested, slashed, burned, and coca being grown in the deforested areas. One of the answers, and I think this is the real answer, is that many of those areas won't support other agricultural products and should be returned to the jungle. And the people, many of whom came from other areas, should go back to those areas. Crop substitution is a possibility in some areas, but in other areas there aren't crops that will sustain the peasants.

Q. *(Dr. Nahas)*   Two questions. First in the case that the United States would come to the legalization of all illicit drugs: What is the attitude of the two great economic competitors, because the United States isn't what is was 20 years ago at the time it was the economic motor of the world. On one side is the EC and the other side is Japan. What would be their reaction to this thing? And the second question is what is the consensus in the United Nations today on this position, is it maintain, continue the fight for the suppression of illicit drugs started by the United States by Theodore Roosevelt at the turn of the century, should we give it up?

Levitsky: I think by the way you asked that question you probably know the answer. There is not a country in the world that says that we should lessen our fight against drugs. Some countries have a different approach and may be effective in some cases, but in the UN there is a broad consensus. We just have put into effect the 1988 UN Convention against Drug Trafficking, which is the strongest document on the books, and it has a strong portion which advocates the criminalization of narcotic drug usage. We have a relationship with the EC—I am going to Rome next week as part of a new consultative mechanism to discuss with the Europeans and others how we are going to work against drug production, trafficking, and abuse; not just in our own societies, but how we, in the developed nations who are basically the consuming nations, are going to assist other countries and coordinate our efforts in dealing with the production. So that both in the UN and in the European Community the attitude against drugs is quite strong. Not that they always agree with the methods we advocate, but basically we have a good consensus and a good coalition with them.

Q.*(Stephen Mugford)*   I hope as a visitor to your country you will forgive me if I appear to be critical. It seems to me . . .

Levitsky: As long as I can be critical of your country. Which one is it?

Q.   Australia.

Levitsky: Okay. I don't have too much to be critical about Australia except that you keep agitating to send us more legal opium.

Q.   We are one of the world's largest producers.

Levitsky: You have a large production of legal opium in, where is it, Tasmania?

Q.   That's right. I think that the United States international leadership in drug trafficking would be given much greater credence if two things would happen. One, if you could prepare to support a rise in coffee prices, because there was an interesting irony at the same time you were attempting to support the Colombian government: There was a driving-down in the coffee prices in which the United States had a tremendous . . .

Levitsky: Could I stop you just for a minute there, please? Because I think that is a bad rap and I am not an economist, so somebody else can explain this better . . . The fact that the coffee agreement went down the drain is not something that was due to the United States. And the fact that we don't have an international coffee agreement now has more to do with the price of coffee now than it has to do with the United States not backing a coffee agreement. So, don't put that on our doorstep. Brazil, talk to the Brazils and other countries in the world as well. Anyway, excuse me, go ahead.

Q. The second thing is that I think I am right in saying that the United States is the world's leading exporter of tobacco which, as I read it, is the world's number-one drug killer and I have to say, and you may correct me on this because I am sure you are more familiar with this than I am, but certainly the impression that I have is that the U.S. Government has taken active steps against those governments who attempted to prevent American tobacco imports. And given that tobacco is the world's leading drug killer, it sits ill when the Americans express concern about health and drug use, but they export tobacco and get upset about other people exporting other substances.

Levitsky: I would say there is a certain amount of truth in what you say. I would say that on a personal basis. On the other hand, tobacco is not a product that is a banned or a controlled substance. So I suppose that in the same way the U.S. Government tries to promote the export of other products that are considered legitimate, as bad as you may consider them, we have an obligation to also do that. I don't necessarily have to agree with that, but luckily that is not my beat either, since we deal with the controlled substances. I would be glad to take a couple of other questions if there are any more. It's up to you.

Q. Doesn't the United States have other, including foreign policy, objectives which incline to contradict you by our policy on drugs?

Levitsky: Yes.

Q. For example, one would be in the case of China. We have an interesting situation with Chinese police who prevent the transfer of drugs into Burma. And on the other hand, cooperation with the Red Chinese police who repress Chinese citizens denying them rights.

Levitsky: Absolutely.

Q. And there are many other cases . . .

Levitsky: There are no, there is almost no policy that does not conflict with another. What you have to do, and that's what government is supposed to do, is weigh the variety of interests that you have. There is no country where you have only one interest, although you have a primary interest. This problem with China—I am glad you mentioned it. Because we have an interesting dilemma. We do want to try to do something against the production and trafficking out of

Burma. Nobody in this world, that I know of, has much influence on Burma. If you can name me a country, we would be glad to approach it. Burma seems to go its own way. Even if Burma, if the government of Burma had ill intentions against the production of opium it would be difficult for it to operate because those areas are controlled by insurgent groups. I flew over Khun Sa's encampment and believe me it looks a lot better than probably what the Burmese army has—airstrips, parade areas and barracks, etc. So there is a problem. And we do have an interest in trying to work with a country like China, which also has a problem with Burma because the route through southern China now is filled with heroin. And the statistics show in southern China that AIDS and drug addiction are both up as a result. So we have to weigh this. And how are we going to do this? We will find a way of having a dialogue with the Chinese that is separate from our other kind of dialogue with them about their repression of the students and other elements of Chinese population. Now some people and some politicians will not like this, just as they do not want us to try to do something with Burma because we stopped cooperating with Burma when they stopped eradicating crops and started eradicating students. So we have to sometimes find a way of balancing our interests. As a narrow-minded drug official, I can tell you that I usually try to say let's find a way of talking with X country, whatever it is, but sometimes I won't win.

Q.   I wonder if you would comment briefly on what you think is the impact of our effort to wage war on drugs. Specifically, the Marion Barry case in Washington.

Levitsky: Well, it created a very big story in Colombia certainly, and many people said that it showed our lack of seriousness. I don't think it did. I think it was part of our system. It was handled in a certain way, and finally when it came out, the people had their say—didn't they? Not the jury, but the people. They did not elect him to the city council. So that has had a certain stir in Colombia as well. I think in cases like that we don't need to be ashamed of our system. We have it and it functions. I don't think it functions perfectly in every case, but we have trial by jury, and he had a trial by jury. It didn't help us in Colombia, but in the final analysis seeing a system like ours work, I think, does help us. '

Q.   Is there a drug problem in the Soviet Union, and do you find the Soviet Union cooperative in the international scene?

Levitsky: There is a drug problem in the Soviet Union and it is illustrative of how supply often creates demand. It started to get worse during the time when the soldiers came back from Afghanistan, where they bought hashish and opium relatively cheaply while they were stationed there. We had a consultation about a year ago. I was in Moscow with the Soviets, and they are concerned, but not quite sure how to cope with it. They had substance abuse, a different kind of substance for quite some time and there is an element in the population that would indicate that they could be very subject to drug abuse since alcoholism has been so high. They have been cooperative in some cases. They have, in fact, recently sent the KGB over to testify in a Canadian case, in a controlled-delivery case. They have been trying to work with us, but I think are still coping with the kind of transition they are in, in terms of what powers the police have and how they can operate. Yes, there is concern. There is a problem. It doesn't seem to be nearly as bad as the one we have, but it is something that they consider significant.

Q. While it is really supply that creates demand, demand also generates supply. I want to pursue the issue of drug policy. We talked about the issue of pushing the drug suppliers around the world. One of the places to push the drug suppliers, if we are going to be successful, is precisely into the United States. When we wiped out the Mexican marijuana fields, we generated a supply in the United States. How do you deal with this problem? The problem as I see it is that the demand may not be for a particular drug. If you look at the history of drug demand it goes through cycles. Cocaine is a drug that we recently . . . it was an old one; it came back. Heroin is now coming back. We may have a methamphetamine or ice demand. How does your policy deal with that and wouldn't we be better off putting the money fighting for the drug policy into demand reduction in the United States?

Levitsky: Well, you know the resources that go into the supply side are really pretty small compared to the amount of effort and money that we put into the demand side. I think we have to have a strong, credible policy of reducing supply, working with other countries to reduce supply as a general principle, but it is never going to be the focus of our policy. If we can so constrict the supply from outside that we force people to produce drugs in the United States, where presumably we have more control than in the Upper Huallaga Valley of Peru, then that is fine, in terms of being able to deal with the problem. You are right. Secretary Shultz always says where there is demand there will be supply. It is true. We are working on the demand side, but we are working on the supply side as well. There is one thing that we have been very much at fault on that we are now beginning to do—we railed against other countries for producing, but didn't do much about our own marijuana crop. Well, we are beginning to seek out the areas where marijuana is being grown, particularly in National Parks, and beginning to eradicate it. So I think that is something that is good.

Q. I would like to follow up. We have indeed reduced the supply of marijuana in California.

Levitsky: Yes, I guess.

Q. No, we have. We have reduced the supply of marijuana. The price of marijuana has risen, but at the same time, over the past few years the supply of crack cocaine has increased. That is, the assumption is that if you get rid of the marijuana you will get rid of drug demands. But that does not seem to be.

Levitsky: Well, no, not necessarily. I am not an expert on why people take drugs, or how many there really are and what kinds of drugs they might take if they didn't have access, and you've got a whole bunch of experts here. You should ask them what they think about that issue. But I think the fact—to go back to the supply and demand question, I don't think there are too many people that will say that, if you are working on the problem, to try to increase the price and to reduce the availability is something that you shouldn't do. That is something that we should do because it will influence not only the people that take it now, but also the people who might try it later, depending on how much is available and how expensive it is. And that is the essence of our efforts. I am not saying that supply reduction is the solution to things. It is a contribution to a general policy. It can be rather significant, but it certainly is not the heart of the problem and we won't solve the drug problem that way.

PART SIX

MEDICAL AND HEALTH IMPLICATIONS

21

MARIJUANA IN A TIME OF PSYCHOPHARMACOLOGICAL McCARTHYISM

Lester Grinspoon

When I began to study marijuana in 1967, I had no doubt that it was a very harmful drug which was unfortunately being used by more and more foolish young people who would not listen to or could not understand the warnings about its dangers. My purpose was to define scientifically the nature and degree of those dangers. In the next three years, as I reviewed the scientific, medical, and lay literature, my views gradually changed. I came to understand that I, like so many other people in this country, had been brainwashed. My beliefs about the dangers of marijuana had very little empirical foundation. By the time I completed the research that formed the basis for a book, I had become convinced that cannabis was considerably less harmful than tobacco and alcohol. The title of the book, *Marihuana Reconsidered*, reflected my own change in view.

At that time I naively believed that once people understood that marijuana was much less harmful than drugs that were already legal, they would come to favor legalization. In 1971, I confidently predicted that cannabis would be legalized within the decade for people over 21. I had not yet learned that there is something very special about illicit drugs. If they don't always make the drug user behave irrationally, they certainly cause many nonusers to behave that way. We are still criminalizing many millions of American marijuana users and arresting 400,000 mostly young people on marijuana charges each year (about the same number who die from the effects of tobacco). What's more, the political climate has deteriorated, particularly in the past few years, to a point where it is difficult to discuss marijuana openly and freely. Surreptitious smokers of the 1960s and early 70s who became more open toward the mid-70s had to go back into their closets during the Reagan years.

One product of the McCarthyite climate of the 1950s was the loyalty oath. Hardly anyone really believed that forced loyalty oaths would enhance national security, but people who refused to take such oaths nevertheless risked losing their jobs and reputations. Today we are witnessing the imposition of a kind of chemical loyalty oath. Mandatory, often random testing of urine samples for the presence of illicit drugs is increasingly demanded as a condition of employment. People who test positive may be fired or, if they want to keep their jobs, may be involuntarily assigned to drug counseling or "employee assistance" programs.

All this is of little use in preventing or treating drug abuse. In the case of cannabis, for example, the test requires analysis of the urine for a breakdown product or metabolite of tetrahydrocannabinol (THC) called THC acid. It is assumed that anyone with THC acid in his or her urine uses marijuana, and anyone without it does not. Clever or well-instructed marijuana users, however, can easily defeat the test by chemically altering their urine or substituting someone else's urine. Even if the urine sample has not been altered, the available tests are far from perfect. Most programs start with an immunoassay, a cheap but inaccurate method that may miss THC acid when it is present and find it when it is not present. Urine that tests positive on immunoassay must be subject to more accurate and far more expensive techniques, such as gas chromatography-mass spectroscopy (GC-MS). Used in this sequence, however, GC-MS of course does nothing to detect false negatives. Furthermore, it is fallible because of laboratory error and passive exposure to marijuana smoke.

Even if there were an infallible test, it would be of little use in preventing or treating genuine drug abuse. The presence of cannabis metabolites in the urine bears no established relationship to drug effects on the brain. It tells us nothing about when the drug was used, how much was used, or what effects it had or has. Marijuana metabolites remain in the urine for days after a single exposure and for weeks after a long-term user stops. Like loyalty oaths imposed on government employees, urine testing for marijuana is useless for its ostensible purpose. It is little more than shotgun harassment designed to impose an outward conformity to certain dominant social passions and prejudices.

Another example of psychopharmacological McCarthyism is the response to a publication in the May 1990 issue of the *American Psychologist*. Two psychologists at Berkeley reported the results of a scientifically rigorous longitudinal study of 101 subjects who had been followed from the ages of 5 to 18 in order to examine the relationship between psychological characteristics and drug use. The data demonstrated that adolescents who had engaged in some drug experimentation (primarily with marijuana) were the best adjusted in the group:

Adolescents who used drugs frequently were maladjusted, showing a distinct personality syndrome marked by interpersonal alienation, poor impulse control, and manifest emotional distress. Adolescents who had never experimented with any drug were relatively anxious, emotionally constricted, and lacking in social skills. Psychological differences between frequent drug users, experimenters, and abstainers could be traced to the earliest years of childhood and related to the quality of their parenting. The findings indicate that (a) problem drug use is a symptom, not a cause, of personal and social maladjustment, and (b) the meaning of drug use can be understood only in the context of an individual's personality structure and developmental history.

The study suggests that current efforts at drug prevention are misguided to the extent that they focus on symptoms rather than on the psychological syndrome underlying drug abuse (Shedler and Block, "Adolescent Drug Use and Psychological Health: A Longitudinal Inquiry." *American Psychologist* 45:612–30, May 1990).

The hue and cry began immediately. The director of a San Francisco drug-prevention program said that it was irresponsible for researchers to report that "dabbling with drugs was 'not necessarily catastrophic' for some youths and may simply be a part of normal adolescent experimentation" (John Diaz, "Furor over Report of Teenage Drug Use," *San Francisco Chronicle*, May 15, 1990). A physician who directs the adolescent recovery center of a metropolitan hospital asked, "What does this do to the kids who made a commitment to be abstinent? Now they're being told they're a bunch of dorks and geeks. You can imagine how much more peer pressure is going to be put on them." An article in *PRIDE Quarterly* (Summer 1990) stated: "Based on the experiences of only 101 subjects, all living in San Francisco, the study drew national attention due to its outrageous conclusion." The article went on to say, "Unfortunately, the permissive thinking which surfaced in the California study will continue to exist in the United States until truly effective drug education reaches beyond the elementary classroom. However, too few educators themselves have seen the latest discoveries about the health consequences of drug use." I am reminded of Soviet party-line criticism of science which led to the phenomenon known as Lysenkoism.

Like *Marihuana Reconsidered* itself, the public discussion of marijuana has focused almost exclusively on its potential harmfulness. In more than two decades of research, I have read and heard little about the value of cannabis. First and perhaps most important, there is its medical potential to be considered. Of all the bad consequences of government harassment of marijuana users, none is more tragic than the medical ban on cannabis. It has been well known for thousands of years that cannabis has more than one medical use. It is far safer than most medicines prescribed by doctors daily, and often works for patients who cannot tolerate the side effects of other drugs. In many cases no other drug will do the job as safely or as well.

Like other psychoactive drugs derived from natural plant sources, marijuana has long been used as a medicine as well as an intoxicant. It was listed in an herbal, published by a Chinese emperor, that may go back to 2800 B.C. In Jamaica, where it was introduced in the seventeenth century by African slaves, it has become the most important popular folk medicine. Cannabis in the form of an alcoholic tincture was commonly used in nineteenth-century Europe and the United States as an anticonvulsant, sedative, and analgesic. It was thought to be a useful appetite stimulant and a milder but less dangerous sedative than opium. It was used to treat tetanus, neuralgia, uterine hemorrhage, rheumatism, and other conditions. Between 1839 and 1900 more than a hundred articles on the therapeutic uses of marijuana appeared in scientific journals. After the introduction of injectable opiates in the 1850s, and synthetic analgesics and hypnotics in the early twentieth century, the medical use of cannabis declined. Even as late as 1937, however, extract of cannabis was still a legitimate medicine marketed by drug companies.

The Marijuana Tax Act in 1937 imposed a registration tax and record-keeping requirements that made medical use of cannabis so cumbersome that it was dropped from the U.S. Pharmacopoeia and National Formulary. The Marijuana Tax Act was introduced under the influence of a growing concern about the use of marijuana as an intoxicant, especially among blacks and Mexican-Americans in the South and Southwest. A strong campaign by the Federal Bureau of Narcotics pushed the law through Congress, although there was little evidence that marijuana was harmful. The legislative counsel for the American Medical Association at the time objected to the law, warning that future investigations in modern clinical laboratories might show even more medical promise for cannabis. The American Medical Association soon changed its stance and for the next 30 years maintained a position on marijuana very similar to that of the Federal Bureau of Narcotics.

The greatest advantage of cannabis as a medicine is its unusual safety. The ratio of lethal dose to effective dose is estimated on the basis of extrapolation from animal data to be about 20,000:1 (compared to 350:1 for secobarbital and 4–10:1 for alcohol). Huge doses have been given to dogs without causing death, and there is no reliable evidence of death caused by cannabis in a human being. Cannabis also has the advantage of not disturbing any physiological functions or damaging any body organ when used in therapeutic doses. It produces little physical dependence or tolerance; there is no evidence that medical use of cannabis has ever led to its habitual use as an intoxicant.

A promising new medical use for cannabis is the treatment of glaucoma, the second leading cause of blindness in the United States. In this disease fluid pressure within the eyeball increases until it damages the optic nerve. About one million Americans suffer from the form of glaucoma (wide-angle) treatable with cannabis. Marijuana causes intraocular pressure to fall and retards the progressive loss of sight when conventional medication fails and surgery is too dangerous. THC eyedrops have not proved effective as a substitute, and as long ago as 1981 the National Eye Institute announced that it would no longer approve human research on these eyedrops. Studies continue on eyedrops containing other natural cannabinoids and synthetic cannabis derivatives.

Cannabis also has a use in the treatment of cancer. About half of patients undergoing chemotherapy for cancer suffer from severe nausea and vomiting, which are not only unpleasant but a threat to the effectiveness of therapy. Retching may cause tears of the esophagus and rib fractures; vomiting prevents adequate nutrition and leads to fluid loss. For about a third of patients, the standard antiemetics do not work. The suggestion that cannabis might be useful arose in the early 1970s when some young people receiving cancer chemotherapy found that cannabis-smoking, which was of course illegal, reduced their nausea and vomiting. There is some controversy about whether THC is best taken orally or smoked in the form of marijuana. Smoking generates quicker and more predictable results in both glaucoma and cancer treatment because it raises THC concentration in the blood more easily to the needed level. Additionally, it may be hard for a nauseated patient in chemotherapy to take oral medicine. Most patients who use THC for this purpose prefer to smoke it in the form of marijuana.

Marijuana is becoming increasingly recognized as the drug of choice for pain that accompanies muscle spasm. This kind of pain is often chronic and debilitating, especially in paraplegics, quadriplegics, other victims of traumatic nerve injury, and people who suffer from multiple sclerosis or cerebral palsy. Many MS victims and others have discovered that cannabis not only allows them to avoid the risks of opioids for pain relief, but also reduces their muscle spasms and tremors, often making it possible for them to leave their wheelchairs and walk. The following account from a patient is illustrative:

> In June 1989, I was a 27-year-old white male who used marijuana off and on for several years as a way to relax and unwind.
>
> I was working as an industrial engineer for the last five-and-a-half years, selling pneumatic and automation equipment to manufacturing plants and factories. I was pretty successful at it.
>
> After a long hard day I would go home, have dinner with my girlfriend, smoke some marijuana, and unwind. I usually spent my evenings in my home office, working at my desk for hours, contemplating strategies to beat competitors. I found that smoking marijuana not only relaxed me—it helped me concentrate on my work.
>
> I would sometimes think that things just couldn't get any better for me. I had a good job, made excellent money, and lived with the woman I was going to marry in a few months. In fact, things didn't get better for me—they got

worse. In June 1989 I suffered an accidental gunshot wound and was instanta-
neously paralyzed from the chest down. I was rushed to a hospital and wheeled
into surgery. I awoke the following evening in a semi-coherent state and very
aware of the pain from tubes in my chest and throat. After ten days in the
Intensive Care Unit, a neurologist told me I was paralyzed and there was nothing
he could do for me. Although the bullet had missed my spinal cord completely,
excessive swelling had left me permanently paralyzed. When I finally realized I
could not be cured, I got angry and that anger never went away.

After two months of watching me try to do the simplest tasks (like dressing,
showering, or just getting in and out of bed), my girlfriend just couldn't take it.
She moved back to her parents' house.

I was no longer able to work, so I subsisted on a meager Social Security
pension. Luckily, I had served four-and-a-half years in the U.S. Navy, and was
eligible to receive medical supplies and care from the Veterans' Administration.

About four months after my injury, I began to experience strange and
somewhat painful sensations known as muscle spasms. At first they only affected
my feet and lower legs, but soon I had spasms in all my paralyzed muscles. I
was given a drug called baclofen but even the maximum dosage suggested by
the PDR [Physicians' Desk Reference] did not give me much relief. I did,
however, experience unpleasant side effects like drowsiness, severe headaches,
excessive sweating, insomnia, and dry mouth.

My spasms became more and more violent. After they caused me to fall out
of bed, my doctors added 20 mg a day of Valium, then another 20 mg. I was
becoming a pharmacological zombie.

There were many other paralyzed patients at the VA Hospital. Some had
been injured for more than 20 years. They told me that they had thrown away
their prescription spasm medications years ago and now used marijuana instead.
They said it worked better and had far fewer side effects. I tried it. After smoking
one marijuana cigarette, I experience relief in ten minutes without the debilitating side effects of Valium and baclofen. Everyday tasks, like showering and
dressing, became remarkably easier to accomplish.

Since then, when I can find marijuana, I smoke three to four cigarettes a
day. I have few or no spasms, and can do away with taking twelve very toxic and
addictive pills a day. I also discovered that I could achieve an erection when I
smoked marijuana; I couldn't achieve an erection before that unless I injected
prostaglandin E directly into my penis.

Approximately 65 percent of the paralyzed patients I've met use marijuana
to control spasticity and pain. Current Drug Enforcement Administration regulations forbid my doctors to prescribe marijuana for me and these other paralyzed individuals, but I do not consider myself or the others to be criminals for
choosing to use the most effective and safest drug for our condition. The DEA
unjustly puts us in the same criminal category as heroin junkies.

The government is now waging a war on drugs, and they are targeting me
and other paralyzed patients, glaucoma victims, AIDS sufferers, and cancer

patients who use marijuana to get relief from their serious ailments. This is not only unreasonable and unfair; it is blatantly immoral.

I am filing an Investigational New Drug Application (IND) with the Food and Drug Administration, the same procedure used by several other Americans who have won the right to smoke marijuana legally, medically. It is my sincere hope that my IND request will be granted. Otherwise, I will risk being unjustly arrested, prosecuted, and jailed.

There are many other possibilities for using marijuana to reduce human suffering at a small cost in toxic side effects. Anecdotal accounts strongly suggest that cannabis may be useful in treating other types of pain, as well as seizure disorders, appetite loss, tumors, and asthma.

If any other medicine had shown similar promise, public and professional interest would be intense. The government, however, in its zeal to prosecute the war on drugs, has been doing everything it can to reduce that interest and prevent the fulfillment of marijuana's medicinal promise. Under federal law cannabis is classified as a Schedule I drug—extremely dangerous and without accepted medical uses. Cocaine and morphine are legally available as medicines; marijuana is not. In 1972 an effort began to put marijuana in Schedule II, a classification that would allow doctors to prescribe it. Finally, in 1988, after years of hearings in which scores of witnesses presented impressive evidence on marijuana's medical usefulness, an administrative law judge ruled that it should be transferred to Schedule II. The Drug Enforcement Administration (DEA) has decided to ignore this ruling, and the decision is presently being appealed.

Meanwhile the medical ban produces absurd and appalling consequences. The most recent is the government assault on Kenneth and Barbara Jenks, a Florida couple in their 20s who contracted AIDS through a blood transfusion given to the husband, a hemophiliac. Both were suffering from nausea, vomiting, and appetite loss caused by AIDS or by the drug used to treat it, AZT; doctors feared that Barbara Jenks would die of starvation before the disease killed her. In early 1989 the Jenkses learned about marijuana through a support group for people with AIDS. They began to smoke it, and for a year they led a fairly normal life. They felt better, regained lost weight, and were able to stay out of the hospital; Kenneth Jenks even kept his full-time job.

Then someone informed on them. On March 29, 1990, ten vice squad cops battered down the door of their trailer, held a gun to Mrs. Jenks' head, and seized the evidence of crime—two small marijuana plants they had been growing because they could not afford to pay the street price of the drug. Cultivation of marijuana is a felony in Florida; the Jenkses faced up to five years in prison. At their trial in July, these dangerous felons used the defense of medical necessity, which has succeeded only three times in the history of the United States. Kenneth Jenks testified that without marijuana Barbara would be dead. Their doctor testified that no other drug controlled the nausea, and that he would prescribe cannabis for them if he could. Since their March arrest, both Jenkses had been losing weight again, and Mrs. Jenks had been hospitalized several times.

The judge rejected the medical-necessity defense and convicted the Jenkses. Although he imposed essentially no punishment (they were sentenced to a year of unsupervised probation and five years of "caring for each other"), they still have no way to obtain marijuana legally. They are now trying to use the only legal means available—asking the FDA for marijuana through a procedure known as the Compassionate IND (Investigational New Drug) application. The government expresses its compassion by subjecting doctors who request such INDs to endless delays and intimidating them with a mass of paperwork. A response could take months; patients have gone blind or died while waiting. Only five or six people in the whole country are now using marijuana obtained by this route.

The arrest of the Jenkses is just one unusually conspicuous result of a policy that is ordinarily disastrous in a quieter way. Sick people are forced to suffer anxiety about prosecution in addition to their anxiety about the illness, with therapeutically damaging effects. Doctors are afraid to recommend what they know to be the best treatment, because they might lose their reputations or even their licenses. Research is suppressed and medical wisdom ignored so that the government can enforce its views on the danger of recreational marijuana use.

The DEA is stubbornly rejecting the dictates of both reason and compassion, not to mention the opinion of its own administrative law judge. It must change or be changed. AIDS treatment is only the latest revelation of marijuana's medical potential, but it might be the decisive one. The protests of AIDS activists have already changed federal policy in several areas of medical research and treatment. Maybe they will also bring the government to its senses on the marijuana issue.

The struggle over medical marijuana use illustrates some important drug-policy issues: self-medication versus government control, pure chemicals versus natural drugs, the historical direction of drug policy and the present minor challenges to it, and the need to find a better balance in making rules about drugs. The potential dangers of marijuana when taken for pleasure and its possible usefulness as a medicine are historically and practically interrelated issues: historically, because the arguments used to justify public and official disapproval of recreational use have had a strong influence on opinions about its medical potential; practically, because the more evidence accumulates that marijuana is relatively safe even when used as an intoxicant, the clearer it becomes that the medical requirement of safety is satisfied. Most recent research is tentative, and initial enthusiasm for drugs is often disappointed after further investigation.

It is not as though cannabis were an entirely new agent with unknown properties. Studies done during the past ten years have confirmed a centuries-old promise. With the relaxation of restrictions on research and the further chemical manipulation of cannabis derivatives, this promise will eventually be realized.

The weight of past and contemporary evidence will undoubtedly prove cannabis and its derivatives to be valuable in a number of ways as a medicine.

If legal, political, and social pressures have hindered recognition of the medical uses of cannabis, they have made public acknowledgment of its nonmedical virtues almost impossible. Despite the hysteria, large numbers of Americans continue to use cannabis regularly. What was once considered primarily a youthful indulgence or an expression of youthful rebellion is now a common adult practice. Millions have smoked marijuana for years, and most of them will continue to smoke it for the rest of their lives. They are convinced that they are harming no one else and not harming themselves as much as cigarette smokers or alcohol drinkers.

The authorities who want to reduce the demand for cannabis have very little idea why that demand is so powerful and persistent. If they did know, they might be less concerned about diminishing the demand and less sanguine about the value of punitive legislation. Our society must make informed decisions based on the fact that tens of millions of its citizens use cannabis. It is important for us to know why those citizens not only like to use the substance, but in many cases believe that it has enhanced their lives.

The best way to learn about cannabis is to let users speak for themselves. In the past few months I have met two artists and a scientist who believe that the use of cannabis is important to their work. The first is a man in his mid-forties who consulted me because, as he said on the telephone, he had a "problem" concerning marijuana. He is a happily married man, the father of two children, who decided about ten years ago that he was sufficiently successful as a painter to give up an ancillary job. He was able to make his living as a painter until eight months ago, when he was forced to give up the use of cannabis because of its illegality. (I cannot provide more details because it would compromise his anonymity.) Before this, his successful painting routine had been as follows: he would take two "tokes" (puffs) of marijuana when he started to paint and another two tokes every two hours as long as he continued to work. He never took more than that. An ounce of cannabis would last him six or seven weeks. He described the effect as follows:

> With it, I get eager, motivated, even excited to paint. My mind focuses on one thing to accomplish at a time. I'm clear of negative thoughts and able to see instantly colors and shapes rather than a subject. I can now see the beauty in something I may have thought of as mundane or boring. My thoughts now seem to be of how precious time is and making the best use of every moment. This leads to greater accomplishments during the day which makes me feel content, satisfied, even happy; self-confidence grows and I want to go after something with a greater challenge.

Since being compelled to cease the use of marijuana, he finds that he sits ". . . for hours before the canvas, unable to accomplish anything. I may look at one painting for an average of 200 hours, and I find myself full of self-doubt and lack of confidence. I may work for weeks on something, only to cover it up later. I waste time, I have no motivation, I get depressed." This man has not produced a salable painting for eight months and his financial situation is desperate. All his technical skills are intact, but he cannot produce paintings of the same caliber that he sold so readily before.

The second artist who finds cannabis important to his work writes as follows:

> Marijuana has over the years served as a creative stimulant to my work as a performer and to my more occasional inspirations as a composer. For me, marijuana is a creative stimulant; almost all my finished choral pieces and songs have been composed partly or wholly under the influence: melodic and rhythmic ideas may just pop into my head during relaxed and happy moments, "points of creative release" one might say. The work of forming these seminal ideas into a whole composition, for me who am not prolific, then takes place over an ensuing period: a few days to a few years (in the latter extreme, intermittently, of course). As a performer I have certainly gained insights into the inner meaning of the musical masterpieces which I play. Practicing new repertoire while intoxicated by marijuana is not a very good nor productive habit: the keen mental concentration of learning notes is not aided and abetted. But once a piece is fluently learned, my understanding of what it means as an entirety is often enhanced. A usual practice day for me is to work in the morning with a few cups of coffee in me. In the late afternoon I often have a little workout in the gym, and this renews me and gets the adrenalin flowing so I can come back to the piano, have a bit of marijuana, and practice very enjoyably and productively for one or two hours. I never try to perform in public when stoned, but as it is well known that marijuana can enhance the pleasure of listening to many kinds of music, I often listen after having smoked some marijuana. And so do many others who I know and have known over the years. WGBH-TV has produced a special on Satchmo, in which his lifelong affection for marijuana is not kept from the viewers. He found it both an inspiration for his music and a balm against life's trials. It seems to work the same way for me; it's one of my best friends, though, as I mentioned earlier, I wish for a better way to partake than by smoking it—pills, cookies, fudge, or whatever.

The scientist, like the two artists, has been using cannabis for years, and he too believes that it contributes to his work:

> As a scientist I have spent literally years training the analytical side of my mind— to be suspicious of my data, to look for order of magnitude arguments to test the reasonableness of my results, to use lateral thinking to try to arrive at the same conclusions by alternative means. This has been an *active* process of mental

discipline: idealizing physical situations, making assumptions to reduce the system to something solvable, and applying logic to determine the outcome.

What has often been neglected in concentrating on only those things I have chosen to think about is an awareness of the wider perspective and significance of the work and the sense of personal wonder which led me into the field to begin with. There have also been many times when the answer to some question was right before me but I was unable to see the "forest for the trees." This is partly due to the same training which enables me to work through complicated analytical problems: in order to concentrate on those pertinent aspects which I have included in the model I will deliberately omit distractions which might perhaps hold the key. This is particularly true of working with computers, which have no tolerance for vague suggestions that perhaps something of importance has been left out of the equations, but will happily spit out results with an apparent accuracy of many decimal digits.

If it were possible, say through yoga for example, for me to turn off the rational side of my mind and think creatively (and randomly) for short time periods, to reverse the training temporarily and see my work in a different light, then it would probably be as productive as getting high (although perhaps not as pleasant). Part of the reason getting high is necessary is the human habit of going over old ground and seeing what you believe to be there rather than what actually exists (the same reason why it is almost impossible to proofread one's own writing).

Obviously it is inefficient for me to try to pursue these new ideas while high, because I am too easily distracted and my analytical capabilities are unquestionably impaired; instead I enjoy the relaxation and keep notebooks recording my unchanneled thoughts in lists and outlines. I would state flatly that both aspects of getting high, namely relaxation and observation of subtle details of problems which I overlook at other times, have been valuable contributions to my work.

It is not surprising that my informants have chosen not to identify themselves. How can we expect people to share these experiences openly in the present atmosphere? The government's newest legal assault includes a fine of up to $10,000 for possession of a single marijuana cigarette. Fear of the law, however, is probably less important than fear of the consequences of being seen as irresponsible and deviant. When homosexuals started to come out of the closet a decade ago, many people were surprised to learn that they were not sick, antisocial, or in other ways "different" aside from their sexual orientation. It was an effective way to reduce this form of bigotry. So, too, cannabis users may eventually have to provide the public with an opportunity to test stereotypes against reality. They, too, are targets of bigotry and may have to adopt the same strategy in their struggle against it.

22

Pharmacologic Assessment of Dependence Risks

E. Leong Way

> It is true that you may fool all the people some of the time; you can even fool some of the people all the time; but you can't fool all of the people all the time.
>
> —Abraham Lincoln

Honest Abe would have been an excellent pharmacologist instead of a lawyer had he chosen to apply his wisdom and common sense to drug problems. By analogy what he said can easily be extrapolated to explain the biologic effects of chemical substances. In any population, humans or experimental animals, a fixed dose of a compound produces effects, beneficial or toxic, on a proportion of the subjects. A low dose of the pharmacologic agent or drug will affect some more vulnerable subjects while a higher dose would be necessary to affect more resistant ones. This dose-responsive relationship is a basic principle usually discussed in the introductory chapter of most pharmacologic texts, and is illustrated by the classic curve shown in Figure 22.1.

When we discuss drugs, therefore, a dose-effect relationship could be applied to mean that many persons may become disabled by licit drugs and that many users of illicit substances do not necessarily become disabled despite propaganda to the contrary. These opening remarks bring us to the topic at hand, concerning drug addiction and drug dependence.

The term "addiction" has varying meanings with different individuals. Before we become embroiled in discussions, permit me to give a definition that has

FIGURE 22.1 REPRESENTATIVE DOSE-ADDICTING RELATIONSHIP
FOR A PSYCHOACTIVE COMPOUND

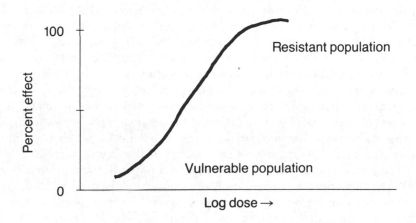

broad implications and extends beyond pharmacology. A pharmacologic definition would restrict drug addiction to be a state where a chemical substance is
used compulsively. Such behavior invariably becomes detrimental to the individual and society. The overwhelming desire to repeat usage results in continual
relapses after treatment or incarceration, and highly motivates the securing of the
compound despite grave medical and social consequences.

There are three major elements of drug addiction, namely vulnerability of
the individual, environmental factors, and pharmacologic components. I shall
dwell only briefly on the first two aspects because those topics would be more
expertly handled by psychologists, psychiatrists, and sociologists. In essence, the
vulnerable person is believed to have underlying psychopathologic problems that
may have genetic and familial facets. Low self-esteem and inability to cope with
stress, environment, peer pressure, and conditioning are conducive to experimentation with and becoming dependent on chemical substances. The compulsive usage of a chemical substance is, therefore, a symptomatic manifestation of
the aberration.

Drug dependence is the pharmacologic facet of addiction. Although vulnerability of the individual is the prime reason that leads to compulsive use of
chemicals, the substance becomes the vehicle for expressing addictive behavior.
Not all pharmacologic agents acting on the brain possess addicting liabilities.
Although there may have been some isolated episodes reported, antipsychotic,
antiepileptic, and antihistaminic compounds have little if any addicting qualities.

On the other hand, certain other substances produce selective effects on mood that tend to promote compulsive usage to varying degrees.

The pharmacologic effects of psychoactive substances that tend to promote dependence are euphoria (a state of well-being), tolerance, and physical dependence. These properties are dose-dependent and are related also to the frequency and mode of administration. Pharmaceutical technology can make relatively innocuous folk practices become harmful vices by enhancing the potency of a product and facilitating its delivery to target sites of action. The habit of ingesting or smoking the dried latex of the opium poppy is hardly comparable to using a syringe to inject heroin, which is the semi-synthetic derivative of morphine, the chief active constituent of opium. Likewise, the destructive attributes of cocaine become increasingly amplified as the mode of administration changes from chewing coca leaves, to sniffing cocaine salt, to inhaling free cocaine base.

The technologic innovations permit the user of psychoactive substances to attain rapid and intense euphoric responses, and the enjoyment or rewarding effect produced by the agent is primarily responsible for its addicting qualities. What is difficult to understand, however, is why the liking for a compound can result in a compulsive usage by certain individuals and why they become obsessed with securing the product, even with a realization of the consequences. More often than not, the drive to maintain the destructive habit leads to the sacrifice of family, position, and prestige, and eventually to criminal activity. Under such circumstances, matter of will becomes subordinated to the need for a substance that has somehow modified physiologic processes. Clearly, much research is necessary in this area to provide a rational explanation; this is a prime mission of the National Institute on Drug Abuse. NIDA not only promotes and supports research on the causes, prevention, and treatment of drug abuse, but also spearheads a program for the development of medications for such purposes. It is hoped that these projects will enable an understanding of the processes involved in addiction.

Psychopharmacologists suspect that psychoactive substances act on the limbic system of the brain because this region also contains the circuitry that regulates the reward system and gives satisfaction in hunger, thirst, and sex. That an alteration in the physiologic processes occurs following sustained administration of certain psychoactive substances can easily be demonstrated clinically, on the street or in the experimental laboratory. This phenomenon, known as physical dependence, is most easily recognized with opiates, but general depressants such as alcohol, barbiturates, and methaqualone (Quaalude) can produce a degree of physical dependence that is more dangerous than that of heroin.

In the case of addiction to an opiate, such as heroin, the discontinuance of the compound after physical dependence has developed is characterized by a feeling of coldness, goose pimples, yawning, and increased secretions from the eyes and nose, following by increased sensitivity to pain, increased respiration, elevated body temperature, diarrhea, vomiting, and muscular aches. This vegetative syndrome is also accompanied by purposive behavior (hostility, pleading, threatening suicide, and so on) to secure a "fix." If allowed to run its course, most of the withdrawal signs subside within a week, but some vague symptoms may persist for months. The period of acute abstinence varies with the opiate, being as brief as one or two days with meperidine and lasting about two weeks with methadone. Although the syndrome is difficult to endure, even highly severe opiate abstinence is not life-threatening if attention is given to replacing body fluids. Moreover, it can be terminated almost immediately by readministration of an opiate.

This is not the case with alcohol and most other general depressants, especially certain barbiturates and methaqualone. During severe withdrawal, the signs include tremulousness, vomiting, cramps, weakness, anxiety, delirium, hallucinations, paranoia, and convulsive seizures. The readministration of a depressant during withdrawal does not terminate the syndrome, although it may allay the symptomology. Physical dependence on alcohol is rather difficult to demonstrate, but once established is extremely difficult to treat. The incidence of mortality in suburban hospitals not equipped to handle abstinence on alcohol may run as high as 15 percent.

The development of tolerance to an addicting substance may accelerate concomitantly its rate of physical dependence development. In instances where the two phenomena appear to be closely related, the need to use higher or more frequent doses to achieve hedonia would serve to intensify physical dependence development. The association between tolerance and physical dependence varies among and within drug groups. With tobacco and cocaine the relationship is difficult to demonstrate. In the case of opiates, however—heroin in particular—tolerance and physical dependence seem to be closely related. Tolerance to the analgetic, respiratory-depressant, diaphoretic, constipating, and miotic effects of heroin can be manifested correspondingly by an overshoot rebound during withdrawal as hypergesia, hyperventilation, hyperthermia, diarrhea, and midriasis, suggesting that tolerance and physical dependence may have some underlying processes in common. Even with opiates, however, tolerance may develop to some actions that are not expressed by an exaggerated abstinent response.

Physical dependence on cocaine or amphetamines has been questioned. However, after sprees on high doses for several days, withdrawal appears to produce exaggerated rebound responses opposite to acute drug effects. In addition to profound depression, such manifestations as fatigue, prolonged sleep, and tremendous appetite may occur to a greater intensity than that observable after prolonged exercise, insomnia, and food deprivation. Physical dependence on tobacco and marijuana is even more difficult to delineate precisely. These findings reinforce the notion that the development of physical dependence is not a necessary accompaniment for producing addiction to a chemical substance. Even in the case of heroin dependence, where the abstinent syndrome is very real and a strong reinforcing factor in promoting addiction, the physical dependency serves principally to provide the excuse for "shooting-up" or getting a "fix." That to avoid withdrawal sickness is a rationalization is indicated by the fact that after the addict is detoxified in a hospital and relieved from physical dependence, craving for the drug is not extinguished. Almost immediately after discharge, the likelihood that the post-dependent addict will soon resort to seeking heroin is extremely high.

From the above considerations, it becomes increasingly obvious that legislative policies on the use, misuse, and abuse of substances have not and are not always based on their pharmacology. Indeed, such aspects are often ignored. The effect of a drug does not become worse if it becomes illegal or better when it is legalized, but to laymen and the media, regulation seems to confer such qualities on chemical substances. Pharmacologists cannot alter facts, but such matters do not seem to faze lawyers.

It always confounds me that lawmakers, for expediency, can decide to define an apple to be a banana and, as illogical as this may seem, an apple can thereafter legally be a banana. To illustrate the point using drugs, based on experimental and clinical observations, pharmacologists group the opiates, marijuana, and cocaine into three distinct classes, but legislators of the 1914 Harrison Narcotic Act made them all "narcotics." Even the lifesaving heroin antidote, nalorphine, which possesses no addiction liability, was legally defined to be a narcotic and subjected to rigid restriction. This categorization remained in effect for over one-half a century and sometimes the law was even enforced to harass physicians. Fortunately, this was changed in 1970 with the passage of the Comprehensive Drug Act, and I was pleased to have had the opportunity as a member of a scientific advisory committee of the Attorney General to provide some input at that time.

The fact that a substance is highly addicting does not necessarily mean that it is the most dangerous to the user or to society. The number of persons heavily dependent on tobacco-smoking exceeds that of any other addicting substance but, despite the numbers, the carcinogenic potential, and the adverse cardiovascular effects of nicotine, there is little concern about the ability of smokers, including airplane pilots, to function effectively while smoking.

Even with heroin, one of the most potent compulsive inducers, chronic use may not be incapacitating. Heroin does not have major effects on the motor and cardiovascular systems and hence, the user can usually function effectively if access to the drug is not prevented. In Hong Kong, high-rise construction workers who are addicts use heroin to calm their fears, and some addicted barbers and tailors use heroin on the job to combat fatigue. The most famous American surgeon, William Halstead, who pioneered many surgical innovations, performed operations while heavily addicted to morphine. In many methadone clinics, the maintenance dose of methadone is four to ten times the analgetic dose and yet many on the program safely drive motor vehicles to and from the clinics.

On the other hand, the use of other substances, even when not addicted, can be dangerous to self and society. The acute effects of alcohol or cocaine place these drugs in a class by themselves. A single pharmacologically effective dose of alcohol or cocaine can be very destructive. The recreational user of alcohol (or certain other general depressants) can be a menace on the road and stimulants, such as cocaine or the amphetamines, may provoke acts of violence. Moreover, the chronic use of these substances results in considerable damage to the brain and cardiovascular system, and alcohol has been especially injurious to the liver. Clearly, then, the pharmacologic and social consequences of addicting substances are not parallel. In enacting legislation against drugs, all their facets need to be scrutinized carefully in perspective.

Proponents of change provide compelling arguments that the potential social consequences of misuse of a given chemical substance should be the prime deciding factor, rather than the adverse pharmacologic effects on the user. Although the acute and chronic harmful effects of an agent cannot be ignored, it is the belief of many that the life-style of the user is self-imposed and if carried out in privacy, without major consequences for society, their inclination would be not to mind the business of others. On the other hand, others would argue there is no assurance that the user in private can control his or her actions. If the habit results in detrimental effects on others, however, punishment could be meted out to fit the crime. Restrictions on a substance, therefore, could be mandated to accord with its harmfulness potential. Sanctions for each compound would need to be considered separately, using the prohibitions placed on alcohol and tobacco as guides. Both these legalized substances now have age and label requirements and restrictions on when and where usage is allowable. In considering sanctions on chemicals, it would facilitate the task if the public and the media could be educated to acknowledge that both substances easily fit the appellation "addicting drug." A harm rating scale, as shown in Table 22.1, summarizing the points discussed above, should be a useful guide for making decisions. The assigned score is arbitrary and is based on the knowledge established on the pharmacologic potency after acute and chronic administration and a value judgment of the indirect consequences.

The idea of considering sanctions for each addicting substance separately has many advocates. Goldstein and Kalant have provided an extensive bibliography and made a very careful in-depth analysis of the benefits and risks for striking the right balance on drug policy. Meyers and his associates also have provided a highly reasoned approach but with somewhat more liberal recommendations on marijuana possession. The late John Kaplan, a highly esteemed scholar and lawyer, provided a balanced analysis of the social and legal issues of drug use and misuse. These are the words of experienced experts in the field, free of piety and

TABLE 22.1. HARM RATING SCALE FOR SUBSTANCES OF ABUSE, BASED ON THEIR
ABILITY TO INDUCE COMPULSIVE USAGE AND THE CONSEQUENCES
OF THEIR ACUTE AND CHRONIC ADMINISTRATION

| | Addiction Liability | | Consequences | | |
	Emotional	Physical	User	Society	Score[a]
Cocaine	5	2	5	5	17
Alcohol	3	4	4	4	14
Depressants	3	4	3	4	13
Heroin	4	3	2	1	10
Marijuana	3	2	3	3	11
Tobacco	3	1	2	1	7

[a]The ranking is based on potency of the pure substance on an increasing scale from 0 to 5, with 5 being the most harmful. Adverse effects on the fetus were not included in the comparison for lack of quantitative and long-term data.

rhetoric; in formulating drug policy, their advice should be given most serious consideration.

Man has learned, since the dawn of civilization, to appreciate the mood-altering effects of the products of certain plants. The use of fermented grain or fruits, latex of the opium poppy, flowering types of marijuana and coca leaves has existed for millenia. It is not very speculative to predict that their usage will continue long after we have departed from Earth. Even if some of us are clever enough to devise means to eliminate the plants that are the source of effects that so many seem to enjoy, not only would such success not solve the problem of compulsive drug usage, more likely it would exacerbate it. One need only point out that the many beneficial drugs on the market today represent improvements from those provided by nature. There is every reason to expect that pharmaceutical chemists can similarly enhance the potency and activity of mood-altering sub-stances derived from plants. Indeed, there are already such products on the scene, as well as "designer" drugs. To be more specific, for example, there are opioid agents available at least one hundred times more potent than heroin. Although such compounds may be more expensive to produce than heroin, their higher potency and the artificially inflated prices of illegal substances would provide the incentive for their marketing in a free enterprise system. Then, even if the budget for interdiction were trebled, it would be difficult indeed to prevent smuggling of substances that could be covered by a postage stamp.

BIBLIOGRAPHY

Blum, R. H., and associates, *Drugs I: Society and Drugs*, Jossey-Bass, San Francisco, 1969.

Blum, R. H., and associates, *Drugs II: Students and Drugs*, Jossey-Bass, San Francisco, 1969.

Brecker, E. M., ed. *Licit and Illicit Drugs*, Little, Brown, Boston, 1972.

Fischman, M. W., and Mello, N. K., *Testing for Abuse Liability of Drugs in Humans*, NIDA Research Monograph number 92, DHHS publication number ADM 89-163, 1989.

Goodman, A. C. G., Goodman, L. S., Rall, T. W., and Murad, F., eds., *The Pharmacological Basis of Therapeutics*, 7th ed., Macmillan, New York, 1985.

Kalant, O. J., ed. and translator, *Maier's Cocaine Addiction*, Addiction Research Foundation, Toronto, Canada, 1987.

Katzung, B. G., ed., *Basic and Clinical Pharmacology*, 3rd ed., Appleton and Lang, Norwalk, Connecticut/Los Altos, California, 1987.

Petersen, R. C., and Stillman, R. C., eds., *Cocaine*, NIDA Research Monograph, DHEW publication, National Institute on Drug Abuse, ADM 77-471, 1977.

The Health Consequences of Smoking, Nicotine Addiction, A Report of the Surgeon General, DHHS, Rockville, Maryland, 1988.

Way, E. Leong, "A Pharmacologist's Concept of Narcotics in Advance in Pain Research and Therapy," *Drug Treatment of Cancer Pain in a Drug-Oriented Society*, Hill, C. S., Jr., and Fields, W. S., eds., vol. II, Jossey-Bass, San Francisco, 1989.

Way, E. Leong, "Contemporary Classification, Pharmacology and Abuse Potential of Psychotropic Substances," *Drugs and Youth*, Wittenborn, J. R., Brill, H., Sonits, J. P., Wittenborn, S. H., eds., Charles C. Thomas, Springfield, Illinois, 1969.

Way, E. Leong, *"Control and Treatment of Drug Addiction in Hong Kong*, L. Wilner, D. M., Kasselbaum, G. G., eds., Jossey-Bass, San Francisco, 1964.

23

DRUG POLICY: SOME THOUGHTS ABOUT STRIKING THE RIGHT BALANCE

Avram Goldstein

I shall address here several points concerning some key drug-policy issues from the perspective of a biomedical scientist (neurobiologist and pharmacologist) who also has hands-on experience in treating heroin addicts. (A recent article expands on these points and others.[1]) Striking the right balance means trying—for each drug separately—to find a set of policies that will minimize, insofar as possible, both the total harm done by that drug and the total harm done by restrictive regulations enforced by law.

In this commentary, I shall try to avoid the kind of hyperbole that has afflicted much of the drug-policy debate. What one sees too often are the exponents of two polarized positions—"prohibitionists" and "legalizers"—each preaching at the other. There is too much rhetoric, and sometimes even invective. An old principle applies here: The less data, the more there is to talk about! What we need is to focus more on data, to seek agreement about the validity of data that already exist, to decide which issues would be clarified by more data, and to agree on what further studies are needed. Then, and only then, can meaningful argument be undertaken about what policy implications may be drawn from the data. For example, a central question—perhaps the single most important question—is the extent to which, for each presently prohibited drug, the user pool would expand if prohibition were relaxed. Here relevant data from history, pharmacology, and economic analysis do exist, and should be subjected to intensive scrutiny and debate.

It is sometimes argued that when an existing policy is doing obvious harm, it is justifiable to make changes without waiting for agreement about the relevant data.[2] This position presumes—what is manifestly untrue—that a bad situation could not be made even worse by ill-advised policy changes.

Drugs are not ordinary commodities. They have profound biologic effects, some beneficial, some harmful. The current debate over drug policy, however, has been virtually uninformed concerning the neurobiology, neurochemistry, toxicology, and medical aspects of the addicting drugs. I congratulate the organizers of this conference for breaking away from that tradition.

All drugs are potentially hazardous, and addicting drugs are additionally hazardous because some people—not all, of course, but also not a negligible number—lose control and develop a pattern of compulsive use. The Pure Food and Drug Laws, dating to the beginning of this century, established the principle that government would both inform and protect consumers against hazards that the average person is technically unequipped to assess. Thus, the most dangerous drugs are restricted to use on prescription or are not approved for medical use at all.

Addicting drugs, even at ordinary doses, can cause *acute* toxic effects on organ systems, like the potentially lethal and unpredictable cardiac actions of cocaine. Acute psychomotor impairment and defective judgment due to the neurochemical effects of ordinary doses of alcohol, marijuana, cocaine, and PCP kill many, many more people than die in the much-publicized street wars over the illicit drug market. Some drugs cause major toxicity on *chronic* use—such as alcoholic liver cirrhosis or the paranoid reactions to cocaine or amphetamines, which afflict every user who is exposed sufficiently to the drug. Fetal damage, as by alcohol or cocaine (the data are not yet clear for marijuana), can result in prematurity and low birth weight and, later, severe learning disabilities.

These and many other harmful drug effects are pharmacologic: "They have nothing to do with quality control or impurities; they occur whether a drug is legal or prohibited. Drug toxicity is extremely variable across people. The *number* harmed is determined by the total size of the user pool. Even with a small *percentage* of toxicity, the larger the user pool, the more heavy users there will be, and the greater will be the total harm.

Without quoting John Donne, let me just say that we are all affected by the consequences of drug addiction, not only through immediate dangers (as from someone driving while intoxicated) but also because we live (I hope!) in a humane and compassionate society. We do not turn our backs on a motorcycle accident because the rider was not wearing a crash helmet. We will not (I hope!) wash our hands of people who have damaged their own health or their babies *in utero* by ill-advised use of drugs. If we are all concerned, and if we are all going to bear the costs, we all have a right to try to minimize those costs. If we accept some role for governmental regulation in this process, the debate can then focus fruitfully on the appropriate degree of regulation for each family of drugs. It seems to me that there is no common ground for discussion with extreme libertarians who equate any governmental regulation to "enslavement."

Drug-related crime is certainly a cause for concern, and it is obvious that drug prohibition—given sufficient demand—fosters a lucrative black market with its associated violence. This aspect of the drug problem is also related to social decay in our inner cities. We need to address that decay, creating legitimate job opportunities for inner-city youth, dealing with the lack of decent affordable housing, overhauling both the welfare system and the education system. Total legalization of the drugs would create new problems while only partially solving existing ones. They key issue here is the extent to which—for each drug—the user pool would be expanded with each degree of regulatory relaxation. It would be a mistake, out of despair, simply to abandon a whole segment of our population to addicting drugs. Our experience with alcohol and tobacco, in regard to the size of the user pool, and the total costs to society, does not offer an ideal model to be copied. It is noteworthy that these two drugs, which are not intrinsically more seductive or addictive than cocaine or heroin, but which are legal, readily available, and cheap, are used by so many more people than use the illicit drugs.

Media sensationalism distorts the totality of the drug problem; that distortion was evident even at this conference. Speakers pay lip service to the fact that alcohol and nicotine are drugs; but then they lapse into discussions that are only relevant to marijuana, cocaine, and heroin. A conference about "U.S. Drug Policy" cannot be restricted to illicit drugs. The common phrases "alcohol *and* drugs" or "tobacco *and* drugs" should be expunged from the language; these *are* drugs, and implying otherwise only serves to reinforce the unwarranted distinctions that are reflected in our regulatory policies. Pretending that nicotine (tobacco) is an ordinary agricultural commodity tends to obscure the hypocrisy of the United States in exporting tobacco products while condemning countries that export cocaine or heroin.

Figure 23.1 gives the most recent official data on the numbers of regular users of addicting drugs. The y-axis is millions of people using at least once weekly. At the extreme left is the estimate for caffeine, which is consumed almost universally (178 million users) but is comparatively benign. Then, from left to right, the bars represent nicotine (Nic), alcohol (Alc), marijuana (Mar), cocaine (Coc), heroin (Her), and all the rest (Oth). Nicotine and alcohol are the addicting drugs that are *by far* our greatest problem from the standpoint of numbers of heavy users and total damage (including deaths) inflicted on users and on society. Knowing the animal and human evidence about the reinforcing properties of the various addicting drugs, it seems quite likely to me that as many people would smoke "crack" cocaine as now smoke tobacco—if the legal status were the same. This conclusion rests also on the social acceptability of smoking (in contrast to intravenous injection), and the rapid entrance of both nicotine and volatile cocaine into the brain after inhalation.

FIGURE 23.1   REGULAR USERS OF ADDICTING DRUGS

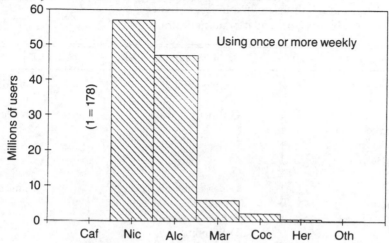

SOURCES: Data for 1990 from several U.S. Government sources. See text for abbreviations. This figure was constructed from Table 2 in Goldstein and Kalant, "Drug Policy."

Total victory in the so-called war on drugs is unattainable; addicting drugs have been with us for centuries, and no government policy will make the problem go away. Research in neurobiology is beginning to teach us why addicting drugs can lead to compulsive use. They all act on a common dopaminergic reward pathway in the brain, a delicate and finely tuned neural system that controls our behavior. Table 23.1 indicates that every addicting drug mimics or blocks some naturally occurring neurotransmitter in this pathway. The receptors for each of these nuerotransmitters are still being discovered; only a few months ago the marijuana (THC) receptor was identified and its complete structure determined.[3]

This brain-reward system was perfected, through evolution, to signal satisfaction from fulfilling basic biologic drives. It is a tightly regulated system, and the addicting drugs not only stimulate, activate, overstimulate, and overactivate it in an artificial manner, but also can disrupt its regulation. Biologists understand, of course, that rats and mice and monkeys are not people; nonetheless, it must be a matter of concern that experimental animals self-administer these same drugs—cocaine most intensively of all—to the exclusion of other activities, and sometimes to the death.

For any given addicting drug, many people use only rarely or not at all, and many use in moderation. However, some people—who and how many is unpredictable—are predisposed to become compulsive users. Compulsive use overwhelms and damages the normal reward functions (perhaps permanently). Whether

TABLE 23.1. THE ADDICTING DRUGS
          (Each drug family mimics, enhances, or
          blocks a particular brain neurotransmitter.)

Drug Family	Brain Neurotransmitter	Effect
Nicotine	Acetylcholine	Mimics
Alcohol Barbiturates Benzodiazepines Volatile solvents	GABA	Enhances
Heroin Morphine Synthetic opiates	*Endogenous opioids:* Enkephalins Beta-endorphin Dynorphins	Mimics
Cocaine Amphetamines	*Catecholamines:* Dopamine Norepinephrine Epinephrine	Enhances
Cannabis: Marijuana Hashish THC	*Receptor just* *identified,* *neurotransmitter* *unknown*	?
Hallucinogens: LSD MDMA ("Ecstasy") PCP Mescaline	Serotonin Serotonin ? ?	Blocks Blocks? ? ?
Caffeine	Adenosine	Blocks

SOURCE: Adapted from A. Goldstein, ed., *Molecular and Cellular Aspects of the Drug Addictions* (New York: Springer-Verlag, 1989), p. xv.

the addict's abnormal neurochemistry is antecedent or consequent to first drug use, the stage of compulsive use defines the user as a victim—the victim of a neurochemical disease. Criminalizing use per se is probably counterproductive, for the many reasons that have been expounded so convincingly by our English and Dutch colleagues.[4,5] Universally available treatment is called for.

Realistic attempts can be made to reduce drug availability, but interdiction at the border is not cost-effective; and even if it were 100 percent effective, novel and more potent synthetic designer drugs could easily be made domestically to fill the gap. The ideal way to ameliorate the drug problem is, obviously, to reduce demand. The present budgetary breakdown for our 10-billion-dollar "drug war," however, is 71 percent for supply-reduction (interdiction and enforcement), and only 29 percent for demand-reduction (prevention education, treatment, and research). These proportions should be approximately interchanged.

The policy debate ought not be about choosing between the polar extremes of prohibition on the one hand and unrestricted legalization on the other. There are many degrees of regulation, and diverse ways of discouraging consumption. In general, we should make tobacco and alcohol more expensive and harder to get. Outlawing cigarette machines would be an effective first step in reducing availability to children. In using increased taxation to reduce consumption, the aim should be to raise the price, but not so high as to encourage a significant black market.

The way stricter regulations on drugs can provide the milieu in which health-oriented prevention-education efforts can succeed is illustrated by the experience of recent years with nicotine. The current salutory reduction in tobacco consumption is coming about in a context of increasingly stringent legal constraints about where and when smoking is permitted. Thus, effective educational efforts concerning all drugs are not alternatives to regulation but supplements to regulation.

If we were to experiment with relaxing prohibitions on any drug, we might begin with marijuana, which appears to be among the more benign ones. Careful planning, of course, is called for. In Alaska and Oregon (often cited by advocates of legalization), penalties for personal possession of marijuana were reduced, but cannabis was not legalized. What the effects of actual legalization would be on consumption over a period of, say, a whole generation, is unknown. Harms caused by greatly expanding the user pool (if that were to happen) are also unknown. Long-term heavy marijuana use is not harmless (here more laboratory and clinical research is needed), and the acute behavioral disturbances can present dangers to others.

Not only with respect to marijuana, but for all addicting drugs, major policy changes should be implemented only when procedures are in place to evaluate the outcome. Adequate research funding, and specification of a rigorous evaluation process, should be part of every budgetary allocation for dealing with the drug problem—whether through interdiction, law enforcement, prevention education, or treatment. Finally, more effective means of detecting vulnerability to addiction (so that preventive efforts might be focused on those most likely to benefit), and the development of novel therapeutic agents, can only come from a deeper understanding of the neurobiology and pharmacology of drug addiction, through intensified research efforts.

NOTES

1. Goldstein, A., and Kalant, H., "Drug Policy: Striking the Right Balance," *Science* 249 (1990): 1513–21.

2. Friedman, M. "The War We Are Losing," Chapter 3, this volume.

3. Matsuda, L. A., et al., "Structure of a Cannabinoid Receptor and Functional Expression of the Cloned cDNA," *Nature*, 346 (1990): 561–64.

4. Turner, D., "Pragmatic Incoherence: The Changing Face of British Drug Policy," Chapter 10, this volume.

5. Engelsman, E., "Drug Policy in the Netherlands from a Public Health Perspective," Chapter 9, this volume.

24

PROHIBITION IS PERVERSE POLICY: WHAT WAS TRUE IN 1933 IS TRUE NOW

John P. Morgan

In January 1930, Harry Gross of Boston perfected an adulteration formula for his brand of medicinal tonic, Jamaica ginger extract. This tonic was widely used, along with other alcohol packaging, to skirt the laws of alcohol prohibition and to deliver beverage alcohol to people of the United States. The two-ounce bottle of ginger extract was, by law, to contain at least 75 percent ethanol. The product had grown in popularity to the point that this single manufacturer-distributor had purchased in one month enough raw material to prepare 500,000 individual bottles, although he shipped some material in barrels as well. Gross shipped the new "Jake" in late January and early February of 1930. By March, newspapers of the "southern rim" (Kansas City, Oklahoma City, Richmond, Cincinnati) reported the emergence of a paralysis caused by adulterant tricresyl phosphate (TCP). Ultimately 50,000 or more people were permanently paralyzed.[1,2] There are many things surprising about the Jamaica ginger episode, but perhaps the most unusual is the minor impact it had on the thinking of the people of the United States. The episode seldom merits a footnote in standard books on alcohol prohibition, and a reading of the documents of the 1930 to 1933 indicates that the sufferers received little sympathy or support, and the ending of federal alcohol prohibition may have had little to do with this devastating event. Those who still account federal prohibition as positive for health do not know of or mention the Jamaica ginger paralysis.

The "Jake" episode illustrates at least four important, even ubiquitous, outcomes of prohibition of drugs and intoxicants:

1. Prohibition engenders criminal enterprises and criminal subcultures.
2. Prohibition generates more potent forms of the forbidden substance.
3. Prohibition enlarges drug toxicity by contamination and adulteration.
4. Those poisoned by interdicted substances in their potent or contaminated forms are blamed for their disabilities, or even their deaths, because they were engaging in outlawed conduct, conduct made outlaw by prohibition.

A RECENT AND RELATED PROHIBITION OUTCOME

On February 4, 1991, the *New York Times* reported a number of deaths and hospitalizations of heroin users in the Northeast (New York City; Hartford, Connecticut; Newark and Paterson, New Jersey).[3] The near-final toll was 17 deaths and 200 hospitalizations in a short period of time. "Heroin" samples sold in street trade carry unusual identifying names. Many of these samples were called "Tango and Cash" after a recent death-and-mayhem movie. Early crime-lab reports identified the drug as an analog of a potent opioid, fentanyl. This particular variant was thought to be a 3-methylfentanyl (TMF).[4] TMF appeared in California as early as 1979, and has been associated with more than 100 deaths there.[5] Fentanyl is a legitimately manufactured potent opioid often used by anesthesiologists during the induction of general anesthesia. The molecule is easily subject to synthetic irregular and illicit manipulation, and a number of slight modifications have led to potent opioid products appearing in street trade, usually sold as heroin. The issue of potency here is both critical and poorly understood. Many opioids are used as analgesics and many have been used as euphoriant-intoxicants. Some are more potent than others in that they deliver analgesia or euphoria in a smaller dose. Morphine is more potent than opium extract, but heroin is more potent than morphine, and TMF is more potent than heroin. A more potent format does not guarantee a greater high nor more analgesia; it simply delivers in a smaller dosage and is therefore a better product for contraband and transportation. When a street product varies enormously in quality and content, which is invariable in an illegal market, the potent product represents a particular hazard. Although street heroin has varied in quality, it is usually of low potency and the usual bag may contain less than 5 percent actual heroin. A user of such material may not be particularly tolerant to the respiratory depressant effect of opioids and therefore at high risk for purer-than-usual heroin or a potent unknown variant such as TMF. The life of a user of illicit opioids may be much different from what we have previously assumed regarding regular use and tolerance. A recent book detailing the lives of a group of injecting addicts would indicate that they spend a significant proportion of time not using and probably not tolerant.[6]

The 1991 episode had been preceded by a similar episode in Allegheny County, Pennsylvania.[7] During 1988, at least 16 apparent overdose deaths were associated with TMF in and around Pittsburgh. Some of these users may have died from other drugs (and other diseases), but the association was shown by conducting the difficult analysis of body fluids for TMF. The article fully describing the Pittsburgh deaths appears in the *Journal of the American Medical Association* approximately three weeks after the *New York Times* reported the deaths in early February. The *JAMA* article contains a sentence that is strangely callous, although in prohibition not unusual. There is, after all, no mechanism to warn or counsel users about such an impending doom:

> Drug abusers in the northeastern United States should be considered at risk for more "designer drug" overdose outbreaks in the future.

One of the interesting features of the media coverage of "Tango and Cash" was the re-emergence of an oft-told myth. In this tale, when drug users hear of overdose deaths, they flock to the site, drawn as if they were flies attracted to honey. This drug tale always includes quotations and opinions from therapists, police, and other experts that users, in searching for the ultimate high, will risk potent drug death to obtain it. The *New York Times* coverage included the heading, "Craving for Better High Is Synthetics' Fatal Lure," and a drug user reportedly said (not about himself), "When an addict hears that someone O.D.'d, the first question they ask is: 'Where'd they get it?'"[8]

Like most myths, I assume that this one is occasionally true, although the quotations seldom come from the risk-tolerant addicts themselves. More importantly, the myth purports to tell us something essential about addicts and addiction. Addicts are inevitably drawn to the greater high. Therefore, attempts to help them by maintaining them with methadone or other clean, standardized opioids are fruitless. Further attempts to reduce harm in a variety of ways by normalizing their lives through supplying drugs, injection materials, and services would be doomed by this "junkie quest." One can imagine the nodding of heads and the clicking of tongues and other communal expressions of conventional wisdom accompanying statements such as, "Ain't that just like those junkies?"

Although these two episodes illuminate the outcomes of prohibition, I'll attempt to amplify these issues further.

POTENCY

Prohibition's chief impact on beverage alcohol was to reduce the consumption of beer. Indeed, Warburton, writing in 1932,[9] believed that the consumption of distilled spirits actually increased during prohibition. Obviously, smugglers and holders of contraband prefer gin to beer, heroin to smoking opium and volatile cocaine ("crack") to cocaine hydrochloride for sniffing. The Jamaica ginger extract (75 to 80 percent ethanol) was more potent than a legal mixed drink before prohibition. TMF may be hundreds of times more potent than heroin. Illegality may lead to infrequent buying, concealment, and rapid consumption—all forces that tend to select for potency. Any attempt to attract consumers to less potent and safer formats requires legal status and control. What we prohibit, we cannot control. Although powerful market forces and even advertising attracted turn-of-the-century buyers to relatively safe beverage cocaine and opium, such market forces cannot operate under prohibition. Outside prohibition, consumers can be attracted to wine and beer as alternatives to distilled spirits. Potency is in part a stepchild of technology and economics. Volatile cocaine enables the seller to package smaller potent units for consumer use. The hard goods may be broken down and sold in smaller units, just like selling individual apartments in a cooperative conversion. Volatile cocaine, in a variety of ways, is a response to forces generated by prohibition.

TOXICITY DUE TO CONTAMINATION

Of course, more potent preparations are inherently more toxic. They are more likely to provide primary toxicity, the pharmacological effect of the drug, such as the overdose deaths caused by TMF. In prohibition, however, secondary toxicities predominate. Secondary toxicity may be more related to the method of use and the drug and nondrug contaminants contained in contraband. Toxicity is generated in prohibition because there is no quality control, no standard of manufacture, and adulteration increases the volume of relatively pure smuggled material and therefore increases profit. The TCP in Jamaica ginger was added because solid adulterants were needed to fool FDA inspectors, who would evaporate the ginger extract and weigh the solid residue. The TCP was also chosen to replace other adulterants because it was less costly and increased profits. Of course, sellers of toxic, adulterated drugs do not face complaint or tort because they are outlaws selling to outlaws.

BLAMING VICTIMS

Both the Jake victims and the TMF-exposed heroin users were blamed for what happened to them. There is, I think, little doubt that the attempt to generate concern and humanitarian services to drug and alcohol users by the discussion of these conditions as diseases does not transform the attitudes held toward them as criminals under prohibition.

It might also be true that the disease model best fits those with middle-class behavior and status. The Jake victims were overwhelmingly poor and nearly universally out of work. Many of those interviewed in Cincinnati had left failing farms and mines in Kentucky and Tennessee and were down and out in urban slums. Most of the northeastern victims of TMF were minority, urban Americans. It is a simple thing to blame them for their lawlessness and assume that they have received nothing more than they deserved. In no instance, however, does the blaming of victims pervade society more than in the treatment of those at risk for or infected with the human immunodeficiency virus—because of injection drug use.

AIDS AS TOXIN AND AS STIGMA

New York City recently canceled its only clean-needle exchange program for injecting addicts[10,11] The Health Commissioner felt that any needle exchange would be "sending the wrong message." This curious phrase is commonly used by those who war on drugs. It may signal that a particular policy has failed in accomplishing any substantive goal but is perversely maintained because it has symbolic and moral value. An important component of the drug problems in the United States relates to the erection of unenforceable and harmful laws just because we want to "send a message." Our laws are generated by a moral repugnance directed at drug use, and we are easily fooled that the moral message sent by the law accomplishes something other than comforting the writers of the laws and their constituencies.

AIDS and the spread of the human immunodeficiency virus (HIV) (secondary toxicity) is a direct result of prohibition. In New York and many other states, not only is heroin illegal (and contaminated), but also the means to deliver it are illegal. Users therefore recirculate needles and syringes contaminated with HIV. Acknowledging that some needle-sharing has grown out of ritual and carelessness, there is overwhelming evidence that a policy of supplying clean needles and syringes will decrease AIDS prevalence in injecting addicts. In Liverpool, England, drug programs committed to the idea that drug-harm reduction is essential while injectors continue to use, have had health workers in the streets distributing bleach, clean needles, syringes, advice, and condoms since the evidence emerged that HIV is spread by injecting addicts. The rate of HIV positivity in Liverpool addicts approaches zero[12] compared with a New York City rate of approximately 60 percent.[13] Again, the needle laws, which do *not* diminish drug abuse, are laws designed to send a message. In this case, the message sent to injecting addicts seems to be, "I wish you were dead." The same message, come to think of it, is always sent to addicts by prohibition. Some critics of needle availability comfort themselves by believing that addict behavior is immutable and that needle supply will not help. The data I have cited above and survey data in New York[13] indicate that such statements are untrue. Society should accept that ethanol and heroin users can change their behavior. The supply of clean needles so that more injecting addicts are not sentenced to death may give them the time to stop being addicts.

CRIMINAL ENTERPRISES

The generation of a criminal enterprise in 1920 to 1930 and today is clear—a result of the value-added tax imposed on drugs by prohibition. The majority of deaths associated with cocaine in New York City are not due to psychopharmacological rage or murderous attempts to gain money to purchase drugs. A New York State drug-research unit estimates that 85 percent of cocaine-associated murder is secondary to turf conflicts and other battles related to drug business.[14] The increase in shooting deaths in New York City might also indicate that the market for volatile cocaine is relatively saturated, concurrent with recent evidence of a decline in use.[15]

Sigma Chemical sells pure cocaine to investigators at $80.40 for five grams ($42.90 for five grams of free base or volatile cocaine). Accordingly, the price of legal cocaine is approximately $14 to $16 per gram. The purchase price of street cocaine may be $100 per gram but this product is 20 to 50 percent pure, so a more correct retail illegal price is $250 to $300 per gram. This precedes the division of the product into small doses of volatile cocaine, further increasing the retail price. The cost of prohibition is determined by multiplying the legal price (which includes, I assume, a fair profit) by a factor of 20 or 25 or more. This range of profit and product desirability generates a criminal enterprise that has always been with us and will always be with us, because it is the cost of prohibition. The perverse nature of prohibition is clear. This phenomenon guarantees profit to those that the policy ostensibly wishes to hurt. The value-added tax is collected only by those engaged in drug business.

When William Bennett, our recently resigned drug czar, was asked about his personal addiction to nicotine, he retorted that despite the addiction, he did not engage in drive-by shootings. If tobacco were illegal, someone would. If tobacco were illegal, there would be an enormous clandestine farming and harvesting effort, the probable manufacture of high-nicotine-content products, and a powerful national distribution system with armed enforcers. The absence of highly potent nicotine and alcohol is a product of their legal status. The absence of a large and important black market is also a product of that legal status.

The continued decline in use and the continued advertising and sale of less potent alcohol and nicotine products also rely on their legal status.

HEALTH AND PROHIBITION

Many of the counterarguments against the ending of prohibition are health-related. Although the discussion and the evaluation of the harm drugs do is important, such discussion has little to do with this debate. The elimination (or modification) of useless and harmful law would not mean that the behavior previously interdicted was condoned, nor would it mean that the now-normalized commodity was safe and approved. Even if I were convinced that illegal drugs did much more harm than is currently apparent, and even if I believed that more of the harm was pharmacological (and not secondary to prohibition), I would still be opposed to the prohibition/criminal justice model. I do not believe that drug use is safe and I am not an advocate of casual illegal or legal consumption of psychoactive drugs. I believe that the best way to make an impact on the drug problems of America is to bring agents under control and not subject them to the wildness of the illegal market. I believe cocaine is entirely too dangerous to be illegal. It was a mistake for those of us who favored the decriminalization of marijuana in the early 1970s to rely so heavily on the safety of the drug. Safety and danger have little to do with neotemperance, which is a moral movement, not an antitoxicity movement.

Prohibitionists are prone (as we all are) to identify as dangerous what is offensive, repugnant, and immoral. Drug misinformation about toxicity is a part of the war on drugs and it serves many purposes. It is frequently stated that marijuana smoke is more carcinogenic than tobacco smoke.[16] This commonly appears in the ads generated by the Partnership for a Drug-Free America. There is actually no proof for such a statement and its origin is largely obscured. The particulate content of inhaled marijuana or tobacco is approximately the same. Marijuana cigarette smokers engage in both deep inhalation and breath-holding, which increase the proportion of solids deposited per cigarette. This finding, in part, led to the above careless statement about marijuana carcinogenicity. Of course, a "heavy" smoker of marijuana consumes 3 or 4 cigarettes per day, while a heavy tobacco smoker may consume 40 or more cigarettes per day. This probably explains the rarity of reported carcinoma in marijuana smokers. If data emerged tomorrow that marijuana could cause carcinoma, however, that would not temper my desire to decriminalize it.

COCAINE

The cocaine and volatile-cocaine issues must be discussed, since some people are convinced that decriminalization of cocaine would lead to unrestrained use because of its enormous seduction and "addictiveness." A number of recent writers about cocaine offer data that belie the distorted claims of media, treatment professionals, and reformed cocaine users.[17,18,19] Both sniffed and volatile cocaine can be used in a nondependent fashion and, as we would expect from previous drug experience, the majority of users do not go on to problematic ("addictive") use. Our usual sources of drug experience confirm this.

In the annual High School Senior Survey,[20] the use of both sniffed and volatile cocaine has recently diminished in the seniors and in an older follow-up group. These data are confirmed by the NIDA Household Survey,[21] Approximately 21 million people in this country have tried cocaine but only 8 million have used it in the past year (before the survey). Three million used it in the past month. Of those 3 million recent users, some 300,000 use it on a daily basis. Therefore, 10 percent of recent users and 1.5 percent of those who have ever tried the drug may qualify as problematic users. Of high school seniors, 4.8 percent in 1987 ever tried smoking cocaine but only 3.1 percent used it in the past year. The percent using in the past month was 1.6. Therefore, of those ever trying this drug in this format, two-thirds have not tried it again in the past year. Cocaine, even in volatile forms, appears to be less seductive than tobacco or alcohol in terms of ability to provoke continued use.

The volatile-cocaine issue typifies a familiar theme. A new drug or drug format (usually potent and exciting to the media and generated by prohibition) is introduced to a small group of Americans. These *avant garde*, usually young and affluent, use the drug and a few have trouble. Although we are concerned about these well-off, experimenting youth, we are not frightened of them. Fear and terror and the call for the crusade come with the democratization of drug use. Just as occurred with heroin users before the 1914 Harrison Narcotics Act, the perceived democratized cocaine user is youthful, urban, male, minority, dangerous, and easily corruptible.[22] The use of criminalization is based in part on a moral repugnance, but also on our attempt to use the criminal justice sanction to control youthful, wanton, underclass behavior related to drugs.

Drug Use after Prohibition

We actually have a series of unplanned (and therefore somewhat unfocused) surveys of post-prohibition behavior regarding marijuana. In the 1970s, a number of state and a few local jurisdictions revised their marijuana laws. Eric Single, who has written extensively about these reforms, notes that they did not decriminalize marijuana, although the 1970s reforms are always referred to with the decriminalization term.[23,24] These laws all reduced the penalties for possession of small amounts of marijuana to less than incarceration. Frequently, the penalties were reduced to small fines and the crimes adjudged as misdemeanors. In every instance, a criminal classification and sanction were retained. Since relatively few marijuana smokers are caught and punished, the actual impact of a reduction in penalties might be minimal. On the other hand, an evaluation of any change following such a law might assess the ability of such a law to send a message, right or wrong.

In Single's words:

> . . . trends in use appear to have been relatively unaffected by the existing criminal laws against possession. Under these circumstances, one would expect "decriminalization" to result in minimal changes in the number of users. . . .

In two American states, Ohio and California, surveys in 1975 and 1976 preceded and followed the decriminalization reform. In Ohio, the law was passed in November 1975. Use in those aged 18 to 24 increased by 6 percent by 1978, and by 12 percent in those aged 25 to 34. In California, the proportion of adult users increased from 28 to 35 percent in the eleven months after decriminalization. This kind of increase, even if real, was thought to reflect the small rate of increase that was already underway in these states, and unrelated to the lesser penalties.

Single discovered an interesting set of "experiments" in the community of Ann Arbor, Michigan. Stuart and his colleagues had analyzed over a period of time self-reported drug use in Ann Arbor during a time of frequent change in the law.[25] During the study, Ann Arbor moved from prohibition to reduction in penalty (still involving possible incarceration), a maximum $5 fine, reinstatement of severe penalties, and "decriminalization" again. Data collected at Ann Arbor and control communities with no change in the law indicated no impacts resulting from these legal changes.

I have previously discussed the annual High School Senior Survey. The authors of this ongoing assessment oversampled respondents in decriminalization states, both those which decriminalized early and late in the 1970s. Their study assessed the time period 1975 to 1980. They identified no impact of decriminalization in comparing these states to others in the sample. Although there was some increasing use,

> . . . any increase in marijuana use in the decriminalization states, taken as a group, was equal to or less than increases being observed in the rest of the country where decriminalization was not taking place. . . .[26]

Further, the most striking demonstration in these surveys is the evidence of the national decline in marijuana use. The national samples of the High School Senior Survey and the NIDA Household Survey show a decline in marijuana prevalence in essentially every age group and parameter of use beginning in 1979 and continuing to the current day.

There were no differences in 1979–80 between reform and nonreform states. All, whether marijuana use has been normalized or not, showed the national decline. This finding would not necessarily indicate that the law had no impact (although in marijuana's case that may have been so); however, the law was less important than a variety of other factors determining use.

DRUG SALES AND PYRAMIDING

The following words are from a slender volume called *Getting Started in the Illegal Drug Trade*:

> When a client comes to you short five dollars for a gram or pays for it with several one- and five-dollar bills . . . he is scraping to get his money together. This will be your first sales representative. . . . When he comes for a gram, pull out an eighth of an ounce, which is three and a half grams, and put a half gram of cut on it for him. . . . You have handed him an amount of cocaine he can sell for four hundred dollars.[27]

This newly franchised dealer will sell to two or three buyers, make his money, and have cocaine for himself. This process is best called "pyramiding." The relatively high price of the commodity means the small-volume user may become a small-volume dealer and *recruit* other users. When any legal supply is absent, the heat of pyramiding is great. The marketing of cocaine more resembles the marketing of Tupperware than the retail sale of other expensive commodities. Prohibition may exert forces such as this one, actually increasing drug use.

ETHANOL PROHIBITION, CIRRHOSIS, AND HEALTH

Recently, a number of writers have emerged, aggressively stating that not all the impacts of federal prohibition of beverage alcohol were negative. Despite the failures of prohibition to control liquor smuggling and trafficking, and despite the evidence that it spawned or at least abetted a criminal enterprise, it still was good for health, they say. The ideas here focus on the belief that prohibition caused a prominent decline in alcohol consumption, and that the decline caused a marked diminution in alcohol toxicities, particularly cirrhosis and alcohol psychosis. These concepts almost always are part of an antireform statement claiming that these laws of the 1920s, like our laws of today, at least diminished use. Aaron and Musto stated this viewpoint in 1981:

> Death rates from cirrhosis were 29.5 per 100,000 in 1911 for men and 10.7 in 1929; admissions to state mental hospitals for disease classed as alcoholic psychosis fell from 10.1 in 1919 to 3.7 in 1922, rising to 4.7 by 1928.[28]

Aaron and Musto relied for their data on a 1932 report by Emerson, which discussed mortality and morbidity in relation to prohibition.[29]

These points and others have been made by history professor John Burnham. He believes that the idea that prohibition did not work and that it abetted the growth of crime constitute a stereotype. He believes that prohibition "worked relatively well":

> Per capita alcoholic consumption declined to very much less than half the pre-prohibition (1910) figure and remained low for decades even after 1933. . . .[30]

Burnham, in another article, discusses the diminished consumption in more detail and illuminates an important confusion about the timing of the decline in consumption:

> The best figures available show that the gallons of pure alcohol ingested per person varied widely over four different periods. In the period 1911–1914, the amount was 1.69 gallons. Under the wartime restrictions, 1918–1919, the amount decreased to .97. In the early years of national prohibition, 1921–1922, there was still further decrease to .73 gallons. In the later years of prohibition, 1927–1930, the amount rose to 1.14 gallons.[31]

Burnham signals the reality, as did Aaron and Musto, that the actual span of federal prohibition, 1920 to 1933, did not solely show decreases in alcohol morbidity and that much of the decline in consumption and cirrhosis *preceded* federal prohibition. If alcohol psychosis dropped until 1922, why did it increase again by 1928? If alcohol consumption declined steadily to 1922, why had it increased again by 1927 to 1930?

A visible and influential defense of prohibition was written for the *New York Times* by Mark H. Moore. In "Actually, Prohibition Was a Success," he describes the decline in alcohol consumption, cirrhosis, and alcohol psychosis previously noted by Aaron and Musto, and adds a decline in arrests for public drunkenness and disorderly conduct, all of which he attributes to prohibition.[32] In Moore's article, it becomes clear that a number of these declines "related to prohibition" began before prohibition and some reversed their declines before the repeal of prohibition in 1933. As previously noted, the decline in cirrhosis began in 1911. The decline in alcohol psychosis began well before 1920, and the decline in arrests for public drunkenness reported by Moore only bridged the years 1916 to 1922.

Aaron and Musto, and Burnham rely for data on the 1932 publication of Clark Warburton. Moore, who does not cite references in his *Times* article elsewhere, also cites Warburton along with Hyman,[33] who also relies to a degree on Warburton.

WARBURTON'S CALCULATIONS

Warburton compiled *The Economic Results of Prohibition* in part under the sponsorship of the Association Against the Prohibition Amendment. Because of this relationship, some have expressed reservations about his data, but many of those who believe in the healthful aspects of prohibition cite him.

Warburton does not generate a unitary thesis about this argument, but his data provide one. There was an apparent decline in alcohol consumption beginning as early as 1907 in the United States. Such a decrease may have related to the temperance movement, state prohibition laws, the growth in wine consumption replacing spirits, and later World War I restrictions, but such decreases had nothing to do with federal prohibition. Warburton also believes that federal prohibition did not contribute to any decline in consumption until 1922 because of the stockpiling of liquor in anticipation of the ban. During prohibition, there was some further decline in consumption but Warburton believes that most of this decline was related to a decreasing consumption of the least potent ethanolic product, beer. Most importantly, based on a variety of indirect evidence, he believes that the consumption of distilled spirits, the most potent ethanolic beverage, increased. One of the indirect measures of this increase was the apparent increase in the incidence of cirrhosis during the later part of prohibition. Table

24.1 reflects Warburton's three-source compilation of cirrhosis incidence, indicating the apparent increase in cirrhosis during prohibition. Figure 24.1 depicts similar trends published by a strong proponent of prohibition, Irving Fisher.[34] All these forces are depicted together by (none other than) Moore and Gerstein in Figure 24.2.[35] The proponents of the view that prohibition was healthy all rely on data that seem quite clearly to portray exactly the opposite.

The decline in ethanol consumption preceding federal prohibition seems likely to relate to the reported decline in cirrhosis and less strongly to some other consequences of alcohol toxicity. Since cirrhosis occurs as a direct result of ethanol-related tissue toxicity, an absolute decline in dosage could have caused the decline in tissue toxicity. Despite this correlation, it is very important to realize that this hazard only exists for heavy drinkers—not the 90 percent plus quotient of ethanol consumers whose dose remains below the threshold of hepatic or other tissue damage. It seems very likely that federal prohibition rather than aiding the previously established decrease in cirrhosis actually *reversed* it. By contributing in a number of ways to forces enhancing the consumption of and marketing of more potent alcoholic products, prohibition caused a rebound in cirrhosis. Prohibition in 1920 to 1933 was a peculiarly perverse, even ignoble experiment. By engendering a shift to more potent and dangerous drugs, it actually enhanced alcohol's pharmacological and toxicological hazards by enhancing potency. Moore, Aaron and Musto, and Burnham all have it exactly wrong. Prohibition was a policy satisfying moral precepts which had nothing to do with diminishing alcohol hazards that it actually enhanced.

CONCLUSION

It is still necessary for those interested in drug-policy reform to spend most time and effort dealing with improper and undocumented claims that support neotemperance. When the untruths regarding marijuana toxicity, the seductiveness of crack, and the economic benefits of urine testing (to those who do not sell urine tests) are dealt with, Congressman Rangel and others begin to ask for specific post-prohibition plans. The political movement to generate such plans has begun. Senator Joseph Galiber of New York has introduced a bill to establish a state drug authority to oversee (and tax) the sale of legal drugs through a state store. Thirty-five percent of Americans, according to a poll of the Drug Policy Foundation, would support legalization of some drugs as an alternative to the continued war on drugs.[36] This poll was conducted by the Drug Policy Foundation, an educational entity dedicated to drug-policy reform and part of the political movement described.

To begin, I would completely decriminalize marijuana tomorrow and require

TABLE 24.1.   PROHIBITION, PUBLIC HEALTH, AND SAFETY:
DEATH RATES FROM DISEASE ASSOCIATED WITH
THE USE OF ALCOHOL, 1900 TO 1930
(RATE PER 100,000 INHABITANTS OR INSURED)

Year	Cirrhosis of the Liver		
	(1)	(2)	(3)
1900	12.9	12.6	
1901	13.6	13.0	
1902	13.9	12.9	
1903	14.5	13.5	
1904	5.8	5.3	
1905	6.2	6.0	
1906	6.4	6.4	
1907	7.3	7.5	
1908	5.0	5.1	
1909	5.1	5.5	
1910	5.4	5.6	
1911	4.9	5.3	4.0
1912	5.3	5.9	5.3
1913	5.9	6.6	5.2
1914	4.9	5.4	4.7
1915	4.4	4.8	4.1
1916	5.8	7.4	5.1
1917	5.2	6.4	5.9
1918	2.7	3.0	1.8
1919	1.6	1.8	1.4
1920	1.0	1.2	0.6
1921	1.8	1.9	0.9
1922	2.6	3.3	2.1
1923	3.2	4.3	3.0
1924	3.2	4.5	2.9
1925	3.6	5.1	3.0
1926	3.9	5.3	3.7
1927	4.0	5.4	3.5
1928	4.0	4.3	3.3
1929	3.7	5.2	3.5
1930			3.2

(1) Registration area of the United States.
(2) Registration states of 1900.
(3) Registration Industrial Department, Metropolitan Life Insurance Company.

NOTE: Death rates, reported from a variety of sources, adapted from Warburton, illuminate a general pattern of decline in cirrhosis from 1902–1903 to 1921; during the period of federal prohibition the decline stopped and may have shown a reversal.

FIGURE 24.1

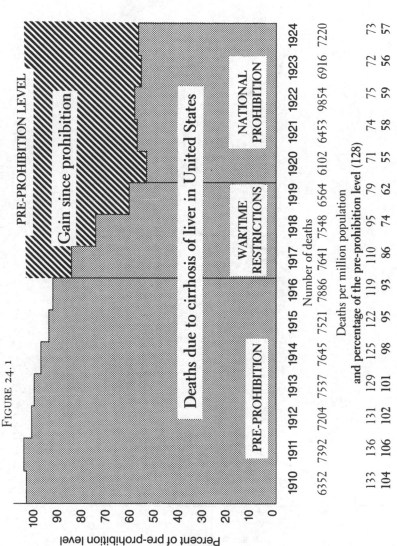

Deaths due to cirrhosis of liver in United States

	1910	1911	1912	1913	1914	1915	1916	1917	1918	1919	1920	1921	1922	1923	1924
Number of deaths	6352	7392	7204	7537	7645	7521	7886	7641	7548	6564	6102	6453	9854	6916	7220
Deaths per million population															
and percentage of the pre-prohibition level (128)	133	136	131	129	125	122	119	110	95	79	71	74	75	72	73
	104	106	102	101	98	95	93	86	74	62	55	58	59	56	57

NOTE: This figure from Fisher depicts, as did Warburton, a decline in cirrhosis death until federal prohibition. As clearly depicted, Fisher claims that prohibition yielded a gain, but the decline cannot be attributed to the federal prohibition of 1920 to 1933.

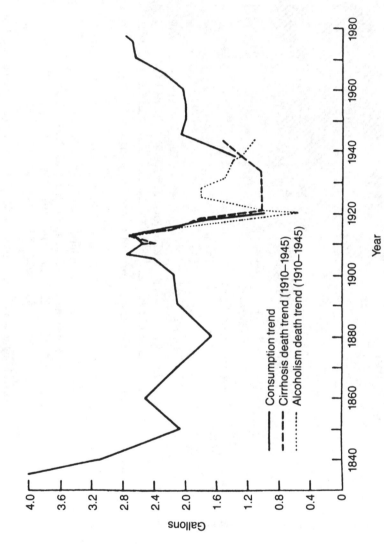

F<small>IGURE</small> 24.2

N<small>OTE</small>: This more modern figure from Moore and Gerstein supports the data presented earlier by Warburton and Fisher. The decline in alcohol consumption and cirrhosis preceded federal prohibition and was not maintained during prohibition.

only that a cigarette weighing 500 mg to 1.0 gram of marijuana would deliver 12 to 20 mg of delta-9-THC. It would be available for purchase to those over 18 with certain restrictions as to time of sale. The use of legal marijuana would be accompanied by strong penalties for driving under its influence. I would encourage the development of alternate delivery systems so that delta-9-THC could be consumed by methods other than combustion, volatilization, and inhalation.

The benefits would be profound. At no cost in increased toxicity, there would be 600,000 to 700,000 fewer arrests in the United States and perhaps $5 billion could be saved in actual police work. Delta-9-THC could be used for its therapeutic effects and we could more easily plan our decriminalization of other psychoactive substances.[37] Those millions of people who would safely use the drug would no longer be exposed to criminals to obtain it. A young man I know would, under amnesty, be released from a life sentence in a federal prison for smuggling marijuana.

Our drug policy is best described as perverse. It promotes what it wishes to stop—the corruption of youth—and it helps those it wishes to punish—retail and wholesale marketers of drugs. The only reason such a policy can continue is that it is not evaluated *as policy*. We could ask for proof of deterrence and evidence of a proper return on interdiction investment, but we do not truly wish to evaluate our drug policy. We continue this "policy" because it is a crusade—a holy war designed to buttress fondly desired moral goals and outcomes. Since drug use is a sin, we must condemn it by law, because making it legal would seem to bespeak a longing for sin. We can evaluate a policy by what it does and accomplishes. We evaluate a crusade by how it makes us feel about ourselves. Ironically, our drug policy, although using the language of health and compassion, is harmful and corrupt.

REFERENCES

1. Morgan, J. P., and Tulloss, T. "The Jake Walk Blues: A toxicological tragedy mirrored in American popular music." *Ann. Intern. Med.* 1976; 85:804–808.

2. Morgan, J. P. "The Jamaica ginger paralysis." *JAMA* 1982; 248:1864–67.

3. Nieves, E. "Toxic heroin has killed 12, officials say." *New York Times*, Feb. 4, 1991: B1–B2.

4. Knopf, A. "Overdose deaths in NYC area blamed on potent fentanyl analogs." *Substance Abuse Report* 1991; 22(4):2–3.

5. Henderson, G. L. "Designer drugs: past history and future prospects." *J. Forensic Sci.* 1988; 44:569–75.

6. Johnson, B. D., Goldstein, P. J., Preble, E., Schmeidler, J., Lipton, D. S.,

Sprint, B., Miller, T. *Taking Care of Business: The economics of crime by heroin users.* Lexington, Mass.: Lexington Books, 1985.

7. Hibbs, J., Perper, J., Winek, C. "An outbreak of designer-drug related deaths in Pennsylvania." *JAMA* 1991; 265:1011–13.

8. Treaster, J. B. "Craving for better high is synthetics' fatal lure." *New York Times*, Feb. 4, 1991: B-2.

9. Warburton, C. *The Economic Results of Prohibition.* New York: Columbia University Press, 1932; reprinted by AMS Press, New York, 1968.

10. Gillman, C. "Genesis of New York City's experimental needle exchange program." *Int. J. Drug Policy* 1989; 1(2):28–32.

11. Purdum, T. S. "Dinkins to end needle plan for drug users." *New York Times*, Feb. 14, 1990: B1-B4.

12. Stimson, G. V., Dolan, K., Donoghue, M., Last, R. "The future of UK syringe exchange." *Int. J. Drug Policy* 1990; 2(2):14–17.

13. Des Jarlais, D. C., Friedman, S. R., Novick, D. M., et al. "HIV-1 infection among intravenous drug users in Manhattan, New York City, from 1977 through 1987." *JAMA* 1989; 261(7):1008–12.

14. Goldstein, P. S. "Homicide related to drug traffic." *Bull. N.Y. Acad. Med.* 1986; 62:509–16.

15. Treaster, J. B. "New York reports a drop in crack traffic." *New York Times*, Dec. 27, 1990: C-1.

16. Tashkin, D. P., Cohen, S. "Marijuana smoking and its effects on the lungs." American Council for Drug Education, 1981.

17. Erickson, P. G., Alexander, B. K. "Cocaine and addictive liability." *Soc. Pharm.* 1989; 3:249–70.

18. Rosenbaum, M., Murphy, S., Irwin, J., Watson, L. "Women and crack: What's the real story?" *Drug Policy Letter* 1990; 2(2):2–6.

19. Cohen, P. *Cocaine use in Amsterdam in nondeviant subcultures.* Amsterdam: Universiteit van Amsterdam, 1990.

20. Johnson, L. D., O'Malley, P. M., Bachman, J. G. "Drug use, drinking, and smoking." National Survey Results, High School, College, and Young Adults Population, 1975–1988. National Institute on Drug Abuse: U.S. Department of Health and Human Services, 1989.

21. Anonymous. National Household Survey on Drug Abuse: Population Estimates, 1988. National Institute on Drug Abuse: U.S. Department of Health and Human Services, 1989 (DHSS Pub. No. (AP) 89-1636).

22. Musto, D. *The American Disease: Origins of Narcotic Control.* New Haven, Conn.: Yale University Press, 1973.

23. Single, E. W. "The impact of marijuana decriminalization," in *Research Advances in Alcohol and Drug Problems*, vol. 6, edited by Y. Israel, F. B. Glaser, H. Kalant, R. E. Popham, W. Schmidt, R. G. Smart. New York: Plenum Press, 1981, pp. 405–24.

24. Single, E. W. "The impact of marijuana decriminalization: An update." *J. Public Health Policy* 1989; 10 (4):456–66.

25. Stuart, R. B., Guise, K., Krell, M. "Penalty for the possession of marijuana: An analysis of some of its concomitants." *Contemporary Drug Problems* 1976; 5:553–61.

26. Johnson, L. D., O'Malley, D. M., Bachman, J. G. "Marijuana decriminalization: The impact on youth, 1975–1980." Monitoring the Future Occasional Paper Series: Institute for Social Research, University of Michigan, 1981 (Paper 13).

27. Long, H. S. *Getting Started in the Illicit Drug Business.* Port Townsend, Washington: Loompanics Unlimited, 1988.

28. Aaron, P., Musto, D. "Temperance and prohibition in America: An historical overview," in *Alcohol and Public Policy: Beyond the Shadow of Prohibition*, edited by M. H. Moore and D. R. Gerstein. Washington, D.C.: National Academy Press, 1981, pp. 127–80.

29. Emerson, H. "Prohibition and mortality and morbidity." *Ann. Am. Acad. Pol. Soc. Sci.* 1932; 163:53–60.

30. Burnham, J. C. "Drug decriminalization." *Science* 1989; 246:1102.

31. Burnham, J. C. "New perspectives on the prohibition 'experiment' of the 1920's." *J. Soc. Hist.* 1968; 2:51–68.

32. Moore, M. H. "Actually, prohibition was a success." *New York Times*, Oct. 16, 1989:A-21.

33. Hyman, M. H., Zimmerman, M. A., Gurioli, C., Helrick, A. *Drinkers, Driving and Alcohol-Related Mortality and Hospitalizations: A Statistical Compendium.* New Brunswick, N.J.: Rutgers University Center of Alcohol Studies, 1980.

34. Fisher, I. *Prohibition at Its Worst.* New York: Macmillan, 1926.

35. Gerstein, D. R. "Alcohol use and consequences," in *Alcohol Public Policy: Beyond the Shadow of Prohibition*, edited by M. H. Moore and D. R. Gerstein. Washington, D.C.: National Academy Press, 1981, pp. 182–224.

36. Drug Policy Foundation. *The American People Talk about Drugs: A Nationwide Survey, 1990.* Washington, D.C.: Targeting Systems Inc., 1990.

37. Randall, R. C. *Marijuana, Medicine and the Law.* Washington, D.C.: Galen Press, 1988.

25

LEGALIZATION OF DRUGS AND BEYOND LEGALIZATION

Kildare Clarke

In September 1989, President Bush addressed the nation on the topic of drugs. If his speech can be taken as an example of either his honest belief or some form of courage, then I can see no reason why in the future we should not look forward to having him declare war on people with diabetes, cardiac problems, or any other medical problem. His speech continues to propose a policy that has miserably failed. The president said, "Drugs are sapping our strength as a nation. The gravest domestic threat facing our nation is drugs. Our most serious problem today is cocaine."

I firmly believe that the president's statement, on strict scrutiny, could not be supported by statistical analysis or casual observation. Yes, there is a problem with drugs but not in the form the president and his drug advisors want the American public to believe.

The president held a plastic bag with some white substance in it and said, "This is crack cocaine, seized a few days ago by the Drug Enforcement Administration agents in a park just across from the White House."

Here I will leave it up to your own imagination as to the sincerity of the agents' ability to find a poor, black person selling crack in beautiful Lafayette Park.

The president had the perfect opportunity to confront the nation with the real drug problem—that we do have a medical emergency on our hands, and if our policy of looking at the problem as a criminal one continues, we will be committing genocide.

The president, instead, did what most politicians whose primary motive is to get elected would have done at the cost of human suffering. He exploited the problem in the same view as he had done in his election campaign, in transforming the image of Willie Horton into an image larger than it should have been. The president and Secretary Bennett's war on drugs is a political war. It is more a war on the people, being waged not by doctors or scientists, but by the street-level bureaucrats (police officers) and the politicians. The story of the so-called drug war only plays to the prejudices of an audience that is somewhat eager to believe the worst that can be said about some people whom they would rather not hear about and their suffering, such as poverty, lack of education, skills, and homelessness express an implied racism (the forgotten group—blacks and hispanics).

The perception of the so-called leaders, who are generally white and privileged, living in safe neighborhoods, who most likely have never witnessed a drug deal or seen a drug addict, with the exception being on TV, is that the drug problem is a black or hispanic creation.

The question we must be concerned about is what is really happening in the world in general, and America specifically? Do we have a drug problem? The answer to that is "yes." When we talk about the drug problem, it is automatically assumed by most people that crack cocaine, ice, LSD, pot, and all the other illicit drugs are the culprits, and their assumptions would be correct. Those people have forgotten that alcohol, tobacco, and the prescribed mood drugs such as valium, librium, demerol, and the like are also drugs—why?

As a physician and a lawyer who is on the front line daily, let me try to put the problem into its proper focus and give credible evidence why there is rational reason for the legalization of drugs, which is long overdue, and the need for the real leaders of society, who are the people and not some mindless bureaucrats, to demand immediate action to stop the war on us, the people, which is being waged now.

Please allow me to start by giving you three examples of what is happening daily, and not some contrived incident to further my political aspirations at the expense of the unfettered human suffering.

In December 1988, I had the unfortunate duty to pronounce the death by gunshot of an eighteen-year-old Hispanic male as his younger brother sobbed and his mother looked on in great pain. She wanted to cry but was unable to do so, being overwhelmed with sad pain. Six months later, the same mother looked on as I pronounced the death by gunshot wound of her second son, who had earlier sobbed over his brother's death. He was seventeen years old and had $7,000 in his pocket. No one had to ask where he got the money.

Sunday, February 2, 1990, six major gunshot wounds and two major stab wounds arrived in the emergency department of Kings County Hospital, victims of the drug war. Among the six was a sixteen-year-old recidivist who had been discharged from the hospital only one month earlier, after suffering three gunshot wounds to his chest and neck. Prominently placed on both sides of his neck were the scars from the surgical exploration of his neck wounds in the successful attempt to save his life. Now he is among the February 1990 statistics with two more gunshot wounds. He is one of the lucky ones that I can write and talk about, but how long will such luck continue before he is included in the statistics of the not so lucky, only to be remembered by a tombstone, at best? (See Table 25.1 and Figures 25.1 and 25.2.)

In our frantic race against time to save his life, his beeper and a substantial amount of money were in his possession. Those who were present as friends of his had major concern about the beeper and the money while his beeper was beeping. These objects were of paramount importance and interest for them to secure, with little concern for his chance of survival.

Our concern was the extent of his damage, and special diagnostic tests were arranged; during this time the patient's concern was focused on other things. His statement to us was, "I just want to get the fuck out of here; I have things to do." Despite our best efforts in reasoning with the patient about his condition and its gravity, and his mother's involvement in the process, it was unsuccessful. She could not control her son's inappropriate behavior; instead she had to agree with him to sign out of the hospital against medical advice, thereby becoming a passive, participating captive of the drug war.

There should be no question in one's mind as to the nature of this young man's urgent business affair which required his immediate attention, forcing him to leave the hospital dismissing all other factors, including his own health status.

J.B. is sixteen years old, arrested for having a loaded gun along with a substantial quantity of crack and money while attending a party. In the hospital the patient was a clean-cut, decent young man, and when asked why a decent young man like him would get involved with drugs and guns, his answer was, "My mother is in jail upstate for drug possession and I have five sisters to care for. I did not want to do anything illegal such as stealing nor do I want to work at McDonalds for $3.50 an hour; therefore, I am doing the thing which can provide for the family."

The gun was given to him by his drug overlord to protect himself against other dealers and robbers, who sometimes prey on younger drug dealers. It is clear that these young entrepreneurs' motive is to achieve the American dream—which is to make as much money as possible through whatever means, because money translates into power. They have learned from the history of Western civilization and, more so, American history that the best way to control any territory is through armed force, even at the expense of death to others. Panama, Grenada, and the Middle East are good examples. These dealers in a sense are builders of the empire in the same order as other barons or superpower countries have done in the past and present.

Why illicit drugs as the means to achieve the American dream and not real

TABLE 25.1. ADULT EMERGENCY DEPARTMENT: GUN-SHOT VS. STAB-WOUND COMPARISON

	Jan	Feb	Mar	Apr	May	June	July	Aug	Sept	Oct	Nov	Dec	Total	Percent
Gun-shot Wounds, 1988	54	39	66	49	71	72	71	86	69	56	36	77	746	61.4%
Stabs Wounds, 1988	36	34	32	37	48	45	43	38	36	35	48	37	469	38.6%
Total	90	73	98	86	119	117	114	124	105	91	84	114	1,215	
Gun-shot Wounds, 1989	68	59	58	58	65	73	69	84	89	94	57	94	868	62.6%
Stab Wounds, 1989	35	31	46	39	41	51	51	49	45	50	35	45	518	37.4%
Total	103	90	104	97	106	124	120	133	134	144	92	139	1,386	
Gun-shot Wounds, 1990	90	67	69	71	82	108	101	85	95	75	—	—	843	63.8%
Stab Wounds, 1990	54	51	43	49	49	47	39	47	56	43	—	—	478	36.2%
Total	144	118	112	120	131	155	140	132	151	118	—	—	1,321	

428

FIGURE 25.1

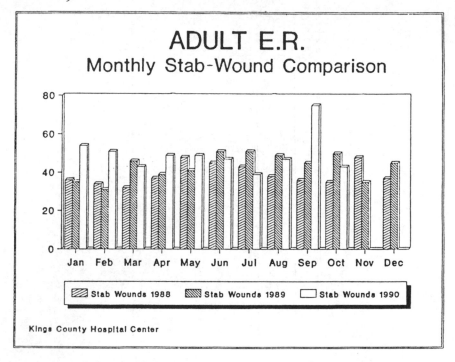

estate, medicine, corporate law, financing, or the like? The answer is academic: The meteoric rise to fame and power is within their grasp, without risk of long-term work under the control of racism, which has provided very little chance of upward mobility as witnessed by their surroundings. The promise of staying in school to become a lawyer, teacher, doctor, or law-enforcement officer seems too remote to be realized. The instantaneous gratification of quick wealth and power dictates the irrationality of delayed gratification to achieve academic greatness and to realize the American dream.

Why such choice by these entrepreneurs? Should society be blamed, or the individual? Instead of looking at whom to blame, as we so invariably do, let us become more expansive and seek solutions other than the current failed drug policy the administration is pursuing.

We as a nation that prides itself as the pacesetter of the modern world should not become egosyntonic to the point of destruction. Even the communist governments of the USSR and other countries have recognized where failure has occurred and the need for change. Can't we arrive at such compelling conclusion of our failed drug policy and stop deluding ourselves, or must we wait until the streets of the suburbs are paved with the blood of the privileged, as is now occurring

FIGURE 25.2

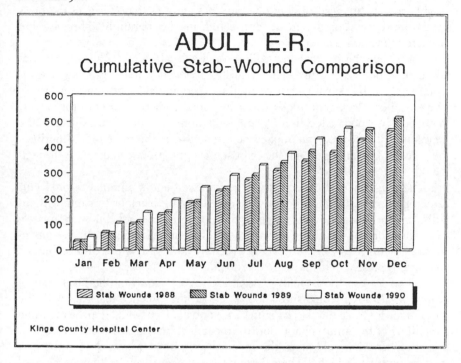

ADULT E.R.

Cumulative Stab-Wound Comparison

Kings County Hospital Center

hourly in the city streets for the poor, before we arrive at the conclusion that legalization of all drugs is the only rational solution to the drug problem?

Let us not repeat another Vietnam experience where the cry of immorality of the war became a concern to the whole nation, and Congress and the president reacted when and only when the sons of the privileged were seeing action, with the coffins containing their remains returning with the grim reminder that their loved ones are now only a memory.

The use of drugs cuts across all ethnic, religious, cultural, sexual, racial, and socioeconomic lines. The huge profits made from drug sales are so inextricably interwoven with this country's economy that it has become impossible to remove drugs without substantial impact on the economy.

Drug use and sales seem to be an urban problem because of focused reporting. This also, although wrong, is understandable. Urban settings are where news gathering is easily done. Most of the major drug hauls, where tons of cocaine are confiscated, do not occur in the ghetto as one would have expected, based on the news reporting. Instead, these hauls are done in the wealthy neighborhoods of Hollywood, Long Island, or Westchester County. Certainly these neighborhoods are not the domain of the poor black and hispanic males who are usually portrayed as the culprits of the drug trade, nor are the drugs found in these neighborhoods financed or controlled by these groups. The focus of the news media, however, is on the urban centers and, maybe, rightfully so because that is where the violence occurs daily.

I must emphasize that my calling for the legalization of all drugs is not advocating the use of drugs. There are those who said that legalizing drugs is tantamount to black genocide; I think those people have glaucomatous vision. The so-called black genocide is occurring now, with the current drug policy. With poverty, poor education at best, and none at worse, no skills and the prevalence of expressed and implied racism as part of the milieu for minorities, the perceived means by which they can achieve the American dream is through the sale of illegal drugs.

The illegality of drugs sets the stage for arrest and a criminal record. This black or hispanic male or female is doomed. Being black or hispanic without skills, unable to read or write properly, and a criminal record almost completely closes him or her out of the job market. Their future is sealed in the pits of continued criminality because they are seen by their past, which also becomes a continuous present. That is the real genocide.

Let us look at the benefits of legalization. By removing the black market profits, legalization would substantially reduce the violence that goes with the illegal trade for turf control (see Figures 25.3 and 25.4). It would stop the maiming and killing of the innocent and not-so-innocent. It would stop the killing of our police officers. It would allow the medical profession to treat drug abuse as a medical problem, which is where it rightfully belongs. By seeing this as a medical problem, we will have better control, thereby reducing death by overdose and from impurities, and the transmission of AIDS from dirty needles. The beneficial effects on communities and families would be just as pronounced. We could provide good role models and preserve our future leaders. Parents who, too often, take orders from their drug-wealthy children would have greater authority to discipline them and convince them to stay in school. Immediately the jail population would be reduced, making room for the real problem-makers of society such as the muggers and murderers. No longer would the faith of these black and hispanic men be blighted by an arrest record for the sale or possession of drugs. One more obstacle in their path would be removed, to be replaced with a productive zeal.

With no more power and prestige and no large amounts of cash coming from drug profits, the dealers' focus would be redirected toward a rational choice of conformity, to an acceptable method by which the American dream can be realized.

I will admit that the legalization of all drugs might cause an initial increase in their use. There are those who say, and will continue to echo as a matter of fact without proof, that legalization will cause a dramatic rise in the use of drugs.

Figure 25.3

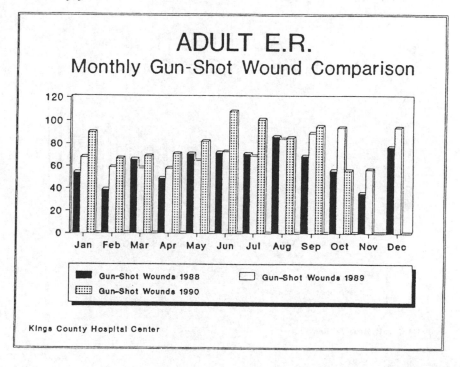

ADULT E.R.
Monthly Gun-Shot Wound Comparison

Kings County Hospital Center

These are the same people who are demanding that those of us calling for legalization (the so-called pro-legalizers) produce statistical and scientific proof to substantiate the claimed benefits of legalization. I would like to remind all that the majority of our technological advancements came about because of creative thinking and foresightedness, and not governance of absolute certainty. If statistical data and proof were the prerequisite for the Wright Brothers' development of the airplane, today we would probably be without an aircraft to zip us across the world. Let's get on with the business of discussing the real issues, which should be the expected and unexpected fallout from legalization. The drug problem can be approached in one of two methods if we intend to be honest, in the true meaning of honesty:

1. Legalization, testing, education, treatment, and prevention
2. Illegality, with criminal sanction, without treatment

The second method, which is basically the current administration policy, to have a combination of illegality with criminal sanction and at the same time talk about

FIGURE 25.4

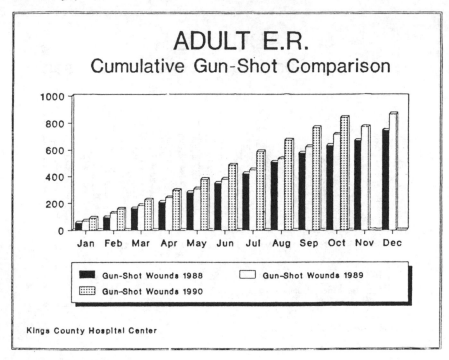

treatment, is begging the question. What is essentially being done is to treat someone's conscience by accepting a quasi-medical model of the problem, yet in the same view advocating imprisonment as the cure. This type of thinking seems schizophrenic; if not, then we should also put people with other medical problems, such as strokes, heart attack, hypertension, AIDS, or cancer, in jail.

I am sure the thought of such action would immediately cause anarchy. If we really accept the current drug policy of illegality, then let's stop wasting taxpayers' money providing treatment and put the users and dealers in prison, allowing the prison to achieve the purpose of confinement, which is punishment and rehabilitation for future productive life. With the legalization model, we can look at drug use the way it should be seen; that is, as a medical problem. Indelibly attached to the medical model is testing for diagnostic purposes with resultant treatment and prevention, the linchpin that drives medicine.

Unlike the non-legalizers' use of the quasi-medical model, the pro-legalizers must respect and accept the medical model in its totality. The medical model would provide an honest approach to the problem of crack babies, which are so often written about. To the delight of all, the medical model would substantially reduce the number of crack babies because the mothers-to-be could now seek early help, either because they have been discovered during testing or on their own accord, without the fear of the unborn child and other children being taken away from them under the rubric of "unfit mother."

The scorn of drug use and abuse would be removed, to be replaced with the same level of care given to all other medical problems. There are those who would oppose the use of testing because of the inherent fear of governmental abuse of power and employers' transgression under the guise of sound business practice. These are genuine concerns that must be put to rest by legislative safeguards. Testing must be purely for prevention and treatment and not for punishment, by express or implied means. To talk about drug legalization without testing is tantamount to a bad surgeon who carries out a colon resection for cancer without first doing a barium enema with G.I. series. The nay-sayers will continue to spread the fear that legalization will be the demise of society. It is important to remind them that legalization is not a fool's folly; therefore, it cannot occur without a certain degree of limit, just as we now have with alcohol.

There must be laws governing the operation of motor vehicles while impaired or intoxicated from drugs. There must be a certain standard to govern the amount of drugs that can be found in someone's system before certain action can be taken against such individual. It will be left to each person to decide what is more important to him or her—drugs or employment.

The outcome of legalization is not destruction, as some would like us to believe. Instead, it is the avoidance of destruction, to be replaced with constructive prevention, such as of early death from guns. There must be laws that focus on the control of guns and severe penalties for those found with such weapons.

With the legalization of drugs and the shift of focus to real crime, the streets would become more available to every citizen without fear of being killed by bullets. The highways and airways must be maintained safe for all users; therefore, the irresponsible drug-users must be punished severely. The issue of roadblocks and checkpoints is a given, as currently practiced concerning alcohol.

All these measures will be necessary to fulfill a rational governmental interest, which is the protection of society without transgression of the individuals' rights.

In closing, I must stress that I have been searching for some recognition by all candidates seeking political office—that the current drug policy is a failure, and the need for a change to look at legalization as a new avenue. Instead, I hear promises to clean up the streets using the same failed approaches, more federal judges, more police officers, more federal dollars, more prison cells.

For me and the rest who are on the front line, such proposals ring hollow. The age of destruction from the bullet is increasing while the suffering climbs in numbers (see Figure 25.5). I realize that no one gets elected to public office by taking the wrong side of controversial issues, but I also recognize that cowardice and myopia rarely lend themselves to great leadership. The onus of responsibility must be placed where it rightfully belongs—on the individual and not the dictate

FIGURE 25.5

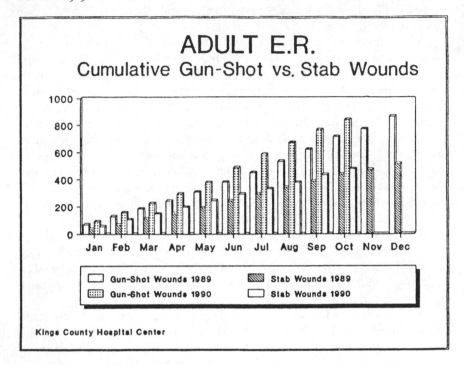

of a select few who decide rightfulness and wrongfulness, generally based on emotional conviction rather than consensus and fact. Let us not be swayed by the wolf-criers. Instead, let us confront the human suffering that is presently plaguing us, as we have done in the past. Let us not be fearful of the unknown; instead, that which is known should be feared as is: currently the case of drug sales with its concomitant violence and death at the end of guns.

We can make a difference by making our voices heard for the legalization of drugs.

COMMENT

Robert B. Millman

I was invited to participate in this meeting to provide a somewhat clinical perspective. What I do most of the time is develop and run treatment programs and treat patients. I will try to confine my remarks according to this limited perspective, this limited vantage point, but it is difficult for me because I am a pretty opinionated person. At the same time, the stridency of a good deal of the discussion in the last couple of days bewilders me as it did Dr. Goldstein. You know, I know that we don't know the answers to many of these questions so it surprises me that everybody seems so sure of what should be done on both sides. What I would like to do is very rapidly go over some of the epidemiologic issues and some of the clinical pharmacologic issues that I think might be important.

As has been mentioned repeatedly, there is good data suggesting that the use of all drugs in the country is declining. Most of the data comes from things like the High School Senior Survey, which in fact is a tour de force, a remarkable survey done all across the country that showed from peaking in 1979 marijuana and all the other drugs seem to be going down. Cocaine peaked a little bit later, in 1984 and 1985, but is still remarkably down. Very interesting—we might ask why it is going down, but we might first ask why did it go up in the first place. Probably in the mid-60s it went up in response to a variety of factors: breakdown of conventional morality, Vietnam war, civil-rights movement, birth-control pills, development of psychoactive medication, better living through chemistry, an altered idea that something could be better from drugs. I think the reason it is going down does not have to do with criminal sanctions. I think it probably has to do with a changed idea, an increase in conservatism in the country, a recognition that things aren't going to change though you take drugs. You still have to get up in the morning and you still have to get a job. There is also a perceived increased harmfulness, I think, in the land. That is another reason why drug use seems to be decreasing.

At the same time it is interesting when you look at the data; it looks as if drug use increases with increasing absenteeism. The number of days absent in each school correlated with the amount of drug use. If we extrapolate that to the inner city, for example in New York City in our local schools, the schools where my clinics are approach 50 percent. That means drug use is going down in the country where people go to school, but we can only guess at what is happening to drug use in the kids who don't go to school—that is, up to 50 percent in New York, Detroit, various other places. What do we know about those people? Very little. Our measures are indirect. We only know about the people who fail. Who fails? The ones who die. Deaths are up. The ones who go to emergency rooms. Requests for emergency treatment are clearly up. Every measure of failure—arrest rates relative to that, births, children born to cocaine-dependent mothers, babies born with cocaine in them—all the indirect measures seem to be increasing so that it looks as if in the inner city drug use is up, cocaine and alcohol use are up, so we might just look more broadly at it, say that drug use has gone from an epidemic situation in our country—epidemic means it sweeps broadly across the population hitting everybody, the rich and the poor, the good and the bad, and the smart and the dumb, and the crazy and the sane—to an endemic situation where it's living in the society and attacking those at risk. Why people take drugs, then, is not the issue. You take drugs because you want to get high, or you want to experiment, or you want to see what is going on. I totally disagree with John Morgan about where volatile cocaine came from. It came because people were looking for better and faster and more efficient ways to get higher and higher. It wasn't a plot; it was a stroke of genius on the part of somebody saying this will get into me a lot faster.

Who is vulnerable? You are vulnerable by virtue of sociologic issues, biologic issues, and psychologic issues. Let me just sketch that out, although most of you in the room would agree with me.

What about sociological vulnerabilities? I think it's obvious. Lack of alternatives. No source of power. A pervasive feeling of weakness. No sense that there is anything in the future waiting for you in these kids. There is no way to get control over your life. It makes sense that many of these kids would at the age of 10, 11, 12 become dealers. Money is the first thing, the impetus at the beginning to get involved in the drug trade, but then soon enough they get interested in getting high. It's a sense of control. It makes you feel good. It's a realistic, rewarding alternative. What we ask, and Dr. Grinspoon asked it indirectly, is how come lots of the kids don't do the drugs, given the grim realities of their lives? Sociologic determinants would be critical, and if we are going to approach the drug problem, maybe we should be thinking very seriously about changing those sociologic determinants—which are very difficult to change. In some ways the discussion ends up being more technological or technical rather than the hard-core difficult problems of how do you provide alternatives to these kids who don't have any.

How about biologic predisposition? I won't belabor that, but there is good and increasing evidence that some people by virtue of genetics or neurotransmitter balance are vulnerable to becoming drug-dependent. I think additional research has to be done on that, but it seems very interesting.

How about psychologic vulnerability? That is very interesting to us in the treatment field. Over the past 20 years, running a bunch of different treatment programs, methadone programs, drug-free, we have seen an increasing severity of psychologic illness in our population. No questions about it. When it was epidemic, we saw lots of normal heroin addicts—people who were psychologically okay and if we could get them off the heroin or control the heroin use through methadone they would be fine. Now we are seeing people who are severely disabled, psychologically disabled, who have multiproblems and methadone is an effective treatment, but they need a good deal more than just the methadone. They need a variety of treatments. Therapeutic communities, I think, are also effective, but they are also recognizing that this is a new population in some ways, requiring intensive psychological care and often medication.

We have thus sociologic, biologic, and psychologic determinants interrelating importantly with pharmacology to cause drug-dependence, and I must say that Dr. Way and Dr. Goldstein stole my thunder. What I was going to say was exactly the same thing they did. I think pharmacologists and clinicians tend to say that ethicists, historians, lawyers don't see the drug users as individuals. They see drugs. They talk about the drug problem. Mr. Meese talks about narcotics. Dr. Grinspoon implies that marijuana relates to heroin. He doesn't really, but you might pick up that implication in his defense of the safety of marijuana, and clearly the drugs are very different. Each has its own ethos. Its own pattern of abuse. Its own pharmacology. Its own adverse effects. And if we are going to talk about the development of a drug policy, we have to know a little bit more about all those things.

I would like to illustrate with a little example; once again Dr. Way did it and Dr. Goldstein did it, but I have to do it as well with cocaine and heroin to explain the differences. Cocaine is not classically addicting. What we say is that it is reinforcing. It has a rapid onset of effects so on the way up you are feeling good, and how fast you go up has to do with how reinforcing the drug is. If you sniff it, you go up slowly, but if you smoke it or shoot it, you go up fast. How fast you go up with drugs and how fast effects wane has to do with how reinforcing they are. Crack is almost the perfect reinforcing drug. Rapid onset, rapid waning of effects. Methadone, for example, would be slower onset, slower waning. Heroin:

rapid onset, moderately fast waning, pretty reinforcing drug. That is what determines in part reinforcement. Anyhow, cocaine: rapid onset, rapid waning, not classically addicting—and what does it do? It leads to alertness or hyperalertness. Everyone who takes it gets a sense of alertness. What is hyperalertness? Hyperalertness is me looking out in the audience and being in a state of vigilance, hypervigilance. I say that Dr. Rosenthal has it in for me. And, in fact, I believe that after a while he is plotting against me and I begin moving back against the wall and I say there are a number of people in this audience who are looking to hurt me and I am huddled up against the wall. You eventually realize that I am paranoid as can be and you take me off to Stanford Hospital. I am saying I am not paranoid; I am hyperalert. I am looking at the cues. Or another way to think about it would be in crossing a street. I know that some guy driving a car could be drunk and if I cross that street, even with the light, I am risking my life because a drunk can come and kill me—so I am afraid to cross all streets. I am hyperalert. You say I am paranoid. The point is that any drug that induces alertness or hyperalertness induces paranoia. That needs to be understood. Cocaine, in a stepwise fashion, induces paranoia in everybody. Everyone has his or her number. For example, I am so healthy I could do huge amounts of cocaine and I would not get paranoid. Some of the rest of you could just do a little bit and you'd be psychotic. The point is, each of us has that number, that capacity.

We thus have a drug that is widely reinforcing, powerfully reinforcing, and at the peak of its reinforcing property induces paranoia or a psychotomimetic. Think about that for a moment if you are trying to develop a distribution system. You give someone the eighth that they get for the eighth. They do the eighth in about four hours, because even if you give it in a safe form it's easy to make it into freebase and you do whole eighth in four hours, and then you come back to the dispensary and you say, "Dr. Millman, I would like my dose." And your eyes are wide and you are hearing voices, and I say to you, "But Mary, you have already had your weekly dose and I can't give you any more." Mary has two choices. She can hurt me or she can buy it out on the street. The point is, because it is so reinforcing and because it is psychomimetic, it is very difficult to figure out a distribution system, and that ends up being a critical question if we are talking about legalizing or decriminalizing drugs.

I won't belabor it, and people discuss the powerful reinforcement of cocaine, but you have to see it to understand it. It is not like marijuana. It is not like other drugs that you know. I did a house call on one young man who is a freebaser, and you just have to see this scene. He lived on the seventeenth floor of a big fancy apartment house in New York City and he had his mattress tented, and sheets all around the mattress, and he had a light set up inside the mattress, and he had disconnected all the electrical appliances, and he had *Playboy* and *Penthouse* magazines under his mattress with this light, and for eight to ten hours a day he would do the freebase pipe and compulsively masturbate and hallucinate. This was a repeated episode. We would bring him to the hospital. It would be a tremendous relief for him. In two days he would be normal again and going back to work as a very rich stock broker, but then for a variety of reasons that I won't go into, we would find him back under his mattress again. Powerfully reinforcing.

Heroin is a very different story. Much more classically addicting. If we all did a dose of heroin right now, we would get high and feel a sense of ease. There would be no violence or paranoia. We would feel like everything is as it should be and we didn't need anything else. Just leave us alone. This isn't such a bad drug at all. Tomorrow morning, if I required you to come back and report, you would tell me about a little bit of irritability. One day's use of heroin or morphine, and you would come back tomorrow and say you felt a little irritable. I yelled at my wife or I yelled at my lover. I kicked the dog. That is one day. If I made you take heroin every day for the next few months, you would come to me with increasing tales of irritability and anxiety—eventually frank with withdrawal, depending on again, set and setting. The individual, his expectations, and the pharmacology of the drug. Eventually you would come in with a profound withdrawal syndrome.

It is interesting that Dr. Way mentioned that it is like the flu and it's not life-threatening. I think that might be a misconception. The physical signs of heroin withdrawal—that's the vegetative signs—*are* like the flu and not life-threatening, but the subjective feeling is a suicidal depression, possibly relating to endorphin deficiency or dopamine excess, but the feeling is one of a suicidal depression. Objectively we say, "Oh, he is just in heroin withdrawal. It's like the flu." But the feeling is, "I can't face the day. I can't survive. I am going to die" and you say "I must get the drug." It is not surprising that someone in that state would go out and hit someone over the head. They are not violent but they might hit someone over the head to get to some more drug to support the habit. Again, when you think of a distribution system related to a drug that is this profoundly dependency-producing, it is difficult. My time is up, and let me close on one final thing. I am chairman of something called the New York Academy of Medicine Committee on Drug and Alcohol Dependence. We have a very prestigious group in New York, and most of the group is against legalization. We are interested in treatment. I was very strongly for needle exchange. I am still for needle exchange or the provision of needles. I am very concerned about the spread of AIDS. Fifty percent of the patients admitted to our heroin programs are HIV-positive. I pushed as hard as I could for needle exchange. My committee defeated me. Many of them dwell on the front line. Many of them are treatment people. Many of them are from a minority community. And they are saying, "No, you are not going to get needle exchange and forget legalization. It's beyond the pale." You must understand I fought hard for needle exchange. I believe it is the correct thing to do, but at the same time the opposition gives you pause. Perhaps they know what they are talking about. It is their community. They tell it to you with great conviction. I think I am right. I am still arguing, but I think it is a message for all of us. That we may think we know what should be done, but we should also be somewhat respectful of the other side.

INDEX

Aaron, P., 415–16
Abortions. *See* Spontaneous abortion
Abstinence, 245
Accidents, drug-related, 103–4, 214–15, 330–31
ACLU, 277, 292, 326
Addiction: behavioral effect of, 78, 179, 392; biologic predisposition of, 8, 403, 436–37; criminal act vs. medical problem, 73, 178; defining, 69–70, 79, 88–89, 390–93; long-run change in, 80–81; measuring degree of, 79–83; neurobiology research on, 401–3; Plato on, 301; religious view of addiction, 38, 180; short-run change in, 80–81; steady-state and, 79–81; treatment specialists on, 240, 331–32; universal impact of, 399–400; of various social classes, 83; vs. drug tolerance, 78–79, 393–94. *See also* Rational addiction model
Addiction Research Unit at London University's Institute of Psychiatry, 232
Addiction-switching problem. *See* Disordered behavior
Addictive goods. *See* Drugs
Addicts: characteristics of, 113–14, 401–2; civil commitment of, 259; decriminalization and, 61, 64–66, 339; as focus of drug war, 256–57; increase of British, 180–81; reaction to drug costs, 80–81; vs. innocent victims, 54, 57–58. *See also* Drug users
"Adolescent Drug Use and Psychological Health: A Longitudinal Inquiry," 381
Adolescents: alcohol and, 338; drug abuse and suicide, 228; psychological characteristics of users, 380–81
Adrian, M., 214
Adulterant tricresyl phosphate (TCP), 405
Advertising: of alcohol and nicotine, 411; as control institution, 38–39, 266–67; legalization and, 63, 314
Advisory Council on the Misuse of Drugs, 181, 183–84, 186
Afghanistan, 374–75
AIDS: in China, 374; as external cost, 103, 217, 319; high Swiss rate of, 334; infants as victims of, 229; legalization and, 430; marijuana and, 385; needle exchange and, 247, 439; prevention policy of Dutch, 173; prohibition impact on, 276, 316; as social cost of heroin, 308; spread of, 261, 409. *See also* Communicable disease; HIV infection
Alaska, 286